MASTERPLOTS
1978 ANNUAL

1978 ANNUAL

MAGILL'S LITERARY ANNUAL
*Essay-Reviews of 100 Outstanding Books
Published in the United States During 1977*

Edited by
FRANK N. MAGILL

SALEM PRESS, Incorporated
Englewood Cliffs, New Jersey

LIBRARY OF CONGRESS CATALOG CARD NO. 77-99209

ISBN 0-89356-078-2

The material in this volume also appears under
the title of *Magill's Literary Annual: 1978*

PRINTED IN THE UNITED STATES OF AMERICA

LIST OF TITLES

CONTRIBUTING REVIEWERS FOR 1978 ANNUAL

ANTHONY ARTHUR
CAROLYN WILKERSON BELL
MAE WOODS BELL
MEREDITH WILLIAM BERG
GORDON N. BERGQUIST
GARY B. BLANK
WILLIAM BOSWELL
JOHN C. CARLISLE
JAMES W. CLARK, JR.
GORDON W. CLARKE
E. GENE DeFELICE
LEON V. DRISKELL
CHARLES ELKABAS
JOHN W. EVANS
KATHRYN FLARIS
GEORGE J. FLEMING
JONATHAN M. FURDEK
BETTY GAWTHROP
ROGER A. GEIMER
LESLIE E. GERBER
LEONARD H. D. GORDON
WILLIAM E. GRANT
ALAN G. GROSS
MAX HALPEREN
STEPHEN L. HANSON
JANET H. HOBBS
WILLIS KNAPP JONES
HAROLD J. JOSEPH
EDWARD P. KELEHER
JOHN R. KELLY
PAUL B. KERN
HENDERSON KINCHELOE
ANTHONY LAMB
RICHARD L. LANGILL
SAUL LERNER
DAVID MADDEN

WALTER E. MEYERS
LESLIE B. MITTLEMAN
KEITH NEILSON
JAMES E. NEWMAN
ROBERT E. NICHOLS, JR.
GUY OWEN
DORIS F. PIERCE
JAMES W. PRINGLE
DAVID L. RANSEL
JOHN D. RAYMER
BRUCE D. REEVES
ANN E. REYNOLDS
ALFRED D. SANDER
MARGARET S. SCHOON
KATHRYN L. SEIDEL
ROBERT L. SELIG
DON W. SIEKER
SOFUS E. SIMONSEN
GREGORY S. SOJKA
JAMES D. STARTT
SHIRLEY F. STATON
LEON STEIN
JOAN HINDE STEWART
JAMES T. SULLIVAN
CAROL WHYTE TALABAY
HENRY TAYLOR
WILLIAM TILLSON
LANCE TRUSTY
HARRY TUCKER, JR.
STUART VAN DYKE, JR.
RICHARD A. VAN ORMAN
JOHN N. WALL, JR.
THOMAS N. WALTERS
ROBERT B. WHITE, JR.
MARY C. WILLIAMS
MARY ANN WITT

EDWARD A. ZIVICH

ix

PREFACE

HERE, in essay-review form, is a survey of the literary year of 1977 comprising a study of one hundred outstanding books published during the year. Represented in this volume are 35 works of fiction, 6 volumes of poetry, 2 dramas, 5 collections of essays, 22 biographies, 10 works dealing with autobiography, memoirs, diaries, and letters, 11 historical studies, 3 books concerning current affairs, 2 volumes of literary criticism, and 4 works which fall into special categories.

Fantasy and folklore enriched the fiction of 1977, contributing a special enchantment to the field of imaginative writing. THE BOOK OF MERLYN, bringing T. H. White's THE ONCE AND FUTURE KING to a close, appeared during the year. In this work the animals that guided the education of Arthur in his youth return to join with Merlyn in an effort to persuade the aging Arthur to forego his battle with Mordred. Their arguments come to naught and Arthur goes out to meet his fate. Tolkien's THE SILMARILLION again demonstrates the breadth of the author's imagination and the power of his words to make us see what he shows us and believe what he tells us. In ANPAO, Jamake Highwater presents a fascinating collection of traditional tales based on American Indian culture, the stories held together by the boy Anpao and heightened by the author's insights through his own Indian tribal heritage.

Another work dealing with the American Indian is Douglas C. Jones's fine novel ARREST SITTING BULL, which depicts the winding down of Indian/white confrontation at the end of the nineteenth century. Out of Australia comes THE THORN BIRDS, set on a Texas-size ranch in the romantic vein, a novel alive with all the ingredients of the popular best seller. With THE THIN MOUNTAIN AIR, Paul Horgan brings to maturity, and to a highly civilized view toward life, the young protagonist of two earlier novels. Other titles of outstanding merit published during the year include John Hersey's THE WALNUT DOOR, John Fowles's DANIEL MARTIN, Jerzy Kosinski's BLIND DATE, Joan Didion's A BOOK OF COMMON PRAYER, Toni Morrison's SONG OF SOLOMON, THE DARK LADY by Louis Auchincloss, HOW TO SAVE YOUR OWN LIFE by Erica Jong, and John Cheever's FALCONER, a metaphorical story of a "solid citizen" who goes to prison for fratricide.

Short story collections were plentiful in 1977, some of the best being THE BOOK OF SAND by Jorge Luis Borges, THE STREET OF CROCODILES by the Polish writer Bruno Schulz, SILKEN EYES by Françoise Sagan, and eighteen stories by Joyce Carol Oates collected under the title of NIGHT-SIDE.

Of the numerous volumes of poetry published in 1977, among the best were THE COLLECTED POEMS OF HOWARD NEMEROV, winner of the 1978

National Book Award for Poetry; DAY BY DAY, Robert Lowell's last collection before his death; SELECTED POEMS: 1923-1975 by Robert Penn Warren, an impressive array; William Stafford's STORIES THAT COULD BE TRUE, a definitive collection to date; and COLLECTED POEMS: 1919-1976 by Allen Tate, which presents Tate's poetic artistry over a period of fifty-seven years.

Few dramas of note saw print in 1977, but AMERICAN BUFFALO by David Mamet, which won the Drama Critics Circle Award for the 1977 season, is one that is worthy of consideration by those concerned with serious dramatic experiences. In a lighter vein are two examples of Tom Stoppard's dramatic vision published under the title of DIRTY LINEN and NEW-FOUND-LAND.

Two excellent studies in literary criticism add to the enjoyment of those who relish in-depth analyses of the works of established literary figures: A. Dwight Culler's THE POETRY OF TENNYSON, and Richard Poirier's examination of Robert Frost and his canon.

Several collections of essays deserve mention, including ESSAYS OF E. B. WHITE; THE HUMAN SITUATION, Aldous Huxley's 1959 Santa Barbara Lectures; LIFE/SITUATIONS by Jean-Paul Sartre; MISSING PERSONS AND OTHER ESSAYS by Heinrich Böll; and Edward Butscher's collection of essays about Sylvia Plath and her work.

Many excellent biographies were published in 1977, studies ranging in time from the fifteenth century (William Caxton, Joan of Arc) to 1977 (Simone de Beauvoir and Jean-Paul Sartre). Literary figures under study include J. R. R. Tolkien, Vladimir Nabokov, Jack London, and Ivan Turgenev, the latter an excellent study by V. S. Pritchett under the title of THE GENTLE BARBARIAN. Political leaders dealt with include Winston S. Churchill, Harry Hopkins, political philosopher Edmund Burke, Jefferson Davis, Adlai E. Stevenson, and Catherine the Great. Military leaders are represented by Robert V. Remini's scholarly study of Andrew Jackson—the first of two volumes planned—and by Frank E. Vandiver's BLACK JACK, examining the life of General John J. Pershing and stressing his military career. Biographies of inventors Thomas A. Edison and Robert Fulton also appeared during the year.

Autobiographies or memoirs, by Will and Ariel Durant, Earl Warren, Milovan Djilas, Anthony Eden, and N. Scott Momaday appeared in 1977 as well as the ninth volume of the Yale Edition of James Boswell's journals, with the subtitle "Laird of Auchinleck, 1778-1782." Also published during the year were Volume I (1915-1919) of THE DIARY OF VIRGINIA WOLFF and volumes of Letters of Franz Kafka, Anne Sexton, and Edmund Wilson.

Interesting works in history are extremely popular in these times and the year 1977 provided its share. Readers who enjoy ancient history will probably be intrigued with THE CELTS by Gerhard Herm. Nearer to our own time is David McCullough's engrossing story of the creation of the Panama Canal in THE PATH BETWEEN THE SEAS. Fritz Stern's GOLD AND IRON is an excellent study of Bismarck's shaping of the German Empire with the financial aid of Gerson von Bleichröder. In THE RIVER CONGO, Peter Forbath provides a fascinating history of this fifth largest river in the world from the time of Prince Henry the Navigator to the twentieth century. MAO'S CHINA and THE CHINESE COMMUNIST PARTY IN POWER, 1949-1976 delineate the progress of

Communist China from 1949 to 1976 and offer new insights to Western readers. THE GULAG ARCHIPELAGO: THREE (Parts V-VII), concludes Alexander I. Solzhenitsyn's monumental report depicting the harsh, inhuman conditions in Soviet Corrective Labor Camps, a work that has moved the conscience of the Western world.

Acknowledged as highly selective because of space limitations, this group of essay-reviews is presented as representative of the years' output of fiction and nonfiction. Some of the books entertain, some instruct, some may serve as links with our almost forgotten past. Whatever the author's purpose, whatever the reader's response, we should all be grateful that no one in our world has been told what he must write and no one has been told that he must read what has been written.

FRANK N. MAGILL

ADLAI STEVENSON AND THE WORLD

Author: John Bartlow Martin (1915–　　)
Publisher: Doubleday and Company (New York). 946 pp. $15.00
Type of work: Biography
Time: 1952–1965
Locale: Illinois, New York, and locations on several world tours

This second volume in Martin's biography covers the years 1952 through 1965 and focuses on Adlai Stevenson's presidential candidacy of 1956, the effects of his party leadership throughout 1952–1960, and his Ambassadorship to the United Nations from 1961–1965

Principal personages:
ADLAI EWING STEVENSON, II, politician and statesman
ARTHUR M. SCHLESINGER, Jr., his adviser
JOHN F. KENNEDY, 35th President of the United States
HUBERT H. HUMPHREY, U.S. Senator, and Vice-President of the United States
LYNDON B. JOHNSON, 36th President of the United States

John Bartlow Martin, the author of this two-volume biography, is eminently qualified as an award-winning journalist, having written many articles on social and political issues since the decade of the 1940's. He is qualified as a statesman, having served as presidential envoy twice and having been Ambassador to the Dominican Republic, and most especially qualified as a close associate of Adlai Stevenson, having worked as his adviser and writer for many years, most notably from 1952 onward. Martin brings all of these faculties to bear and, with the help of voluminous written data gathered from personal records and many public papers, has produced a highly detailed, nearly day-by-day account of Adlai Stevenson's hectic public and social life.

This second volume is divided into two phases of Stevenson's public commitment, titled simply "The Nation" and "The World," by which author Martin indicates that during the decade of the 1950's, Stevenson's major impact was in national politics, while after 1960, his achievements were in the field of international diplomacy. Hence, *Adlai Stevenson and the World* recounts the years of most prestige, most popularity, most challenge, and most fulfillment for this important American who became a world leader.

During the thirteen years covered in the second volume, Adlai Stevenson enjoyed ever-increasing world renown. He was always traveling, meeting with associates and friends, giving speeches—an informed, delightful, articulate, and inspiring spokesman for his political party and for his nation. His trips abroad were numerous, lengthy, and wide-ranging, during which he visited with most of the dignitaries on every continent. The quality and quantity of honorary degrees he began receiving became noteworthy. And yet, his career was paradoxical.

Despite having been twice defeated for the Presidency in 1952 and 1956, and not winning his party's nomination as candidate in 1960, Stevenson seems never to have been regarded as a loser, but rather as a shining paragon of high-

1

mindedness in public service, one of the most noble figures on the political scene, here and abroad, the like of whom, incidentally, we have not seen since. Reasons for this good opinion of him, according to biographer Martin's suggestion, include the probable fact that Eisenhower's popularity was unbeatable anyway and so to lose to him was no disgrace, and more specifically, the fact that Stevenson's courage and determination were indomitable in the face of his upsets, becoming a sort of trademark of his, as he smilingly, gallantly, and eloquently continued the pursuit of important national and international goals.

Even though Stevenson was not in public office during 1952–1960, he affected public policy. Beginning shortly after the 1952 elections, in the spring of 1953, the political advisers of his first presidential campaign set about immediately after the defeat to remain in his service, and that of their party, by continuing to study major issues of the day and to draft position papers for Stevenson to present in speeches as the spokesman for the Democratic party, now that they were out of office and ex-President Truman had officially retired from active politics. These advisers included Kenneth Galbraith, Arthur M. Schlesinger, Jr., George Ball, Averell Harriman, Chester Bowles, and Tom Finletter, among many other experts in several fields. They became known as the Finletter Group, met periodically for four years or more, and served their party and the nation well by researching and speaking out on important issues. Martin indicates that such assemblages of political adivsers as the Finletter Group, and other groups who continued during the entire eight years of the Eisenhower Administration, actually established critical attitudes in the nation and were responsible for many of the policies which later became enacted, especially under the following Democratic presidents, John F. Kennedy and Lyndon B. Johnson. Therefore, as a figure about whom others gathered, Stevenson was both a catalyst and a prime mover himself, whose party leadership engendered many beneficial effects, even though he held no policymaking office in the federal government during these years.

A great part of Adlai Stevenson's later life was taken up with campaigning, a facet of his endeavors which Martin knew intimately, and which is therefore reported here in the presidential election years of 1956, 1960, and to a lesser degree 1964, when one reads of the exhaustive travel and speechmaking schedule which national campaigning required. Stevenson not only accomplished these taxing assignments but seems to have thrived on that kind of public exposure, because even in off-year elections he was always ready to stump for the party candidates throughout the country; and he did so with verve, resilience, and, generally, widespread success. And yet, paradoxically again, although a fully committed national politician, his scope was never limited to this nation alone.

Frequent trips abroad to all parts of the world, coupled with a lifelong interest in world affairs, made Stevenson ever aware of international politics. It is the international scope of his endeavors which he seems always to have cherished.

Foreign affairs were the aspect of the presidency of this country in which he was apparently most interested, as can be quickly corroborated by noticing the internationalistic tone of all of his speechmaking. At the advent of President Kennedy's election, the cabinet post of Secretary of State was Stevenson's prime desire; and his disappointment at not getting that post was only partially mitigated by his acceptance of President Kennedy's appointment of him as the U.S. Ambassador to the United Nations, taken only after assurances that he would be allowed to help make policy and not merely be a spokesman. During the years 1961–1965, Adlai Stevenson was a firm, patient, successful negotiator, working together brilliantly with two United Nations Secretaries-General, Dag Hammarskjöld and U Thant, and achieving much in prestige and good will for his country and the free world during very difficult and varied world crises. They now read like a recital of horrors: strife in the Congo, Angolan independence, the Berlin Wall, Formosa, Red China's admission, the Bay of Pigs, Cuban missiles, Khrushchev's attacks, NATO, constant disarmament talks, Dominican Republic intervention, Vietnam. During all of this extreme international tension, we had a most respected and capable world diplomat as our representative. His record in the UN is enviable; his counsel to two presidents on international diplomacy was consistently wise. Even though Martin indicates in the subtitle of the first chapter of this volume that the period of 1952–1955 was his "finest hour," that may be hyperbole and a Churchillian echo for dramatic effect, because a very strong case can most assuredly be made for the position that his UN years were the culmination of a lifetime of internationalist tendencies and that Stevenson's most important contributions were his positive effect on the rest of the world.

Nowhere are paradoxes more evident than in the social aspect of Stevenson's life. Martin provides us with an objective recounting of social events and some of the man's personal habits. We appreciate, for example, that although generally considered an intellectual, Stevenson very rarely read; instead, he gathered information by association with many intelligent colleagues and friends who discussed issues with him, thereby becoming more of a "broker of ideas" than a creator of them. His speeches, as an indication of this, were generally prepared by others; he would then edit and re-edit them up to the last minute before delivery.

In a similar fashion, one is surprised to realize that despite nearly continuous movement, constant traveling, and extremely intermittent interaction with people, Stevenson nevertheless inspired great loyalty and admiration from many gifted and dedicated persons. His admirers reacted emotionally to him as well as intellectually, in that they felt affection for him as well as respect. It is stated that he almost never terminated a friendship but continued them until, in only one or two instances, the friends reluctantly separated from him. Such constancy occurred either in spite of his lifestyle or because of it.

Many of his closest friends were women who fit into a discernible pattern:

they all were quite intelligent, very sensitive, openly and unashamedly flattering to him, usually married, many older than he, some quite wealthy and influential. He carried on enduring associations with Alicia Patterson (Mrs. Harry Guggenheim), Jane Dick (Mrs. Edison Dick), Agnes Meyer (Mrs. Eugene Meyer), Barbara Ward, (Lady Jackson, wife of Sir Robert Jackson), and Marietta Tree (Mrs. Ronald Tree), the latter of whom was out briskly walking with him in Grosvenor Square, London, the morning in July, 1965, when he died suddenly of a heart attack. Mrs. Eleanor Roosevelt was a close and venerated friend continually until her death in 1963. All gave Stevenson valuable assistance, support, and advice, and campaigned for him. It could be said, therefore, that he held the deep affection of several women. It might also be said that he had no lasting intimacy with any one woman, inasmuch as divorce followed a shattering marriage that ended with the mental deterioration of his wife, Ellen Borden Stevenson, so that he was never again willing to remarry.

Throughout this biography, we read, predominantly, excerpts from Stevenson's speeches, his correspondence, daily appointment calendar, and travel notebooks, including the realistic touches of his abbreviations and occasional misspellings. Martin explains in the biography's "Source Notes" at the end of the volume that he has spent the past twelve years culling over speeches, press conference transcripts, public statements, program papers, lectures, law-firm records, and the private effects which he himself helped catalog. Therefore his method has been to set down the chronological series of events with such excerpts. Actual conversations with others are paraphrased rather than re-enacted. He states, "I have let the material speak for itself." But while such techniques are not only defensible but desirable as the journalist's stock in trade (apparent objectivity being the means to promote complete believability), in any creative literary endeavor, such fact-gathering and reporting seems singularly one-dimensional, and in a biography can be unnervingly superficial and unsatisfying.

Some critics of this work have said that it contains too much detail and that its style is ponderous. Closer scrutiny discloses that the rub comes from the fact that its length does not seem to reward the reader with fresh insight about this public figure. An objective compilation of source data with interpolation of narrative is a worthwhile technique, but readers require help in being able to decipher the public and social pose in order to get to the man within. After insisting, in the "Acknowledgements" section at the end of this second volume, that Stevenson was complex and sometimes ambiguous, Martin states: "But I think that the important questions have been answered." Not only have they not been answered, they have not even been asked in these volumes.

One thoroughly respects Martin's disinclination to delve into psychological and moral dimensions which he may feel inadequate to discuss; such may be, after all, completely out of his domain. But what is a biography if it is not an appraisal of the protagonist's substance and essence? One reviewer praised

Martin's stringent lack of sentimentality in this work. It is true that one is supposed to be convinced of Martin's impartiality toward his subject by recognizing his meticulous avoidance of anything resembling prejudice favoring Stevenson, but the sheer physical evidence, the years of study, of patient sifting of data, of careful elaboration of two long volumes, all combine to overwhelm us in exactly the opposite direction: this biography has to have been a labor of devotion. And that being so, it hardly seems worth the effort for Martin to have denied the obvious and to have composed a concatenation of outward activities with little or no depth into the character he knew very well.

Martin states in the "Acknowledgements" that the interpretation of Adlai Stevenson in these volumes is his, yet that is precisely what is lacking—his unique interpretation of one of this century's most interesting public figures. The facts of his life are masterfully given, but no interpretation of them is offered, and the facts do not always speak for themselves. Stevenson was anything but obvious; he was never deceitful, with himself or with others, but he *was* multifaceted, variegated, ambiguous whenever the situation defied resolution, a dynamic criss-cross of influences and ambitions, inspiring yet needing inspiration, courageous and yet vulnerable, disappointed on occasion but not daunted for long. So, while this two-volume work can well be pointed to as an outstanding example of a political biography, it is not a personal one.

Adlai Stevenson and the World is nevertheless a very valuable and penetrating examination of recent political history in this country with many informative and enlightening passages concerning the interworkings of the federal government and the international diplomacy at the United Nations. Perspectives are given which show how policy becomes determined under the pressures of state, and many revealing glimpses of famous people are intertwined in the narrative.

Anthony Lamb

THE AGE OF UNCERTAINTY

Author: John Kenneth Galbraith (1908–   )
Publisher: Houghton Mifflin Company (Boston). Illustrated. 365 pp. $17.50
Type of work: Current affairs

A historical and philosophical analysis of changing political and economic institutions throughout the world, focusing on the problems and changes in American capitalism

Those who are familiar with John Kenneth Galbraith and his works think of him as the economist who attacked the large producers, large buyers, and large unions which exert substantial economic power. Others think of him as a radical in his profession who attacks traditional economic theory and prefers the development of a large and active public or government sector in America to solve its problems. Galbraith is a Professor of Economics at Harvard University and former chairman of the Americans for Democratic Action. However, it is frequently overlooked that Galbraith is an exceptionally talented literary artist as well as a contemporary political philosopher and historian who would probably much prefer to be compared to John Locke or Karl Marx than to Paul Samuelson or Simon Kuznets.

Galbraith has published a series of books, several of which have gained popular acclaim. He is probably best known for two books that have generated considerable controversy: *The Affluent Society* (1958), in which he argues for a strong public sector, and *The New Industrial State* (1967), in which he argues .that the traditional businessman has been replaced by a technostructure of specialists in the modern corporate world. Whether or not one accepts Galbraith's views, there is no question that he raises provocative issues and provides insights as well as informative material in an interesting and understandable style. It is this particular quality that makes his books so popular and pleasurable to read. *The Age of Uncertainty* is no disappointment in this sense.

As a matter of background, *The Age of Uncertainty* is a consequence of the effort to develop the film series of the same title, which was produced by the BBC and shown throughout the United States on the Public Broadcasting System. For his pilot attempt with the new media, Galbraith proceeded to write a series of concise essays that focused on a single contention: that there is worldwide tension which results from the "shaking up" of traditional political and economic doctrines. In other words, Galbraith examines the contrasts between the certainties of the past century with the uncertainties of our time. Capitalism, with its well-defined theory of markets and profits, was certain of its success, yet now we are witness to the uncertainty of its future. Socialism was certain of the rightness of its views; now it is haunted by uncertainty. Imperialists, certain that colonialism was the proper way to deal with underdeveloped societies, are now being toppled in many places throughout the world. These are the issues that Galbraith approaches in his typical evolutionary style. As would be expected, much of his material is derived from his earlier works. Indeed, parts of this book are taken directly from earlier publications. But for those who are familiar with Galbraith, *The Age of Uncertainty* will not be a disappointment. Galbraith pursues his challenge to the powers of the marketplace and questions the assumed dangers of the State. He also takes a position that appears to have substantial public sympathy, in favor of increased government involvement in economic affairs.

Galbraith's approach is methodical and thorough. First he examines the political-economic philosophers in a detailed, comprehensive way and discusses their impact on the political-economic systems. From the viewpoint of an economist, he outlines the evolution of economic thought and history. Galbraith is able to present his information in a way that is generally appealing and fascinating, by blending details with interesting anecdotes and major historical events to provide pointed insights and reflections into the evolution of historical episodes over the past two hundred years.

Purely by coincidence, 1776, the year of the American Declaration of Independence, is also the year that Adam Smith published *The Wealth of Nations*, a treatise that has come to be accepted by economists as the origin of modern economic thinking. Smith concluded that the wealth of a nation results from the independent pursuit of each of its citizens to seek his own interest; Galbraith takes the reader through the more familiar episodes and examples in Smith's classic work in order to set the scene for the events of that era and to contrast the view of Adam Smith with our current economic structure, with its conglomerates, multinational corporations, and international labor unions. He pursues what he calls the "tyranny of circumstance," contrasting the historical situation with the theoretical interpretations. He explores such events as the New Lanark experiment near Glasgow, Scotland, where David Dale, a Scottish capitalist and philanthropist, attempted a new social order where children were taken from orphanages to go to school and to work in his cotton mill. He then looks at the New Harmony experiment in Indiana operated by Robert Owen, Dale's son-in-law, as an attempt at a new social and economic order.

In exploring the influences of Thomas Malthus, best-known for his essays on population and his doctrine that it is generally possible to have an overproduction of goods, and the arguments of David Ricardo, who argued against that possibility, Galbraith recalls the famines that have plagued the world. He includes an impressive pictorial supplement interspersed in the narrative. This section is masterful in its ability to focus on persistent problems and relate these problems to our present age of uncertainty. Another particularly interesting essay deals with the lifestyle and morals of the rich, focusing on Herbert Spencer, an English philosopher and pioneer sociologist who applied the phrase "survival of the fittest" to account for the position of the successful and the wealthy. Galbraith analyzes the rich in America and argues for the important role of the railroads in maintaining a wealthy class. Recalling the struggle for the railroads and their control, he weaves a net of events while highlighting important problems and concepts; he includes the Church in his explanation of the power wielded by the rich. A particular example is Galbraith's treatment of Thorstein Veblen, the son of poor Norwegian immigrants, born in Wisconsin, and known to economists for his depiction and analysis of what is called "conspicuous consumption." Galbraith not only explores Veblen's background but also illustrates the theory of conspicuous consumption with a pictorial barrage depicting the parties of the rich, the Riviera, gambling, and other exhorbitances familiarized to moviegoers in *The Great Gatsby.*

Probably the most fascinating section in *The Age of Uncertainty* deals with Karl Marx. Having laid an adequate background, Galbraith characterizes Marx as a social scientist, brilliant journalist, and historian, but not as a revolutionary. A startling reminder to the Capitalist world are some of the demands of *The Communist Manifesto,* such as progressive income tax, abolition of inheritance, a national bank with a monopoly of banking operations, public ownership of transportation and communication, extension of public ownership into industry and the cultivation of idle lands, better soil management, work by all, free education, and abolition of child labor. Galbraith points out how many of these demands have been and are being met, but not without some conflict and opposition. Again, the author supplements his treatment of Marx with pictorial images of the revolutions and analyzes the rationale for opposition to these social reforms, evidenced by our own prejudices to social changes when identified as "Communist." Galbraith discusses these issues calmly and rationally, defining the basic ingredients for a successful revolution as determined leadership with a vision and a specific plan, dedicated followers, and a weak opposition; he also identifies the nemesis of revolution as reform and nationalism.

Galbraith then examines one last "certainty" of the past: Imperialism. He examines the Spanish empire in some detail to demonstrate fully the implications of colonialism, and discusses changing attitudes toward attempts to govern indirectly and to shape the political development of distant lands. He points out that what were once the colonial powers are now identified as "developed nations," while what were once the colonies are now referred to as the poor "developing nations." In order to appreciate fully recent developments, Galbraith next elaborates on the major events of Lenin's career. He focuses on such concepts as the territorial imperative; what he calls the "stupidity problem," typified by leadership stemming from tradition or social rank rather than ability; and the "rogue reaction"—those actions such as general strikes which lack direction and predictable results. The author points out Lenin's need for a highly disciplined, loyal, and committed group which does not involve the general population in the revolution. His detailed treatment of and anecdotes about Lenin are an especially interesting aspect of the book.

Galbraith also attacks another less obvious "uncertainty" of our age: the role of money. In exploring the origins and role of money, Galbraith focuses on the historical importance and prosperity of Amsterdam. Pointing out both the prosperity and the abuses that arise from banking, he cites the familiar fate of the Dutch East Indian Company and the ensuing "panics" in the Western world. By examining the revolution of paper money and centralized banking, and detailing the conflicts of Andrew Jackson and Nicholas Biddle, the author centers focus on the uncertainty implicit in paper exchange in a very enlightening fashion. He also offers an interesting interpretation of the contemporary economics figure, Sir John Maynard Keynes, and looks at the weaknesses of the Keynesian theory and the chronic problem that arises from its practice: deficit spending can be a cure for unemployment under *certain* circumstances, but the theory does not explain what to do under a variety of *other* circumstances.

Using his own experiences in Germany before World War II, Galbraith next deals with the Cold War. Depicting the Cold War as a moral crusade with a focus on liberation and a rolling back of the iron curtain, he addresses some of the consequences of its tactics, including the behavior of the CIA, the American episode with Cuba, and the Vietnam War with the unprecedented demands which it placed on our economic resources.

Finally, no work by Galbraith would seem complete without an analysis of the large corporations and the technostructure he has often written about. The corporation is typified as a purely economic entity and is rationalized on economic grounds as an amoral entity with no higher purpose; but Galbraith illustrates the falsity of this picture by showing us examples of fights for extended power by corporate heads with self-aggrandizing motives. He presents his near-classic case of the James B. Glow Company, a seemingly insignificant competitive butcher shop on the south side of Chicago that had a weak reputation in the industry for quality and business ethics, yet which grew to become Unified Global Enterprises, a large conglomerate with extensive overseas operations and earnings, now centered in New York. Galbraith emphasizes that the capitalist "uncertainty" is epitomized by UGE, which he argues is neither a powerless and passive instrument of market forces nor the passive servant of the stockholders.

It is important to recognize Galbraith as a social philosopher and literary artist in order to place his work in honest perspective. *The Age of Uncertainty* is not light reading—the subject matter does not lend itself to simplicity—but it is more correct to consider *The Age of Uncertainty* as a learned book, written in a style both interesting and readable, and buttressed by a strong central theme and purpose.

Jonathan M. Furdek

ALL THE YEARS OF AMERICAN POPULAR MUSIC

Author: David Ewen (1907–   )
Publisher: Prentice-Hall (New Jersey). 850 pp. $19.95
Type of work: Music history
Time: Colonial times to the present
Locale: The United States

A comprehensive chronological survey of American popular music from Colonial days, with a much-needed emphasis on the new musical trends of the last two decades

All the Years of American Popular Music is rumored by at least one source to be David Ewen's eightieth book. Whether or not the figure is actually that high, there is absolutely no doubt that Ewen is the most prolific writer on music in history. This latest work in many respects caps a career that has spanned most of the twentieth century. It might be better named "All the Years of David Ewen," for it is very much a product of the author's earlier works as well as a lifetime of experience.

Born in 1907 in Lemburg, Austria, Ewen was introduced to music through private instruction in piano, harmony, and music theory. He completed his education in New York City at C.C.N.Y. and Columbia University. His first book, *Unfinished Symphony: A Story-Life of Franz Shubert* was published in 1931 and was praised by the *New York Times* as a product of "earnest and painstaking work." After that the books kept coming. His second book, *Hebrew Music,* came out the same year, and 1933 saw the publication of *Wine, Women and Waltz; A Romantic Biography of Johann Strauss, Son and Father* and *From Bach to Stravinsky: The History of Music by Its Foremost Critics. Composers of Today* followed in 1934 and a second edition appeared in 1936. 1936 also witnessed Ewen's marriage to Hannah Weinstein, a New York teacher.

Although still publishing books, Ewen expanded his horizons in 1937 to become music editor of *Cue,* a New York music magazine. In 1938 he became record editor of *Stage* and in 1940 editor of *Musical Facts.* The author took time out for service in the United States Army in 1944-1945, and in a radical departure from his prior literary subject matter, he wrote the authorized history of paratroopers. After the war, he became director of Allen, Towne and Heath Publishing Company—a position he held until 1950 when he published his thirtieth title, *The Story of Irving Berlin.*

Now, thirty or forty titles later, Ewen's career reaches its pinnacle with *All the Years of American Popular Music.* This massive 850-page volume is a stunning work of research and writing. With almost fifty years of music study behind it, this volume is in some respects a rehashing and collating of previous Ewen books, but its major strength is that its one-volume format convincingly and dramatically demonstrates how American popular music has developed out of the experience, tragedy, soul, and passions of the people of all races who came to this country. It has become an accepted fact that American music even at its poorest is reflective of the manners, customs, and habits of common people to a degree of precision unmatched by more scholarly music. Thus, Ewen makes no apologies for his serious treatment of popular music, but treats it as a form of folk music that is, in his mind, much broader than the traditional rural material that has been long viewed as forming the basis of such music. *All the Years of American Popular Music* is a comprehensive, well-documented sourcebook on every kind of popular music written, played, danced to, or sung by Americans from the Puritans and their hymns to the rock phenomena and the currently frenetic pop music scene.

Ewen's vast chronological narrative contains a tremendous array of names, facts, titles, stories, anecdotes, and critical assessments. The book effectively revives songs, singers, and composers long forgotten. When our country was young, our popular music consisted of the patriotic and political type; such songs had a national rather than an individual orientation. Among our early songs were many borrowed from England, including "Yankee Doodle" and the "Star Spangled Banner."

As the country expanded, Ewen notes that songs relating to pioneering became popular, particularly nostalgic tunes of home and family. Songwriters like Stephen Foster and James A. Bland were popular during this period. Songs of transportation, still popular today, also got their start at this time with writers addressing horse and buggys, railroads, steamships, and the bicycle.

American music became more leisurely in the "Gay Nineties" and represented life in an innocent and unhurried stage with major emphasis on a somewhat artificial sentimentality. The waltz was the predominant form of musical expression, and popular songs told a story usually of frustrated love. The advent of ragtime, however, in the early years of the twentieth century expressed a gradual protest against such leisurely living and music and popular arrangements developed some excitement culminating in the elaborate embellishments of jazz.

Following World War I, music became unrestrained, and very few aspects of American life evaded the attention of musicians and songwriters. Our clothing, our games, our slang, and our dances were celebrated in music. Even national events inspired songs. It has been estimated that Lindbergh's flight alone encouraged the publication of over one hundred now forgotten (except by Ewen) songs. For the most part, though, the author attempts to deal with musical pieces that were the "standards" of their period. A "standard" is defined by Ewen as being the popular music equivalent of a "classic" in serious music. For the music of the twentieth century, Ewen is able to detail fully names of composers, lyricists, circumstances surrounding the composition of a piece, its performance history, major productions of the tune on the stage or in motion pictures, and all relevant additional historical information.

About a third of the book deals with people and events occurring after 1960. Ewen treats "Rock 'n' Roll" with a certain respect, even while a certain pessimism regarding its survival seems to come across in some of his comments.

He concedes that this form is now the dominant mode of musical expression and thus cannot be ignored. The result is that Rock and its practitioners are treated in a more objective and meticulous vein than in many works by so-called historians of that music.

While *All the Years of American Popular Music* is, on one level, a history of American popular music, its major value in the long term will be as a source book. Ewen has generously strewn his history with thousands of names and dates which are made accessible through a seventy-one-page index in which the reader can discover, for example, who composed "A Summer Place." He can also learn that John Denver was once Henry Deutschendorf, Jr. But this points up a weakness of the book: there is little, if any, cross-indexing. One cannot look up Henry Deutschendorf, and find out that he grew up to be John Denver. Cross-indexing would have made more of the minutia contained in the book accessible to readers.

Although Ewen shows genuine enthusiasm for the progress of American popular music and has compiled much interesting material, his book may well be of little interest to serious music scholars. *All the Years of American Popular Music,* like Ewen's earlier efforts, is plainly written for popular consumption and, as such, is less concerned with being a specialized and scholarly piece of work. Its size, while lengthy, is still too small to permit in-depth discussion of all the important phases of our musical history. The catchy title is a snap judgment that proves untrue for a scholar desiring the final word on a musical topic. The serious student will also be disappointed by the lack of treatment given to some major but peripheral areas of popular music in the United States. American scholars and critics of popular music, for example, are given no systematic discussion, and some important ones are neglected entirely. Additionally, there is little discussion of the progress of musical education in addressing the many issues involved in the appreciation of popular music. In a volume which attempts to be as extensive as this one does, there will naturally be some omission of this kind, and some topics will be treated in a more superficial manner than others.

One major area where Ewen's book is impressively strong is that of music biography. The author is well known for his biographical treatments of musical artists, and he maintains his reputation in his latest work. He presents clear and interesting pictures of the men and women who have made a permanent contribution to our nation's musical life through their compositions, orchestrations, and performances. He also does not hesitate to mention artistic defects where they are relevant to the discussion of an individual's musical development.

The biographical materials in the book are not devoted exclusively to the musicians and composers of yesterday. A significant portion of the book contains biographical material treating those artists who still have significant meaning to music lovers. The younger musicians, particularly those involved in

Rock whose music is new and vibrant and vital, are given serious and objective treatment as well.

As a reference work, this book has some limitations and is not as all-encompassing as the title would have us believe. The arrangement is of necessity historical and designed for popular appeal, but it also collects and makes available to the more serious reader much valuable material. If it is accepted for what it is, it will prove more stimulating and useful as time goes on. *All the Years of American Popular Music* succeeds admirably in its attempt to trace the growth and interest in musical activity in America from the beginning to the present. Unexpected but greatly appreciated is the attention the work pays to the phenomenal developments in the music of the last two decades. While in the final analysis the book does not claim to be the counterpart for popular music of *Grove's Dictionary of Music and Musicians*, it is one of the few books which attempts to deal with the whole spectrum of American popular music.

Stephen L. Hanson

AMERICAN BUFFALO

Author: David Mamet (1947–   )
Publisher: Grove Press (New York). 106 pp. $2.95 (paperback)
Type of work: Drama
Time: The present
Locale: Chicago

A tense, provocative drama about three men planning the robbery of a valuable coin collection

> Principal characters:
> DON DUBROW, a man in his late forties, the owner of "Don's Resale Shop"
> BOB, his young friend
> WALTER ("TEACH") COLE, a petty crook, Don's friend and associate

Ever since Samuel Beckett demonstrated with *Waiting for Godot* in 1954 that an intense exploration of a static situation, replacing the conventional causal plot, could not only be philosophically provocative, but dramatically exciting as well, the modern theater has been glutted with such "situational" or "metaphorical" plays, ranging in quality from unquestioned excellence to thorough mediocrity. Thus, the basic situation in *American Buffalo* has been exploited by a score of contemporary dramatists to the point that it has almost become a cliché.

Two or three men wait somewhere for something or to *do* something. While waiting, they fill the time with apparently aimless dialogue, act out their idiosyncrasies, and play "games" with themselves and their surroundings. Their concealed and not so concealed prejudices, dislikes, and perversities surface and clash with those of their associates; tension mounts as whatever they are waiting for fails to arrive or whatever they are to do becomes increasingly delayed, difficult, or unlikely. Eventually the conflicts either erupt into violence or nearviolence (Harold Pinter's *The Dumb Waiter* or *The Caretaker*) or they simply unwind and dissipate (as in Beckett's *Waiting for Godot* or *Endgame*).

To present such a play in 1977, twenty-five years after *Waiting for Godot*, required audacity leavened with folly. Not only to succeed, but to do so with originality in a form that would seem to be dried up, requires an exceptional talent indeed. Echoes of the contemporary masters—especially Pinter—are present, of course, but Mamet's vision and vocabulary are his own and *American Buffalo* is as fresh and unique a product as any on the recent American stage.

The primary reason for Mamet's success is probably that, while Absurdist ideas and techniques have been in the dramatic atmosphere for more than two decades, attempts to harness it to the American experience have been largely unsuccessful, Edward Albee's periodic forays into the area notwithstanding. David Mamet is really the first dramatist to weld the force of the situational play to the American environment with a characteristically American rhythm and diction (although two other fine young playwrights, David Rabe and Sam

Shepard, have utilized absurdist materials quite effectively. Rabe's plays are, however, more conventionally experimental and essentially realistic, while Shepard's are wildly powerful in language and image, but generally lack the focus needed for a coherent theatrical experience).

As in all effective examples of the situational approach, the setting of *American Buffalo* is crucial. Mamet's three would-be felons wait and plan in Don's Resale Shop, a crowded, messy junk shop that becomes a metaphor for the lives of those characters that inhabit it. Its claustrophobic density suggests their narrow, trapped lives. The various objects that are piled and jammed aimlessly together are all bits and pieces of the American culture turned to worthless scrap. These "things" (the word takes on ominous connotations during the play) have little present value, but retain the dangerous capacity to stimulate the thoughts, false expectations, and absurd dreams of these three sad men who sit amidst the clutter.

It is not stretching the metaphor too far to see the characters themselves as "junk objects," as individuals outside society, whose only connection to it lies in those distorted expectations and fantasies it induces. Perhaps such vague hopes and unlikely dreams can even have a positive value in such lives as they blunt the dismal reality of the bleak present and negative future. But, given the stimulus that opens up a glimmer of real possibility—however far-fetched—to these longings, they can potentially provoke violence and destruction. This is the simple dynamic that animates *American Buffalo*.

Don Dubrow, middle-aged owner of the salvage shop, discovers a gem in his trash, or, rather, has it discovered for him. A well-dressed stranger walks into his shop, spots a buffalo-head nickel and, after a short negotiation, buys it for ninety dollars. This sudden, amazing profit awakens Dubrow to the possibilities of coins. With his young friend and helper Bob, an addict painfully trying to stay clean, Dubrow develops a crude plan to rob the dealer of his entire collection. Uneasy about his dangerous project, he mentions it to another friend and "business associate," Walter "Teach" Cole, a petty crook and second-rate gambler. Teach quickly convinces Dubrow that the job is too complex and risky for Bob and so replaces him as the would-be thief.

Thus, the play in many ways resembles Pinter's *The Caretaker*, but with an emphasis and twist that makes it distinctly American. As in the Pinter play, an ambiguous, subtle relationship between two men is threatened by the intrusion of a third male figure, a volatile, manipulative character who would use and then sacrifice the others to his own needs and desires. The pending crime, however, makes the conflict more than simple manipulation; it becomes a test of all the individuals concerned. It also establishes a social and psychological context for the play that is distinctly American (as Pinter's work is distinctively British).

The relationship between Dubrow and Bob is undefined, but strong. Dubrow clearly enjoys his dominance over the younger man, and Bob expresses no resentment as a dutiful, subservient "gofer." He has a real need, both practical and emotional, for the older man, although the precise nature of the need is not clear: father and son? Lovers? Both? It is hard to say, but, whatever it is, Mamet is able to suggest a real emotional bond between them with a minimum of verbiage.

Teach is the dynamic center of the play (as is Davies in *The Caretaker*), a volatile, self-pitying, grandiose paranoic, whose mounting frustrations and desperate manipulations increasingly threaten to explode into violence. He is also a catalog of American clichés, prejudices, anxieties, dreams, and hates. A small-time sneak thief and chiseler, Teach sees himself as the epitome of the American system and defender of free enterprise, which he defines as the freedom to do whatever one wants in order to make a quick profit. He refers to his petty thefts as "business enterprises," and sees the coin collection as his one shot for success. Thus, the play becomes a kind of parody of the American Dream story, the Horatio Alger tale of success which goes to those daring enough to recognize and seize that sudden opportunity when it appears. But all three characters are comically inept as thieves; they are clowns, but desperate clowns. The real driving force behind their potential crime is not greed, but fear and hatred; fear that they are indeed thorough failures, and hatred toward the coin dealer for his success, the apparent ease with which he makes money, his snobbishness, his lifestyle, the sexiness of his girl friend.

As Teach's bragging becomes more extreme, his fears, cruelty, and suppressed violence become more overt and dangerous. His hostility, especially toward the mild and inoffensive Bob, intensifies; his paranoic fears become more open—he quakes whenever a police car passes by; and his ridiculous incapacities, as well as his own awareness of them, become more blatant and desperate. His irritation sharpens when Dubrow decides to bring in another crook, a slightly more skillful thief-gambler named Fletcher, actually to steal the collection. Teach's desperation and paranoia are made concrete when he produces a gun, and after the whole project is aborted (when Fletcher is mugged and hospitalized), his rage strikes out at Bob. He gets the sudden delusion that the mugging is fake and that Bob and Fletcher have somehow managed to steal the coin collection out from under him.

Teach's violence is, of course, a product of his frantic attempt to preserve his ludicrous self-image as a skillful, respectable "businessman" whose lack of material success can be attributed only to bad luck. This one job is vital to both Teach and Don because it will prove that they are not the mediocre failures that, inside themselves, they know they are. Put to the final test it is obvious that they lack both the intelligence and the nerve to carry out the robbery; they can turn their hostility only towards each other. Don is actually relieved by Fletcher's mishap, which both aborts their plans and gives them an excuse for it. But Teach, forced to a final acceptance of his failure, cracks completely. After hitting Bob he goes on a rampage, shouting and raging around the junkshop.

But if Teach is thoroughly broken, Don and Bob are somewhat restored and their relationship is repaired. Of the three, only Bob was never actually absorbed into the "dream." His willingness to attempt the crime, as well as his disappointment at being replaced by Teach, was a product of his devotion to Don, not his greed. On several occasions he attempts to borrow money from both Don and Teach. Knowing of his drug problem, we assume he wants it for dope. But in the end he produces a buffalo-head nickel for Don which, we learn, he has purchased. Seeing how the previous coin has become a symbol for Don, he tries to replace it. This final act of love forces Don to see how distorted his perceptions and values had become and enables him to come to terms with his failure. Thus, a modicum of meaning and dignity is salvaged from the fiasco.

All of which may not sound like the sort of tragic insight that great drama is made of. Admittedly the three characters in this play are neither admirable nor likable, although both Don and Bob have redeeming qualities. But—and this may be the special power of such a play—the audience identifies not so much with the characters as with their situations. The world of Don's Resale Shop is not an especially pleasant one, but, as Mamet presents it, a very real one. We feel the frustrations and fears of the characters and we can understand their inarticulate and even foolish dreams. By reducing the conflict between them to the most basic primal urges (fear, greed, frustration), reinforced by powerful cultural myths, underscored by a vivid setting and reinforced by a potent, almost incantory speech (liberally sprinkled with four-letter words) that sounds like "authentic" Chicago dialect, but has a simplicity, repetitiveness, and rhythm that is closer to dramatic verse, Mamet is able to draw us into this barren, squalid, primitive world for an impressive and lasting dramatic experience.

American Buffalo won the Drama Critics Circle Award as the best American play of the 1977 season.

Keith Neilson

ANDREW JACKSON AND THE COURSE OF AMERICAN EMPIRE, 1767-1821

Author: Robert V. Remini (1921–   )
Publisher: Harper & Row Publishers (New York). 502 pp. $15.00
Type of work: Biography
Time: 1767-1821
Locale: The United States

The first volume of a scholarly two-volume biography of one of the most important early American presidents

> Principal personages:
> ANDREW JACKSON, lawyer, judge, Tennessee politician, general
> RACHEL JACKSON, his wife
> WILLIAM BLOUNT, his early political friend
> JOHN COFFEE, his friend, business partner, and military associate
> AARON BURR, former Vice-President who led a conspiracy against the
>   United States government
> JOHN SEVIER, his early political rival
> JAMES MONROE, President of the United States, 1816-1824
> JOHN QUINCY ADAMS, U.S. Secretary of State during the Florida
>   conquest

Robert V. Remini is a Professor of History and Distinguished Professor of the Humanities at the University of Illinois, Chicago Circle. He is best known within the historical profession as a leading scholar of the Jacksonian Era. He has chronicled various aspects of Andrew Jackson's America, both as author and editor, in seven previous books. *Andrew Jackson and the Course of American Empire, 1767-1821* is the first volume of a two-volume biography of Jackson. With this work, Remini begins the first full-length scholarly biography of Jackson to appear in recent decades. The book is a signal work by a significant historian.

Andrew Jackson was born on March 15, 1767, the son of Scotch-Irish immigrant parents who had settled in the Waxhaw Settlement, South Carolina. He received his small amount of youthful education during the late 1770's. In 1780-1781 he served in the American Revolution, an experience marked by extreme difficulty; he was wounded, captured, and imprisoned. When released in an exchange of prisoners, his health had so deteriorated that he came down with the fearful smallpox, a disease that almost claimed his life. The tragedy was compounded by the 1781 death of his mother.

Yet, from these harried aspects of Jackson's youth emerged a man who would indeed be a towering figure in early United States history. After a brief career as a schoolteacher, Jackson studied law, and eventually became a licensed attorney. The legal profession gained for him entry into the world of the frontier courts, both as attorney and judge. More importantly, the law provided Jackson with significant opportunities to fulfill his single-minded ambition. He moved to Tennessee, where newer settlements meant opportunity for advancement, and became a gentleman in Tennessee society. He engaged (sometimes disastrously) in the massive land speculation that played such a key role in the Western territories, and he served Tennessee as representative and senator to the federal government. Like many other prominent Westerners, he was drawn into the famous Burr conspiracy, but he learned a valuable lesson when Burr's plot was unmasked—that Western interests could only be served with the backing of the United States.

To further those Western interests, which centered on elimination of the Spanish and Indian barriers to white American settlers, Jackson became an officer first in the Tennessee militia, later in the U.S. Army. He finally gained national prominence during the War of 1812. He conducted successful campaigns against the Creeks, and led American forces at the Battle of New Orleans. His victory at New Orleans assured him of a heroic place in American history. General Jackson was the winner in a climactic, epic battle during the war that fused American nationalism. National acclaim and gratitude were his. Jackson capped his military career during the years covered in this volume by "removing" major Indian groups from the old Southwest, and by securing Florida for the United States by invading that Spanish possession. Western interests had indeed been fulfilled, using the legitimate power of the Army.

Remini proves to be a historical traditionalist when constructing his description of Jackson's personality. He chooses not to employ any shaky theorizing from the recently developed field of psychohistory, although Jackson certainly is an inviting case to study. While acknowledging psychohistorical approaches in a footnote, Remini maintains the traditional approach to historical biography, by drawing his information from the extant primary sources. Readers will find little innovation in his study of Andrew Jackson's character. Remini describes—he does not theorize.

And Remini's descriptions of the Jackson personality are overly restrained to the point of distortion. The obvious profanity of Jackson's language is indicated, but Remini discreetly eliminates even low-key examples. In addition, Jackson's whiskey drinking is relegated to a footnote, except for vague references in the text. The author has stripped Jackson of a coarseness that was an essential part of the general's character.

Remini is more successful in presenting Jackson's boundless ambition, which was such a driving force in his early career. Remini also clearly shows Jackson's deliberate use of anger and rage (expletives deleted) to obtain the results he wanted. Feigned anger worked well in most situations, but real Jacksonian anger was not to be countered—nobody crossed Jackson when he had " 'shoot' blazing in his eyes." Yet, Jackson the firebrand had a strikingly different side to his personality, a side marked by genuine tenderness, warmth, and generosity. Remini reveals this aspect of the future president's makeup by quoting his letters to his wife and family, documents that show Jackson could be a truly gentle man. Remini also includes the story of an incident during the Creek War. While fighting what was clearly a war of extermination against his Indian foes, Jackson encountered an Indian infant in the arms of his dead mother on the battle site, and the destroyer of the Creeks adopted the baby boy. Remini satisfactorily presents the two sides of a personality which was complex, paradoxical, and contradictory.

Remini's volume is rich in the military history of the period. The battles of the Creek campaign, including the famous Battle of Horseshoe Bend, are reconstructed in vivid detail. The monumental Battle of New Orleans is given a properly expansive account, as is the campaign against Spanish Florida. In this respect, Remini contributes a significant, exciting book to the literature of military history through his study of a military man.

The author also unravels the evidence surrounding Rachel's date of divorce from a prior husband. Jackson and Rachel did begin a life together before she was legally divorced. Yet, the evidence suffered from the controversy about the divorce raised by Jackson's opponents during his presidential campaigns. Remini presents a reasoned account, outlines several alternative theories, and resolves this often-muddled question.

The biographer also includes useful geneological tables in the book, as well as maps which enhance the military accounts of the volume. The section of illustrations is well chosen.

The most significant contribution that Remini makes in this book lies in the realm of historical interpretation. He finds that the fortunes of Andrew Jackson and the early United States were clearly linked—that Jackson influenced for all time the direction and course of U.S. expansion on the North American continent. He demonstrates that Jackson was involved in the expansionist sentiments and politics that surged through the early American frontier areas. Indeed, Jackson's personal ambition placed him at the head of that movement. The War of 1812 proved to be crucial. Attempted expansion into the northern part of the continent—British Canada—never materialized, despite the fervor of "War Hawk" congressmen. Campaign after campaign was bungled by less-than-competent generals. After the Treaty of Ghent, which ended the war, the Canadian-United States border was finalized with the sole exception of "Oregon" in the extreme Pacific northwest. In effect, the War of 1812 and its aftermath barred United States territorial expansion to the north.

But the situation was very different in the old Southwest during the war. With Jackson at the head, the Army smashed organized Indian resistance to white American penetration and conquest. The Battle of New Orleans gave the United States its most important victory of the war. Jackson's postwar drive against Spanish Florida gained support in Washington. What Remini argues is that these Jacksonian triumphs set the course of future U.S. territorial expansion. While Canada was closed to American expansionism, the old Southwest was definitely open to U.S. advances. Jackson not only crushed the Indians, but broke the weak Spanish hold on Florida. Later, from his position of military strength, he negotiated huge cessions of Indian land to white American land speculators and settlers. After ending effective Indian resistance, Jackson "removed" the remnants of Indian settlements to territory west of the Mississippi River. United States territorial expansion would subsequently follow a westward rather than a northward path. The westward direction of American conquest was assured because victory against the "hated dons" and the "savages" had been demonstrated clearly and forcefully. Andrew Jackson had seen to that.

Edward A. Zivich

ANNE SEXTON
A Self-Portrait in Letters

Author: Anne Sexton (1928-1974)
Edited by Linda Gray Sexton and Lois Ames
Publisher: Houghton Mifflin Company (Boston). Illustrated. 433 pp. $15.00
Type of work: Letters
Time: 1928-1974
Locale: Newton Lower Falls and Weston, Massachusetts

A collection of the confessional poet's letters from 1948 to 1974 with editorial comment by her elder daughter and her close friend

Principal personages:
ANNE GRAY HARVEY SEXTON
ALFRED MULLER SEXTON II, her husband
LINDA GRAY SEXTON, her elder daughter
JOYCE LADD SEXTON, her younger daughter
ROBERT LOWELL, a poet, critic, teacher, and friend
GEORGE STARBUCK, a poet, critic, and associate at Boston University
W. D. SNODGRASS, a poet, critic, and friend
STANLEY KUNITZ, a poet, critic, and friend
JAMES DICKEY, a poet and critic
C. K. WILLIAMS, a poet and friend
MAXINE KUMIN, a poet, collaborator, and confidant

The hand that stilled the heart could not stifle the voice. Since Anne Sexton's suicide in 1974, the literary world has received a legacy in three posthumously published works. *The Awful Rowing Toward God* (1975) and *45 Mercy Street* (1976) complete her volumes of confessional poetry. But nothing has augmented her poetical gifts more than *Anne Sexton: A Self-Portrait in Letters* (1977) edited by Linda Gray Sexton, her elder daughter, and Lois Ames, her biographer. The letters themselves show the richness of Sexton's life as poet, critic, philosopher, friend, lover, wife, and mother. They show the complexities and difficulties of Sexton's playing all these roles in one brief lifetime of forty-six years.

Linda Gray Sexton, perhaps more than anyone else, knew her mother and shared her most intimate thoughts for twenty-one years. Linda was sometimes a mentor, sometimes a sounding board, often a cause for concern, but always an understander of "the language." This perception not only has made Linda Gray Sexton a poet in her own right, but it has made her a highly qualified editor of this collection.

Lois Ames, too, knew Anne Sexton well before her suicide. First introduced to her as Ames was searching for biographical information on Sylvia Plath, Ames became a correspondent, traveling companion, and confidante to Sexton, sharing the last nine years of her life. While Lois Ames and Linda Sexton's compiling this collection was obviously a "labor of love," it was more accurately an attempt to share with the literary world this very special woman with whom they were on such intimate terms.

The paradox of Anne Sexton's being so special is that in so many ways, she was so ordinary—a daughter anxious for parental approval, a mother delighted with and sometimes depressed by two daughters, a true wife (although she "loved" many people), a suburban housewife who pecked out the moments of her existence with two toddlers running in circles around her.

And yet, Sexton was far from ordinary. Her accomplishments include nine published volumes of poetry, a collection of letters, several children's books; the Pulitzer Prize in Poetry in 1967 for *Live or Die,* an honorary doctorate from Tufts University, Fairfield University, and Regis College; an honorary Phi Beta Kappa from Harvard and Radcliffe; a guest professorship at Colgate University; and a professorship at Boston University.

Sexton's friends and acquaintances are as extraordinary as her list of credits: Robert Lowell, George Starbuck, Maxine Kumin, Elizabeth Bishop, W. D. Snodgrass, Tillie Olsen, Anthony Hecht, Sylvia Plath, Ted Hughes, Louis Simpson, Kurt Vonnegut, Stanley Kunitz, and James Dickey. These people were among her best friends as well as her most severe critics. Vast numbers of letters attest to the special camaraderie Sexton shared with some, the special antipathy she had for others.

The attraction of Sexton is this unique blend of special and ordinary. She was the self-made woman who, with little "formal" education, was a professor at Boston University. She was simply a mother who found time to pour her soul into numerous volumes of poetry with children underfoot. She was a sharer of fragmentary thoughts and joys with those she loved and respected. She was open, very honest, and sometimes silly. Sexton was casual, conversational, and yet sometimes censorious simultaneously. This blend of so many polarities was the Sexton intrigue.

A large part of the Sexton mystique stems from her suicide itself, the constant wondering of "when" and "how," the desire to see precisely what went wrong and where. The mystique is the search through the letters and poems for clues to the tragedy of October of 1974. The end of *A Self-Portrait in Letters* is itself the answer. The suicide was deliberate, planned, a composite of many years of deciding on the tools. "But suicides have a special language./ Like carpenters they want to know *which tools.* They never ask *why build.*" ("Wanting to Die" from *Live or Die*).

And yet so much of Sexton's work is filled with life, a celebration of her own existence and the existence of others. Her letters are a testament to this. To a stranger in need of encouragement, a mental patient, Sexton writes, "So I say live, because of the sun, the dream, the excitable gift" ("Live" from *Live or Die*). Sexton observes life and blooming all around her and participates in that growth as in "Little Girl, My Stringbean, My Lovely Woman." "My daughter at eleven/ (almost twelve) is like a garden./ . . . where apples are beginning to swell./ . . . But what I want to say, darling,/ is that women are born twice." Not only is Sexton's love affair with death part of the intrigue, but so is her exuberant celebration of life.

These major themes of life and death are prevalent in her letters. While she rejoices at the rebirth of Linda and Joy at adolescence, the birth of eight Dalmatian puppies, the births of new collections of poems of W. D. Snodgrass *(Heart's Needle)* and C. K. Williams *(I Am the Bitter Name),* Sexton spends considerable time dwelling on the death of her mother ("The Division of Parts" from *To Bedlam and Part Way Back*), her father, Sylvia Plath, Joan Sexton, and herself.

Another major, related theme is illness, especially her own. Sexton gives detailed accounts of her hospitalizations for mental as well as physical problems: her dilation and curettage and her broken hip. She discusses her medication, Thorazine, which stifles her creativity and makes her sensitive to the sun she loves so much; her psychiatrists, Martin, Deitz, and Chase; and her close encounters with death. Many letters, especially those to closer friends such as Anne Clarke, a California psychiatrist introduced by Tillie Olsen, and W. D. Snodgrass, in early years, portray her deep depression and fears. Letters to Kayo Sexton written from Europe dwell on fears of being away from him, of not knowing what he is doing, of being in an unfamiliar environment. As Anne Sexton fluctuates between states of normalcy and illness, so her letters reflect it.

Many letters requesting love, encouragement, and help are inextricably bound to these mental states and represent another major motif in Sexton's correspondence. She begs for letters from her family to ease her loneliness as she tours Europe on a grant from the American Academy of Arts and Letters. She corresponds with James Dickey, hoping to learn the cause of his repudiation of her poetry. As books of poetry are about to be published, she writes to her poet-friends expressing anxiety, almost begging for reassurance that she is indeed a good writer. To unknown and known writers, she sends fan mail, the probable by-product of which is a complimentary letter in return. This is not to imply that she was ungenuine: she was totally honest, but also insecure.

Sexton was anxious about money, and her protests about her poverty become yet another prominent thread running through her correspondence. To George Starbuck she complains that she should be a full professor and not simply a lecturer at Boston University. To Thomas Alexander of Cape Cod Community College she comments that James Dickey received $900 for a poetry reading while she was offered $775. Sexton mentions that Houghton Mifflin pays her smaller advances than other poets and worries about a daughter ready to enter college. She argues with her psychiatrist, Dr. Chase, about a fee increase. This anxiety, too, contributes to her insecurity.

An additional major idea reappearing throughout Sexton's letters is that of faith. Her initial doubts are discussed with Brother Dennis Farrell, a fan from a California monastery with whom she developed a long relationship via letter. To Anne Clarke she writes "God? spend half time wooing R. Catholics who will pray *for* you in case it's true. Spend other half knowing there is certainly no

God." Sexton's ambivalence is evident as she expresses to Erica Jong the thought that no poem is written by any writer, no poem is singular, all is part of one vast poem written by God.

Sometimes Sexton is not so philosophical. Her thoughts are not of God, but of her swimming pool, her girls and summer camp, and her vacations with Kayo. She is just plain Mom. A significant amount of correspondence shows her in this role. She loves Linda, Joy, and Kayo. Letters are filled with the girls' antics and their importance to her. She advises them at camp by letter on every subject from birth control to psychiatric help. But always, Sexton's pet names, "Bobolink," "Linda Pie," "Joy Ball" hint at the extreme closeness of their relationships. Kayo, too, is "Boots" and she is his "Princess" and "Button." Theirs is a language of love and caring.

Life and death; her own illnesses; her need for love, encouragement, and help; her need for financial security; her reflections on God; and love of family are all major thrusts throughout Sexton's letters. Over and over again, through years of correspondence, these themes resound, reflecting her current mental, physical, emotional, and intellectual states. The abundance of major themes is suggestive of the variety of letters present in the collection.

The style of Sexton's correspondence, too, is varied. Letters are composed often of fragmentary sentences, sometimes incomplete in meaning. Ellipses follow many sentences, allowing the letter's recipient to supply the remainder. While this is sometimes difficult for the Sexton reader, it is not difficult for the Sexton friend who can predict her intimate thoughts. Letters to close friends rarely stay on a single subject or maintain an even tone. Their intent is to suggest Anne-sitting-at-her-typewriter-right-at-the-moment-talking-person-to-person, and they accomplish this goal. These familiar letters are filled with myriad misspellings and typographical errors, a Sexton stock-in-trade. Only after hiring a "girl Thursday" with money received from a grant do the letters become more readable to the outsider. Nevertheless, even dictated, the letters are still delightful.

To people with whom she has not yet established a correspondence, Sexton writes letters that are more complete and even in tone. She stays on a single train of thought more readily, but like in her letters to close friends she still reveals a significant portion of humor, love, respect, and craft. While these are the easier type of letter to read, they are not the more revealing.

The principal strength of this volume is that the correspondence does reflect Sexton's life intimately; the letters offer a look at her soul. Because they are chronologically arranged, one can see the progression of mental states, creativity, honors, love, and friendship. While the letters have been selected, they are in every sense complete, not even omitting details that are deprecatory or personal because these details are Anne Sexton. The goal of the editors is an objective presentation of Sexton's life and in this goal, they succeed. In addition, the reader is treated to a collection of photographs that spans Sexton's life, and can associate faces, names, and letters—the outcome of which is more personal interest and involvement in the volume.

An additional strength of *A Self-Portrait in Letters* is its inclusion of individual poems which greatly augment the text or serve to foreshadow a stage in the poet's life. For one who is not a Sexton reader, the poems are still sufficient to grasp the greatness of the poet. For one who is already familiar with her work, the poems recall the best of the best. The poetry is reprinted chronologically throughout the book of letters, and, juxtaposed with the letters, it becomes more meaningful.

Also accompanying the letters is thorough and excellent explanatory material that prefaces the major divisions of the book as well as some individual letters. When letters themselves do not reveal enough, Linda Sexton and Lois Ames supply the details, adding continuity to the volume. Hence, the reader does not get fragments, but a whole.

A further editing bonus is that Linda Sexton and Lois Ames have included in brackets within individual letters the titles of books in which specific poems being discussed are printed. This aids the Sexton researcher, as does the index, which is significant, comprehensive, and complete. It allows this collection to be a major text for students of confessional poets of the last three decades.

Linda Gray Sexton and Lois Ames have taken their craft seriously, a legacy they inherited from Anne Sexton.

> Writing a poem is a lonely thing, each word
> ripped out of us . . . and you know . . . and then
> later on the wrong things start to happen;
> you get to be fashionable or 'a new kind of
> orthodoxy' and the only way to prevent your-
> self from going sour or becoming an art climber
> is to go back to your desk.

Anne Sexton: A Self-Portrait in Letters has been back to the desk.

Carol Whyte Talabay

ANOTHER WORLD: 1897-1917

Author: Anthony Eden (1897-1977)
Publisher: Doubleday and Company (New York). Illustrated. 175 pp. $7.95
Type of work: Memoir
Time: 1897-1917
Locale: England, the Western Front

An account of Anthony Eden's childhood and experiences in World War I, as well as a tribute to the generation which suffered in the trenches of the Great War

Before his death in January, 1977, Anthony Eden composed a charming memoir of his earliest years and joined to it a sober rendition of his experiences as a young officer in World War I. The result, published posthumously as *Another World: 1897-1917*, offers an intimate glance at both the personal life of one of England's leading twentieth century politicians and an aristocratic way of life which is now as far in the past as the *Ancien Régime* of France. Eden's description of that life reminds one so much of Talleyrand's observation on eighteenth century France that it could be paraphrased to read, "No one who was not a member of the English upper class in pre-1914 Britain knows how sweet life can be." It was the catastrophe of World War I, along with more prosaic economic changes, which destroyed this world, and Eden is an example of how one of its most illustrious members faced the destruction of his civilization.

It is rare for a world leader to write with the tenderness and insight about his childhood which Eden does. When it happens, it is revealing about both the man and his country. In Eden's case it unveils a sense of humor, modesty, enthusiasm, innocence, discipline, and generosity. In fact, he comes across as an extremely sympathetic person. Those with an inclination to view life cynically might regard him as a bit of a do-gooder, while his stiff upper lip in the face of enormous personal and national loss appears almost inhuman, but all in all Sir Anthony Eden was one of the most natural and sensitive men ever to achieve supreme political leadership. The fact that a man with such qualities could be rewarded with the highest office of his country attests to the continuing English tradition of emphasizing human values as much as sheer power.

Eden's political career was not uniformly successful, and to his permanent disgrace, he left office in the wake of the humiliation of the forced retreat from Suez in 1956. The triumphs, though, outnumbered the defeats. Entering Parliament in 1923, he made a mark with his speeches on foreign policy and was soon rewarded with sub-Cabinet governmental positions. From this vantage point, he was able to participate in European diplomacy in the 1930's, building up a formidable expertise and firsthand contact. When Stanley Baldwin appointed him Foreign Secretary in 1935, he became the youngest man to hold that office since the eighteenth century.

Diplomacy in the 1930's was extremely contentious business, with unsavory Fascist dictators strutting on the stage, small East European states bickering about their borders, an uncertain and threatening Communist regime in Russia, and civil war in Spain. Eden's constant exposure to this mixture convinced him that England must stand firm and deal from strength, although he was not opposed to all negotiation. When Neville Chamberlain became Prime Minister and began acceding to the demands that Mussolini and Hitler were making without receiving any *quid pro quo,* his Foreign Secretary disagreed vehemently and resigned in protest in February, 1938. This was Eden's finest hour, and Winston Churchill later wrote, "he seemed to me at this moment to embody the life-hope of the British nation."

Eighteen months later, after war had broken out, Eden rejoined the cabinet. With Churchill's appointment as Prime Minister, he was elevated to Minister of War and then Foreign Secretary again. In this position, he worked extremely closely with the often irascible Churchill, and for six long years devoted himself heroically to the defense of his country. He fully supported the Prime Minister's emphasis on the American alliance, smoothed the path to wartime cooperation with the Soviet Union, and then tempered Churchill's enthusiasm for his Eastern ally as its postwar ambitions became more apparent. He was also instrumental in bringing France back into the war as a full-fledged member of the alliance. By all accounts, Sir Anthony was a gifted diplomat, and even figures as difficult to deal with as Charles de Gaulle paid him tribute.

The elections of July, 1945, brought the Labor party to power, and Eden stayed in opposition until the Conservatives came back in 1951. With Churchill still in command, Eden returned to the Foreign Office. From 1951 to 1955, he showed a deft hand by outwaiting the anti-British Mossadegh in Iran, re-negotiating with the Egyptians, and helping to terminate the French war in Indochina. In April, 1955, he became Prime Minister after Churchill turned the government over to him.

The complex Middle East situation grew more tangled in 1955 when the newly emergent Nasser signed an arms deal with Czechoslovakia. To retaliate, the United States and Great Britain withdrew their offer to fund the Aswan Dam project and Nasser in turn struck back by nationalizing the Suez canal in July, 1956. The canal was a vital link for British oil supplies and trade with India and the Far East; it was as sensitive an issue for Britain as the Panama Canal has been for the United States. In addition, drawing on his experience from the 1930's, Eden equated Nasser with Hitler and believed that a refusal to act would lead to a collapse of Britain's position in the world. As a result, he joined France and Israel in an attack on the Canal in October, 1956, but the hostility of the Superpowers forced all three to withdraw their forces. Faced with a recurrent intestinal illness, Eden resigned in January, 1957. In this way, the distinguished career of a statesman known for his morality and contributions to peace ended unhappily.

In *Another World: 1897–1917,* Sir Anthony Eden, Earl of Avon, returns to his childhood and young manhood and provides the background which places his years of political activity in perspective. His heritage was uncommon. On his father's side, the Edens had been landowners in County Durham for four centuries, a remarkable achievement which made Anthony feel the responsibility of upholding a tradition which would be tested during his lifetime more severely than at any point since the Napoleonic Wars. The Edens were no ordinary landowners, and their manor, Windlestone, was an enormous nineteenth century mansion situated in a beautiful park. Having the run of such a place was a delight to a young boy, and he describes in detail its world. Sir William Eden, Anthony's father, genuinely headed a small kingdom, with its numerous tenant farmers, laborers, woodsmen, craftsmen, blacksmiths, gardeners, and keepers of the stables and hounds. The agent who took care of financial matters was himself the brother of an Admiral, and there was an intimidating second-in-command who directed the foxhunts among other duties. The household staff, too, was quite an affair, with valets, cooks, butlers, chauffeurs, maids, nannies, and the governess "Doodles." His mother's side had the political connections. She was a Grey; her father had been Governor of Bengal; his uncle was the celebrated Lord Grey who had passed the Great Reform Bill of 1832, while Edward Grey, Foreign Secretary at the outbreak of World War I, was his mother's cousin. Reared in this environment, there could have been no doubt in Anthony Eden's mind about what the future might hold for him.

Yet, somehow, it did not go to his head. For one thing, his father was an unusual and apparently difficult man. He was an artist who spent much of his time buying paintings, and he frequented a set including the novelist George Moore and the painter Walter Sickert. He paid very little attention to his four sons and made Anthony feel that he was "a plodder of conventional ability and tolerable good looks, taking after my mother's family and not very exciting." Lady Eden, a beauty, also had trouble relating to her children. She was a believer in duty, founding a local hospital, visiting the tenants, and supporting old soldiers with generous gifts. Educated at Eton, Anthony Eden certainly enjoyed the best England could offer—wealth, connections, culture, and a moral sense of purpose. While he may not have received all the love he could have wanted, he was a happy child, close to his younger brother Nicholas and entranced by the world.

In the summer of 1914, though, war swept across Europe, and Eden, along with millions of other Englishmen, responded to the challenge with exemplary courage. His eldest brother, Jack, was killed in October, 1914, and Nicholas, only sixteen, went down with his destroyer at the Battle of Jutland. Anthony's third brother, Timothy, was interned in Germany the length of the war and his only uncle, Robin Grey, was shot down and put into solitary confinement because he was the cousin of the foreign secretary. To add to the family's bereavement, Sir William Eden died in 1915. (Anthony Eden's oldest son died in action in World War II.)

Such tragic loss is overwhelming, and one can only admire the stoic determination which animated men such as Eden. The second half of his short volume depicts the war as he knew it. World War I remains the pivotal historical experience of twentieth century Europe, and *Another World: 1897–1917* may be one of the last firsthand accounts of it which will be written. Although Eden's description does not have the demonic force of Robert Graves's *Goodbye to All That*, it does not minimize the brutality, confusion, and slaughter which were the hallmarks of the conflict. As befits a statesman, however, Eden brings some order to the telling of the experience.

The author left Eton a year early in the summer of 1915 to become an officer in a regiment. The following spring his platoon was sent to Flanders, where it was decimated in the battle of the Somme. Re-formed by new recruits, it spent a year in the trenches, where Eden participated in the Messines attack under General Plumer. He received the Military Cross for the rescue of a wounded comrade in no-man's-land, and in May, 1917, he was promoted to the staff at Second Army headquarters. For the most part, life at the front was a tedious routine, with the constant threat of death from snipers and shells, and combat restricted to risky patrols at night into no-man's-land. Once every six months or so the great offensives would be organized with hundreds of thousands of troops attacking the enemy lines. These were the periods of complete hell, when in a matter of days, if not hours, the strength of a company might be halved or worse. Like most in his generation, Eden felt the comradeship of arms strongly, calling it "the finest form of friendship." The war taught him the irrelevance of class distinctions; it tempered him, but left his illusions intact.

Eden's background, with its artistic as well as political influences, plus its infusion of duty, helped produce the morally upright, sensitive, and self-assured statesman who directed British foreign policy for two decades. It was the strength of his own character, though, which enabled him to withstand the shocks of World War I and emerge from it with a continued belief in the value of civilization and a readiness to lead the fight for it twenty years later.

Stuart Van Dyke, Jr.

ANPAO
An American Indian Odyssey

Author: Jamake Highwater
Publisher: J. B. Lippincott Company (Philadelphia). Illustrated. 256 pp. $8.95
Type of work: Folklore
Time: From the beginning to the present
Locale: North America

The story of Anpao, who wanders in search of his heritage so that he may attain wisdom and marry the maiden he loves

Principal characters:
WASICONG, a holy man who tells the story
ANPAO, an Indian boy who cannot remember his origins
KO-KO-MIK-E-IS, the girl he wishes to marry
OAPNA, Anpao's twin brother and mirror image; the other half of himself
THE MOON, estranged wife of the Sun
THE SUN, who loves beautiful women and has spoken for Ko-ko-mik-e-is
OLD MAN, creator of the visible universe
GRANDMOTHER SPIDER, who raised Anpao and Oapna
AMANA, a girl who saves Anpao's life
RAVEN, from whose people came the deer and buffalo
MORNING STAR, child of the Sun and the Moon
SMALLPOX, a missionary who brings death to the people
THE BIG KNIVES, who come from the east

Western civilization has long since lost its most basic heritage. Several thousand years ago the precursors of that civilization still lived in harmony with their universe and were as much an integral part of it as the stars or the grass. As millennium succeeded millennium and Western culture became more and more urbanized, giving greater attention to technological advancement, the links with origin were gradually severed. The universe required more interpreters and its interpreters became of necessity more sophisticated; in time it assumed an adversary role and was no longer a mystery to contemplate but a puzzle to be solved—and an entity to conquer as well. Mere acceptance of it was no longer possible.

Western man continues to invent tools of astonishing complexity in his search for final answers, but the universe tends to ignore him. Each solution has to be discarded in its turn and ultimate understanding remains elusive. That cheerfully iconoclastic observer of scientific achievement, Charles Fort, once observed that looking for a final answer to anything is like searching for a needle that was never lost in a haystack that isn't there. The essential truth of his remark is becoming more obvious to us. Although our endless research has brought about a vast increase in knowledge and material benefits, its dividends in terms of wisdom and human happiness are relatively obscure. Each fresh discovery carries with it the dual potential of technical advancement and widespread disaster; these dilemmas have proliferated until Western man finds himself living in a world of perpetual crisis, with his survival resting in precarious balance on a razor's edge of human frailty. It is a vicious circle from which he cannot escape.

This position is rendered more intolerable by long alienation from the need to live in harmony with a surrounding universe, and modern man now finds himself without an anchor. Religion, undermined by various discoveries, no longer affords the authority and support he once depended upon; and in many cases the replacements he has devised have closed the door to that refuge with grim finality. Modern man has become a stranger in his own universe, and he is homeless in the truest sense of the word. It is no wonder that loneliness and isolation are the demons that torment him.

Until quite recently, Western man has described those cultures which developed along lines other than his own as primitive. This is a misnomer, for all cultures are complex and highly developed, regardless of the course their development may have taken. While it is true that the effect of Western civilization upon cultures it considered primitive was often calamitous, verifying an obvious technological advantage, it has become evident to us that they were not inferior in any other way. It has also become increasingly clear that inheritors of Western culture are not as happy, or perhaps as fortunate in the human sense, as those of the cultures it has destroyed or assimilated. These vanishing peoples were consciously an integral part of a sentient and harmonious universe: they belonged to one another and to everything around them. Western man belongs only to himself or to his sociopolitical group and suffers from feelings of inadequacy; he has rejected the ancient concepts so long ago that he can no longer understand the nature of such cultures, though he envies them even as he destroys them.

In spite of the extent to which they have suffered at the hands of those who gradually conquered them, the Indians of what is now the continental United States were fortunate in many ways. They never found it necessary to concentrate themselves in urban developments or to organize themselves on a large scale; their technology was adequate for survival and for their social requirements; their warfare was limited and was a game that never proliferated into wholesale slaughter as we know it today. Their social organization had its catalog of restraints, codes, binding traditions, and customs, but they enjoyed a high level of personal freedom. Of greatest importance was their close relationship to the world around them. This link with the infinite has never been broken, although the destructive pressures of a civilization that has overrun their own are making inroads more and more difficult to resist.

Although the culture of the American Indian has had many recorders and interpreters among non-Indians during the past five centuries, such efforts have been in many ways inadequate. The author of a recent book on Frederic Remington states that the artist was a bigot, principally because Remington remarked that the white man would never understand the Indian. This is the sort of gratuitous accusation currently fashionable in intellectual circles, and it reveals an ignorance of both artist and subject. Remington's conclusion was both perceptive and honest, and any Indian would have agreed with him. He admired and respected the Indian for qualities of strength, intelligence, competence, and courage; that attitude is reflected in his work, for his portrayals of Indian warfare are graphic and impersonal, and when he shows us the Indian in defeat, he does so with implied compassion or regret. The same author goes on to mention other white artists who have studied Indian culture exhaustively and to equate their work with genuine understanding, but this is erroneous. Appreciation, admiration, and respect it is and should be; understanding, it is not.

It is never really possible for the inheritors of one culture to understand those of another. The effort to do so is of necessity superficial, however intensive or dedicated it may be. Hearn so steeped himself in Japanese culture that he considered himself to all intents and purposes a Samurai, but no authentic Samurai would have been deceived for a moment. The accumulated nuances of millennia are not assimilated in a decade or two. Eliot and James, endeavoring to be more British than the British, had the advantage of a partially shared heritage but even so were not entirely successful. Such assumed identities are at best an illusion. White men who lived with the Indians, intermarried with them and were adopted into the tribes, were accepted but never made any pretense that they were really a part of the culture. They enjoyed and appreciated the lifestyle and they learned a certain wisdom from it, but that was all.

If true understanding of the American Indian and his world is not entirely possible for outsiders, the reasonable approximation afforded through enjoyment and appreciation is well within our capabilities; and the best approach to any culture, if our goal is at least a partial understanding of the people themselves, is through its literature. This is the key to an entire heritage, and if the literary tradition is an oral one, it contains little that may be regarded as insignificant. The American Indians never found it necessary to develop a true written language, and the art of storytelling was an important part of their education. Although each gifted storyteller developed an individual style, the stories themselves remained essentially intact from one generation to the next; as in the case of Icelandic saga, everyone in the audience knew each tale by heart, and the teller was corrected if he strayed from accepted fact. Oral traditions of this kind often produce a people notable for the beauty and eloquence of their formal speech, and many white men have paid tribute to the oratorical and poetic powers of the Indian.

Ideally, one who interprets a literature should belong to those who produced it and should also be educated in the culture of those for whom it is being interpreted. Jamake Highwater is eminently qualified for such a task. His own tribal heritage is Blackfeet and Cherokee, and his degrees in cultural anthropology and comparative literature provide him with a broad basis for intercultural communication. An added bonus is the fact that he is a superb storyteller in his own right.

Anpao is a good collection of the traditional tales, retold by Highwater and arranged in roughly chronological order from ancient to modern. They are linked by the character Anpao, whose pilgrimage serves as a narrative thread which ties the stories together. Anpao is Highwater's own creation, but is so skillfully employed that he is not perceived by the reader as a superimposition. The tales themselves include samples of various literary categories, ranging from theology to history to humor; they are told with freshness and enthusiasm, and to read them is a delightful experience.

Highwater has provided a brief essay in the form of an appendix, entitled "The Storyteller's Farewell," which should be read first as an introduction to the tales. Although not necessary for enjoyment, it is essential to full appreciation of their significance and forms a very necessary bridge. In addition to discussion of sources and some evaluation of earlier collections, Highwater explains a number of elements that would otherwise be puzzling to the general reader. He also points out the impropriety of describing traditional literature as myth, a term that connotes lack of authenticity or presupposes an inferior spiritual concept.

The reader of *Anpao* will immediately recognize that sense of oneness with the total environment which has already been noted. To the Indian, the universe and all things in it are alive and sentient; all are closely related and there is communication between them. Most of the people Anpao meets during his journey are personalities who wear the forms of various animals, although some appear as natural forces. These entities provide him with knowledge, assistance, entertainment, and wisdom: through their guidance he traces the heritage of his people and, in the end, achieves his destiny and wins his heart's desire.

Most memorable of all the tales, perhaps, is that of the Creation. Old Man, who builds the visible universe, is not quite the great spirit who pervades all things but rather its focal point. He is motivated by curiosity and delighted with the things he invents, being both artist and experimenter, and he is not immortal. He ages as he continues to create, and many of his discoveries are accidental— among them death. His love for all creatures could not be better exemplified than in the special honor he confers upon that humblest of waterfowl, the coot.

Some of the stock characters in Indian literature have their counterparts in the folklore of other cultures, as might be expected. The most notable and amusing of these is Coyote, the wily and clever rogue who shares obvious affinities with Reynard the Fox. Coyote does not always fool the other person but he always makes the attempt; and even when the joke is on himself, Coyote remains optimistic and irrepressible.

Literature of the American Indian is an important part of our national heritage and deserves to be much more widely known and studied than it is. The work of Jamake Highwater will do much to correct that deficiency. He has already provided important bridges to other aspects of Indian culture: his first widely acclaimed book, *Song from the Earth,* explored contemporary Indian art and artists; a second major contribution, *Ritual of the Wind,* surveyed Indian music, ceremony, and dance. He has also published articles in various magazines. *Anpao* is an equally important introduction to the rich treasury of Indian literature and will, it is to be hoped, constitute the first volume of a series. In addition to its other merits, the book is handsomely and appropriately illustrated by the well-known Luiseno artist Fritz Scholder; however, the reader will wish that more of Scholder's artwork had been included.

It is not surprising that interest in American Indian culture is growing steadily among non-Indians, particularly the younger generation. Many, reacting to the pressures of a civilization that is increasingly less human, search for simpler and more natural ways to live. That they should investigate Indian crafts and lifestyles, and find them compatible, is not surprising. Perhaps in time they will even regain an approximation of that intimacy with the universe their culture enjoyed in the beginning, but abandoned so long ago.

Although understanding may never be complete, it can be much closer than it has been in the past. If Jamake Highwater continues his efforts and others take up the challenge he has provided, a much closer bond between the two peoples, red and white, may not be far away. The bridges are being built; if all are as revealing and as rewarding as this one, the traffic over them can only increase.

John W. Evans

ARREST SITTING BULL

Author: Douglas C. Jones (1924–   )
Publisher: Charles Scribner's Sons (New York). 249 pp. $8.95
Type of work: Novel
Time: December, 1890
Locale: Standing Rock Indian reservation, North Dakota

A novel which explores the nature of nineteenth century Indian and white violence, and the catalysts that incited it

> Principal characters:
> SITTING BULL, medicine chief of the Hunkpapa Sioux and veteran of Little Bighorn
> JAMES MCLAUGHLIN, career Indian agent in charge of Standing Rock
> WILLA MAE FAVORY, schoolteacher at Standing Rock day school
> STANDING ELK, a bright young agency policeman

Douglas C. Jones is the author of two earlier books, a factual work, *The Treaty of Medicine Lodge,* and a historical fantasy, *The Court-Martial of George Armstrong Custer.* In his current work he combines the meticulous research of the historian displayed in his first book with the literary flair and pace of his fantasy, to create the best kind of historical novel. Jones is a professional artist and journalist; these disciplines serve him well as he reconstructs each ambience with the eye of the artist and the ear and voice of the journalist—a happy amalgamation of talents.

Jones builds a flawless novel around the nucleus of the arrest of the recalcitrant Sitting Bull, the Sioux leader in the last days of the white man's war with the Indian. He molds, polishes, and defines characters who spin around the central act of the arrest, each personality a clear, believable part of the whole, each adding his bit of energy to the relentless vortex that is pulling a people toward disaster. The incidents fit neatly into the total story; each is a carefully measured and complete statement, adding to the plot as closely as stones mesh in a flagstone walk. The themes of displacement, alienation, ambition, frustration, rebellion, acculturation, and loyalty are dealt with realistically and with remarkable insight.

Billed on the dust jacket as a "spine-chilling novel of death and deception, of misunderstanding and bureaucratic bungling, of attempts at conciliation and of burning hatred—all of which combine to sow the seeds of disaster," it is certainly more than that; it is a study of the motives behind a conquered people's last desperate attempt to resist change, of white men and women unsuccessfully attempting to penetrate the mystique of the Indian by using the Anglo-Saxon measuring stick, of the Sioux' naïve attempt at blending their old beliefs with those promulgated by the Christian missionaries, of old enmities and loyalties, of the inner ideological struggle of the Indians serving as the white man's police force.

The time of the novel is December, 1890. There is unrest on the Indian reservations in the Dakotas. Seasons of drought have depleted the grain and cattle on the land to which the Indians have been assigned. The supplementary rations provided by the government have been drastically cut by a penny-pinching Congress in a classic case of bad timing. Anarchy rules on some reservations, and wily old Sitting Bull takes advantage of the situation to foster as much dissension and resentment as he can. He encourages the spread of the ghost dance, a virtual religion promising an Indian Messiah who will free them from the white oppressor. The old warrior has no faith in the cult, but he uses it as a convenient device to harass those in authority. He knows, too, that his stirring up of the ghost dancers may lead to his arrest, an action that he hopes will instigate violence on the part of his followers.

James McLaughlin, Indian agent at Standing Rock reservation, does all in his power and wisdom to head off an uprising, but he knows an explosion is inevitable. He plans to delay it by arresting Sitting Bull, for he knows only too well that the canker of rebellion is nourished by the old man's vitriol. Hastening the urgency of the arrest is General Nelson Miles, an Army officer insensitive to the wishes of the agent and the mood of the times. Miles wants to make the arrest his way, inviting unnecessary violence in so doing. McLaughlin must act summarily to prevent Army intervention; the arrest ends tragically in a way neither McLaughlin nor Sitting Bull had anticipated.

On one level this book is a fast-moving western with all the prerequisites, even an understated romance. On the more significant level, Jones makes the important statement that despite their overt differences, both Indian and white man share a common humanity—one of accomplishment and frustration, love and hate, heroism and weakness. He makes it clear that both are diminished by their condition; the white man is robbed of his morality as he robs the Indian of his identity.

Sitting Bull symbolizes man's violent response to loss of self-esteem through loss of dignity. His resistance to change, and the manifestation of that resistance, is treated with understanding—Old Bull's wily manipulation of his followers, his realistic assessment of conditions but refusal to accept them, have earned the grudging respect of the author. Jones sees both sides of issues and does not lose his perspective. While Sitting Bull does loom large in the narrative, it is those around him who are more memorable.

Agent James McLaughlin typifies the ideal government employee, a bureaucrat in the better sense of the word. Called "Whitehair" by the Indians who respect age and wisdom, he is recognized as firm but fair, and even loved by some. McLaughlin knows that he is more than the voice and hand of the Bureau of Indian Affairs; in his own eyes, and those of the people, he has proved himself a friend. A career employee of the Department of the Interior, he has been with the Bureau most of his adult life, surviving changes of administration because he is good at his job. Like anyone involved with topheavy management, he is frequently frustrated by the workings of bureaucracy. One of his keenest annoyances is the tendency of top level politicians in the Bureau to play it safe, and let the Army solve militarily what the Indian Bureau should be doing for itself. Jones has McLaughlin rant, "These gutless bureaucrats . . . . Pass the buck . . . . The Army, the Army, the Army, at the first sign of discontent on the reservations." He always points out that, ":You have to keep soldiers and warrior societies apart. When they rub together, you must expect a little disaster now and again."

McLaughlin feels that the ghost dance will run its course, and the Indians will cause no problem, if there is no intervention. It is to the south, where political appointees have caused things to get out of hand, that there is trouble, not at Standing Rock. Jones sums up McLaughlin's attitude: "Even as President Benjamin Harrison sends troops into the reservations to the south and the newspapermen flock there and the politicians wring their hands, Standing Rock remains the domain of Whitehair. His Indians know it and so does the Fort Yates commander, Colonel Drum." Unfortunately General Miles does not see it that way. The character of McLaughlin rings true. He is not Solomon, but he is wise; he is human enough to grit his teeth in annoyance when his Indian policemen refer to Sitting Bull as "Old Uncle," despite the fact he is aware that is what they call most older men in the tribe; he rails at bureaucrats even though he is one himself; he enjoys making pompous Buffalo Bill Cody look silly, and foiling General Miles.

Willa Mae Favory, agency schoolteacher, is depicted as finding her solace in religion, but not fanatically so; she is aware of an undefined lack in her life; she has never had the reassurance and support of family ties. Her father, a widower and a career sergeant in the Tenth Cavalry, had taken her with him from post to post—the only real warmth she remembers is a period in her childhood when the troopers under her father's command played with her, made toys for her, and generally spoiled her, as soldiers away from home have always done. At age twenty-nine she applied for a teaching position with the Indian Bureau and was assigned to the Standing Rock day school. The reservation was the home of the Hunkpapa Sioux and of their chief, Sitting Bull. Soon after her arrival in the summer of 1890, she realized she had moved into a gathering storm of rebellion. Willa Mae does not really understand the Indians, although she has lived among them as long as she can remember; she cannot measure their actions and motives by any but her own standards and background. Jones makes clear her inability to assess the essential truth of her relationship with them—she fails to understand that people so savage in war can at the same time be so considerate of another's feelings, that their apparent deception may be a desire to avoid offending. Willa Mae is puzzled by her reaction to young Standing Elk, an agency policeman who comes to her to learn to read and write; she does not recognize love, for she has never experienced it. Willa Mae and Standing Elk provide the tentative, barely suggested romantic interest—a welcome softening of the edges of what is, by design, a lean, hard, spare narrative.

Standing Elk himself comes through as an essentially tragic figure, a symbol of innocence and human dignity trying to accept the restrictive forces about him without denying his heritage. He recognizes the greatness in Sitting Bull, yet he realizes that some of the greatness has been created in the minds of the Sioux by the old man himself. He recalls the songs and stories of his childhood that soothed him and made him feel secure. Now they come to trouble him, no longer pointing the way, for they have become riddles. He recalls the legend of the pipe woman who came from the sky, warning the warriors that no one could smoke the pipe if he had murdered another Sioux, yet he knows many who have murdered their brothers and still smoke the pipe. Even as the stories of the old ones confuse him and make him feel alienated, he wonders at the white man's religion; it does not show much evidence of consistency, either. Standing Elk senses that his contentment is increasingly threatened by his exposure to the white man's mores and the reading lessons, lessons that tell him about things he must think out, somehow. He does not know how to deal with his own frustrations; Standing Elk, white man's policeman, attracted to a white woman, finds himself still emotionally tied to the old way of life, afraid to go near the ghost dance for fear of being affected by it, afraid to be in the presence of Sitting Bull, for fear the old man's magnetism may cause him to be drawn away from Whitehair. He agonizes, "I do not think my spirit is ready yet to become a white man." Ironically, when he dies, it is carrying out a white man's orders and at the hands of one of his own people.

Standing Elk's death presents a moral problem for another Sioux. Old Gall, a convert and an Episcopalian to the best of his understanding, secretly buries Standing Elk with traditional Sioux ritual, his love for the young warrior winning out over his newfound religion and his loyalty to Whitehair. The personality of Gall, who fought at Little Bighorn along with Sitting Bull, is the antithesis of that of the old dissident; through these two aging warriors, Jones clearly defines the extremes of response by the Indian to the encroachment of the white man.

Gall's burial of Standing Elk gives an excellent detailed picture of traditional Plains Indian rites; the chapter dealing with the burial is one of the most moving sections of the book. There is detail and symbolism in the account—the use of the old doeskin jacket, brittle old moccasins, fringed leggings, all treasured things from Gall's past, placed on the body along with a loincloth of trader's blanket and the elaborate headdress given to Gall by the agent; he no longer has need for these things. The old man pulls the hide from the cabin door. "It is the only thing left of the buffalo," he says, as he and his wife wrap Standing Elk's ceremonially garbed body in the robe. Young Standing Elk, whose spirit was not ready to be a white man, is laid to rest as he would have wanted to be.

Despite earlier qualms, once the burial is completed Gall is at peace with himself; he is glad of the evidence of Standing Elk's courage—the pistol in the dead man's hand had been empty, the wounds in his body were in front. Jones develops the poignancy of such an experience. With a vestige of the old warrior still apparent, Gall thinks, "That is a good way to die. Dying with one's face toward one's enemies." Gall soliloquizes:

> What I have done is good, as well. Whitehair will have to know. What is important has already been done . . . the funeral conducted as it would have been in the old days. . . . And now I stand before the white man's God. He will forgive me. . . . But even without that there is a goodness within me. . . . As if my fathers were smiling down on me. . . . There is a feeling like the old days, when we ate buffalo tongues and fought the Crow and killed Custer at Greasy Grass. It is hard to come completely away from those times.

There are subordinate characters who exemplify types that shaped the history of the period; standing out among them are General Nelson Miles and Sergeant McSweeney. Miles typifies the rigid military mind, a man in the position of authority who yields to a sense of power and forces his methods on others. He wants action, and he will get it if he has to go to the top to procure it; arrogantly contemptuous of politicians, he uses them, nonetheless, to gain his ends. Foiled in the first attempt to force his will on McLaughlin, he plans to strike again, totally unable to understand the possible consequences of his arbitrary decision. Miles is unable to relate to Sitting Bull's refusal to relinquish his code under pressure, not able to understand that the motivation behind the old warrior's stance is one of maintaining his dignity—living by that code, or dying by it, if need be. In his own way, Miles is as unyielding as Sitting Bull; the two are more alike than either would believe. A more sympathetic treatment of the military is presented in the vignette of Sergeant Major McSweeney. A tough, earthy, responsible man with pride in his cavalry outfit, he is everywhere; shaping up the troops, settling their brawls, cursing or encouraging the men as the need arises.

This book is as instructive as it is entertaining. The author's sense of drama makes history live, breathe, and speak. The past becomes as clear and vital, and sometimes more credible, than the present, in this highly successful view of a complex period in our nation's history.

Mae Woods Bell

BLACK JACK
The Life and Times of John J. Pershing

Author: Frank E. Vandiver (1925–   )
Publisher: Texas A&M University Press (College Station). 2 vols. Illustrated. 1,178 pp.
$35.00
Type of work: Biography
Time: 1860–1948
Locale: The United States, the Philippines, Japan, Manchuria, Mexico, and France

Although considerable attention is given to Pershing's relationships with family and friends, the focus of this minutely detailed biography is on his military exploits

Principal personages:
JOHN J. PERSHING, Commander-in-Chief, American Expeditionary Forces, 1917–1919
FRANCES WARREN PERSHING, his wife
FRANCIS EMORY WARREN, his father-in-law and United States Senator from Wyoming, 1890–1893 and 1895–1929

By any quantitative measurement *Black Jack: The Life and Times of John J. Pershing* is a monumental biography. Eleven hundred pages of text describe a life that spanned eighty-eight years, almost half of which were devoted to active service in the United States Army. Frank E. Vandiver spent eighteen years in research and writing about his subject. His bibliography, which runs to twenty-four pages, includes an impressive list of unpublished sources. Vandiver acknowledges by name over one hundred and eighty people who at various stages of the project lent assistance. It is hard to imagine that any scholar will soon attempt to duplicate this effort.

Despite these impressive credentials, *Black Jack* is on balance a disappointment. It tries too hard to be magisterial. The attempt fails because there is insufficient grist in Pershing's life to merit a multivolume study. Longevity notwithstanding, Pershing's fame is anchored almost entirely in two events: the Punitive Expedition against Pancho Villa in 1916–1917 and the United States participation in World War I. The Punitive Expedition, while interesting, was a military failure. It is generally considered today as one of those bizarre episodes that marked American imperialism in the twilight of the Monroe Doctrine. As for World War I, it must be kept in mind that the direct American military contribution to the Allied war effort was slight. American troops were present in force only during the last half year of the fighting. Thus it seems fair to conclude that the basis of Pershing's fame is highly confined. That Black Jack became a hero to his age reflects more on the needs of that age than it does on Pershing.

All of which is not to say that Pershing is undeserving of serious investigation. The essential point is that the substance of his life does not warrant Vandiver's extended treatment. It hardly seems necessary to devote the first third of this biography to a career that appeared to be dead-ended in the rank of captain. Yet it is not until page 402 that the reader is told that Pershing's jump promotion to brigadier general has been confirmed by the Senate. One of the unfortunate results of this expansiveness is that much of the writing is excessive. One suspects that Vandiver has employed conspicuous language to compensate for a lack of inherent significance in Pershing's early career. In any event, words such as "thrilled," "zestful," and "throbbed" abound. "Glee" and "gleeful," the worst offenders, appear dozens of times. This tendency toward overwriting is most evident in descriptions of Pershing's private life. One example will suffice to illustrate the problem. The setting is Zamboanga, the Philippines. Pershing's wife, Frankie, has just surveyed the family's residence on the military base. Her reaction is described as follows:

> An obvious advantage teased Frankie's femininity. The house shrieked for renovation. As her eye swept the maze of rooms, Frankie's fancies soared—endless changes beckoned. Clearly care had been lavished in creating this dowdy edifice, but additions and remodelings had spoiled an old simplicity. The place now brooded in slovenly pretension.

In addition to a distracting wordiness, the narrative also suffers from misleading generalization. Vandiver writes, for example, that prior to the outbreak of the Spanish-American War Spanish officials were puzzled by the hostility of the United States. Since Spain had conceded autonomy to Cuba in November, 1897, these officials could only conclude that the United States "simply spoiled for a fight." This observation neglects the very important fact that "autonomy" was a sham, known to be so by the Spanish as well as the Cubans and Americans. The Spanish concession excluded control over all matters relating to the military, foreign affairs, and the administration of justice. Thus the conflict between Spain and her colony (and ultimately the United States) after November, 1897, was substantial rather than casual and largely emotional, as Vandiver implies. His treatment of Woodrow Wilson is equally defective. Any serious student of Wilson will wince at the following assessment: "With a zealot's simplistic eye, he saw government as moral trust, denied the need for political maneuver." Later on, and less justifiable still, Vandiver compares Wilson's optimism with that of Candide. The suggestion of such similarity is, at the very least, gratuitous. What is particularly disturbing about the foregoing examples is that they suggest a greater concern for verve than for accuracy.

If one is willing to take the time and effort, important information about Pershing can be gleaned from the detail provided by the author. A particularly decisive moment in Black Jack's career came in 1901. After moving laterally through a variety of assignments since his graduation from West Point, he was sent to the Philippines where he demonstrated considerable perception in volunteering to lead a pacification mission in Mindanao, home of the wild Moros. Mindanao was far from the amenities of Manila and thus considered by most an unattractive assignment. Pershing, however, shrewdly calculated that Mindanao offered a likely prospect of military action, action that promised visibility. His technique in pacifying the Moros displayed solid common sense. Less truculent natives were separated from the "hostiles" by offers of protection and even-handed justice. The intransigents that remained were then sought out and subdued. Pershing's efforts were made easier by the Moro habit of making last-ditch stands from primitive forts where their swords and rifles were no match for the army's artillery. Hand-to-hand combat was mainly avoided, with the result that few Americans were seriously wounded or killed.

Pershing's initial exploits in Mindanao (he subsequently returned as commander of the Department of Mindanao and governor of Moro Province) were instrumental in his dramatic promotion to brigadier general. In the absence of more exciting action elsewhere, Pershing's successful forays against a barely civilized people in an exotic part of the world attracted attention. Even President Roosevelt took note. This fame, combined with the influence of Senator Francis Warren, Pershing's father-in-law and chairman of the Senate Military Affairs Committee, was sufficient to obtain a much sought-after promotion from captain to brigadier general. Such leapfrogging, while not unprecedented, was unusual. Raised eyebrows and jealous recriminations notwithstanding, the promotion was confirmed by the Senate. Without this stroke of good fortune it is doubtful that Pershing would have received the command position that he needed to demonstrate his ability.

The second volume of the biography is dominated by Pershing in the role of Commander-in-Chief of American Expeditionary Forces in Europe. The period from the spring of 1917 to the spring of 1919 witnessed the apogee of Pershing's long career in the military. Vandiver writes this section with a surer hand than elsewhere. The quiet strengths of Pershing's character are revealed by the pressures of fighting a determined foe and cooperating with headstrong allies. In order to prepare American recruits for a combat role as quickly as possible, Pershing shuffled personnel, conducted on-site inspections, and listened without prejudice to criticism. Meanwhile he struggled with the French and British on issues of strategy. Generals Foch, Pétain, and Haig worked tirelessly to persuade Pershing to permit the assimilation of American units into their armies. He resisted all of their blandishments, and, when sufficient numbers of doughboys were ready for battle, they joined the conflict as a separate force. While Belleau Wood, Château-Thierry and Saint Mihiel came late in the war, the results of those engagements removed any doubt about the quality of American soldiers.

Vandiver's coverage of the remainder of Pershing's life is mercifully brief. After the signing of the Armistice, ceremonial duties increased enormously. There were celebrations to be attended and monuments to be dedicated. Although Pershing became Chief of Staff, a position that he coveted, in 1921, the glory days passed with the war. In subsequent years he devoted much time to the American Battle Monuments Commission. But by the late 1930's he had become chronically ill and infirm. After lingering through another war—one which he was powerless to affect—Pershing died in 1948.

Upon reaching page 1,097 of *Black Jack*, this critic was convinced that a biography half that length could have been much more successful. By including too much material, some of which is extraneous and distracting, Vandiver fails to delineate a three-dimensional personality. With the possible exception of the period of World War I, Pershing seems to pass through his life leaving only surface impressions behind. In the final analysis, *Black Jack* demonstrates the proposition that in biography detail is an inadequate substitute for definition.

Meredith William Berg

BLACK ORCHID

Authors: Nicholas Meyer and Barry Jay Kaplan
Publisher: The Dial Press (New York). 310 pp. $8.95
Type of work: Novel
Time: The late 1800's
Locale: Manaus, Brazil, along the Amazon River

An adventure novel centering around Harry Kincaid's attempt singlehandedly to break the Brazilian monopoly on rubber by smuggling out some seeds

> *Principal characters:*
> HARRY KINCAID, a cynical adventurer
> PROFESSOR LONGFORD, his companion, a botanist disguised as his valet
> PIERRE COUTARD, the foppish, dissipated heir to a rubber fortune rivaling that of the Mendonças
> MERCEDES COUTARD, Pierre's sister, the cold, ruthless power behind the throne
> COLONEL ARMANDO MENDONÇA, a dying rubber magnate trying to keep his empire together
> DOLORES MENDONÇA, his headstrong daughter, bethrothed to Pierre Coutard but in love with Harry Kincaid
> IQUITOS, an Indian reared by Colonel Mendonça

Nicholas Meyer and his co-author Barry Jay Kaplan are popular novelists. Nicholas Meyer is the better-known, having recently written *The Seven-Per-Cent Solution* and *The West End Horror*. Before coauthoring *The Black Orchid*, Barry Jay Kaplan had written and published numerous romances and gothic novels under various pen names. Both authors are thus well equipped for this present task—the creation of a historical potboiler which presents itself firmly as light reading and looks fondly toward film sale.

The *donnée* of this adventure story is its Brazilian setting—the city of Manaus, the center of the late nineteenth century rubber monopoly, and the adjoining Amazon River. Manaus is truly extraordinary—the result of the attempt of suddenly rich rubber magnates to create a European city and culture on the sweltering banks of the Amazon. Electric trains, copies of European architecture, an opera house, and cobblestone streets are part of the physical imitation; fashionable clothing, French food, and the latest dances are part of the cultural. Everything—the marble, the food, the cobblestones—must be imported. And the effort is a gigantic failure, a case of substance without spirit.

The phenomenon of Manaus is by no means treated seriously. In fact, the details seem conveniently woven into the novel from note cards gathered specifically for the purpose: "The Hobby Horse Quadrille (the latest New York rage) was succeeded by the Alice Wonderland Quadrille, which was in turn supplanted by the first waltz of the evening, regarded as slightly daring in Manaus." This short passage taken from the costume ball scene is one of many examples of pointless attention to detail. It is bad enough that it is unconnected with plot or character; it is worse that it makes little sense to call a waltz "slightly daring" in a society as dissipated as that of Manaus. The authors know the names of some popular dances; they know that the initiation of the waltz created a mild sensation in Europe. Mindlessly, they combine these facts into a pointless and inappropriate sentence. It is this continual name-dropping which is, in fact, the novel's chief means of suggesting historicity.

The defender of light adventure fiction might well answer that such name-dropping is a harmless, painless method of education: a bit of history has been woven into an exciting format. One may be permitted some doubts. The authors have not attempted to give history life, but have used history for their own melodramatic purposes by making "free with events and dates, telescoping time willy-nilly." And one wonders too whether the details are really accurate, or just seem so. When we are asked to eat in a "formal *salle à manager*" or to heed to the views of *"grandes homens,"* we may well be taken aback. If the other details of the novel are as uneven as the authors' French, perhaps none are reliable.

The City of Manaus is the centerpiece of the novel, but the Amazon River dominates the opening scene as well as the exciting close of the story. In their use of the river, the authors are far more successful in integrating setting and plot. The size and menace of the Amazon are effectively conveyed. One can feel the stifling heat, the constant annoyance of insects, and the incredible width of the river. The menace of the Amazon is also very clear: alligators, piranhas, killer ants, and the thick jungle that reaches to the water. The climax of the book—a chase down the river—weaves all of these elements into an exciting, suspenseful series of episodes. Of course, even in this, the novel's climax, some may entertain skepticism concerning the authors' true inventiveness. They trot out a piranha episode, an attack by killer ants, and so on, in faithful sequence, almost as if they were following a list entitled "useful melodramatic dangers."

If the novel's setting is largely original, the characters are largely stereotyped and threadbare. At the center of the novel is Harry Kincaid, an American adventurer in his mid-forties starting out on what he hopes will be a profitable last adventure—breaking the Brazilian rubber monopoly by the smuggling of rubber seeds for germination in English hothouses and later transplantation in Malaya. He is entirely cynical; when offered a better price, he is quite willing to betray his original employers. In one of the novel's few attempts at wit, Harry, attending a costume party in evening dress, is twitted about being out of costume. "Oh, but I am," Kincaid countered . . . . "I'm here disguised as a gentleman." Near the novel's end Harry decides to bury his companion-in-adventure, Longford, killed in a horrible accident. High motives are ascribed to him, but Harry knows better: "he had insisted on the burial not because his feelings for Longford were so great, but because they were so little." Finally, in a blinding flash of synthetic insight, he realizes that he is "imitating a human being . . . his entire existence (is) nothing more than a sustained attempt to flee from his own absence."

Nothing of this fashionable cynicism prevents Kincaid from being an adventurer who earns the admiration of friends and enemies for his skill at his chosen trade. He thinks of every eventuality. For example, when he realizes that a hydrogen balloon has the ability to track the vessel in which he plans to escape, he cuts it from its moorings on the fateful night. When he rows back alone to send an encoded cable, he immediately afterwards cuts the cable line, but in two places—one visible, the other hard to find. Moreover, his prowess is not limited to adventure, but also includes romance. An otherwise unapproachable dancer yields to him with few preliminaries. Both of the novel's heroines seduce him.

To some extent, the novel is built on fantasies of seduction. Partly these fantasies are male-oriented. Harry is irresistible; women, despite their better instincts, throw themselves at him. Of these fantasies Harry's relationship with Dolores Mendonça is the apotheosis. She develops a schoolgirl crush on him that disappears when she realizes his true purpose in Manaus. Nevertheless, ultimately her knowledge of his true character awakens in her a passion far deeper and far less eradicable than the first. But the novel's fantasies are not entirely male-oriented. Dolores and her sister-heroine, Mercedes Coutard, are not the wispy, receding heroines of romantic fiction. Mercedes is ruthless and aggressive; Dolores becomes ruthless and aggressive as the novel progresses. Thus we have fantasies created to please not only male readers but female readers who like to think of themselves as assertive but not unfeminine.

Male-female relationships, however, are only peripheral to the plot of *Black Orchid;* central to it is the fantasy of a single adventurer pitted against the collective power of the rubber barons: Colonel Mendonça and Mercedes Coutard. Mercedes, realizing that Colonel Mendonça is old and dying, anxiously plans to gather all power for herself. In pursuit of this end, she organizes a civil war to destroy the Colonel's rubber plantation. The Colonel, equally ruthless, but obviously in the old style, proposes a marriage between the Coutard and the Mendonça families as a way of bringing a final and lasting peace. Both of these schemers—Miss Coutard and Mendonça—are equally reprehensible because their power rests entirely on the virtual enslavement of the Indian population on whose misery the splendor of Manaus depends. But if the reader thinks that this novel is going to offer him a special insight into the workings of power, the injustices it perpetrates, and the means of dealing with it, he is mistaken. Social injustice and corporate power are introduced only to foster melodramatic encounters between the lone adventurer and the forces bent on destroying him.

In the end, *Black Orchid* is not a novel of character or of atmosphere but of plot. On reflection, this plot may seem mechanical; much of it can be anticipated. However, there is no denying the sheer ingenuity with which the authors arrange the novel's incidents. Let one example suffice. An aerial balloon is introduced quite naturally as a tourist attraction at the rubber convention. Surely, the reader thinks, the balloon must be an important prop in the plot. This impression is confirmed when Harry Kincaid takes a well-planned and thoughtful ride in the device. However, the reader's expectations are defeated. During the costume ball, the balloon is noticed, rising, freed from its moorings. This is Harry Kincaid's doing, but the balloon is not a direct part of his escape plan. Harry, forever ingenious, has realized that the vehicle could be used to track the steam yacht in which he escapes. We are suitably impressed by Harry's skill and by the authors' also; they have surprised us in any ingenious way.

One would like to feel that *Black Orchid* could stand by itself as an interesting light fiction on the strength of its exotic setting and its mechanical and exciting plot. It should then make no difference that the book is little more than a motion picture scenario, slightly fleshed out. Why should we ask more of it than of the film it yearns to be? Precisely because it is a novel, and, in the nature of things, we expect more of a novel than of a motion picture. Adventure films can be enjoyably watched in a state of diminished attention, while *Black Orchid* demands our full attention. Nevertheless it gives us little in return because it is not so much written as manufactured. It insults the cultivated reader and provides strong evidence to those concerned about a general debasement of taste.

Alan G. Gross

BLIND DATE

Author: Jerzy Kosinski (1933–   )
Publisher: Houghton Mifflin Company (Boston). 236 pp. $8.95
Type of work: Novel
Time: The present
Locale: International

The chronicle of the adventures of George Levanter, a modern picaro who uses disinterested, diabolical cleverness to outwit his antagonists

Principal characters:

> GEORGE LEVANTER, a private investor who travels in search of business, adventure, and romance
> PAULINE, his last lover, a famous concert pianist
> JACQUES MONOD, his friend, a dying scientist
> ROMARKIN, his friend from school days in Russia
> SERENA, his lover, a high-priced prostitute
> FOXY LADY, another lover, a transsexual
> MARY-JANE KIRKLAND, his short-lived wife, a rich heiress
> OSCAR, a young rapist

Readers of Kosinski's *Blind Date* will not be surprised to discover the same heights of stylistic achievement as well as the familiar depths of sexual perversion that critics have praised and damned since the appearance of his first work, *The Painted Bird* (1965). *Steps* (1968), *Being There* (1971), *The Devil Tree* (1973), and *Cockpit* (1975) all portray a terrifying vision of a world dominated by barbarism, sadomasochism, and violence; Kosinski's art reveals itself not in his endless chapters of scenic cruelty but, in the manner in which he arranges, conveys, and describes these experiences to the reader to achieve maximum dramatic impact.

George Levanter, *Blind Date*'s protagonist, is a private investor whose business ventures take him from Russia to New York, from the Alps to Los Angeles; however, his East European heritage, especially the trauma of being a Russian Jew in Nazi Germany, constantly surfaces into his consciousness. Levanter has clearly descended from the ten-year-old boy of *The Painted Bird* (a victim of World War II Nazi atrocities), "Chance," the main character of *Being There,* and Tarden, *Cockpit*'s antihero. All these heroes are individuals who learn quickly to survive in a world devoid of justice and morality. As a result, Levanter lives as a picaresque con-man whose good and evil acts are purely serendipitous. Early in the novel, he blackmails a despicable corporate chairman; shortly thereafter, he becomes victimized by the prosecutor of a divorce case. Chance, not justice, prevails.

Levanter is a picaro in both the traditional and modern sense. Like Gil Blas, he is a rogue, but unlike Le Sage's protagonist, he does not come from a low social level. He deals with people from all classes and different locations and quickly learns their foibles and frailties. Kosinski's picaro also bypasses the line between petty rascal and criminal which places him in the distinct American picaresque tradition initiated by Herman Melville's *The Confidence Man*. Like Melville's work, *Blind Date* often surpasses the satiric humor of the traditional picaresque rascal and progresses into pure vitriol and pessimism; the laughing is replaced by horror.

The picaresque hero defines the book's structure: a loosely connected series of adventures, many quite impossible to conceive as happening in one man's life, with a cumulative effect rather than a resolving conclusion. Levanter's journeys have no goal. Yet, the novel's episodes consist overwhelmingly of scenes of manipulation. As the dust cover (a man controlling a number of individuals as so many puppets bound by strings, yet his own movements are also controlled by attached strings) suggests, free will and dignity are rare commodities in a world shaped by whimsey. The central metaphor for the entire novel, the "blind date," is what Oscar, a youthful rapist, calls his attacks upon helpless young women; since the victims never see their assailant who attacks them from behind with scientific proficiency, the brutal impersonality of the acts remains intact. When young Levanter finally brutalizes a young girl he calls "Nameless," Oscar is jailed for the one crime he did not commit; the irony of injustice increases.

This metaphor of impersonality is reinforced by the numerous disguises and masquerades which Levanter perpetrates in the novel; at various times he charades as a Russian government official, a secret agent from the American Council for Global Security, and an Eskimo. He gains personal satisfaction or revenge through each of these ploys. For example, he double-crosses a Communist agent by posing as an agent; thus, he avenges the death of his friend, a fencing champion, by impaling the treacherous agent on a sabre. He also kills the Deputy Minister of Internal Affairs from a kingdom which tortures intellectual dissidents. Afterward, Levanter feels elevated by executing such seldom-seen justice. Another attempt at mercy backfires, however, as his release of other political prisoners results in the death of an innocent translator. Such are the brutal ironies of Kosinski's fictional universe.

Sexual identities also become merged in this fictional universe which confuses illusion with reality. Levanter becomes enamored of "Foxy Lady," whose sexuality seems satisfying but ambiguous to him. She, unlike other women, seems to understand "everything he wanted." He feels cheated upon discovering that Foxy Lady did not have a tumor but a penis removed in recent surgery. Later Levanter marries Mary-Jane Kirkland, a rich widow whom he meets on a legitimate blind date. Her death by cancer is clearly foreshadowed by the appearance of Levanter's article in *Investor's Quarterly* concerning the "role of chance in creative investment." The hero's one true attempt at emotional investment with love extending beyond mere sexual gratification ends in emotional bankruptcy. This metaphor of life as a game where victory is sweet, but where defeat is inevitable, accounts for the death of Kosinski's protagonist. The last skier with a chance of a solo run on his favorite range which he could ski "blindfolded," he becomes lost in an icy fog and succumbs to the indomitable will of nature despite an admirable struggle.

Levanter's demise answers the death wish of the novel's epigraph from Jonathan Swift, who asks: "Remove me from this land of slaves,/Where all are fools, and all are knaves,/Where every knave and fool is bought,/Yet kindly sells himself for naught;—" Through this struggle to assert his individual will upon the people and circumstances that surround him, George Levanter becomes the first Kosinski character to approach heroic stature. His triumphs and defeats illustrate the author's conception of life as a "blind date" where chance prevails.

Blind Date is not, however, entirely free from those gratuitous parables which dull Kosinski's other works. For example, Levanter becomes enamored of a woman who has no body; a bone disease has withered all her limbs into vestigial stumps so that she must be wheeled in a baby carriage or carried from place to place. Levanter desires this woman since "she had incorporated her deformity into the totality of her life." Luckily, she rebuffs his advances to prevent the description of a truly bizarre seduction.

Kosinski wisely offsets such solipsistic parables by skillfully weaving true historical characters and incidents into the fabric of his fictional narrative. While teaching an investment course at Princeton University, Levanter rents a home next door to Svetlana Alliluyeva, Stalin's daughter. The shock of this situation—a Russian refugee living next to the daughter of the former Russian dictator—stops Levanter from speaking to her in their native Russian tongue. His friend Romarkin shakes his head at this coincidence and observes that "anything can happen." "Anything" can and does occur in the novel to verify Levanter's father's claim that "civilization is the result of sheer chance plus a thousand or two exceptional men of ideas and action." Levanter meets one of these famous "investors"—people who utilize personal energy and means to aid civilization—Charles Lindbergh. When they meet, Levanter mentions the aviator's citation from Hitler and participation in keeping the United States out of World War II as great blows to his faith in human wisdom. Lindbergh defends his interest in Germany as a model technocratic society; he overlooks its racial hatred as merely a temporary aberration. The mass atrocities, of course, prove him wrong.

The most effectively utilized historical incident, and perhaps the best executed section of the novel, involves the Manson murders. Kosinski introduces the re-creation of this brutal act through a Russian woman whom Levanter encounters in Cannes; she was the lover of "Woytek" (Wojiciech Voityck Frykowski), a man whom Levanter brings to America against her wishes. Levanter enlists "Gibby" (Abigail Folger), a rich American heiress, to look after the Russian immigrant. They move to California and stay in Beverly Hills with their pregnant friend, "Sharon" (Sharon Tate, wife of director Roman Polanski). Levanter plans to join them, but a baggage mixup delays his Los Angeles arrival and, ultimately, saves his life. As news reports of the tragedy flood his consciousness, Levanter reimagines the crime from Woytek's point of view; the result is the best descriptive writing in the entire novel. These scenes read cinematically faithful to the facts presented by Vincent Bugliosi's *Helter Skelter,* and their emotional impact parallels scenes in Truman Capote's *In Cold Blood* for terror and veracity. These murders also restate Kosinski's chief thematic thrusts: the role of sheer chance upon men's lives, the brutality of human nature, and the defeat of rational man by blind nature.

Other scenes dramatize science's attempt to influence life's outcome. Levanter visits a famous immunology research laboratory, where thousands of mice are caged and diligently monitored to prevent contamination. When he tries to convince his guide that a mouse runs loose in the room despite reliable, responsible scientists, the man will not believe his claim. Upon seeing the mouse, the scientist reports its existence to a young research assistant who also denies its existence. Only when all have witnessed the mouse scampering across the floor will they admit a "human error" has occurred. In another instance, when Levanter learns that Jacques Monod, an esteemed French biologist who discovers how the living cell manufactures the substance of life, is actually being deprived of this very substance, he is stunned into silence at life's cruel ironies. Monod tells him that "blind chance" determines each random event of life. An orderly predetermined life scheme "bypasses the drama of each unique instance of man's own existence." Monod, the author of the appropriately titled work *Chance and Necessity,* accepts his fate, but Levanter leaves him "mute and dispirited" at life's injustices.

In the novel's other epigraph Jacques Monod asks who can "define crime" and distinguish "good" and "evil" when the "traditional systems" place ethics and values "beyond man's reach?" George Levanter lives in this world of moral ambiguity: his life is a succession of "blind dates" which rarely gain profits for their investor. He lives by his wits and dies knowing that he has done his best. His death is not a surrender to the blizzard which freezes him, but merely an "acknowledgment of its might." He "scores quite well in the games he plays"; even if "few others . . . would ever want to learn to play his game."

Gregory S. Sojka

A BOOK OF COMMON PRAYER

Author: Joan Didion (1935–   )
Publisher: Simon and Schuster (New York). 272 pp. $8.95
Type of work: Novel
Time: The present
Locale: The fictitious Central American country of Boca Grande with flashbacks to San Francisco and various cities of the American South

A realistic narrative of what it is like to live in the contemporary world, which is teetering absurdly on the edge of spiritual collapse

> Principal characters:
> GRACE STRASSER-MENDANA, the narrator, a sixty-year-old American woman
> CHARLOTTE DOUGLAS, an American woman in her early forties
> WARREN BOGART, her first husband
> LEONARD DOUGLAS, her second husband
> MARIN, their eighteen-year-old daughter
> VICTOR, Grace's brother-in-law, the Defense Minister of Boca Grande, one of Charlotte's temporary lovers
> GERARDO, Grace's son, a young international playboy and supporter of Victor's overthrow, another of Charlotte's lovers
> ANTONIO, Grace's other brother-in-law, a "sociopath"

In the preface to her well-regarded essay collection entitled *Slouching Toward Bethlehem* (1968), Joan Didion recounts that the title essay about the subculture of the Haight-Ashbury district of San Francisco was the first time she "had dealt directly and flatly with the evidence of atomization, the proof that things fall apart." She continues to investigate this contemporary phenomenon in *A Book of Common Prayer*, her third and best novel. In this clarification exercise on the contemporary milieu—a world of shorn values, smashed hopes, and harsh realities—Didion through her setting, her central character, and her narrator informs the reader of the desperate state of contemporary life, of the desperate attempts of those who try to live decently on the edge of the yawning void.

Ironically, Didion's representations of the great cosmic chill usually are set in subtropical climates—Los Angeles, Las Vegas, New Orleans—and the setting for *A Book of Common Prayer* is perhaps the most fitting of any for her themes. Boca Grande squats on the equator, its humid days and nights passing in a monotonous, forgettable succession of seeming changelessness. But change of one sort or another is always occurring—bacteria flourish, reproduce, and die; the natural cycles of innumerable insects continue; rust destroys automobiles and tin roofs; vegetation grows over the $34 million road built into the interior. Much is growing, but much more is rotting, from the vegetation and the cars to the people and their institutions. The country's history, like its landscape, is utterly forgettable. Governments are overthrown so frequently and with so little meaning that only the disintegrating ruins of the monuments of previous administrations and the memories of a few people attest to their existence. Throughout all the cycles, one senses no evolution, no progressive pattern, no purpose or design to the growth and the rot, a sameness of prodigality and waste. With Boca Grande, then, Didion creates an effective metaphor of the modern environment—a world characterized by great growth and great disintegration but by no design.

To such a country comes Charlotte Douglas in search of asylum, peace, and purpose, in search of a retreat from her history. What better refuge from flux than a world that seems not to change? What better haven from a past than a country that seems to lack one? Charlotte is on the run from emotional involvements—from her former husband, Warren Bogart, a profligate parasite who, unknown to Charlotte, is near death; from her present husband, Leonard, a lawyer who seems too busy with Third World countries and leftist clients to have much time for her; from the newspapers and F.B.I. men who have constantly been hounding her for information concerning her daughter, Marin, a Berkeley dropout turned inchoate bomb-thrower; and from the baby that Charlotte had to replace Marin, a baby who was born prematurely, hydrocephalic, and who died in the parking lot of a Coca-Cola bottling plant in Mérida, Mexico. From all of this, Charlotte retreats into a dream of life, a life of delusions which ironically lead her into an accidental entanglement in a political overthrow and her purposeless death. She had not expected this; she had not really anticipated any of the nightmares that afflict her; she had been unprepared for almost everything, especially the equatorial nothingness and absurdity of Boca Grande.

True, "as a child of comfortable family in the temperate zone she had been as a matter of course provided with clean sheets, orthodontia, . . . one brother named Dickie, ballet lessons, and casual timely information about menstruation and the care of flat silver"; but she never developed much clearsightedness. So naïve does Charlotte seem that her typical response to any personal, political, or historical difficulty is that everything will turn out all right in the end. "Immaculate of history, innocent of politics," possessing instead of knowledge a great faith in the inevitability of progress and "the generally upward spiral of history," Charlotte Douglas typifies the *norteamericana*. And her reaction to her own past is typical also. Instead of developing a realistic outlook, Charlotte decides instead to manipulate her history to eliminate thinking of the horrible events of her life; to stay sane, she erases rather than reconciles the pain of her betrayal of her husbands, their betrayal of her, Marin's disownment of her, and the loss of her baby. Those that she cannot erase, she revises into delusions, myths built from fragments of reality, dreams, lies, and wishes.

Her reaction to Boca Grande is rather typical of her reactions to her past. She refuses to see it as it really is—an absurd, rotting, purposeless world—and attempts to revitalize it: first through letters she tries to sell to *The New Yorker* about Boca Grande as a " 'land of contrasts,' " as the " 'economic fulcrum of the Americas,' " as one marked by "the 'spirit of hope' "; then through her ideas of establishing an annual international film festival in the country, of opening up a fashionable boutique there, of caring for the sick, and of providing birth control information to the natives. These notions and actions came to nothing.

Her letters are rejected; no film festival is ever seriously considered; her boutique, a shabby hole-in-the-wall, becomes a meeting place for political plotters; her attempts to immunize the populace from cholera are stopped by the government; no one bothers to come to her clinic; and she is finally killed during a political upheaval called the October Violence after refusing to leave when she had the chance. One could assume from all of this that Charlotte is only a naïve contemporary American, foolishly optimistic, that she is only a rich, deluded do-gooder. But if one investigates her more carefully, a more pitiable and somewhat heroic person emerges.

Charlotte is on the run from her history. To prevent it from impinging on her and ultimately destroying her, she has sought escape into another country, literally and metaphorically. In Boca Grande, she immerses herself in projects, routines, and affairs that offer some distraction, some escape from the Eumenides of memory. That she is partially successful is reflected in a scene in which the narrator says of Charlotte's stay in the Hotel del Caribe, "You're at the mercy of the maids." Charlotte responds, "They're very nice here" and "Actually I'm never depressed." But throughout the novel, she also reveals that her attempts at forgetting, erasing, and revising are futile. Her desires to re-create a life, to establish order, and to forget seem halfhearted, tentative, their actor detached, separated, an outsider. From spending hours reading and rereading newspapers and books written in Spanish and not understanding a word of them to having affairs both with Victor, the Defense Minister, and with Gerardo, Charlotte seems inattentive to the realities of her situation and surroundings. Her actions, then, some of which appear vacuous, overly idealistic, or childish—those of "an outsider of romantic sensibility"—reflect detachment from the present and the impossibility of complete divorce from the past.

Not seeing clearly her present reality, covering up the anguish of memory, Charlotte must create fictions of both. Boca Grande would be famous for its film festival; the people would use IUD's and diaphragms to ease the population increase; she would one day at the Boca Grande airport see Marin returning to her. Delusions coupled with a country that "seemed not to demand attentiveness" produce such a seeming obliviousness in Charlotte that she appears to walk unknowingly to her death by AR-15 submachine gunfire during the October Violence. She is, however, perhaps a stronger, more perceptive character than one would like to believe. She shows some remarkable toughness in spots—at one point killing a chicken by breaking its neck cleanly with her bare hands, at another saving a man's life by performing an emergency tracheotomy with a boning knife—and there is evidence that she purposely stayed in Boca Grande and incited the guerrillas to shoot her, in short planned her own death rather than pulling the trigger herself. Her character, then, is complex, ambiguous: she is not just a deluded American fool, but a woman trying to forget the past through an unrealistic clouding of both memory and reality, a person who has finally confronted the realities of nothingness, of rot, of the past and has taken the option of death, the only exit.

The ambiguity of Charlotte's fascinating character is made possible by the point of view Didion employs. A *persona*, Grace Strasser-Mendana, is Charlotte's witness. Interestingly enough, Grace, while attempting to narrate with the precision of a research chemist, actually creates uncertainty about Charlotte's ultimate nature. A year after her death, Grace now feels that she has gathered enough evidence to tell accurately Charlotte's story. Trained as an anthropologist and then switching to biochemistry because the former did not yield conclusive enough evidence, Grace establishes very early in the novel her objectivity. Applying the scientific methods of biochemistry, a "discipline in which demonstrable answers are commonplace and 'personality' absent," the narrator observes acutely and reports flatly, the product being rather brutal but accurate treatises about Boca Grande, its people, its history (or lack of it), and the past and present life of Charlotte, the narrator's chief concern.

From her initial view, the reader perceives Charlotte to be a rather deluded, driven woman, one who dreams her life away. As Grace is detached from any illusions about life, so too is the audience detached from Charlotte, seeing her through the vital data found in passports, entry visas, and the contents of her handbag. The narrator also relies on much hearsay evidence and her own personal observation to construct Charlotte's history, one which initially appears silly but pathetic. As the novel proceeds, however, Grace realizes that her scientific method does not seem to be producing conclusive results about the main character's nature; tempted once to use the word "unstable" to describe her, Grace pauses and then comments that she is "less and less convinced that the word . . . has any useful meaning except insofar as it describes a chemical compound." At the end of the work, Grace finally admits, "I also recognize the equivocal nature of even the most empirical evidence" and that "I am less and less certain that this story has been one of delusion. Unless the delusion was mine." As the narrator loses faith in her method, the reader's perception and understanding of Charlotte's character become simultaneously and paradoxically clearer and more ambiguous. Charlotte Douglas appears not as silly and pathetic, but as a confused mixture of strength and vulnerability, passion and detachment, delusion and realism.

As Grace fails in the final analysis to understand unequivocally Charlotte's nature and motivations, the reader ironically is presented a portrait that in its complexity and ambiguity seems closer to the realities of human existence, Didion's technique moving the novel one step closer to the accurate portrayal of life. One cannot know through objective analysis the essence of a total person. Even one small aspect, fear of the dark, is remarkably complex, consisting, as Grace says, of "an arrangement of fifteen amino acids." No human, then, can ultimately be charted, diagrammed, and absolutely known, as the narrator has attempted in the novel. What appears instead is only a somewhat confusing re-creation of a personality, but as close to the essence of Charlotte Douglas as one may come, as close to one who lives on the edge of despair and oblivion as one can get.

The style through which the author communicates her vision is somewhat loose, quite pure and simple, the unadorned reportorial voice of the author of *Slouching Toward Bethlehem* mixed with the *persona's* Flaubertian and somewhat cynical habit of recording simultaneously the grotesque and the romantic in the same sentence. When asked whether she had a technical intention for the novel, Didion remarked, "Yes, I wrote it down on the map of Central America. 'Surface like rainbow slick, shifting, fall, thrown away, iridescent.' I wanted to do a deceptive surface that appeared to be one thing and turned color as you looked through it." So, too, with the reader's perception of Charlotte, the narrator, and the country. Through them, Didion in *A Book of Common Prayer* creates simultaneously both a vision of and a prayer for all caught in the age of dysfunction, of disintegration, of the cosmic chill. One understands a bit better our fragmented world after reading this fine novel.

Harold J. Joseph

THE BOOK OF MERLYN

The Unpublished Conclusion to *The Once and Future King*

Author: T. H. White (1906–1964)
Publisher: University of Texas Press (Austin, Texas). Illustrated. 158 pp. $9.95
Type of work: Fantasy
Time: The legendary past, on the eve of the battle between Arthur and Mordred
Locale: Salisbury Plain and Cornwall

The concluding book of White's treatment of the Arthurian legend, in which he brings Merlyn back to his former pupil

> Principal characters:
> ARTHUR, the once and future king
> MERLYN, his magician-tutor
> T. NATRIX, a snake,
> CAVALL, a hound,
> BALIN, a falcon,
> ARCHIMEDES, an owl,
> GOAT,
> HEDGEHOG, and
> BADGER, members of the Committee on Might in Man

T. H. White's *The Once and Future King,* published in 1958, has the distinction of being a work from which not one but two movies have been made. Walt Disney adapted the animated cartoon *The Sword in the Stone* from the first book of White's tetralogy, and Alan Jay Lerner and Frederick Lowe freely selected material from it for their musical success, *Camelot.* But despite the popularity of *The Once and Future King,* it was not until 1975 that the extent of White's plan for the work was rediscovered: *The Once and Future King,* as White wrote it, was composed not of four parts, but of five. *The Book of Merlyn* is the fifth part, the conclusion to that work.

A prologue by the British novelist Sylvia Townsend Warner outlines the ironic history of *The Book of Merlyn* and its thirty-three-year disappearance. Apparently White had no ending firmly in mind when he began his retelling of the Arthurian legend, yet historical forces were already in action that would lead him to a conclusion. He completed the first book of the story, *The Sword in the Stone,* in 1938. The book was immediately successful both in England and America, but White's enjoyment was diminished because his mind, like those of most Englishmen, was fixed on Hitler's threat to the peace of Europe. Although Prime Minister Neville Chamberlain's appeasement bought a temporary respite from war fears, it was clear to many, including White, that a conflict of monstrous proportions was inevitable.

In January 1939, while working on *The Witch in the Wood,* the second book in the series, White accepted an invitation to spend some time in Ireland. His diary reveals the turmoil in which he found himself in 1939: at one moment he planned to become a conscientious objector, at another to enlist in the armed forces, at still another to seek some kind of defense work. In a revealing

comment to a friend he wrote of his hatred for war and his judgment that he
would find being a coward more endurable than being a hero.

The fighting had already begun when White started work on the third part of
his theme, *The Ill-Made Knight*, which he finished quickly. By November of
1940, he was well into the fourth part, *The Candle in the Wind*, and out of his fear
of war and his fervent pacifism an idea for the conclusion of the whole series was
beginning to take shape. The end of *The Candle in the Wind* depicts Arthur on
the night before the battle with Mordred, his nephew and son. The old king has
seen the failure of all his plans to civilize his people and bring peace to the
realm; his life has been spent in vain. But with this picture of Arthur in mind,
White devised a new ending for his story, one that seemed appropriate not only
for Arthur's times but also for his own.

White came to see the whole Arthurian legend as a search for a means of
preventing war, and decided to organize his five-part work around that theme. In
the fifth and concluding book, he would have Merlyn return to Arthur on the eve
of the last battle, and bring the despondent king to the committee of animals
who had helped guide his education as a youth. Placing the main part of the final
book in a badger's den had two advantages for White: first, the book would end
as it had begun, emphasizing man as a part of nature, not as something above
and separate from it. Second, and more important, the badger's den provided
White with an apt setting for an examination of man as a political animal.

Any discussion of the nature of man, given what was occurring in Europe at
that time, was bound to be profoundly pessimistic, and White's discussion is no
exception. We must make allowances for the sincerity of the author's pacifism; it
seems heartfelt and profound. But after that allowance is made, there remains
the nagging thought that *The Book of Merlyn* is in part self-justification for
White's departure from England. This thought arises from the air of unreality
that hangs over White's endeavors in 1940–1941. No Englishman needed to have
the horrors of war preached to him while the Battle of Britain was raging in the
skies over his head. Anyone in the streets of London was much more keenly
aware of and involved in man's brutality to man than was White, sheltered in the
safety of Ireland. What could the author realistically hope to accomplish with an
antiwar novel when a German invasion was expected at any time? The answers
to questions like this will have to await a complete biography of T. H. White.

If we do not now have that biography, at least we have all of *The Once and
Future King* as White intended it to be, and no future discussions of the story will
be complete without taking *The Book of Merlyn* into account.

If *The Book of Merlyn* would not bring peace to England, and White could
not reasonably expect that, at least its arguments could bring peace to his mind.
Having decided on the theme of the story as a whole, White realized that some
early parts would need to be rewritten. The revisions, together with the
manuscripts for *The Candle in the Wind* and *The Book of Merlyn*, went to the
publisher in November of 1941. It hardly need be stressed that antiwar tracts did

not find a congenial reception in England in 1941. Yet White insisted that *The Once and Future King* should be published as a five-book whole, or not at all. Unsurprisingly, the decision was made not to publish it at all.

Sylvia Warner's brief preface to *The Book of Merlyn* does not answer an interesting question: in 1958, *The Once and Future King* was published, but only in four parts—*The Book of Merlyn* was omitted, although some of its material appeared in earlier books. But to what degree was White involved in this truncated version? Why had he relaxed his earlier objection to partial publication? Once again, we do not know. In any case, the manuscript for *The Book of Merlyn* was sent, with the bulk of White's papers, to the archives of the Humanities Research Center at the University of Texas at Austin. There it was discovered in 1975, and, after being prepared for publication, saw print in 1977.

In the context of the preceding volumes, *The Book of Merlyn* comes as an abrupt change in tempo. Every version of the legend of Arthur is filled with incident and action. That was surely the case with White's primary source, Thomas Malory's *Morte d'Arthur*, and it is likewise the case with those parts of *The Once and Future King* that faithfully follow Malory. Even those parts of his work which are White's original inventions make their points primarily through what the characters do, not through what they say. In the first two books, Merlyn is a good teacher not because he lectures Arthur wisely but because he places the boy in situations from which he can gain a surer and more lasting lesson. But White's method changes in *The Book of Merlyn;* what we have is, for the most part, a monologue. Merlyn has many words to say, and the animals join in from time to time, but the voice is always that of White, heaping condemnation on the human race, whose only defender is a rather slow-witted Arthur.

White himself may have felt that the change in method was too abrupt. Perhaps in an effort to enliven the static situation of the book, he brought to it two episodes from earlier parts. In these, Arthur is changed by Merlyn into first an ant, and then a wild goose. As an ant he learns what life is like in a totalitarian state, where everything not forbidden is compulsory. As a wild goose, he learns the arbitrary and artificial nature of human boundaries, the natural aristocracy of the capable, and, surprisingly, the sanctity of private property. The two parts contain some of the most vivid scenes and powerful arguments of the whole work, but they are only parts. The rest of the book depends entirely on ideas for whatever liveliness it may possess.

When the debate begins, the Committee (Merlyn and the animals) has been debating the proper adjective to describe human beings. The members reject the term *homo sapiens* since *sapiens* means wise and is therefore unsuitable in the light of human history. The first suggestion is *homo ferox; ferox,* ferocious, seems appropriate since man is unique among animals, they argue, in killing for pleasure. Merlyn describes every animal fleeing in terror at the approach of a human being. At this point it may occur to the reader that we do not *know* that other animals do not take pleasure in killing, nor do domesticated animals flee from man. But the only defender of the human race present is Arthur, and the deck is stacked against him. Effective counterarguments do not occur to Arthur, here or elsewhere.

After a short discussion of the applicability of *stultus*, foolish, to the human race, Merlyn changes Arthur into an ant, and at the end of the lesson, supplies the moral for him. In reducing every member of the species to absolute equality, the ants have made themselves slaves. Any society that denies the uniqueness of the individual (here he names fascism and communism) approaches the society of the ant. And the magician further argues that any society with aspirations toward democracy will inevitably follow down that path. Merlyn reads "Liberty, Equality, Fraternity" as "Liberty, Brutality, and Obscenity."

In its disgruntled view of human nature, the book may at this point remind the reader of nothing so much as the fourth book of *Gulliver's Travels*. Swift is in White's mind, to be sure: at this low ebb in Arthur's spirits, White has the king refer to humans as yahoos. With the king almost despairing, Merlyn changes him into a wild goose. His sojourn with the geese does not have the expected result. Rather than desiring to return to human society full of insight, the king wants only to stay with the geese. Merlyn has to bring him back forcibly in order to continue the lecture. The cause of war, the magician tells him, is nationalism. The cause of war is the desire of groups of humans to lay claim to some part of the earth as their communal property.

White has the easiest of tasks—arguing for a proposition that most people already agree with. Yet he makes Merlyn sound curiously inept in his discussion of nationalism, since his examples come as a shock: "The petty and driveling advocates of Irish or Polish nationalism: these are the enemies of man." More than anything else, White seems out of touch. If his examples lack force in 1977, how ludicrous might they have seemed shortly after Russia and Germany had torn Poland in half for no other crime than existing? And the inclusion of the Irish is at best ungrateful, coming from a man who, at the time he wrote those words, was spared the fury of air bombardment only by the Irish nationalism of which he complains.

In the last analysis, White's argument is overwhelmed by the particular. It is easy to argue against war in the abstract, to argue against the idea of war. But in the midst of a specific war, those arguments may or may not have a purpose. Arthur, after all the wrangling, returns to the battlefield out of duty and there meets his fate. It is cold comfort for him and the reader to be told that ten thousand years may breed the desire for war out of the race, but that is the only consolation and hope that White extends. And if the far future is not a comfort, neither is it a guide to present action. If one agreed entirely with White, what was he to do at that time, when British nationalism, which the author despised, stood in opposition to antlike fascism, which he also despised? In short, what does one do when there is no Ireland to run to? Clearly, White preferred Britain to Hitler's Germany, if only as the lesser of two evils, and the book closes with a request for prayers for the soul of Thomas Malory and T. H. White, his humble disciple, who, he says, "now voluntarily lays aside his books to fight for his kind." But he did not. White remained in Ireland and returned to England only after the war was over.

Walter E. Meyers

THE BOOK OF SAND

Author: Jorge Luis Borges (1899–   )
Translated from the Spanish by Norman Thomas di Giovanni
Publisher: E. P. Dutton (New York). 125 pp. $7.95
Type of work: Short stories

A collection of thirteen stories by the Argentine master recalls the Borges of the intricate, ironic stories of Ficciones *and* The Aleph

Jorge Luis Borges, who will turn eighty next year, has been writing and publishing for fifty-six years of his life. Because of the widely held belief of many readers in the United States that nothing of any literary consequence has been written in Spanish since *Don Quixote,* Borges was not "discovered" until the 1960's by the English speaking world. Some tardy discoverers refuse to recognize the South American origin of Borges and continue to place him in anthologies and works of criticism dealing with modern European fiction and literature, but both Borges' life and literature remain very much Latin American. Just as the Nicaraguan Ruben Dario revitalized Spanish poetry in the nineteenth century, so Borges renovated the prose idiom of the Spanish language.

Borges is the chronological father of modern Latin American writing as well, a paternity readily admitted to by such progeny as Gabriel García Márquez *(One Hundred Years of Solitude),* Carlos Fuentes *(The Death of Artemio Cruz, A Change of Skin, Aura),* Julio Cortázar *(Hopscotch, Blow-up),* and still others less famous or less translated. His late appearance made him anachronistically a contemporary contributor to that explosion of novels, short stories, and poetry starting in the mid-1960's in Latin America known as the "boom." Ironically, most of Borges' influence and fame rests upon a corpus of essays *(Inquisiciones,* 1925; *Evaristo Carriego,* 1930; *Discusión,* 1932; *Other Inquisitions,* 1952) and short stories *(A Universal History of Infamy,* 1935; *Ficciones,* 1935–1944; *The Aleph,* 1949) that generally appeared between 1925 and 1952. As with any writer as productive as Borges there have been ups and downs of critical success. In fact, after the publication of *Doctor Brodie's Report* (1970–Spanish, 1972–English), a new style and somewhat new subjects emerged, indicating an unexpected and regrettable change toward narrative simplicity. Fortunately, Borges has forsaken his flirtation with Rudyard Kipling and has returned to his stock of doubles, Platonic archetypes, mirrors, dreams, repeating patterns across time, and literary works-within-works in *The Book of Sand.* The same economical style and the same thematic preoccupations here echo those of the 1930's and 1940's.

The Book of Sand's thirteen stories explicitly and implicitly avoid, even disclaim novelty. In "The Congress" the aging narrator states that "novelties— maybe because I feel that they hold nothing essentially new and are really no more than timid variations—neither interest nor distract me." Borges' specific usage of the adverb "essentially" underscores his point that attempts at originality and newness are only pale reflections of eternal essences. With the possible exceptions of "The Bribe," by his own admission a psychological story, and "There Are More Things" (also the title in the original), a tribute to and pastiche of the horror fiction of H. P. Lovecraft, these compact narratives constantly stir up memories of plots, themes, and lines of earlier stories and essays and further heighten the Platonic effect so dear to Borges that "to know is to know again."

Among the themes that Borges has used in the past those of the double, time, pantheism, and the existence of a magic word that expresses everything reappear singly or in combination in these stories. "The Other" employs the double. This initial story resembles "The Circular Ruins" of *Ficciones* and the poem, "Borges and I." "Ulrike" uses cyclical time as the characters perform fundamental timeless acts. In "Ulrike" life imitates literature as it did in *Ficciones'* "Theme of the Traitor and Hero" where the narrator suspects the "existence of a secret form of time, a pattern of repeated lines." In this instance, however, the Colombian narrator imperceptibly becomes Sigurd and Ulrike, Brynhild, characters of the Volsungs Saga. Apparently casual allusions to De Quincey and his Ann of Oxford Street, the Niebelungen, Henrik Ibsen, and William Morris, both of whom wrote versions of the Volsungs Saga, enrich the structure of this work and make it typically Borgesian. In this and in other stories of the collection the characters tend to disintegrate, one character blending with another, or often they remain nameless like their fictitious narrator.

Personal time, the important theme in "Avelino Arredondo," contrasts Arredondo's personal experience with a rigorous, unrelenting, external chronology. "Utopia of a Tired Man" uses the voyage in time to take the narrator out of the present and set him down into the distant future. This situation provides Borges with a vehicle for satirizing the ephemera of the present with the nightmarish reduction and simplification of the future. The narrator returns to the present with proof of his journey, a very small painting which "represented, or suggested, a sunset and which encompassed something infinite." It is no accident that his painting reminds us of Coleridge's dream flower or H. G. Wells's wilted flower of the future. The old narrator of "The Night of the Gifts" remembers and relives in the retelling two fundamental eternal acts, love and death, which he experienced in his youth. The two most ambitious stories of the book deal also with forms of time. "The Congress," which bears no small resemblance to *Other Inquisitions'* "A New Refutation of Time," attempts to relate how a given moment, an imminence of eternity was experienced and how imperfectly words describe it because the successive nature of language contradicts the concept of the eternal or the intemporal. "The Book of Sand," the closing story, postulates the existence of a monstrous book that contains nothing less than infinity between its covers. Borges' peculiar irony, making it both the last story and the title of the collection, should not be overlooked.

Language becomes the theme of "Undr" and "The Mirror and the Mask," although language's inability to express adequately man's thoughts and feelings figures as a leitmotiv in several other stories. In "The Mirror and the Mask," the poet in three successive attempts refines his poetry from his initial lengthy panegyric, to an ode, and finally to a single line of spoken verse. The poem devastates two men: "not venturing to repeat it aloud, the poet and his king savored it as if it were a secret prayer or a blasphemy." His one verse, much like the book of sand or the painting from the distant future, encompasses all experience. The bard admits to the origin of the poem in a dream (remember Coleridge and Caedmon, who also received their poems in dreams) and, in a Borgesian sense, he becomes the vocal instrument of something quite beyond him and the confines of this world of substance. The poet kills himself; the king wanders his kingdom as a beggar never daring to repeat the poem.

"Undr" shares in the same search for the poem that contains all experience. Set in the eleventh century, Ulf, a poet of the race of the skalds, seeks the Urns, a race whose poetry consists of a single word. The skalds, as any knowledgeable reader of Borges' *Literaturas germánicas medievales* (1966) or of Scandinavian literature would know, were poets who multiplied and combined lengthy recondite metaphors known as *kenning* in their verses. Ulf witnesses the death of the Urn king who hears the Word from his court poet, but the Word eludes him. The Urn poet, forbidden to reveal this word, urges Ulf to search for it. After many adventures and years, Ulf returns to the Urns' village only to find his poet friend dying. Ulf, after retelling "in exact order and with a great many details" what he experienced, hears the waning voice of the Urn sing one word, "undr," meaning wonder. That one word reveals to Ulf everything that he is and has done. Signaling his understanding, Ulf picks up the harp and sings to a different word which, of course, is not disclosed to the reader. There is in this concept of the single word or in the picture or in the book composed of infinite pages the pantheistic theme which finds repetitions scattered throughout the pages of this collection. In "Undr" the dying bard reveals how "life gives everything to everyone, but most men are unaware of it." Poetry and the poet do make men aware. This same expression reoccurs in "The Night of the Gifts" where "all things are revealed to all men—or, any way, all those things it's granted a man to know." And again in "The Sect of the Thirty" a fragment of an anonymous ancient manuscript reveals that at the Crucifixion of Christ there were intentional and unintentional participants: the two intentional ones were Christ and Judas, and all of the rest of mankind were the unintentional. The nameless author relates that members of the abominable, heretical sect worship Christ and Judas equally and forgive all the others, since "there is no one culprit. Everyone, unwitting or not, is an agent in the scheme laid down by Divine Wisdom. All of them now share the Glory." This pantheistic reduction helps to explain Borges' lack of strong individual characters and the consequential difficulty of remembering them since they all fuse together.

These themes encountered in *The Book of Sand*, of course, are not unique to Borges, but the mode in which they find expression is. Borges is very much a stylist. Even in translation the special quality of his prose emerges. The very fact that writers and critics now speak of plots, phrases, and so on as distinctively Borgesian indicates how remarkable is his style. The allusion, the dream entering the real world, irony, the juxtaposition of opposites ("secret prayer or a blasphemy"), the voyage in time, the story-within-a-story narrated by receding first-person narrators, the disturbing mixture of reality with fiction, all are his stock-in-trade.

Borges' essays resemble fiction or certainly allow the welcome incursions of the fictional world to intrude upon the real one; his fictions acquire a veneer of reality by imitating the objective essay, the book review, or the scholarly commentary. For example, "Undr" and "The Sect of the Thirty" appear to represent fragments of ancient manuscripts glossed by an anonymous neutral researcher. In the latter story, however, the authenticity of the nonexistent manuscript is provided by a deceptively casual reference to its being mentioned in one of the footnotes of Gibbon's fifteenth chapter of *The Decline and Fall of the Roman Empire*. The fifteenth chapter, indeed, deals with the early Christian heretical sects, but there is no such footnote. Borges uses the apocryphal reference to legitimize his fictional world.

Fully ten of the thirteen stories are first-person narratives, told generally by anonymous men, or nearly so, and quite advanced in age. Often one narrator cedes his function to another and he in turn to still another. "The Night of the Gifts" provides a good illustration. Embedded within the story are no less than three different narrators, each retelling an episode from many years before. This concatenation of time and events draws the reader into Borges' fictional world, making him lose his own sense of time and reality. The distant memories and dreams of the telescoping narrators create similar effects in the other stories.

It would not be difficult to detail at some considerable length the delightful ironies, the clever allusions to other literatures, the sources, and the metaphors so patent in Borges, but it would defeat one of the avowed intentions of the author, who, in his Afterword, hopes that "these hasty notes . . . do not exhaust this book and that its dreams go on branching out in the hospitable imagination of those who now close it." Indeed this volume, like the book of the title story and like the sand, has no beginning and no end. In a very genuine sense *The Book of Sand*, borrowing from Borges' own lexicon, vindicates his reputation as one of the most important and influential writers of the century.

John R. Kelly

BOSWELL
Laird of Auchinleck, 1778-1782

Author: James Boswell (1740-1795)
Edited by Joseph W. Reed and Frederick A. Pottle
Publisher: McGraw-Hill Book Company (New York). 570 pp. $19.95
Type of work: Journals
Time: 1778-1782
Locale: Edinburgh and Scotland; occasionally London and England

The ninth and most recent volume in the Yale Edition of The Private Papers of James Boswell, *this book covers the period when Boswell had settled in Edinburgh with his family, was attempting to establish and extend his law practice, and finally came into his inheritance as Laird of Auchinleck*

> *Principal personages:*
> JAMES BOSWELL
> MRS. BOSWELL, his wife
> LORD AUCHINLECK, his father
> LADY AUCHINLECK, his stepmother
> SAMUEL JOHNSON

James Boswell was a constant embarrassment to his family, and, when he died in 1795, so the story went, the family burned all of his papers so that he could cast no further disgrace on the family honor. The early twentieth century view of Boswell was essentially that of his family, reinforced by the sneering Victorian estimation of Macauley: that James Boswell had been a vain, loose, superficial, foolish social climber who had, by some process not well understood, ingratiated himself with the great Dr. Samuel Johnson and had stumbled onto the writing of the world's greatest biography, *The Life of Samuel Johnson.* Then in the third decade of the present century, through a series of remarkable accidents, discoveries, and manipulations, the fact that the Boswell papers had not been burned came to light. Then the papers themselves were acquired from the Boswell descendants through some devious financial operations, and, by the combined efforts of Yale University and McGraw-Hill publishers, these papers began to appear in well-edited and annotated form to an eager audience. The present volume is the ninth in a series presenting Boswell's private diaries and journals for our examination.

Boswell was just twenty-two when, in 1762, he left his native Edinburgh behind and set out to see the world, especially that great and wonderful center of British civilization, London. As his journey began he made several resolutions. He was, he thought, going to meet people, important people. James Boswell of Scotland was going to be known among the salons of Europe and to all the important members of those select groups, for most of all, except perhaps for wine and pretty women, Boswell craved fame with an intensity that bordered on obsession. Furthermore, Boswell was convinced his adventures would be of such significance that he should keep a journal from day to day in which he would record his actions, feelings, intentions, and impressions. This habit of maintaining a daily journal, begun in his youth, prevailed throughout almost the entirety of Boswell's life. With amazing candor he entered everything, leaving himself utterly exposed to a curious world when these papers began to be published a few years ago. Everything is here: the excessive drinking bouts and the hangovers and remorse that followed in their wake; evenings spent with Samuel Johnson, Sir Joshua Reynolds, Oliver Goldsmith, and other famous men of the time; intrusions into the privacy of anyone of sufficient importance that Boswell would wish at a later time to drop their names in casual conversation; the sights, sounds, and smells of the bustling metropolis of eighteenth century London; and, of course, escapades with various ladies of various degrees of virtue, escapades followed not only by remorse but occasionally by attacks of venereal disease as well.

And yet the reader of the early volumes in this series is entertained with a lively sense of narrative and with a vivid sense of background: the eighteenth century comes alive under Boswell's touch. We meet Dr. Johnson face to face, informally and unbuttoned. And the brash young man did have something apparently; he was, after all, admitted, and at times welcomed, into the company of writers, artists, philosophers, and statesmen with impeccable credentials. And so the image of Boswell was revised, and he began to be seen as urbane, witty, sophisticated, and in every way the superior of the character who had emerged from Macauley's critical observations. He had his foibles, of course, but then so has everyone; and to be sure one can find redeeming qualities in anyone welcomed by the great Samuel Johnson. And, too, out of these accounts of his conversations with Johnson came the revisions that passed through a series of metamorphoses to become the *The Life of Samuel Johnson,* one of the world's great books.

Through the efforts of modern editors, Boswell's private journal covering a period of more than twenty years has now appeared. He may be seen as a gawking young man from the provinces just entering London, and then learning his way thoroughly around that great town. His visit to Holland in 1763-1764 followed next; he then took the Grand Tour through Europe, intruding on Voltaire, visiting the Corsican patriot General Paoli, conversing with Frederick the Great. This journey took him three years and into Germany, Switzerland, Italy, Corsica, and France. The well-traveled Boswell, now twenty-six years old, returned to search for a wife and to attempt to establish himself in his chosen profession, the practice of law. He was not a highly successful lawyer; indeed, he experienced several years of growing family and financial distress. And so he is to be found in 1778, at the beginning of the present volume, anxious concerning his meager legal activities and troubled with a host of other problems.

The text of the present volume is quite a different thing from the text of the first volume. Boswell, obviously, is older now and is beset with all the problems that growing old involves. His family is growing, and with it his expenses and worries. He no longer has the leisure for maintaining his journal that he had earlier; many of his entries, therefore, are highly abbreviated reminders to himself, presumably for future expansion which never took place. Many entries are made several days after their nominal date when Boswell had forgotten many of the details of a particular day's events. Thus the lively narrative character of the earlier volumes is quite lost here, and the reader is given, instead, a series of discrete moments, some quite vivid and others without color and detail. Many entries are cryptic, and the reader can but guess at the meaning with the editor's assistance. There are numerous gaps of days or even weeks in this manuscript which the editor often attempts to fill out with interpolated quotations from *The Life of Samuel Johnson,* if an allusion to the missing events should be found there, or with passages from other journalists who were present at the same events. In some instances there are no alternative accounts, and the gaps simply stand with no clarification. As in the earlier volumes the reader is given a view of a vast panorama of places and personages, but the landscape of Edinburgh pales beside that of London and Europe; and there is no Dr. Johnson, or Oliver Goldsmith, or Voltaire, or Rousseau in Edinburgh, though some of the Englishmen who enlightened the pages of earlier volumes do recur here during Boswell's occasional short trips to London. But by and large the narrative and the colorful backgrounds of the earlier volumes are no longer noticeable.

If this book lacks narrative structure and the interesting anecdotal material of fascinating persons, besides Boswell himself, of course, it does have several threads of thematic material running through it that tend to give it structure and unity of a quite different order. Perhaps the most prominent, as well as the most interesting, of these unifying and ordering themes is that of Boswell's relationship with other members of his family. There are distinct gradations, including his attitude toward his wife and children, toward his aging father and his father's second wife, toward his brothers, and toward a host of distant relatives. A second pervasive theme running through the volume is that of Boswell *vis-à-vis* his chosen profession, the bar. This theme is inextricably bound up with the conflict in Boswell's own heart between his affections for his Scottish homeland and his conviction that everything worthwhile lies south in London. A third theme involves Boswell's relationship with himself and his aspirations to be "a considerable figure" in the literary world. And finally, there is the kaleidoscopic view of Boswell in his many manifestations as man of the world, rake, socialite, traveler; graceful, charming, witty, or debauched, with debauchery always followed by black remorse and vows to leave off this aspect of his life.

Despite his avowed belief in concubinage and his almost obsessive trips to the stews, one cannot doubt the sincerity or the depth of Boswell's affection for his wife and children. By August, 1778, when this volume begins, Boswell's wife was obviously consumptive; she suffered from fits of violent, racking coughing spasms and spitting up blood alternating with periods when, in Boswell's words, "she never looked better." Boswell's own spirits vacillated wildly between hope and despair with the cycles of his wife's health, but tragedy always lurked in the background. Death, or the threat of it, runs throughout this book. Boswell's wife and father were both very ill, Dr. Johnson was growing old, and the deaths of at least a dozen friends and relatives found their ways into these pages. Boswell is very fond and proud of his children, chronicling each new word which enters the vocabulary of the youngest. The older ones often read scripture in the evening, and their father is always pleased with the performance.

Boswell's relationship to his father has been a constant theme in the journals, and now he is old and agonizingly ill. Boswell loved his father and desperately wished to be loved by him. But the old Laird of Auchinleck regarded his eldest son as a profligate wastrel; yet Boswell was the heir of entail. He had to inherit the family estate by law, and the old man seemed to resent this fact. He has kept his son on a very meager allowance for many years, even against the advice of his friends. He considered, with no evidence whatever to support such an opinion, that Boswell's wife encouraged Boswell in his spendthrift ways, and his treatment of his daughter-in-law and his grandchildren, to Boswell's great distress, was often cold and almost cruel. Boswell was anxious to succeed as Laird of Auchinleck and was concerned that his wife "might perhaps die before my coming to the estate . . . which would place her in a situation which she so well deserves." He was even driven at one point to confide in his journal that he "could not help viewing his [his father's] death as a desirable event." Yet when the old man did die, near the end of this volume, and Boswell became in fact the Laird of Auchinleck, the difficulties he had encountered on the way rendered the event of very little satisfaction. Lord Auchinleck was agonizingly ill; Dr. Gillespie had to empty his bladder three times each day by catheter. The old man, in his frugal Scots way, had settled an annuity on the doctor in order to guarantee his services, and Boswell saw this as an erosion of his future estate and wondered if he could modify the bequest when he became Laird.

Lord Auchinleck's second wife, Boswell's stepmother, was another source of difficulty. She tenderly cared for the old man, seeing her role as one who would protect him from a son who would ruin him; Boswell, on the other hand, considered her to be an obstinate obstacle to the establishment of a better relationship between him and his father. Fortunately, however, these two later came to understand each other better and to share a genuine mutual fondness.

Boswell's law practice had never been extensive, but its decline during the period covered here was cause for anxiety not only because of the resulting financial problems, but also because he was forced to admit the connection between his declining law practice and his father's less and less frequent appearance on the bench in the Court of Session. He longed to transfer his practice to London, "yet feared I should not be able to rise to any eminence there." Yet, if he did leave Scotland, he would forfeit all his income except for the parsimonious one hundred pounds a year his father allowed him. But in his fantasies London remained always a possibility, and he begged his friend Edmund Burke to seek an appointment for him. He was constantly torn in two directions: he wanted very much to assume his inheritance as Laird of Auchinleck, but he also yearned to go to London, hopefully to sit in Parliament. The invitation from Burke never came, and Boswell never resolved the conflicting desires in his own heart and mind.

Of more importance for readers today than Boswell's legal career was his literary life. By now, he had a substantial reputation; "I am," he observed quite accurately, "better known in the world than most of my countrymen." We see him at work on his *Hypochondriack* essays, searching Edinburgh libraries for apt mottoes and quotations. His anonymous pamphlet to Lord Braxfield was very well received, and Boswell never tired of asking various persons who had not pierced the cloak of anonymity what they thought of the pamphlet, just to hear himself praised. He had a series of letters in the *Public Advertiser;* his editorials were printed in the *Caledonian Mercury;* and he wrote rather mediocre occasional verse. Several years earlier he had toured the Hebrides with Dr. Johnson, and during the period covered in this volume, he was revising his notes on that adventure into what would become a very well-known travel account. He was also planning his *The Life of Samuel Johnson*, which would become his greatest work and, in the estimation of many, the greatest biography in the world. "I told Erskine," he recorded, "I was to write Dr. Johnson's life in scenes. He approved."

And so the Boswell who emerges from these pages is a continuation of the Boswell of the earlier volumes. He is older now; he has troubles as well as responsibilities. He still has his foibles, but they have become less youthful amusements and more flaws of character. Yet his perception of life is maturer and his intellectual grasp is strengthened. If he is no longer as amusing and entertaining as he once had been, he is nevertheless more human and more genuine.

Robert B. White, Jr.

CATHERINE THE GREAT

Author: Joan Haslip (1911–   )
Publisher: G. P. Putnam's Sons (New York). 382 pp. $12.95
Type of work: Biography
Time: The eighteenth century
Locale: Russia

The story of one of Russia's most colorful, ambitious, and accomplished rulers

Principal personages:
> CATHERINE II, Empress of Russia, 1762–1796
> CATHERINE DASHKOVA, her friend, co-conspirator, and director of the
> Academy of Sciences
> GREGORY ORLOV, her lover during the first decade of her reign
> STANISLAUS PONIATOWSKI, another lover and later King of Poland
> GREGORY POTEMKIN, another lover, administrator of New Russia
> PETER ULRICH (PETER III), Emperor of Russia (for six months) and
> Catherine's husband

The life of Catherine II of Russia is fascinating enough to command a regular and secure place in the book trade, and every four or five years a new popular biography appears. Joan Haslip's volume is the latest offering, and it meets all the requirements of the popular genre. Haslip faithfully recounts Catherine's string of romances and sexual encounters, her correspondence with great literary and royal personages, and her major foreign policy triumphs. However, the author builds the story on the often repeated and long outdated secondary accounts of Brückner, Soloveytchik, and Walezewski, plus some gossipy diplomatic dispatches. As a result, we get no new information or interpretation.

It is unfortunate that Haslip took this easy route, when, with a little extra effort, she could have produced something fresh and valuable. In the past fifteen years American, British, and French scholars have published a number of original monographs and shorter studies opening whole new lines of inquiry and discovery, and they have substantially modified the previously accepted knowledge about Catherine's reign. Haslip gives us none of this. The professional historian will certainly be dismayed to find how little of hardwon scholarly research gets translated into popular history. To her credit, Haslip writes with flair, and readers with no previous knowledge of the topic or period will profit from this entertaining introduction. They may, however, miss entirely the true reasons for Catherine's greatness.

The focus throughout this book remains on Catherine the woman of insatiable sexual appetite, Catherine the witty correspondent of philosophers and kings, Catherine the imperial conqueror of Turks and Poles. To judge from this account, about the only serious work she did on her own was identifying and buying major collections of Western art. This treatment trivializes Catherine both as a person and a ruler. One can scarcely come away from this book without feeling that Catherine was a nymphomaniac. Time and again we hear of lovers staggering out of her bedroom in complete exhaustion, pumping themselves up on aphrodisiacs, and seeking escape from her constant need for genital stimulation (we are at least spared the story of the horse). In reality, Catherine's love life was prosaic. She worked hard at the job of reigning and ruling, often twelve to fourteen hours a day, and sex was merely her way to relax and let off tension. But a woman ruler who scorned the expected prudish standards and who was clever and powerful enough to thwart the designs of foreign representatives and their masters could scarcely avoid being a target of slander. The stories of Catherine's sex life were largely the fantasies of frustrated men. Such tales were naturally picked up and peddled by popular book sellers. They sold well then, and apparently there is still a market for them today.

Haslip writes history in the grand manner. In her pages the "great person" theory is alive and well with an almost made-for-television baldness. Nothing of importance happens without the personal intervention of a heroic character. A typical case is the description of the 1771 bubonic plague epidemic in Moscow. The favorite Gregory Orlov was sent to deal with it, and, according to Haslip, his "boldness and decisiveness . . . cleared the city of the pestilence." As simple as that. Of course, no one then knew anything about the etiology and treatment of plague; its abatement was a function of changes in the weather and the rat-flea vector. Orlov just happened to arrive at the right time to take credit for it.

The book assigns too much power and influence to the Orlov brothers generally. They provided the muscle for Catherine's *coup d'état* in 1762, and in the early years she was indebted to them and dependent enough not to want to alienate them. But there were three loci of power in eighteenth century Russia: the imperial guards (where the Orlov strength lay), the Senate (seat of the leading families), and the court parties. Haslip gives the impression that Catherine did not believe she could rule without the support of the Orlovs, which falsely diminishes her stature. While no ruler could act effectively without the cooperation of these three institutions (as Peter III learned too late), Catherine was an astute politician who well understood how to manipulate this political configuration and keep its various elements in check.

Perhaps the biggest problem with popular history is its uncritical acceptance of any good story. Haslip's first chapters rely heavily on Catherine's famous memoirs, a source written with an obvious political purpose and reworked several times. Haslip simply accepts it as a true account, not merely repeating Catherine's self-serving portrayal of her husband as a dangerous madman, but even elaborating on it with a little popular psychology of her own. Yet there is no evidence that Peter was deranged. He was a drunkard, and his boorish and occasionally even silly behavior is fully explained as the actions of a drunken man. Catherine's effort to convince us otherwise by recounting each incident in lurid detail does not succeed, even if we can sympathize with her need to justify an act of usurpation and regicide.

At one point, however, Haslip declares her independence of Catherine's interpretation. This is on the issue of the paternity of her son Grand Duke Paul. Despite Catherine's hints that the real father was not Peter Ulrich but Sergei Saltykov (her first extramarital lover), Haslip grants the honor to Peter on grounds of supposedly similar physiological and personality traits. She adds the interesting suggestion that Catherine denied Peter's paternity in order to exonerate herself before her grandchildren for having condoned her husband's murder. Haslip may be right about Catherine's conscious bending of the truth here, but the empress' motives were no doubt different. One of the chief elements in Catherine's justification of her power seizure was the need to protect her son Paul, whom, she argued, Peter intended to get rid of. Raising doubts about Peter's fatherhood made the threats to Paul more credible. As for the question of paternity, it is far from clear that Catherine herself knew who the real father was.

The superficial treatment of most events described in this work leads to some serious misrepresentations of the workings of Russian politics. An obvious example, and one that scarcely requires any special analytical ability, is the cliché about Alexis Orlov acting for Catherine in killing Peter III, the implication being that Catherine had all but ordered the killing. In fact, Catherine had no need to do or say anything about Peter's fate. His continued existence posed a greater threat to the Orlovs and other conspirators than it did to Catherine, since his return would certainly have brought them to the scaffold and probably only landed Catherine in a convent. Peter's end would therefore have come soon enough without any complicity on Catherine's part.

Most distressing, on any issue of real importance to the social and political development of Russia, Haslip falters, if indeed she tells us anything at all. In regard to the secularization of church property, a major reform begun by Peter III, she speaks of a "storm of protest from all classes of people," when in fact what was most striking about this reform was the virtual absence of any protest. By the late eighteenth century the church stood in such abject dependence on the state that protest from within was unthinkable. Nor could an institution that provided little by way of social, intellectual, or even spiritual refuge expect the defense of its interest by other classes. About the only reaction to the reform came from the enserfed peasantry, which saw the "liberation" of ecclesiastical peasants (as well as the freeing of the nobility from obligatory state service, which occurred in the same year) as a harbinger of their own emancipation from bondage to the landed nobility. When this promise failed to materialize, the serfs interpreted the overthrow of Peter III as a plot by the "evil boyars" to suppress the manifesto granting their freedom, and, not surprisingly, they soon discovered Peter III's (twenty-three of them, in fact) living in the villages and ready to lead the serfs to victory over the usurpers.

The most successful Peter III was Emelyan Pugachev, whose peasant war of 1773–1774 engulfed vast areas of central-eastern Russia and threatened to ignite rebellion in Moscow itself. This last great social upheaval of the early modern era—Haslip inexplicably calls it the first—destroyed the walls protecting Catherine's compulsive personality. It is a tribute to the quality of Catherine's public relations that Haslip could be led to assert that during the crisis "only the empress kept her head." In reality, she came altogether unglued, babbled about leading the gentry on the battlefield, and then sank into a period of prolonged despondency.

Much to Catherine's credit, after recovering she quickly polished up and began implementation of a major reform of the provincial administration, a measure she had been perfecting for more than a decade. The reform was her crowning achievement as a ruler. With it she did what Peter the Great had long struggled in vain to accomplish: create a domestic administration separate from the armed forces. This meant that the next time Russia went to war its provincial administration did not evaporate and with it the government's capacity to collect taxes, muster recruits, and, not least, to contain peasant insurgencies and thus forestall another Pugachev rebellion. Catherine's government reforms established the basic framework of Russian administration until the emancipation of the serfs in 1861.

These reforms were not Catherine's only claim to greatness. Her tolerance and encouragement of public discussion, even to the point of subsidizing independent journalism, gave impetus to a budding intellectual life and provided Russia with the greatest freedom of expression it was to enjoy at any time prior to 1905. She also granted to the nobility and towns corporate rights, which, however fragile and circumscribed, were the first recognition in modern Russia of the notion that citizens could exercise rights against the state. Finally, there was Catherine's remarkable ability to select the ablest field commanders (P. Panin, Suvorov, Rumiantsev, Repnin, Kutuzov) and some of the most skilled government ministers (N. Panin, Viazemskii, Teplov, Bezborodko) of modern Russia. These were the true sources of Catherine's greatness and her legitimate claim to that title. Any history that neglects these aspects of her work and dwells on her supposed need to be physically subjugated by men, her insatiable sexual demands, her art collecting and monumental building projects greatly diminishes its subject and misses much of the point of studying the life of Catherine II.

David L. Ransel

THE CELTS
The People Who Came Out of the Darkness

Author: Gerhard Herm (1931–   )
Publisher: St. Martin's Press (New York). Illustrated. 312 pp. $10.95
Type of work: Archaeology and history
Time: c. 2500 B.C.–A.D. 1000
Locale: Western Asia, Central and Western Europe, and the British islands

A survey of the Celtic peoples from their presumed origins, through the height of their civilization, to their eclipse in the early medieval period in Western Europe

Principal personages:
BRENNUS THE ELDER,
BRENNUS THE YOUNGER,
DUMNORIX,
VERCINGETORIX,
CASSIVELLAUNS,
KING ARTHUR,
QUEEN MAEVE,
CÚ CHULAINN,
ST. COLUMBA, and
CONOR MAC NESSA, Celts
DIODORUS SICULUS,
POLYBIUS,
POSIDONIUS, and
STRABO, Greeks
CAIUS JULIUS CAESAR,
TACITUS, and
LIVY, Romans

Most of our conceptions and misconceptions about the early Celts, until quite recently, have been based on a few scattered reports of ancient Greek and Roman writers, and on the myths and legends of the Celts themselves. All of these sources mixed fact and fancy to varying degrees. Not until the late nineteenth century did serious efforts to sort out the truths about the Celts begin. Scholars in several disciplines—archaeology, history, linguistics, and the physical sciences—have conducted extensive and intensive research into what the Celts were truly like. Many of the old notions have been revised and today we probably have a better understanding of the ancient Celts than their contemporaries did. There is much that is still puzzling, but the curtain of mystery has been somewhat lifted; the Celts have partially come out of the darkness.

Gerhard Herm is not himself a trained archaeologist or historian; he is a professional writer with an interest in ancient history. One of his previous books, a popularized study of the Phoenicians, has been translated into twenty-four languages and seems to have been widely read. To gather materials for *The Celts,* Herm traveled through Europe studying the sites of Celtic settlements, and he has also drawn substantially upon the writings of such authorities in the field of Celtic studies as Nora Chadwick, Jean-Jacques Hatt, and Kenneth

Jackson.

Always intriguing are the researches of scholars into the possible origins of various human societies. As to the origins of the Celts, Herm finds plausible a current theory which suggests that the Celts—and all Indo-Europeans—emerged from certain tribes living in the steppe lands of the lower Volga River around 3000 B.C. One archaeologist has called those particular tribes the Kurgan (mound) people, and has found that they were taller, more long-headed and possibly more graceful than the squat, round-headed, Ukrainian tribesmen who inhabited the same general area. Some linguists consider it possible that the Kurgan tribes spoke what is known as the "Ur-language," the supposed ancestor of the later Indo-European tongues. By c.2400–2300 B.C., the theory continues, the Kurgan people had domesticated horses and, hitching those animals to their carts, the tribes began migrating eastward and westward, probably impelled by population pressures. Those who migrated eastward came into contact with the Sumerian and Akkadian civilizations of the Fertile Crescent, adopted elements of civilized life from those more advanced societies, and then migrated on further to Iran and India.

The tribes which traveled to the west settled in the plains and mountains of Bohemia and central Germany where they found copper and tin which they used to make bronze. The Bohemian bronzemakers established the Unětice culture which, at its greatest extent around 1500 B.C., included much of central Europe. Two subsequent Indo European cultures probably emerged from the Unětice: the Urnfield in northern Europe and, later, the Hallstatt in Western Europe, differing from the Unětice in the kind of burial for the dead they used, and probably in the languages they spoke. The Urnfield and Hallstatt cultures by c.1000 B.C. resembled what is known to be the Celtic way of life at a later date: ironmaking had appeared, people resided on solitary farms rather than enclosed villages, had more interest in raising animals than in the cultivation of the soil, included a warrior class which used two- or four-wheeled chariots and fought with battle axes, and priests who sacrificed to sun gods.

It seems likely that Celts or Proto-Celts shared in and learned these cultural features, and that sometime between 1300 and 600 B.C. a distinctive, identifiable culture which can be called Celtic evolved. However, scholars will surely never be able to say "suddenly the Celts arrived" because no people come out of the darkness into history with a full panoply of the national customs, language, and culture already intact. As Herm puts it, rather picturesquely, the Celts appeared when the first man said "good morning" to his wife in Celtic, but no one will ever know just when that happened.

In the mid-nineteenth century, at a site in Switzerland called La Tène, archaeologists uncovered a rich store of various artifacts dating from the fifth century B.C.—swords, spears, tools—many of them decorated in almost naturalistic patterns which came to be known as the La Tène style, which is now regarded as uniquely Celtic. The Celtic artists were eclectic, taking motifs from the arts of the Mediterranean and from the splendid artwork of the Scythians who lived to the east. Over several centuries following the early La Tène artifacts, Celtic artists and craftsmen produced numerous practical and decorative objects, many of which were brilliantly executed and technically perfect.

From Bulgaria and Rumania in eastern Europe, to France and the British islands in the west, investigators have found many other indications of Celtic culture since the first finds at La Tène. These later discoveries show that from the fifth to the first centuries B.C. the Celts acquired a wide variety of civilized skills. They learned to inlay metals, and could cast soft iron. They knew how to enamel and to make ornamental glass. The weaving and dyeing techniques they used produced excellent wearing apparel.

In the same period (450–50 B.C.), Celtic towns sprang up; some ninety Celtic *oppida* have been located in ancient Gaul alone. Trade routes joined these to other Celtic towns from the Atlantic to the Carpathians. One of the most impressive archaeological finds of recent years is the discovery of a large Celtic community on the Danube River in Bavaria near the village of Manching. Excavations at Manching began in 1955 and are not yet completed, but enough has been revealed to show that the Celts had a good-sized community there, and that it was a major trade and industrial center for much of Celtic Europe. The town covered some four hundred hectares contained within a four-mile-long defensive wall. Within the town were hundreds of mud-faced stone dwellings, numerous shops and workplaces including iron and glass works, potteries, goldsmiths, and bronze foundries. Herm, upon visiting the Manching town site, finds it astonishing that some Celtic prince, whose name we do not know, was able to organize, discipline, and direct his barbarian tribesmen to erect such an establishment as Manching town. The town was conquered by the Romans about A.D. 15, and its end was violent as attested by many split skulls found among the ruins. Still, the fact that it did exist, and flourished for many years, is evidence of considerable cultural advances by some of the Celts since the pre-La Tène era.

One of the more interesting chapters of *The Celts* deals with the Druids, "the authentic and most important representatives of the Celtic people." It was in respect to the Druids and their functions that the contemporary Greek and Roman writings about the Celts were often most in error. That the Druids were priests (called "miraculix") who performed ceremonies in oak groves using golden sickles, branches of mistletoe, and white cloths, and that sometimes those ceremonies involved human sacrifices, was known to the Romans. But the Druids were more than priests; they were seers who knew the past and the future, medical healers who, over generations, had acquired an extensive and efficacious pharmacopeia, and they were students of nature and the seasons; "they were university, church and court of the realm all in one." Some Celtic scholars find parallels between the Druids of Western Europe and the Brahmin ruling caste of Aryan India, both groups having roots in the "shaman" of the early Indo European tribes. Like the Brahmins, the Druids were poets who sang the songs and told the legends of their people, and they were students and teachers of the law. No class or group had more influence among the Celts than the Druids, not even the tribal kings. It is not surprising, therefore, that when the Romans conquered the Celtic tribes, the Druids and their practices were banned for political and moral reasons.

The Romans first met the Celts around 400 B.C. when the Gauls, as the Romans called them, migrated into the Po River valley. Diodorus Siculus gives a description of the striking and terrifying appearance of the Celts at this time: "like wood-demons . . . hair long and shaggy and bleached white . . . those of high rank shave their cheeks but wear a moustache . . . the way they dress is astonishing." They wore brightly colored shirts and trousers, and striped or checkered cloaks. Some of the warriors wore bronze helmets with horns to make themselves taller and more ferocious, and covered themselves with chain armor, but "most of them went naked into battle."

Around 390 B.C. hosts of these blond giants led by Brennus the elder with wild singing and horrible yells advanced on Rome. They overwhelmed the defenders and captured the city. After months of negotiation, Brennus agreed to accept a tribute of one thousand pounds of gold and declaring "woe to the defeated," returned north with his army. The Romans rebuilt their city, but the scars of fear and hatred for the Celts never healed.

Not until three and a half centuries had passed did Romans repay their enemy with the conquest and subjugation of Gaul by Julius Caesar. A substantial portion of *The Celts* is devoted to Caesar's Gallic Wars. Those wars culminated in the battle at Alesia in central Gaul where the Celtic chief, Vercingetorix, had assembled some eighty thousand warriors of several tribes for what proved to be the last defense of their homeland. After resisting the Roman siege for several months, the starving Celtic warriors surrendered. Vercingetorix was taken to Rome to adorn Caesar's triumph and then executed. All Gaul became a Roman province. The Gallic Celts merged and blended with Romans in the generations after Caesar's conquests, and lost much of their special way of life.

Across the Channel in Britain, however, the Celtic tribal kingdoms kept their independence and identity for a longer time. It was not until a century after Caesar that the emperor Claudius undertook the invasion of Celtic Britain and began the "campaigns at the world's end." Those took many years and were never fully completed, for the Celtic Scots and Irish could not be brought under Roman sway. In Scotland and Ireland, the Celts and their culture survived on the fringes of the Roman empire.

For many readers the final chapters of *The Celts* may be most interesting. There, Herm delves into the lost world of Celtic Ireland and Britain, retelling the stories of the fabulous Irish hero Cú Chulainn, of the fascinating Queen Maeve, and of the great King of Ulster, Conor Mac Nessa. And he tells of the British war chief who fought the invading Saxons and defeated them many times before he was slain; and then of the mythic transformation of that chief into the most remembered of all the Celtic heroes, King Arthur.

More significant historically than these legends, however, was the conversion of the Irish Celts to Christianity in the fifth century A.D. After that conversion, there emerged in Ireland a remarkable period of learning, literature, and art, and out of the Irish monasteries then went missionaries to bring the gospel of Christ to Celts and non-Celts in Britain and all over Europe.

The Celts is a competent work of historical popularization. Herm's intention was to provide an introduction for the general reader to the history of the Celtic people; seemingly he has succeeded, since the book is said to be a bestseller in Germany, where it was originally published. The English translation has produced an occasional odd sentence structure and clumsy syntax, but many portions are clearly, even lyrically, expressive. The photographic illustrations are few and not particularly illuminating, and some of the maps are not well juxtaposed with the text. The organization of the book is rather confusing with some of the early chapters out of chronological sequence; to help clarify matters, Herm has wisely provided a list of dates and events in an appendix.

James W. Pringle

THE CHINESE COMMUNIST PARTY
IN POWER, 1949-1976

Author: Jacques Guillermaz
Translated from the French by Anne Destenay
Publisher: Westview Press (Boulder, Colorado). 614 pp. $24.75
Type of work: History
Time: 1949-1976
Locale: The People's Republic of China

A narrative account of Chinese history since 1949 which emphasizes the role of Mao Tse-tung in directing the Communist Party and establishing the policies of the People's Republic

For the first time in the memory of Chinese living in the early 1950's, China had begun to experience a period of unification, peace, adequate food, economic growth, and international respectability. A century and a half of decline and disorder had abruptly come to an end with the emergence of a formidable Communist movement that came out of the fields and paddies of China's agrarian society. The challenges at the time were enormous. War with Japan and civil war with Chiang Kai-shek's nationalists had left China devastated. Public works were destroyed, fields were left unattended, and starvation was rampant. China's deprivation, however, brought on the anguish and despair among its people that facilitated the Communist Party in setting up a new government and a new society.

In viewing the events that followed "liberation," Guillermaz narrates, in great detail, the Communist Party's policies and methods of implementation. He is particularly interested in identifying the problems that beset the Communist leadership and the role of Mao Tse-tung in seeking solutions within the context of Marxism-Leninism. Obviously focused in the author's mind is an answer to the question: How has the Communist Party been able to maintain effective control over such a large nation under the trying conditions that beset China in 1949?

The problems were widespread. China's population, Guillermaz considers, is the most important. Without an accurate tally, no effective means to check population growth, and inadequate agricultural technology, a substantial shift in the country's food-people ratio could result in disaster. A second problem given the Party's attention is economic development. In this area, the Communist government has sought to devise policies which would expand both agriculture and industry, interrelating their expansion. Third, to bring about extensive political and economic change in China, the Party has experimented considerably with policies that would create an egalitarian society to break class distinctions and "elitism." Guillermaz, however, detects residual strength in family and clan ties, as well as the prevalence of materialism and individualism of Chinese tradition that impedes the development of a "new society." A fourth problem is to overcome factionalism which has historically plagued Chinese politics. Power struggles have continued to play a role in the casting of

Communist directions, especially in the shifting between moderate and radical leaders. Guillermaz, however, could not unwrangle Mao's last days. When the book was completed in 1976, Mao was still alive and the "Gang of Four" leftists had not yet been incarcerated; and the unsettled political scene at this juncture did not allow the author to assess accurately China's future political course.

The assertive hand of Mao Tse-tung in China's socialist transformation is evident throughout the upheavals of the Communist experiment. The "Hundred Flowers" campaign (1956), seeking the adulation of China's intellectuals; the "Great Leap Forward" campaign (1957-1958), China's fanatical drive for instant communalization and industrialization; and the "Cultural Revolution" (1966-1969), Mao's effort to make his revolution and "Maoism" permanently ingrained in the mind of every Chinese, were all part of Mao's strategy. The fact that they failed to achieve their objectives is not important. What is significant is that the movements were part of the Maoist brand of Communism that differed from the Soviets' and brought Maoism to an equal footing (at least in Chinese eyes) with Marxism and Leninism.

Guillermaz envisions Mao as "compliant and inflexible" and yet as one who contributed seriously to Communist doctrine and who had an influence on the international movement. Nevertheless, the author regards Mao as a leader who outlived his usefulness as a nation-builder and confused the past with the future. The watershed was the Cultural Revolution, according to Guillermaz, as the cyclic phenomenon of revolution was too disturbing to peace, order, and planning; and he questions the "seriousness of [the] Maoist vision." More credit should be given to Mao. While his tactic might have been overdrawn, his vision was not. He knew the difficulty of erasing old traditions in China, and he was fully aware of the "capitalist tendencies" that forged an emphasis on consumer production in the Soviet Union. He earlier expressed his concern to visiting American journalist, Edgar Snow, that China's youth might some day lose their revolutionary zeal. Mao was looking beyond Mao and *his* revolution.

In his analysis of the success of China's Communist Party to maintain effective control, despite periodic convulsions that threatened stability, Guillermaz generally presents balanced and well-reasoned views. Despite his recognition of the continuity of tradition in China's Communist state, he sees the necessity of the new institutions created by Mao and the Party's control of the media and the educational system to mold new thoughts and practices among the people. The task, he believes, was not difficult. Facilitating rapid changes in Chinese thinking was the small middle class, the lack of China's experience in political democracy, limited religious sentiment, the subordination of the individual to clan and family requiring only a transfer of loyalty to Party and state, and the search for new values by China's youth. The intensity of the Communists' psychological techniques used to accomplish "ideological remolding" does not figure in Guillermaz's analysis. This is unfortunate, because an account of oppressive tactics and China's legal system that places a defendant at the mercy of the state would render a more accurate view of the human cost of Mao's revolution.

The key to understanding Mao's success in establishing a viable government out of the ashes of chaos lies in the highly centralized administration of the People's Republic. Supported by most writers of the Communist period, Guillermaz believes that China's leadership of dedicated adherents to the Communist creed who could effectively command a loyal and disciplined cadres were most responsible for the new government's success.

China's yearning for a decent livelihood in 1949 commanded the attention of Mao and the Communist Party. While all aspects of economic improvement were sought, the communalization of the Chinese countryside was a prime target for Mao's Communist experiment. Despite Guillermaz's critical view of the Great Leap failure and the chaos it caused, he regards the Communist economic programs, both in food production and industrial development, generally successful. Considering the odds—diverse and difficult topography, uneven distribution of resources, the lack of a modern scientific tradition, and poor transportation—China's achievement has been great. Placing this economic gain in its proper perspective, Guillermaz observes that China has really "not yet emerged from its backward condition." While optimistic about China's future, the author believes that the nation can no longer experiment with risky shortcuts to bring about rapid modernization.

An important observation made by Guillermaz is that when China experienced periods of political stability and economic progress, it appeared strong internally and influential in its foreign affairs. Periods of rapid communization, however, disturbed the equilibrium and led to disaster. Despite the turmoil, the Communist experiment did not collapse. Rather, it hastened the decentralization process which Guillermaz regards as necessary and advantageous.

Ever since its inception, China's Communist government made changes in Chinese society. Western observers have speculated on how much has actually changed. Recognizing the thoroughness of certain institutional changes, Guillermaz sees many remnants of the past and does not feel that the Chinese spirit and lifestyle has been undermined. The Chinese reasoning by means of analogy, the coexistence of opposites, and ways of doing things are familiar. The Chinese remain industrious and frugal. The homes in which they live, the food they eat, the transportation they ride, and the tools with which they farm would easily be recognized by a returning Old China Hand. This is an observation reported by many Americans who have been to China in recent years.

Guillermaz substantiates his positions very well and presents a rational analysis, but a few of his contentions can be questioned. For example, he sees the Korean War in political terms for its value as a "mass campaign" to unite the people more firmly behind the new Communist government in China. He regards the war as an "unfortunate mistake" because it led to the strengthening of Western defenses in the Pacific, delayed China's entrance into the United

Nations, and encouraged China's doctrinal intransigence. While the war may have indeed been a mistake for North Korea and its Soviet backers, the China involvement was essential for its own security. In its consolidation phase, China's Communist government was too preoccupied with internal affairs to prepare schemes of foreign ventures for its propaganda benefits. The security needs of China that require friendly states on its borders have always been a primary concern of that nation's foreign policy.

In his discussion of Soviet relations, Guillermaz explains that China could not accept *détente* as it would seriously weaken her position in the socialist camp and in the world generally. China, he believes, also feared *détente* because it would "lead to a progressive liberalization within the socialist camp as a whole." He points out that China was undergoing "a hard period, a phase of great internal tension" and that a relaxation of its hard line was unacceptable. China's opposition to *détente*, however, is complex, involving historic, ideological, and territorial disagreements. Consequently, the severity of China's disdain for its northern neighbor has been consistent since 1956 regardless of whether its internal policies have been "hard" or "soft."

During the pragmatic years of Liu Shao-ch'i in the early 1960's, Chinese enmity toward the Soviet Union intensified to the point of including racial overtones. The resumption of moderate policies under the leadership of Hua Kuo-feng, Teng Hsiao-p'ing, and Li Hsien-nien (which Guillermaz had not witnessed when he completed his book) brings no change to Chinese fears and suspicions about Soviet intentions. Whether China's leadership is moderate or radical, the depth of the Sino-Soviet schism is likely to prevent *détente* from becoming a viable alternative to public denunciation, armed borders, and military clashes.

Guillermaz pays little attention to cultural developments, especially painting, in China under Communism; and when he does, he discards its value as a serious creative contribution to art. He regards painting as having come to an end with Hsü Pei-hung, who died in 1953. The rest is mediocre, socialist realism portraying base and insignificant subjects. This is too simple an explanation, however, as it overlooks other fine talents. In general, Chinese artists painted in the socialist mold during periods of harsh political policies such as the Great Leap and Cultural Revolution eras; but when moderate leadership relaxed the hard line, they took advantage of the situation and exhibited their creative talents. Sometimes they felt compelled to include a subtle political overtone in their predominantly traditional painting, while on other occasions only the native tradition is evident. Ch'i Pai-shih and Fu Pao-shih receive a mere mention, but they deserve more. They painted in ink (rather than Western oils) and used such traditional themes as Fu's "Poets of the T'ang." In addition, how can we overlook Yu Fei-an ("Pigeons and Plum Blossoms,") and Wu Tso-jen ("Thundering Yaks")? And how can we find anything political in Lin Feng-mien's "Cormorant in Flight"? In addition to painting, porcelain, lacquerware, and embroidery were produced—admittedly, with an eye on the Hong Kong tourist market.

This excellent, detailed account of the history of the Chinese Communist Party in power is a worthy reference for any interested reader. What few flaws the book has are not so serious as to mar its value; they merely provoke new considerations about China's myriad faces. The narration ends just before Mao's death in October, 1976, but the history of Chinese Communism continues to be written.

Leonard H. D. Gordon

CIRCLES
A Washington Story

Author: Abigail McCarthy (1915–   )
Publisher: Doubleday & Company (New York). 251 pp. $7.95
Type of work: Novel
Time: 1976
Locale: Washington, D.C., and campaign sites across America

A novel based on an incident which occurred in the 1972 presidential campaign, which follows the brief but intense presidential aspirations of Senator Sam Nordahl and his supporters

> *Principal characters:*
> SAM NORDAHL, United States Senator
> ALICE ANN NORDAHL, his wife
> JEFF STREATOR, a television documentary producer
> SARAH STREATOR, his wife
> TIANA BRIGGS, a political columnist
> LAURA TALBERT, a widow living in Washington, D.C.

The political novel, a once respected genre produced with sophistication and style by such writers as Bulwer-Lytton and Anthony Trollope, has in recent decades become almost exclusively the province of the hacks, who churn out massive volumes in which potential disasters and personality guessing games take precedence over any feeble attempts to explore the real nature of power or the consequences of power on the human personality. Perhaps because she came to fiction-writing late in life, and perhaps because she is a wise and gifted individual, Abigail McCarthy has written one of the finest political novels to appear in many years. As the wife of a former United States senator and presidential candidate, Mrs. McCarthy had the opportunity to observe the national political scene in a way few authors outside of politics can hope to. (This may also be why so many political novels are written by reporters, rather than by experienced novelists.) But what she made of this material can only be the product of her own special sensibility and talent. In *Circles: A Washington Story,* McCarthy is first a novelist and secondly a social commentator.

Many readers will, no doubt, enjoy *Circles: A Washington Story* because of its insider's point of view and its shrewd observations and comments about the most minute aspects of political and social life in Washington, but the book offers greater rewards than that. Although the author is brilliant when dealing with the desperation inherent in Washington social circles, she is equally sharp when writing of the changes which have taken place in Washington over the years, from decade to decade, administration to administration, election to election, crisis to crisis. The changing styles of social form and political ambition are all clearly delineated with the economy of words of a skilled craftsman. McCarthy's observations—or those of her characters—about the factors which make or break politicians ring true. This is not a book of scandalous revelations, but it is one which only a person who has spent years on the scene could have written. One feels certain that this picture presents Washington as it is.

But, more than merely satisfying the reader's curiosity about the workings of national government and the secrets of power-trading, *Circles* offers an intelligent woman's concern with moral issues that go beyond political games to the profound concerns of all human beings. McCarthy probes old suppositions, stereotyped opinions, and irrational but stubborn myths. In the pages of *Circles,* the values and moral righteousness of Western materialism are confronted by a shrewd mind and unjaded moral sense.

The narrative is refracted through the points of view of several characters. Although the story is of Senator Sam Nordahl's attempt to win the presidential nomination, he actually is not the central character, except in that his personality acts as both a catalyst and a mirror for the other characters who revolve around him. The men and women surrounding Nordahl see what they want to see—what they *must* see—in his handsome, bland features. The press representatives, the other politicians, and his wife, all find themselves confronting new visions of themselves, as well as of their candidate. This gradual stripping of layers is what this fine novel is all about.

The story is framed by the reflections of Laura Talbert, a genteel lady of the old school, a woman who has spent most of her life in Washington, part of the inner circle for decades, but now gradually receding into the background. Rather wistfully, Mrs. Talbert ponders her fate, the fate of many a Washington widow. She is not bitter about the outcome of her life, but she wonders just what it all has meant. There have been undeniable satisfactions, but at times she is inclined to wonder what her destiny might have been if she had chosen a different, more aggressive, pattern for her life, one not so much in the shadow of her husband. For it is a fact that any small influence that she had, any brief power or long-lasting respect that she achieved, was due to her primarily as the wife of a man who possessed power and commanded respect. The situation of Laura Talbert reflects but one aspect of the position of women in Washington circles. Gradually, with infinite subtlety, McCarthy exposes additional layers of the lives of women in Washington, both directly involved in government and on the sidelines. But her interest is chiefly with the wives, with the women who are expected to be always attractive and on duty, to serve and wait until needed to serve again, but who hold no official offices and receive no pay. Laura Talbert represents but one facet of this complicated and fascinating picture.

Laura Talbert's personality is sharply and subtly revealed in the opening chapter as she begins telling her own story. The reader comes to understand gradually what makes this woman as she is, and to pick up bit by bit the various aspects of her life. Her need for discretion is fundamental, yet she has lived a life not without its secrets. She is not ashamed of having had an affair many years before, and she is rather proud of the discreet way in which she carried it off, hurting no one. She is somewhat shocked when she looks around her at the world of the 1970's, when people are more blatant about their lifestyles. She sympathizes with the needs of younger women to express their own personalities, but only up to a certain point.

Alice Ann Nordahl is the perfect candidate's wife, attractive, intelligent, charming, and poised, yet she too is not immune to the new trends and alterations in the roles of men and women. Why can't a woman be affirmative in her choice of marriage and homemaking as a way of life, she asks? Yes, she admits that there are injustices, that women should receive equal pay for equal work and should have economic equality on all levels, as well as opportunity when they desire it. But what will all of these changes bring, she asks? The fact is that life is a matter of choices and chance, and there is no point in making choices on the basis of what ought to be, rather than what is. Here, we come close to the heart of the novel, for the narrative, with its many threads, is really about choices, and about the incidents which compel those choices, right or wrong, to be made.

But perhaps the novel is most biting and poignant when dealing with the character of Tiana Briggs, a political columnist whose struggle for professional success has led her to the inner circle, but at a cost that only she knows. A vividly conceived, brilliantly drawn character, Tiana represents the career woman of the past thirty years who was forced to make sacrifices if she chose to compete in a "man's world." The women who have come after her and built on her success cannot imagine the difficulties and pains that she has had to overcome to reach her level of power and respect. The contrast between her life and that of young Sarah Streator and the other women belonging to later generations is startling.

However, McCarthy may hit closest to home when dealing with the political wives and the condescension with which they are viewed by both the press and male Washington. There can be a very positive role for a political wife to play, as Alice Ann Nordahl explains, if she enjoys a variety of people and is good at campaigning, but that only works if the husband can accept her help and her sharing; some men cannot. Some women feel exploited when forced into that role, others relish it. The family is supposed to be the center of life in America, and the political wife is supposed to represent the best features of this vision; it is an unfair position for anybody to be placed in, and one almost impossible to live up to.

As Sarah Streator reflects when she has tried to rebuild her own career, after giving it up for marriage and family, one must have one's own identity. One is what one does. She sees, among the faces at the farewell luncheon for Laura Talbert, the faces of women who never woke up to their full potential, the faces of women whose lives ended before they really had begun. The thought is intolerable to her, yet many of those women do not even realize what they have missed. They never learned to recognize themselves as separate, responsible individuals; they always were the lesser part of a team. The subtle variations between the conditions of these different women are skillfully pinpointed and analyzed by McCarthy; it is here that her artistry reaches its peak.

Older women are seldom seen sympathetically in fiction and are not supposed to be noticed in an America which worships youth. Yet the older women portrayed in this novel are rich and rewarding characters, among the best in the book. They are drawn with affection and understanding and more than a little compassion, in all of their complexity and diversity. They make clear the great loss that we all suffer by the current preoccupation in our society and literature with the concerns of youth.

With this book, McCarthy has confirmed her position as a writer of skill and distinction. First in her well-crafted autobiography, *Private Faces/Public Places,* and now in *Circles,* she shows both insight and precision in detailing the insecurities and ambiguities that gnaw at the women whose lives are sacrificed to the pursuit of power—usually a power which they can only share in the most minute way. She has shown in both books the subtle techniques of these women who alternately follow behind and deftly lead their political husbands. *Circles* portrays more accurately than any male-authored Washington novel the social life by which the politicians, journalists, lobbyists, and bureaucrats seek to manipulate one another and the fate of the country. For it is a fact that the cocktail and dinner parties, the luncheons and teas, the carefully prepared social functions and apparently accidental encounters all affect the country's political course.

Circles is quiet in tone, but it is all the more effective for that. Abigail McCarthy may lack a flair for the emotional, but her clear, lucid style and sharp intellect make vivid the dilemma of the contemporary political woman. Everyone, even the political male, who reads this novel should understand the conflicts and recognize the frequently devastating results of these conflicts on human lives. For all of its quiet tone, this is, at last, a deeply moving novel.

Bruce D. Reeves

COLLECTED POEMS: 1919-1976

Author: Allen Tate (1899-   )
Publisher: Farrar, Straus and Giroux (New York). 218 pp. $12.50
Type of work: Poetry

The volume which sums up the life's work of one of America's foremost poets and men of letters

Allen Tate, American man of letters, critic, commentator on the literary and social scene, is first and foremost a poet. Associated from the beginning of his career with the movement that created a truly modern American literature, he is one of the few still with us from that exciting time in the 1920's and 1930's when Hemingway and Faulkner in prose and Eliot, Ransom, Tate, and Warren in poetry broke new ground in the handling of language in imaginative literature. He has also been connected with two other movements which have, in greater or lesser ways, shaped our sense of ourselves and our society. The first was the New Criticism, which taught us to read our literature with great care and precision, and which taught us to discover in that literature the great riches of the English language. The second was the Southern Agrarian movement, which called to our attention the cost in social and personal terms of the technological revolution. Now, at the end of a long and distinguished career, during which he has received most of the honors which America can bestow on its men of literature, he has been given the opportunity to sum things up, to bring together his past achievements and indicate those things which he wishes to be remembered for. The most notable of these summary volumes is his recent *Essays of Four Decades* (1968), a compilation of those essays in literary criticism which he feels are worthy of preservation. His *Memoirs and Opinions* (1975) is a more relaxed volume, a collection of informal essays and memoirs, which gives us more of the reflective Tate, the great writer who is also a gentleman.

The present volume, however, is the central one, the one which informs the others, which makes clear the source and power of Tate's reputation, his place in twentieth century American literature. For it is his poetry, after all, that has built Tate's reputation, that has given his opinions on other matters their value and authenticity. And it is a tribute to Tate's faith in the quality of his work, and in the perceptiveness of generations of readers to come, that for *this* volume, uniquely among his summary volumes, he has chosen to avoid the route of selectivity. Instead, he has taken the risk of giving us everything, a collected poems rather than a selected poems. All the familiar great works are here—"Ode to the Confederate Dead," "Cold Pastoral," "The Swimmers," "Seasons of the Soul"— but there are all the minor poems and very early poems as well. In fact, the poems in this volume range in date from 1919 to 1976; to read them in order of their composition, which one can easily do since each poem is carefully dated, is to trace the development of one major poet in his sureness and confidence in handling his language, forms, and themes. Tate's corpus is not large—in all about one hundred and twenty poems—but what strikes the reader is the high quality of so much of this work, a richness and a complexity of language and vision which we can ill afford to be without in our day.

If there is a central quality to all Tate's work, it is what we might expect from a close student of T. S. Eliot and an associate of the New Critics Cleanth Brooks and Robert Penn Warren—a pervasive sense of irony. The New Critics taught us that irony is at the heart of poetic language, an irony which derives initially from a sense of the distance between the ideal and the real, and which usually expresses itself in Tate's poetry in a juxtaposition of unlikely elements. In his "Mr. Pope," the central figure strikes fear because his "tight back was rather a goat's than man's." On broader, and more thematic level, Tate's poems generate an irony of perspective by juxtaposing again and again the present with the past. In his most famous poem, "Ode to the Confederate Dead," the sacrifices of the past, and the agonies of defeat, are presented to challenge us to see ourselves in their light. In other poems, the past to be juxtaposed with the present is specifically the classical past, as Aeneas is conjured up to pay a visit to Washington and New York. In other poems, the classical appears only as an allusion, a brief of passing reference, but still generates a perspective from which to see, and judge, our present situation.

What the poet gives us is precisely, therefore, a way of looking at ourselves and our present, a perspective which calls us to depths of seeing, to a range of vision, which is often rare in our age. When Tate first joined with the other agrarians in questioning a naïve faith in progress and in future hope, his voice seemed bitter, acerbic, cynical. In the face of what we now know about the costs of "progress," we may hear him again as a more familiar voice, one which sees the hollowness at the center of so much that we may hold dear, and yet does not despair. What may seem obscure in Tate, his range of learning and his depth of classical allusion, can now seem a reminder of the riches we still have access to. His sense of the value of community and tradition may call us to rediscover them for ourselves. His confidence in the value of poetic language may be seen as an act of faith in man the poetic maker, who may use his skills both to show us painful realities and to cure us of holding on to false hopes.

There is development in Tate's poems, a movement which this volume makes accessible. The early "Elegy" conjures up dark images of the "dry hollows of the mind," an image close to Eliot's "Hollow Men," which will recur in more subtle form in Tate's later poetry. In the imagery, more generally considered, there is also movement, from what is little more than ordered prose to a richness of expression that often seems remote and obscure, but turns into powerfully moving and evocative language on closer examination. Tate's early work shows a tendency to create a poetic world remote from the realities of his existence; locales of Greece and the Orient seem far from Nashville, Tennessee. The later poems, however, and his best, fuse poetic vision with a deep sense of place, of real places—the Confederate graveyard, the subway, Christmas Day—to create a moving and profound sense of the heights and depths of reality.

But there is wit here, too, wit and an ability to laugh at human pretension, as in his "Two Conceits," which builds on the nursery rhyme "Sing a Song of Sixpence": "Sing a song of London/Paris and Berlin/Washington and Moscow/ Where the Ids are in/When the I's were opened/They saw ne'er a thing/But Phoenix in the Turtle/The Turtle on the Wing." Such moments give Tate's work a delightful variety to complement its overall richness.

That Tate's poetry has been so much in the mainstream of modern literature in America, and his politics and social views so much of the minority, suggests something telling about the role of art in our culture. So much of our attitude toward the present and the future is bound up in a naïve optimism about the value of progress, an approach to life that crumbles quickly before any sensitive man's reflection. As a result, much of our art has been an act of dissent, whether a naturalistic call to see life as it is really lived, a revolutionary plea for rapid social change, or an impassioned cry for what is being lost. Whether the criticism is launched from the left of the political spectrum or from the right, it has the quality of dissent in common with other acts of artistic expression. The response of Tate and many of his fellow Southerners to the coming of industrialization in the South was the creation of a world of value in art, especially in poetry. In this way, if not politically, Tate and the other agrarians, such as John Crowe Ransom and Robert Penn Warren, have reshaped American thought in significant ways. In so doing, they are linked with that other American so ill at ease in our technological society, T. S. Eliot. Tate the Southerner and Eliot the expatriot Midwesterner shared their sense of dissent from the mainstream of twentieth century American life; both men sought in tradition and in hierarchically organized society a sense of order and stability, a richer sense of humanity, to serve as an antidote for the rootlessness and restlessness of much of American society. It is Eliot's shadow that stands just behind so much of Tate's poetry, but to say that is to take nothing from the younger man, just to locate him in a realm of common voices. Tate's sense of history, his sense of time, of the realities of human life, of loss, of tragedy, of the value of community and tradition—these are the distinctive marks of his poetic vision. It is a vision for which we must be deeply grateful. In the midst of our own second thoughts about the nature of progress, the cost in personal and global terms of our technological society, Tate's poetic voice seems no longer reactionary, if it ever did, but prophetic. In an uncertain future, we will be grateful to him for it.

John N. Wall, Jr.

THE COLLECTED POEMS OF HOWARD NEMEROV

Author: Howard Nemerov (1920–   )
Publisher: The University of Chicago Press (Chicago). 510 pp. $20.00
Type of work: Poetry

The Collected Poems, winner of the 1978 National Book Award for Poetry, testifies to Nemerov's depth of insight and breadth of experience, as well as to his ability to write both rarefied poetry and a more accessible variety

Howard Nemerov's poetic achievements, it is quite safe to say, are fully insured against a future loss of immediacy and damage done by hostile critics. Though very much the poet of twentieth century America, he addresses age-old problems and concerns with rigor and notable insight. His subjects and themes are drawn from the many ages of man, his audience is universal, his imagery, Daedalian, and his capacity for satirical comment, memorable—at times, Swiftian. This volume of verse, his *Collected Poems,* is a compilation of distinguished Nemerov collections beginning with *The Image and the Law* (1947), proceeding through *Guide to the Ruins* (1950), *The Salt Garden* (1955), *Mirrors & Windows* (1958), *New and Selected Poems* (1960), *The Next Room of the Dream* (1962), *The Blue Swallows* (1967), *Gnomes & Occasions* (1973), and ending with his latest volume, *The Western Approaches: Poems 1973-75* (1975).

To examine critically Nemerov's success as a poet, it is instructive to look toward the major themes, then toward Nemerov the intellectual poet and satirist.

Three themes recur in *The Collected Poems:* time's mysterious passing, war, and the natural world. Returning to childhood for clues to his meaning and for emotional sustenance, the poet faces the harsh truth expounded in "An Old Photograph" that "No one escapes the perjury of time." After all, it is time itself (rather than any mere reexperiencing of childhood moments) that the poet is after. It is time, variously described and decried as a thief and liar, that tricks all of us and steals from us our most valuable, painfully earned lessons—even our fondest memories. Time conquers. As the poet, surveying the New Jersey boardwalk in "Elegy of Last Resort" finds, "We enter again November, and the last/ Steep fall of time into the deep of time,/ Atlantic and defeated. . . ." Together with time, we experience the descent into the void from which there is no escape and no awakening.

Many Nemerov poems have to do with the mystery involved in time's passing. As an American living in the Northeastern states, this poet knows well his seasons; yet the one season he writes about more than others is that quiet, ominous period between fall and winter when the bite of time is felt most acutely by the perceptive observer. Like the "cinnamon moths" of the poem "The Rent in the Screen," who, upon being awakened from cocoons by the treacherously "sweet mildness of the late December day," fly "Across the gulf of night and nothingness" into "The falling snow, the fall, the fallen snow," we too make our yearly and all-too-brief flight into hopes and dreams, lulled by the summer's heat, only to fly into the sad and puissant arriving winter. Like the *persona* in "Observation of October," human beings have that "old desperation of the flesh" when confronted by the annual drying up of the easy and free times of spring and summer.

Time, that implacable enemy against which there is no weapon to employ, is, to the poet, an "angry wheel" that "might burn away in air," giving the thoughtful individual very few quiet meditative moments of genuine insight before forcing him on to do battle with the encroaching tide of everyday duties. In "A Harvest Home," the *persona* is able, if only for the briefest time, to bask in the august stillness of "the long field in fall," reflecting upon the sun's silent bending of earth toward afternoon. This momentary blessing is, however, nothing more than one of time's confidence tricks, "a snare/ For time to pull from and be torn/ Screaming against the rusty brake." Or time may be cast in the image of an ocean voyage from which there is no return and it may be found in the painting, "Triumph of Time," by Pieter Brueghel, wherein time is depicted as a great elephant bearing a trumpeting angel which tramples the books and crowns and kings to dust.

Nemerov is much like certain anonymous artists of the Middle Ages whose paintings portray the victory of the grave over worldly ambitions and hopes and yet, unlike them, he is unable to paint the companion scene: that of the uncorrupted body rising to the New Jerusalem.

Poetry is the poet's chief bulwark against the aggressor, time, who must in the end conquer all. And yet, the poet questions the efficacy and enduring value of what he writes, knowing full well that he cannot hope to compete with the ancients, the old masters like Homer whose poetry had a sufficient, sustained vision of life and a wholeness destined to survive the centuries.

In addition to time, Nemerov is obsessed by another destroyer: modern warfare. Having participated in World War II, the poet knows well what that conflict said about us and our technological world, what it elucidated for us, what ambiguity of response it and other wars manifest within us.

Modern warfare cannot be sung in the manner of Homer or Virgil: it is more cruel than ancient warfare because it is more mechanical, more difficult to conjure up because it is too awesome a phenomenon. And yet, Nemerov, working with isolated memories of conflict, makes the attempt to tell what war is really like without saying too much in the process. In one of his earlier poems, "For W___, Who Commanded Well," the poet speaks of the ironies inherent in being an officer in charge of men in an era when the individual soldier or officer no longer matters—an era when technology decides outcomes of battles and big money interests control wars. This theme is vividly reiterated in other creations such as "September Shooting" (ostensibly about bird hunting, but actually dealing with modern warfare) in which the poet finds that "death comes quickly/ And is not famous nor ever identified. . . ." It is a time when, "The anonymous bullet flies out of/ An irrelevant necessity, and knows no evil."

But it is the smaller things that say as much about Nemerov's view of war as anything possibly could: those mummified blue eyeballs ripped from a dead enemy soldier that his killer keeps in his pocket as rattling souvenirs. Without God and without any great faith in the motivations of fellow men who always have in them the capacity to rip out the eyeballs of others for a joke, Nemerov frequently finds some measure of solace in the one place poets have traditionally sought comfort: nature. Although his finest collection of nature poems is found in *The Salt Garden* volume, poems honoring nature's moods are scattered freely throughout *The Collected Poems*.

As has been previously noted, nature is both a mirror and an agent of time. Those seasonal changes mirrored in meadows, woodlands, and beach areas seem to push the poet relentlessly toward his death. And even spring, portrayed as a "powerful bear,/ Drunken with deathlessness" in the poem, "Zalmoxis," instructs the poet in the vagaries of human fortunes and gives him powerful intimations of his mortality. In the lyrical "Dandelions," for instance, spring brings those small yellow flowers that delight everyone but the most hardened lawn enthusiast. But dandelions, like everything that lives, change, becoming the "Stricken and old, ghosts in the field . . ." that the poet depicts withering away in the most merry of seasons. Like the dandelions, it is inferred, we too will become, with horrifying rapidity, like those ". . . ruined spinsters," who sway in the field parading "ghostly hair."

Destruction is a part of Nemerov's summer as well as his spring. For summer is the time when the sun beats hardest upon creation, drying flowers and plants, while encouraging the rankest and ugliest weeds to grow. In "Midsummer's Day," the poet surveys an abandoned farm that bakes in midsummer heat, noting, "that fate runs/ Wild as the summer—Babylon and Rome,/ As ruin remains brought in a sense home."

Autumn is, as has been noted, a time for people to reflect upon the fleeting pleasures they experienced in the summer (whether such pleasures are real or imagined, the poet does not say). It is, as always, the melancholy season when even a falling leaf offers an intricate lesson to the perceptive onlooker, who sees in its slide to earth, "An old story;/ How youth may go from glory to glory/ Changing his green for a stiff robe of dry/ Magnificence. . . ." And it is a time to store sheaves of wisdom and memory for the coming of the dark, ancient ceremonies of winter when visual inspiration will be all but gone until spring's return.

"The Pond," one of Nemerov's most anthologized, most important poems, speaks of winter's taking of a young boy's life. The boy (named Christopher) is an unwitting victim of thin ice on the pond, and his death's dignity and significance is almost erased by the winter's apathy: its blank ice sheet's stare, the dead woods, and the silent, uncaring surrounding terrain. Winter is eternal (or so it first appears): cold, dark, static, unknowing, a perfect void. But juxtaposed against the implacable, deadly face of winter are the awakening cries of spring's first birds, summoning life from the apparent grave and bringing hopes to a once hopeless world. Nature—more specifically, nature as she is found in the Northern United States—is a creation whose seasons serve as reminders to man of his fate and yet are also providers of hope and joy.

Nemerov has been saddled with the appellation "academic poet," the implication being that his is a pedantic poetry, a stale product of the "academy." Nothing could be further from the truth. His lifeblood is, admittedly, the world of ideas, for he is essentially an intellectual poet (as opposed to a poet whose horizons are established by an amorphous and mythical "academy"). He is familiar with the world's greatest movers and shakers—those artists and thinkers who have pointed the way: Homer, Virgil, Dante, Lu Chi, Brueghel, Shakespeare, the English metaphysicals, Vermeer, Valery, and Rimbaud, to name but a few. To understand Nemerov, one must have more than a surface acquaintance with the literary, religious, and artistic traditions of both East and West, for Nemerov is one of this century's "difficult" poets, in a league with poets such as Pound, Yeats, and Breton who write for the tiny minority of poetry readers. Yet, this is not to say that he cannot be earthy and concrete, because one of his strengths lies in his ability to be both abstract and concrete in the same poem.

Nemerov writes about all sorts of things, both private and public, earthy and ethereal. He can, for instance, illuminate Mafia "cement-overcoat" killings and Sunday papers strewn across a floor, the horrors associated with suburban lawnmowers and suburban social functions, the meaning of a rotten-in-the-grill Cadillac prowling American city streets, as well as discuss Plotinus or the *ars poetica*. His far-searching poetic vision is often reminiscent of the later Yeats: "And man, geometer, construes his arcs/ And angles to cathedral poise, of which/ Sunday's massive reserve composes still/ Continuous limits of the possible." Increasingly, however, his poetry turns from abstraction to concreteness; his language becomes more "common" and his images more accessible as one moves from his earlier poems to his later ones. Of football on a television screen, he makes vivid what he sees, speaking of "a spaghetti of arms and legs/ Waving above a clump of trunks and rumps" and of ginkgo trees, he notes, "fallen yellow fruit" that "mimics the scent/ Of human vomit. . . ."

Nemerov's poetic voice very often is spoken of as something detached and lordly, somehow quietly ironic—and, for the most part, this is true. Nonetheless, his measured, calm language increasingly gives way to the more colloquial language of his later volumes in which lines like the following turn up (this passage is taken from his "Ozymandias II"):

> I met a guy I used to know, who said:
> 'You take your '57 Karnak, now,
> The model that they called their Coop de Veal
> That had the pointy rubber boobs for bumpers.'

Yet, at his most characteristic, Nemerov remains the poet assuming a traditionally aloof narrative tone that keeps his verse impersonal and authoritative:

"You will remember, Theseus, that you were/ The Minotaur, the Labyrinth and the thread/ Yourself; even you were that ingener/ That fled the maze and flew—so long ago—/ Over the sunlit sea to Sicily."

Known for his lyrical evocations of time's passing and nature, Nemerov also has a reputation of being a satirist of the first rank, who, with the usual moralistic undergirding of the true satirist, judges his own society and finds it lacking in many crucial ways. His satirical poems evince a sensitivity toward destruction, hatred, bigotry, war, and the human suffering they create.

In "A Negro Cemetery Next to a White One," the poet expresses profound indignation over the plight of black people in this country by speaking of black ghosts turned away from heaven by a blond angel; or a university museum exhibit in which a decorated pottery skull serves as the very emblem of the artist's own vanity and essential emptiness and preciousity; or of the platitudes recalled after a commencement ceremony wherein a new generation of young people was stuffed with clichés and lies.

In all, Nemerov's satire has become more powerful and less enigmatic in the last three volumes of his poems than it was previously. He has mastered the most demanding of satirical devices: the epigram (or, as he might call it, the "gnome"). Worthy of Swift or Wilde is the gem called "The God of This World" in which God "smiles to see His children, born to sin,/ Digging those foxholes there are no atheists in." His wit, particularly when presented in so compact a vehicle, is devastating.

As a portrayer of the ironies and ambiguities of our time, Howard Nemerov has few—if any—equals. His line of vision, hitched as it is to his proper, poised, and classical tone, is an expansive and encompassing one. Sufficiently humble to take lessons from past and present masters and sufficiently outspoken and self-assured to denounce present-day mediocrity, cruelty, and waste, this poet has achieved something few poets ever do. His achievement resides in the fact that for over thirty years, he has exhibited a capacity for intellectual growth as well as an unruffled—even majestic—ability to say important things crisply, nobly, memorably. His is a unique and forceful American voice.

John D. Raymer

CONFLICT AND CRISIS

The Presidency of Harry S Truman, 1945-1948

Author: Robert J. Donovan (1912-   )
Publisher: W. W. Norton & Company (New York). 473 pp. $12.95
Type of work: History
Time: 1945-1948
Locale: The United States

A history of the first administration of Harry S Truman, which saw the origins of the Truman Doctrine and the Marshall Plan as outgrowths of the developing Cold War with the Soviet Union

> *Principal personages:*
> HARRY S TRUMAN, President of the United States, 1945-1953
> DEAN ACHESON, Under Secretary of State, 1945-1947
> JAMES F. BYRNES, Secretary of State, 1945-1947
> CLARK M. CLIFFORD, Special Counsel to the President, 1946-1950
> JAMES V. FORRESTAL, Secretary of Defense, 1947-1949
> GEORGE C. MARSHALL, Secretary of State, 1947-1949
> JOHN W. SNYDER, Secretary of the Treasury, 1946-1953

Harry Truman has become something of a folk hero in recent years. A factor in forming this popular image of Truman has been a tendency to compare his bluntness and lack of pretense to the manipulation and deception characteristic of Nixon's "imperial presidency." This view of the man has been reinforced on the stage and in the media by presentations based on Truman's self-serving recollections as recounted in Merle Miller's *Plain Speaking.* This is not the Harry Truman who emerges from Donovan's well-researched and ably written account of the postwar President's first administration.

Robert Donovan was particularly well equipped to write this book. The Truman period is ripe for serious historical analysis because of the availability of source material. The death of Truman resulted in the opening of many of his private papers which had been closed to researchers, and coincided with the opening of State Department files and even some of the records of the National Security Council. In addition to these advantages which are available to all Truman scholars, Donovan had the opportunity to observe the events he describes as a White House correspondent during the Truman years. In addition, for this book he has recently interviewed many of the men he knew then to fill out the written record.

Truman was one of our least prepared Presidents, yet the problems he faced were probably greater than those encountered by any modern president with the exception of Franklin Roosevelt. He was a small-town politician who had grown somewhat during eight years in the Senate, but he had not gone to college, had no training in policymaking or management, and had no diplomatic experience. He liked to say that being President was not much different from running Jackson County, Missouri, but this was more of a rationalization for his meager background than his honest perception of the presidential office. Truman had only conferred with Roosevelt twice while he was Vice President, and these were political or social discussions rather than policy sessions. As a result, Truman knew virtually nothing of the current concerns or plans of the Administration. He did not even know of the work being done on the atomic bomb.

Being new to executive work and having little background on which to draw, it is little wonder that he stumbled badly. Because of his lack of preparation he was forced to rely on his advisers, but most were Roosevelt's appointees and few of these could imagine anyone else being President, particularly Harry Truman. Most soon quit or were fired. As a result he had virtually a new cabinet within a year. He tried to learn. Conscientiously he read everything given to him, but he had so few people on his staff who were experienced enough to sort things out for him that this task became an excessive burden. Though blessed with extraordinary physical stamina, some feared he would break under the strain of trying to do too much himself.

Through his many years of experience in Washington, Roosevelt had acquired a knowledge of the federal government which was as great as any of his subordinates'. By drawing on this knowledge and developing a network of contacts throughout the federal bureaucracy, he was able to preside over and control the tremendously expanded executive branch which developed during the New Deal and World War II. With none of these advantages Truman had to rely on an enlarged White House staff to manage the bureaucracy he had inherited. Though he eventually developed a competent corps of aides by the time he left office, it was a slow process. Eventually Clark Clifford, John Steelman, and Charles Murphy provided the kind of White House staff that succeeding Presidents have found essential.

In many ways the immediate postwar period has been a watershed for our own times. It was then that the Cold War with the Soviet Union began and that tension is still one of the most significant influences on our lives. The reconversion of the industrial system from war production to consumer items has served as the basis of the country's postwar economy and foreign trade. The essence of Donovan's book is an analysis of Truman's impact on these developments.

In the process of facing and attempting to dispose of these monumental problems, Truman drew on inherent traits of courage, humor, and capacity to learn. He was never able to overcome entirely, however, his basic provincialism, ineptness, impetuosity, and crudeness. In making his decisions he was ever conscious of maintaining the power of the presidency intact as well as keeping a personal political advantage.

Truman has been more severely criticized by historians for his part in the origin of the Cold War than any other single development during his presidency. While most of his contemporaries applauded his leadership in foreign policy, the historical record has brought many of these decisions into question. In his treatment of these controversial decisions, Donovan typically provides the available evidence for the reader and then gives his own, usually judicious, explanation of Truman's actions.

Many revisionist historians have pointed to Truman's hard-line attitude toward Soviet actions in Poland in April, 1945, as a significant milestone in establishing a climate of tense relations with Russia. They usually attribute what appears to be a radical shift from Roosevelt's policy to Truman's inexperience, his provincial anti-Communist attitude, and a desire to show that he was tough and capable of being President in his own right. Donovan does not think Truman was trying to establish a new policy because there had not yet been time to even consider such a change. Rather he believes that Truman was simply trying to adhere to Roosevelt's policy as interpreted for him by his diplomatic advisers. Donovan does not seem to consider seriously the possibility that these advisers had not agreed with Roosevelt's policy and took advantage of Truman's ignorance to establish a more uncompromising attitude toward the Soviets. In advancing this interpretation, Donovan demonstrates that his views have not been much influenced by the revisionist writings of the 1960's and 1970's.

Similarly, Donovan explains Truman's decision to use the atomic bomb as a continuation of what he believed Roosevelt's attitude to have been. Some revisionists have seen the dropping of the bomb in Cold War terms, and concluded its main purpose was to impress the Russians with our new weapon rather than to force Japan to surrender. Donovan sees it in essentially a political context. Truman, as a new accidental President, could not hope to challenge the unconditional surrender doctrine handed down by Roosevelt even if he was inclined to do so. Also it appeared that the Japanese would not surrender unconditionally without an invasion of the home islands. The atomic bomb represented an alternative to the huge loss of American lives anticipated in such an invasion. Needless loss of American life would be a heavy burden for any politician to carry. On the evidence he submits, Donovan concludes that the "simple" reason Truman dropped the bomb was to save lives by ending the war quickly. He admits, however, that Truman's advisers were "sophisticated enough" to realize that a demonstration of the bomb's potential would increase American leverage in postwar negotiations.

Revisionist historians have also pointed to the announcement of the Truman Doctrine—and the accompanying exaggeration of the Soviet threat which was used to get Congress to accept it—as the American declaration of a Cold War on the Soviet Union. It was this announcement which established the American policy of intervening in any country that was perceived as being threatened by Communism as a device for containing the Soviets. Donovan's account of this development follows the orthodox view and does not add anything to our understanding of it. Nor does he ever deal with the question of Truman's role in the origin of the policy. This gap must be considered a major flaw in the book.

Donovan does break new ground in his analysis of Truman's attitude toward, and his role in, the establishment of the new state of Israel. It is a tangled web of

State and Defense Departments' opposition to the Zionists for strategic reasons, the efforts of Truman's old haberdashery partner Eddie Jacobson to serve as a conduit into the White House for Israeli views, and the significance of the Jewish vote to a Democratic president in a particularly difficult election year. Donovan skillfully blends the documentary evidence with information obtained through interviews with some of the principals in telling his story. He concludes that in spite of all the unique factors in Truman's situation, after "the full disclosures about the gas furnaces it is inconceivable that any president of the United States in office in May 1948 would have done essentially other than that which Truman did."

It is in his treatment of domestic politics and problems that the author is most effective and original. Yet even in this area, Donovan is much more descriptive than he is analytical and the reader must search for his interpretations. For example, he describes Truman's close friend, Secretary of the Treasury John Synder, as having a typical banker's view of the economy. He adds that Truman's economic instincts were very similar to Snyder's. This would imply that Truman did not really believe in the Fair Deal that he proposed and presumably advocated it for political reasons alone, but Donovan does not explore this theme further.

Truman's twenty-one point message delivered to Congress on September 6, 1945, laid the basis for the Fair Deal. It was written primarily by Roosevelt's old speechwriter Sam Rosenman, who was anxious to commit the new President to a liberal course. Rosenman had gone to Potsdam with Truman and was able to take advantage of the voyage home to counteract some of the President's conservative instincts and commit him to a continuance of the New Deal. Rosenman later believed it was the most important thing that he did during his work with Truman. When Rosenman began to prepare the message for Congress, the President's conservative advisers tried to dissuade him from delivering it. Curiously, in view of the significance of this first statement of domestic policy of the new Administration, Donovan drops the story at this point. Perhaps this is where the historical trail ends, but the reader is entitled to the author's view of why Truman stood firm in his support of the message.

In a sense the twenty-one point message was characteristic of the basic political strategy that Truman used during most of his first term and the election of 1948. In this message and many others he asked for much more than Congress could deliver even if they had been sympathetic with the proposals called for. It was a way of making a political record without worrying about the consequences or the costs. It might win elections, but it produced little in the way of concrete legislation. When the Republicans gained control of the Eightieth Congress, Truman pursued this strategy with a vengeance. He was thus able to gain the initiative and blame Congress for all the country's problems because they would not accept his recommendations.

Donovan feels that the election of 1948 with its whistle-stop campaign changed Truman's public personality and established the "Give 'em hell" image which he sought to live up to ever after. Egged on by desperation, Dewey's unaggressive campaigning, and the enthusiasm of the audience, Truman went into his act and threw out any charge that came into his head. Prominent among his targets were the "do-nothing" Republican-controlled Congress and Herbert Hoover. When told that Hoover had been hurt by his irresponsible charges, Truman admitted privately that he had not meant a word of it.

Realizing that he was behind Dewey, Truman desperately searched for some dramatic gesture to give his campaign a shot in the arm. Some of his political advisers suggested a peace mission to Stalin. Truman accepted the idea and pressured Chief Justice Fred Vinson into undertaking the task. Such a move would have undercut our allies and circumvented the United Nations at a critical time. It was only when Marshall put his foot down that Truman reluctantly dropped this very risky injection of politics into diplomacy.

Conflict and Crisis is a book which is rich in personal detail and perceptive character sketches which reflect the author's intimate observation of the times he describes. While probably not the definitive history it strives to be, it is the best so far on the early Truman years and will become the new standard. One hopes that Donovan is now at work on a second volume which will complete the story It will be eagerly awaited.

Alfred D. Sander

DANIEL MARTIN

Author: John Fowles (1926–   )
Publisher: Little, Brown and Company (Boston). 629 pp. $12.95
Type of work: Novel
Time: 1930's to the present
Locale: England, chiefly Oxford and London, and California

The story of a man's renewal of a relationship with a long-lost friend and lover

Principal characters:

DANIEL MARTIN, an English playwright and Hollywood scriptwriter
NELL RANDALL, his former wife
CAROLINE MARTIN, their daughter
ANDREW RANDALL, an English country squire, Nell's present husband
ANTHONY MALLORY, an Oxford professor of philosophy and college friend of Daniel
JANE MALLORY, Anthony's wife and Nell's sister
BARNEY DILLON, another Oxford classmate of Daniel, now a television personality
JENNY MCNEIL, a young English actress working in Hollywood, Daniel's current mistress

John Fowles's novels have always been splendid stories, richly written, capable of setting a mood and sustaining it over long pages of narrative. Yet there has always been something mysterious and almost surreal about them. *The Collector,* a story of human possessiveness, parallels the hobby of butterfly catching; *The Magus* describes an encounter with other-than-ordinary knowledge and power; *The French Lieutenant's Woman* is an attempt to re-create the ethos of Victorian England and to explore the labyrinths of Victorian sexuality. All these novels are at the fringes of reality, all in the twilight world where the ordinary shades into the mysterious, and the imagination seeks to create worlds of meaning and significance from the most ephemeral of evidence. *Daniel Martin* is quite a different book, a book set in the full light of day, in the full realities of our time and our world. The novel begins with the phrase, "Whole sight; or all the rest is desolation." The rest of the book is an attempt to see life, one life, whole, and thus to recover it from desolation, to retrieve it for meaning, for significance, for what it can say to others.

The life is that of Daniel Martin, Oxford graduate and serious playwright turned Hollywood scriptwriter with no illusions about the social value of his profession. He who was a husband and father is now turned casual lover and serial polygamist, and is currently having an affair with a young English actress the same age as his daughter. The son of an Anglican vicar steeped in the traditions and landscape of his native England, Martin is now an expatriate, living in the quintessential American landscape of Southern California. He is, therefore, Everyman who feels cut off from past, from origins, who is in exile from all that was, who flees into and thus is prisoner in the present, the momentary, the transitory, the ephemeral.

But the movement of this novel is a turning-back and a turning-within. Because Martin's affair is with Jenny, an English actress, he is turned back toward his origins. And in the midst of their relationship comes a transatlantic telephone call from his former wife Nell to say that an old Oxford classmate, Anthony Mallory, is dying of cancer and wants to see him before the end. So the journey backwards begins. It is a journey that will take him back to the old country, to old friends, to lost but not forgotten issues, hurts, loves, passions. In his research for a movie on the early twentieth century British hero Kitchener, it will take him back to the realities of the British past. Finally, on a trip to Egypt, it will take him back to the beginnings of human history. But the physical journey only parallels a deeper journey, a journey into self, into the origins of values and emotions and feelings, into the realities of love and death, of brokenness and forgiveness, of reality and illusion. Fowles sets out in this novel to present a man struggling to see himself whole; the result is a remarkable literary achievement, a book almost unique in our time in the richness and complexity and power of its vision.

The plot is simply told: Daniel and Anthony had been friends at Oxford, where Anthony had taken a first in philosophy, and Daniel, a fourth in literature. While there they had met two sisters, Nell and Jane. After college, Nell and Daniel married, had one daughter named Caroline, and, in the course of things, were divorced. Nell remarried another Oxford classmate named Andrew, and now lives with him in his family's country estate. Daniel went on to a string of casual and not-so-casual liaisons with a wide variety of women. Anthony and Jane married after college, had several children, and are still married when the novel opens. They are still in Oxford, where Anthony has become a professor of philosophy. But this marriage, too, has gone sour; Jane has a lover, while Anthony is dying of cancer. There is but one complication in what is an all-too-conventional and ordinary situation; once, before any of them left college, Daniel and Jane had a brief, one-day-long affair, a sign that there was more to their relationship than just friendship, more that could not be accommodated into the ordinary interaction of potential brother-in-law, sister-in-law.

This is the past that Daniel flies back to in response to Anthony's plea for a final visit, a past clouded by ill-feeling over Daniel's breakup of his marriage with Nell. And what Anthony, on his death-bed, calls Daniel to is a redemption of that past, an overcoming of estrangement, a renewal of relationships, a forgiveness of past differences. Specifically, he hopes that Daniel can do something for Jane, something to make up for what Anthony feels are failures on his part in their marriage. This task Daniel undertakes, first through spending time with her on a visit to the home of his former wife, then through inviting her to visit his English country retreat, and finally through taking her on a ten-day cruise on the Nile while he investigates potential locations for a projected movie on the English colonial experience in Northern Africa.

What Daniel discovers while getting to know Jane all over again after so many years is that in some strange way the working-out of his life, the finding of meaning in his life, is bound up in his relationship with her. She has become a profoundly withdrawn woman, defeated and hard to reach. But in the time he spends with her, he finds her introspection conducive to his own self-reflection; as he gets to know her, he discovers himself. From somewhere early in the book, we get the suspicion that in some way Daniel and Jane will discover a future together, in spite of the fact that everything seems to be against such an eventuality. Gradually, however, impediments fall away: her current lover deserts her, her own resistance to going on the trip with him dissolves, her reluctance to enter into anything other than casual conversation with him gradually melts. And yet what is finally left is the past, the past that both unites them and separates them. How all that will work out gives the book its suspense and tension, which Fowles orchestrates marvelously. He gives his novel the qualities of a mystery story, a narrative that moves at a leisurely pace, yet sustains interest and builds tension to hold and involve the reader.

Daniel Martin, therefore, is that sort of book for which one does not want to give away the ending; each reader deserves the pleasure of seeing the final working out of all the strands of the narrative, and experiencing the final splendid pages. What a reviewer *can* do without depriving potential readers of the novel of that experience is to point out a few elements that contribute to the overall impact of this major literary work. One of these is the drawing of Fowles's minor characters. Caroline, Daniel's daughter, now having an affair with Barney Dillon, yet another Oxford classmate of Daniel, is deftly presented. She is yet one more aspect of Daniel's past with which he must be reconciled, one more person who forces him to reexamine his present situation. Her relationship with a man old enough to be her father is too close to Daniel's relationship with a woman young enough to be his daughter, and so he is forced to reconcile his feelings about both relationships. As usual in this book, the resolution cuts both ways; he finds he must give up his mistress, but he must also accept what his daughter decides to do. Barney himself, a writer with pretensions to seriousness, now become little more than a television personality, forces Daniel to reevaluate his own commitment to a profession equally transitory, equally destructive to the lives of those involved in it. But the minor character most fully drawn because she is allowed to speak for herself is Jenny McNeil, the young British actress with whom Daniel has an affair. She, too, is in the process of discovering herself and the reality of her humanity. The high value which she places on Daniel is occasionally a corrective to Daniel's self-deprecation. She must lose him, finally, but our sense is that their relationship has been good for both of them and has made possible the future which must separate them.

Even as Jenny emerges in the book through letters she writes to Daniel in England, so does a major theme about the relationship between art and life. Over and over, the book draws our attention to itself as a book, as a work in the process of being written. The speaker throughout is Daniel, except for an occasional chapter written by Jenny; he, on occasion, tells us of his reactions and second thoughts about what he has just written. At the end of the book, Daniel knows that the novel he wants to write, and has thought about writing, can never be written; the speaker, describing himself as Daniel's "ill concealed ghost," says that he has made the last sentence of Daniel's never-to-be novel the first sentence of this one. What happens in this book is that the real story of Daniel's self-discovery becomes the novel we read; in other words, his story becomes real for us because it has become art. If we are to learn from the book, therefore, we are called to see the process of self-understanding, the task of creating our own lives, as in some way parallel to the novelist's task of creating the lives of his characters. Fowles and Martin are not the same, but we must suspect that the process of writing this book was one of self-discovery for Fowles as well.

For what this book is finally about is nothing other than the nature of human life. It is about learning that hardest of human lessons: that true love of another human being comes not through loving in them what we are or what we can make them into, but through knowing them as they are, and letting them be themselves. What finally happens between Daniel and Jane happens because Daniel learns who she is, and convinces her that he loves that person, and not someone else. Such is the freedom that love brings, such is the freedom that makes real loving possible. One testimony to the value of *Daniel Martin* for our age is that in the midst of a culture that values youth above all else, that finds itself progressively more and more cut off from intergenerational experience, here is a book that makes one feel good about being over thirty, that argues that knowing one's past sets one free in the present. It is a celebration of humanity, a defense of humanism. As such it is an enormously valuable book, a book to delight in because it helps us value who we are and what we can do. *Daniel Martin* is a major literary event because it affirms the value of our humanity and enriches our experience of ourselves and those we know. At the same time, it teaches us the value of art, its power to show us ourselves, to help us understand ourselves.

John N. Wall, Jr.

THE DARK LADY

Author: Louis Auchincloss (1917–   )
Publisher: Houghton Mifflin Company (Boston). 246 pp. $8.95
Type of work: Novel
Time: From the 1930's to the 1950's
Locale: New York City and its suburbs

A novel of manners that explores the multifaceted consequences of one woman's self-focused drive toward the limelight, in which she gains her objective with tragic consequences for the three persons closest to her

Principal characters:
> IVY TRASK, editor of the fashion magazine *Tone*
> ELESINA DART, former actress rescued from alcoholism and obscurity by Ivy Trask
> IRVING STEIN, investment banker, art connoisseur, and master of Broadlawns
> DAVID STEIN, Irving's youngest son
> ELIOT CLARKSON, David's best friend and second cousin

A modern day novelist of manners, Louis Auchincloss is frequently compared to Anthony Trollope. As a recorder of a way of life the comparison is valid; however, he seems less inclined to show us the flair, the wit, or the good warm blood of his characters that marked Trollope's style. It is as though, because they are of his milieu, he wants to shield them from the probing and critical eyes of the non-U and the unwashed. Over a decade ago, S. K. Overbeck wrote of Auchincloss, "Aside from its inventive ironies, Auchincloss's prose is all polish and no spit. . . ." (*Newsweek,* March 27, 1967.) It is unfortunate that the same can be said of Auchincloss' later work, including this novel; he seems to be observing from a distance, not coming close enough for the reader to feel, taste, or smell the realities he intends to convey.

The outsiders seem more real than the highborn, wealthy WASPs in many of Auchincloss' novels, and this is no exception. Ivy Trask, a successful self-made woman, is one of the more memorable of Auchincloss' characters. The author often exploits the hand-in-the-velvet-glove ploy; this time there are two—both Ivy and her protégée Elesina Dart are classic examples of the strong, manipulating, singleminded woman.

Ivy is at heart a driven, insecure, unloved, and unloving woman. Auchincloss has her fill her emptiness by living vicariously through well-born, lovely Elesina, an actress she rescues from alcoholism brought on by two destructive marriages and a fading stage career. As Ivy succeeds in strengthening Elesina's position, she diminishes those around her. The ultimate irony is exemplified by the fact that Elesina fares so well under Ivy's sponsorship that eventually there is no longer room for Ivy in the world she has built for Elesina.

Early insecurity has made Ivy into a snob, and although her position as editor of *Tone* should be assurance enough, she revels in her close association with Clara and Irving Stein. Stein, a lawyer and former surrogate judge, is now an investment banker and art collector. As a member of the Stein inner circle, Ivy uses the devices at her command to make herself indispensable to Clara in much the same way that she did earlier to the relatives who took her in as an orphaned niece. Eventually she begins to sense a subtle change in the Steins, fears they are beginning to take her for granted, and may soon hold her in contempt. In a calculated attempt to prove she can produce something of value on her own, something to enhance her standing in their eyes, she proposes a visit to Broadlawns of her actress friend, Elesina Dart. Through the consequences of this act, an act which precipitates changes of lifestyles and a breakdown of family ties, friendships, and a marriage, Auchincloss becomes a moralist. He turns moralist, too, in his treatment of Irving. Elesina is maneuvered into a loveless marriage to Irving after Ivy sets about breaking up his marriage to the colorless Clara. In a departure from the traditional view that it is the woman who pays, he condemns Irving to a life of invalidism and impotency soon after he and Elesina take the vows.

Continuing to hew her path of disaster through the lives of those she touches, Ivy focuses on David, the Steins's youngest child, the one who means the most to Clara. She encourages an affair between Elesina and David—to hurt Clara as much as to gratify her grand plan for Elesina's happiness. By the time her husband dies, Elesina, who has become as pragmatic and callous as her mentor, gives up David for the material security bestowed by Irving's will. She has proven herself the woman that Ivy sees in her.

Elesina is goaded, by her own mother's contempt, into recognizing that she is becoming a harder and more self-focused individual than even Ivy has envisioned, but it does not bother her. Always the actress, she craves more and more attention and applause; indeed, she needs it for survival. She is certain that she has always been in control of her own life. She is convinced that if Ivy has exerted influence over her, it is because she, Elesina, has allowed it. In a revealing statement, she admits that " . . . If I was going to the dogs, it was because I wanted to. Because barks and bites attract me. . . . There's always been a streak of cruelty in me. . . . It's not attractive but I face it. . . ." Elesina is reaching the stage where she, like Clara, no longer needs Ivy. As she overcomes political obstacles in her ambition to stay in the limelight, Ivy realizes she is losing her influence over the strong-willed Elesina; she painfully admits that Elesina no longer needs or wants her. Elesina's rejection of her ill-advised help in a touchy political situation leads Ivy to commit suicide. Even then, Elesina seems little moved by another's pain. Both Ivy and Elesina are typical of the women in Auchincloss' work, who are frequently much stronger and far less admirable than his males.

Irving Stein is not portrayed with any complexity. He exemplifies the manifestation of the merchant prince mentality, although he is a lawyer. He was born to Orthodox Jewish parents, but his pursuit of beauty through art has led him to abandon his religious heritage. Irving as a young man fantasized his union with Clara Clarkson as more than it really was—a marriage for social .advantage. Quite predictably, in his middle years he indulged in a series of extramarital affairs that had about them an aura of exploitation, since most were with the wives of impecunious artists who neeeded his help.

When Elesina arrives on the scene, he is ripe for the plucking, as Ivy is well aware. When Irving plans to make Elesina his mistress, he does so in the conventional manner; however, Ivy sees this as the time to suggest a more permanent arrangement. Through Ivy's astute scheming, Irving begins to think of Elesina not as his mistress, but as rightful mistress of Broadlawns—as his wife. He is moved by the revival of his youthful dreams of a happy master of the manor displaying a beautiful wife on his arm.

A memorable character, although not completely limned, is Eliot Clarkson. Eliot is David's second cousin, but more particularly his champion and friend. His story is another of the well-plotted ironies familiar to Auchincloss' readers. Eliot's friendship with David begins during a nasty anti-Semitic contretemps at prep school. Eliot's attraction is intense and on his part homosexual; he visualizes the two of them against the world, but knows this is an unrealistic dream. Accepting the fact that he must share David with others, he wonders "bitterly in time if his own intransigency had not done more for David's social career than all of Irving Stein's ambition." After David is rejected by Elesina, the two men enlist in World War II. David is killed and Eliot survives. Here the symbolism becomes obvious; a Jewish lamb sacrificed to the Nazi guns that others might live. Eliot, stationed in England, goes through the war physically unscathed. He becomes a politically radical, left-wing professor of law during the hazardous days of the McCarthy reign of terror. In his compulsion to keep alive David's memory, Eliot edits and publishes *The War Letters of David Stein*. To the readers of the book, David becomes a hero, and the mysterious woman who sent him off to war and to death becomes an anonymous symbol of hate. Elesina is not free of his influence, even in death.

Despite overplotting and contrivances, Auchincloss has succeeded in staying close to his theme of ambition to be realized at any cost. The book can be classified as predictable Auchincloss with two exceptions: he abandons his usual good taste when he caricatures, to the point of cruelty, the homosexual minority; and when he casts Jews into a pejorative, stereotyped mold. On the whole it exemplifies what one has come to expect of this writer: a somewhat humorless, urbane, ironic approach to the plight of the upper-middle class, a group, he leads one to feel, who are as much survivors in their milieu as are the guttersnipes of the urban ghetto. The sad thing is that while these characters interest one briefly, Auchincloss does not succeed in making one really care about them.

Mae Woods Bell

DAY BY DAY

Author: Robert Lowell (1917–1977)
Publisher: Farrar, Straus and Giroux (New York). 137 pp. $8.95
Type of work: Poetry

A collection of sixty-six poems, Lowell's last before his death, which continue in the confessional mood of his recent volumes

In a poem called "Our Afterlife I," Robert Lowell tells his old friend, fiction writer Peter Taylor, "This year killed/ Pound, Wilson, Auden . . . / promise has lost its bloom." Later, in "Our Afterlife II," he observes that "even cows seem transitory" and "The old boys drop like wasps / from windowsill and pane." This book is valedictory; intimations of mortality crowd the pages—not allusions to death in the abstract but a deep-gut sense of things passing away. Lowell will not prettify the process of aging and death. In a poem near the end of the collection, he makes "Thanks-Offering for Recovery" and considers taking with him to church a grotesque shrunken head. But he doubts any church would accept the head, and concludes the poem: "This winter, I thought / I was created to be given away."

Lowell's death in a taxicab between Kennedy Airport and Manhattan on September 12, 1977, lends poignance to *Day by Day,* in which the reader often sees the poet at airports—leaving someone, or being left, escaping his native Boston, or returning to it. In retrospect, Lowell's entire career seems predicated on almost equally strong desires to escape and deny, on the one hand, and to return and affirm, on the other.

Since 1944, Robert Lowell has published no fewer than seventeen books, including plays and translations. During that time, he has refused to be shelved, demurely, as befitted a Boston Lowell; instead, his political activism often attracted the glare of public notice. In 1943, he was sentenced to prison for violation of the Selective Service Act. In 1965, he publicly refused an invitation to the White House, because, as he said, artists "cannot enjoy public celebration without making subtle public commitments." He admitted his "dismay and distrust" of American foreign policy in 1965, and in December, 1968, the Justice Department included him with other intellectuals suspected of conspiracy against the draft. In January, 1968, Lowell had been refused a visa to attend a Cuban Cultural Conference, because, as a passport official said, "We did not believe it was in the interest of the United States. . . ."

Nevertheless, Lowell's poems rarely treat politics overtly and directly. His chief concern has seemed to be reconciling the dream with the reality of twentieth century American life, and, on occasion, his work has satisfied even the demands of patriotism. When Lowell, in *Day by Day,* asks how often his antics, his "unsupportable, trespassing tongue" have "gone astray and led me to prison . . . / to lying . . . kneeling . . . standing," he recalls his public as well as his private life. The poem quoted, called "The Downlook," celebrates the end,

or at least the diminishment, of yet another of Lowell's personal relationships
That poem comes close to starting the collection's theme; "the downlook"
between lovers leaves no greater happiness "than to turn back to recapture
former joy."

Many of the poems in *Day by Day* turn back, but they do not recapture any
great amount of joy. They confront the same doubts and uncertainties, the same
monsters from within, that have haunted Lowell's verse almost from the start
and have become more insistent since publication in 1959 of his famous *Life
Studies*. By now, Lowell's themes are familiar, for the so-called "Confessional
School of Poets," of which Lowell's was an early and compelling voice, has come
close to dominating contemporary verse. Confessional poets—W. D. Snodgrass,
Anne Sexton, John Berryman, Sylvia Plath, and, of course Lowell—do not
always show their readers either beauty or truth. They show themselves.

It would be inaccurate to sum up the confessional poets under any single
explanatory word or phrase. Alcoholism and mental disorder are as misleading
as father-complex and existential despair. Still, when Lowell writes about
reading an article on John Berryman, "as if recognizing my own obituary," he
establishes kinship with the author of the *Dream Songs*. The article, Lowell tells
us in "Unwanted," says Berryman's mother, "not mine," lacked an affectionate
nature—"so he always loved what he missed."

Lowell has said that his *Life Studies* resulted from his impatience with prose
methods in an autobiography. To a major extent, he has been writing his
autobiography ever since but without the transitions and sequential logic prose
requires. In *Day by Day*, the poet's earliest experiences find a place next to his
present-day sensations. Poems about his fatherhood mingle with those about his
uneasy sonhood. He addresses all three of his wives, apparently still wishing to
understand the earlier relationships with fiction writer Jean Stafford and critic
Elizabeth Hardwick as much as his latest marriage to Irish-born Caroline
Blackwood. The book's final section, dedicated to Caroline Blackwood, provides
the book's tentative sounding title. Some poems address her by name, but even
those and others set in England, where he lived with her and their small children,
betray the constant tug of the American scene which engrossed Lowell while it
repulsed him.

Day by Day has its storyline, and doubtless Lowell's intimates follow it all.
Perhaps it tells of the poet's return home, metaphorically as well as physically, or
perhaps it does no more than tell of his resignation, if not acceptance, in the face
of age and death. No matter what the central story, the reader is likely to feel like
the *voyeur* character in Lowell's celebrated "Skunk Hour," out spying on lovers
in parked cars. Those explicit accounts of "downward looks" between lovers and
what they meant tell more than the reader may want to know. Two poems
associated with airports ("Logan Airport, Boston" and "Morning After Dining
with a Friend *(Some Weeks After Logan Airport")* hint at the problem: in the
first, Lowell says he cannot "bring back youth with a snap of my belt, / I cannot

touch you." In the second, "waking wifeless" has become a habit.

A poem like "Home," with its implicit complaints to a "you" who considers the speaker's illness a desertion, speaks of London and apparently alludes to Lowell's third wife. The poem's final lines mingle the religious and the secular: "The Queen of Heaven, I miss her, / we were divorced." Does Lowell, converted to Catholicism in 1940, the year of his marriage to Jean Stafford, and lapsed from the faith and divorced from Stafford, mean the Blessed Virgin—or a woman? Whoever, she had faith that the "divided, stricken soul / could call her Maria, / and rob the devil with a word." No matter whom the poem means, it cries out in pain and absence.

Lowell's personality emerges in *Day by Day* with all the engaging qualities of the familiar boyish photographs of him, and the critic tells himself in vain that liking the poet is *not* the point. Poetry as subjective as this invites the reader to take sides—to hope at the very least the poet will learn something from what is happening to him. In short, when the poem's subject is unabashedly the poet himself, its quality depends upon how rich, how varied, how intrinsically interesting the poet really is. Robert Lowell's self proves sufficient to sustain yet another book full of what an earlier time would have judged fit to be told only to one's priest or analyst.

Its classical title aside, the opening poem of the volume invites application to Lowell's life. "Ulysses and Circe" is ostensibly third-person, but the poet's voice intrudes in the fifth line to ask "Why should I renew his infamous sorrow?" When the first section ends with the hero's boast that "by force of fraud," he has done what no one else could do, one wonders if Lowell means himself. In "Unwanted," he calls his poetry a "farfetched misalliance / that made evasion a revelation." An important recurring word here is "misalliance"; in his "Epilogue," Lowell says "All's misalliance."

In Sections II–IV, Ulysses is a fugitive in Circe's "exotic palace," where "he dislikes everything / in his impoverished life of myth." The poet's, or Ulysses'? Ulysses speaks in Section V, but it is Lowell's preoccupation we hear: "Age . . . the bilge we cannot shake from the mop." In the sixth and final section of the poem, Ulysses returns to Ithaca and Penelope; or does Lowell return to America and to Elizabeth Hardwick, his wife of twenty-nine years? "Off Central Park" celebrates (one presumes) a return to Hardwick's apartment where, "The old movables keep their places; / . . . confidently out of style."

In "Ulysses and Circe," the lines "Nobody in Ithaca knows him, / and yet he is too much remarked" perfectly sum up Lowell's anonymity and fame. Early in the poem, "ten years to and ten years fro" and, at the end, "ten years fro and ten years to" document Lowell's comings and goings—tedium. The heroic subject diminishes with the image of the hero's gills—"Unnatural ventilation—vents / closed by a single lever / like cells in a jail." Ulysses—or Lowell?—is an oversized shark, "a vocational killer / in the machismo of senility."

The second poem, "Homecoming," reiterates the idea of the poet's "lost love hunting / your lost face" and retains the Homeric allusion. In a "town for the young" who break themselves against the surf, the aging speaker is homeless: "No dog knows my smell." Another poem, "Suburban Surf," associates Caroline Blackwood with surf, partly through its subtitle *("After Caroline's return"),* partly through images. "Lake Walk," set in Ireland, again speaks of disillusion. Seven years dwindle to "a diverting smile"; and "the misleading promise" appears "nomadic as yesterday's whirling snow, / all whiteness splotched."

Some, but not many, poems in *Day by Day* mark Lowell's strides toward quieting the old terrors, but mostly they reveal him continuing to "freelance on the razor's edge." Measuring his life in leavings and returnings, Lowell, still the little boy, registers surprise when things do not remain as he left them. The smarts to his ego during schooldays ("St. Mark's, 1933") remain as fresh as if administered yesterday; "To Frank Parker," a recollection of an evening with a friend forty years ago, comes out all sour. The June night in Massachusetts reminds him that grass and pollen produce "the asthma of high summer— / the inclination to drink, not eat." Age crops up again—"another species, / the nothing-voiced." Even survival seems of dubious value, "if two glasses of red wine are poison."

In poems to his parents ("To Mother" and "Robert T. S. Lowell") as well as in "Unwanted," Lowell peels additional protective layers from the "public man," until he touches his nerve—and the reader's. Regularly, Lowell's poems earn a tang of reality—at once local and particular and larger-than-life. Whatever else Lowell's autobiography-in-progress (now ended) may have done, it never hacked at the surface of life. Perhaps, though, Lowell should have recalled that he, not the critic, wrote the line in *The Dolphin* (1973) which undoes it all: "Everything is real until it's published."

That is the flaw in confessional poetry, even in a poem like "To Mother" with its apparent gain in compassion and understanding. At last, better than twenty years after his mother's death in 1954, Lowell can say that she is "as human as I am . . . / if I am." Was that final twist for the sake of the poem, or did the twist *really* arise from a felt change? In the long run, many of the poems here teeter between mere excellence of craft and genuine achievement, and too many of them smack of the child's "they'll-be-sorry-when-I'm-dead" line—said too late.

"Unwanted" ends with questions: ". . . will mother go on cleaning house / for eternity, and making it unlivable?" and "Is getting well ever an art, / or art a way to get well?" The possibility of mother's making eternity unlivable creates a fine ambiguity, but the final questions seem easy. Lowell practiced his art assiduously and well, but, from the looks of *Day by Day,* art did not provide a way to get well. Getting well is an art in itself, maybe impossible to achieve. The poem "Art of the Possible" proves that point.

Lowell knew the answer, or he discovered it in his "Epilogue," where he complains that his "blessed structures, plot and rhyme" will not help him make "something imagined, not recalled." He says that what he writes turns into snapshots, "lurid, rapid, garish"; the example of a painter like Vermeer reminds that "We are poor passing facts" and must give "each figure in the photograph / his living name."

Lowell is here, in this sometimes lurid, rapid, and garish photograph called *Day by Day*. And he has his living name by virtue of recording, in pain, much of America's collective anguish. His name and what he told, from 1944 through 1977, will stand among the glories and reproaches of America up to, and past, her bicentennial.

Leon V. Driskell

THE DESTINIES OF DARCY DANCER, GENTLEMAN

Author: J. P. Donleavy (1926–   )
Publisher: Delacorte Press (New York). 402 pp. $9.95
Type of work: Novel
Time: World War II
Locale: Ireland

A comic novel about the growing up and misadventures of Darcy Dancer

Principal characters:
> DARCY DANCER, the hero of the novel, an adolescent open to experience
> MR. ARLAND, his tutor, a sensitive man in love
> CROOKS AND SEXTON, two comic servants
> FOXY, a rascally neighborhood lad
> LOIS, an artist friend of Darcy

The Destinies of Darcy Dancer, Gentleman is J. P. Donleavy's seventh novel. Written in the comic spirit, it understands the difference between the serious and the solemn. The novel is about the joy and agony of growing up, but the joy is not elevated to spirituality and the agony is not uplifted into tragedy. Men and women suffer and die, but suffering and dying are not dwelt upon. Nothing, in fact, is allowed to interfere with the hero's zest in his encounter with life, nor the author's zest in his encounter with the reader.

This zest is interwoven in the novel's fabric, part of which is made up of Darcy's stream of consciousness:

> Darcy Dancer leaving the dining room. Chin down. Spine bent. Step back up these few carpeted steps. Treading on the wool woven roses. Go out. Not know where I'm going. Nor care. Why she adored. Walk. On these night time streets. Away through one's crashing dreams. Under lamplight. On the grey speckled blocks of granite. Leave the fence at Trinity. A pub Lincoln's Inn. Big closed back gates of the college. Light in the porter's lodge. Turkish turrets across the street. Down Westland Row. Stone pillars of a church. Iron pillars of a bridge. Train chugging over. Every part of her comes haunting. The slap she gave me in the face. The album of her castles. The ballrooms. The waltzing ladies and gentlemen. Charging at me on her rearing horse. All the way to the moored looming shadowy ships on this black river flowing through this black city.

The syntax of this passage is full of interest. Despite the fact that it represents Darcy silently speaking his inmost thoughts, it is in the third person. Having just seen the woman he is convinced he loves "adoring" another man, Darcy is fighting despair by distancing himself from himself: hence the third person. Verbs are also cunningly used, imperatives like "walk" indicating self-commands of actions ordinarily automatic, participles indicating continuously observed actions. Finally, the variation of sentence fragments and whole sentences—the syntactical rhythm—is part of the meaning. The whole passage consists of fragments except for brief imperatives, until "Every part of her comes haunting." Again the fragments trip over one another until the gloomy poetry of the final sentence.

Up to the sentence "Every part of her comes haunting," Darcy is preoccupied with getting out of the dining room, away from Miss von B's presence. His task is difficult to manage because his feelings keep breaking through—"Why she adored. . . . Away through one's crashing dreams." Finally Darcy seemingly masters himself and we see and hear only his observations on his nocturnal sojourn. But self-composure is impossible.—"Every part of her comes haunting." No more perfect image of lost love seems possible. The catalogue that follows is a mere smattering of this onrush of images, dissolving in the final dark sentence that irretrievably sums up Darcy's mood.

This paragraph certainly could not exist if it were not for Faulkner's and Joyce's experiments with stream of consciousness. But Donleavy's stream of consciousness is only one step removed from first-person narrative. Darcy, although perhaps not in full control of himself, is certainly in full control of the narrative. The keenness of his sensations give even his despair a buoyancy. So close to himself, he will never escape into real despair. He creates out of his anguish a poem that more than half comes to terms with anguish. Even in emotional pain, Darcy has not lost his zest for life.

Donleavy's brilliant adaptation of stream of consciousness technique is matched by his brilliance in the use of dialogue. In a boy's school, Darcy, who asserts himself against the tyranny of the other boys, is about to be punished by them. First, however, they must get a hold on him:

> Touch me and each of you will regret it in turn.
> Grab him.
> Let go of me.
> Hold him, for god's sake, hold him.
> Christ he's strong.
> Hold him, get his head in a lock. Get him down, down.
> Bloody hell don't let him loose, knocking over the candles.
> Get him . . .
> O christ, where the hell is everyone.
> I've got him.
> No you haven't, you've got me . . .
> A newspaper is alight.
> Put it out you sod.
> I can't while this . . . (Darcy) is loose
> I've got him.
> You've got me again, you sod.

Two points should be made about this dialogue. First, it is natural. Donleavy has a good ear for the vocabulary and speech rhythms of these adolescents. Second, the dialogue is self-sufficient; it carries along the narrative. We can see Darcy standing before his juvenile tribunal; we can see them grapple with him; we can see the candles knocked over in the struggle; the blind grappling in the dark; the resulting conflagration. True, the dialogue contains stage directions— "knocking over the candles"; "A newspaper is alight"—but they are a natural part of the dialogue and do not intrude on its elegance and economy.

Brilliant as these two passages are, they are not in themselves comic; to be seen as part of the comic spirit, they must be viewed in the context of the whole novel. Darcy's stream of consciousness despair is real, but shortlived. Two pages later he blackmails an acquaintance on an adulterous fling, meets "Ronald Ronald Ronald," a con man, and starts on a new adventure. In the case of the dialogue in the boy's school, it looks as if our hero's comeuppance is near at hand; he is about to be hurt and humiliated by a group of sadistic fellow students, boys he has come to detest after only one day in attendance. However, the struggle so feelingly described, and the conflagration so cunningly alluded to provide sufficient confusion for Darcy to effect his escape, armed only with sets of long underwear and a carton of fudge filched from a less than generous new acquaintance.

Thus comedy does not exclude seriousness, but keeps it in check. For the main characters of the novel are unabashedly serious. Mr. Arland, Darcy's tutor, Miss von B, the housekeeper who initiates Darcy into the mysteries of life, and Darcy Dancer himself. Mr. Arland is clearly intelligent and sensitive and unfortunately in love with a young woman who rejects him. Finally he finds what he thinks is happiness with a woman named Clarissa, and is transformed. In Clarissa's presence, he says to Darcy: "And now what would you like in the way of sandwiches. How about a smoked salmon, eh." Darcy observes: "Never before in my entire knowledge have I ever heard Mr. Arland utter the word eh. Something has distinctly changed. Even his crossed leg has his foot jiggling up and down. A movement he told me no gentleman ever makes." The affair ends unhappily. Clarissa seems unfaithful; he rejects her; she kills herself; he disappears.

This tale is hardly comic. Nevertheless it should be noted that Mr. Arland's first, rejecting sweetheart is a participant in a series of comic adventures that make clear her complete unsuitability as his future bride. Moreover, Darcy hears about Clarissa's death in the least solemn of circumstances: in the midst of a comic misadventure with a woman who, as it turns out, is Clarissa's sister.

Neither is Miss von B's story of violation, destitution, and bare survival in wartorn Poland the stuff of comedy. Still, her affair with Darcy is laced with the comedy of her snobbery punctuated by her not-quite-successful attempts at learning colloquial English. Finally, the last scene between Darcy and Miss von B is not their sad parting, but an accidental meeting where she has clearly overcome her sorrow for him in her adoration for another man.

But it is Darcy himself who is the hero of the tale. In some sense his story is that of the romantic hero growing into manhood. In his search for maturity he reaches after schooling, love, career. These are all serious matters, but Donleavy does not treat them seriously. Darcy's formal schooling is a matter of one day: his search for love is a series of comic misadventures, and his chosen career is that of the idle rich. Oddly, he succeeds at this last. After running up his bogus credit to monstrous proportions at the best Dublin shops, hotels, and restaurants, he attends the races, bets on a long shot on a tip from a casual acquaintance, and wins a fortune on a horse that is the progeny of the stallion Dancer. The accident and the coincidence are doubly absurd. Darcy does not earn his success, except by effrontery; he is Horatio Alger in reverse.

The novel's title refers to Darcy's destinies. One meaning of these destinies is undoubtedly Darcy's seemingly infinite possibilities stemming from his youth and his pluck. Another meaning is the number of "lives" he lives as a result of his comic journey. He starts out as a member of the gentry, becomes a lower and then an upper servant to the *nouveaux riche* class, and ends as an impecunious and finally a well-fixed gentleman. In part these changes in class are stages in Darcy's education. As a result of his adventure as a servant, "Never again shall I treat the servants of Andromeda Park in a thoughtless and uncaring manner." However, such insights are by the way. The main point of all these changes is to wring the last bit of comedy out of the novel. Darcy's insight into social conditions is followed by a comic encounter. Darcy as an ill-kempt servant delivers turf to the drawing room, picks up a current magazine and plops himself down on the sofa. Enter the lady of the house.

Donleavy's most recent comic novel makes delightful reading. Donleavy is a master of narrative, but he is more than that. His most important characters have the vividness of real people. They are firmly anchored in flesh and blood concerns of loving and living. However, they are not so firmly planted in seriousness as to make *The Destinies of Darcy Dancer* anything but a comic novel. Finally we are left with the author's sense of fun, his feeling for the absurdities of life and the ability of the comic spirit to overcome them.

Alan G. Gross

THE DIARY OF VIRGINIA WOOLF
Volume I: 1915-1919

Author: Virginia Woolf (1882-1941)
Edited by Anne Olivier Bell with an Introduction and notes by Quentin Bell
Publisher: Harcourt Brace Jovanovich (New York). 356 pp. $12.95
Type of work: Diary
Time: 1915-1919
Locale: London

The first of a projected five-volume edition of the complete diary of Virginia Woolf which documents the emerging reputation of both Virginia and her husband, Leonard

For most of its length there is a peculiarly insulated quality to the first volume of Virginia Woolf's diary. We find little suggestion of her buried or imaginative life, almost no mention of the novel (her second, *Night and Day*) that she was writing through much of this period, only the briefest of critical comments on her reading, a minimum of reference to the larger social and political issues that consumed the energies of her husband, Leonard—in fact, if it were not for the occasional air raid warning and the sight of German prisoners of war, the reader would scarcely be aware of the fact that England was lost in the dark, bloody tunnel of World War I. For all of their crochets, the letters currently being published provide us with a much fuller sense of Woolf's life during the period covered by the present volume.

Indeed, the first two-thirds of the volume gives us only the barest outline of Woolf's days and ways. So reticent is the diary at this early stage that Woolf's biographer, Quentin Bell, may be correct in suggesting that the diary was initially intended for therapeutic purposes, "partly as a sedative, a way of proving to herself how normal she was." Certainly there seems to be an air of determination and self-congratulation in the keeping of the diary, an air that the diary itself scarcely seems to warrant. But, given the fuller and more complex entries in the closing pages of the volume as well as the selections already published by Leonard in *A Writer's Diary,* later volumes should prove extraordinarily interesting both to the careful critic and the gossipy reader.

Nevertheless, even through the reticence several things begin to emerge. There is, for example, the closeness of Virginia and Leonard, marked, among other things, by the frequency with which they simply went walking together: "After lunch we took the air in the Old Deer Park"; "we noticed the damaged Bridge as we walked to Kingston this afternoon. . . . We had a very good walk." However, Virginia's interest in Leonard's outside concerns could not even be termed marginal, so that they separated often enough when Leonard went to the London School of Economics, to a meeting of the Fabian executive, to groups promoting the League of Nations and the cooperative movement, to editors, to the offices of publications he himself edited, to the innumerable lectures he was called upon to give as his fame and expertise grew. She could take only a limited supply of the Sidney Webbs: "L. went to the Webbs, & I came home." Nor did she cotton much to her in-laws: "L. went to see his mother; I called on Jean." But when, in London, they went their separate ways, they met regularly for lunch or afterwards; when left at home to write, Virginia was likely to meet "L." en route so that they might walk home to Richmond together. Often enough, Leonard's moods and needs were registered in the diary along with her own: "amused me, but bored L. I'm afraid." And more than once we find the crisp comment: "We wrote all the morning." Clearly they created an atmosphere for each other in which they could work independently, possess their own souls and moods, and at the same time rest in each other.

There were differences enough, of course, and some of them, when pulled out of context, must have seemed insuperable. Virginia registered several quarrels— "We quarrelled almost all the morning!"—and no doubt there were some that she did not register. Her comments on Leonard's family and on Jews in general could, at times, be downright anti-Semitic: "I do not like the Jewish voice; I do not like the Jewish laugh," comments that Leonard must have read. There were also, of course, her recurring madness and daily fear of madness. Poignantly, the first segment of the diary lasts only six weeks, for it was interrupted by a bout of violent, screaming lunacy that, among other symptoms, took the form of a raving antipathy to Leonard himself. On February 13, 1915, she wrote: "I met L. at Spikings & we had tea, and were very happy." Two days later, the diary breaks off, not to be resumed for two and a half years.

While asserting over and over again her lack of interest in social, political, and economic matters—the very staff of life to Leonard—Virginia did accompany him now and then to some of the meetings he addressed, and she was suitably impressed by his ability as a speaker; in 1913, in fact, she had joined him on a ten-day tour of the industrial north. For four years she presided over monthly meetings of the local branch of the Women's Co-operative Guild held at Hogarth House. But, aside from Leonard's participation, she tended to find political meetings amusing at best, dreary at worst. As for the women of the Guild, "it always puzzles me to know why the women come. . . . They don't pay much attention apparently." To her, the audience at one public gathering "all looked unhealthy & singular & impotent." When Leonard spoke at Hampstead, she found the audience too "clean, decorous, uncompromising." Politics in general she saw as "an elaborate game" designed for men trained in the sport. And despite the coaching she must have had on all sides—"everyone makes the state of the country his private affair"—she insisted that she could make little sense of Labour Party politics, as immersed as Leonard and other Fabians were in the party. As for women with public missions, "their eccentricities keep me amused, when to tell the truth, I've ceased to follow their plots and denunciations"—though, conceivably, some jealousy might have been involved in the remark since Leonard, perforce, spent a good deal of time in the company of such women. Part of her feeling, perhaps, was due to the sad sense of what political and social responsibility did to one's feelings of youthful elasticity: "So we all step into the ranks of the middle aged, the responsible people, the burden bearers. It makes me a little melancholy." Despite it all, the central fact of her existence remained her relationship with Leonard.

Unmistakable, however, was her need for as many friends and acquaintances as she could muster, whether they were taken singly or in groups. The published correspondence testifies to its function in helping to spin a dense social web of those who outlined her world, and the diary takes careful note of days when no letters arrive. A party at Gordon Square was described as presenting Virginia with "2 hours of life." Another gathering, while composed of "the same party as usual," was "as usual, to my liking; so much alive, so full of information of the latest kind; real interest in every sort of art; & in people too." She assumed, in passing, that her feeling would not be shared by Leonard. Certain of her friends were particularly capable of making her vibrate in sympathy: Clive Bell, for one; Lytton Strachey, for another. If Lytton "were to walk in at this moment we should talk . . . as freely as we ever did, & with the sense, on both sides I think, of having hoarded for this precise moment a great deal peculiarly fit for the other."

There is, in fact, a fascinating entry for January 22, 1919: "How many friends have I got?" She sorts them, first, chronologically, according to their association with various stages of family history and then, over a period of a month, attempts to define the peculiar qualities of certain of them.

Indeed, we find a gallery of pungent character portraits in the diary. There is Katherine Mansfield who, on first meeting, seemed to stink "like a—well civet cat that had taken to street walking." Even at the first meeting, however, Virginia conceded that Mansfield would no doubt repay friendship, though as late as 1919 she was wondering whether she might list the author among her friends. There is Lady Ottoline Morrell, everyone's favorite comic target, spotted in the street, "brilliantly painted, as garish as a strumpet," perceived more sympathetically at times, but almost always condescendingly: "to me she always has the pathos of a creature vaguely afloat in some wide open space, without support or clear knowledge of its direction." There is Roger Fry, "in his wideawake hat," carrying a number of French books under his arm, hurrying to his editorial office at an art-history magazine, concerned with the production of a play designed by the Omega Workshops, run by Fry, and yet, in his enthusiasm, persuading Virginia into a nearby bookstore where she purchased a new French novel with money intended to pay for watch repairs. There are the many young men and women moving in and out of the Bloomsbury orbit—"cropheads" or "Bloomsbury bunnies," according to Virginia. And there are the many odd relationships and *ménages* forming the subject of delighted gossip: "Indeed I see the plots of many comedies brewing just now among our friends." And there are, of course, others: T. S. Eliot: "sharp, narrow & much of a stick"; Maynard Keynes, "a little inhuman," but "like quicksilver" in his conversation.

But, despite parties, meetings, visits; despite hours and hours of extended conversations; despite long walks and days of househunting and shopping; despite enforced periods of rest, during which her writing was carefully restricted—despite all this and much more, an enormous amount of work was produced at the Woolf household. Their famous Hogarth Press consumed great quantities of time and effort. Articles and reviews poured out of both Leonard and Virginia, the latter noting, on one occasion, that they were earning a tidy sum by their literary journalism. Virginia, at any rate, was capable of turning out an astonishing number of rapid reviews. Immediately after completing her essay, "Modern Novels," for the *Times Literary Supplement,* she submerged herself in the novels of Daniel Defoe for still another article: "I have to read one book a day in order to start on Saturday—such is the life of a hack." The next day, however, she failed to complete *Moll Flanders* because she spent the day in London, where, meeting E. M. Forster and learning that he had never read Defoe, she commanded him to do so. Nevertheless, her article, "The Novels of Defoe," appeared in less than two weeks. Of course, the most important aspect of her creative life, the production of the novel *Night and Day,* receives almost no mention in the diary, except for an occasional statement to the effect that a slight break in the flow of review books had given her time to pursue her novel. Only when it was completed could she bring herself to comment on it and, in the privacy of her diary, announce that she found it good: "I compare for originality & sincerity rather well with most of the moderns."

Max Halperen

DIRTY LINEN and NEW-FOUND-LAND

Author: Tom Stoppard (1937–   )
Publisher: Grove Press (New York). 75 pp. $6.95; paperback $2.95
Type of work: Drama
Time: The present
Locale: London

A brilliant, farcical drama about sexual scandal and political hypocrisy in the House of Parliament, coupled with a short play on English tradition and the American landscape

Principal characters:
Dirty Linen
MADDIE GOTOBED, secretary of the Committee and the object of their investigation
WITHENSHAW, M.P., Chairman of the Select Committee on Promiscuity in High Places
COCKLEBURY-SMYTHE, M.P.,
MCTEAZLE, M.P.,
CHAMBERLAIN, M.P.,
MRS. EBURY, M.P., and
FRENCH, M.P., Members of the Committee
New-Found-Land
BERNARD, a very old Home Office Official
ARTHUR, a very young Home Office Official

Line for line, word for word—and this is a "words" play if ever there was one—*Dirty Linen* along with *New-Found-Land* may well be Tom Stoppard's liveliest and funniest work, if not one of his deepest or most ambitious. From the opening lines—five minutes of clichés in foreign tongues—the play sizzles with a continuous flood of one-liners, comic monologues, outlandish puns, extravagant metaphors, hyperbolic rhetoric, double entendres, verbal duels, sophisticated witticisms, and ludicrously corny jokes. In all, Stoppard overwhelms us with a comedic verbal dexterity, punctuated by adroit bits of physical farce, which is almost unique on today's stage, although it has many predecessors: Congreve, Sheridan, Wilde, Shaw, George S. Kaufmann, and even the Marx Brothers.

Dirty Linen and *New-Found-Land* is really a sandwich of a theatrical evening; the second shorter play, a dramatic duet actually, is inserted about three-quarters of the way through the action of the first one, prior to the working out of the main play's "problem"—although the basic conflict in *Dirty Linen* is, at best, an extremely thin one. Indeed, although the actual resolution of the play occurs offstage, during the *New-Found-Land* interlude, this indirect climax is perfectly appropriate to a play whose impressiveness derives from its wit and ideas, rather than its conflicts.

What is the play about? Political hypocrisy and pomposity, especially the British parliamentary variety, the absurdity of traditional forms and rituals, of moral double-think, of the journalistic need to make something out of nothing in order to fill space, sell papers, and "compete," the artificiality and irrelevance of both politics and journalism to real life, and, above all, the split between what is actually done and the nonsensical, cliché-ridden language we invent in order to describe and conceal the doing of it.

Dirty Linen involves the attempt of a parliamentary sub-committee (the "Select Committee on Promiscuity in High Places") to submit a report on the recent and extravagant extracurricular sexual activities of that august body:

> McTEAZLE: . . . there is no phrase as certain to make a British sub-editor lose his sense of proportion as the phrase "Mystery Woman." This Committee was set up at the time when no fewer than 21 Members of Parliament was said to have been compromised. Since then rumour has fed on rumour and we face the possibility that a sexual swathe has passed through Westminister claiming the reputations of, to put no finer point upon it, 119 Members. Someone is going through the ranks like a lawn-mower in knickers.

Their fact-finding and reporting are greatly complicated by the fact that all save one of the male committee members can be included among the fallen and that their new secretary, Maddie Gotobed (Stoppard has never been a slave to subtlety), is, indeed, the "Mystery Woman," having risen in the ranks with remarkable speed despite dubious secretarial qualifications (Q: "You do speedwriting, I suppose?" A: "Yes, if I'm given enough time," or, Q: "Do you use Gregg's or do you favour the Pitman method?" A: "I'm on the pill").

Most of the play's humor, in the best farce tradition, comes from each committee member's attempt to keep his relationship with Maddie secret from his colleagues. As McTeazle puts it:

> . . . the tragedy is, as our luck would have it, that our gemlike love which burns so true and pure and has brought such a golden light into our lives, could well become confused with a network of grubby affairs between men who should know better and some bit of fluff from the filing department—

This speech indicates, however, a degree of self-control that is quite beyond these men when they actually come in contact with her. Their public images collapse and their "private" selves break into their every speech and gesture. For her part, Maddie reacts to the mens' moral gyrations with a combination of eager helplessness and naïve disregard, as her physical actions continually contradict her verbal protests of innocence, and her "knickers" (underwear) are scattered about the stage like confetti.

The major conflict in the play comes from French, a "puritan" committee member, the only one (excepting Mrs. Ebury) who has not had previous contact with Maddie. His intervention threatens to abort the whitewash, as he demands an honest report, put together by gathering evidence, hearing witnesses, and tracking down rumors. He insists that they "name names," unaware of the fact that all of his male colleagues will be among those named. But his conversion, which occurs offstage during the *New-Found-Land* interlude, is never really in doubt. Maddie Gotobed is a power that no mere man could possibly withstand. Indeed, the author of the final committee report is Ms. Gotobed herself.

And that is altogether appropriate, since Maddie not only represents the positive virtue of honest sexuality, but Stoppard's other ideas as well. Throughout the play her common sense is constantly juxtaposed against the hypocritical clichés of the MP's. From the beginning of the drama she is openly puzzled by the committee's purpose and she becomes more heated on the topic as the drama progresses. It is she who ascribes this public over-concern with politicians' private sex-lives to an essentially frivolous journalistic establishment. Although only talked about, the press is probably a more central target of Stoppard's biting wit than the politicians.

While French is being overcome by Maddie offstage, the second play, *New-Found-Land,* takes over the stage. Two Home Office civil servants appear, ostensibly to discuss the naturalization request of an American. This American, a dubious "artistic type," is presumably the real-life theatrical director Ed Berman, whose pending British citizenship occasioned the plays in the first place. *Dirty Linen* was originally intended as a tribute to the event, but soon grew away from the topic. Thus, Stoppard wrote and inserted *New-Found-Land* in the body of the play as his personal accolade to his friend, colleague, and the play's director, both in London and on Broadway.

While even less of a "play," *New-Found-Land* is, perhaps, even funnier than its companion piece. It actually consists of two verbal arias, a lengthy paean to "old traditional England," as personified in Lloyd George, by Bernard, the ancient, doddering civil servant, followed by an even longer and funnier travelogue about America delivered by Arthur, his young companion. The former is amusing, the latter hilarious, and between them Stoppard sketches an instant portrait of America that is perceptive and biting. But it is Arthur's "Greyhound Tour" of America from coast to coast, a collage of every media cliché, motion picture vignette, travel poster, popular gossip, and comic book, that is the most brilliant comedic set piece of both plays. Arthur's ebullient tirade goes on for a good fifteen minutes of uninterrupted monologue, ending in a final, wonderful effusion.

This extravagant verbal feat, the high point of a most verbal pair of plays, well demonstrates the paradox of Stoppard's successful plays in particular and the current British theater in general. In a theatrical era where text is minimized, ignored, or used, at best, as a blueprint, where the playwright is accorded a minor role in favor of director and actor, where language is increasingly treated as simply one of many useful devices, where improvisation is employed and disciplined classical acting thought passé, where ideas are considered irrelevant, Stoppard insists on the primacy of the text, the centrality of language, and the necessity for ideas, and his plays are resounding successes, both artistically and commercially.

Language, wit, ideas—these things have brought Tom Stoppard to the forefront of contemporary British theater, a theater that has established itself, in this period of antilanguage, as one of the most literate and verbal in the history of the English stage. Stoppard, Pinter, Storey, Bond, Osborne, Beckett—all are, in their unique ways, masters of the verbal idiom at a time when the vitality of the British stage is satisfying, exciting, and provocative.

Keith Neilson

A DUAL AUTOBIOGRAPHY

Authors: Will (1885–   ) and Ariel Durant (1898–   )
Publisher: Simon and Schuster (New York). 420 pp. $12.95
Type of work: Autobiography

The story of the Durants, individually and as a couple, in which they discuss their personal lives and opinions as well as their professional lives as writers and their writings

Will and Ariel Durant have spent their lives bringing the gifts of philosophy and history to thousands of people in the form of their books and lectures, and their dual autobiography may be the best gift of all. They have described here the joys and the sorrows of their journey across so many decades. We are treated to stronger and more personal opinions than they often have expressed in their public speeches and written words.

The book is arranged chronologically with Will and Ariel alternating in the narrative. Much of the story is devoted to their personal lives and their infatuation with each other, but a great amount of space is also devoted to the social and political events that influenced their intellectual development. The contrapuntal arrangement of their observations gives rise to something of a dialogue and is far less distracting than may be supposed. That they chose to present a dual autobiography is not surprising, for the last several volumes of *The Story of Civilization* were a joint project. It might be, in fact, very difficult for this inseparable pair to produce individual autobiographies.

Perhaps the most inviting and intriguing chapter is the first, where Ariel, without much of Will's editorial hand, describes her childhood and adolescence. Ariel comes across as part feminist/radical socialist and eventually part dutiful wife in the old style, a fascinating combination. Her political fires seem to mellow as her attention and energies have turned more and more to the "family business" of writing books. Throughout the remainder of the work, those sections written by Ariel that alternate with the sections written by Will have come under his polishing pen, and her thoughts frequently reach us through his graceful style. That Will seems to have taken on the general editorial duties is also typical of their roles in life, ever since they became acquainted as teacher and pupil at the Ferrar School in New York so long ago.

By all rights the Durant marriage never should have worked. There is a thirteen year difference in their ages. Will was well educated and well read when they met, while Ariel was just discovering books and ideas. Will had been reared in a strongly Roman Catholic family, Ariel in a less strongly Jewish one. But their love was strong enough to overcome such inauspicious circumstances, and to abide through the weeks of loneliness and separation that they endured for so many years while Will was on the lecture circuit. In our day of all too frequent divorces it is heartening to find a pair that could overcome a number of formidable obstacles and remain so devoted.

Nevertheless, this autobiography does not exclude some moments of doubt and accusation—Ariel's terrible loneliness while Will was away, for example, or a number of petty jealousies. These are all honestly, if blushingly, shown in excerpts from their correspondence. In this regard, the Durants play Everyman and Everywoman for their readers. In the end, they have come through it all, given patience and perspective, with a rock-solid marriage, and in so doing may shed a positive light on similar experiences for others.

Will's concern for his repudiated religious beliefs is a theme that is recorded throughout his life. He began firmly grounded in the Roman Catholic Church, so firmly grounded, in fact, that the natural course of his life led him into a seminary to study for the priesthood. As he read more and more theological and philosophical works, he came to value the creative wonder that is man's mind more than the dogma of his Church. He left the seminary and rebounded into the radical socialist libertarian Ferrar School as a teacher. By comparison to many others connected with this institution he discovered that his views are really fairly moderate. Thus began a lifelong reevaluation of his personal religious faith and his political preferences against a background of intellectual exercises and discoveries as well as more personal and emotional experiences. Thousands of his readers have experienced similar struggles, many while officially adhering to a particular faith or political stance.

This aspect of the autobiography is not as overburdening as it may sound. It is, rather, a great strength in the story to watch Will Durant struggle with so many doubts and conflicts and yet resolve them into a philosophy of optimistic patience and perspective. It is refreshing and almost amusing to watch as he discovers, in his summation, that his idealistic socialism has mellowed into more idealism than socialism.

Will particularly celebrates the abilities of the human mind. Many reviewers and historians have complained that Will Durant is a popularizer of history, and Durant has spent considerable effort to answer that charge. What his critics seem not to have comprehended is that such a designation should carry no negative connotations. He writes for a different audience from that envisioned by the academic historian, but his audience is no less valid. He explains it best in the preface to *The Story of Philosophy:*

> Perhaps each kind of teacher can be of aid to the other; the cautious scholar to check our enthusiasm with accuracy, and the enthusiast to pour warmth and blood into the fruits of scholarship.

And yet the question remains why so few people read the scholars, and so very many read the Durants?

What seems to have started Will Durant's success and continued it, is his ability to share with his readers his own enjoyment of historical research and his curiosity and excitement over what he discovers. He reads and distills his readings, putting them into a larger context, and then shares with a very personal pleasure his findings. It is this enthusiasm for his discoveries that engenders a like enthusiasm for history and philosophy on the part of his readers.

While enthusiasm is the key ingredient here, it would be of no consequence were he not a very good and hardworking writer. In this synthetic approach to the recordings of civilization the Durants interpret the events and movements of history, art, science, and philosophy for the reader in order to draw these various aspects into one cohesive picture, illuminated with many biographical essays. The term "synthetic" often has a negative connotation suggesting that which is not real, and to use it without a word of explanation would be a disservice to the Durants. Something that is synthetic, in the true meaning of the word, is a combination of various elements drawn together into a cogent whole. Theirs is a synthetic autobiography just as their books were synthetic, or integral, history.

Aside from its great worth as the autobiography of a fascinating pair, the book includes many short biographies of leading writers and public figures of the last several decades, since many of them were friends or correspondents of the Durants. Luckily, these persons are all represented in the index to the book, which was thoughtfully provided to make these items retrievable.

The Durants take a genuine delight in laudatory reviews of their work and share thank-you notes from the great and glorious of our time in such an innocent way that it almost seems that they are surprised to have been the objects of such attention. There are moments in the work that this emphasis on the positive becomes almost smug, even though they do quote generously from negative reviews as well. The deceivingly smooth flow of their lives from year to year is perhaps a function of Will's pen gliding over the final draft of most of the chapters. This makes the book very pleasant to read, but it might have been a little more fun if more of Ariel's pithiness had been interspersed as in the first chapter.

The Durants each wrote an ending to the book. Will once again synthesizes the more dominant elements in his life into a typically philosophical essay. Ariel, as is her wont, admits more poignancy to her summation, emphasizing again the great love that has sustained them throughout. Ariel is quite correct in closing with the observation that they have led enchanted lives. From inauspicious beginnings, through the uncertainties of social change, depression, and wars, they have stayed together in a wonderfully close and stable relationship and managed a family "business." Their life's work is something which they enjoy immensely, and they have made a great deal of money doing it. Moreover the fruits of their labors have brought understanding and pleasure to thousands of people.

Margaret S. Schoon

EDISON
The Man Who Made the Future

Author: Ronald W. Clark
Publisher: G. P. Putnam's Sons (New York). 256 pp. $12.95
Type of work: Biography
Time: 1847–1931
Locale: The United States

A biographical study of the life of Thomas A. Edison which focuses primarily on Edison's professional career as an inventor and business entrepreneur

> *Principal personages:*
> THOMAS A. EDISON
> ALEXANDER GRAHAM BELL, inventor of the telephone
> HENRY FORD, organizer of the Ford Motor Company

Ronald Clark's excellent biography, *Einstein: The Life and Times,* has raised expectations far beyond the level that has been attained in Clark's study of *Edison: The Man Who Made the Future.* The latter, generously sprinkled with quotations, is a narrative account of Edison's life with little attempt at sophisticated or critical analysis of the biographical activities and events and with only brief efforts at comprehending the real man as distinguished from the legend. Clark has constantly before himself the subtitle of his book, "The Man Who Made the Future," and takes pains, often unconvincingly, to demonstrate the validity of this interpretation.

Thomas Alva Edison was born in Milan, Ohio, on February 11, 1847, to Samuel and Nancy Edison. Early in life, he exhibited considerable interest and skill in reading such works as R. G. Parker's *Natural and Experimental Philosophy,* the writings of Thomas Paine, and Newton's *Principia,* which convinced him that "I am not a mathematician." Indeed, Edison proved to have much more interest in practical experiments than in theories. Clark contends that even as a boy, Edison manifested three characteristics that were to remain with him all of his life: "They were quickness at turning chance circumstance to his own benefit, a refusal to be deterred, and a relentlessness—some would say ruthlessness—in exacting as much payment for a job as traffic would stand."

Edison's early successes came as a result of opportunities presented to telegraph operators during the American Civil War. During this period, he moved from community to community filling one telegraphic position briefly before moving to the next. By 1865, he had worked in a half dozen towns and cities and in the next few years would continue to stay in a job only until he had learned what he could from it and then seek to expand his knowledge elsewhere.

Soon after he went to Boston in 1868, Edison invented the automatic vote recorder and an improved stock ticker. He then began to work on a multiplex telegraph to send multiple messages over a single telegraph wire. In 1869 he went to New York City and, in the view of Clark, turned his full attention to becoming a professional inventor, eventually setting up Pope, Edison and Company to provide inventions and instruments for "the application of electricity to the Arts and Sciences."

Through this company Edison produced his Universal Stock Printer, brought out a new "gold printer," and rented the latter to various agencies. The sale of this service to Western Union provided him with money to undertake additional experimentation. Moreover, General Marshall Lefferts of Western Union began financing some of Edison's research. Money received from improvements to Western Union equipment permitted Edison to establish workshops and research laboratories in Newark, New Jersey, where he brought together a competent staff who became devoted to him. At this new facility Edison improved the automatic telegraph, which permitted high speed transmission, and invented the quadruplex telegraph, making possible the sending of multiple telegraph messages simultaneously over a single wire. As a consequence of the quadruplex Edison was involved in his first legal suit. He had received financial and other support from Western Union and had promised the invention to them, but instead had deviously negotiated with and sold it to Jay Gould's Atlantic and Pacific Telegraph Company. A spectator at the trial recorded in his diary the observation that Edison "has a vacuum where his conscience ought to be." Clark points out and then attempts to soften the charge of duplicity, but the case remains a blot which Edison himself recognized. Legally Edison was permitted to sell to whom he chose, but his negotiation with Gould was of questionable morality.

Also during this time in his career, Edison was hired to find ways around patents, which says much about the business practices in the mid-1870's and the 1880's. Businessmen who did not wish to pay for patents but who wished to profit from the ideas, sought out inventors such as Edison to evade patents. In his work of evading patents, Edison often provided excellent inventions and improvements, for the work required a thorough understanding of all aspects of the technologies and physical principles involved in the inventions.

In 1876 Alexander Graham Bell invented the telephone, and Edison began working on the apparatus to improve it. He undertook significant changes which revolutionized the device and made it practical as a popular means of communication. Constructing an effective carbon transmitter, Edison gave Western Union a communication system with which to challenge Bell. The fight between Western Union and Bell, in which Edison was directly involved, raged on both sides of the Atlantic, while both men provided inventions to give advantage first to one side and then to the other. Finally in England on June 8, 1880, the competing corporations merged into the United Telephone Company.

While the Edison-Bell feud was being fought, Edison was busily involved with other inventions such as the electric pen, which eventually led to the duplicating machine; he also improved the typewriter and made it into a working instrument. In 1876 Edison moved his workshops to Menlo Park, New

Jersey, where he assembled an outstanding staff of dedicated workers and inventors. The climate he generated at Menlo Park was intellectual, stimulating, and infused with a spirit of community and mutual support, and the result was a constant stream of inventions and patents in a wide variety of areas. Here Edison astonished his staff with the invention of the phonograph, and in 1878 he created the Edison Speaking Phonograph Company. The phonograph caught the public interest and soon, throughout the United States, audiences sat in rapt attention listening to recordings of all manner of sounds. Although much of Edison's fame came from this invention (he was asked to demonstrate it for President R. B. Hayes), he lost interest in it soon after its successful demonstration.

Edison had for some years believed that electricity could be employed in the service of humankind to revolutionize life and ease its burdens. He first acted in the area of the use of electricity in lighting, beginning his study of the problem in 1878. The prevailing lighting systems of the day were gas or the electric arc, with gas representing almost a monopoly of the lighting industry. As Edison approached creation of an incandescent lamp, the first problem was that of what material and shape would be most effective for a filament. The Edison Electric Light Company was established to facilitate Edison's work. Patenting a bulb with a platinum filament in 1878, Edison continued his experiments. In October, 1879, Edison succeeded in producing a bulb with a carbon filament that lasted for about forty hours. He obtained a patent and the press spread the word throughout the United States. Edison used light bulbs to illuminate his home and other buildings at Menlo Park. Since the Pennsylvania Railroad ran tracks to Menlo Park and visitors often came, the spectacle of such illumination proved very impressive and was clearly a triumph for Edison.

His success with lighting convinced Edison that he was launched on an exceedingly significant development and that he should undertake a more difficult and more significant effort—the wide distribution of electricity from a central generator. Effective lighting depended on this. Improvements in the light bulb went forward in the period, so that sales of bulbs had reached 45,000,000 by 1903. From new offices in New York City, Edison attempted both to manage his corporate empire and continue his interest in invention, particularly in a central generating station.

Part of the development of the generation system was undertaken in the early 1880's when Edison divided up a district into a number of small areas, each served by feeder wires; this avoided the need for long feeder wires. Copper was further reduced by a three-wire system. Edison and his Menlo Park staff next worked out an insulation system to prevent electricity in buried wires from seeping into the ground, and then developed a large dynamo. The problem of consumers overloading the system was solved by the invention of the fuse. Edison also produced a working electric meter to determine the amount of electricity used by customers. In order to move ahead in these and other areas, Edison created the Edison Lamp Company, the Edison Machine Works, the

Edison Shafting Company, the Thomas A. Edison Construction Department, and the Edison Electric Illuminating Company of New York. Edison's corporate empire grew as his interest expanded. His generating station proved effective enough to found the Edison Isolated Lighting Company, created to install such stations across the United States.

The organizational structure of Edison's corporate empire was leaving him little time for invention; he needed help. In 1881 Samuel Insull was hired by Edison and eventually brought order to his empire. With corporate and financial matters securely in the hands of Insull, Edison turned to the considerable problems of developing his electrical system. He achieved international success in establishing electric lighting systems in Belgium, Holland, Italy, and England. Dynamos were developed for shipboard use. Constant improvements outdated equipment rapidly but pushed electrification ahead. On September 4, 1882, at 3:00 p.m., the J. P. Morgan Company on Wall Street was, amid ceremony, lit with some four hundred electric bulbs. Soon thereafter Edison started the first hydroelectric plant. Moreover, some three hundred generating plants were operating by early 1883. Uses other than lighting were also developed for electricity, such as electric fire alarms and electric railways.

After filing a number of patents relating to an electric railway, Edison joined in 1881 with S. D. Field to form the Electric Railway Company of America. Together they installed a demonstration track at the Chicago Exposition and established the practicality of the electric railway system; but, practical or not, the public and Edison lost interest in the system for more than a decade after its invention.

Clark contends that in the decade between 1880 and 1890, Edison crossed the border between the famous and the celebrity. The decade was also important because Edison's failure rate increased. The author argues that "whatever the cause, genius began to flicker." In this period, Edison purchased a home in West Orange, New Jersey, a suburb of Newark. The laboratories of Menlo Park were left to fall into disuse and ruin while new laboratories and research facilities were constructed near Edison's new home. Affiliated companies were constructed near his West Orange home. The National Phonograph Company, the Edison Business Phonograph Company, the Edison Phonograph Works, the Edison Manufacturing Company and others were soon constructed. Also from 1885 onward Edison was involved in initiating some two hundred lawsuits at a cost of two million dollars to protect his patents. Increasingly Edison was also involved in generating publicity. The most determined of his propaganda campaigns involved his stubborn support of direct current in opposition to alternating current. The difficulty with direct current was that it could only be effective at a limited distance, and, as use of electricity grew, direct current ran into problems. Nikolas Tesla supported alternating current even though he worked for Edison. Becoming infuriated with Edison's tactics, he quit and went to work for George Westinghouse. At Westinghouse, Tesla produced a practical system of alternating current that eventually replaced Edison's direct current. The Edison propaganda campaign had failed.

By 1888 Insull's organizational efforts resulted in the formation of the Edison General Electric Company, and Edison surrendered control of much of the industrial complex he had fathered. By 1889 his name was dropped from the company and he emerged an embittered and, for a time, almost unbalanced man. Unfortunately, Clark does not go into the details of this period, which, one suspects, might have been very useful in understanding his subject's personality.

Meanwhile, Edison again returned to improvement of the phonograph. He recognized that the primary use of the phonograph would be the recording of music, but, as in his advocacy of direct current, he again backed a loser: he insisted on the cylinder over the flat record even though the cylinder had far more limited use than the record. Only in 1913 did he give in to the record—but not before it was clear that "The Man Who Made the Future" had guessed wrong again. In the late 1880's, Edison had turned to moving pictures and by 1888 had taken out a patent on the kinetoscope. Several improvements were made in the 1890's, but by 1896 he lost interest, ceased development, and turned his attention elsewhere.

The next problem with which Edison became involved was extracting iron from low grade iron ore deposits. He planned very expensive and complex industrial installations which became models for uranium extraction in the United States in the 1940's. The installations were brilliantly conceived and technically a triumph. Unfortunately, the discovery of rich deposits of iron ore in the Mesabi range of Minnesota made the installation irrelevant and Edison, after losing some two million dollars, closed his plants. Edison next turned to cement houses which he successfully developed, but which the public refused to purchase. Again guessing wrong, Edison collaborated with Henry Ford to produce an electric automobile. Although contributing significantly to the development of the battery, Edison eventually had to recognize that the gasoline and not the electric automobile represented the wave of the future.

Edison's work during World War I was involved with providing synthetic substances to aid the war effort, the most important of which used carbolic acid and benzol. He was able to develop techniques for producing these chemicals, and also to aid the Navy with torpedo detection, more efficient periscopes, and other improvements in equipment. The end of the war brought a period of real decline for Edison, and Clark has little of substance to say about the inventor until his death in 1931.

Ronald Clark has written a rather dull account that provides the details of Edison's inventions, but little insight into Edison the man. Lacking dates at critical points and jumping, regardless of chronology, from issue to issue or invention to invention, the story is difficult to follow. Finally, detailed descriptions of important events, such as Edison's loss of control of his corporate structure, are too often lacking. The interesting subject and handsome format of this book have not been matched by the writing of a biographer from whom readers have come to expect more.

Saul Lerner

ESSAYS OF E. B. WHITE

Author: Elwyn Brooks White (1899–   )
Publisher: Harper & Row Publishers (New York). 277 pp. $12.50
Type of work: Essays

A collection of essays originally published over a span of more than forty years in which one of America's most celebrated prose stylists writes about country and city, man and nature, the remembered past and the world of tomorrow, and writers and writing

The warm reception of *Letters of E. B. White* in 1976 has led to the most welcome publication of a collection of thirty-one of White's essays, most of which appeared originally in *The New Yorker, Harper's,* and other magazines over a span of more than forty years. The essays range in length from the two-page "Riposte," answering J. B. Priestley's assertion that Americans believe hen eggs are good only if they are white, to a twenty-six-page account of a voyage, remembered many years later, by a youthful and naïve Elwyn Brooks White from Seattle to Alaska and back in 1923. The arrangement of the book, as White says in a brief Foreword, is "by subject matter or by mood or by place, not by chronology." There are seven groups of essays: "The Farm," "The Planet," "The City," "Florida," "Memories," "Diversions and Obsessions," and "Books, Men, and Writing." Several essays have not been published before in book form.

"A loose sally of the mind," wrote Dr. Johnson defining *essay* in his *Dictionary,* "an irregular indigested piece; not a regular or orderly composition." The form (or lack of form) permits quick shifts from one topic to another and, in White's practice, not only allows veering or tacking as with a whimsical wind pushing his sailboat on Penobscot Bay, but also includes many parenthetical interruptions not limited to a mere word or phrase. White likes parentheses, and his frequent use of them helps to make his essays sound like amiable talk from an intelligent, urbane man with some interesting comments to make and an often amusing way of making them. In "Coon Tree" he remarks that his doctor has ordered him to put his head in traction for ten minutes twice a day, and he parenthesizes: "Nobody can figure out what to do with my head, so now they are going to give it a good pull, like an exasperated mechanic who hauls off and gives his problem a smart jolt with the hammer."

White's parentheses usually contain no more than one sentence, if even that, but occasionally he needs more room. In enumerating and describing the changes that have "modernized" his old kitchen in Maine, he complains that there is no longer a tub to wash his dog in. Then he adds a parenthesis: "I give our current dachshund one bath a year now, in an old wash boiler, outdoors, finishing him off with a garden-hose rinse. He then rolls in the dirt to dry himself, and we are where we started."

White has often been praised for his prose style, which is so easy and flowing that it seems effortless, but the casualness is deceptive; it has been carefully attained. Literary echoes sound occasionally, yet they are natural, not pretentious. As he listens to a farm helper spading rocky earth for the burial of a pig that has died after long suffering, White says somberly to himself, "Never send to know for whom the grave is dug, it's dug for thee." One winter in Maine he recalls how a Florida beach he used to enjoy visiting has been "developed" and thus has been ruined for him, and he indulges in a rueful biblical pun, "And if the surf hath lost its savor, wherewith shall we be surfeited?"

White's occasional figures of speech reflect his experience of both rural life and city life. He looks at bundles of fir-balsam wreaths ready to be trucked from Maine to Boston or New York for the Christmas trade, and to him they are "aromatic dumplings [for] hungry dwellers in cities." Young firs are also ready for the long haul, "standing as close together as theatergoers between the acts." On another occasion he watches an old gander that has lost a fight with a young gander and has sat alone in the hot sun for two hours. "I felt deeply his sorrow and his defeat," writes White. "I had seen his likes often enough on the benches of the treeless main street of a Florida city—spent old males, motionless in the glare of the day."

When he was young, White tried writing verse and once had published in a Louisville newspaper a sonnet on a horse that won a race at Churchill Downs (beating a horse that White had bet on). In later years White occasionally returned briefly to verse, several examples of which he reprinted in *The Second Tree from the Corner* (1954), but he recognized early that his normal medium was prose. Yet the music and even the rhythm of poetry still sound in phrases and sentences of his later prose, as in "A Report in January," written from his Maine home in 1958:

> The days ahead unroll in the mind, a scroll of blessed events in garden and in barn. Wherever you look, you see something that advertises the future: in the heifer's sagging sides you see the calf, in the cock's shrill crow you hear the pipping egg, in the cache of topsoil down cellar next the furnace you see the seedling, and even on the darkest day the seed catalogue gives off a gleam from some tomato of the first magnitude.

White and his beloved wife Katharine, who, following a long illness died shortly after *Essays* was published, had a number of homes during their forty-eight-year marriage. There were several apartments in New York—the opening essay, "Good-Bye to Forty-Eighth Street," describes the leaving of one of these—but "home" in the essays usually means the white farmhouse in North Brooklin, Maine, which the Whites bought in 1933 and in which White still lives, having, as he remarks in the Foreword to *Essays,* "finally come to rest." This farm house is the scene of many of the best pieces in *Essays,* whether they were written there or not.

Readers of White's volume of letters or of most of his earlier books may remember that he finds nature's creatures—from insects all the way up the evolutionary ladder to man—by turns entertaining, amusing, or enlightening and sometimes saddening or almost maddening. Animals and birds, both wild and domesticated, often appear as characters, either major or minor, in his verse, his fiction, and his essays. He once wrote a seriocomic ode on a cow that had died from a bee sting, and the protagonists of all three of his books for children are nonhuman, although Stuart Little combines the appearance of a mouse with the speech and other characteristics of a highly intelligent and well-mannered boy.

In the early 1930's White had a Scotch terrier named Daisy ("an opinionated little bitch") who purportedly wrote several letters to Mrs. White reporting on the activities and troubles of her husband. One of Daisy's newsy letters is included in *Letters of E. B. White,* and her obituary appears in White's *Quo Vadimus?* (1939). Of the whole series of dachshunds that show up in White's writings over the years, Fred is the chief, an energetic, troublesome, and yet endearing dog (Fred's dead now, dammit, as White once wrote) who is as unforgettable to White's readers as he is to his former master. Fred furnishes the comic relief in "Death of a Pig," which is reprinted in "The Farm" section of *Essays.* The piece is a sad and ironic story of a pig which is bought to be fattened and then slaughtered for his pork but which White goes to extraordinary trouble to try to save from dying of an undetermined illness that finally destroys him. During the several days and nights of the struggle, Fred is all over the place, observing and supervising ("his stethoscope dangling") as White and two veterinarians try vainly to cure the pig; and Fred staggers along behind White and his helper Lennie as they drag the pig's body to its burial place. "The grave in the woods is unmarked," writes White in conclusion, "but Fred can direct the mourner to it unerringly and with immense good will, and I know he and I shall often revisit it, singly and together, in seasons of reflection and despair, on flagless memorial days of our own choosing."

A mother raccoon plays the principal role in "Coon Tree," a little nature comedy enacted mostly in or on the trunk of a tree in front of White's Maine home. As White meticulously describes the coon's "thorough scrub-up" before her nightly foraging and her slow and careful descent of the tree, one is reminded of the close and patient observation of animals and birds by Henry David Thoreau—one of White's favorite authors—who in the nineteenth century found in nature the same kind of pleasure that White has experienced in the present one. Another comic nature essay is "The Geese," though it ends in pathos. White ingeniously arranges to have eggs from a super-laying goose hatched by her less productive sister and then somewhat later observes sadly as the elderly gander who fathered the goslings is beaten and run away by the goslings' young and vigorous uncle on the maternal side.

White is skeptical about much of what has been and is being done by modern scientists and technologists, and he wonders about their predictions regarding the kind of world that is being projected for future generations. "I would feel more optimistic about a bright future for man," he says, "if he spent less time proving that he can outwit Nature and more time tasting her sweetness and respecting her seniority." Again, in "Sootfall and Fallout," in which a troubled, anxious, fearful tone predominates, he comments, "I hold one share in the corporate earth and am uneasy about the management." Even as early as 1939, when he wrote "The World of Tomorrow," a report on the New York World's Fair, he complained that there was too much technology and too little life in what he saw.

"Here Is New York," one of White's best-known essays, was written in the summer of 1948 and appeared first in *Holiday* in 1949 and later as a small book. Although it pictures a New York quite different from the present one, White has included the essay in his collection because he remembers the former city "with longing and with love." It is a beautiful memorial to a city that was.

White goes back to the 1920's to compose a fond memorial to the Model T Ford in "Farewell, My Lovely," which was first published in *The New Yorker* over the pseudonym Lee Strout White. Suggested by a manuscript sent in by Richard Lee Strout, the essay nevertheless draws largely upon White's own memories of the Ford, since he and a friend, Howard Cushman, traveled across the United States in 1922 in a Ford roadster that White had bought for about four hundred dollars. White comments on the many gadgets that could be bought from Sears Roebuck to equip or decorate the car, which "was born naked as a baby"; and he mentions some of "the lore and legend that governed the Ford," including what to do about the "extravagantly odd little device" called a timer. White once tried spitting on his timer to remove a possible hex. The essay will stir the memories of those who drove the old Model T, and it may pique the curiosity of jaded younger drivers bored by the modern car, which needs only a turn of the ignition key to start and which then moves forward smoothly to driving speed without even a manual changing of gears.

The three authors White recalls with affection and respect in his final group of essays are Don Marquis, Will Strunk, Jr., and Edward Howe Forbush. Marquis was the creator of Archy, a poetic cockroach who typed his poems in lower case because he couldn't manage the capital key, and Archy's racy feline friend Mehitabel, whose mottos for living were "toujours gai" and "wotthehell wotthehell." The essay was first written as an introduction to a 1950 edition of *the lives and times of archy and mehitabel.*

Will Strunk was the professor who taught White English usage and composition at Cornell, using his own little text, *The Elements of Style*, and issuing his oral imperatives in triplicate, as when he laid down Rule Thirteen: "Omit needless words! Omit needless words! Omit needless words!" White's adulatory essay on Strunk led to a publisher's request that White prepare an updated edition of *The Elements of Style*, and the book has enjoyed considerable success as a text.

Edward Howe Forbush was an ornithologist who died in 1929 just before completing his master work, *Birds of Massachusetts and Other New England States.* In "Mr. Forbush's Friends" White writes of his pleasure and profit from "reading around" in his set of *Birds of Massachusetts* over two decades. He particularly enjoys Forbush's "immense enthusiasm for anything that has feathers," the abundance of well-organized information he gives, and the use the author makes of his "large company of informers, or tipsters" who feed him such information as that furnished by a Massachusetts lady who heard a catbird sound "Taps" and who "Believes bird picked it up from hearing it played at burial services in nearby cemetery."

E. B. White will never win a Nobel Prize for Literature. As he says in his Foreword, essayists are considered second-class citizens. White has won a whole group of lesser awards, however, the earliest being several honorary degrees in the 1940's and 1950's and the latest a special Pulitzer citation in literature and the arts in April, 1978. He richly deserves every award.

Henderson Kincheloe

THE FACE OF BATTLE

Author: John Keegan (1934–   )
Publisher: The Viking Press (New York). Illustrated. 354 pp. $10.95
Type of work: Military history
Time: 1415, 1815, and 1916
Locale: Agincourt, Waterloo, and the Somme

Through accounts and analyses of three battles, the author tries to understand better what the experience of battle is really like

Principal personages:
    HENRY V, King of England
    ARTHUR WELLESLEY, Duke of Wellington
    SIR DOUGLAS HAIG, later Earl Haig

John Keegan is Senior Lecturer in War Studies at the Royal Military Academy, Sandhurst (the British equivalent of West Point). He admits in the very beginning that he has never been in battle, nor near a battle. In those two statements is an opening key to this book. *The Face of Battle* is an effort to derive from the historical sources a better understanding of what it is like to be *in* battle—not just to narrate the events, but to come closer to a realization of what the participants felt. The method is a description and analysis of three battles: Agincourt, Waterloo, and the Somme. Keegan surrounds the battle accounts with an introductory chapter and a conclusion, which provide much of the value of his work. The method is justified, for not only are the battle accounts fascinating and innovative in themselves, but they demonstrate the observations made in the more general portions, and bring the analyses to life.

Keegan's introduction is in large measure a study of military history, at once a defense and a critique, but also an effort to rescue the genre from its limitations. The authors of military history have been largely staff officers intent on "lessons," teachers in the military schools with much the same attitude, and amateur students of history, or of battle, or of both. The limitations derive from these facts, but lie deeper. The writers of military history have rarely gone beyond the fighting; they have taken what Keegan calls the "win/lose" approach, which isolates the military story from the rest of history. He likens this method to the English and American trial by jury, which he calls "accusatory," an aggressive process intended to reach a verdict. The alternative approach is the French "investigatory" proceeding, in which the judge has wide powers of interrogation and investigation to aid in arriving at truth. Whatever the merits of the two legal procedures—a matter for serious thought—the analogy is a valuable stimulus to an examination of the preconceptions behind historical writing, especially but not exclusively military historical writing. The implication is that practicing historians, military and otherwise, may not be fully conscious of the theoretical underpinnings or ramifications of their procedures.

Keegan's point, however, is especially applicable to the battle historian; if battle is not a crime, it is at least a definite event, and therefore possessed of parallels. In the "court of history," the question is always, Who was guilty of the result, if it was defeat, or responsible for the result, if it was victory? This commonest of approaches makes statements such as, "If General A had not extended his flank . . . ," or, "If General B had moved up five minutes earlier. . . ." Obviously, this is too narrow an approach. Not only is it unsafe to assume that the result of battle hinges on some single decision, but it is also true that not all battles have clear victories or defeats for which credit and blame can be distributed. Deeper and more important, if the historian looks only for guilt or innocence, blame or responsibility, he will not reach an understanding of the total event or process in all its background and complexity.

Keegan uses two examples to illustrate typical qualities of military history writing in the past; one is the English "philosopher of war," Sir Edward Creasy, the author of *The Fifteen Decisive Battles of the World,* first published in 1851 and often reprinted, extended, and imitated. Creasy, accepting the Victorian aversion to war but fascination by it, concentrated only on those battles which, as his title indicates, decided the course of history.

The second example is Julius Caesar and his *Gallic Wars,* which is illustrative, perhaps originative, of much battle writing. Not only Caesar's but most succeeding battle accounts are from the view of the general, whether or not written by him. The resulting difficulties are obvious: the tendency to self-glorification; the limits, both physical and intellectual, of the view; and, more important to Keegan's argument, the creation of a seemingly clear and simple picture out of a very complicated and confused set of happenings.

For the main body of his book, Keegan has chosen three battles, all English, and all told from that point of view: Agincourt (1415), Waterloo (1815), and the Somme (1916). The accounts are not typical battle narratives; we have little of the generals' plans and orders, though the successive movements are described. Rather the emphasis is on what actually happened, so far as it can be discovered, and that means what the men in battle did. There is attention, for instance, to the soldiers' condition before the battle. At Agincourt and Waterloo, they were tired with marching, and at Agincourt, with waiting in line; at Waterloo, many had spent the night in the rain. Keegan suggests the probability in many cases that they were sustained by liquor, perhaps actually drunk—a probability he supports from the record, but one which is rarely mentioned in conventional accounts.

The character of the troops and their relationship with their superiors at Agincourt are obvious concerns. Knights and men-at-arms, for instance, were unlikely to feel any desire for combat with mere archers; there was neither profit nor prestige in such a confrontation. Class lines distinguished officers from enlisted men at Waterloo, and usually at the Somme, but with somewhat different results. Methods of recruitment are taken into account at the Somme especially, where many outfits came from the same town and even the same civilian occupation. Keegan offers realistic appraisals of the encounters, framed in terms of the arms involved: for instance, infantry and cavalry against archers at Agincourt; infantry and cavalry against artillery at Waterloo, infantry against machine guns at the Somme. The author successfully captures the mood of confusion, noise, mud, falling comrades, enemies, and horses dead, wounded, or riderless; it is all pictured, vividly but in a low key. The rhetoric is not that of a battle piece; Keegan's treatment is basically analytical, not narrative.

Keegan asks practical questions. Why was the British square used and what was it like to be in it? What were the trenches, and complexes of trenches, and how do soldiers go about taking them? And, especially, how did men behave, and why? Why did some individuals and some groups go forward under fire, and others not? Why did men break—or more realistically, perhaps, why did more *not* break? What part did the hope of gain play—ransom for prisoners taken at Agincourt, looting at Waterloo? How much influence had the respect of fellow-soldiers, how much the leadership of officers? What effect had patriotism and self-esteem? How often was physical compulsion used—some Waterloo troops were driven forward by their officers' swords. What actions were due to fatigue? To shock?

The answers are sometimes speculations, sometimes a convergence of modern experience and theory with what is known of the contemporary conditions. The experts, each in his separate world, no doubt will have objections to Keegan's method—the battle historian to details of his accounts, the military men to his judgments of discipline or the lack of it, the psychologists and sociologists to his theories about men in groups and men under stress. What is important about Keegan's book is that, while the questions it asks are not the usual ones, they do seem to be the ones historians *ought* to ask.

In his summary, Keegan moves toward the present and the future, and discusses the ways in which mechanization, and the elaboration of modern technology, have changed battle, and the ways in which the impact of war falls on total populations, not on the military alone. There is the suggestion that the strain of battle, and the fear of it, may grow—may eventually even render it obsolete. It is an intriguing discussion, related to the historical analysis, but not necessarily validated by it.

In fact, one of the values of the book, but also one of its peculiarities, is the range of subjects treated in a comparatively brief space. The author displays considerable literary skill, particularly in his ability to include a wide and, at first glimpse, seemingly unrelated, set of interests or facts. The Somme account, for instance, includes not only some notion of trench warfare in general, and of the English society from which the "Kitchener army" came, but a note on the Russian front, and a discussion of the literary aftermath of the battle and the war.

The peculiarities and limitations of *The Face of Battle* are minor compared to the value of the book. It is cleanly and attractively written, and it rests on the solid foundation of its sources; both general reader and historian can enjoy it and profit from it. Two groups especially should have this book recommended to them: those interested in military history, whose usual version of it is the location of X division on the left flank, and the nonmilitary historians, who regard it not as unimportant, but as beneath the dignity of the intellectual and professional. Both may have their eyes opened; some may be moved to plow farther and deeper the ground which has been opened. History could be enriched; and it is possible to hope that increased and enriched understanding may eventually help toward an abolition of battle itself.

George J. Fleming

FALCONER

Author: John Cheever (1912–   )
Publisher: Alfred A. Knopf (New York). 211 pp. $7.95
Type of work: Novel
Time: The present
Locale: Falconer prison

A middle-class, middle-aged professor, a drug addict who has slain his brother, tries to adjust emotionally, sexually, and spiritually to life in prison

Principal characters:
    ZEKE FARRAGUT, a professor, drug addict, and fratricide
    MARCIA FARRAGUT, his bisexual wife
    JODY, a prisoner, Farragut's lover
    CHICKEN NUMBER TWO,
    CUCKOLD,
    RANSOME,
    STONE,
    TENNIS, and
    BUMPO, other prisoners
    TINY and
    MARSHACK, guards
    CHISHOLM, Deputy Warden

The New Yorker goes to the jailhouse. That's not too surprising. Writing all those masterly *New Yorker* stories, as moralist in residence, in suburbia, in Ossining, near Sing Sing Prison, about upper-middle-class *angst,* Cheever must have finally felt obliged to commit one of his characters to prison, to imagine "how it would be." Fortunately, prison life itself is not finally Cheever's subject; he seems to assume his readers know all about that, as, in every sense that matters, they do.

Farragut, forty-eight, impulsively kills his brother Eben in a fit of rage suppressed since childhood. The nature of the killing, the brevity of the novel, and Farragut's "passion for blue sky," like Meursault's, may remind one of Camus' *The Stranger.* But Cheever's readers will recall more aptly his interest in relationships between brothers in "Goodbye, My Brother," one of his best stories, in "Brother," and in *The Wapshot Chronicle* and *The Wapshot Scandal.*

Cheever often delineates the special contradictions and absurdities in the character of the upper-middle-class male. Moving in an ambience of nostalgia and sentimentality, his characters often escape through dreams and prolonged waking fantasies from the monotony of routine lives and settled psyches; those escapes result in nightmare disruptions that are occasions for the stories. Disillusionment, emptiness, *ennui,* and loneliness break out in tentative or bizarre, joylessly calculated, or impulsive rebellions. Now one of those men, a man of privilege, of the professions (a teacher), a drug addict since his army days, goes to prison, leaving his son and his bisexual wife behind in suburbia.

Fiction, says Cheever, should "reflect the exaltations, the discursiveness, the spontaneity and the pratfalls one finds in a day." In *Falconer,* prison-pent feelings, routines, customs, ceremonies, and rituals become parallels that offer perspectives on everyday life in the "free world." The effect of this novel is suggested in what Auden said of Yeats: "In the prison of his days, teach the free man how to praise." Imprisonment of the self in one's own emotions—Cheever has often implied that metaphor; now he turns it around. Either way, the metaphor is trite, but Cheever's explorations make it richly suggestive. Is Falconer a regular prison, like Sing Sing, or an asylum for the criminally insane? Cheever is generally ambiguous enough to allow either possibility. Falconer sounds like another name for Farragut. What one reviewer said of a certain kind of Cheever story applies to *Falconer:* "It is as if Marquand had suddenly been crossed with Kafka."

So, from a fresh perspective, *Falconer* is another of Cheever's social satire, comedy-of-manners fables, and prison is a metaphor of the suburban human condition. But more aptly and originally, prison is a metaphor for sexual limbo. Melancholy is the predominant mood of all Cheever's stories—even when he is being cheerful. He leaves us with a sense of mortality, mutability, and pathos on the verge of collapse into bathos. His style, even in his frequent witty moments, is suffused with sadness, as if written during a hangover the morning after a cocktail party.

Two elements seldom found in a typical *New Yorker* story dominate *Falconer*—profanity and raunchy sex, almost entirely onanistic/homosexual. Prison life is an incessant see-saw of tumescence-detumescence. Just as Farragut must have his allotted drug fix every day, he must also have Jody, his young conniving lover, an addiction acquired in prison. Humiliations related to food, shelter, and sex are routine. Nude searches are frequent; the final section begins: "So they were naked again." Group masturbation in the "Valley" is another haunting metaphor of sexual pathos.

In their imaginative flights and escapes, Farragut and Jody are a sort of composite Icarus figure. Cheever's richly ambiguous style and his way of presenting characters and events prevent one from being absolutely certain that the escapes literally occur. After a long build-up, Jody escapes in a visiting bishop's helicopter, disguised as an acolyte; it is a very brief scene that takes one's breath. The point of view then abruptly shifts from third person, focus on Farragut, to focus on Jody, outside Falconer. Although he usually focuses on one character, Cheever is almost always a modified Trollope-like omniscient narrator. But this shift is disruptive, *unless* we enjoy the possibility that in the scene outside Falconer, Farragut imagines himself to be his lover Jody.

The progress of Farragut's own escape is more prolonged, more suspenseful, more imaginative, more darkly comic—he replaces his dead cellmate in a canvas sack. The possibility that both escapes are imagined justifies and gives continuity to Cheever's point of view strategy. And one feels the exultation Hermann Hesse provides in "My Life: A Conjectural Autobiography," in which

Hesse paints on his prison wall a blue train, already half inside a tunnel, and, before the eyes of his jailors, boards it and rides away.

Whether the escapes are literal or imagined, or intended as deliberate ambiguity to suggest both simultaneously, the novel's ending is not only unfashionably happy, it is ecstatic:

> Stepping from the bus onto the street, he saw that he had lost his fear of falling and all other fears of that nature. He held his head high, his back straight, and walked along nicely. Rejoice, he thought, rejoice.

Cheever trots out the usual rogue's gallery of convicts and guards, but filtered through Farragut's sensibility, they look and sound more interesting this time around. Ransome killed his father. A criminal organization pierced Stone's eardrums with an ice pick, framed him, and gave him an expensive hearing aid. Tennis claims to have won the Spartanburg doubles, twice in a row. "I'm listed in the sports encyclopedia. . . . I'm here because of a clerical error." Bumpo, "the cellblock celebrity . . . was supposed to have been the second man to hijack an airplane." Chicken Number Two was a jewel thief. "I was very charming. Everybody knew I had class. And . . . I had willingness." Cuckold, cellblock merchant of contraband, "iced" his wife by mistake the night she told him none of the three kids were his. He tells Farragut long stories about his promiscuous wife and about a brief encounter with a homosexual in a motel. Chisholm, Deputy Warden, "gets his kicks out of watching men in withdrawal" from drugs. Marshack is a guard with the instincts of a born killer. He shaved his head to enhance his image. " 'The shaved skulls,' Farragut thought, 'will always be with us.' " Tiny is an obese guard who slaughters twenty cats when one of them eats his London broil. "There were more cats in Falconer than convicts."

Leaving out details or even a sense of Farragut's life as a professor (what did he teach?) may seem to some readers less like authorial strategy than caprice. Why delay Farragut's memory of the scene in which he killed his brother? Because he couldn't face it? But that explanation isn't conveyed. "Why did you kill your brother, Zeke?" asks Chicken. Why at that point, near the end of the novel? It seems contrived. Does Cheever assume a convention of delay? The flashback exposition is interesting in itself, but Cheever deals it out in discrete blocks.

The structure of *Falconer* is justifiably anecdotal and episodic. The tonal shifts from satirical to lyrical to realistic to ironic are effective because Farragut's mind, emotions, and imagination are adrift, sometimes wilfully. Never fatal or tragic, the irony is sometimes the arbitrary irony of transient literary effect. Many of Cheever's stories—and certainly this novel—are governed by original concepts that he executes with a mingling of conventional and surprising literary elements and devices. We feel the energy of imagination in every line.

Readers may sometimes wish Cheever would express emotions and ideas in dialogue and scenes more than in commentary. It is difficult to remember what happened. Cheever is so good at the commentary technique that *what happens* is a mood, an impression, and usually that is enough. Sometimes he offers a preposterous or out-of-key line or episode the reader cannot believe but likes so much he *makes* it fit, or accepts it as *lagniappe*. For instance, Eben tells Farragut that his wife watches television so catatonically that one time, to make her see him, he went on the game show *Trial and Error;* following that rather far-fetched anecdote, Farragut kills his brother, a scene full of off-key notes, as when Eben kisses the living room rug.

Cheever's two *Wapshot* books were too long for his talent. *Bullet Park*'s 245 pages came closer. *Falconer* is the perfect length for a man who has written more than one hundred *New Yorker* stories (see his seven short story collections). *Falconer* is a long *New Yorker* story, a little longer than a novella. Cheever writes a Chekhovian kind of story, suffused with a Proustian preoccupation with the past, memory, and nostalgia. Like Faulkner, he has created his own world in his stories and novels. Some readers may compare him with two other *New Yorker* writers, Salinger and Updike, and perhaps with James Gould Cozzens and Louis Auchincloss, but such comparisons leave Cheever's special qualities untouched. He is at once the most typical of the *New Yorker* writers and the least stereotyped, the least often predictable.

Despite his three earlier novels, one thinks of this writer, whose first story appeared in 1930 when he was eighteen, as a short story writer of great variety and even, for him, an experimental venturesomeness. When we list major American writers, we do not include those who are mainly short story writers. But like Peter Taylor, Katherine Anne Porter, J. F. Powers, and Frank O'Connor, Cheever is a major writer. He is not a public figure. He has never been involved in the social and political movements or aesthetic controversies of the past five decades. Even in *Falconer* the infamous Attica prison riots and slaughter only hover over Farragut's cellblock in rumors and radio waves. Cheever has only tenuous associations with academia. He has, quite simply, been a professional writer all his adult life. As early as 1964, John Aldridge called Cheever one of our "most grievously underdiscussed important writers." Despite some popular and critical success and the *Newsweek* cover story when *Falconer* appeared, that assessment remains accurate.

A genuine product of New England upper-middle-class traditions in life and literature, whose formal education ended with his expulsion from Thayer Academy at South Braintree, the sixty-five-year-old Cheever seems to be one of the most socialized, domesticated of men, retaining the innocence of the insulated. One imagines, however, that beneath the pretense and disguise is really a Martian whose effort to remain coolly detached is often discouraged by ineffable sadness that in his many reports he tries to make effable.

Like Horace, who delighted as he instructed, Cheever is a dark moralist who creates stories in a cheerful mood of play. He tells us he was taught, in his Puritanical family, "that a moral lies beneath all human conduct and that the moral is always detrimental to man." His aim as a writer has been to "record a moderation" of the teachings of his family. Cheever delineates the nuances in the tensions between the Blakean poles of innocence and experience in each of his characters. The tension and the contrast between Cheever's superconscious omniscient voice and the characters' intermittent self-scrutiny, that result in partial insights which undermine motivations and behavior, produce ironies the reader knows only Cheever can conceive. His compassion is spiked with ridicule, his fables collapse, at moments, deliberately into farce.

Cheever tells us that he "attempts to celebrate a world that lies spread out around us like a bewildering and stupendous dream." He writes fiction to confirm his feeling "that life itself is creative process." He is a prophet of the apocalypse who reveals a sometimes disconcerting power of positive thinking. "Literature as I see it is more a giving than a diminishment." Like Bellow's, Cheever's vision is affirmative, seeing something in us that transcends our self-made limbos. He writes with one foot on the narrow, wobbly plank world of Harlequin, the other in the brooding world of Hamlet. But finally, his imagination neither profoundly disturbs nor transforms our consciousness. In describing upper-middle-class life as faithfully as Balzac, he does not seem to attempt, or presume, like Rilke, to say, "You must change your life." But one cannot ask, even of a major writer, everything.

David Madden

THE FORK RIVER SPACE PROJECT

Author: Wright Morris (1910–   )
Publisher: Harper & Row Publishers (New York). 185 pp. $8.95
Type of work: Novel
Time: The present
Locale: The borders of Nebraska and Kansas

A witty and imaginative domestication of the science fiction genre, in a mysterious and suspenseful fable about the triumph of the imagination

> Principal characters:
> KELCEY, a writer
> ALICE, his wife
> HARRY LORBEER, a plumber, proprietor of Fork River Space Project
> DAHLBERG, a house painter and onetime author

Since publication of his first novel in 1942, Wright Morris has been moving toward consummation of his hero-witness theme by means of his ordinary but strange characters, his witty, resonant style, and his mind-expanding conceptions. *The Fork River Space Project* is as quiet and meditative as *Fire Sermon* (1971) and *A Life* (1973), his two recent novels, and as eerie and bizarre as the novella *War Games* (1972) and several stories in *Real Losses, Imaginary Gains* (1976).

Morris first gave us "The Word from Space" in 1958, delivered by a cosmic mailman. That fantasy begins: "What reassured me was how normal everything looked." A similar tone is sustained throughout *The Fork River Space Project,* which is a sort of literary UFO approaching the Science Fiction galaxy. Having explored inner and outer territories, starting from Nebraska, Morris suggested in 1967 that he might take us into orbit. *In Orbit* examined the varying effects on many different kinds of people of a twister and a kid (who resembles a space man) on a motorcycle, as these two happenings simultaneously hit a small Midwestern town.

In *The Fork River Space Project,* Dahlberg, a house painter and onetime writer of semi-science fiction, and Harry Lorbeer, a plumber and proprietor of "The Fork River Space Project," change the lives of Kelcey, an aging writer of "humorous, fantasy-type pieces," and his young second wife, Alice. This short novel is Kelcey's witty and lyrical meditation on a constellation of images that revolve around two mysterious and suspenseful questions: Did the population of Fork River, Kansas, vanish in a twister or a spaceship? Are Dahlberg and Harry planning a space trip, and will Alice go with them? Though Kelcey is more interested in mulling over the implications of these questions than in answering them, and though the story elements are filtered through Kelcey's musings, *The Fork River Space Project* may prove to be Morris' most accessible fiction since his first, *My Uncle Dudley,* and may attract the wider public he has always hoped to reach—and which he deserves.

Near the end of the novel, Kelcey finds Dahlberg meditating nude in the ghost town schoolhouse that houses the space project. "I've been giving some thought to it," Kelcey tells him. Increasingly, his life turns on "speculation." "How explain it?" he asks, rhetorically. What we have been experiencing is Kelcey's almost total articulation of his thoughts, as if the novel were a long essay by Loren Eiseley, Morris' late good friend. We have collaborated with him in fusing thought and feeling through images, body wisdom, intuitions, reasonings, moments of pure being, visions, and, above all, imagination. All those categories of perception and modes of thinking are integrated in Kelcey's sensibility, his conceptual imagination.

In different ways, Harry and Dahlberg become heroes to Kelcey and Alice, their witnesses. Alice's response is to become Dahlberg's lover. Alice is a further refinement of Morris' wisecracking, audacious woman-as-catalyst, beginning with the Greek in *Love Among the Cannibals,* continuing with Etoile in *Ceremony in Lone Tree,* Cynthia in *What a Way to Go,* and Joy in *Fire Sermon.* Kelcey discovers Alice and Dahlberg alone: "They were in orbit. They were where everybody wanted to be." Later, he thinks: "Some people are determined to get into orbit. Was it so unusual that one of them was my wife?" As he approaches the lovers, Alice says to Kelcey: " 'You look far away!' Was I wrong in thinking that she liked that better?" He keeps telling himself "it's her own life," not his. He sees "her face tilted upward, as I had often seen it, radiant with expectations"—that he knows he cannot fulfill. Kelcey is older than Alice; she was a young commercial artist when she met him on a summer cruise. Kelcey's response to Harry and Dahlberg is to transform himself through his imagination. Harry "started me thinking—or should I say seeing? On the mind's eye, or the balls of the eyes, or wherever it is we see what we imagine, or imagine what we see." Dahlberg's father, an early inventor of a space rocket, and Harry's father, a railroad magnate who opened the West and built Fork River to glorify his wife, passed on to their sons a tendency to blend fact and fiction. Dahlberg wants *"to restore awe . . .* without awe we diminish, we trivialize, everything we touch." Kelcey quips, "My heart belongs to Harry," the visionary. And Kelcey feels "a surge of warm fellow feeling for Dahlberg," under whose Buster Keaton deadpan, "I see his brain pan twinkling like a constellation." Dahlberg tells Kelcey, "This is *your* project as much as it is *my* project."

Imagination is Kelcey's state of mind, in which what he sees is less important than what he imagines. What he hears and sees "boggles the mind" and gives "cause for wonder"—two of many clichés whose original freshness Morris resurrects in lively contexts. Kelcey closes his eyes "to see more, as well as less," one of several paradoxes that aid perception and energize Kelcey's rhetoric. His overexcited imagination also produces dreams that reach back to prehistory and project into the space age. He cautions Alice not to look at anything too closely. "The jig is up as soon as" a UFO, for instance, "is identified." She takes his advice, follows the wisdom of the body, and goes into love orbit with Dahlberg, causing psychological space to expand between herself and Kelcey, to whom she begins to seem like the first visitor from space.

Kelcey achieves the state of awe, but for him "the experience of unearthly, celestial transport is a matter of imagination"; he doubts the astronauts had it, and Morris suggests the experience of Alice and Dahlberg and Harry, in space, or in love, are not as varied and intense as the ones Kelcey conjures in the sanctuary of his imagination, simply by closing his eyes.

Kelcey's hero-witness relationship with Dahlberg and Harry teaches him how to expand his imaginative powers until he can have their experiences, including Alice's, vicariously while deepening his own. Their effect on his imagination makes him feel weightless in space, buoyant, transformed. "Somewhere between where was I, and where I am, is where I am." Outwardly, Kelcey shows affection by teasing, emotion by obviously withholding it, conviction by sarcasm. But now he has new emotions, and enjoys the full bloom of his feelings. Near the end, he experiences pure being: "My sensations were so primal I lacked a word for them. A plant might feel as much, or as little, as I did. There was not a shred of consciousness in it. I was in the world like a stalk of celery." Constantly stimulated superconsciousness enables him to reach that state, wherein he is cleansed and rendered receptive to rarer sensations later.

To focus and give a comic perspective on these concepts about the workings of the imagination, Kelcey gives us, twenty pages from the end, the story of Taubler and Tuchman, which he had promised halfway through. (Morris made earlier use of this set-piece device in *Ceremony in Lone Tree* and in *One Day.*) In the summer of 1939, when he was a student in Paris soaking up culture, Kelcey met Taubler, a crazy genius who "preferred the illusion to the reality," and "who was the space trip of my life." The empty plains of Kelcey's childhood in Nebraska was the physical preparation for Taubler, and Taubler and Tuchman were the metaphysical preparation for the imaginative space flights Dahlberg and Harry inspire.

Kelcey went to Paris to be "flabbergasted," a word that burlesques Dahlberg's concept of awe. A fortune cookie told him he would make new friends and begin a new life; but that new life does not begin until decades later with Dahlberg and Harry, who parallel Taubler and Tuchman. Taubler thinks Americans are a hoax invented by movie producers; Dahlberg years later declares, "Life on this planet is a hoax." Having transformed Parisian scenes in his artistic imagination and thus made them his creations, Taubler signs his work by painting his name on walls all over Paris; Dahlberg paints Kelcey's sun deck, making it a launching pad for the imagination. When Taubler showed him the earth through a telescope, all Kelcey was capable of seeing was his own lashes. Taubler had painted on a wall the earth as seen from space; Harry offers a similar view in Fork River and teaches Kelcey to see it. Tuchman tells Kelcey that Taubler has his "own system . . . and you'd better believe it." Years later, Harry says, "You better believe it . . . or it's not going to happen." "I could believe it. Hadn't he already painted me into it?" Kelcey says of Taubler, and that's true of Harry and

Dahlberg, too. Tuchman, himself a witness to Taubler, explains to this new, young witness, "You've got to make your own world, then live in it." Having told us that story, Kelcey suggests that his own experiences tell him that it is better to imagine a space adventure than to experience it, or that only by imagining it can one experience it.

Although *The Fork River Space Project* is a short novel, it is abundantly and complexly image-laden, thought-provoking, and poetically suggestive. Through his imagination, expressed in a witty, paradoxical, punning style, Kelcey ponders the nature of human perception and experiences intuition in rarefied moments that Morris embodies in charged images. "The way to change the world was to change one's perspective." "All perception was extrasensory." He meditates on images of space and of twisters. "The view *from* space compels the awe that will enlarge man's finite nature." He feels he shares "the cosmos with the vast indifference of the prime mover." A sense of time permeates the novel. He imagines and dreams images of prehistoric man in caves at Stonehenge (he is partial to the Ice Age), of pioneer American history.

To enhance those abstract concepts and science fiction itself, our most bizarre genre, with a sense of everyday reality, Morris domesticates them with such images as these: "I . . . stood for a moment in the draft from the refrigerator, the chill, impersonal winds of space blowing into my face." A space ship will give off "a whirring sound like a musical top." In the note she leaves Kelcey before soaring off with Dahlberg, Alice asks him to get the lights and phone disconnected at the now totally abandoned Fork River.

Two major motifs that characterize the American experience throughout history are the expectations aroused by the landscape, with its prospects for spiritual and physical development, and the long waiting for those expectations to come to pass. Those two concepts, often repeated with many variations, illuminate the vision Harry and Dahlberg and Alice share, but it is Kelcey, the most imaginative witness, who has the talent for waiting, satisfied meanwhile with what those expectations stimulate in his imagination. One of the qualities Kelcey has that the others lack and that prevents him from being a true believer and from attempting to act out expectations, visions, and dreams, is his sense of humor. Dahlberg tells him that he is a very funny man. As a type, Kelcey was in the cave back in the Ice Age. "And I am there at the fringe of the circle gawking." As witness, he tells Dahlberg: "If anything should happen, somebody should be there to report on it."

A possible objection to the meditation technique may be that what the reader experiences is Kelcey's total articulation of every element in the novel; by mulling everything over himself, he may leave too little for the reader to experience and imagine, and thus undercut the mystery and awe. The meditation technique allows Morris to justify his use of the old device of stimulating suspense, then delaying the next narrative stroke by exposition or meditation.

Even for so short a novel, *The Fork River Space Project* may strike some readers as underpopulated; outside the depopulated town of Fork River (except for Harry, Dahlberg, and Lindner, who is a kind of caretaker) the world consists only of Kelcey and Alice and two minor characters, Miss Ingalls, a librarian, who provides Kelcey with information about Dahlberg, and Dr. Fred Rainey, a weather seer, who provides Kelcey with scientific explanations and further information about Harry. But this paucity of people lends an aura to the novel that enhances Morris's effects.

The Fork River Space Project is the seventh of Morris' nineteen novels to be told in the first person, a point of view perfectly suited to a book that demonstrates the power of the imagination, leavened with lucid intelligence. Unvarnished, Morris' style is grainy, textured. As Kelcey says of Dahlberg's style, "you have to let him tell it." In his own way. And Morris' way is elliptical. You have to let him meditate on people, situations, concepts, images. But the reader must collaborate. The reader's active participation is built into the dialectic of Morris' style.

In his lamentably neglected book *About Fiction: Reverent Reflections on the Nature of Fiction with Irreverent Observations on Writers, Readers, and Other Abuses* (1975), Morris talked about style, among other things. Having noted that "the facts, so called, are in: the imagination is out," Morris invokes the spirit of Yeats: "As I altered my syntax," said Yeats, "I altered my intellect." We observe that process in Morris' works, and in Kelcey's mind as he meditates. But for the reader who has not learned to read (as the writer has learned to write), the syntax may be difficult to follow. "Nothing is explained, or will be explained: what is shown must be perceived, apprehended," says Morris of Camus' *The Stranger*. "The reader's pleasure is often in proportion to what is left unsaid, or ambiguously hinted." To read such fiction well is to grasp some of the skills involved in its creation. Later, he says, "What we choose to call 'style' is the presence in the fiction of the power to choose and mold its reader."

The Fork River Space Project is Wright Morris' finest novel since *In Orbit*. Ultimately, space is "the territory ahead" that Huck Finn sets out for at the end of Twain's classic. In each of his novels Morris has been heading for that space behind the eyelids where imagination, mystery, and awe make everything possible. In Fork River, he satisfies the great expectations his earlier novels have raised, and at least for a season, and perhaps for decades, the image of the American experience Morris has captured will haunt us.

David Madden

THE GENTLE BARBARIAN
The Life and Work of Turgenev

Author: V. S. Pritchett (1900–   )
Publisher: Random House (New York). Illustrated. 243 pp. $10.00
Type of work: Critical biography
Time: 1818–1883
Locale: Western Russia and Europe

An account of the life and writings of the Russian novelist and short story master which ranges from his youth on the vast 5,000-serf estate ruled by his tyrannical mother to his death near Paris

> *Principal personages:*
> IVAN TURGENEV, Russian novelist, playwright, and short story writer
> VARVARA PETROVNA, his tyrannical mother
> PAULINE VIARDOT, a Spanish-born opera star
> LOUIS VIARDOT, her French husband
> LEO TOLSTOY, Russian novelist

In its history, the novel has undergone many permutations; different authors have molded the form to suit the needs of their particular geniuses. Sometimes, in different localities, it developed in quite opposing directions, only again to be transformed by the genius of one person or of a group of writers. In England, the novel originated in the middle-class realism of Richardson and Defoe, while in Russia it can be traced back to the quite different prose and verse novels of Pushkin, with their highly romantic, vividly tapestried, Oriental qualities. These contrasting beginnings determined the later developments of the novel form in these two countries. The English novel always seemed to be rooted in the details of everyday life, while the Russian novel was inclined to fly off into explorations of the supernatural, the bizarre, the psychologically unexpected, and the politically dangerous. But there have been exceptions, the writers who sought to emulate the quiet, reasoned manner of the Western European writers, who were influenced more by the realism of the English novel and the style of the French writers; perhaps the foremost example of the "Europeanized" Russian writer is the "gentle barbarian" about whom Pritchett has written so sensitively and well: Ivan Turgenev.

The work of Turgenev seems more contemporary than ever before; a hundred years after they were written, his novels and stories speak to readers with a freshness and significance that perhaps even his contemporaries did not feel. While we admire the genius of many of his colleagues, often while reading their books we must make concessions to the passage of time from when they were written to our own era, but this is seldom required with Turgenev's works. Why does Turgenev seem to be "modern" in both subject matter and style? V. S. Pritchett addresses himself to this question, among others, in this extraordinary discussion of the man, the writer, and his times. *The Gentle Barbarian* may be the definitive study of Turgenev; seldom has there been such a perfect union of literary biographer and subject as in the case of V. S. Pritchett and Ivan Turgenev.

For decades, Turgenev seemed the least important of the four great nineteenth century Russian writers, less profound and obviously great than Dostoevski, with whom he quarreled, Tolstoy, for whom he prepared the way, and Chekhov, whom he influenced. He was the aristocratic, self-conscious artist whose gentle love stories and carefully constructed, exquisite novels drew prose pictures of the strange world of the Russian country gentry and their serfs. But if Turgenev was all of this, he was, of course, much more. He was committed as few writers ever have been to telling the truth. Apolitical, he did not avoid writing of political subjects, but when he did, he nearly always brought down upon himself the wrath of the opposing factions, each believing that he was prejudiced against them. His enemies, and often his friends, could not understand his determination to analyze all aspects of a situation and to present what he found, without holding up any side as right or wrong. You must be committed, they told him. He *was* committed, more than they knew, but to a higher principle than political dogmas. His integrity was pure in relation to his art, and his discipline was awesome.

Pritchett is fascinated by the process by which a great writer such as Turgenev is created. Certainly, Turgenev was molded to an extraordinary degree by the strange and difficult relationship he had with his terrifying, sadistic mother. Without overemphasizing the point, Pritchett makes clear the influence of Varvara Petrovna on Turgenev's later life, on his work, the fact of his bachelorhood and his love affairs, even on his psychological makeup; a case in point, for example, was the fact that Turgenev felt that he needed to be a possession, to *belong,* to any woman in his life, as he and everything else on the great estate had belonged to his mother. She was a tyrant, ruling her estate like an absolute monarch. She enjoyed punishing her serfs for mistakes, either real or imagined, and was capable of completely gratuitous cruelty. Ivan Turgenev's distaste for the system of serfdom was born in the years during which he watched his mother's cruelty. When Ivan's older brother married against her wishes, she cut him off without any money, not relenting even when he gave her three grandchildren. She remained unmoved even when the three children all died during one terrible year.

Ivan was Varvara Petrovna's favorite, but she found ways of hurting him, too, chiefly by inflicting pain on the serfs whom he tried to defend from her wrath. Everything in the miniature world of her estate belonged to her, the thousands of "souls" who worked for her, the forests and fields, the villages, the huts in which the peasants lived, everything. Even Ivan belonged to her, and although he lived many years after her death, he never married; he was unable to overcome the feeling that he still was part of her inventory.

However, he did love other women, and the relationship that meant the most to him in his life was the affair with the famous opera singer, Pauline Viardot.

Over many decades, his relationship with the temperamental Spanish singer had many fluctuations, but always he returned to her and her husband. The oddest aspect of this affair was that Turgenev was good friends with Pauline's husband. It is probable that for most of the duration of the relationship between Turgenev and Pauline Viardot, it was a platonic, romanticized affair in which he worshiped the great singer and was friend more than lover. Pauline, who was the model for the singer in George Sand's famous novel *Consuelo,* both stimulated and interfered with Turgenev's writing. He claimed that he could not write unless he was in love, but when he was with her he tended to fritter away his time on petty duties for her or her children. The most satisfactory arrangement seemed to be when they were apart, bound together only by the florid letters which he wrote to her; it was at these times that he created some of his finest works.

Pritchett chronicles with economy and shrewdness the changing fortunes of Turgenev's friendships with Tolstoy and Dostoevski. He was a good friend to the young Tolstoy, who was a decade younger, and helped the beginning writer to get started. He later devoted much time and energy to assisting Tolstoy and many other Russian writers to get translated and published in Western Europe. Almost singlehandedly, Turgenev made the nations of the West aware of Russian literature; yet his friends seldom realized how diligently he worked for them and how well he represented their works to the Western European literary world.

The literary history of Russia is filled with quarrels, with hysterical scenes and duels and tearful reconciliations. Pritchett brings some sense and tact to his recounting of the literary battles in which even such a restrained individual as Turgenev was involved. He explains the paranoia that drove Goncharov to quarrel with Turgenev and practically everybody else; more importantly, he discusses the ups and downs of Turgenev's relationship with his revolutionary-agitator friends Bakunin and Herzen. Perhaps the most famous literary quarrel dealt with in the book is the one between Turgenev and Dostoevski over the Slavophile movement and Turgenev's expatriot way of life. Beyond slogans and ideology, Dostoevski resented Turgenev's wealth, his elegance of manner and speech, his affectation (as Dostoevski called it) of European styles. He did not see how Turgenev could continue to write about Russia if he lived in Europe. Turgenev apparently was more affected by Dostoevski's remarks than he cared to let most people know.

Pritchett perhaps is at his best in discussing Turgenev's genius as a writer. He indicates the subtleties of Turgenev's style, the techniques which he employed to capture the layers of nuance for which he is famous. He labored to hold the moment between noticing and not noticing; this, he felt, was art, not just recounting what one nakedly saw. He was fascinated by the waywardness and timelessness of seeing, by the light and shadow of seeing, and by the playing over of what had been seen. In his fiction the past and present mingle in a stream.

There are two masters of seeing in Russian literature; Tolstoy and Turgenev. But, while Tolstoy sees vividly, as if he is an animal, Turgenev, who is equally exact, makes it clear that what is seen already is changing. This aspect of his writing creates a feeling of poignancy in many of his stories and novels.

When Turgenev began writing, there was no established tradition of storytelling or novel-writing in Russian literature. He was forced to be a founder and innovator; he was at the beginning of that series of great novels which paralleled the awakening of the Russian people. Behind him was only the work of Pushkin, notably *Eugene Onegin*. Turgenev was only slightly drawn to French models; he did not like Balzac and had not yet encountered Flaubert. He did admire Gogol, but his temperament would not let him write in the grotesque vein of the author of *Dead Souls*. He possessed a natural tendency to write in scenes; his novels, therefore, are structured like plays, and they influenced writers such as Chekhov. Through diligence and singlemindedness of purpose, he helped to create the Russian novel.

From his first stories, one is amazed at how much Turgenev conveys of the subterranean emotions, especially in his scenes of country house life. The watchful, timeless silence of Russia permeates his fiction. He is perhaps most famous for his love stories, for the tenderness and sadness of his descriptions of young love. The permanence of his love stories is dependent on his sense of love as a spiritual test, as a test of moral character, as well as a diagnosis of the spiritual condition of each generation.

Early in his career, the notion of the "extraordinary man" fascinated Turgenev. This subject runs through his work like a theme, culminating in his most famous novel, *Fathers and Sons*. But even when he dealt with large themes, he tended to underplay them; he shrank fastidiously from Balzac's coarse exuberance. The approach was everything, the style the necessity which guided the work. His portraits are not only of his heroes and heroines, but of particular epochs. He observes and listens, presenting characters who are many-faceted, complex, real. His work is never didactic, but is rooted in his deep commitment to truth.

V. S. Pritchett, himself a talented novelist and short story writer, as well as a shrewd critic and literary commentator and a student of Russian literature, has explored with subtlety and compassion the interplay between Turgenev's extraordinary life and his writing. This biographical essay will be read and appreciated for decades to come.

Bruce D. Reeves

THE GIANTS
Russia and America

Author: Richard J. Barnet
Publisher: Simon and Schuster (New York). 190 pp. $8.95
Type of work: History

An account of how Russia and America emerged as the world's two superpowers after World War II, and an analysis of their present relationship to each other

Those familiar with the style and substance of Richard Barnet's other works, *Global Reach* (with Ron Müller), *The Roots of War,* the *The Economy of Death,* and *Intervention and Revolution,* may be somewhat disappointed by this latest book. *The Giants: Russia and America* possesses none of the trenchant criticism of United States foreign policy that distinguishes these other works. The dominant tone of this work can only be described as sober and subdued. Not that Richard Barnet has suddenly converted to orthodoxy and shed his role as a revisionist critic of U.S. foreign policy; the ideas expressed in *The Giants* are perfectly consistent with the author's previous positions taken over the years. It is simply that the tone of this latest book is much more moderate and balanced than one would have expected from an analysis of Barnet's other works. No doubt part of the reason for this balanced judgment is due to the fact that when it comes to parceling out blame for continuing the arms race, there is plenty of criticism to go around on both sides. The foreign policy elites of both superpowers have generally operated under the assumption of the worst possible case.

What does Barnet attempt to do in *The Giants*? First, he briefly describes the changes that have taken place over the past sixty years of peaceful coexistence with the Soviet Union. What Barnet finds unique about the present age is not that all the Cold War stereotypes have disappeared, but that both sides are getting to know their counterparts better. Representatives of the Soviet and American governments have met each other numerous times across the negotiating table. These contacts have been useful in gaining a more realistic perspective of the opposition. While there is some danger that these contacts may lead to new misconceptions of the opposition, this situation is certainly preferable to the one which prevailed during the height of the Cold War when neither side talked directly to the other.

Second, Barnet describes how *détente* came about, focusing mainly on that "correlation of forces," as Kissinger used to call it, which was responsible for the change of policy toward the U.S.S.R. Barnet leaves the impression, however, that *détente* began with the election of Richard Nixon to the White House in 1968. While the process of *détente* was certainly strengthened by the Nixon-Kissinger Administration, the roots stretch back much further. From the Soviet perspective, Malenkov's speech before the Supreme Soviet in August, 1953, can be considered a turning point in U.S.-Soviet relations. It was in this speech that

Malenkov enunciated the doctrine of peaceful coexistence with the capitalist West which forms the basis of the Soviet view of *détente.*

Barnet next attempts to define what *détente* means in the contemporary environment, and he identifies it with the series of wide-ranging agreements that have been negotiated between the United States and the U.S.S.R. The most important of these agreements include SALT, the Berlin accords, and a 1972 agreement negotiated between Nixon and Brezhnev in which the parties pledged themselves to consult with each other concerning "the development of situations capable of causing a dangerous exacerbation of their relations." As part of this agreement, the two nations recognized "a special responsibility . . . to do everything in their power so that conflicts or situations will not arise which would serve to increase international tension." As Barnet correctly points out, it is this latter agreement that has engendered so much controversy in the West. *The Giants* leaves several important questions unanswered. For example, under the rubric of *détente,* does the United States have the right to expect that the Soviet Union and her allies such as Cuba will not encourage and support revolutionary movements in Africa? What about the widespread violation of human rights in the Soviet Union directed against Jews and dissidents which threaten to make a mockery of the Helsinki accords? How should the United States react to such problems? Unfortunately, Barnet never makes it sufficiently clear whether *détente* should be conditioned by Soviet behavior in these two areas.

Fourth, Barnet sketches the image of the enemy that exists in the minds of Soviet and American decision-makers. Not surprisingly he finds these images distorted by years of misperception. Although there is nothing new in this presentation, it is nevertheless important to be reminded of the impact which false images have had on foreign policy formulation.

Surely one of the most crucial issues that exists between the United States and Soviet Union concerns the nature of the strategic military balance today. Barnet reviews in depth the main components of this balance—strategic nuclear forces, the Soviet and American navies, and conventional military forces that each side has stationed in Europe. He finds American power sufficient in every field to deter the Soviet Union from mounting an attack against the United States or her NATO allies. He agrees that the relative power of the Soviet Union has grown substantially over the past several years; the significance of this increase, however, is subject to interpretation.

Barnet, for example, does not believe that the national security of the United States has been endangered by recent increases in military spending by the U.S.S.R. He does not see the Soviet leadership trying to achieve a "theoretical war-winning capability" that would enable them to fight and win a nuclear war with the United States by striking first and holding back a retaliatory force sufficient to blackmail the United States into submission. Such alarmist fears expressed by Paul Nitze and others associated with the Committee on the

Present Danger are, he believes, not warranted.

Finally Barnet examines the role that foreign trade plays in the U.S.-Soviet relationship. He points out, for example, that American multinational corporations played a major role in helping to foster *détente* with the U.S.S.R. Economic titans such as Donald Kendall, David Rockefeller, and Armand Hammer urged closer U.S.-Soviet relations in order to create the kind of political environment in which it would be possible to promote greater trade with the Soviet Union. From the Soviet side, the stimulus for closer economic relations with the United States came from top Soviet leaders who were interested in accelerating the transfer of new technology to the U.S.S.R.

From a policy standpoint, the most crucial issue concerns the political wisdom of technology transfers to the U.S.S.R. Opinion in the United States is sharply divided over this controversial issue. Those who favor technology transfers usually argue that these links will help the United States maintain some leverage over the Soviet economy. As the Soviets become increasingly dependent upon these technologies, their behavior at home and abroad should be moderated. Skeptics of *détente*, on the other hand, maintain that the transfer of sophisticated technology to the U.S.S.R. should be resisted since this has profound security implications for the West. Barnet eschews simplistic explanations of this complicated problem. He recognizes the very real dangers of sharing our knowledge of computers and electronic equipment with the Soviets. At the same time, however, he sees the U.S.S.R. as becoming part of a more interdependent world and finding it more difficult to return to outmoded economic conditions.

The basic thesis of the book is succinctly stated when the author writes, "There will be no possibility of a lasting detente without a fundamental change in the military relationship." What troubles Barnet and other scholars is that the process of *détente* has not penetrated very far, and foreign policy elites on both sides are still prisoners of the past. How to breakdown the cycle of fear and distrust that plagues the U.S.-Soviet relationship is the crucial issue facing the two superpowers. Barnet has a more ominous fear that the "Giants" may stumble into war by miscalculation. As the Soviets attempt to flex their muscles as a world power, the danger of confrontation may grow. Unlike the past when the Soviet Union was relegated to a position of inferiority, today they have achieved parity with the West in nearly all fields. In a future crisis situation, Kremlin leaders may choose not to back down from the brink as Khrushchev did in the Cuban missile crisis. If this happens, the two superpowers may find themselves in a war that no one wants and neither side can win.

Although this book was written during the early days of the Carter Administration, Barnet strikes a prophetic note on the future of U.S.-Soviet relations when he sees the Carter Administration as downgrading the importance of *détente* with the U.S.S.R. Not even Barnet, however, could have projected how far relations between the two countries would degenerate since the heyday of *détente* in 1972. While we are in no immediate danger of going to war with the Soviet Union, our relations with the Kremlin are being increasingly strained by what we perceive to be Soviet meddling in African politics. In the latest crisis in Zaïre, President Carter has even suggested that congressional restraints on his ability to conduct foreign policy should be reviewed. If this is done, it might mean a return to the interventionist policies of the past with all the potentials for miscalculation that Barnet and others fear.

In conclusion, *The Giants* is an important book for those concerned about the present state of U.S.-Soviet relations. Barnet not only helps to demolish many of the myths that continue to plague American relations with the Soviet Union, but he also places these relations in perspective.

Richard L. Langill

THE GINGER TREE

Author: Oswald Wynd (1913–   )
Publisher: Harper & Row Publishers (New York). 294 pp. $10.00
Type of work: Novel
Time: January 9, 1903 to August 20, 1942
Locale: Aboard a ship en route between England and China; Peking and Tokyo

A recounting through letters and journal entries of the tale of a very proper young Scottish girl who goes to China just after the Boxer Rebellion to become the bride of the military attache at the British Embassy in Peking

Principal characters:
> MARY MACKENZIE, a Scotswoman living in Asia
> RICHARD COLLINGSWORTH, her husband and military attache at Peking
> COUNT KENTARO KURIHAMA, a Japanese aristocrat and Mary's lover
> MARIE AND ARMAND CHAMONPIERRE, French Embassy personnel
> ALICIA BASSETT-HILL, a spinster missionary
> AIKO SANNOTERA, a Japanese aristocrat and liberated woman
> BOB AND EMMA LOU DALE, an American couple living in Tokyo
> PETER NASSON, Mary's friend and lover

This novel narrates the tale of a young, sheltered, very proper Scottish girl who has been reared by a rigid, self-righteous, reticent widow in South Edinburgh. The girl is sensitive, compassionate, and by nature drawn to people. She finds the restrictions and repressions imposed upon her life intolerable when she moves to Peking and marries a very proper and sexually repressed man. The confinement of the life of the embassy personnel in the period following the Boxer Rebellion, plus the discomforts of the change of lifestyle, and the strangeness of the foreign land and customs, all combine to make her feel lonely and depressed. The lack of communication with her husband and her ultimate realization that there is really no love between them increases her sense of isolation, which is intensified by the spectacle of the warmth and affection so openly shared between Marie and Armand when she accompanies them on a holiday to the Western Hills near Peking while her husband is away on duty.

Mary's impulsive love affair with Count Kurihama which occurs at this point is delicately narrated, and seems, strangely enough, quite a natural thing for this lonely, frustrated, generous young woman to do. The event is decisive in determining Mary's future. She is henceforth bound to the Orient both by her affection for her lover and by her blood ties to their son, Tomo. At first she feels totally alien in Japan, where she has no friends, no relatives, no knowledge of the language, and no control over her own destiny. Later, when she takes charge of her own life and moves to make a career, a home, and a set of friends for herself, she adapts herself increasingly to Japanese ways and adopts the attitude that Japan is now her home, despite her British citizenship.

In the final section of the book, Mary sees herself as akin to the ginger tree, the alien plant which has taken root and flourished in the Japanese garden, but which the gardener dislikes, calling it a foreign thing which can never be a suitable plant for an authentic Japanese garden. She acknowledges that she will never be accepted truly by the Japanese, despite her love of Japanese culture and her attempts to conform and to preserve their traditional culture and heritage against the inroads of Western concrete, electricity, and industry. She regards her deportation from Japan as exile from her home, rather than as a return to her home. The poignant final scene is deeply moving in its warmth, tenderness, and utter finality.

The author has told the entire tale as a series of journal entries and letters from Mary to her mother and to her friend Marie. This method of narration is difficult to handle, but the author has done so very capably. The sense of immediacy and intimacy is heightened by the device of the journal-letter format. The limited point of view of the girl, her speculations, errors of judgment, and hopes and fears, all function as elements in the shaping of the point of view and in the emotional tone of the narration.

Not that Mary, the journal and letter writer, ever goes into detail in describing her own emotions or even her general emotional state very often. Her Scottish upbringing and proper Victorian reticence combine to make it impossible for her to communicate such intimate details as her private emotions and still remain true to her character. Happily, the author has conveyed such authenticity of Mary's character, that he can leave the reader to guess, or to infer, those things which Mary cannot bring herself to write. Mary's reticence is not dissemblance, though. She is honest in her thoughts, in her actions, and in her relations to others. She admires this quality in others too, although she often suspects others are not entirely honest with her. This suspicion occasionally causes her to misjudge others and to make mistakes, which she stolidly records without excuse or apology, accepting her errors and limitations of judgment just as she has accepted her "errors" in behavior.

Mary is the soul of humility, acknowledging her passiveness, her sinfulness, her helplessness, and her lack of insight into others as well as herself. But this humble, realistic appraisal of herself is leavened by a defiant, cool assertion that whatever she is, she will survive and make the best of what comes.

And indeed much does happen to Mary Mackenzie. She is embroiled in the political and social upheavals of early twentieth century Asia in a very personal and inextricable way. The Boxer Rebellion, the rule of the Empress Dowager Tsz'e Hsi, the Japanese-Russian battles, the Emperor Meiji's death, World Wars I and II, various major earthquakes, fires, *tsunamis*, and even the depression of the 1930's are all important elements affecting the life of this remarkable woman. She is at times passive, yielding, and buffeted by dynamic forces around her. But she gathers strength and determination from such episodes, and emerges with new courage, new independence, and new decisions about what to make of her life. The sheer magnificence of her survival and the unfolding of her career despite the rejection, ostracism, impediments of sex, language, culture, and society are developments fascinating to watch.

Mary begins as an occasionally defiant and willful girl, but one strongly imbued with traditional ideas of Presbyterian and Scottish Victorian morality and duty. She appears to undergo a sea change with her transport to an alien culture on the other side of the globe, and finds that she no longer fits into the tiny bastion of Victorian propriety which is the Embassy Compound in Peking. Mary's growth, her increasing development of a capacity for love, understanding, patience, and forgiveness, and her courage in the face of shocking and unpredictable events and losses make her finally emerge as an exceptional woman, but a wholly believable one.

The character of Kentaro as perceived by Mary is admittedly incomplete, but probably represents a fair depiction of Japanese character as revealed to "foreigners" who cannot truly participate in Japanese life and culture. Mary's relationships to other Japanese, such as Aiko, her employers, maids, and neighbors, give further insights into personalities shaped by so different a culture. Indeed, the entire range of characters other than Mary is that of a gallery of portraits viewed through her eyes, and reflecting therefore her limitations of vision. The characters have life, but they lack somewhat in depth and solidity. In contrast to all of them, Mary emerges as a towering figure of great strength and courage, but resigned to her small weaknesses. One such weakness is her initial suspicion of overtures of friendship. But then her enthusiastic warmth and delight in people seems all the more charming when she finally allows herself the luxury of openness and trust.

The language, the narrative style, and the tone of the book are for the most part a triumph for Wynd. It is a difficult task for a male author to try to narrate an entire novel through the personality and the language of a woman, and yet the language and the characterization ring true. One can believe that such a woman as Mary Mackenzie would have written in such a way. Occasionally there are peculiarities of syntax which may cause a momentary confusion to the reader. But these are rare, and probably reflect the bilingual background of the author.

The novel is enjoyable for the characterization and for the storyline, which moves briskly enough to assure the reader that each chapter will contain exciting, important episodes in the story. More than that, the depiction of scenes limning the cultural milieu of China and Japan in the early part of the twentieth century is fascinating, and these images come to life with a carefully detailed series of vignettes and descriptions. Such descriptive passages are concise and always smoothly employed in the amplification of the storyline. None could be deleted without diminishing the story in a real sense.

This novel charting the development of the mind and character of a young girl from innocence through much adversity, occasional joy, and great loneliness, accomplishes its task with skill and conviction. But it simultaneously charts the attitudes which the Japanese adopted toward foreigners and things foreign during the same span of time: their pride, running to arrogance; their rejections of foreigners as intimates, and adoption of Western techniques and mechanization; and their driving determination to achieve dominance in Asia and thus gain recognition as a power in the world. All these attitudes and more are revealed and brought to life as vital shaping forces in the evolution of world history, made concrete through the actions of characters in the novel. In a very real sense, the book becomes a personalized history lesson, a look at how the dynamics of the large social forces at work in the world impinge on the small private world of a woman seeking to survive in an alien land.

The world of Mary Mackenzie is a personally ascetic one. There is little description of luxuries; and architecture, clothing, food, and scenery in general are touched on rather lightly, leaving much to the imagination of the reader. Rather better, though, are the descriptions of natural scenes and phenomena. The tremor of an earthquake, the swell and surge and crash of a *tsunami*, the raging terror of Tokyo afire, are envisioned meticulously and evoke a sense of the reality and immediacy of the event which transcends the printed page.

The book is in many ways a commentary on the social and moral values of the period, both Japanese and Western. Mary was rejected, despised, and cruelly deprived of her children by both cultures. She was never able to establish herself as a socially acceptable person in either world, despite her manifest talents and successful business career. Mary's growth with respect to personal relationships is largely demonstrated in her relationships with men. Her relationships with women characteristically begin with some suspicion and reserve and move to an acceptance and lasting friendship, but she maintains a clear-eyed sense of the women's strengths and limitations. With men, there is a decided difference. Mary begins her journal with an ill-defined romantic idealization of her fiancé. She never comes to know or understand this man who becomes her husband. Her rather uncritical admiration of Armand, her impulsive and unexamined attraction to Kentaro, and her passive acceptance of the decisions men make on her behalf during her early years only gradually change as she matures and establishes herself in the business world. Here she finds that she can and must act independently, and defy the attempts of men to manipulate her and keep her in a subject position.

Her success in doing this brings a measure of anguish and social approbation which she had not anticipated, but just as she has endured the rejection she suffered by taking a lover, so she endures the scandal which results when she asserts herself in the business world. From strength and conviction gained by such experiences, she comes more and more to deal with men as equals, bargaining with the banker for a favorable arrangement in setting up a business, ignoring the advice of her lawyer to follow her own hunches about how she should invest her money, and declining to marry Peter, because, finally, respectability is less inviting than personal independence. She even declines to marry Kentaro because the marriage cannot be on her terms, with her son returned to her and acknowledged as their child.

The Ginger Tree does not have a happy ending. There is little of happiness throughout the novel, and that little is dearly bought. But adversity becomes Mary Mackenzie. She thrives on it. And she takes comfort and joy in small things, like a letter from a friend. Or like the stubborn presence of an alien ginger tree in a Japanese garden.

Betty Gawthrop

GOLD AND IRON

Bismarck, Bleichröder, and the Building of the German Empire

Author: Fritz Stern (1926–   )
Publisher: Alfred A. Knopf (New York). Illustrated. 620 pp. $17.95
Type of work: History and biography
Time: 1815–1945, with a concentration on the period 1859–1893
Locale: Germany

A pioneer study in which Stern analyzes the joint work of Otto von Bismarck, the Prussian statesman, and Gerson von Bleichröder, the Jewish banker, in forging German unification and in shaping the destinies of the German Empire

> *Principal personages:*
> OTTO VON BISMARCK, Minister-President of Prussia and Chancellor of the German Empire
> GERSON VON BLEICHRÖDER, Bismarck's personal banker, adviser, and confidant
> WILLIAM I OF HOHENZOLLERN, King of Prussia who was proclaimed German Emperor in 1871
> WILLIAM II OF HOHENZOLLERN, King of Prussia and German Emperor, 1888–1918
> BARON JAMES DE ROTHSCHILD, Head of the Paris Rothschild bank who corresponded frequently with Bleichröder on political and financial matters of interest to the French and Prussian governments
> ADOLF STOECKER, Court chaplain of the Hohenzollerns and outspoken anti-Semite
> HEINRICH VON TREITSCHKE, prominent historian and outspoken anti-Semite

Fritz Stern, Seth Low Professor of History at Columbia University, is a leading authority on modern German history. His earlier books in this area include *The Politics of Cultural Despair: A Study in the Rise of Germanic Ideology* and *The Failure of Illiberalism: Essays on the Political Culture of Modern Germany.* Now, to these impressive works he has added the monumental *Gold and Iron: Bismarck, Bleichröder, and the Building of the German Empire,* the first study of Gerson von Bleichröder, Otto von Bismarck's personal banker and confidant. Stern spent almost two decades in researching the book, which is based primarily on Bleichröder's voluminous correspondence with Bismarck and members of his family and with the House of Rothschild in Paris. As the title indicates, the central theme of the book is the joint work of Bismarck and Bleichröder in shaping the destiny of Germany at the moment of its great upsurge of power.

In its overall scope, the book is divided into three areas of concentration. Part One deals with the rise to prominence of Bismarck and Bleichröder and Bleichröder's role in helping the Prussian statesman bring about the unification of Germany. The second part analyzes their multifaceted collaboration in shaping the domestic, financial, and foreign policies of the new German Empire.

The concluding part deals with the Jewishness of Bleichröder in relation to the Jewish community, to German society and politics, and, above all, to German anti-Semitism. In the last third of the nineteenth century anti-Semitism in Germany and other countries was undergoing a transformation from a passive, "respectable" brand characterized by mere social prejudice toward a clannish group, to a more aggressive type whose proponents demanded curbs on the growing power of the Jews. Ironically, Bleichröder's very service on behalf of the recently unified Reich combined with his own social prominence and financial prestige contributed immensely to the emergence of this new, more intolerant anti-Semitism.

Bismarck chose Bleichröder as his personal banker in 1859, just three years before his own appointment by King William I as Minister-President of Prussia. By 1864, Bleichröder had become a member of Bismarck's inner circle of advisers, a prestigious position which he would hold for the next twenty-five years or so. During this period, in which he was often referred to as the German Rothschild, Bleichröder's responsibilities grew steadily as did his own personal wealth and power. He served Bismarck not only as his personal banker but as his political adviser as well, and all of Europe came to know him as Bismarck's secret agent. Bleichröder's numerous financial and political contacts throughout Europe comprised an intelligence network whose effectiveness was frequently superior to the official state intelligence agencies. In particular, he maintained a voluminous correspondence with Baron James de Rothschild, who was head of the Paris Rothschild bank until his death in 1867. Baron James frequently transmitted to Bleichröder valuable information on financial and political matters that touched the delicate and declining relations between France and Prussia during the 1860's. Bleichröder also used his sources of information on financial matters to build up personal fortunes for himself and Bismarck. Despite the tangle of public and private business between the two protagonists, Stern concludes that Bismarck did not formulate policy in order to advance his private interests.

According to Stern, one of Bleichröder's most important services to Bismarck was his effort to secure financial backing for the first two wars of German unification; namely, the Danish War of 1864 and the Seven Weeks' (Austro-Prussian) War of 1866. Together, these wars enabled Bismarck by 1867 to unify the German states north of the Main River under the Prussian-sponsored North German Confederation. Bismarck's desperate need for money to finance these wars—a need which Stern notes has been totally ignored by later historians—became apparent to him in 1863, when Denmark proclaimed the incorporation of the Duchy of Schleswig, thus severing that territory's traditional union with the neighboring Duchy of Holstein, itself a member state of the German Confederation. Bismarck intended to go to war if necessary to drive Denmark from Schleswig, but he was unable to secure from the Prussian Diet the necessary funds for military expenditures. Consequently, Stern writes, Bismarck turned to Bleichröder and used his connections—among them, the Rothschild banking houses throughout Europe. Bleichröder did indeed have "connections" with the Rothschilds, but no money was forthcoming from them, for, as Stern quotes Baron James de Rothschild, "it is a principle of our Houses not to advance money for any war." Stern, furthermore, is vague in describing precisely how Bleichröder went about financing the six-month Danish War while it was being waged. The author's most concrete reference to Bleichröder's activities in this regard is that he "seems to have urged that the government mortgage the bonds of a loan, already authorized by the [Prussian] Diet for railroad construction," to bankers who would supply the government with immediate funds. Otherwise, throughout the chapter on the Danish War, Stern repeatedly informs the reader that Bismarck still needed money, thus leaving some doubt as to how effective Bleichröder's quest for capital actually was during the course of the war.

Stern leaves no doubt, however, about Bleichröder's success in raising money for the Seven Weeks' War. In July, 1865, as relations between Austria and Prussia steadily worsened, the Prussian government and the Cologne-Minden Railroad signed an agreement, arranged by Bleichröder, that provided Bismarck with much of the money he needed in order to meet the military expenditures of an Austrian war. The agreement, Stern notes, was the outcome of protracted negotiations, in all of which Bleichröder was involved as both the company's banker and one of its directors. Under terms of the agreement, the Prussian government renounced its prior right to purchase the stock of the railroad, in exchange for thirteen million talers. In addition, the government was no longer obliged to maintain a large guarantee fund which had been set up to provide backing for minor lines associated with the Cologne-Minden Railroad and to cover possible interest payments on the railroad bonds. The elimination of this fund thus freed another seventeen million talers for Bismarck's use. After the successful conclusion of the Austro-Prussian war in July, 1866, Bleichröder provided further assistance to Bismarck by collecting the indemnity imposed on Saxony, an ally of Austria. In a similar fashion, Bleichröder was instrumental in arranging the transfer of the French indemnity after the Franco-Prussian War of 1870–1871.

Bleichröder, by arranging the funding of Prussia's great victory over Austria, not only contributed to German unification but also, at least indirectly, to the end of the constitutional crisis which had plagued Bismarck on money matters since the beginning of his ministry in 1862. The liberal opposition to Bismarck's foreign policy collapsed now that he had broken Austria's historic influence in Central Europe. Finally, then, on September 8, 1866, the Prussian Diet voted to accept the government's bill of indemnity, which gave retroactive assent to previous governmental expenditures that had been made without parliamentary consent.

Despite his close collaboration with Bismarck and his acquisition of great personal wealth and power, Bleichröder embodied what Stern refers to as "the ambiguity of Jewish success." For all of his public and private success, he was never quite able to obtain full respectability and acceptance from those whom he served. It is true that in 1872, at Bismarck's urging, William I ennobled Bleichröder, the first Prussian Jew to be so honored without converting to Christianity. Bismarck, however, made his recommendation orally, not in writing. The formal patent of ennoblement, moreover, was amended so as to delete the customary reference to those "who sprung from good families." Emperor William simply could not bring himself to proclaim that Bleichröder had sprung from what Prussians would call a good family. Ironically, Bleichröder had been raised to the ranks of the nobility because he had undertaken to salvage the fortunes of Prussian Junkers who had lost money in the collapse of some railroad projects in Rumania. Far from appreciating his efforts on their behalf, the Prussian aristocrats considered him little more than an embarrassing necessity.

Stern leaves the reader with a depressing portrait of Bleichröder: a man totally blind by 1880 who sought to emulate the values and lifestyle of his pseudolegal nobilitarian peers, whose acceptance of him was at best conditional. Most of the old Junker aristocracy, who would not have anything to do with Bleichröder socially, bitterly condemned members of the Bismarck family for attending the banker's lavish parties. Interestingly, their denunciation of Bismarck's relations with Bleichröder found its parallel in the new anti-Semitism that was unleashed during the 1870's.

Stern treats Bleichröder as the hostage of the new anti-Semitism which arose in Germany in the years of depression following the great financial crash of 1873. The very term "anti-Semitism," as the author points out, was first coined in Germany at this time; its adherents propagated the myth that the Jews, because they were now the true power in Germany would, if unchecked, corrupt the German character. Consequently, anti-Semitism demanded that the state should revoke or restrict the rights of Jews. Bleichröder's financial power and his recent elevation to the nobility made him the most obvious target of the new anti-Semitism. In Bleichröder, the anti-Semites found the living embodiment of all the Jewish stereotypes: the Jew as promoter and plotter, as corrupter, as one who amassed a fortune on the stock exchange instead of earning his daily bread by the sweat of his brow. There was, then, as the author demonstrates, a violent anticapitalistic sentiment in the new anti-Semitism. But this sentiment was not confined to the anti-Semites; they simply exploited the view held by many observers that the evil forces of materialism, greed, and moral decay were endangering the fabric of society in the new Empire. In time, more people were prepared to blame these manifestations of corruption on the Jews. Bismarck's enemies went so far by the mid-1870's as to insist that the chancellor was under the influence of a Jewish conspiracy to dominate the state that was masterminded by Bleichröder.

The author describes in considerable detail the difficulty which Bleichröder encountered in coping with the increasingly vicious anti-Semitic attacks on the Jews in general and on himself in particular. It was bad enough to be attacked by such anti-Semitic popularizers as Adolf Stoecker, the court chaplain of the Hohenzollerns, and Heinrich von Treitschke, the prominent historian. But what hurt Bleichröder even worse was that none of his contacts—he never had any real friends—in the ranks of the Prussian elite and Bismarck's entourage came to his defense. Rather, they maintained an embarrassed silence where he was concerned. What is more, during the 1880's, the Bismarck regime began a policy of covert discrimination against the Jews that the civil service continued under Emperor William II. Tragically, then, the very state which Bleichröder had helped create came to adopt or at least condone anti-Semitic attitudes. His detractors continued to heap insults on him to the very end of his life in 1893.

In the eighty odd years between his death and the publication of *Gold and Iron,* Bleichröder remained, in spite of his important contributions to Germany, what Stern calls an "unperson" in German historiography; he represents, in the author's words, "everything that has been left out of German history." Bismarck himself set this pattern by making only one passing reference to Bleichröder in his three volumes of memoirs. Subsequently, the editors of Bismarck's collected works did not publish so much as a single letter of the chancellor to his banker. German historians have focused exclusively on one of the two protagonists of Stern's account, writing some seven thousand volumes on the Iron Chancellor since his death in 1898.

Hence, Stern's book, though marred by a repetitive writing style, assumes great importance not only for its contribution to German history but to German historiography as well. As history, *Gold and Iron* provides the reader with an in-depth study of a critical period in the development of modern Germany. In this context, Stern's discussion of the character of late nineteenth century anti-Semitism is particularly illuminating. Historiographically, Stern weaves a biographical portrait of Bleichröder into an analysis of the social and economic life of the German Empire. This technique is something of an innovation in itself, for as Stern notes, contemporary German historians have tended to shun the importance of the individual in history, and their fascination with the structure of society often dulls their concern for the spirit that animated it. Henceforth, historians will be obliged to take into consideration the role of Bleichröder in financing the unification of the nation that chose to vilify and ultimately forget him.

Edward P. Keleher

A GUIDE FOR THE PERPLEXED

Author: E. F. Schumacher (1911–1977)
Publisher: Harper & Row Publishers (New York). 147 pp. $8.95
Type of work: Philosophy

A short, difficult book which reveals the spiritual and metaphysical basis underlying the author's famous work Small Is Beautiful

Anyone who collects evidence to prove that great achievements can come late in life needs to consider the case of E. F. Schumacher. Born in 1911 in Bonn, Germany, Ernst Friedrich Schumacher intended to become an economics professor like his father. To that end, he studied at Bonn, Berlin, Oxford, and Columbia University in New York. He began teaching at Columbia, but the intense thirst for practical work which marked his whole career made him increasingly discontented with academic life. Repulsed by Hitler's Germany, he settled in England in 1937 and went into business. When war broke out, Schumacher—like most German-born subjects—was interned; the government required him to labor on a Northhamptonshire farm for two pounds a week. But he soon gained release and worked both as a journalist and an associate of Lord Beveridge, a principal architect of the British welfare state. Following the war, "Fritz" Schumacher returned to Germany as an economic adviser to the British Control Commission. In 1950 the Labour government named him an economics adviser to the National Coal Board, which operates Britian's nationalized coal mines; he eventually became head of planning.

Schumacher remained in this post for twenty years, all the time contributing editorials for *The Times, The Observer,* and *The Economist.* His position with the Coal Board provided him with a variety of important challenges. He found himself embroiled in a portentious debate on the future of energy resources; his unorthodox analyses led him to predict a petroleum crisis, and he thus opposed those economists who in the late 1950's were calling for the closing of the mines. Schumacher also observed the tendencies of a key large-scale nationalized organization. Accepting the NCB's right to exist, Schumacher nevertheless supported efforts to decentralize the coal industry, devolve decision-making, and strengthen viable low-level organizational forms. Some of Schumacher's inspiration here came from the British Guild Socialist tradition—especially R. H. Tawney—and Roman Catholic social thought. (Schumacher converted to Catholicism and associated himself with such left-wing Thomists as Jacques Maritain and Etienne Gilson.) The Coal Board also sent Schumacher on numerous missions to Third World nations, and he became increasingly preoccupied with the question of the relevance of Western models for economic development. In 1965 he established the Intermediate Technology Development Group, a private company which assists developing nations to create the sort of technologies appropriate to their abundant-labor, low-capital situation.

Had Schumacher singlemindedly channeled his efforts into the Intermediate Technology Group, his influence outside the narrow world of "development economics" probably would have been negligible. But in 1973 Schumacher assembled a series of his papers, lectures, and essays; these he published in England and America under the odd title *Small Is Beautiful: Economics as if People Mattered.* While the book caused some excitement in Britain, American reviewers largely shunned it. Three years later, as the nation—stunned by the Vietnam defeat, an oil pricing crisis, and a general erosion of institutional authority—began to seek new perspectives, Schumacher's book was rediscovered. Elliot Richardson, Ralph Nader, Governor Jerry Brown, and other luminaries testified to the book's brilliance. By mid-1976 some ten thousand copies a month were being sold; ultimately the book, translated into fifteen languages, became a world bestseller. Said Peter Barnes in *The New Republic,* "I had never heard of E. F. Schumacher before reading this book. After reading it I am ready to nominate him for the Nobel Prize in economics." Many noneconomists echoed similar sentiment, for the work possessed an extraordinary cross-disciplinary relevance.

What was Schumacher's message? In fact, to those who listened closely there were two quite distinct messages, one socioeconomic and the other moral-philosophic. The first of these took the form of trend-identification and analysis. Schumacher often called attention to four closely related tendencies, the first of which is the ever-increasing size of everything in industrial society: organizations, machines, transport and communication systems, cities. "We suffer," he wrote, "from an almost universal idolatry of giantism." Nearly lost is the wisdom that for every activity there is an appropriate scale, and that for psychological vitality a society needs a rich variety of small, personalistic groups. The second tendency is the victory of complexity over simplicity in most spheres of existence. Is it written, asked Schumacher, that machines and organizations *must* be sources of bewilderment for their beneficiaries? Can't some of the ingenuity expended in their making go towards rendering them intelligible? Like social theorist Ivan Illich (whose ideas resemble those of Schumacher in a number of ways), Schumacher frequently pointed to the maddeningly complex and quite uneconomic structure of modern food transportation networks to illustrate this point. A third trend is the high capital intensity of most productive undertakings. To enter any significant area of production one must control a vast amount of capital. This requirement consigns energetic persons of modest means to the role of subservient "job holders," unable to exert their creative powers. Lamentably, this trend is increasingly evident even in Third World areas, where indigenous capital is in short supply and small labor-intensive enterprises are desperately needed. And finally, Schumacher pointed out the escalating violence of man's technologies. Epitomized by long half-life pesticides, the proliferation of nuclear power plants, and the adaptation of agriculture to machine imperatives, such violence begets equally violent "ecological backlashes."

In very general terms, Schumacher's proposed solution for these problematic tendencies is a radical orientation of scientific and technical inquiry. The aim must now be to "make things small, so that small people can make themselves productive." The new slogan must read: "production by the masses, rather than mass production." Elegance, grace, proportionateness, simplicity, energy-efficiency, nature-enhancement—these qualities can be embodied in a new generation of tools, insisted Schumacher. On the organizational plane, large impersonal corporate structures (both public and private) need to experiment with devolutionary and federalistic schemes. The firm of the future might well be "a well-coordinated assembly of lively, semiautonomous units, each with its own drive and sense of achievement."

But to give technology "a human face," one must first understand what it is to be human. It is at this point that Schumacher's second message was spoken, a moral and philosophic Word which dwelt intriguingly amid all the words about economics and society. In chapters dealing with such prosaic topics as land use, intermediate technology, the role of economic theory, and nuclear energy, readers found themselves face to face with notions like "levels of being," "cardinal virtues," "the principle of subsidiarity," "the exclusion of wisdom." They heard the heretical claim that economics ought to be less concerned with the wealth of nations and more with the health of human character. For man is not the self-gratification machine that classical and contemporary economics takes him to be. Man, Schumacher boldly affirmed, is the pinnacle of creation, made for fellowship with God, suited to a calling higher than that of "consumer/profit maximizer."

Although Schumacher invoked Buddhism, Gandhi, and "the traditional wisdom of mankind" in his polemic against "economics" (which economics? one wonders), it is clear that his main inspiration is Roman Catholic moral philosophy. Those familiar with the political writings of such neo-Thomists as Maritain, Gilson, Pope Pius XI, and Heinrich Rommen will find Schumacher's writings to be less original than many have thought. Like Schumacher, the leaders of the Thomist revival in this century have accused capitalism of possessing the same materialist metaphysics that Marxism openly embraces. Like Schumacher, they too see positivism, pragmatism, the idea of natural selection, and the Freudian emphasis on unconscious motivation as belittling and cheapening the human self-image. What must be restored, they argue, is a panoramic image of man's high place in creation. Or, in Schumacher's words, "It is only when we can see the world as a ladder, and when we can see man's position on the ladder, that we can recognize a meaningful task on earth."

In *Small Is Beautiful*, Schumacher's philosophic and religious standpoint guided his analysis of concrete issues; but except for the famous chapters on "Buddhist economics" and education, it largely remained implicit and undefended. Pressed by admirers to issue a more detailed statement of his *Weltanschauung*, Schumacher completed *A Guide for the Perplexed* in 1977. He did not live to witness its reception, for a stroke ended his life on September 4 of that year. As that reception has been largely unfavorable, and as Schumacher revealed himself to be more an eclectic sage than a philosopher, some providence may perhaps be divined here.

To call Schumacher a sage rather than a philosopher is not to gainsay the value of his work. *A Guide for the Perplexed* is in many ways a striking synoptic vision of man's place in nature. Yet a vision is not the same thing as an argument; true argumentation has the immense virtue of bringing conflicting syntheses to bear critically on each other. Schumacher abhorred Cartesian dualism, positivistic science, behaviorism, all forms of materialism, pragmatism, skepticism—in short, modernity. But rather than expose the shortcomings of these positions through analysis and careful reasoning, he was content to denounce them, ascribe to them dangerous consequences, and then invoke "the ancient wisdom tradition of mankind." The latter he was more concerned to describe and praise than defend. Thus, his attack on modernity has a distinctly reactionary quality about it.

Recognizing these limitations, we may still appreciate his reconstruction of "the wisdom tradition." In Schumacher's view, the tradition rests on four principal convictions. First, nature is hierarchically structured, with each level being ontologically discontinuous with what is above and below it; further, the macrocosmic world's hierarchies correspond to a natural hierarchy of human faculties. The third conviction is that knowledge is fourfold and includes these distinct yet complementary fields: self-knowledge, knowledge of the inner life of others, knowledge of the self as an objective phenomenon, and knowledge of the world apprehended as casually determined. Fourth, determinism and freedom are two necessary modes of viewed reality, with the acknowledgment of freedom entailing a recognition of a group of insoluble existential problems.

Schumacher's hierarchic vision—he praised the venerable notion of the "Great Chain of Being"—restores to the universe *inherent* values. Empiricists begin with a world of pure fact, brute matter; they are thus forced *a priori* to distinguish facts from values and consider values to be nonmaterial, subjective phantoms. The empiricist starting point ignores the "grades of significance" displayed in the world. Creation contains meaningful progressions: from lifeless *materia,* through sentient organic life, to intelligent and then self-conscious existence; from common (natural elements, microorganisms) to rare (the fully self-conscious man); from outer to inner; from beastly to angelic; from passivity to activity; from necessity to freedom; from disintegration to unity.

Cognate progressions can organize personal development, so that anyone who would truly imitate nature moves beyond sensuousity to rational discipline, innerness, and philosophic contemplation. This right developmental pattern is self-vindicating, for the person discovers that when he exercises his higher faculties (reason, virtue), corresponding realities in the cosmos are opened to him, realities which he "needs" (in a nonphysical sense) to experience. Or, as Aristotle put it, "Contemplation is the highest form of activity, because the intellect is the highest part of our nature, and the things apprehended by it are the highest objects of knowledge. . . . Therefore the activity of contemplation will be the perfect happiness of man."

For Schumacher, as for Aristotle and St. Thomas, the cultivation of the contemplative faculty reveals to the philosophic soul the divine character of reason itself. Man is both brutal and angelic, but the inherent bias in nature is "upward" and "inward," so it is correct to say that man's true destiny is the beatific vision of God. The human task then is to become progressively freer of the domination of reason by the senses. Small wonder, then, that Schumacher was fundamentally opposed to the ideology of economic growth; for by making growth the highest goal, entire societies are consigning their citizens to arrested development. Instead of weaning them from excessive reliance on physical gratification, they transform consumption into man's highest and most "natural" art.

It is telling that for Schumacher the mystic is very nearly the model of the fully actualized human being. His book quotes from a wide variety of mystical sources, and even retells the curious story of Therese Neumann, a celebrated German mystic who, after thirty-five years of living only on the daily Eucharistic meal, died in 1962 at the age of 64. The work properly observes here that such liberation from material constraints cannot finally be attributed to any spiritual exercise. "Only when the striving for 'power' has entirely ceased and been replaced by a certain transcendental longing, often called the love of God," may such "higher powers" be acquired. The beatific vision is a divine gift, not a human production. Schumacher's intense admiration for the mystic was qualified only by his belief that the fourth field of knowledge—causal inquiry—is too often ignored by those engrossed in the Way. In general, though, when Schumacher spoke of the need for a "new model of civilization," he meant that the present model is defective because the highest human type, the mystic, is effectively banished from it.

By now the range and general character of Schumacher's ideas are clear enough. That the author never acquired the famous British distaste for grand syntheses is also plain. Complains Harvey Cox, "The trouble is that Schumacher violates his own best advice. He goes big. He pours on too much and therefore is not persuasive." There are other irritants. In his haste, Schumacher lumped together his (mostly unidentified) intellectual opponents, labeling their work with fuzzy pejorative names like "scientism" and "evolutionism." His conception of science was based on such ideologues of science as August Comte and Vilfredo Pareto; he seemed quite unaware of the revolution in the understanding of the scientific enterprise since Einstein and Heisenberg. The very opaque distinction he drew between descriptive and instructional sciences makes his other commentary on this subject seem entirely suspect. Like all those who enthuse over the perennial philosophy, Schumacher overlooked the strong internal tensions in that philosophy, such as the tensions between immanentalist and transcendentalist, Gnostic and non-Gnostic, Platonist and Aristotelian.

The perplexed shall not, therefore, gain much specific guidance from this book. But they may be stimulated by it to consult Schumacher's excellent sources or intrigued enough to turn back to *Small Is Beautiful*, where Schumacher's vision found its ideal context.

Leslie E. Gerber

THE GULAG ARCHIPELAGO: THREE
Parts V-VII

Author: Alexander I. Solzhenitsyn (1918–   )
Translated from the Russian by Harry Willetts
Publisher: Harper & Row Publishers (New York). 558 pp. $16.95
Type of work: History and autobiography
Time: 1918–1956
Locale: The Soviet Union

> *The continuation of the history of the Corrective Labor Camps in the Soviet Union, to which is added the story of the Special Camps, hard-labor institutions for political prisoners, and the practice of exile to desolate regions within the country*

The Gulag Archipelago: Three is the conclusion of the massive work that Alexander Solzhenitsyn planned in penal servitude and wrote from 1958 to 1967. The first four parts of the work appeared in English translation as Volumes I and II in 1974 and 1975, and were chiefly concerned with the Soviet system of the Corrective Labor Camps, the means by which the Communist Party under Stalin enslaved uncounted millions of innocent people.

The person who has faithfully read through the first two volumes will nevertheless find some surprises in this conclusion to Solzhenitsyn's epic history: despite the manifold cruelties of the slave-labor camps described in the earlier parts, the Corrective Labor system was not the worst that the Soviets could devise for their own countrymen. The penal system had still more chains it could hang on its prisoners, and especially on those unfortunates convicted under Article 58 of the Criminal Code—the political prisoners. Those chains are shown to the world in Part 5, "Katorga," and Part 6, "Exile."

Although history will classify the twentieth century as the most barbaric and bloody ever recorded, those who hope for the future of the human race will find a few shreds of comfort in Solzhenitsyn's work. We find in Volume III that dictators are as fallible as democrats, and in this volume, for the first time in this epic of pain, a few beams of light break through. *Katorga,* the title of Part 5, means "hard labor," and designates yet another chain of islands in the Archipelago of punishment that stretches through the Soviet Union. In 1943, Stalin decided to segregate the politicals and certain other types of prisoners, taking them out of the Corrective Labor Camps and moving them to Special Camps, institutions of hard labor where, it was thought, they could be more effectively controlled and exploited. But rather than placing still another burden on the inmates, the hard labor camps proved a means of unintentionally lightening their load.

Stalin's plan was crushing enough in its conception: it provided for twelve hours a day of back-breaking work on an inadequate diet; it provided for locking the prisoners into their huts at night, without access to latrines; it provided for them to be held almost incommunicado from the outside world, from their friends and families; and finally, it provided as usual that their guards could shoot them down for the slightest infractions, or even for no infraction at all, without fear of punishment. In some places the plan did not work, though, with the harshness its developers desired, for two reasons.

First, the segregation of the prisoners turned out to be a great blessing. In Volumes I and II, Solzhenitsyn recounts story after story of the persecution of the political prisoners, not through the unaided efforts of the camp administrations, but through the use of prisoner informers. The administrations had a second ally in the thieves, the professional criminals in the camps, who regarded the politicals as their legitimate prey, and plundered them with the unofficial blessings of the jailors. When the politicals were removed to the hard labor camps, the numbers of the professional criminals among them were at least diminished. For the first time, the politicals could achieve something of a feeling of solidarity, a feeling of united rather than individual suffering under their oppressors.

The second reason is the more important. The katorga system began in 1943, and a different kind of political prisoner was being sent to the camps. Prior to World War II, the political prisoner was often a Communist Party member caught in one of the numerous purges, or a member of one of the several leftist, but non-Bolshevik parties. But now the camp numbers were swelled with returning military men who had been captured and imprisoned by the Germans; with whole cadres of members of nationalist movements, especially Ukrainians; with those Russians who had administered territories under the German occupation. These new convicts were frequently men with experience of resistance, or at least with experience of disciplined group behavior. For the first time there came to be organizations and lines of authority separate from those imposed by camp discipline.

Solzhenitsyn is particularly concerned in this volume to answer those critics who ask why, if life in the camps was as brutal as he depicts, no one tried to rebel. His answer is that they did try; that they rebelled singly and in groups; and that their resistance was continual, and took many forms.

He begins on the level of individuals and small groups. Thus in these pages we find the first stories of successful resistance to the ravages of the thieves; eventually this resistance, by ones and twos, leads to the forming of underground prisoner organizations who reply to the thieves in kind, visiting rough retribution as well on informers and stool pigeons. He discusses many escape attempts, some of them successful despite enormous odds against them. A prisoner contemplating escape more often than not had to plan for a trek across hundreds of miles of trackless desert, in the face of propaganda that had made him appear a savage to the civilian population. He could expect anyone he met to hand him over to the authorities without hesitation. And there is a kind of wistfulness to these tales of escape, too; despite all their experience in the system, the prisoners tried to escape not to Japan or India or Western Europe, but often simply to return to their homes. Nevertheless, there were prisoners who mounted try after try, ending only with their freedom or their death.

Solzhenitsyn proceeds to large-scale revolts, hunger strikes, and work stoppages, culminating in the armed rising at Kengir, which held the camp against the authorities for forty days. However, the result was the same in each case: first, some initial, limited success, then ultimate failure. And the author draws two conclusions from these histories: first, when challenged, the system would grind to a halt. The successes of the revolts depended on uncertainty in the administration of the MVD, which ran the camps. The rulers of the camps faltered, especially after the execution in 1953 of L. P. Beria, the head of internal security. Prior to his death, camp leaders knew they could murder the striking prisoners in safety; after it, they were not so sure for a time.

The second conclusion is more sobering; the final failure of the prisoner revolts resulted from their betrayal by high party officials. The word of the government, solemnly pledged, could not be trusted. And it could not be trusted because public opinion did not and does not exist in the Soviet Union. With complete control of all forms of communication, the government could prevent any word of the revolts themselves from ever reaching the attention of their own public or the attention of the West. An investigating committee from Moscow could promise whatever it liked to the prisoners, secure in the knowledge that no one would hold its members accountable for the fulfillment of those promises.

But these stories of battles against hopeless odds hold the same lesson as does the story of the rising of the Jews of the Warsaw Ghetto against Hitler's SS: no power can ever repress people in absolute security. And the stories have an additional, special lesson for Americans: the event that sparked hope among the prisoners of the Archipelago was the outbreak of the Korean War. They thought it meant the beginning of a third World War; readers of the book in America need to ponder how far a human being must be pushed before he will welcome an atomic war. And we need to reflect also whether some kinds of existence are not worse than the threat of atomic destruction. The politicals thought so.

Katorga is the subject of Part 5; Part 6 takes up exile, the third prong (after the Corrective Labor Camps and the hard-labor Special Camps) on Stalin's pitchfork. The system of exile, like so many of the repressions detailed in the whole work, began in the 1920's and 1930's with the deportation of anyone branded a *kulak*—not only prosperous peasants, but also unsuccessful peasants—anyone who would not join a collective farm. The sweep included millers, blacksmiths (reclassified as *petit bourgeois*), anyone that a bureaucrat held a grudge against; and the total reached fifteen million from this source alone. The exile was not a relocation to some settled rural or urban community, but often it meant that a group of people with hardly anything but the clothes on their backs would be dumped on the barren bank of some subarctic river. In circumstances like this, it is not surprising that a sentence of exile was often indistinguishable from a sentence of death; it just took a little longer to execute.

One could be exiled for several reasons: for being of the wrong nationality, for instance, or for having served a term in the camps, or even for living in the wrong place. The first of these Solzhenitsyn discusses as a reverse migration of nations, for whole peoples were moved from the west to the barren central and eastern parts of the Soviet Union. In this way the Volga Germans were deported, and Greeks who lived in the Caucasus. The list of those removed goes on and on: the Chechens, the Ingush, and Karachai, the Balkars, the Kalmyks, the Kurds, the Crimean Tartars—all names almost unheard of in the West, and all forcibly deported from their homelands. To these must be added those who simply resided where there was a partisan movement: the Ukraine, or the Baltic states of Lithuania, Latvia, or Estonia.

And to these, but later, are added those men and women who served their ten- or twenty-five-year sentences in the camps. Solzhenitsyn himself, after serving out his sentence, is not released to resume his life in freedom, but is exiled to Kok-Terek, a miserable mud-hut village of four thousand in northern Kazakhstan. The exiles who are ex-prisoners find themselves stuck in still another Catch-22; they cannot establish a legal residence in their places of exile until they have jobs, and they cannot get jobs until they have legal residences. Therefore the lot of the more "fortunate" of them is much like slavery: if they do find work, their employers realize that they can squeeze their workers as much as they like; if the ex-prisoners quit, or are fired for complaining, they will starve.

To add to all this, there is an alternative to exile—banishment. The difference is that one can be banished (and subjected to all the disgrace and hardship of exile) without even the kangaroo trials the exiles usually undergo. One can be banished by "administrative action," as many were for the crime of being Moslems or Baptists.

The concluding part, "Stalin Is No More," briefly discusses the changes in the system since 1953, especially those since the Party Congress at which Nikita Khrushchev denounced Stalin's reign as the "Cult of Personality."

Since those events, there have been changes; thousands were released from camp or exile, and rehabilitated. But rehabilitation does not mean an admission that the government was wrong, and the prisoner was innocent, but only that his crime was not so bad. Those who were responsible for all the false imprisonments and deaths were not punished, but either remained at their posts or retired on government pensions. In 1953, the secret police, the KGB, was abolished; it was replaced six months later by the MGB with the same personnel.

Solzhenitsyn has just a single point to make in the final part, and it is this: although things have changed, they have changed only in practice, not in principle. Instead of thousands of political prisoners sentenced under Article 58 there are relatively few; there are still political prisoners, although their sentences have been camouflaged under other sections of the Criminal Code—a trumped-up charge of rape is as easy to process as a trumped-up charge of treason. If their numbers are fewer, there are still plenty of political prisoners in the camp system. And, more important, there are no safeguards that the same thing will not happen again. Solzhenitsyn demands that the guilty be punished; partly, of course, his cry rises from the yearning for an abstract justice. But there is a still more practical reason: until an open and full accounting of the Gulag system is made, and until those responsible for its erection and administration admit their guilt, it can happen again. It can happen until the Communist Party admits that it is both fallible and responsible to those it governs. Had those two obvious truths been accepted in 1917, *The Gulag Archipelago* would never have had to be written.

Walter E. Meyers

HARRY HOPKINS
A Biography

Author: Henry H. Adams
Publisher: G. P. Putnam's Sons (New York). Illustrated. 448 pp. $15.00
Type of work: Biography
Time: 1890–1946
Locale: Iowa, New York City, Washington, D.C., London, Moscow, Casablanca, Teheran, Yalta

Adams tells the life story of the principal relief administrator of the New Deal, and one of its most controversial figures

> *Principal personages:*
> HARRY L. HOPKINS, FERA-WPA administrator, Secretary of Commerce, presidential assistant
> FRANKLIN D. ROOSEVELT, President of the United States
> WINSTON CHURCHILL, Prime Minister of the United Kingdom
> JOSEPH STALIN, dictator of the USSR
> HAROLD L. ICKES, Secretary of the Interior, PWA administrator

Henry H. Adams, a former professor of English, has written a four-volume history of World War II, and this biography reflects the background knowledge which that task provided. The material on Hopkins comes mainly from the Hopkins papers on microfilm at the Roosevelt Library in Hyde Park, and Adams' extensive research makes it unlikely that more new information about Hopkins' life and work will be forthcoming. After the preliminaries, Averell Harriman's Foreword, and a Prologue built around Hopkins' resignation from the Cabinet in August, 1940, Adams' account is basically chronological, and divided into two sections, the shorter dealing with Hopkins' prewar career and the longer with his last crucial services. The proportions show the author's assessment of the relative importance of the two periods in his subject's life.

Authors are not responsible for publisher's blurbs, but somebody should be held to account for a wrapper which reads on the front under the title, "The life story of the man behind FDR, the New Deal, and Allied strategy in World War II." Hopkins was tremendously important, as Adams' whole account proves, but that importance is obscured, not shown, by hyperbole. Better testimony is Harriman's opening in his Foreword to Adams' biography: "If Sir Winston Churchill had been asked which two Americans, other than President Roosevelt, had done the most to defeat Hitler, he would have unhesitatingly replied, 'Among the military, General Marshall, and among the civilians, Harry Hopkins.'" What kind of man could evoke such a tribute?

Hopkins' beginnings were ordinary: an Iowa birth and for the most part youth, a father who was a harness maker and salesman, and a mother who was a former schoolteacher intent on the education of her children. He attended Grinnell College and achieved no high record of scholarship, but developed an interest in history and politics, and benefited from the influence of a professor who taught "Applied Christianity." It was apparently this professor who steered Hopkins into his first career by recommending him for a counselor's post at a New Jersey summer camp for poor boys. Adams suggests that Hopkins took the offer because it would give him a chance to see the East; he did stop on the way— it was 1912—to see the Republican Convention in Chicago and the Democratic Convention in Baltimore.

Throughout this early account, Adams is sparse with analysis and explanation; the absence of documentation is almost certainly the reason. Yet some speculation occurs: not merely one professor, but the whole "Progressive" idea, and the growing importance of social work, might well turn an Iowa boy of 1912 in that direction. At any rate, as Adams tells it, the experience of the summer camp was Hopkins' introduction to urban poverty and to urban ethnicity—the boys came from New York slums. Hopkins went from summer camp to a New York settlement house, and from there to the world of professional social work in the metropolis.

Several things are implied, though not stated, in Adams' account of Hopkins' career from 1912 to the Depression. He worked for the Association for Improving the Condition of the Poor, for the city government, for the Tuberculosis Association, for the Red Cross—a variety of mostly private agencies and organizations. He became an organizer, executive, and expediter, rather than a case worker. He developed a reputation for getting things done, but in his own way, not always by the rules. And in the "prosperity" of the 1920's he was never out of contact with those who did not share the prosperity. Not, Adams' account makes clear, that he was poor or monkish. Hopkins liked the company of the rich; he liked to live well. The point, rather, though Adams does not express it, is that Hopkins was never able to accept the prosperity as being the prerogative only of the rich.

Hopkins' second career began during the Depression, when Roosevelt, as Governor of New York, put Hopkins in charge of a temporary relief project which provided work for the poor. When Roosevelt went to Washington, in the midst of all the emergencies of the Hundred Days, he accepted a plan largely conceived by Hopkins for grants-in-aid for work relief, and made Hopkins administrator. Hopkins said he expected to last six months; he lasted almost six years. Under a variety of names and acronyms—FERA, WPA—the organization he directed spent money to relieve unemployment; it did not simply offer "relief," but jobs.

Thereupon hangs Hopkins' first great reputation. The jobs were of all sorts, for the unemployed were a varied mass of people. Streets and bridges were repaired and forests replanted, and there were also theater and art projects, and the great writers' project of collecting massive amounts of material for American history and folklore. Hopkins' job as he saw it was to keep the money flowing and the men and women working. He dealt with state and local politicians often desirous of building a machine out of WPA workers; he persuaded the budget authorities and the Congress to come up with at least some of the money; he faced a horde of critics, including most of the press, whose definition of WPA work was leaf-raking and shovel-leaning.

And he feuded with Harold Ickes, or Ickes with him. Adams' tone is generally sympathetic to Hopkins, but sober and factual. Ickes, of course, was anything but sedate, and he was in competition with Hopkins for money, prestige, and power. His Public Works Administration was supposed to undertake the larger, long-range projects, while Hopkins worked on the smaller and less expensive ones. But the lines were never clear, and Roosevelt's administrative style confused them further; Ickes was convinced Hopkins was undermining him, and put his suspicions into his diary. Adams does not take Ickes' complaints too seriously, although he does admit in some passages that Hopkins could be a ruthless and skilled adversary in bureaucratic in-fighting. Basically, however, he is portrayed as an informal, red-tape-cutting administrator who had enormous energy and drive and a full command of his responsibilities.

In other areas the author's treatment seems on the bland side. We are given the facts of Hopkins' first marriage, divorce, and second marriage, but little beyond bare facts. The picture of Hopkins the race track and party frequenter, perhaps overdone by his opponents, is barely acknowledged. Instead of personal information, Adams stresses the accomplishments of Hopkins' agencies (especially in emergencies such as the 1937 and 1938 floods), Hopkins' increasing rapport with the President, and his political ambition. The highest ambition was for the presidency in 1940; there can be no doubt of Adams' evidence that Hopkins wanted the presidency and thought he had a good chance, and no doubt that Roosevelt encouraged him, both privately (the evidence is necessarily by Hopkins' own account), and publically (by appointing him Secretary of Commerce). The question is, how deeply committed was Roosevelt, who was never one to give himself away? Also, one has to wonder whether a Democratic party which had defeated most of Roosevelt's efforts to eliminate unsympathetic senators and representatives in 1938, and which proved so reluctant to accept Henry Wallace for vice-president in 1940, would have nominated Hopkins. In any case, the ambition was never tested; Hopkins' serious illness, which led to his resignation from the Commerce position, also ended his presidential hopes. It also opened the way to his most important achievement, which is Adams' principal story.

Hopkins stayed at the White House; he was Roosevelt's manager, in fact, for the third-term nomination at Chicago; but as the war in Europe and in Asia grew more desperate with the fall of France and the air assault on Britain, it became Hopkins' preoccupation, as it became the President's. Hopkins' official title was Presidential Assistant, and he also became a powerful member of the numerous committees set up first for the defense effort and Lend-Lease to Britain, and later for the United States war effort itself. He was expediter and allocator of supplies, breaker of bottle-necks, and constant gadfly. He was also Roosevelt's personal emissary first to Churchill and then to Stalin. Again, supply was his great concern. His questions to the British and Russians were: What do you need and how much? His questions to American industry were: What can you produce and how soon?

Beginning with the trip to England in January, 1941, Hopkins flew when necessary to the British Isles and to Moscow. He accompanied Roosevelt to the wartime conferences. Adams is detailed and clear about the trips, and about Hopkins' continuing ill-health and near-exhaustion; the picture of his subject's dedication and great output of energy is one of the best he draws. Along with it is the picture of a man of very great ability. Adams several times emphasizes Hopkins' grasp of complicated processes of supply, and retention of the masses of facts and figures necessary to enable him to see to it that the job was done.

And yet, it is no contradiction of Adams' account, nor any diminution of Hopkins' dedication and ability, to suggest another context. Hopkins' success in speeding the production of ball bearings came not from any official position, and only in part from his powers of persuasion, but in considerable measure because his phone call began, "This is Harry Hopkins from the White House." Even more, his importance to Churchill and Stalin was that he represented Roosevelt. What he said represented Roosevelt's thought; what they said to him would be reported directly and accurately to the President. The service was enormously important, but it depended on the relationship of the two men, and there was never any doubt who was chief and who was subordinate. One point, however, should be made: Hopkins had the ability to reduce matters to essentials, to find the knot that untied the whole complicated issue, to strike through to the point. Particularly in wartime, this was a most valuable asset.

Adams' book clearly reflects this and other qualities. The private Hopkins is talked about, not conveyed; maybe he cannot be. The public Hopkins and his achievements we see largely as he himself saw them, but that is a necessary limitation. Hopkins was an important figure, and this book helps us to understand how and why.

George J. Fleming

HEARTS AND MINDS
The Common Journey of Simone de Beauvoir and Jean-Paul Sartre

Author: Axel Madsen (1932–   )
Publisher: William Morrow and Company (New York). 320 pp. $10.95
Type of work: Biography
Time: 1905–1977
Locale: France

A new look at the lives of one of the most important and celebrated couples in the history of French letters

> *Principal personages:*
> SIMONE DE BEAUVOIR, French feminist, fiction writer, and essayist
> JEAN-PAUL SARTRE, French philosopher, playwright, fiction writer, and political essayist

When Jean-Paul Sartre was asked last year if his works would have been any different had he not known Simone de Beauvoir, he answered that everything he had written before he met her contained the essentials of his thought. He added, however, that because of their fifty-year close friendship, his writings certainly bear the impact of their common experiences and struggles. Axel Madsen's *Hearts and Minds* is neither a literary promenade nor another investigation of philosophical debates. It attempts to uncover the affinities between Beauvoir and Sartre as individuals and as writers, to show how the two reacted to a particular political and intellectual milieu, and to present the reader with simple yet human facets of their longtime liaison.

Some readers may be confused, at first, by the book's title. Those who remember the 1975 documentary on Vietnam, *Hearts and Minds*, could mistake this new book for the script of the film by Peter Davis. Perhaps to avoid any ambiguity, a subtitle has been added with specific references to the author's main objective: to depict the relationship between Beauvoir and Sartre. The parallel between the film and Madsen's book cannot naturally be perceived on the level of substance but rather in the intentions of both director and author. Through a montage of interviews and newsreel footage, Davis had created a powerful visual essay whose purpose was to understand the attitudes and beliefs of a generation: the Westmorelands and the Rostows, the Ellsbergs and the Stones. By adopting a similar title, Madsen sets the tone for his book. He interviews his main subjects, Sartre and Beauvoir, looks into their writings, immerses himself in the France of the postwar era, and attempts to grasp the attitudes and feelings of that period.

Sartre and Beauvoir met in 1928 as students of the prestigious Ecole Normale Supérieure in Paris, where they studied philosophy, Greek, logic, and psychology. The following year, they took the difficult state examination for the *agrégation*, a competition in which Sartre's name was listed first. Beauvoir ranked second. Music, writing, American novelists, and cinema brought them even closer, and before he was off for his military service, Sartre proposed a two-year negotiable contract which would bind them, yet which would safeguard each one's freedom. At a time when the education of respectable bourgeois girls was geared towards motherhood and rearing a family, Beauvoir opted for a lifestyle that went against the grain. Feminism was either a taboo word or unheard of in most parts of the country, and her rejection of accepted social conventions (an attitude seen by her critics as a sign of eccentric tendencies) expressed one woman's desire for self-fulfillment and control over her own destiny. Ironically, the man who was to become her life partner was a *machismo* until the age of fifteen, as Sartre would concede later. He was surrounded for many years by a group of women composed of his mother, grandmother, and their friends; his father died when he was two years old. It was in this milieu, encouraged by a domineering grandfather, that he learned the superiority of man over the "second sex." If his liaison with Beauvoir did not turn into a battle of the sexes, it was often put to the test, and it endured in spite of their outside paramours, or as Beauvoir liked to call them, their "contingent love affairs." For those who perceived Beauvoir's dependence on Sartre as paradoxical with her outspoken stand on feminism, she would answer that the fact that she recognized and admired his superior political activity in no way downgraded her nor weakened her rapport with him. In effect, their relationship was long-lived because of their mutual respect. She was his best and most useful critic and vice versa.

One of the virtues of this book is that the biographical data does not take over the narrative completely. Madsen, the accomplished biographer of another statesman of French letters, André Malraux, relates the chronological events of Sartre's and Beauvoir's lives to other significant contemporary incidents. Thus, the reader is offered a comprehensive and dynamic picture of France, and enabled to see the two authors' main works in their context, set against the background of wars, political polemics, and intellectual currents.

Sartre dominated the Parisian intellectual scene for more than a decade in the postwar years. Almost every aspect of French letters is affected by his thought, whether it is the novel, the drama, or the philosophical essay; a score of articles and prefaces add to his already voluminous production. Except for two or three of his popular works, Sartre is not widely read in France nowadays. The diminishing interest in his writings among French scholars and students alike in his own country can be traced to various factors, one of which is the loss of actuality. Sartre's popularity was no doubt the result of his intellectual versatility, but it also resulted from his ability to fill the void created by World War II. He grasped the contemporary mood and responded to the individual's pessimism by confronting it with the notions of freedom, responsibility, and *engagement*. Beauvoir's novels and other writings often echoed Sartre's concepts of existentialism or expanded his theories. In *Hearts and Minds,* Madsen gives us a useful account of the two writers' production and is able to show with clarity the gradual progression of their thought as well as the context of some of their most important works. His study goes even further by emphasizing their individual political consciousnesses.

In about forty years, France had witnessed the occupation of its territory by the Nazis; the ineffectiveness of succeeding governments in dealing with economic matters; the debacle of its foreign policy in Indochina and its agonizing involvement in Algeria; the emergence of General De Gaulle from his retreat and the birth of the Fifth Republic; the May, 1968, events; and the downfall of the man who had solved the Algerian question. While most intellectuals espoused causes and joined political parties, Beauvoir and Sartre stood away almost suspiciously from any group that might hinder their independence. Their apparent aloofness, which brought them criticism from the left and the right alike, meant only that they were willing to engage in any worthwhile mission as long as it did not impose the dictates of either a government or a political party, or the dogmas of a religion. Indicative of this independent stand *vis-à-vis* any ideological or institutional group are Sartre's indifference for the much coveted *Légion d'Honneur*, his lack of interest in a potential professorship at the prestigious Collège de France, and his categorical refusal of the Nobel Prize.

Probably the most vociferous attacks on Sartre came from the French Communist Party (P.C.F.), which singled him out first as an *agent provocateur* during the German occupation. Sartre had managed his way out of the German camps and joined forces with a group of intellectuals in writing anti-German propaganda for a clandestine newssheet. Rumors originating with the P.C.F. soon spread that he could not be trusted, on the grounds that his means of escape from the camps was not very clear. Curiously enough, it was during his years of imprisonment at Stallag XIID at Trèves that he wrote a little-known play set in Jerusalem, *Bariona*, in which he vents his hatred for the Nazis. In spite of the ill-founded accusations, Sartre favored a *rapprochement* with the French Communists and would eventually lend them his support by working with the Comité National des ecrivains. As a Communist sympathizer, he was tempted at times to join the Party, but felt that being one of them would mean the deprivation of his individuality and free choice, which he was not ready to relinquish for the sake of belonging to a group. Sartre's existentialism came under vigorous scrutiny by the Party ideologists and intellectuals, who described it as anti-humanist or as being the product of a foreign influence: that of Heidegger's "naziism." Moreover, it was feared that his theories either discouraged or prevented people from joining the Communist Party. Surprisingly, it was in 1952 with *The Communists and Peace* that Sartre demonstrated his ardent support for the P.C.F. and world Communism. It was not that he now espoused Marxist dogma, but that he believed sincerely that the P.C.F. offered the best solution for France. On the other hand, he could not be against the proletariat, a group in which he placed much of his faith. The Russian intervention in Hungary in 1956, however, dealt a severe blow to his friendly relations with the Communists. He criticized vehemently the Soviet invasion, and called for the Soviet writers to denounce publicly their government's maneuvers. Most important, in the Revue *Les Temps Modernes,* of which he was the Director, he summarized the thirty years of the P.C.F. as years of hypocrisy, and he demanded the de-Stalinization of that Party.

Had his amicable ties with the P.C.F. not been severed in the aftermath of the Hungarian tragedy, they most certainly would have been on the Algerian question. While the Party adopted an ambiguous position in this instance, Sartre from the beginning was firm and decisive in his antiwar stand, and he made no secret of his sympathies for the National Liberation Front of Algeria (F.L.N.). For the one million *pieds-noirs* (as the French community in Algeria was designated then), the return of De Gaulle to active politics in 1958 was interpreted as the pursuit of past colonial policies and a reassurance that *Algérie française* would remain as such. An *Algérie algérienne* was the more inconceivable in many French minds, particularly for the economists in the government, since the loss of that territory would be translated into a loss of what France needed most: natural gas, agricultural products, new markets, and, of course, cheap labor. Peace with the F.L.N. would also cause a massive exodus of fearful Frenchmen: a situation France never envisaged when it sent its troops to that part of North Africa in the nineteenth century. Thus, economic factors played the larger role in constructing French foreign policy; perhaps this was De Gaulle's thinking when in Algeria, he shouted to a delirious crowd of *pieds-noirs* his famous: "I have understood you."

France was slowly entangled in its own version of Vietnam, and the war she was to confront for almost a decade carried its toll of innocent victims on both sides. Sartre wrote in that period what many consider his best drama. Set in postwar Germany, *The Condemned of Altona* alluded to contemporary political incidents in France and Algeria by discussing among other things the question of guilt as well as the demystification of military heroism. His solidarity with Algerian fighters took one more practical step when he met in Rome Frantz Fanon, a Martinican psychiatrist and member of the Algerian provisional government. Subsequent to their talks, Fanon's *The Damned* included a violent preface by Sartre in which he declared his total support for Algerians and other colonized people. Beauvoir took up the case of a young Algerian terrorist girl, Djamila Boupacha, indecently tortured by French soldiers. Besides attracting public attention, the article she submitted to *Le Monde* recounting the matter caused some embarrassment to the French government, which retaliated by having that newspaper's overseas edition suppressed in Algiers. Never before had Sartre and Beauvoir been involved so wholeheartedly in a cause as in the Algerian affair, and never had their personal lives been so much at stake. (Sartre's apartment was bombed twice.) They spoke at rallies against torture and torturers, voiced total disapproval of their government's policies, and signed the Manifesto of the 121 at the risk of a five-year imprisonment. This document, an appeal to the French left to make known their unconditional support for the

Algerian movement, denounced the war and even encouraged the draftees to disobey. It is, no doubt, this equal belief in human justice that prompted them to participate later in the Bertrand Russell International War Crimes Tribunal, to approve of the student riots in Paris in May, 1968, and, in the case of Sartre, to take in 1970 the directorship of the government-banned Maoist newspaper, *La Cause du Peuple.*

Age is putting an end to their combative temperaments. But only a few years ago, Beauvoir signed the Manifesto of the 343 and campaigned for an appropriate abortion bill, and Sartre talked to the workers of the Renault automobile installations. Both were seen on boulevards handing out banned newspapers, before being picked up by police vans.

From political indifference to commitment to radicalism, and finally, to militancy: these have been the major steps in Beauvoir's and Sartre's half-a-century "common journey" as suggested by the reading of *Hearts and Minds.* Much has been written on the two authors individually, but Madsen adopts a distinct new approach by composing a dual portrait which vividly illustrates how intensely their lives have been interrelated. *Hearts and Minds* is not a large book, unfortunately, and on occasions one has the impression of reading through condensed data. Although most of the material here is familiar, Madsen's study is nevertheless commendable for its vivid, honest, and objective portrayal of a revered couple whose liaison has almost become a legend.

Charles Elkabas

HITLER'S WAR

Author: David Irving (1938–   )
Publisher: The Viking Press (New York). 926 pp. $17.50
Type of work: History
Time: September 3, 1939, to April 30, 1945
Locale: Europe

This analysis views Hitler as a man of great military ability who was nevertheless surprisingly weak in imposing his will on his subordinates

Principal personages:
ADOLF HITLER, the Führer
MARTIN BORMANN, his powerful secretary
JOSEPH GOEBBELS, Gauleiter of Berlin and Reich Propaganda Minister
HERMANN GÖRING, Commander in Chief of the Luftwaffe and head of the Four-Year Plan Office
HEINZ GUDERIAN, famous German tank commander
WALTHER HEWEL, liaison officer at Hitler's headquarters
REINHARD HEYDRICH, SS General who was the brain behind the extermination camps
HEINRICH HIMMLER, SS Reichsführer
ALFRED JODL, Chief of the OKW operations staff and Hitler's closest military adviser
WILHELM KEITEL, Field Marshall and Chief of OKW
ERICH VON MANSTEIN, Field Marshal, Hitler's favorite offensive general
THEO MORELL, Hitler's doctor
ERICH RAEDER, Grand Admiral and Commander in Chief, Navy
ERWIN ROMMEL, Field Marshal and charismatic general
ALBERT SPEER, Hitler's scheming Munitions Minister

During 1942, Adolf Hitler praised a biography of William II written by an Englishman and expressed the opinion that foreigners sometimes made very objective historians. He went on to remark that he was having transcripts made of all his important conferences and that some day perhaps an "objective Englishman" would write his story. As David Irving relates this incident, it is clear that he wants to be the objective Englishman Hitler prophesied. The result is a controversial and sometimes vexing book.

In Irving's approach to his subject, pride of place goes to the eleven years he spent going through the primary sources. Great emphasis is placed on sources he located which no one else has utilized; in fact, this sometimes seems to be his main criterion in judging the importance of a source. He writes history as scoop. Irving wants to escape from the incestuous relation between historians who trade the same stories back and forth, and so he has spurned published works on Hitler. Irving's object is to reconstruct the war as Hitler viewed it. He does this with a careful, almost day by day, analysis of Hitler's orders, the intelligence reports he was receiving, the transcripts of his war conferences, and diaries of people closely associated with him, some of them used here for the first time.

Irving empathetically rethinks the war from Hitler's perspective, a bold approach from which most historians have been deterred by the repugnance of the subject. Irving is able to accomplish this because his Hitler is completely sane and turns out to be not so bad as we had imagined.

Irving's method imposes a very narrow focus on his book. It begins abruptly with the invasion of Poland and the reader flounders for many pages before he gains his bearings. The book ends without conclusion 823 pages later with the suicide of Hitler. Irving is totally preoccupied with Hitler's day by day military and political decisions, so there is no room in his long book for such crucial factors as the role of ideology or a systematic analysis of Hitler's personality. Naturally, an account based entirely on the "nuts and bolts" decisions Hitler had to make once he had started his war places him in his most pragmatic light, yet this narrow focus also distorts the image of Hitler and is the most serious weakness of Irving's book.

The author's most controversial conclusion is that Hitler did not order the extermination of the Jews and indeed did not even know about it until at least October, 1943, and may not have learned about it until SS General Ernst Kaltenbrunner told him one year later, in October, 1944. Irving's argument is partly one of silence. No document has ever been discovered in which Hitler ordered the massacre of the Jews and Irving has been unable to find any mention in any of the diaries he has read that anyone ever discussed the matter with Hitler. Irving buttresses his argument of silence with circumstantial evidence. On several occasions Heinrich Himmler stated that he had taken on himself the responsibility for the final solution, statements which Irving interprets to mean that Himmler made the decision himself. Hitler himself said late in the war that the whole matter was Himmler's business. Moreover, all of Hitler's explicit references to the Jewish problem referred only to the deportation of the Jews to the east. On November 30, 1941, Himmler telephoned SS General Reinhard Heydrich from Hitler's headquarters and ordered him to stop liquidating the Jews. Irving believes this proves that Hitler was actually insisting the Jews not be exterminated, and he attaches such importance to the episode that he includes a facsimile of Himmler's telephone note recording this call. That the extermination of Jews was suspended after Kaltenbrunner conferred with Hitler in October, 1944, confirms to Irving that Hitler never wanted the final solution during the war.

For Irving, then, the final solution was partly the initiative of a crackpot, Heinrich Himmler, and partly an *ad hoc* solution adopted by local authorities to the near insuperable problem of what to do with the millions of Jews dumped on them from all over Europe. Irving argues that only about seventy people knew what was happening and Hitler, who was completely absorbed in the war and had abdicated his authority in other areas, was not one of them.

Throughout the book, Irving scrupulously sticks very close to his evidence, so much so that the reader yearns for a perspective in which to place and evaluate the evidence. It is only in the matter of the final solution that Irving endeavors to extract an interpretation from the evidence that many readers will find remarkable. His reason for this is that this argument is the keystone to two of his main conclusions—that Hitler was sane and that his authority during the war was surprisingly limited.

Himmler was a crackpot; Hitler was not. Irving is convinced Hitler was a pragmatic man who would never have wasted scarce resources for such an irrational purpose as killing Jews. Hitler's idea was to make use of the Jews as forced laborers and as hostages; killing them defeated both purposes. Irving acknowledges that Hitler was indeed ruthless and brutal. Deporting the Jews was bad enough, and his violent anti-Semitism, which Irving labels pathological, created the atmosphere in which the extermination of the Jews could take place. Hitler ordered the liquidation of Communist political commissars and pitiless reprisals against the partisans. But these atrocities had some purpose to them and were not different in kind from the terror bombing tactics of the British air force sanctioned by Winston Churchill. Irving's contention that Hitler was a normal wartime leader is an effort to deal a knock-out punch to the psycho-historians.

What kind of wartime leader was Hitler? Irving finds him quite ineffective. He was unable to assert his authority, and as he became increasingly enmeshed in the minutiae of tactical military decisions, his authority in other matters slipped away. His orders to develop a fighter-bomber jet plane which would be effective in thwarting an amphibious landing on the Atlantic coast were ignored and it was too late when he discovered the jet propulsion program had constructed only a fighter plane. He was consistently misled by Albert Speer and the Peenemünde rocket scientists about both the progress and the potential of the A-4 program so that he committed resources to that program which could have been more useful elsewhere. Even in military affairs, his generals frequently ignored his orders. This erosion of his authority was a pity, since Irving believes he was usually right and his subordinates wrong. Many of Hitler's plans bogged down in personal rivalries between Albert Speer, Hermann Göring, Martin Bormann, Joseph Goebbels, and Heinrich Himmler. Irving views Hitler's inability to get a grip on the machinery of state and party in Nazi Germany and the resulting slackness of effort and inefficiencies as his greatest failure.

Irving believes that Hitler as a military leader tended to lose his nerve and never mastered the ability to deploy effectively large armies; but despite these reservations, his admiration of Hitler's military gifts shines through. He believes that Hitler had gained great technical mastery through an impressive systematic reading program and that he knew by heart the great works of military strategy by Frederick II, Moltke, Schlieffen, and Clausewitz. His instincts were almost always right and his generals were by no means as perspicacious as they claimed after the war.

Time and again the author confounds the conventional wisdom about Hitler's military mistakes. He shows that Hitler was receiving intelligence reports of ominous military preparations in the Soviet Union, and presents Hitler's attack in June, 1941, as a preventive war instead of a gratuitous military blunder brought about by an irrational obsession for *Lebensraum.* Given the fatal underestimation by German intelligence of Soviet military capacity, Hitler's decision to attack was perfectly reasonable and his optimism was shared by the entire army. Only Göring and Admiral Erich Raeder had misgivings.

Irving believes that Hitler's plan to encircle Moscow was much sounder than the direct assault favored by General Brauchitsch and the army. If Hitler had not been ill at the crucial moment, the generals might not have been able to subvert his plans and Moscow might have fallen. That winter, during the crisis of the Soviet offensive before Moscow, it was Hitler who saved the day by his determination and courage, which prevented his dispirited generals from retreating. In the summer offensive of 1942, General Bock repeatedly resisted Hitler's orders to move his armored divisions south, and a chance to encircle the Russian army was lost. Hitler was frequently betrayed by German intelligence, which grievously underestimated Russian reserves and which completely failed to predict the Soviet summer offensive of 1942, despite Hitler's gravest misgivings and explicit requests by him to be alert for an offensive.

Irving argues that the monumental catastrophe at Stalingrad was a shared responsibility, but, as in so many things, after the war it was blamed on Hitler through fudged memoirs, fake diaries, and tampered OKW diaries. Hitler's mistake was to brag prematurely and publicly about the fall of Stalingrad, and this made him loathe to abandon the effort. Once the Soviets had encircled the city, Hitler, contrary to postwar reports, was surrounded by optimistic generals who believed that the Soviet encirclement was temporary. By December 18, breakout had become a logistical impossibility and so all the talk about Hitler's blind refusal to allow it lacks substance. Moreover, the Sixth Army was tying down seventy Soviet divisions which could have jeopardized the entire southern front if released.

Irving shows that it is a myth that Hitler never allowed strategical retreats. It was not until 1944, after Russian troops had entered German territory, that he issued a no retreat order. He repeatedly urged on his generals his prediction that the Allied invasion would be in Normandy or Brittany, but they ignored him in favor of their expectation of a direct cross channel invasion. Then German intelligence vastly overestimated Allied reserve strength, causing Hitler to hesitate to commit his reserves because of his fear of a second invasion in another place. The collapse of the eastern front in the summer of 1944 was abetted by defeatist generals who advised their men to surrender. Only Hitler prevented a complete collapse; without him, Irving believes the Russians would have been on the Rhine within a month.

Irving does not believe that Hitler's hope of reversing the course of the war during the last year was mere fantasy. He had ordered the Luftwaffe to build up a secret reserve of fighter planes which would enable him to throw two thousand planes into the struggle for France at one stroke. One hundred and fifty new Mark XXI submarines were to be ready by the end of 1944. The disagreement over Poland between the Allies lent substance to the hope that the Soviet-Anglo-American alliance would split if Germany could gain time. Irving believes Hitler could have reaped the cold war benefits that fell to Konrad Adenauer if he could have prolonged the war another year or so.

This notion that the Allies might have come to some sort of accommodation with Hitler, despite all that he had done, is a remarkable one to say the least. It is reflected in perhaps its most vexing form in Irving's idea that Churchill's policies were unfortunate for Britain. Irving continually emphasizes that Hitler had no designs on the British empire. He seems to agree with Hitler that it would seem more natural for Germany and England to be fighting Bolsheviks and the Yellow Peril together instead of Germany and Japan fighting Great Britain and Soviet Russia, to the mutual ruin of European supremacy. Without ever quite saying so, he leaves the impression that the Duke of Windsor, with his pro-Fascist leanings and his hopes to mediate between Great Britain and Germany, understood British interests better than Churchill.

Such eccentric judgments only detract from the real value of Irving's book. His meticulous analysis of the decision-making process in Germany during the war is an indispensible antidote to the self-serving memoirs of Speer, General Heinz Guderian, and Field Marshal Erich von Manstein. No other book provides a closer examination of Hitler as a war leader. Irving's persuasive demonstration of the limitations of Hitler's authority should lay to rest once and for all the Hitler-as-scapegoat school of history. His portrayal of Hitler as a man whose decisions were always rational and usually right but who failed because he was an ineffective leader who was unable to impose his will on his subordinates is an important revision of the conventional view and deserves consideration. But Irving's narrow focus prevents a definitive portrait of Hitler, and his curious lack of understanding about the meaning of the war will leave some with the impression that he goes beyond revision to exoneration, and this fault may prevent the book from receiving a serious hearing.

Paul B. Kern

HOW TO SAVE YOUR OWN LIFE

Author: Erica Jong (1942–   )
Publisher: Holt, Rinehart and Winston (New York). 310 pp. $8.95
Type of work: Novel
Time: The 1970's
Locale: New York, Hollywood

A sequel to Fear of Flying *which traces the protagonist, Isadora Wing, as she flies west to Hollywood, migrates back to New York to leave her husband, and then soars westward again to a new lover*

> Principal characters:
> ISADORA WING, the heroine
> BENNETT WING, her husband
> JOSH ACE, her lover

In *Fear of Flying* Erica Jong created a female protagonist who tried to rid herself of the trappings of home, husband, and security when she ran off on a journey through Europe with Adrian Goodlove, a British, nonchalant, often physically impotent psychiatrist. Although Adrian and Bennett Wing, Isadora's husband, shared the same profession, Adrian was more exotic than her Chinese spouse because he was so unpredictable. After Adrian left her in Paris, however, Isadora returned to Bennett's hotel room to take a bath. *How to Save Your Own Life* begins three years after the events of this first novel. It is obvious that Isadora needed more than a physical cleansing, and, unfortunately, the prose and ideas offered in Erica Jong's new novel are tepid, like bathwater that has been sitting for too long.

As *A Chorus Line* is a Broadway musical about the problems that dancers face when trying out for such a production, so *How to Save Your Own Life* is a novel about the personal and professional difficulties that a famous novelist encounters when she achieves fame. In the middle of this novel she announces to her readers that her next book will be entitled *How to Save Your Own Life;* this is the book we are reading. Who has created these pages—Isadora Wing, Erica Jong, or the fictitious Candida Wong of the equally fictitious *Candida Confesses* that is related somehow to Isadora Wing of *Fear of Flying?* The identification crisis that Isadora Wing grapples with in the text when she tries to disassociate herself from Candida Wong presents serious difficulties for the reader who tries to discern who is the "amanuensis to the Zeitgeist?" Perhaps, Ms. Wong-Wing-Jong has revived the mixture of autobiography and fiction that was so popular during the 1920's in American literature. After all, F. Scott Fitzgerald purportedly lifted passages from Zelda's diary as well as excerpts from their lives when writing his short stories and novels; certainly, the same literary license should be available to a female writer of the 1970's. Besides, now someone might write a sympathetic biography of Mr. Jong's life.

In the novel, the problem of merging autobiography and fiction is one with which Isadora and Bennett must deal, but which they never really resolve. From a female writer's point of view, Bennett is exposed as a husband who can come to terms with his wife's spiritual and sexual undressing, but forbids her and threatens to leave her if she uses his past experiences in her new novel. Isadora resents and refuses to tolerate this attitude. She writes, "It is one thing to demythicize women, to expose one's self—but it is quite another to demythicize men, to expose one's husband. A man's hypocrisy is his castle." It is this hypocrisy and the hypocrisy of others that greatly disturb Isadora. Bennett is constantly being praised for putting up with a wife who has written a book that confirms that not only do heroines actually have sexual fantasies, but that they also confess them. The thought that he is now telling her what to write and what not to write about infuriates her artistic sensibilities. She is tired of the patient, humorless husband role that Bennett has chosen to play, and she desires to become the wife who threatens to embarrass him professionally.

Although Candida confessed openly, Bennett has waited several years to reveal his longterm love affair with Penny Prather. Isadora is personally hurt when she discovers that he could feel passion for another woman; however, when she realizes that Penny and Bennett had been using her study—where she wrote her first poems and stories—for their assignations, she is professionally outraged. Her anger is intensified by the realization that they had been reading her unpublished manuscripts after coitus. Such castles of hypocrisy must be torn down with waves of prose. And so she writes, and often writes well, even though Bennett warns her at the end of the novel as she leaves him that she can never do so again without him.

Personal and professional hostilities mesh and embitter Isadora, too, as she remembers Bennett insisted that she use his name at the end of her poems and on the cover of her novel. Isadora, before overcoming her fear of flying, was troubled by what name to use. At first, she signed her poems with her maiden name, "Isadora White," but Bennett was disturbed and disappointed and characteristically reacted as a Freudian psychiatrist would—such a choice obviously pointed to a preference of father over husband. Isadora, too, responded in a characteristic manner by feeling guilty. Now, though, with newly discovered fame and hostility, she resents his having his name emblazoned upon jacket covers and gilded editions, and being listed in *Who's Who*. Her name has been lost, while his has been made famous by her efforts.

Isadora's successful efforts and notoriety, however, are often troublesome to her. At a writing conference in Chicago, she dislikes being committed to obligatory publishing parties where she receives distasteful sexual propositions and tiresome requests to read manuscripts written by some stranger's nephew. Although she can remember when she thought of editors and publishers as demigods, she is not ready for this kind of acceptance. Alone in her hotel room, she is physically, mentally, and emotionally frustrated. Isadora masturbates and relieves one of her anxieties, but two others remain. While she lies in bed, she imagines that a series of critics, like a chorus in a Greek play, enter her room and pronounce her work "dead." However, it is her heart, not her mind, that seeks flight. She feels as if she is dying, and, after some hesitation, places a call to Bennett. This interruption of his sleep annoys him, and he cryptically tells her to write a poem.

The professional psychiatrist gives the advice of a professional writer, while Isadora, the professional writer, acts as a psychiatrist to the authors of fan letters that resemble those of a "Miss Lonelyhearts" column. One such letter is included in the novel, complete with mental and written replies. What Isadora thinks, in this case, is not what she writes. The interchanging of roles between Isadora and Bennett is like the streamers of a mismanaged Maypole: they keep passing one another while weaving a web of misunderstanding in the rite of marriage.

Like Johann and Marianne in Bergman's *Scenes from a Marriage*, Isadora and Bennett have stopped speaking the same language. Their conversations are filled with deception and lies. Since the reader is allowed to see what Isadora is actually thinking and can with some imagination assume what Bennett is thinking, an end to this relationship is welcomed, but it is very slow in coming. First, the female protagonist feels drawn to recount the details and circumstances surrounding Bennett's affair with Penny. The living conditions in an Army camp in Germany during the late 1960's, the disastrous skiing trip that resulted in Isadora's breaking her leg, and her frequent conversations with a male friend all help Isadora to put together the pieces of a past that make her present seem less fragmented, yet neither complete nor solidified.

Before she plunges herself into the past, she attempts to formulate a picture of herself through the network of her friends. To avoid seeing Bennett, she visits with all seven of them. Through these characters, the reader is given some glimpses into Isadora's past self and present personal problems. Gretchen Kendall, a feminist lawyer, tells her that she's heard this "I'm leaving Bennett" routine before and encourages her this time to do so; Hope Lowell, her fairy godmother and muse, says the same thing—only more poetically (what else would you expect from a muse?)—and reaffirms the beauty of love; Abigail Schwartz, her shrink, helps Isadora to uncover past repressions; Jeffrey Rudner, a doctor and her lover, offers her sexual gratification; Jeffrey Roberts, a writer for cosmetic advertisements, offers the same on a permanent basis; Holly, an artist and cultivator of ferns, tells her to live and love because she is a mammal, not a fern; and, Michael Cosman, a general practitioner from Great Neck, helps her to become hysterical and then advises her to return after she is more rational. Isadora states that writing takes an enormous amount of energy. How can she have any left after all these conversations, all of which belabor the issue of her leaving Bennett?

Sprinkled throughout the pages that explore Isadora's hesitation about leaving Bennett are explicit passages of their sexual encounters; however, none are as detailed nor as sensual as the excerpts which describe her lesbian affair with Rosanna Howard before her trip to Hollywood or her participation in an orgy at Rosanna's home after her journey to the Coast. To Isadora, lesbianism is exciting, sexually fulfilling, but distasteful. The orgy helps her to link up with anyone—except Bennett. Both provide her with brand new experiences in her life that now excludes Bennett.

Sandwiched in between these encounters is a *bona fide* love affair. In Hollywood, Isadora meets and loves Josh Ace, a twenty-six-year-old bearded screenwriter. Isadora and Josh speak the same language, and often they stay up all night doing so. He loves her writing and does not want to become a mere character in her next novel. Josh desires her life and gets it.

Something peculiar happens to Isadora's observations in this celluloid area of Hollywood. The castles of hypocrisy are now real ones, but she does not desire to destroy any of them. She becomes extremely visual and studies outward appearances like the eye of a camera. Colors, textures, sizes, and shapes assume an unaccustomed importance. Palm trees, pink hotels, big cars, parties, drugs, Jacuzzis, posh apartments, mansions, and Olympic-size swimming pools are the accoutrements that accompany this change about people and things. Feminism is metamorphosed into femininity, as even the act of coitus has lost its former significance. In addition, she is duped by a slick female producer who wants to make a film of *Candida Confesses.* Beliefs and artistic sensibilities, which were once of supreme importance, become in California quite meaningless. So, when she returns to New York on business she writes to Josh and ultimately leaves Bennett.

How to Save Your Own Life, then, is anything but a novel about how to do so. Jeannie Morton, Isadora's friend who commits suicide the summer before the protagonist's journey to California, advises her to live. Yet, Isadora relies more on other people's advice, security, and chance meetings than she does upon herself in her how-to-do-it-yourself manual. She does not leave Bennett until she is reassured of Josh's love, and in this new affair, she succumbs to the power of the male-dominated relationship. She moves to Hollywood to join her lover and previously mailed poems, which are included in this text. Although passages from this novel are as powerful as those found in her first, it seems that Isadora Wing has conquered her fear of flying, but is now afraid to tread alone on the ground.

Kathryn Flaris

HUGO BLACK AND THE JUDICIAL REVOLUTION

Author: Gerald T. Dunne
Publisher: Simon and Schuster (New York). Illustrated. 492 pp. $12.50
Type of work: Biography
Time: 1886–1971
Locale: Clay County and Birmingham, Alabama; Washington, D.C.

A biography which illuminates Hugo L. Black's influential personality while it stresses his part in altering the role of the Supreme Court and the doctrines of constitutional law

> *Principal personages:*
> HUGO LA FAYETTE BLACK, United States Senator from Alabama and
>   Justice of the Supreme Court of the United States
> FRANKLIN D. ROOSEVELT, President of the United States
> WILLIAM O. DOUGLAS,
> FELIX FRANKFURTER, and
> ROBERT H. JACKSON, Justices of the Supreme Court
> EARL WARREN, Chief Justice of the Supreme Court

Justice Oliver Wendell Holmes is reported to have attributed much of John Marshall's greatness to the fact that he was *there*—present in the early shaping years. It is also true of Marshall, Holmes himself, and a number of other notable justices that they were there for a long time. The serious-minded ought not assess such statements too lightly, but they are justified in noting other characteristic qualities of great justices, such as intellectual power and clarity; the courage of conviction; an instinct for essentials; and persuasiveness with brethren of the Court, the bar, and the public.

By such criteria, Hugo Black belongs in the category of influential judges, and high on the list. Gerald Dunne's account uses still another basis to judge Black's importance: Black as Justice was participant, protagonist, and sometimes driving force in great changes in the thinking of the Supreme Court.

One of the virtues of Dunne's account is his emphasis on the complexity of and the contradictions in Black's character. In so much writing about the Court, its work, and its divisions, justices are forced into categories—liberal or conservative, activist or defender of the status quo—and it is a matter of relief, even rejoicing, to find a biographer who understands that paradoxical, shifting human qualities cannot be thus constricted. Black the man, not just Black the Justice, is Dunne's subject, and the paradoxes and contradictions abound.

By inference rather than explicit statement, Dunne links Black's character to his background and development. Born in the hill country of Clay County to a storekeeping father and given a strict Baptist upbringing by a family very concerned about education, Black earned a law degree at twenty, and built a career in Birmingham as a lawyer for unions and the poor, a prosecutor, and a police-court judge. Ambition, intelligence, and combativeness were notable traits in his personality; so was a strain of thought and behavior most easily classed as Populist. Ambition and demagoguery, Dunne suggests, were not absent, but they were not the whole story.

The climax of Black's early career was election to the United States Senate, after a campaign marked by energy, skill with publicity, and appeal to the poor and unprivileged. His newspaper advertisements, in an obvious thrust at the lists of notables sponsoring opponents, read "Paid for by himself." Black's election was also important for an episode that was later to create great difficulty and controversy in his career. The Ku Klux Klan was a power in Alabama politics, and Hugo Black, for whatever reasons, joined; he resigned in time for the Senate campaign, but the resignation (accusers could say) reads like a formality, and he unquestioningly had Klan support.

The new Senator made something of a reputation as a radical, and began a course of self-education. He also faced, in 1928, a severe test for a politician in officially dry, Protestant, Klannish Alabama: the nomination of Alfred E. Smith of New York, an urban Catholic. Black's Senate colleague, J. Thomas Heflin, probably the most notorious of anti-Catholic prominent politicians, left the party. Black formally endorsed Smith; but he had not attended the convention that nominated him, and he remained quiet through the whole campaign, as Dunne emphasizes.

The significant Senate career of Hugo Black began with the Depression and with the election of Franklin Roosevelt and a Democratic Senate and House. Black's reelection in Alabama gave him a new position in the Senate; his main attention was on the recovery and reform of the crippled economy. He sponsored labor bills and he joined with George Norris in the battle for the Tennessee Valley Authority—a continuation of an old feud with Alabama Power. But his notable success, according to Dunne, was not legislative, but investigatory.

In fact, Black's conduct of Senate inquiries is, with the Klan episode, a major thread in Dunne's outline of his subject's career. Certainly, it gave Black his first national reputation. Chairing a committee investigation of public utilities, he displayed all the prosecutor's skill in finding the weaknesses in the testimony of hostile or reluctant witnesses, and revealing their confusions and contradictions. Witnesses and their friends complained of browbeating, and many people questioned the legality of Black's methods in acquiring private papers, and subpoenaing whole categories of telegrams from Western Union.

Dunne also points out that, if the ostensible purpose of the inquiries was legislative—writing laws to prevent repetition of the abuses of the 1920's—its main result, and quite possibly Black's objective, was to focus public attention on the abuses, and direct public anger against the utility magnates, lobbyists, and their political servants whom he accused of perpetrating them. For this, not the judicial or the legislative but, rather, the prosecutor's role was required. Even more, says Dunne, what it required was skill in reaching public opinion—in other words, using the media, which in the 1930's meant to some extent radio and motion pictures, but mainly the newspaper and magazine press. This skill, Dunne argues, Black had in a high degree—in fact, next to the master himself, Roosevelt. A certain cynicism goes with this—Dunne more than once quotes

Chairman Black to the press outside the hearing room, "Come on, boys; the show's going to start."

The conduct of the utility hearings made Black known and, in the expected circles, hated. It also made him one of the most reliable and outspoken New Dealers. Dunne even speculates on his chances for the 1940 Democratic nomination, at least for the vice-presidency. In Roosevelt's word, that one is "iffy," but it suggests something of Black's record and repute, and helps explain the shock-effect among the opponents of the New Deal when Roosevelt gave his first Supreme Court appointment to Black, and in circumstances embittered by the recent ill-fated proposal to "pack" or "reform" the Court. However, the tremors were nothing compared to the revelation, after Senate confirmation, and after Black had privately taken the oath, of his past membership in the Ku Klux Klan. Dunne tells the story early, out of chronological order, but effectively, and again stresses Black's talent for using the media, in his account of the radio address in which Black defended himself, and, apparently, closed his side of the controversy.

The real story of Hugo Black, and the meat of Dunne's book, begins here. Justice Black left much more of a mark on the nation than Senator Black, and his judicial career was even more subject to controversy than his senatorial one. There were arguments over constitutional law, and over the policies the law inhibits or permits; there were (at least in the gossip columns) personal antipathies and conflicting ambitions among the "brethren" (as the justices call one another); there was the sometimes underlying and frequently dominating issue of the stance and function of the Court itself. In other words, Black was at the center of what Dunne rightly calls a judicial revolution. Its exact nature, and its intertwining with the forces suggested above, and still others, is examined. And the author is too careful, too aware of the complexity of his subject, to oversimplify or generalize.

In the 1920's and 1930's, the Supreme Court had been accused of substituting its judgment of policy for that of elected legislatures. This was especially the case in the use of the Fourteenth Amendment to limit the states' power to regulate business and industry, and to protect both property and contract. The dissents of Holmes and Stone, particularly, accused the majority of reading their social and economic preconceptions into the Constitution. The "Roosevelt Court," whose reconstitution began with the Black appointment, reversed that trend. Though some decisions of the term preceding began the reversal, no longer was New Deal legislation constantly running the risk of unconstitutionality. Many of the same commentators and justices, however, who had condemned the use (or abuse) of the Fourteenth Amendment in economic matters, and who had called for self-restraint by the Court, had also wanted a more active Court in defense of individual rights and liberties.

Here were great problems for the Roosevelt Court, which were to be inherited by the Warren Court of the 1950's as well. The legal problem, which Dunne explicates by cases rather than abstract exposition, is twofold. First, to what extent can the Court make the Bill of Rights bind the national government? The issues are not only of First Amendment freedoms of speech and religion, but of procedural rights, and protection from self-incrimination, search and seizure, and the like. Here Black's position was emphatic, and many thought extreme: he read the Constitution literally. The second issue concerns the states. Traditional doctrine held that the Bill of Rights bound the Congress, not the states, and that the Fourteenth Amendment had not fundamentally changed the rule. Black and others began to hold the "incorporation" theory—that the Fourteenth Amendment made the other amendments binding also on the states.

In addition to a full examination of Black's judicial record, Dunne relates the clashes of principle and of personality on the bench and in chambers that Black had with other justices, notably Robert Jackson and Felix Frankfurter. The charges leveled against Black and the majority of the Court were similar to those brought by earlier critics of the "conservative" Court: the justices were making law and policy, not judging; they were writing sociological, not constitutional, opinions; they were usurping the place of the legislatures; they were moving into a political thicket. Throughout the public issues, however, Dunne's focus is always on Black. The picture he paints is of a man aggressive in the Senate and in judicial argument, as well as on the tennis court, yet noted for charm and kindliness; acclaimed by the liberals, yet old-fashioned in his patriotism and even more in his unsophisticated, literal view of the Constitution.

Hugo Black and the Judicial Revolution is not a book only for scholars; Dunne's remarkable achievement is that his interpretation, for all its insistence on complexity, is clear. Any layman with a reasonable knowledge of recent history and constitutional government will benefit from this lucid and intelligent account.

George J. Fleming

THE HUMAN SITUATION
Lectures at Santa Barbara, 1959

Author: Aldous Huxley (1894–1963)
Edited by Piero Ferrucci
Publisher: Harper & Row Publishers (New York). 261 pp. $10.00
Type of work: Essays
Time: The twentieth century

A series of lectures which examines the planet on which we live and our place in the ecology as well as man's relationship to his society

Aldous Huxley was one of the great minds and writers of the twentieth century. A Britisher educated at Eton and Oxford, he turned to literature in his twenties, becoming internationally known as a novelist. Although his work as a novelist still tends to overshadow his other writings, he was also the author of essays, biography, drama, poetry, and short stories. Prior to World War II he migrated to the United States, where he lived until his death. According to his editor, Piero Ferrucci, Huxley delivered the present series of lectures, or ones very like them, at a number of institutions, including the Massachusetts Institute of Technology and the Menninger Foundation. The editor reports that he chose the series delivered at Santa Barbara for the University of California because that series was the most comprehensive.

This series of essays includes sixteen of the original seventeen; the editor omitted the eighth lecture, entitled "The Future Is in Our Hands," because it was but a summary of the preceding ones. Of these lectures Huxley wrote, early in January, 1959, to Matthew Huxley, that he intended beginning with the biological foundations of the human situation, such as the state of our planet, population problems, and the relationship of heredity to environment. He said he would then proceed to treat of techniques in every field of human endeavor and how such activity affected the social and political order. Finally, as he put it, he would discuss the individual human being and his potentialities. Of the task he had undertaken Huxley commented, "It is an impossibly large project—but worth undertaking even inadequately, as an antidote to academic specialization and fragmentation." Few persons living in the twentieth century could do what Huxley did in these essays, for he called upon a wide-ranging experience and knowledge to help his readers better understand the problems human beings share with one another. Although eighteen years elapsed from the delivery of the lectures by Aldous Huxley to their publication in 1977, they remain surprisingly adequate and up-to-date; pieces of information contained within them have become outdated, but the essays themselves remain remarkably pertinent for their readers. Huxley set out to build bridges between art and science, between objectively observed facts and immediate experience, and between morals and scientific appraisals; he styled himself, indeed, *pontifex*, or bridge-builder. He believed that the man of letters can perform a valuable function by bringing together a great many subjects, showing the relationships among them. Our educations, as much now as when he spoke, lead us to keep separate what we learn from our immediate experience.

Before such interests were as popular as they are today, Aldous Huxley began his series of lectures by looking at the relationships between mankind and our native planet. In "Man and His Planet," Huxley ranges through some of the effects man has had on our environment, some of them good, but many of them destructive. He notes that we have deforested huge areas of the world in the interests of agriculture, only to have faulty agricultural practices ruin the soil over the centuries. He reminds us that the forests of Europe, which once covered most of the continent, were also devoured for such reasons as building houses, heating buildings, constructing ships, making glass, and smelting metal ores. What we do and have been doing, he rightly tells us, makes a gloomy picture. We need, he suggests, to see the use of the environment in more than a purely practical way, to look at it from a moral and aesthetic stance—as he puts it, "with a philosophical trend in our mind." In "More Nature in Art," the next essay in the series, he states that we have the necessary information and knowledge to prevent further ecological damage, even to repair much past damage, but that there is a gap between what can be done and the likelihood of its being done, for changes in our treatment of our world involve hundreds of millions of people. New ideas must be communicated to those people and, even more difficult, they must be persuaded to adopt ideas and methods which, if imposing temporary hardship, insure long-term benefits. Committed as we are in Western civilization to education, persuasion, and democratic methods, we nevertheless find the task of changing people's ways more difficult than if we adopt coercion. Huxley makes the interesting and unusual point that our art could help, if artists working in all media returned to representational modes from their present use of abstract forms. Such a realistic art, combined with a good ethic and a good philosophy, would, he suggests, greatly enhance our chances of salvaging, even improving, our planet.

Of all the essays in this present collection, perhaps "The Population Explosion" will seem most relevant two decades after it was written, if for no other reason than that its topic has been one which has had considerable public attention. But the chief interest in this essay ought to be on what Huxley says about the relation of population to human well-being and human values in general. Population figures are for most persons difficult to understand fully; the meaning of some of Huxley's examples may escape both our understandings and our imaginations—such examples as that in early Paleolithic times the total human population on earth was probably less than twenty million, or that in the fifteenth century there were fewer than a million Indians in North America east of the Rocky Mountains. Even such a recent change as the more-than-fifty-percent increase of the population of the United States since 1940 is a difficult concept to understand, even among people old enough to have experienced and observed the change. But the real thrust of Huxley's essay is not statistical: he asks first of all what the practical alternatives are. He suggests that one choice is to let nature solve the problem, through starvation, disease, and warfare. Another choice is to increase industrial and agricultural production, but it appears already that we must collectively work harder to stay where we are. His third alternative is to increase production while at the same time trying to reestablish the balance between birth and death rates by intelligent and humane methods. Huxley understands the difficulties, which he terms colossal, in limiting population, for controlling the birth rate is a problem involving medicine, chemistry, biochemistry, physiology, sociology, psychology, theology, and education. One specific problem, he tells us, is that some worldwide, or at least regional, agreements on birth control will be necessary for success, but that political leaders do not think in biological terms. Furthermore, the rapid population increase makes educating people and raising the material standard of life almost impossible.

When Huxley moves to looking at the individual human being, he becomes most interesting, for he espouses causes which he knows have not found favor in many quarters. His positions sometimes run counter to ideas which have become institutionalized, so that his positions threaten vested interests. For example, Huxley takes to task the behavioral psychologists, including J. B. Watson and B. F. Skinner, pointing out that they have clearly tended to eliminate hereditary factors as influences on human behavior, without regard for what geneticists have proved to be true. Huxley also suggests that modern psychiatry has neglected the genetic influence on mankind because its practitioners and theorists have simply paid no attention to the human body. Huxley's conclusion is that to make the most of the genetic variability which exists in humankind we must improve the environment, but that we can disregard genetics only if we are willing to imperil our values. He develops a monistic view which insists on bringing mind and body together, not separating them, as philosophers and theologians through the ages often have done.

The lectures contained in *The Human Situation* were given in two groups. In the group delivered in the spring of 1959, Huxley tried to look at the future of the world, suggesting that the most prominent view of the world is one of tempered optimism, but that nuclear weapons, especially the hydrogen bomb, have reintroduced the old idea that the world could end abruptly and catastrophically. Following the lead of Bertrand Russell, Huxley looks at three short-term possibilities. One is nuclear war which eliminates mankind; the second, nuclear war leading to a return to barbarism because of the breakdown of the complicated industrial and communications systems; the third, the creation of a single world state. While Huxley sees the third as the only desirable alternative, he recognizes that there are many vested interests which militate against its happening by any democratic means. But for the short-term in our future Huxley says he hopes for more attention to basic scientific research, for he stoutly believes that we stand on the threshold of profound discoveries about our human nature and external nature.

In the lectures delivered later, in the autumn of 1959, Huxley turned from the world as a whole to looking at individual human potentialities. He believed it important that we recognize the profound difference between the generalizations we can make about societies and the generalizations we can make about individuals. In "The Individual Life of Man," Huxley tries to prove that the single human being's life lies quite largely outside the history of a given time, outside the activities which historians later see as significant. Huxley cites Vasili Rozanov's view of private life: "picking one's nose and looking at the sunset." Huxley calls this a beautiful definition, given the interpretation that private life consists in enjoying one's own physiological reactions and one's own aesthetic and inspirational reactions. One result of our focus on private life, he insists, is that we do not experience progress subjectively, although we may observe it, either at firsthand or through our reading. A second result of the focus on private life is that we interpret the world in terms of the individual's life, which is nonprogressive; old people going down find it at least difficult to see the world around them as going up.

In the latter lectures of the series which deal with the individual human being it is a different Huxley speaking from the one in the earlier lectures, or at least a different Huxley from the one known to readers of his novels and other earlier work. In the latter lectures he turns, in part, from science to mysticism, from observation to vision. Over and over, the reader sees him trying to unite the realm of common sense with the realm of vision. In the essay entitled "The Ego," the author reviews conceptions of mankind from Homer to the present, and proposes that our physical constitution equals our unconscious, that we are the kinds of individuals we are because of our very organisms. For the most part, he bases this view on his understanding of William H. Sheldon's work in describing human beings psychologically, as well as physiologically, in terms of their being combinations of three physical types: the endomorph, the mesomorph, and the ectomorph.

So, too, in "The Unconscious," Huxley takes an uncommon view. He deplores the refusal of openminded scientific people to consider such phenomena as telepathy, clairvoyance, and precognition. He insists that we must learn to think in terms of parapsychology, even though, as he puts it, in academic circles parapsychology is regarded as a kind of intellectual pornography. Huxley also espouses a positive view of visions in the "Natural History of Visions." He examines the induction of visions by isolation, hunger, and drugs, and speaks with great sympathy of inducing visions by changes in body chemistry through the use of drugs. Rather than seeing such use of drugs, whether natural or synthetic, as distortions of the human organism, he praises the distortions as mind-expanding and transcendent. Further, in his final lecture he speaks glowingly about using drugs to enable persons to achieve their potentialities in the material world as well as in a world of visions. He hopes that pharmacological means can be found to increase human efficiency and endurance, to give psychic energy, and to enable us to endure sustained tension. It was this interest in consciousness-expanding techniques which gave Huxley a new career and new fame late in life, as an exponent of psychosynthesis.

Gordon W. Clarke

I HEARD MY SISTER SPEAK MY NAME

Author: Thomas Savage (1915–   )
Publisher: Little, Brown and Company (Boston). 242 pp. $8.95
Type of work: Novel
Time: The present, with flashbacks
Locale: Crow Point, Maine; Seattle, Washington

A genealogical tracing of a family through four generations, culminating in the reunion of brother and sister

> *Principal characters:*
> TOM BURTON, a successful novelist
> AMY McKINNEY NOFZINGER, his sister adopted at birth by the McKinneys
> ELIZABETH (BETH) SWERINGEN BURTON, his mother
> EMMA SWERINGEN, THE SHEEP QUEEN, his grandmother

Tom Burton, the central character of Thomas Savage's tenth novel, is patterned very closely on the author. They are the same age, and both are novelists with the same publisher; their immediate families are also similar. Whether the rest of the novel is factual is not relevant, for Savage writes convincingly of the forebears of the fictional Tom Burton. In a novel whose title gives away its punch line as this one does, it is difficult to maintain suspense, but the intricate weaving of the many strands of the story keeps the reader wondering how the various parts will ultimately fit together. The book achieves its intrigue through the author's juggling of several storylines, switching from one time and locale to another, without supplying the necessary connections until the pieces begin falling into place by themselves. Gradually all coalesces at the end.

The book opens with a description of Tom Burton and his family in their home at Crow Point, on the Maine coast. We learn of Tom's career as a novelist and of his novelist wife and grown children. We also get a hint of his family heritage from his comments that his aunts could not understand why he would leave the Rocky Mountains, and that he wanted to get as far as he could from the Montana ranch of his youth where his "beautiful, angel mother" was so unhappy. This idyllic introduction is abruptly dropped as the next chapter begins the apparently unrelated episode of a young twenty-two-year-old mother giving up her newborn child in the year 1912. This child turns out to be Amy McKinney.

Amy McKinney's life is then related in detail. She is adopted by the McKinneys to replace their own son who had been killed by being thrown from a horse. The McKinneys were good, ordinary, uninspired people. Amy's life is only briefly disturbed when a malicious child acquaintance mentions that she is an adopted child. But Amy quickly recovers from the shock and accepts her foster mother's reassurances. After the death of her adoptive parents she goes through a rather loveless and sterile marriage with Philip Nofzinger, followed by a very amicable divorce.

Throughout his description of Amy's life, Savage's keen sense of family ties is evident. That is, Amy's whole existence, though not marred by any overt tragedy, comes across as a very dull, uninspiring, almost emotionless affair. She feels no real sense of belonging to a family, and since she has no siblings, the death of her parents ends any sense of belonging. Her cousins feel that the family's prized silverware should go to real family rather than to the adopted outsider. Savage is guilty of stacking the cards against Amy. The McKinneys are not consciously comparing Amy to their own lost child and thus depriving her of a normal childhood; they are giving her the best of which they are capable. They are simply a stodgy couple who keep to themselves and would rear any child to be dull and emotionally deprived.

It is only after her divorce that Amy seriously thinks of the note her father had left in his safe deposit box for her. Mr. McKinney had believed in the right of an adopted child to learn of her real parents despite the laws to the contrary, and being a lawyer he had had the wherewithal to procure the name her mother had signed on the release papers. With the help of a lawyer Amy discovers the real names of her mother and father, and after a fruitless search for her father (she was directed to a deceased derelict with a similar name), she is apparently reconciled to never discovering who her real parents are. With this the story of Amy gives way to a new set of characters.

The second section of the book is set in the small, dying mining town of Jeff Davis Gulch where one of the last remaining prospectors, George Sweringen, discovers gold. George and his family are dropped while the narration picks up Emma Russell, who "quite a long time ago" left Illinois for Idaho Territory to teach school. In Idaho, the plain but highly intelligent Emma marries Thomas Sweringen, the son of George, who had invested his gold in property and had begun a dynasty. The major portion of the book deals with Emma, whose shrewdness and luck in business results in her increasing the family's holdings and becoming known as the Sheep Queen. All through the relation of these events the reader is kept guessing what each segment of the story has to do with the others; and unless he is keeping track of the names and the confusing chronology of events, he will not see the connection. It is part of Savage's technique to give clues by reference to historical events such as the inaugural date of Benjamin Harrison and the date on which Idaho became a territory; and the reader must keep track of the complex time sequence.

The Sheep Queen and her family, especially her daughter, Elizabeth, are lovingly and minutely described. Elizabeth is much more attractive than her mother; she is her father's favorite child and is given the best education possible. When the story is picked up, she is promised to a young man of good family whom she does not love. Here, family ties are strained. Her father sympathizes with her lack of love for her fiancé, but her mother is more concerned with amassing new family ties as if they were another piece of property. This is the only lapse the family suffers. In years to come the family's members go through many divorces, possibly because they find their own company so much better than that of anyone else. Through all, the family sticks together. Their clannishness extends to a kind of ancestor veneration because "We felt our ancestors were worth worshipping."

In this case Elizabeth disappoints her mother by forsaking her fiancé for the traveling salesman, Ben Burton. At this point, the names and events start falling into place. These are the names Amy learned of as being her parents. Yet, there is the improbability of a married couple giving up a firstborn child for adoption and keeping even the existence of such a child a closely held secret within a family that is so close.

Back in the present time, Amy's interest in her ancestors is reawakened and she gets in contact with Tom Burton's aunt expressing her belief that she is the daughter of Beth Sweringen Burton. Knowing as much as he does about his ancestry, Tom Burton of course denies the possibility. How could his mother have had a child and no one of the close-knit family known of it? Then, like a detective story gradually revealing one clue, one hazy memory of the past after another, the pieces start to fit together.

Tom's mother, Beth, who had been resigned to marry the young man of her mother's choice, decided instead to run off with the traveling salesman whom she married. Tom discovers that his mother and father, Ben Burton, were married at the time Amy was born, adding to the improbability of Amy's being an abandoned sister of his. It is impossible for him to accept that his mother could have given up a legitimate child. Illegitimacy is the only reason he can think of for a mother to give up her child, and he could not imagine his own mother could have been guilty of such a transgression. Savage cleverly depicts Tom's gradual acceptance of the fact that Amy may be the daughter of his "no good" father and another woman; he has come to believe his family's description of his father who had divorced his mother when he was two years old. His one meeting with his real father had convinced him of Ben's unreliability and phoniness. So, he is ready to accept that Amy may be his half-sister, but nothing yet can convince him they have the same mother, for Beth had signed a fictitious name to the release.

In a long, rambling letter to Amy after he has pieced things together, Tom Burton recounts the death of his mother ten years earlier. He relates that his grandfather had outlived the Sheep Queen as well as Beth, and then he states, "But there was an earlier death that accounted for the sadness that never left my mother's face even at the end." That death was of the Sheep Queen's favorite, her son Tom-Dick, who was her hope for the future of the Sweringen family. He died while his sister Beth was pregnant, and a few weeks later Beth gave birth to her first child, a girl. And because that child was a girl, Tom Burton says, his mother gave her up "to show her mother a woman could survive a loss greater than her own, greater because it was voluntary." Although this solution is highly improbable, it is due to Savage's skill as a writer that he manages to bring it off. He never even brings up the question of how Ben Burton would have taken to his wife's sacrifice; it is unlikely that a father would stand idly by and allow his flesh and blood to be given up. That the birth could have been kept secret from him as it was from Beth's sisters is more unreasonable for the reader to accept.

This highly improbable sequence of events is explained by the family's closeness. But, the point of the sacrifice seems lost if no one in the family was aware of it. (Beth's sister vaguely recalls a letter referring to a miscarriage.) If the family is so close that one member would sacrifice so much, it is small wonder that the Sweringen family is so riddled by divorce. Besides, the child itself is part of that family, and Savage does not explain how such a callous act can be reconciled in a family of such strong instincts.

Another improbability is the way Savage handles the last section of the book. When all the pieces to the puzzle have fallen into place for him, Tom Burton does not telephone as the average person would; instead he writes a letter to Amy. And this twenty-six-page letter reads more like a novel than a letter, holding off the crucial revelation until the very end, making it unlikely that the recipient would very easily follow all the details since she has not been privy to all that has gone before in the book. Yet, in spite of these minor lapses, the book succeeds in keeping the reader entertained and interested until the very end. The most serious drawback of the novel is the tremendous demand it places at times on our credulity.

Roger A. Geimer

THE ICE AGE

Author: Margaret Drabble (1930–   )
Publisher: Alfred A. Knopf (New York). 295 pp. $8.95
Type of work: Novel
Time: The present
Locale: England and Wallacia (a fictional Balkan country)

A novel whose characters lead lives disrupted by catastrophes common to our time, and thus display the problems of an iced-over England

> *Principal characters:*
> ANTHONY KEATING, a property developer
> ALISON MURRAY, his mistress
> MOLLY, Alison's ten-year-old, brain-damaged daughter
> JANE, Alison's nineteen-year-old daughter
> LEN WINCOBANK, a former property developer, now in jail
> MAUREEN KIRBY, his mistress
> GILES PETERS, Keating's partner
> KITTY FRIEDMANN, a friend of Anthony and Alison

Events associated with the characters of Margaret Drabble's latest novel when listed off seem bizarre: a mother has borne one brain-damaged child and another, now a teen-ager, who has been imprisoned in a Balkan country behind the Iron Curtain; a woman has had her foot blown off by an I.R.A. bomb in a London restaurant; a property developer has been imprisoned on fraud charges; a fairly young television executive turned property speculator has both lost his fortune and suffered a heart attack. But as the novel develops, one sees that their stories are meant to appear not freakish but representative—representative, that is, of the troubles that are afflicting British citizens and, in fact, Britain itself. Most of the exciting events have happened just before the novel begins, moreover, so that it is mainly concerned with a time of passivity and waiting; the characters are, one might say, iced in.

Like her last novel, *Realms of Gold,* Margaret Drabble's book focuses chiefly on two lovers in midlife but intertwines their story with a number of others. It is much more obvious in this novel than in the previous one, however, that the characters are types chosen to illustrate contemporary English life and the vicissitudes peculiar to it. Fortunately, Drabble's ability to develop believable and sympathetic characters and to write well in a lowkey, finely ironic style prevents the book from being boringly schematic. Moreover, her inveterate cheerfulness keeps *The Ice Age* from becoming a gloomy catalog of disasters.

Yet such a catalog may be inferred from the characterizations, events, and commentary of the novel. London is a "sinking ship," spilling over with people, garbage, and motor vehicles. Masses of concrete buildings stand empty, having proved not to be what anyone wanted to live in or rent for offices; in fact, belief in growth as an ideal to strive for has also been a casualty of the slump. No ideal or vision has replaced this belief; there is instead fear and despondency, disgust with corruption, and lack of confidence. Economically there is a slump, yet inflation accompanies recession. There is random terrorism: death can strike anywhere at any harmless, goodhearted person. Accidents, it seems, are becoming more frequent and more intense. Of course there are physical ills characteristic of our time: the heart attack that strikes a young businessman; cerebral palsy; breast cancer. Also, cracks and decay appear in domestic as well as public life: children reject old traditions, taking to drugs and easy sex; wives are dissatisfied, and both husbands and wives are unfaithful; divorces are common, so common that some people have several. Homosexuality surfaces. God is out of date, and mysterious influences from outer space are in. Intellectually there is a change, too: a classicist, committed to preserving the tradition of scholarship, finds that students are no longer interested and that in the end he has lost interest himself both in classics and in composing poetry; like a dryad in a myth he seems to have been changed into a tree.

As the list shows, Drabble has attempted to be impressive but not comprehensive. Cold War difficulties and political prisons are introduced through the scenes set in Wallacia, but international problems are otherwise omitted, as are the dangers of pollution, the evils of political corruption, the problems of dealing with labor unions, racial problems, energy problems and many others. She is suggesting a variety of typical problems of life in England today; however, she is most interested in stressing the emptiness, the lack of social values and ideals, the boredom, the selfishness, the depression, the insecurity of individuals.

As *The Ice Age* begins, its characters and England itself are sunk in depression, bogged down in problems they do not know whom to blame for and don't know what to do about: "A huge icy fist, with large cold fingers, was squeezing and chilling the people of Britain, that great and puissant nation, slowing down their blood, locking them into immobility, fixing them in a solid stasis, like fish in a frozen river." But as the novel moves along, things appear to be improving somewhat, although perhaps at glacial speed; and the end of the book is positively hopeful in a qualified way. Two-thirds through, a nightclub entertainer who specializes in insults and black comedy is introduced so that his point of view may be rejected. The English have lost their feeling of innate superiority, and they no longer deserve to be insulted and knocked about. At this point England is portrayed as not frustrated, not stuck fast, but "passing through some strange metamorphosis, through the intense creative lethargy of profound self-contemplation." Finally, the last sentence of the book assures us that "Britain will recover."

Anthony Keating is the character from whose experiences a reader can most readily discern Britain's problems and anticipate her recovery. At the beginning of the novel, Keating is on ice at his country home, High Rook House, recovering from a heart attack. He has been forbidden excitement, whiskey, cigarettes, and sex; he is quite alone and very bored. He is worried about his mistress and his business, now near bankruptcy, and his problem of how to pay for High Rook, which was bought as a refuge for simple living and loving. But, he tells himself, it appears to have been purchased too late. Perhaps Drabble is suggesting that we cannot accept the modern world, and that when we have got what we want, we retire to the life characteristic of some earlier age.

Anthony, who is thirty-eight, comes from solid, middle-class Yorkshire stock and was provided with a public school and university education. But he broke away from the tradition when he rejected the Church, rejected the idea of a profession, and went into an industry peculiar to our time, television. Eventually he found himself bored and directionless. He had no political or religious creed and nothing either calling him or driving him. At this point he rebelled even further by casting aside his career and pension and entering the risky business of buying and developing tracts of property. Drabble, who deals heavily in symbols, uses two to suggest Anthony's attitudes and problems; one is the Imperial Delight Company, and the other is his heart attack.

The name of Anthony's firm, the Imperial Delight Company (named after a candy company whose site he took over), gives a sense of the power and pleasure he felt in his new enterprise. In this novel adults love developing property as children love to eat candy. Property speculation is a romantic and exciting game to be played for personal, not social, reasons. On one piece of property is an old gas storage tank; Anthony's heart soars like a bird at the sight of his derelict gasometer. But there is no solidity either to his existence or to his business interests. In good times he felt himself to be "a modern man, an operator, at one with the spirit of the age"; when the balloon burst, the general emptiness left behind affected him as well as the age itself. An abandoned, empty gas storage tank, stripped of its romance, is emblematic of what is left.

The heart attack that lays him up is, of course, real, but it is also symbolic of the uneasiness that has attacked Anthony. He finds himself not really suited to the sharp dealings and gambles of his business and perhaps not entirely suited to Alison, his mistress. (For, like other modern men, Anthony has divorced his wife Babs, easygoing mother of his four children, and taken up with someone else.) His period of enforced physical idleness is succeeded by a protracted alcoholic debauch before the final action of the novel which leaves Anthony physically but not spiritually imprisoned. He is still iced-in, but his heart has recovered.

Len Wincobank (note the significant name) is another property developer who is now on ice in Scratby Open Prison. He and Giles Peters, one of Anthony's partners, serve as foils for each other and for Anthony. Len has made his way up from a background of mean poverty. Giles, on the other hand, is very wealthy and in fact something of a rebel in that he is refusing to be a third-generation dilettante. One has a sense of viewing a British television documentary in which persons interviewed have been carefully selected to represent the upper class, middle class, and the lower class. Both Len and Giles love risky deals. Giles is a floater who cannot sink; he grabs at anything. Though he has known Anthony since university days, he has no compunction about cheating his old friend. Len, a more attractive character, is the new businessman of the 1960's. Although he has been convicted of fraud, he is still a person of more scruples than Giles and is, furthermore, a man of greater vision. The vision, however, is not of human happiness and comfort in an enormous expanse of buildings but simply of the buildings. He lost out because lazy, complacent, stick-in-the-mud Porcaster (yes, Pork City) rejected his vision of its rebuilding and renewal. Len's mistress, Maureen Kirby, also came from a poor family; she made her way up through hairstyling, shorthand, and sex to a fine life with Len. There was a Rolls-Royce, plenty of money, luxurious travel, lots of good times. Though delighting in this childish carnival existence, Len and Maureen could hardly believe in it—luckily, because they both lost it. Though Giles, Len, and Maureen are all temporarily down, they are all resilient and at the end of the book they are all about to bounce back. Their values are selfish and their standard of conduct not high, but all have energy and intelligence, and Len and Maureen are goodhearted and exceedingly sympathetic.

"These are terrible times we live in," Kitty Friedmann, wrote to Anthony. She, too, is laid up; she lost a foot and her husband was killed when an I.R.A. bomb went off in a restaurant in London. The fearful injustice of such terrorist attacks is emphasized by Kitty's simple, generous, and friendly nature. But, like most of the other characters, she, too, is recovering.

An unhappy situation from which there is no release, however, is that of Alison Murray, a woman who has not managed to define herself or her role properly or to find emotional satisfaction. Once an established actress, she willingly renounced her career in order to be a good wife; that is, she refused to be more successful than her husband, from whom she is now divorced. When her second child, a cerebral palsy victim, was born, Alison concentrated her love on this deprived child. Her older child, in her turn deprived, grew up hostile, resentful, and self-pitying. As the novel begins, this daughter, Jane, is in prison in the Iron Curtain country of Wallacia, charged with drug possession and with killing two men in an automobile accident. This little family is thus representative of several of the disruptive ills of modern domestic life. Jane at the end of the novel will emerge from prison and show signs of abandoning her stance of determined alienation. But Molly will be forever locked in the prison of her jerky, retarded self. Finally, Alison, who has lost Anthony, appears to have invested her intelligence, her energy, her love without any emotional return. Drabble seems to suggest that Alison, like Molly, is permanently iced-in. Her suffering is simply painful; it will not open up any new life for her.

Drabble's broad canvas, her well-developed and sympathetic characters, and her technique of occasionally addressing her readers directly give the book some of the comfortableness of a nineteenth century novel. Her unobtrusively witty style, realistic detail, and ear for conversation make the book a pleasure to read. Unfortunately, the representative nature of the characters and the heavy symbolism are at times too obvious. Conversely, the basis for the author's optimism about Britain is too vague. Her faith appears to be placed in British courage and fortitude and in a Puritanical belief that suffering can sometimes be useful. Through Anthony she suggests a spiritual change; predictably this is expressed partly through symbols. The book begins as a pheasant falls; like Anthony, it has been struck by a heart attack. At the end of the novel a rare bird, a tree creeper, rises up toward the snowy mountain heights. Through disappointment and suffering, Anthony's heart has been renewed. This suggestion is nebulous but reassuring. Britain, too, one may hope, will not only survive the ice age but emerge regenerate.

Mary C. Williams

IN MEDITERRANEAN AIR

Author: Ann Stanford
Publisher: The Viking Press (New York). 88 pp. $5.95
Type of work: Poetry

Poems in six thematic divisions which are lyric without tight structure, dramatic without direct conflict, and narrative without complex plot

"One Swallow does not make a Winter" was a witticism of the 1940's inspired when Ivor Winters' disciple Alan Swallow devoted his small press to an exclusive group of poets; Ann Stanford was one of the poets who studied under Yvor Winters at Stanford, and she published her first volumes with the Swallow Press. She has since won many prizes, appeared in the Borestone "Best Poems," been included in anthologies and a variety of magazines from fugitive to slick, received fellowships, and published critical articles and books on, among many other things, women poets such as Ann Bradstreet and May Swenson.

The first poem, "Glimmerglass," sets the tone in a timeless place, the center from which the circular plot with its portraits and landscapes emanate, the ring of house, lake, and shore, outside of which is the "unbroken forest" where "the enemy waits." The last verse, "Listening to Color," reveals "My message keeps/ turning to yellow where few leaves/set up first fires over branches/tips of flames only, nothing here finished yet." The *personae* throughout are the central and informing intelligence of the poet, as spy, as observer in many guises. Stanford's method is classical in its restraint, using varied tempo, cadenced rather than stressed stanzas, and modulated rhythms. Imagist with played down metaphors, the poems are distinguished by their original idiom.

"Our Town" and "On Music" furnish echoes of Robinson and Dryden with remarkable variations in modern instances which give the reader pause. They are celebrations of technical excellence almost as abstract as music, the latter poem translating the idea of "Song for St. Cecilia's Day" through Purcell into Benjamin Britten. The same feeling persists in what might almost be called a transliteration of Euripides into "The Burning of Ilium" with a riposte as current as news from Israel, Cambodia, Ireland: the streaming refugees, "the dust of cities falling," a dead child in a mother's arms. The theme is extended in "Libraries" to include the greater vandalism in almost Pindarian terms of ideas and intellect destroyed yet nurtured still.

Quite opposite in feeling is a group of portraits, especially of owls. Old Owl appears in a verse as prelude to a section of bestiary pieces, in which all the creeping, flying, scampering creatures rejoice in his disappearance, while the *persona* wishes or calls for his return as muse: "Come soon, sweet Owl./I miss your velvet note/ and the soft slip of your wing." "The Owl Inside" follows as in a nightmare exploding into color and sound, then recalled in "The Message": ". . . Not to wake/ while owls rummage the trees/search runnels of grass, not seen,/heard, heard into dream." Other birds appear in other poems, always exactly described but extended to symbol not exact, the unresolved mysteries celebrated yet not understood. The key to this dilemma appears in "Language" as it does in a previously published "The noun/is what is feared . . ." that is, how to make the naming intelligible beyond language. More explicit portraits leave no doubt; "Prophet" is John the Baptist, Cellini imprisoned seeks light as artists' only tool, all the women in the Perseus series speak exactly. Perseus, after his conquests, wonders if he is a hero in a poem of existential inauthenticity and anguish.

There is no title poem, but the sequence under that heading, the eleven verses whose *I* is the abstracted pursuer, the *We* either those spied upon or the power behind the chase, has all the elements of a Delamare landscape and a Robbe-Grillet plot, with their sharp focus on unresolved terror. The locale shifts from a mysterious, apparently Italian villa, to the forest, a train, a city largely seen through the eyes of a counterespionage agent, blundering, fearful, lonely, astute, alienated—anything but the stereotypical spy, since he has no idea of his mission, has lost contact with his leader, and longs to join and embrace those he is terrorizing. They in turn fumble with fake maps, act out their roles as if coconspirators. The mood is dominated by the Sirocco, the heat penetrating and undermining both statuary and morale. The plot takes a Kafkaesque turn to irresolution which carries over to the next section of poems, especially "Exiles," in which the actors in the drama cannot go home again:

> We sort out noises at night
> watch where we walk by day.
> But the sky lurks like a spy. Our words
> turn against us, what we keep is a threat.
> They're bound to be after us.

This is a chilling scenario where nothing happens, where terror is the final moment, where the cast is galvanized into inaction.

Dream and memory alternate to create a dual point of view in the reassuring poems of other sections. The most striking example of twin focus is in "Mr. D.," where death takes a brief holiday, seen through the rattling eyes of the collaborator as a comforter, a nurse in tweed, who "told me how to dream without dreaming/like roots under the snow in winter./Dark, and knowing that darkness, warm/and held like a comfort around me." There is no autobiography, no hint of the confessional poet's stance, either here or in "After Exile" where dream and memory reach a resolution of faith:

> It was not the dream that did it.
> It only reflected
> the serpent of power rising
> from the roots of earth
> into the head where the hair
> flew out like sprays of a flowering tree.
> Blossoms falling wherever the feet
> half-touched the ground
> the girl with new-risen breasts

> running through doorways
> into the green garden
> where trees grew overnight
> placing themselves in trim rows
> and the blooms of azaleas, acacia,
> and pomegranate split the air with color,
> whole skies of blooms covered the ground
> but it was the fountain that rose like a serpent
> ricocheted over every tendril of the green garden.

The remembered roots, the dream of life prevailing in a kind of epiphany make of this cadenced poem of stress and unstress an epitome as well. The same sense of mystery is apparent in another dreamed remembrance of things that are not past or present but eternal: "There was a man unseen/before, shone on the porch of dream/the light behind him bright/ his face seen and never seen/ before" suggests the ineffable. Yet the settings of the poems are often specific, such as a ranch in California, where the reality is so strong that she believes things will never change if she revisits the past: "Whatever I do, my uncle is going to be here/smoking his cigarette, talking of shorthorn cattle. . . . If I come back, things will start again." This poetic affirmation, a license never to be revoked, is the celebration of life while being lived, the affirmation which Ann Stanford proclaims.

The Stanford seasons have, however, some discontent. Heat is often insufferable; cold is too often numbing. "The trouble is we are always reminded of something/beside the point" which kills "that old child's morning game of resurrection." The doubt is not enough to make the sun and moon go out, as Blake said it might, but it gives a slight edge to the mood of the poems.

William Tillson

JACK
A Biography of Jack London

Author: Andrew Sinclair (1935–   )
Publisher: Harper & Row Publishers (New York). Illustrated. 297 pp. $12.95
Type of work: Biography
Time: 1876–1916
Locale: The United States (including Alaska and Hawaii), London, Japan, Korea, the South Pacific, Australia, Mexico

A major new biography which tells the absorbing story of a self-made author and political radical whose rise to fame and wealth was followed by long suffering and apparent suicide

Principal personages:
> JACK (JOHN GRIFFITH) LONDON, journalist, novelist, short story writer, essayist
> FLORA WELLMAN LONDON, his mother
> BESS MADDERN LONDON, his first wife
> CHARMIAN KITTREDGE LONDON, his second wife
> JOAN LONDON, his older daughter
> ELIZA LONDON SHEPARD, his half-sister
> GEORGE STERLING, a poet, bohemian, and friend of Jack
> ANNA STRUNSKY, friend and lover of Jack

In histories of American literature and studies of American fiction Jack London is usually considered a minor figure in the development of literary realism and naturalism in the early years of the twentieth century. Arthur Hobson Quinn in 1936 dismissed him quickly with the comment that he was a journalist who wrote "too hastily and too often" and whose vogue was passing, "for there is something impermanent in the very nature of the literature of violence." A decade later, Robert E. Spiller remarked that London was a "vigorous, naïve, and prolific" writer who personified the romantic impulses of the new century and who left "a small body of writing which, for sincerity and vitality, deserves to be rescued from the oblivion to which his artistic faults threaten to condemn it." George F. Whicher was less favorably impressed and wrote in 1951 that London had "little sense of the artistic sincerity of his work and was never unwilling to combine his poetic memories of the great open spaces with popular and highly profitable sentimentality." Edward Wagenknecht, in *Cavalcade of the American Novel* (1952), called London "a hack writer of genius" whose writing "was never more than a means to an end, and the end was material advancement." The general public in America perhaps remembers London now only as the author of *The Call of the Wild* and *The Sea Wolf* and of several Alaskan stories such as "To Build a Fire" and "Love of Life," which have been reprinted in many high school and college textbooks and collections of short stories. By contrast, he is reportedly the most popular of all American writers in Russia, and in France a publisher has recently been reissuing his complete works.

Andrew Sinclair's major new biography of Jack London tells the life story of an amazing young man who fought his way upward from illegitimacy as an infant, through rough and dangerous experiences in a great variety of occupations, to an immensely popular success as a novelist and considerable notoriety as a political radical, and who died, an apparent suicide, at the age of forty. Sinclair also attempts to correct some false impressions about London that can be traced back either to Jack's myths about himself or to earlier biographers who lacked access to many materials that were made available to Sinclair.

London was born in San Francisco in 1876, the son of Flora Wellman, a spiritualist, and John Chaney, a vagabond and astrologer, who had deserted Miss Wellman after she refused to have an abortion. When the baby was only a few months old his mother married a widower, John London, who gave his name to the child. The boy was always called Jack to distinguish him from his adoptive father. Jack did not learn the identity of his real father until he was almost a man. He wrote to Chaney then and felt intensely the sting of rejection when Chaney denied the paternity and refused to see him. Jack achieved a minor sublimated revenge in an early story entitled "A Thousand Deaths," in which a son kills his probable father who has cruelly tortured him. The stigma of Jack's origin was not exorcised, however, and it contributed to his later mythmaking about his family background. Jack's sense of rejection had earlier been instilled by his mother's having neglected him for other interests, one of which was lavishing on the young son of her stepdaughter Ida the affection she had denied her own son.

The poverty of his family led Jack to drop out of school at thirteen and take a series of jobs requiring long hours of often hard physical labor and scant pay. He became an oyster pirate in San Francisco Bay, joined a gang of delinquents in the city, sailed as a seaman on a sealer bound for Japan, nearly died of shingles on the way back, hoboed across the United States, was arrested as a vagrant in Niagara Falls and jailed for a month, and then decided at nineteen that he would return to school and get the education which would enable him to escape the hard and perhaps derelict life that must otherwise almost certainly be his fate.

Jack became interested in books in his early schooling but later had had little time for them until his return made him determine that through both intensive and extensive reading and study—up to nineteen hours a day—he could make up six years of school in two. After a year in high school and five weeks in a cram school, he studied independently with furious application and was admitted to Berkeley as a special student; but he left after his second semester and thus ended his formal education. His continued voracious reading for the rest of his life, however, influenced his thinking and his writing.

Among authors Sinclair cites as exerting a literary influence on London are Kipling, Stevenson, Twain, Milton, Dante, Poe, and Wells. As early as 1900 Jack admitted to a friend, "I would never possibly have written anywhere near the way I did had Kipling never been." Three years later he published an essay, "The

Terrible and Tragic in Fiction," in which he praised Poe's use of terror in his writing, terror such as Poe himself had known. Jack had experienced similar fears in troubled dreams and frightening nightmares, and he felt a psychological kinship with Poe. In a footnote to his *The Iron Heel* London wrote that H. G. Wells was "a sociological seer, sane and normal as well as [a] warm human." Sinclair sees the novel as possibly deriving from London's reading of Wells's "When the Sleeper Wakes" and "A Story of the Days to Come." The Wellsian influence is also present, thinks Sinclair, in London's *Before Adam*.

Other writers who helped to direct or develop Jack's views and his philosophy of life were Karl Marx, Charles Darwin, Thomas Huxley, and Herbert Spencer. Through them and through friends he met during what he later called his "frantic pursuit of knowledge," London became a socialist but, as Sinclair puts it, "of his own special persuasion." He believed in a socialism that was both evolutionary and revolutionary, and he believed also that it would be established by the white race, which he considered superior to others. Because he wrote so rapidly and because he churned out so much of his fiction and so many of his essays to meet the continuing demand for money to pay for his extravagant style of living, he was often inconsistent. It did not disturb him that he wrote for a capitalist like William Randolph Hearst while he remained a Socialist Party member. Nor did it bother him that he so often championed individualism whereas orthodox socialism taught that the individual should be submerged into the group. Some of London's later views derived from Friedrich Nietzsche, Sigmund Freud, and Carl Jung, all of whom, London believed, helped him to understand himself as well as other people better.

After Jack left Berkeley he planned to write for a living, and he began to produce a stream of essays, stories, and poems that in turn brought a horde of rejections from editors. In desperation he worked briefly in a laundry for thirty dollars a month and then, with his stepsister Eliza's elderly husband, James Shepard, he joined the Klondike gold rush in 1897. Shepard turned back because of ill health, but Jack continued the journey, suffered physical hardships, contracted scurvy, was frustrated in his search for gold, kept a log of the whole trip, and finally returned to San Francisco a year after he had left, bringing only $4.50 worth of gold dust and, though he did not know it at the time, enough memories and observations to provide him much of the wealth he was later to gain from writing about Alaska.

Jack turned to hack writing to escape starvation, was encouraged by a publisher's offer to bring out a volume of his stories, fell in love with Anna Strunsky, a young Russian Jewish girl whom he had not money enough to marry, and then married a poorer girl, Bess Maddern, whose fiancé had just died. For a while the companionate marriage seemed happy enough but, though Bess gave him two daughters, she could not offer the emotional and intellectual stimulus he needed. For such stimulus and for entertainment as well he soon turned to a young poet, George Sterling, and a bohemian group called the Crowd, which included Charmian Kittredge, who would become first Jack's lover and later his wife.

The Crowd for a while provided an outlet for some of London's boundless energy. In childhood he had scarcely known what it was to play with other children. He and the Crowd now indulged in physical sports, practical jokes, and picnics. But he soon realized that he must escape from such play; it amused but it led nowhere. He disciplined himself to write a thousand words a day. There were constant demands for money for both his own household and his mother's, and selling his writing was his only means of getting the cash.

Jack also rebelled increasingly against his loveless marriage to Bess. He began a love affair with Anna Strunsky, accepted an offer to report post-Boer War conditions in South Africa, got only as far as London when the offer was withdrawn, and stayed to investigate slum conditions in London in order to write *The People of the Abyss*. He then returned to try to patch up his marriage, drove himself to write two novels, escaped again on a sloop voyage with a friend, and then began an affair which would culminate in his marriage to Charmian Kittredge the day after his divorce from Bess.

Before marrying Charmian, however, he had traveled to Japan and Korea to report the Russo-Japanese War in 1904, published his tremendously popular *The Sea Wolf*, had another brief love affair, begun to write *White Fang*, and bought a California ranch.

Though now a famous writer and capitalist landowner of sorts, Jack still retained his socialist views; he preached his socialist doctrine in numerous lecture halls, announcing the future takeover of governmental power by his socialist "comrades." He published in 1907 *The Iron Heel*, a sensational futuristic novel predicting the domination of North America by a Fascist-type dictatorship in the United States and a similar domination of the Far East by Japan.

Finally tiring of the notoriety he had gained and the pressures of his life, Jack planned for himself and Charmian a seven-year round-the-world voyage which would provide education, adventure, and new sources of writing material. Temporarily interrupted by the San Francisco earthquake, the uncompleted voyage on his expensive boat, the *Snark*, finally proved a disaster. The *Snark* was sold for a fraction of its cost, and Jack returned home suffering from various maladies including yaws, the treatment of which was to give him permanent arsenic poisoning from salvarsan. To allay the pain from his decaying body, of which he had earlier been so proud and even boastful, he managed to endure the few remaining years of his life only because of the massive amounts of drugs he consumed.

Despite his sufferings he continued his writing, publishing *Martin Eden*, a largely autobiographical novel which ends in suicide for its protagonist, and *John Barleycorn*, another autobiographical account, which pictures his struggles with alcoholism. To pay off his many debts he also turned out a mass of inferior writing. He brought on more debts through additional land purchases, lavish entertaining, and attempts at scientific and technologically progressive farming. Though money poured in, it also drained out rapidly while London fought, through constant medication, to stave off the final loss of mind and body. He died November 22, 1916, apparently from an overdose of morphine and atropine. Whether the overdose was intentional or not has been argued since by biographers and others. Sinclair believes that if it was intentional, Jack did not plan his death, but instead either decided impulsively to end his long torture, or possibly tried merely to deaden his pain with no terminal result intended.

In chapter-by-chapter notes at the end of *Jack*, Sinclair has well documented his absorbing biography of London, and he has supplied an excellent index for students and other readers seeking information on particular aspects of London's life and work. Interest in the biography may well lead to a revival of interest in London's best writings as well as some of his less-known works.

Henderson Kincheloe

JEFFERSON DAVIS

Author: Clement Eaton (1898–   )
Publisher: The Free Press/Macmillan Publishing Company (New York). 334 pp. $12.95
Type of work: Biography
Time: 1808–1889
Locale: Mississippi, Washington, Richmond

A biography of Jefferson Davis, a major figure in the history of the American South, by a senior Southern historian

> *Principal personages:*
> JEFFERSON DAVIS, President of the Confederate States of America
> ABRAHAM LINCOLN, President of the United States
> ROBERT E. LEE, Supreme Commander of the Confederate Army
> SARAH TAYLOR, daughter of Zachary Taylor, Davis' first wife
> VARINA HOWELL, Davis' second wife

Suppose that Pickett's gallant charge at Gettysburg had succeeded, and Lee's army had swarmed through the trenches and destroyed Meade. That major Confederate success in Pennsylvania, a northern state, could well have devastated the North's will to win. The "Peace of Washington of 1863" would have brought acceptance, if not recognition, of the Confederate States of America, and Jefferson Davis' life would today be viewed quite differently. In the C.S.A., historians would eulogize him as a great nationalist, war leader, Founding Father, and Savior of the Republic. Northerners might regard him balefully as a successful foreign despot. The aristocratic, conservative, and individualistic South that he epitomized would today be admired throughout half of North America.

Pickett failed, of course, and the Confederacy, its way of life, and Jefferson Davis were relegated to the dustbins of history. The man recently resurrected by Clement Eaton is a curious antique, a sire of lost causes, filed away in the American pantheon somewhere between the awful Benedict Arnold and the saintly Virginian, Robert E. Lee.

There is a lesson in all this: historians have contrasted Davis with his nemesis Lincoln for over a century, from which something can indeed be learned. But it is far more revealing to compare Davis and his Confederacy with George Washington and the Second Continental Congress. Essentially the historiography of the Revolution is based on the fact that it succeeded. We revere the seminal events of the years 1775–1781 with an enthusiasm that dwells heavily on great images of victory: the embattled farmers of New England, Saratoga, John Paul Jones and ship-to-ship duels, and the final surrender at Yorktown. Our filiopietism beclouds hard truths. Was there ever a feebler organization than the Second Continental Congress? Why did Washington's army freeze, starve, and desert to the brink of dissolution at Valley Forge amid the fattest barns in the world? Yet studies of the Confederacy seem to emphasize such weaknesses, inabilities, and, of course, its ultimate failure, perhaps proclaiming a preordained destiny. Historians have frequently ratified results with the dictum of inevitability, but generals and politicians are more succinct: "There is no substitute for victory."

What sort of man was Jefferson Davis? His biographer has wisely permitted his contemporaries to dissect him at length, and they broadly agree on his nature and ways. Physically he was, like Jackson, Lincoln, and Calhoun, a tall, spare man. Like Calhoun too, he was a fine *pater familias* who could always vent his spleen on a congressional colleague. He was an egotistical, monumentally self-assured, true prima donna who required careful handling, obsequious approaches, and frequent praise. Eaton suggests that Confederate Secretary of the Navy Mallory survived on competence alone, but Judah Benjamin lasted largely because he read his man carefully and preened him frequently.

Davis was a first generation aristocrat, like Calhoun, who fashioned his conduct on an eighteenth century model. But he equals his namesake and inspiration only in his dedication to patriotic duty. Davis developed an early and extremely Southern sense of honor, and, though he never fought, ardently defended the code duello. His nouveau "Cotton Snob" touchiness was revealed in the army when he ignored the direct command of a superior, and later successfully defended himself before a courtmartial with the observation that no gentleman could accept that officer's haughty tone of voice. He was, concludes Eaton, high-minded, strong-willed, icy, proud, and dedicated to principle. Jefferson Davis was also a pivotal figure in the history of the South. Was there a warm human being lurking somewhere behind that official exterior? Probably not. He was not a *likable* person: Clement Eaton found no evidence of the existence of a single close friend. He was, in fact, what he seemed: an earnest Southern Victorian gentleman, whose personal and public lives were one.

Davis was a fine example of those addicted to the nineteenth century neo-Roman school of oratory. His speaking style, after years of evolution from the ornate, became direct and dignified, delivered *ex tempore* in a clear, penetrating voice. A little imagination from his audience could well conjure up a toga and a broken column on which to rest his noble arm.

He was born in 1808 (a year before Abraham Lincoln) to a relatively prosperous semifrontier Kentucky family, the last of ten children; his father, a Pennsylvania-born veteran of the Revolution, puckishly gave him the middle name Finis. Davis' youth was spent on farms in Kentucky and Mississippi; Transylvania College later placed him in contact with the scions of the planter class and the academic lucidity of the New England mind. Mississippians were citizens of a new and raw state, but eager to absorb the ways of Virginia and Carolina, and by 1824 Davis had become quite the young aristocrat.

The death of his father and an appointment to West Point channeled his career away from the law, toward the military arts. His cadet career was mediocre, and Eaton records evidence of wildness in the young man. Skipping chapel was one of his minor sins; he also received numerous demerits, arrests, and even a courtmartial at "The Point." Still, he managed to graduate with his class, though in the nether ranks. The presence of Cadets Robert E. Lee, Joseph E.Johnston, Albert Sidney Johnston, and Leonidus Polk possibly determined his class rank as much as his personal activities.

Davis' subsequent service was unsatisfying. Like Grant, he served his military apprenticeship at distant Western forts, and he resigned his commission in 1835, having gotten a low opinion of Indians, a high opinion of himself, and the hand of Sarah, the daughter of Col. Zachary Taylor. Sadly, she died within the year of malaria. He also gained superb horsemanship, a proud military bearing that well suited his invisible toga, and a lifetime of poor health from a bout with pneumonia.

Davis quietly farmed and prospered in Mississippi for the next decade. In 1845 he married the bright, verbal, but stuffy Varina Howell. Later that year he won a Democratic seat in the House of Representatives, and so launched his national political career.

Biographer Eaton considers Davis' first term in Congress revealing, but finds no overt indications of a great future in the bookish and earnest Southerner. Davis reflected his family's political heritage as a dutiful expansionist Democrat in an era when his class spoke through Whiggism, but he was no rough-and-tumble politician. Eaton's analysis of antebellum Mississippi elections reveals a predilection for demagoguery, humbug, and dirty tricks; the Redneck had arrived with statehood, not Reconstruction. Davis did precipitate a disagreement on the house floor with another young Congressman, Andrew Johnson of Tennessee, by arguing without forethought that West Pointers would serve the army far better than tailors. Johnson, equally thin-skinned, took umbrage, and characterized Davis in turn as one of "the illegitimate, swaggering, bastard, scrub aristocracy." They would cross swords again.

The war with Mexico provided a short but pivotal interlude in Congressman Davis' life. Resigning his seat at the first whiff of gunpowder, he returned home and was soon elected Colonel of the elegant First Mississippi Rifles. Off to war they went, rather like the Rough Riders of another day, clad in hunting clothes, armed with new percussion rifles and Bowie knives. In the vanguard Colonel Davis stylishly rode a blooded Arabian, faithful servant at his side.

In Mexico he fought under his former father-in-law, now General Taylor, who unlike Davis affected old clothes and ran his battles perched sidesaddle on the broad quarterdeck of his reformed plowhorse, Old Whitey. At Buena Vista Davis demonstrated the Kiplingesque style that thrilled his times by leading a brilliant cavalry charge against the Mexicans. Brevetted Brigadier-General of Volunteers by Polk for his exploit, the prickly Davis declined the commission, claiming that only the state of Mississippi could make such an appointment. He returned home shortly thereafter, accompanied by 376 survivors of the 926 who had marched away a year earlier, to be honored as the "Hero of Buena Vista." Davis' brief command of a volunteer regiment against Mexico in 1847 established his reputation as a leader of men, secured him a Senate seat immediately, and a presidency fourteen years later.

During the next three years Davis gilded his image, though he was still no political chieftain. He bravely opposed Calhoun in favor of Polk and advocated the annexation of Yucatan, though not of all Mexico (on racial grounds). He demanded the admission of Oregon in its entirety but denied Congress' right to exclude slavery from the north woods. Yet Davis also endorsed a compromise line between the sections running west to the Pacific. His advanced concept of Southern rights was clear by 1851, when he was induced to resign his seat by a sorely rattled Mississippi Democratic leadership, and sought the governorship. Losing to an old enemy, Henry Stuart Foote, Davis returned quietly to his plantation, Brierfield, and his role as patriarchal master.

How stood Davis on the Negro? Eaton treats the subject fully, if traditionally, with a summary of the present state of historical thought on racism and slavery. The writings of Stampp, Genovese, and Fogel and Engerman are reviewed with care, though Eaton's personal view seems to catalogue him as a progressive follower of U. B. Phillips. Davis' antique racial ideology and his acceptance of the "curse of Noah" as the ultimate "divine decree" on race are analyzed fully. One trusts that God knows what Noah's curse was, because man does not. Davis also defended the peculiar institution on other grounds, and, with a view apparently endorsed by Eaton, defended the "Great Plantation" as a proving ground for future black advancement.

Davis was a good massa, and, though occasionally a seller of intractable slaves, a practicer of absentee ownership, and a frequent user of overseers, Jefferson, we are assured, was much loved by his loyal servants. Eaton assures us that he and his brother Joseph hunted "companionably" with them while Varina sewed clothing for them with her own hands. Eaton notes early in the book how much Jefferson loved his faithful Jim (*almost* like a brother); much like Calhoun, Davis "spoiled" his "people."

Was Davis a true ideologue, a fugitive professor of political science like Calhoun, barking abstractions at a room full of pragmatists? Or was he a man cleverly defending his cause against a growing opponent, seizing on "eternal truths," simply because he would lose on every vote? Both sides of Davis appeared in the turbulent 1850's. As Secretary of War in the Pierce administration, he, alone among Southern leaders, advocated a transcontinental railroad, authorized a route-finding expedition, and through Pierce, pushed the Gadsden Purchase through Congress. Eaton considers this period in Davis' career as "forward looking."

His second term in the Senate, commenced in 1857, plunged him into new circumstances. The older generation of Unionists (the likes of Clay, Webster, Calhoun) had been supplanted by fire-eaters from all sections (Seward, Toombs, and their ilk), and he discovered himself amidst what historians have termed a "blundering generation." Surrounded by men who preferred posturing and scoring points to discussion and compromise, the monumentally inflexible Davis fell heir to Calhoun's mantle. He remained a faithful Democrat and a philosophical defender of slavery and Southern rights, but he was no fire-eater. He accepted the right but not the necessity of secession. Jefferson Davis spoke for much more than party or state; he had evolved into a leading Southern nationalist, but his reasonable ideal was a great and equal South, *in* the Union.

For the next three years Davis debated an endless variety of abstractions, symbolic issues, and concrete sectional differences. The territories, fugitive slaves, popular sovereignty, the Dred Scott decision, and the future of the sections occupied his mind. Douglas' Freeport Doctrine seems a reasonable solution in retrospect, to the present, but polarization had by then blinded men to reality, and the Union foundered in a sea of dividing houses, irrepressible conflicts, higher laws, and impending crises.

When the crisis came Davis fought secession manfully, endorsing a Democratic compromise candidate, Horatio Seymour of New York (whom Eaton rather casually brands a "doughface"). But, like Washington and Lee, Davis went with his state, and in January, 1861, with a powerful farewell address, ended his career in the United States Senate.

Ex-Senator Davis fully expected war, and anticipated that he would become the George Washington of the Confederacy. He was in his garden at Brierfield cutting roses when the message arrived announcing his nomination as provisional president of the Confederate States of America (to be confirmed by popular vote a year later). Saddened, he accepted his duty and prepared an inaugural address which reiterated the Anglo-American principles of consent of the governed, the social contract, and the right of revolution, while simultaneously calling for peace with the United States. It was a Declaration of Independence *and* a new government in one.

Was Davis a good president? Eaton carefully weighs the testimony of his contemporaries and later writers with his own careful judgment. He concludes that Davis was a capable, if not great, war president, and repeats Gorgas' question: *"who could have done better?"* Wielding power over an unready and untested nation, Davis grew even as it shriveled, from advocate of states' rights to nationalist, from brigadier to strategist, and from racial conservative to emancipationist. His nationalism became too fierce and consistent for the deep South, and gradually the fire-eaters turned against him. His labors to keep the war a contest among white Christian gentlemen failed, and he shifted toward abolition and the enlistment of black soldiers. He—like the Continental Congress—wisely sought salvation in foreign intervention, and, invoking the powers of King Cotton, attempted to lead Great Britain and France into his camp. But Lord John Russell was no Count Vergennes, and King Wheat and the growing Union blockade gradually removed any control over foreign affairs from his hands. He was no politician, yet he worked wisely with the South's emerging nationalists versus states' rights party system by judiciously balancing appointments from each. In the process he confounded his states' rights opponents and their potential leader, Vice-President Alexander Stephens. Eaton sympathizes with Davis' appalling problems, comparing him to a leader of an underdeveloped nation making war on a larger, more advanced one.

Some of Davis' presidential difficulties were the products of his austere, rigid personality. He disdained propaganda, public relations, and the press, in equal measures. He failed to foster teamwork and cooperation among the leaders of his revolutionary government; he simply was not inspirational. He bogged down in administrative detail, declined to delegate responsibility, misjudged political associates, and feuded with everyone. Davis' interchanges of letters invariably terminated with an expression of righteous outrage over his correspondents' conduct in some matter.

President Davis' relations with his Congress were formal, aloof, and ultimately counterproductive. The Confederate Congress performed somewhere between the Continental Congress and an interstate debating society, rooted to a man in their respective states. That Congress required the likes of a Jackson, Roosevelt, or Wilson. It needed strong, inspired leadership, but received only stern lectures on duty.

Cooperating with the governors of the Confederacy was even more difficult. Frank Owsley's epitaph for the C.S.A., "Died of State Rights," is not much exaggerated, notes Eaton. Davis crossed swords with nearly every governor, but his personal demon was the feisty Joseph Brown of Georgia. Brown, a man at least as egotistical as his president, was also a populist, demagogue, and Georgia nationalist, and fought Davis step by step throughout the war. Brown "won" when Lee surrendered; Georgia's army was still fat, well-armed, and in Georgia.

Eaton's review of Davis' direction of military affairs is necessarily cautious and balanced, for if he lost, he also nearly won. Much of Eaton's material comes again from Davis' contemporaries, and reminds us that the last century was an era of excessive personal vanity among public and military men. Time and again duels were fought to the death over some real or imagined slur. Generals resigned or sulked in their tents until stroked by presidents, captains led suicidal charges to clear their names of some innuendo. Commanding such men required skills beyond mere diplomacy.

Commander-in-Chief Davis did some things rather well, some badly. He maintained political supremacy over the army until the end. He determined the overall Southern military posture—defensive war, interior lines, endure to the last—that supported the Confederacy's basic "leave us alone" political position. With brilliance he directed smaller armies and green troops against a rapidly evolving Northern war machine. He opposed the election of officers and argued against short term enlistments. He supported West Pointers unstintingly, and above all, he believed in the peerless Lee.

Davis' military limitations were also notable. Armed with an inflated opinion of his own military prowess, Davis personally directed the war effort until events forced him to name Robert E. Lee General-in-Chief. He began the war trying to defend too much with too little, using territorially autonomous armies unable to draw on one another. He retarded the advance of able generals and retained incompetents in command positions. Eaton praises Davis' order bringing Johnston's Valley force "on the cars" to Bull Run, thus presenting Beauregard with victory, but accuses him of practically abandoning the vital city of New Orleans to Union capture.

By 1864 Jefferson Davis had been reduced to faith, perseverance, and a stiff upper lip that fought spreading pessimism. His last card was a treaty between God and the Confederacy: the cause was just, therefore—somehow—victory must emerge. Certainly he could do no more, except silently bear the growing if unjustified hatred of his beloved South. For the war was going badly, and presidents must pay. Davis became the national scapegoat, overseer of disaster, and, ultimately, gloomy despot.

Were the charges fair? To be elected president of a new union composed of states' rights fanatics was challenging; to fail, perhaps understandable. Could another man have gotten more from that land of philosophers and fire-eaters, of individualists and romantics? Those very centrifugal forces that made the Confederacy possible also destroyed it, and Jefferson Davis was both creator and victim.

Comparisons between the two war presidents appear throughout Eaton's text. Davis was a conservative, old line gentleman, no politician, and certainly no democrat. Aloof, reserved, and proper, he probably would have been simply embarrassed by one of Father Abraham's "little stories." Lincoln was likable, egalitarian, and casual. Nowhere is the contrast between them more apparent than in their mental processes in debate. Davis invariably presented his ideas as finished philosophical constructs, take them or leave them. Lincoln talked, thought, debated, reconsidered, and only toward the end, reached what he termed the "nub" of a question. One knew, the other sought. Yet both were great nationalists, racists, and interestingly, neither ever executed a deserter who appealed for executive clemency.

Over the years Southern hatred for Davis melted into sympathy, then admiration; his manacled term in a dank casemate in the walls of Fortress Monroe affected millions in all sections. Freed in 1867, he became the martyred symbol of the Lost Cause, and dropped from history. He spent his days at Beauvoir on the Gulf coast of Mississippi, traveled, and wrote his memoirs on behalf of Southern rights. Even his sympathetic biographer recognizes the irrelevance of this late effusion. Acceptance finally came, and Davis died a reconstructed unionist in 1889.

Clement Eaton is perhaps our most eminent contemporary Southern historian. A native of North Carolina, educated in South and North, this child of the last century has followed a distinguished teaching career and written several master works, particularly his *Freedom of Thought in the Old South* (1940). His biography of Davis is a balanced and mature work that rarely strays from its subject, the public man, Jefferson Davis. Most of the book is a narrative of the war years, and only fourteen pages carry Davis from 1865 to 1889.

Does Davis come to life in this biography? No, but he was not a lively man. Eaton accurately presents Davis as a bundle of abstractions (planter, husband, parent, senator, president). Probably Eaton's style is well suited to its subject, and one senses that Davis would like the book. Eaton eschews the colorful activist authorship of a Catton or Morison, preferring the cool, neutral style. Eaton's *Jefferson Davis* is probably not a definitive work, but it is a solid, well-researched, and workmanlike volume that will serve our time well.

Lance Trusty

JOAN OF ARC

Author: Edward Lucie-Smith (1933–   )
Publisher: W. W. Norton Company (New York). 327 pp. $10.95
Type of work: Biography
Time: 1412–1431
Locale: France

A biography which only partially succeeds in its attempt to disclose the human woman behind the legendary figure through use of objective historical techniques

Principal personages:
JOAN D'ARC, the French national heroine
DUKE OF ALENÇON, a French commander who believed in Joan's mission
JEAN D'AULON, master of Joan's household
ROBERT DE BAUDRICOURT, French commander at Vaucouleurs
CHARLES VII OF FRANCE
PIERRE CAUCHON, the Bishop of Beauvais, Joan's enemy
COUNT OF DUNOIS, BASTARD OF ORLEANS, the leader of the French forces defending the beseiged city of Orleans
JEAN D'ESTIVET, the Canon of Beauvais, and Joan's inquisitorial prosecutor
BROTHER MARTIN LADVENU, a sympathetic Dominican priest

Even so distinguished an author as Edward Lucie-Smith, English poet, art and literary critic, and author/editor of some thirty books, must answer the question: Why another biography of Joan of Arc? She is the best-documented historical figure of fifteenth century Europe. Thanks to the careful recordings of the ecclesiastical Trial of Condemnation (Rouen, January-May, 1531) at which Joan was questioned, tried, and sentenced, and to the recordings of the three series of investigations comprising the posthumous Trial of Rehabilitation (1450; 1452; 1455–1456) designed to reverse the earlier trial's condemnatory verdict, we have today Joan's own words and those of over a hundred people who knew her. Translations of these Latinate documents were first made available by the great nineteenth century scholar Jules Quicherat, and more recently by Pierre Tisset and Yvonne Lanhers. As a result of these easily accessible primary materials, as well as of the fascination of the myth itself, there are today well over twelve thousand published items on Joan of Arc. These include many standard biographies such as those by Francis Lowell (1896), Andrew Lang (1908), Albert Paine (1925), Michael Monahan (1928), Vita Sackville-West (1936), Jules Michelet (trans. A. Guerard, 1957), Régine Pernoud (1962), and Frances Winwar (1948). Even more formidable to a biographer are the well-known literary portraits—Joan as a witch in Shakespeare's *Henry VI;* an object of ridicule in Voltaire's *La Pucelle;* a spiritual savior in Schiller's *Die Jungfrau von Orleans;* an apotheosis of chastity in Mark Twain's *Personal Recollections of Joan of Arc;* a saccharine saint in Anatole France's *Life;* a doughty Protestant heroine in Shaw's *Saint Joan;* a common-sensical mystic in Anouilh's *The Lark.*

Lucie-Smith's answer to the question of yet another biography of Joan is that such portraits as those referred to above when not dull are biased: the woman's face is obscured by the opinionated controversies her name has always aroused: Devil or saint? Royalist or revolutionist? Feminist or traditionalist? Realist or romanticist? Therefore, Lucie-Smith's purpose as he informs us in his "Introduction" is to present an objective study, based solely on the historical evidence, that will reveal Joan's human face. Though his aim is laudatory, the result is a failure. The trouble is that by sticking to historical "facts" and thereby ducking the larger political and social issues, Lucie-Smith's *Joan of Arc* becomes a series of discrete surfaces which suggest, but do not make sense of, her complex and puzzling nature.

Moreover, contrary to Lucie-Smith's asseveration that he holds no opinions, no preconceived theories about Joan, he in fact does. His unquestioned assumption is that mystical or out-of-the-ordinary happenings can be explained naturally—by which he often means psychoanalytically. The extraordinary becomes an aberrant, abnormal reaction resulting from repression of unconscious fears and desires. For example, Joan's famous Voices, appearing to her from her thirteenth year onward, in the guise of St. Michael, St. Catherine, and St. Margaret, and impelling her five years later to seek out King Charles VII, to raise the seige of Orleans, and to insure the King's coronation at Rheims, are patronizingly dismissed as "obsessions," mere hallucinations familiar to twentieth century doctors. Similarly, Joan's father's dream that his daughter would eventually go away with men-at-arms is reduced to a subconscious, incestuous fantasy. Even more unsatisfactory is the explanation of Joan's predictions, made on separate occasions, of the deaths of two enemy soldiers who had taunted her. Their subsequent seemingly accidental deaths by drowning, Lucie-Smith says, can be interpreted as an attempt at intercourse since water signifies the womb. Less baffling, if equally reductionist, is the author's interpretation of Joan's prevision that a sword destined to be hers was waiting hidden by the altar at Sainte-Cathérine-de-Fierbois: Lucie-Smith says she must have seen it before and that it must have registered on her unconscious. This sword, found where she said, became Joan's victory weapon at the battles of Orleans, Jargeau, Meung, Beaugency, Patay, Troyes, and Rheims. She carried it until, in the abortive attack against Paris in the fall of 1429 when her triumphs were turning to defeats, she snapped the blade by hitting its flat against a camp harlot's back. Finally, Joan's accurate prophecy on May 13, 1430, in Compiègne that she had been sold, betrayed, and would be delivered to death (she was captured in battle by the hostile Burgundians ten days later, sold to the English, and burned at the stake May 30, 1431) is described by Lucie-Smith as a "paranoid outburst." The author's method of deflating prophecy to paranoia, visions to vacuousness, flattens many-dimensioned humanity into Michael Foucault's one-dimensional man. We wonder how such an undistinguished, distracted girl-next-door could stir the timorous Charles, inspirit a French nation, and create a myth now five centuries old? At issue here is not Lucie-Smith's admirable aim to explain events rationally or "naturally." Rather, at issue is his too narrow interpretation of "natural." Reducing "rational" to "psychoanalytical" shears Joan of her powerful charisma, just as his substitution of historical facts for a central organizing viewpoint of relevant issues strips her of coherent meaning. Lucie-Smith's *Joan of Arc* is an unfortunate example of the twentieth century axiom that the perspective of the viewer always influences what is viewed; every generation sees Joan in its own image. His Joan reveals the impoverishment of our mechanistic, pseudoscientific mind-set.

Yet the author's noninterpretive objectivity is not without merit. His facts are always trustworthy. In *Joan of Arc* no speech of Joan's, or of anyone else's, is invented; no action is recounted that cannot be verified. If the author's style is not as flexible and felicitous as that of his other critical works, we can infer that this, too, is in conformity to his criterion of objectivity. Because he does not embellish or proselytize, his narrative conveys an authoritative historicity.

Furthermore, his narrative method of stringing together vignettes of Joan in a particular time and space indicates, even if it does not illumine, just how complicated a person she was. Her girlhood as the daughter of a comfortable peasant-farmer accounts for her extreme piety (she attended church at every possible chance) and for her nationalism. At this time France was, of course, torn by the Hundred Years' War. Her village, Domrémy, though loyal to the French King Charles VII, lay in the midst of squabbling feudatories dominated by the Burgundians. Normandy and Bordeaux were controlled by the English who, allied with the Burgundians, controlled most of northern France. The indecisive Charles huddled in the south of France.

Consistent with his factual method, Lucie-Smith refuses to dramatize Charles' and Joan's famous meeting when the King tested her by hiding himself among his courtiers. Undeceived, Joan bypassed the flamboyantly dressed nobles and bowed before the "Dauphin." Granting Joan to have been extremely sensitive to other people's inadvertent gestures, Lucie-Smith comments that surely she would have known beforehand of Charles' small eyes, his droopy nose and knock-kneed, shambling gait. Perhaps, but his explanation leaves us not quite satisfied.

So, too, are we dissatisfied with his treatment of the much debated historical crux—the Sign by which Joan was supposed to have convinced Charles of the divinity of her mission. Having summarized other historical views, the author adds his own: Because of Charles' great susceptibility, Joan was probably able to convince him that he heard and saw, if only momentarily, her own Voices. However it was done, Joan did persuade the King of the sanctity of her three mandates: God would deliver France from its enemies; Joan, the messenger of God, would lift the siege at Orleans; and Charles would be coronated at Rheims. Some three months later (May 1429) Joan, the French commanders, and— thanks to Joan's fame—a swelling soldiery approaching 12,000 men, lifted the seige of Orleans, the gateway of the Loire.

The account of the days of skirmishes, charges, and countercharges at Orleans is among the more valuable sections of *Joan of Arc*. Lucie-Smith's careful detailing lets us understand just how the English with their circlet of outer fortifications managed to effect a slow strangle-hold on this vital river city.

Then, too, the glimpses of Joan in battle enable us to understand why she was admired, obeyed, and even venerated more often than she was liked or trusted. For example, her matchless courage and bravery are evinced again and again: leading a small band, Joan forays into the midst of the English forces to escort to safety a band of priests; when her forces must retire, she is always among the last to leave, fighting a rear-guard protective action. (A year later she would be captured doing this.) But alongside her bravery, we see her pride. Arriving at Orleans, Joan tongue-lashes the French commander Dunois for failing to position his troops properly. "The counsel of the Lord God is wiser and surer than yours," she scolds. Yet her arrogance is seemingly justified. As Joan berates Dunois, the wind shifts, allowing the French barges to float down to the city.

Lucie-Smith catches the essential haphazardness of war when he describes how the French won their decisive victory at Orleans. Evening had come on and the trumpet for a French retreat actually sounded when Joan noticed her beloved standard in strange hands. (She was unaware that, in order to climb a ditch, her standard bearer had entrusted the banner temporarily to a friendly Basque.) Alarmed, Joan tried to wrest the banner from the Basque; the resultant tug-of-war so fluttered the flag that Joan's army, about to retire, interpreted this as a sign to rally and recharged the bastion, the Tourelles. Thereupon the French in Orleans took heart and assaulted this key fort from their side. The English, caught in the middle, were at last routed.

The coronation of Charles in the cathedral at Rheims two months later was to be the apex of Joan's career. During the ceremony she stood beside the King, holding her standard. But her subsequent attack on Paris was aborted by Charles' Machiavellian hesitations. According to the author, the King deliberately delayed Joan while he secretly attempted an accommodation with the enemy. Lucie-Smith's fine portrait of this elusive King makes us wish that he had written Charles' biography instead of Joan's. Neurotic Charles—weak yet intelligent, stubborn yet mutable, always reluctant to act—lends himself more readily than mystical Joan to psychoanalytic insights. Evidently Charles manipulated his phobias and compulsions to suit his own purposes, even while apparently under their control. It is a surprise to realize that this supposedly weak failure of a king ruled for forty years, and was dubbed "The Victorious." As Lucie-Smith remarks, Charles was a more formidable and less pitiable man than most historians would make him out to be.

Joan's disastrous campaign against Paris took place in the fall of 1429; in the spring of 1430 she was captured fighting a sortie at Compiègne. Taken to Rouen, she was tried for sorcery and heresy in the inquisitorial court headed by her enemy, Pierre Couchon, the Bishop of Beauvais. What was remarkable about this Trial of Condemnation, of course, was that for five months, from January to May, 1431, a nineteen-year-old peasant girl held at bay a formidable phalanx of doctors and divines. Her presence of mind, unfailing memory, and sharp common sense are all evidenced by her pithy responses. For example, when asked by her judges why her standard was allowed at Charles' coronation when others were excluded, she replied: "It had borne the burden and it was right that it should have the honour." Again, when asked if she believed she was in a state of grace, she avoided the trap of damning herself if she said she was not, or damning herself for presuming to know God's mind if she said she was. She answered, "If I am not, may God put me in it; and if I am may God keep me in it." So consistent was she that the original seventy charges against her had eventually to be reduced to twelve, and the charge of sorcery dropped. But the charge of heresy—that is, refusal to submit to the Church and so deny her Voices—was to prove fatal. Ironically, this charge would be phrased in her own words: she did "not wish to submit herself to the judgment of the Church militant or to that of any man in the world, but to God alone." From a twentieth century perspective, it is difficult not to hear the incipient voice of Protestantism here. Yet Joan was a devout Roman Catholic throughout; two of her hardest burdens during these last black months were that she was unable to confess—she had found out that her confessor-priest was a stool pigeon—and that she was forbidden to go to Mass because she wore men's clothes.

Indeed, the issue of men's clothes is perhaps the most intriguing of all. For, along with heresy, the second charge on which she would be condemned was the wearing of men's clothes. In part, of course, such a charge belongs to a long tradition of misogyny, a tradition especially blatant in the medieval Church, which held women to be vastly inferior to men. Lucie-Smith points out that Joan's clothing, along with her masculine pudding-basin hairstyle, would cause her judges uneasiness because it symbolized a claim to male potency that they had renounced.

The issue of male clothing also raises the question of Joan's sexual nature. Lucie-Smith speculates that this "man-woman," as he terms Joan, was probably uncertain about her own sexuality. The fact that she wore men's clothing, did not menstruate, and preferred to sleep with women, especially young women, indicates a latent homosexuality, a need to take on a new sexual identity. Obviously for Joan male clothing was intimately connected with her mission to deliver France. She had dressed like a man since setting out for Chinon in 1429; until her death in May, 1431, she was to return to women's dress only once—after her abjuration.

Lucie-Smith covers the several possible explanations for Joan's abjuration—the renunciation of her Voices and of male attire—as well as her subsequent recantation of the abjuration, but the matter probably will always remain something of a mystery. In any case, having once more donned men's clothing,

Joan's confidence and courage flowed back. She announced herself ready to die for her beliefs. With only a cross made of two sticks and her Voices for succor, Joan died a slow death by burning at high noon in the Rouen marketplace.

Lucie-Smith's biography ends here. For an account of the Trial of Rehabilitation held some quarter century later reversing Joan of Arc's condemnation, we can turn to Charles Lightbody's cultural history, *The Judgements of Joan* (1961). And we need only remind ourselves of Joan's beatification by the Roman Catholic Church in 1909, and her canonization in 1919, to substantiate the axiom that each generation will see and use Joan according to its own vantage point. The pity is that Lucie-Smith's *Joan of Arc* so clearly reveals both the advantages and disadvantages of our nonjudgmental, factual, impersonal age.

Shirley F. Staton

JOHN L. LEWIS
A Biography

Authors: Melvyn Dubofsky (1934–   ) and Warren Van Tine
Publisher: Quadrangle/The New York Times Book Company (New York). Illustrated.
  619 pp. $17.50
Type of work: Biography
Time: 1880–1969
Locale: Iowa, Illinois, Washington, D.C., and various coal regions of the United States

A biography which analyzes the influence of a dramatic and powerful labor leader within the context of his times and the history of the labor movement

> Principal personages:
> JOHN L. LEWIS, President of the United Mine Workers and founder of the CIO
> WILLIAM GREEN, President of the American Federation of Labor
> PHILIP MURRAY, President of the Steel Workers and the CIO
> FRANKLIN D. ROOSEVELT, President of the United States

During the coal miners' strike in the winter of 1978, a reporter interviewed a retired miner, who said in effect, "It would not have happened while John L. Lewis was president. He would never have allowed the men to reject a contract he negotiated." In its way, that statement says more about Lewis than more conventional characterizations, which however, may still be necessary for the generation that did not know Lewis. John L. Lewis belongs to the top ranks of any list of leading figures in American labor history; and in his day, he was always in the very top ranks of best-loved and most-hated public figures.

Dubofsky and Van Tine have done thorough research, which took them to the archives of both government and labor bodies, to the manuscript census reports (for Lewis' family), to private papers, oral history reports (which they find of limited value), and the contemporary press. The nature of these materials is important, because it very largely determines the nature of the biography. Lewis left little in the way of family and personal papers, and even much official union business apparently is unrecorded. Careful biographers of a figure such as Lewis are therefore limited in what they can say about their subject's private life, about his motives, and even about some of his maneuvers. Gaps must be filled by speculation, but this is kept to a minimum, and when it is indulged in, it is labeled as such. Dubofsky and Van Tine also spend considerable time in the process of demythologizing; text and footnotes are full of corrections of past sources. Saul Alinsky's "unauthorized biography" of 1949, for example, suffers greatly; but it is apparent that the principal mythmaker was Lewis himself.

His early life, for instance, is very difficult to trace. As his name would suggest, his parents were Welsh, and, like many Welsh immigrants to the United States, they had experience in the coal mines. They came, after journeys not altogether traceable by the authors, to Lucas County, Iowa, where Lewis was born. Rural Iowa in the 1870's and 1880's was partially coal country. The

Lewises moved around; John attended high school but probably did not graduate (the records are not clear). He worked in the mines, and took a prominent role in local theatricals. He also served briefly as officer of the local union.

His real career, however, began, after a long sojourn in the West and a business failure, with his move to Illinois and his rise in the local and district union there. Dubofsky and Van Tine, admitting that Lewis' motives were speculative, put his resultant success in perspective. Lewis brought with him his father and brothers, a sizable nucleus for an organization; they were English-speaking and Protestant, which gave them an advantage over newer immigrants. Also, Lewis' skills of oratory and manipulation were already developed. Within a decade, Lewis had risen in the union hierarchy. Dubofsky and Van Tine point out that his career was not so much in the mines or in an elective union office as in the bureaucracy, as paid organizer for the United Mine Workers and the American Federation of Labor, and aide to Samuel Gompers, then president of the AFL. "Bureaucrat" is their term, and it rightly distinguishes Lewis and others from the rank-and-file; his actual work, however, was not so much that of a deskbound official as of an evangelist or traveling salesman.

By a succession of appointments and resignations in 1917-1918, Lewis became acting president of the UMWA without an election. Once arrived, he consolidated his position to win the next election—and he continued to be re-elected for years thereafter. The authors suggest that Lewis' methods in achieving such success were ruthless.

The history and situation of the United Mine Workers afford some under-standing of Lewis' rise and of the problems of his presidency. Coal mining was notoriously, undeniably, hard and dangerous work. Relations between operators and miners had rarely been serene, and were often violent. Within the union, ethnic and religious divisions, factionalism, bitter feuds, and accusations of misuse of union funds or of "class collaboration" (serving the bosses rather than the workers), were constant. In addition, Lewis, as President, had to deal with the impact of World War I and the postwar adjustment of the economy and of the coal industry. Himself a Republican, at least officially, Lewis had to face the individualistic and frequently antiunion mood of the prosperous 1920's. His contacts with the administrations, and especially with Herbert Hoover as Secretary of Commerce, won advantage neither for the union nor for himself (he apparently would have liked to be Secretary of Labor).

The low point for the union and for Lewis, the authors feel, was the Great Depression. Coal, already a distressed and depressed industry, could not support the army of miners, certainly not at union wages. Union membership declined, and only the New Deal, and in particular Section 7A of the National Industrial Recovery Act guaranteeing the right of collective bargaining, saved the union.

It was at this point in his career that Lewis began his important drive to modify the structure of the American Federation of Labor to accommodate the new mass-production industries, whose workers accounted for a large portion of the labor force. The United Mine Workers was one of a few exceptional industrial unions in that it was organized on the basis of all workers involved in mining, rather than on the basis of crafts. The unionization of many of the newer and larger mass industries, such as automobiles, steel, and rubber, was hampered by the insistence of the craft unions that their jurisdictions be recognized and the workers divided. Lewis and others, notably Sidney Hillman and David Dubinsky of the garment workers' unions, worked within the AFL to develop an organizing campaign in the mass industries. The result, as Dubofsky and Van Tine relate in meticulous detail, was a struggle with the dominant forces within the Federation. When the industrial organizers lost, they seceded from the AFL to found the Congress of Industrial Organizations (CIO).

These were days of high drama, and in many ways were the high point of Lewis' career. Auto workers discovered a new tactic: instead of picketing from outside, they "sat in" the plant. In the negotiations, which involved not only the workers and General Motors, but the courts, Governor Frank Murphy of Michigan, and President Roosevelt, Lewis was a key and much-publicized figure. The organization of steel, which had failed in the 1890's and again in 1919, was eventually a success, but only after the tragedy at Republic Steel in South Chicago on Memorial Day, 1937, and only after private arrangements, not involving the rank-and-file, had been made between Lewis and Myron Taylor of U.S. Steel. Plainly, throughout this story, the sympathies of the authors are with Lewis and his followers. The old leadership of the Federation are portrayed not only as lacking in vision, but also as stubborn and selfish; President Green in particular is viewed as weak and obstinate. "I've been exploring Bill Green's mind for years," Lewis told one advocate of reorganization; "I can tell you there's nothing there."

Yet their sympathy is not unalloyed. Lewis, they point out, had a long history of anti-Communist pronouncements, and they believe him sincere; yet he was willing to use Communists as organizers and aides without apparent qualms. Also, despite the original dependence of the organizing drives on the New Deal, Lewis' relationship with Roosevelt deteriorated. Ambition, and perhaps disappointment—the CIO had backed Roosevelt's reelection in 1936 and expected to be rewarded—as well as the difference of personalities and styles, all played a part. The authors point especially to the personality factor: Lewis, in public at least, was grim and angry and spoiled for a confrontation, while Roosevelt was always adept at compromise, and usually seemed agreeable even when not agreeing.

For Roosevelt, labor support was vital, but he was not strategically disadvantaged by the division of the AFL-CIO; to Lewis, this was black ingratitude. Moreover, while Dubofsky and Van Tine do not take Lewis' Republicanism (until 1932) too seriously, they do stress his essentially capitalistic viewpoint. That he liked limousines and large offices, that he blended well with the rich and mighty at luncheons and cocktail parties, and rarely "socialized" with fellow labor officials, is significant, but it is not the whole story. Lewis believed, the authors argue, in competition, but like the businessman, he sought competition that minimized losses. He saw the union as a business, not as a force for social change; a better share for the miners was his objective, rather than any radical changes in social structures. Some of the liberal New Deal ideology was bound to be in disagreement with such an approach.

But the real root of Lewis' opposition to Roosevelt lay in foreign policy. The experience of World War I, along with a heritage of Midwestern isolationism, made Lewis a vigorous and genuinely convinced adherent of neutrality, and an opponent of Roosevelt's foreign policy from 1939. It was this position that led him to oppose Roosevelt's third term in 1940, and that led to his resignation from the CIO presidency after labor, torn between two loyalties, chose Roosevelt.

Dubofsky and Van Tine next detail the following years, with their drama and frustration. Lewis retained control of the UMW, and led it in confrontation with mine operators and with the government, and thereby earned a reputation for lack of patriotism in many circles. His catch-all District 50 of the United Mine Workers, organizing a wide variety of nonminers, threatened other unions, but their power was not great enough to form a third force in competition with the AFL and CIO. Nor did Lewis' efforts at unity have the results he desired; the UMW rejoined the AFL, and in a few years "disaffiliated."

Lewis retired from the UMW presidency in 1960, and died in 1969, a largely forgotten figure. It was an inevitable consequence of the passage of time—Lewis was eighty-nine, and had been out of the public eye for a decade—but it was an ironic and somewhat bitter ending for so dramatic and dynamic a personality.

Van Tine and Dubofsky, in opening and in summary, relate Lewis' regime and methods to the later history of the United Mine Workers, and in particular to the killing of Joseph Yablonsky in 1969 when Yablonsky was challenging Lewis' successor in command. Throughout, they offer strong grounds that suggest the unscrupulousness of Lewis' methods; the dictatorial character of his rule over the union; the probability that he made private "deals" with some operators; and, toward the end, that he used pension funds and the union's relation to banks in which he had an interest to his own ends.

It is not a pretty story; but there is another side, and the authors do it justice as well. Lewis' leadership of the miners depended on more than manipulation; the miners held a genuine affection for their leader, and appreciated the material gains the union brought them. And Lewis, it is plain, never lost sight of the primacy of the union's goals, whether from commitment or shrewd self-interest. He survived, they also make clear, because of his intimate knowledge of the coal industry and his sense of the limits it could bear in labor costs, but even more because of his realization of the pragmatic need for cooperation in what were frequently depressed and over-producing enterprises. The authors insist, as well, on Lewis' genuine concern for the safety of the mines and the health of the miners.

This account is balanced, thorough, and even-handed; the analysis is penetrating. The story is a fascinating one, and well told; if occasionally the prose is stiff, it may be the price of care and accuracy.

George J. Fleming

KITH

Author: P. H. Newby (1918–   )
Publisher: Little, Brown and Company (Boston). 143 pp. $7.95
Type of work: Novel
Time: 1941
Locale: Cairo, Egypt

The story of the passionate obsession of a young British soldier for his uncle's Coptic wife

Principal characters:
DAVID COZENS, a young medical orderly in the British army
RAYMOND FOULKES, his uncle
NADIA FOULKES, Raymond's Coptic wife
MR. GUIRGIS, Nadia's father
RONNIE PENHALIGON, an American chaplain in the British army

In this, P. H. Newby's eighteenth novel, the author appears to be scraping the bottom of the barrel in drawing upon his wartime experiences in Egypt. Two of the main characters embody two aspects of his previous occupations as British soldier and as lecturer in English literature in Cairo. The book recounts the experiences of David Cozens, nicknamed Tishy, a young medical orderly with the British army, eager to exchange his noncombat status behind the lines for active duty. The story is told by David more than twenty years after his tempestuous, incestuous relationship as a nineteen-year-old with his uncle's young Coptic wife, a woman presented through the narrator's eyes as an overpoweringly sensually attractive, yet unattainable woman. "Writing about her is the only way to possess her. No one did really, certainly not Uncle Raymond, or me, or all those others." "Those others" refers to officers, for Nadia is rumored to be a prostitute specializing in British officers. She does this to humiliate her husband, Raymond, who married her without informing her that he had been married to another woman whom he had divorced.

The book opens with the elderly David trying to describe the spell woven by Nadia, his uncle's wife: "When you consider what Nadia eventually became it is extraordinary anyone ever thought she once tried to throw herself off the Great Pyramid." David's obsession is such that it is difficult for the reader to ascertain whether Nadia is all he implies she is or whether the narrator is still under the romantic spell of his youth. His first meeting with her is beguiling and frustrating. Shortly after he is stationed in Cairo, he receives word that his uncle, a lecturer at the university presently holding a commission in the British army, is seriously ill. When he visits Uncle Raymond, he is asked to look up Nadia and inquire after her welfare. He is told that the authorities have been unable to contact her. Uncle Raymond forbids him to ask about his past, of which David is totally unaware, since it has been considered a taboo subject in David's home—at least for the youthful lad.

Gradually Uncle Raymond fills David in on the details of his first marriage and subsequent divorce and his present marriage to Nadia, an ex-student of his.

It comes out that Uncle Raymond's troubles with Nadia, besides the difference in age and background of the elderly English gentleman and the beautiful young Coptic woman, is that she had not been informed of his first wife until after their marriage. For this reason she looks upon herself as being Uncle Raymond's concubine, and insists on believing he considers her the same.

David's attempts at carrying out his uncle's wishes are met at first with rebuffs from Nadia; she completely refuses to answer her door. When he finally arranges to meet her, his sexual attraction is heightened by a "clumsy attack" of an ineffectual old man who is beaten off with a single blow smashing his dentures. The old man turns out to be Nadia's father who is in the habit of hiding outside her door and accosting visitors.

It is in the portrayal of Nadia, central to the novel, that Newby's powers wane. Nadia represents for David all that Cleopatra was. She is exotic, beautiful, and intelligent; she quotes Henry James and Karl Marx, showing what an apt student of her husband she has been. But her actions leave the reader wondering whether she is cleverly inscrutable, as was her immortal forebear, or simply mad. For example, from the first page Newby speaks of her apparent attempt to commit suicide by the improbable means of jumping off the Great Pyramid. This occurrence takes place in the morning after their first night together. She had claimed that his sleeping with her is further proof that the English consider her to be a concubine rather than a wife, and she had disappeared from her apartment before David awoke. The entire question of whether she did or did not jump, and if she did, what her motives might have been, is left up in the air. David's only answer is "She's an Egyptian and she thinks she's the Sphinx." It is through incidents and comments like this that Newby tries to convey the exotic inscrutability of a culture alien to Western standards, but the reader is never quite sure if Newby expects him to take his comments about Nadia literally or as the biased interpretation of the once romantically involved David.

The love affair, if it may be so termed, is portrayed as an almost totally physical one. Although she possesses a keen intellect and a fierce sense of independence, Nadia's attractiveness to David derives from her sensual charms combined with her frequent rejections of his advances. Again, one is reminded of the games Shakespeare's Cleopatra plays with her lover/competitor Mark Antony.

As is usual in books dealing with people of widely divergent cultures, Newby tries to explore the relationships between these peoples. In the person of Nadia's father, Guirgis, we get the proponent of the philosophy that national characteristics are meaningless, that all people share a common humanity. This idea is hotly disputed by Nadia, who claims that the only ones who defend such a proposition are non-Europeans speaking to Europeans. She very plausibly suggests that such a philosophy is simply a device for the subjugated race to prove it is not inferior. Ironically, her father himself, despite his pathetic aping of English interests in reading P. G. Wodehouse and playing golf, disproves his own theory when he advises David that the country will not let him marry Nadia as he intends. He argues that the Egyptians are "prisoners of history" and cannot improve their condition. He then tells David that his original meaning was misinterpreted; he simply meant that one had to act as though there were no differences among various peoples. This, he says, is what great writers such as Shakespeare have always done.

David's Uncle Raymond adds a similar commentary on the differences of the races when he speaks of the failure of his marriage. He attributes it to Nadia's nationality: "Always been something *odd* about Egyptian women. St. Antony thought so. It influenced his thinking." Uncle Raymond later speaks of the peculiarity of Egypt as "a mixture of pride on the one hand and degradation on the other." The central incident of the book is an illustration of this dichotomy: Nadia's sense of pride has been offended by the knowledge of Raymond's first wife. That she is of another background leads her to the outraged feeling that she has been compromised, and to get revenge she degrades herself to the status of a prostitute serving the English. The very degradation of her position salvages her sense of pride. She is trying to humiliate her husband; if she is his concubine, she is also concubine to others, and that redounds to his greater shame. Eventually she is successful and Raymond is rendered impotent.

Another closely related aspect of these differences is the natural inability of humans to communicate with one another. Raymond blames his situation on the Arabic language which confuses its extravagant descriptions of reality for reality itself. Significantly, despite his many years of residence in Egypt, he has never bothered to learn Arabic because there is no great body of literature at the end to reward such study.

But, regardless of national differences, there is a communication failure among the characters. David's difficulties arise from his youthful impetuosity and his inability to see others' points of view. As might be expected, his relations with Uncle Raymond are affected by his feelings of guilt, but he is also repeatedly on the verge of being arrested for breaking army regulations. For example, he commits the offense of dressing in an officer's uniform and frequenting places restricted to officers. In such a precarious circumstance he dares to get involved in a dispute with another officer to the extent of jeopardizing his future. He debates the American chaplain, Major Ronnie Penhaligon, on the nature of evil. Penhaligon maintains that the war has its good side in that "Captain" Cozens is engaged in an unequivocal fight of good against evil. David maintains that nothing is clear-cut about the war, especially the question of good and evil. His thoughts about the war are mixed up with his guilt feelings about his relationship with his uncle and aunt. He feels that one has to be evil to understand it, and that he is as capable of evil as Adolf Hitler. In this debate David sounds like a typical youth arguing with his elders. Penhaligon, a self-righteous spokesman for formal religion, fails to see David's point that in fighting the Nazi army they are also fighting the evil which is within every man.

Penhaligon's anger leads him to charge David formally with treason to the Assistant Provost Marshall. It is only through Uncle Raymond's peacekeeping efforts that David is not arrested for impersonating an officer.

Although Newby does raise serious questions of communication among people of wide cultural differences and of the nature of evil within each of us, the novel fails in its portrayal of the central conflict, largely through the confusion regarding the main character and Nadia. It might seem that *Kith* is about the coming of age of David, except that Newby suggests much more with Nadia as the heroine and with the serious repercussions that result from her character and behavior.

The novel ends with the narrator recounting his experiences in the twenty-some years which have lapsed since the affair. His last recollection of Nadia had been of thugs who set upon them and knocked him unconscious, and, he had supposed, killed Nadia. His beating resulted in "hysteric dumbness" which did clear up in time for him to take part in the Normandy invasion. Afterwards his interest in sex had disappeared for twenty years. After all these years he discovers Nadia is still alive and has married an Ethiopian Prince. When he meets her, he finds her totally committed to her new life while he has wasted the last twenty years of his. He thinks of his cuckolded uncle and his talks about Alexander and Antony, realizing that what Uncle Raymond was saying was that one could not escape the role in which he was cast. David understands now that he does not know how to get away from himself. That part of Newby's message is clear.

Roger A. Geimer

LANCELOT

Author: Walker Percy (1916–   )
Publisher: Farrar, Straus and Giroux (New York). 257 pp. $8.95
Type of work: Novel
Time: The present
Locale: A plantation up the river from New Orleans

A modern novel about a man whose quest for evil results in his participation in it, for only by participating in evil can he understand what went wrong in his family situation in particular and in the modern world in general

> *Principal characters:*
> LANCELOT, the narrator, a cuckolded husband, failed lawyer, and ex-grid star
> MARGOT, his wife
> PERCIVAL, the priest who acts as a sounding board for Lance's monologue

Lancelot is made up of the ramblings of a madman in search of evil. Lancelot Andrewes Lamar, a cuckolded husband who has slit the throat of his wife's lover and blown up his Belle Isle plantation home with his wife inside, narrates Walker Percy's fourth novel from a "nuthouse."

Similar to his three earlier novels, *The Moviegoer* (1960), *The Last Gentleman* (1966), and *Love in the Ruins* (1971), *Lancelot* is packed with philosophical and theological questions, questions debated in his essay collection *Message in the Bottle* (1975). Lancelot is another of Percy's alienated characters who has lost himself to everydayness, sex, consumerism, newspapers, and television. He is jolted out of his alienation only by catastrophe: his wife has been unfaithful—his daughter is not his. Percy, a Christian novelist, uses violence, shock, and the bizarre as a catalyst to promote a self-directed search. Lancelot, like the characters in Percy's earlier novels, undertakes the search only after catastrophe occurs.

In a series of fragmented flashbacks, Lancelot, failed lawyer, ex-grid star, Rhodes scholar, and madman, travels through his memory in an attempt to discover what went wrong. He relives the past, while rambling in a monologue to a silent priest who acts as a sounding board, from the Institute of Aberrant Behavior where he has been confined since the Belle Isle fire and murder.

The search begins, as in Percy's earlier novels, by confronting the haunted past, because only by understanding the past can Lance contemplate the future. In doing so he must, as Percy has suggested in his philosophical essays, "stand in front of the house of his childhood in order to recover himself." Once there Lance discovers his father was a crook. He must then not only become aware of sin, of evil, but he must also see it and experience it. What he sees is his wife committing adultery, his daughter participating in an orgy, and his son admitting his homosexuality. The issue is twofold: first Lancelot must see his wife's unfaithfulness; then in his quest for sin, he must experience evil—he must kill. While searching for evil, he discovers that "sexual sin was the unholy grail I sought." Because his wife's unfaithfulness jolts him out of his ordinary existence, he questions whether "good can come from evil," and he undertakes a search "not for God but for evil." "Dishonor," Lancelot learns in this first-person narration, "is sweeter and more mysterious than honor. It holds a secret," and he is determined to discover the secret.

So, the protagonist experiences evil and discovers despair. But for Percy, a follower of Kierkegaardian philosophy, despair is a stage toward hope. Lancelot despairs of the modern world, "The great whoredom and fagdom of America." But he visualizes a new life, a new order of things; "there will be a tight-lipped courtesy between men. And chivalry toward women. Women must be saved from the whoredom they have chosen." His new life, as he visualizes it, involves a retreat to "a cabin and a barn and fifty acres in the Blue Ridge not far from Lexington, Virginia." Joining him, he assumes, will be Anna, a victim of gang rape, who along with Lance is a patient in the institute. Lance links his future to Anna's.

Percy, termed a stylist by many, has progressed in his style; the monologue device spans the novel. Yet he takes this novel one step further than *Love in the Ruins*, where the main character awaits the end of the world. Here Lancelot ends the modern world for himself and plans to start a new one. Again, as in his earlier novels, Percy reverses the traditional ways of making do in the modern world. Average happiness is conceived as despair, sin is better than indifference, forgetting better than remembering, wonder better than certainty, tragedy better than an ordinary day, and madness better than sanity.

The new novel, with Lancelot rambling to a priest in confessional fashion, breaks from Percy's previous style. The monologue, which pretends to be a dialogue, is similar in tone and style to Camus' *The Fall*, except that it is broken at the novel's conclusion when the priest answers "yes" to Lance's newfound understanding and ability to change, to heal his broken self, as Percy has all his characters do at the conclusions of his novels. Percy, a Catholic, always incorporates religion into his novels, and Percival, the priest-psychiatrist, echoes Father Rinaldo Smith and Kev Kevin of *Love in the Ruins*.

The protagonists in Percy's four novels all seek alternatives to their present alienated existence, alternatives which will enable them to function in a fragmented and empirically oriented society. Consequently, the fragmented self exemplified by Binx of *The Moviegoer*, Will of *The Last Gentleman*, Dr. More of *Love in the Ruins*, and Lance in this novel is reunified in varying degrees by the novels' ends. Other similarities also exist between *Lancelot* and Percy's previous novels. Binx is a moviegoer in that novel; Lancelot is a television watcher, while Margot is an actress with a company filming a movie in Belle Isle. Lancelot realizes, as Binx eventually did, "that the movie folk were trafficking in illusions in a real world, but the real world thought that its reality could only be found in illusions." Percy also repeats his intrigue with catastrophe as a means of "rendering the broken self whole" in *Lancelot*. Binx in *The Moviegoer*, Sutter

Vaught in *The Last Gentleman,* and Dr. More in *Love in the Ruins* realize that "only in times of illness or disaster or death are people real."

Although Percy continues to pose philosophical questions in *Lancelot*—can good come out of evil, does tragedy heighten reality, how is one to live in the modern world—he has not progressed in developing new characters and ideas. They all echo and re-echo his last three novels as well as his philosophical essays. *Lancelot* continues a progression in Percy's writing, for Lance, like the other protagonists, undertakes a search—in this case, a search for evil. He begins a new world for himself by personally and symbolically trying to destroy the modern world, by understanding evil through his participation in it.

The fragmented digressions of Lancelot's mind are the vehicle Percy uses to convey his philosophy. But the reader gets bogged down in the author's philosophical gymnastics over questions of the significance of the past, the question of good and evil, and the alienation and fragmentation of modern man. Those who have read and enjoyed Percy's earlier novels will find *Lancelot* tedious at times.

Janet H. Hobbs

LETTERS ON LITERATURE AND POLITICS
1912-1972

Author: Edmund Wilson (1895-1972)
Edited by Elena Wilson
Publisher: Farrar, Straus and Giroux (New York). Illustrated. 768 pp. $20.00
Type of work: Letters on literary and cultural history
Time: 1912 to 1972
Locale: The Eastern United States

A collection of letters which traces the involvement of Edmund Wilson in the cultural and political life of the United States from before World War I to 1972

Edmund Wilson's *Letters on Literature and Politics* selects from the vast number of available letters those dealing with his close involvement with the cultural, literary, and, to a lesser extent, political life of America from the early twentieth century to his death in 1972. The book was edited by Wilson's widow, Elena, and it includes an excellent index, judicial footnotes, a sympathetic Introduction by Daniel Aaron, and a Foreword by Leon Edel. The arrangement of the letters is also unusual and intelligent. It breaks the usual rigid chronological arrangement to focus on significant events or relationships. As a result, we retain a sense of overall development and change and a fuller understanding of Wilson's involvement with the Dead Sea Scrolls, Russian politics, or his relationship with F. Scott Fitzgerald and John Peale Bishop. The apparatus is not only thoroughly professional but it is also accessible to the specialist and the common reader alike, an achievement that Wilson would have appreciated.

The reader may, however, wonder why such pains should be taken to present the letters of a man who was not an esteemed writer of imaginative literature, nor a wit, nor a person who led an exciting or adventurous life. Wilson was no Byron, Keats, or even a Lady Mary Wortley-Montague. Nor was he given to confessional outbursts or revelations of the heart. Indeed, we find him referring to his marriages in such casual sentences as these:

> I got married last February to a girl named Margaret Canby (she was formerly married to a cousin of Henry Seidel).

> I'm married to a girl named Mary McCarthy, who has done some writing for *Partisan Review* and *The Nation.*

However, if we find out little about the inner man in this volume, we do see the public Wilson, a man who was involved in nearly every new book, new idea, new movement of the twentieth century. And we do see him—or hear him—as his contemporaries did. Wilson had a commanding presence, and the letters are often harsh and tactless, but always confident in the midst of various cultural breakdowns.

The first letter in this collection is vintage Edmund Wilson, even though the author is a sixteen-year-old prep school student:

> In short, with the exception of two chapters which pleased me very much, *The Naulakha* seems to me to be only a tolerably interesting and fairly readable potboiler. Your enthusiasm about it surprises me.

The tone is positively majestical; it shows Wilson's easy grasp of the problem, an easy dismissal of the offending book, and a typical blast at the deficient taste of a reader. These Wilsonian traits remained until his death sixty years later, as we can see in a 1969 letter about Wallace Stevens:

> Have you looked into his letters, which seem to me deadly? The idea of the Hartford insurance man who has never been abroad but fancies himself as a wistful Pierrot inhabiting the *fin de siècle* I have always found somewhat repellent. His early book *Harmonium* has some nice—purely verbal—writing, but his more pretentious stuff bores me . . .

As the style and sweeping judgments suggest, Wilson was a popular rather than a scholarly critic; he was very much in the mold of Matthew Arnold or Samuel Johnson. He performed a necessary function in introducing difficult, *avant-garde* writers, often from non-English nations and languages, to the American public. He championed the cause of Joyce, Eliot, the French Symbolist poets, and many others before it was fashionable to do so. He was not as close to these artists as Ezra Pound was and perhaps did not understand them as completely. But his reviews, his encouraging letters to readers and reviewers, and his books, especially *Axel's Castle*, made many of the great moderns available to educated people of the day.

He had, it is true, some blind spots which marred his otherwise impressive record of correct judgments. For example, he could not tolerate Robert Frost: "Frost and Amy Lowell I never cared for at all, but I did like *Spoon River Anthology.*" He dismissed D. H. Lawrence in his later years: "I've always been meaning to read Lawrence's novels—other than *Lady C.*—but have never got around to it. I met him once and thought him ill-bred and hysterical, and his writing mostly affects me in the same way." But Wilson was open to different literature; indeed, the more difficult, the more readily did he accept the challenge to read, understand, and elucidate the text for others. So while we must acknowledge Wilson's influence, we need to notice that his criteria for excellence in literature were, at times, rather narrow. Some examples of such criteria are his demand for exact rather than half rhyme in poetry and his insistence on sufficient motivation for fictional characters and realistic detail. Wilson could also be cruel in seeking out lapses in books by his friends or enemies which often provoked sharp answers to the criticism and amazed replies from the critic.

> In regard to my criticisms in general, they were stimulated, not by preconceived ideas about metrical rules, but by the fact that I stumbled over certain lines in the poem. Then, when I wrote you, I analyzed them to see what was the matter.

Nor was Wilson tactful in writing to friends on subjects other than literature. His letter to Allen Tate on the occasion of Tate's conversion to Catholicism is a good example of this trait: "I hope that becoming a Catholic will give you peace of mind; though swallowing the New Testament as factual and moral truth seems to me an awful price to pay for it." Tate was, it seems, enraged at Wilson's lack of feeling.

Another disconcerting characteristic of Wilson was his inevitable revision of his earlier positive opinion of a writer; few escaped his shifting tastes and judgments. Even Joyce was finally brought low: "About *Ulysses:* It is certainly true that parts of it—especially toward the end—are just incredibly dull." Even the majestic Eliot is found wanting: "As I was saying to you, I think, there is a scoundrel and actor in Eliot. It was the young scoundrel who wrote the good poetry, and it is now the old scoundrel who is putting on the public performance." Perhaps more is involved here than a change in taste or even a reevaluation. Wilson was a maker of reputations, especially from 1914 to 1939. He must, therefore, abandon his previous discoveries to free himself to praise and call attention to new writers. He had to be *au courant* to justify his reputation as the Dean of American Letters; he could not afford to spend his time going deeper into established modern or ancient writers. This trait is also seen in his personal relationships. The early letters to, for example, Christian Gauss, are respectful, even humble. In a few years, however, even the learned and honored Gauss is being corrected and instructed. Wilson needed to dominate the books he read and the people he knew, and he managed to do just this with almost every book or person he met.

Wilson's own attempts at fiction, poetry, and drama were, for the most part, failures. The poetry, an early volume, lacked the true poetic voice that was so evident in his friend, John Peale Bishop, which may explain Wilson's gentle treatment of Bishop. The fiction, as he admits, lacked the lifelike quality of the novels of his other friend, F. Scott Fitzgerald. None of the plays was successfully produced. The desire to be an artist rather than a man of letters is hardly a desire that is confined to Wilson, but one wonders how a critic as tenacious in investigating a text, and so harsh and comtemptuous of second-rate work, could allow such works to be printed.

Wilson was too much a man of letters to become deeply involved in politics. He remained aloof from both World War I and World War II, and despised those who were propagandists for either war. His one close brush with politics was with the cause that captured so many intellectuals in the 1930's: Communism. Wilson's experience was representative. In 1935, he defended the mass murders to a very skeptical John Dos Passos: "In regard to Russia, it seems to me a mistake to form any too definite opinion because we really know nothing about it. I don't see any reason to disbelieve that they had a counterrevolutionary conspiracy backed by Germans on their hands, as they said they did." Wilson did, however, go to Russia in the 1930's, and, while he remained generally sympathetic, he was disturbed by the treatment of the proletariat. By 1938, he had changed completely; he condemned the Moscow trials as "clearly frame-ups designed to divert attention from the real causes of the system's working badly. . . ." He was never again to be tempted in the coming years by a political ideology.

Wilson's direct influence upon literary taste and judgments seemed to wane after 1939. The *avant-garde* was now the Establishment, and there was less need for a cultural arbiter. In these circumstances, Wilson turned to other areas where discoveries could be made and passed on to the public. He learned Russian and encouraged us to read Pushkin and Pasternak. He read and wrote about Haitian and Canadian literature. He even learned Hebrew and went to study the Dead Sea Scrolls. This was significant and important work, but somehow, with the exception of the work on Russian literature, it did not have the impact that Wilson's earlier work did. We have not embraced Canadian or Haitian literature, and Christianity seems to have gone beyond the effects of the Dead Sea Scrolls with its own internal reforms. Wilson ended his career with a memoir, *Upstate*, a prelude to the diaries and letters that have come forth after his death.

It is, perhaps, appropriate to ask: What is the permanence of Edmund Wilson? He was, it is clear, essential to Anglo-American culture in this century. He was a graceful writer, but he is not likely to be remembered as a stylist. His major criticism has, for the most part, been absorbed into the culture. His life is fascinating to us because of his closeness to the cultural center of this country, but he did not possess or display the deep humanity that, say, Samuel Johnson did. And so he will most probably in the long run be considered a minor figure who nevertheless contributed to the success or failure of figures more important than himself.

James T. Sullivan

LETTERS TO FRIENDS, FAMILY, AND EDITORS

Author: Franz Kafka (1883–1924)
Translated by Richard and Clara Winston
Publisher: Schocken Books (New York). 509 pp. $24.50
Type of work: Collected and edited correspondence
Time: 1900–1924
Locale: Various European cities

> *A translation of the correspondence published in German by Max Brod in 1958, but also including material which did not appear in that edition*

The appearance of this book is an important publishing event, bringing to completion the translated letters of Franz Kafka, except those to his sister Ottla. The milestones in this undertaking are the *Letters to Milena* (1953), the *Letter to His Father* (1966), and the *Letters to Felice* (1973). The correspondence, of course, complements the publication of Kafka's works in English translation, including the diaries, so that very nearly all of his output—literary works, diaries, and letters—is now accessible to those unable to read the original language. Nor, except to specialists, is reference to the original language absolutely necessary: Kafka's influence in the non-German-speaking countries began in the 1930's and has steadily continued since then. Although it is true that no translation can retain the inherent nuances and shades of meaning of the original text, literate persons everywhere, scholars among them, first become acquainted with "great authors" through translations. Although certainly the best approach to an author is to read his works in their original language, this does not mean that a reader loses critically through an accurate and sensitive translation: Dante became known in America through the English of Henry Wadsworth Longfellow. The several merits of *Letters to Friends, Family, and Editors* include just this: Richard and Clara Winston have outstandingly performed the task of rendering into colloquial and idiomatic English the 1958 edition by Max Brod of Kafka's correspondence, including some letters not in that text (see the Preface).

A spot comparison of the translation with the original language shows that the Winstons have closely adhered to the sense of Kafka's German, and that their English idiom is at once extensive and precise enough to lend accurate expression to German locutions. The English-speaking reader, therefore, ignorant of German, can gain practically as much from the correspondence here presented as from the original edition published by Brod. In fact, and another reason to welcome this publication, it is rather a rule of thumb that the wider the appeal an author gains through translation (which is an underpinning of comparative literature), the greater his influence upon other societies and times. In German literature of this century, the translations especially of Thomas Mann and Hermann Hesse illustrate this transcendence of national and continental boundaries.

The Winstons' handsomely bound and printed book consists essentially of 524 letters to forty-eight different addressees, making up 415 pages of text. This is followed by a little more than seven pages of "conversation slips," the written utterances of Kafka made during his final illness. The correspondence is admirably annotated in seventy-two pages of meticulous references to the letters arranged by year; the notes clarify and identify allusions in the letters (some of them obscure: for example, "Ohropax" is identified as a brand of ear plugs, while the "composing hut" turns out to be Gustav Mahler's summer residence). A chronology of six pages provides the essential facts concerning Kafka's life; and an adequate index of some seven pages completes the book, which is very nearly free of misprints. In sum, *Letters to Friends, Family, and Editors* is an exemplary product of translating and editing, very professionally done, and should be in the library of every person and institution having an interest in this major author.

The letters themselves reveal Kafka as being all his life, or at least since 1900, a sociable and outgoing person, far more concerned with his relationships with those individuals to whom he was attached by family ties, friendship (the majority of the letters are addressed to Max Brod, Oskar Baum, Robert Klopstock, and female friends), or the prospects of publication of his works (letters to Ernst Rowohlt and Kurt Wolff), than with social and political events (from these letters, one would hardly know that World War I occurred). The one exception is Kafka's consciousness of his Jewish heritage, and the position of Judaism in the world of his time. His consciousness of being Jewish is traceable here and there throughout the correspondence; and, in fact, most of the people with whom he either had or formed ties were Jews (such as Martin Buber and Franz Werfel). Otherwise, Kafka gives the impression of a man who needs to communicate and to write; who is very sensitive to details of his environment; who is restless, yet afraid of change; who has a constant interest in current literature and in the literature of the past; who suffers illness and occasional despair; and who, late in life, contracts a fear of people. This is the man who, finally, in spite of all the pressures with which he had to contend, could still write to Robert Klopstock in October of 1921 that "In ordinary daily life the only real comfort is the experience that, incredible as it is, one emerges time and again from the bottomless pits of so many a moment."

Harry Tucker, Jr.

LIFE/SITUATIONS
Essays Written and Spoken

Author: Jean-Paul Sartre (1905–   )
Translated from the French by Paul Auster and Lydia Davis
Publisher: Pantheon Books (New York). 216 pp. $8.95
Type of work: Essays

A translation of Sartre's latest book, Situations X: Politique et autobiographie, *which contains three interviews in which Sartre takes an intimate look at himself and his work, and four essays on political topics*

Jean-Paul Sartre, whose heyday as the "high priest of existentialism" is long past, has never settled comfortably into the role of an *éminence grise.* Each decade has seen him at once thoroughly engaged in the affairs of the moment and developing as a creative philosopher. He abandoned his career as a writer of "literature" with his last play, *The Condemned of Altona* (1959) and his autobiographical *The Words* (1964). Since then, he has expressed himself in philosophy *(Critique of Dialectical Reason),* literary criticism (the monumental studies of Genet and Flaubert), and in the ten volumes of essays, primarily on literary and political topics, which he calls *Situations.*

In Sartre's first great philosophical work, *Being and Nothingness,* "situations" refer to the ways in which an engaged consciousness structures the world in which it finds itself. Writing on theater, Sartre calls the dramatic situation a "trap" from which a character, in asserting his freedom, creates an exit. The essays are aptly titled in that they represent ways of being engaged with the world and new developments of ongoing philosophical concerns.

The translators of *Situations X* have chosen to put the autobiographical interviews ("spoken essays") before those on politics, reversing the order of the original. This no doubt reflects the fact that American readers will tend to be more interested in the personal and general topics Sartre treats in the interviews than in his more strictly French or European oriented political concerns. Sartre has never spoken about himself more freely or candidly than in "Self-Portrait at Seventy," an interview with Michel Contat which first appeared in *Le Nouvel Observateur* in 1975. In a much briefer interview with Simone de Beauvoir, he attempts to explain his position, and earlier lack of position, on the feminist movement. In another interview with Contat, and with Michel Rybalka (who are collecting and editing Sartre's complete works), Sartre comments on *The Idiot of the Family* and on the interests which led him to study Flaubert.

"Self-Portrait at Seventy" reveals almost immediately why the interview has become an important means of expression for Sartre. Since his vision is almost totally gone, he must now rely on the spoken word for all communication. Although he admits that not being able to read and write in one sense "robs me of all reason for existing" he seems to accept his condition with equanimity. Simone de Beauvoir reads him newspapers and books, he converses with his intimates and with others who wish to see him, he listens to music a great deal, and he is preparing, with others, a series of broadcasts for television. What he cannot work on in preparing speeches, he says, is style: for that he would have to be able to see the writing on the page. He admits to problems of adaptation which come with old age—he cannot adjust to the tape recorder. And while he acknowledges that many contemporary young people are scornful of preoccupation with style, he admits to an ongoing concern with literary manners of presentation.

In spite of this difficulty, a clearly Sartrean style still emerges from the pages of these *situations*. One does sense the lack of the striking metaphors which characterized Sartre's novels and even his philosophical works, but the sharp, direct Sartrean voice is there. An ideal which Sartre still holds, and which he expresses here more directly than elsewhere, is that of complete candor: not sincerity, which involves "bad faith," but transparency. He "can imagine the day when two men will no longer have secrets from each other, because no one will have any more secrets from anyone, because subjective life, as well as objective life, will be completely offered up, given." Such a condition is not possible in the present state of society, but one can strive for it. The interview seems as good a vehicle as any.

Sartre's views on himself, fascinating enough to those who have followed his life and work, are further enlivened by Contat's occasional disagreements with them. For example, Contat refuses to accept Sartre's characterization of himself as "just anybody" and points out that he has had various difficulties in adjusting himself to fame. In conformity with existentialist beliefs, Sartre refuses to "be" a famous man or an old man. He acknowledges the characteristics and the problems which old age gives him (one might say the *situation* of old age), he views his past life with a certain new serenity and acceptance, but he feels most comfortable and most creative with young people around the age of thirty.

Sartre also, of course, refuses to "be" an existentialist, a label which, he says, is now only used in textbooks, "where it doesn't mean anything." And yet, if one must have a label, Sartre would prefer "existentialist" to "Marxist." Freedom, the overriding theme of his life and works, continues to be his major concern. Sartre still feels that existentialism can exist legitimately within the larger framework of Marxism. His political goal is "to point out, emphasize and support . . . whatever aspects of a particular political and social situation can produce a society of free men." In the present world context, the only such society possible will be a socialistic one. This society does not yet exist—certainly not in the USSR and not even in China; it is still to be created.

Simone de Beauvoir begins her questioning of Sartre with the observation that although he has consistently spoken out for oppressed groups (workers, blacks, Jews), he has never spoken of women as a group. In response to this, Sartre reflects on his past life and finds that he has always viewed women as individuals, never as a class with common interests or problems. Under further questioning, Sartre admits to a certain amount of *macho* in his life and works but says that he had assumed it to be an individual rather than a male trait. His awareness of women as a group or movement which intersects but does not correspond to the traditional class struggle between bourgeois and proletariat has thus constituted a kind of awakening.

Sartre's analysis of *how* women constitute a common-interest group nonetheless seems somewhat dated; it is based on a view of women in traditional roles which have already altered radically in the past few years. The bourgeois woman, for example, is seen as bourgeois only through her husband—she has no direct relation to capital. The relations between such a woman and her maid are closer, of a different order, than those between worker and boss. Workingclass women need to be awakened to oppression at home, through their husbands, as well as to oppression through their class. Such a view does not account for the growing number of women at all social levels already in the work force. Simone de Beauvoir's concern about what kind of work successful women will do—whether they will be preempted by existing male values or use their situation to transform society by working for feminist needs—seems more to the point. Sartre concurs that at the present stage women need to accept positions in the existing power structure.

Whatever the contradictions have been, one cannot in the end doubt the reality of Sartre's commitment to feminism. His relationship with Simone de Beauvoir, although exceptional, is certainly, as she herself indicates, a case in point. At a time when many male intellectuals found the woman question laughable, Sartre supported de Beauvoir in her writing of *The Second Sex* and maintained with her a relationship in which the equality of both partners was never in question.

In speaking about *The Idiot of the Family,* Sartre must deal with the problem of implicit self-contradictions in his lifestyle and work. How can someone who said farewell to literature to devote himself to militancy involve himself in the exhaustive study of a nineteenth century literary figure? Sartre acknowledges that his aims are ambiguous: he is engaged both in a kind of escapism and in a search for a method, along with a redefinition of *engagement,* which will have contemporary implications. Sartre declares himself in opposition to the fundamental premise which unites most of the recent crop of critics in France and their disciples: he is completely opposed to the notion of a "text." What interests him is the old critical idea of elucidating "the relationship between the man and the work." The methodology which proceeds from this idea, however, is uniquely Sartrean: it combines the Marxist premise of a study of economic and ideological influences on the writer with the existential question of how the individual deals with his "situation" and forms his unique project.

At the end of the interview on *The Idiot of the Family* Sartre asks himself the question, "How can a political writer make himself understood by a popular audience while carrying out an idea to the very end?" The problem approached here, that of the relationship of the militant intellectual to the popular masses, is one dealt with more directly in his four political essays, "The Burgos Trial," "The Maoists in France," "Justice and the State," and "Elections: A Trap for Fools." In the second and third essays, in particular, Sartre discusses his role as editor of the Maoist *Cause du peuple* and his hopes for a publication which would permit workers and "country people" (a rather quaint translation of *paysans*) to speak directly to each other in their own language, without the intermediary of bourgeois expression. Sartre is always rather tiresome when he speaks with guilt about his inevitable bourgeois background, but in these essays he speaks more positively than usual of potential future alliances between workers and intellectuals.

The four essays, written in the early 1970's, all betray the influence of the somewhat euphoric hopes which swept over Sartre and other members of the extreme left in the wake of May, 1968. The promise of the creation of an entirely *new* society, neither bourgeois democracy nor a staid and stale Communism, seems at hand. The spontaneous, popular, creative character of the May uprising signified, for Sartre, an announcement that bourgeois society was doomed. After May, 1968, Sartre tells us, he was able to formulate for himself the difference between a codified, permanent system of justice controlled by the state and an "irregular and primitive" popular justice in which the people protest the injustices they have suffered through oppression. This constitutes the theme of "Justice and the State." One must choose between these two forms of justice, Sartre says, and May, 1968, enabled him to choose the latter.

Each of the essays takes a particular case as a point of departure and develops an aspect of a general theme: the "mystifications" perpetuated by bourgeois democracy and exposed by genuine popular needs. In "The Burgos Trial" Sartre reflects on the Basque uprising in Spain and its brutal repression by the Franco regime. He argues that suppression of nationalist movements within existing states is not merely a result of Fascism, as we would like to think, but inevitable even in democracies such as France which insist on treating men as abstract entities in a state rather than concrete members of a Basque or Breton community. The revolt against internal colonialism, which the Basque struggle exemplifies, is part of a popular movement and a claim to genuine, nonabstract identity. Similarly, in "Elections: A Trap for Fools," Sartre argues that elections, which give people an abstract identity as voters, or citizens, rob them of their true identity and encourage them to betray the community or class to which they genuinely belong. Sartre opposes the condition of "seriality," in which one assumes the characteristics of a statistical member of a group as defined by Others (a driver, a soldier, a television viewer, a voter) to those of genuine collectivity, popular sovereignty. Elections in no way offer people a chance to influence politics, but only to perpetuate the system of nonrepresentative democracy.

Sartre's concept of a true socialist society seems in these essays rather vague and utopian. In the end, he reveals his true colors as an anarchist. The final words of the book (in the arrangement of the translators) are indicative: "We must try, each according to his own resources, to organize the vast anti-hierarchic movement which fights institutions everywhere." The anarchic political position is perhaps after all the most consistent with Sartre's philosophy.

The English translation of these interviews and essays reads well. With the exception of a few inaccuracies ("social sciences" for *sciences humaines*) it follows the French closely, and gives the French term when the translation cannot be exact. The American reader will find here a rich personal, philosophical, and political portrait of a man whose self-examination reveals an ongoing moral lucidity.

Mary Ann Witt

MAO'S CHINA
A History of the People's Republic

Author: Maurice Meisner (1931–   )
Publisher: The Macmillan Company (New York). 416 pp. $17.95
Type of work: History
Time: 1949–1976
Locale: The People's Republic of China

An interpretive history of the major political, social, economic, and intellectual developments of China's Communist government

The title of Maurice Meisner's comprehensive assessment of the first quarter century of China's Communist government sets the tenor of his book and the Chinese revolutionary experiment in proper perspective. In strategy, ideological growth, and personal leadership, Mao's presence dominated the major changes that have taken place in China since 1949. Viewing the motivations behind Chinese Communist policies, Meisner offers many salient comments to explain Mao's—and by inference, China's—contribution to the ideological development of Marxism-Leninism. So extensive has Mao's imprint been that a third component added to the Marxist-Leninist lexicon, identified as "Maoism," is justified.

While Mao developed *his* views on Communism and its application to the Chinese scene in the early 1940's at Yenan, his basic concepts had already been formulated two decades earlier. Meisner contends that when Mao became an avowed Marxist in 1919, his thoughts that would later guide his interpretation of Marxism and revolution were already present. It is axiomatic that Mao then believed that the course of history is determined by men and that their revolutionary thoughts were most important in directing their actions. Mao could see during the New Culture Movement of the early 1920's that organization and activism were effective means for bringing about political, and possibly institutional, change. It is precisely these ideas that led Mao to take his dramatic steps in launching the Great Leap Forward campaign (1957–1958) and the Great Proletarian Cultural Revolution (1966–1969), the first to accelerate the pace of communization and the second to challenge the party's implementation of Marxism-Leninism.

Although Mao recognized Communism as a world revolutionary movement, he departed from traditional Marxist thinking to see the special role of China in it. Nationalism was prominent in Mao's thoughts, and at the root of it was the Chinese hatred of imperialism. This widespread Chinese sentiment, Mao believed, would unite the people behind the revolutionary cause. In search of this mass support, Maoism inevitably assumed a populist role; and the countryside, where the vast peasantry lived, became the object of China's Communism. Mao's nationalist and populist role, contends Meisner, had a profound influence on "the manner in which he adapted and employed Marxism." His basic departure from Leninism was Mao's disinterest in the urban working class and in his understanding of the nature and role of the party. The peasant masses, Mao believed, bore a "revolutionary consciousness" rather than the party. While Mao's strategy was unorthodox, Meisner correctly points out, his goals were in accord with orthodox Marxism.

Important to the determination and success of Chinese Communism was the commitment of the Maoists to the vision of a "socialist future" once a Communist government had been established. The Communist movement in China, Meisner contends, was not led by power-hungry men using Marxism as an ideological disguise for their ambitions, nor were they solely nationalists or modernizers, but they were devoutly committed to liberating those who were oppressed and exploited. Consequently, no matter to what extent Chinese Communist revolutionary strategy may have strayed from classical Marxism-Leninism, China's leadership never abandoned its socialist objectives, as evident in the social and economic policies of the People's Republic.

To achieve Mao's goals in a large country, with yet unknown millions of people, speaking various dialects, amid squalor, destruction, and disorder, was no simple task in the early years after victory. The restructuring of China in a socialist mold required intense discipline and strict governance to weed out disruptive elements. Despite Mao's preference for "democratic" methods of "persuasion," it became apparent in the period 1949–1953 that the new Communist state resorted to oppression. A virtual "reign of terror," sanctioned by Mao, against intransigent landlords opposing the new regime, resulted in the deaths of at least two million people.

Meisner suggests that this harsh policy was a nervous reaction to external threats emanating from the Korean War, a policy which subsided as the threat of a direct American attack on China receded. His explanation, however, may be too simplistic. While foreign threats were used to rally support for the new government's policies, the oppression was likely a response to more urgent needs. When the Communists seized power, relatively few Chinese were acquainted with the objectives of Maoism; and at least one segment of society (the landlord class which the Communists despised) was hostile toward any government that threatened their wealth and position. To consolidate their control, some swift and decisive measures were natural for the Communist leadership. Mao had shown in later years his propensity for rapid change; and when asked about the brutality of the revolutionary process, he noted that revolution was not the same as going to a dinner party.

Emphasizing the rapidity of change, Meisner, at another point, notes that the Communists had brought more fundamental changes in China's social structure in the first three years of their rule than had occurred in the previous two thousand years. While China changed modestly over two millenniums, this is an exaggeration. China had indeed experienced great changes and sometimes rapid change in its social structure. Such diverse events as the introduction of Legalism in the brief Ch'in dynasty (221–206 B.C.) and Buddhism, which nearly replaced

Confucianism (third–sixth century A.D.), were as earthshaking in their time as Communism today. More importantly, the continuity of tradition in today's China in farming techniques, personal lifestyles, and ways of thought suggest that not everything has changed.

With the emphasis on rural China, Mao found urban society and the bureaucratic and intellectual elements there a frustrating obstacle to his egalitarian objectives. Moreover, by 1956 he grew concerned about the Communist Party resisting his radical social and economic policies and feared that the party was degenerating into a conservative and routinized bureaucracy. While it is not entirely clear what motivated Mao to launch the "Hundred Flowers Campaign," Meisner believes that uneasiness about the Party may have been Mao's primary concern, and he discounts the possibility that Mao was merely setting a trap to expose intellectual dissenters. In order for the party to flourish, Mao believed that Marxist ideas had to be challenged with "incorrect" ideas from the outside.

The mounting criticism, especially from young people, gave Mao his first serious jolt. They were regarded as antisocialist attacks and led to an "anti-rightest" campaign to quench the opposition. The witchhunt gave renewed emphasis to the need for ideological purity within Maoism; and, according to Meisner, this experience caused China to abandon the Soviet model and begin the Chinese (or Maoist) road to socialism.

Mao's emphasis on bringing about rapid institutional change, now in the context of China's socialist course, led to the "Great Leap Forward" campaign in 1958. Maoists believed that socialist ends could be attained only by socialist means, and this meant that the countryside would have to be industrialized. The object of the Great Leap Forward, which was basically an intensification of the second Five Year Plan to expand industry and bring communization to rural China, was to create a technological revolution in a still underdeveloped society and to mark China's passage from socialism to Communism.

Meisner offers a clearer explanation of the results of the Great Leap Forward than most writers who appear content to regard the episode a failure, a utopian effort with unrealizable goals. The author disagrees with this assessment and contends that the goals of the Great Leap Forward were attainable but that the problem lay in the "irrational fashion in which Maoists attempted to implement those policies." Moreover, he correctly points out that the "failure" of the Great Leap Forward was far from complete, and many aspects of the program survived. While the "backyard furnaces" disintegrated into oblivion, the rural communes continued in one form or another. In addition, some water conservation projects, such as dams and canals, were another lasting contribution.

The most traumatic episode of the Communist experience in the People's Republic was the Cultural Revolution. Completely anathema to Communism is a challenge to the supremacy of party authority. In the late 1960's, however, there was not only an attack on the party, but it was led by those who helped to build and direct the party. So devastating was the movement against the party that near-chaos reigned over China until the army, once allied with the Cultural Revolution, had to stop the rampaging students from causing further excesses. Mao, who initiated the movement, called it off and condemned the extremists as "ultra-leftists."

A revival of the party and return to "normalcy" has suggested to many writers that the Cultural Revolution was a failure, except that Mao had regained his power. Meisner, however, places the Cultural Revolution in better perspective by noting more lasting social changes that resulted from the movement. While the egalitarian ideas of the Cultural Revolution penetrated the countryside belatedly and more slowly than in urban centers, it is among China's peasant masses that the social transformation can be seen. The peasants, especially the poorer ones, have gained a greater voice in making local economic and social decisions.

The social gains in China's countryside have occurred in several areas. First, there has been a shift of industrial resources to the rural sector in which industries serving agricultural needs (for example, tools and farm machinery) have been developed. Second, the "barefoot doctors" with limited training have brought a degree of medical care to areas which formerly had none. Mao, in 1965, had already seen the need for expanding China's medical care to the rural regions and declared that doctors with minimal training were better than no doctors or "quacks and witch doctors." Third, a radical reconstruction of China's educational system, while it disrupted advanced training in the cities, brought more practical training to rural youth and greater opportunities for those who had no hope for an education in the past. Fourth, labor and industry became less bureaucratic and more egalitarian as bonuses and rate wages were eliminated.

Despite these gains in what Meisner terms Mao's experiment in "mass democracy," the author believes that the main failing of the Cultural Revolution was that it did not go far enough. Popular and democratic political institutions, allowing workers to acquire control over the means of production and gain their own socioeconomic freedom, did not occur. Meisner's assessment is correct, but to place the Cultural Revolution in full perspective, it can be said that it failed in its primary objective, but succeeded in selected areas furthering the Communist process. Since the completion of Meisner's book, however, there has been some further retreat from the "social gains" of the Cultural Revolution. Agitation for pay raises brought wage increases for lower income workers in the fall of 1977, and the revolutionary committees were formally brought to an end at the Eleventh National Party Congress in August, 1977, when strict party discipline was restored. Nevertheless, the gains of the Cultural Revolution in the countryside are not likely to wither away entirely.

Meisner concludes that Mao and the Communist leadership have been successful in creating a modern nation-state but not quite so successful in accomplishing the ultimate socialist goals. Because the Maoist doctrine requires "continuous" revolution and the successors of Mao are not seen as likely (according to Meisner) to check the bureaucracy as Mao had done, the struggle for an ideal socialist society should continue, but actual attainment is questionable. We can only conclude that without Mao, Maoism will be slowed.

Leonard H. D. Gordon

THE MEMOIRS OF EARL WARREN

Author: Earl Warren (1891–1974)
Publisher: Doubleday and Company (New York). 394 pp. $12.95
Type of work: Autobiography
Time: 1900–1970
Locale: California and Washington, D.C.

An autobiographical account of the public life of Earl Warren with references to major political and legal events pertaining to his professional successes as a District Attorney, Attorney General and Governor of California, and Chief Justice of the Supreme Court

> *Principal personages:*
> EARL WARREN, politician and jurist
> MR. AND MRS. MATHIAS WARREN, his parents
> NINA ELIZABETH MEYERS (*née* Palmquist), his wife

In addition to this posthumous memoir, the published writings of Earl Warren consist of *A Republic, If You Can Keep It* (1972) and *The Public Papers of Chief Justice Earl Warren* (1974). In all three publications, objectivity is evidenced by the selection of issues of central political and social importance, in the case of *The Public Papers,* and by the dedication to major civil responsibilities for good citizenship, in the case of *A Republic, If You Can Keep It.*

Earl Warren was a respectful figure in American national life and it is not surprising to find that his own narrative of major events in his career is calm, rational, even sobering. What may be surprising to some, however, is that the somewhat methodical recounting of the wide variety of national interests and influences during the last four decades by a structured, legal mind can bring with it a steadying confidence in this nation's people, values, and governmental processes. There could be no better counterbalance to the despair generally occasioned by the misadministration of Richard Nixon than this autobiographical account of the buoyant career of one of the most important and effective mid-twentieth century politicians and jurists, whose ethical career is all the more remarkable for having endured extremely unethical times. At each of the important stages of his professional life, Warren exemplified the benefits of moderate and virtuous paths of conduct and the salutory results of actions based on such ethics.

The purpose of these memoirs, as stated tersely at the end of the preliminary chapter, is educational, in that the Chief Justice intended them to be instructive for those who might wish to learn from a career such as his. This same purpose seems to have been the inspiration for all three of his published writings. Warren's public life appears to have been a steady, sure, charmed rise in political popularity in ever-widening spheres of state and national prominence, during which, in these memoirs as in fact, one appreciates his very capable handling of increased responsibilities. To be sure, the Republican ticket in 1948 lost, but this defeat could in no way be considered personally his. Every biographer agrees that the hearty, robust physical appearance of the man, coupled with his innate courtesy, personal warmth, and instantaneously communicated integrity made Earl Warren deservedly popular and thoroughly respected. At each new undertaking, moreover, Warren brought steadfast determination, hard work, and practical aims to bear on each situation, with the result that every post he held became expanded in scope and function. Never content with the *status quo,* he took what was and improved it.

In order to learn from such a career, it is necessary to observe Warren's courage in success, his self-reliance and confidence. What he said of his state at one national convention was true of him, that he represented "the great, hopeful, energetic West where there is little fear of failing and no fear of trying." But, these are not pages from which one witnesses triumph over adversity. We are not told of any experiences which he thought of as serious setbacks or discouragements. Even though many thought Warren ambitious for the presidency, there is no suggestion here either of that specific ambition or of any disappointment at not being nominated. There is no remorse expressed over the 1948 elections; his reference to it merely states some probable contributory factors, such as taking the election for granted, not working hard enough, and not facing main issues.

The didactic intention of these memoirs has greatly conditioned their structure and the selection of events to be mentioned. The beginning chapters provide somewhat sporadic information as to the formative process of this important man's character. There is sustained effort to select serious examples of the hardships of life in those days, such as the painful, lingering death of a neighbor child, the horror of a cock fight, a savage rabbit kill, the severities of strikes, a shootout on the streets of his hometown, and the personal tragedy of his father's murder, bludgeoned to death by an unknown assailant. In these passages, we appreciate that Warren thought such cruelties of life played a part in his own formation, perhaps in determining his characteristic seriousness of nature.

Frivolity is scrupulously avoided in these pages; there are no remembrances of playfulness, outings, social events, dating, family or personal enjoyments, even idle moments, either as a boy or as a man. If Warren mentions playing the clarinet, which he did throughout high school and college days for pleasure and profit, it is stated to be only a means of making extra money. If he mentions experiences at work, it is only to point out the valuable lessons derived therefrom, even to stretching the point by saying that delivering ice could certainly be considered as performing a humanitarian service. College days, when he got away from home for the first time, were not spent in any social experimentation or carousing, but rather in friendly conversations, good reading, and an occasional beer with his friends.

The two people he mentions most are his father, who was his educational benefactor and stalwart example of practical determination, and his wife Nina, apparently the most wholesome and encouraging life companion that he could have wished for, to judge from his frequent remark, and this book's dedication, that she was "the best thing that ever happened to me."

The good humor associated with Warren throughout his public life is nowhere present in these memoirs. One might be tempted to impute a purpose to such an omission by assuming that he stifles his wit for didacticism's sake, but the truth is closer to the observation of other biographers who aver Warren to have been devoid of facetiousness. On the one hand, it is certainly true that he exuded good fellowship, good will, good humor; on the other, it is equally accurate to note that he was not witty, not humorous. In fact, one suspects he rather disapproved of such tomfoolery. When he relates a mildly comic schoolboy scrap for which he was punished, he congeals our sympathetic smile by adding that on the whole he profited from the experience. And when he tells of his London hotel stay for Queen Elizabeth's coronation in 1952 and hears singing and joke-telling coming from the sidewalk spectators who had gathered forty-eight hours ahead of the event and were amusing themselves during their wait, he reacts by informing us that their din did not really bother him that much. An enterprising student of Warren's California political days culled well over three hundred of his speeches and found jokes nearly completely absent (there was one, perhaps). In this regard, therefore, we can conclude these memoirs to be faithful to the man himself.

We should hasten to consider, however, that the same mental attitude or character trait which disinclined Warren to flippancy must also have been a factor in preventing him from ever having been inane, superficially entertaining, fanciful, or, as an extension of such tendencies, devious. During his career he displayed candor, a strong sense of honor, and a no-fooling-around knack of getting to the heart of issues. In his memoirs he performs the same surgical feat, and does so with no posturing, no petulance, no recriminations, and no glorification of prideful moments of his career, which were many indeed.

The general scheme of the book is one of annotation of Warren's successive achievements: winning cases while District Attorney, winning executive and legislative actions while governor, winning decisions while Chief Justice. The sections dealing with his years as Assistant D.A. and D.A. of California's third most populous county take place during prohibition and the post-prohibition eras; they are exciting samples of an energetic program of law enforcement and prosecution during gangster days. We follow several cases and observe Warren's basic method of direct confrontation successfully determine convictions in many cases concerning bunco artists, official bribes, fraud, graft, even gambling ships and murders. The section dealing with his three terms as governor recounts major programs he initiated; it was a powerful record of achievements at a time when California's popularity and concurrent population boom were expanding greatly the problems and opportunities in that state. One thinks now of the role of leadership California has enjoyed in many state functions and can trace their impetus to Earl Warren's administration. There were great strides made then in public health care, including mental hospitals (the "snakepit" conditions inspired Warren to take California out of the asylum age), in state corrections systems, the highway program, expanded university system, and in conservation efforts. He was a forward-looking governor and ahead of his time, as such programs as his advocacy of a health insurance plan and a state Fair Employment Commission will attest.

The deep sense of pride with which Earl Warren assumed his duties as Chief Justice of the Supreme Court is vividly brought out by these memoirs because the very first passage in the book describes the majesty of the Supreme Court building and expresses the author's awe and abiding devotion both to the creed of "Equal Justice under the Law" and to the solemnity of purpose which the position inspired in him. The later section dealing with the Chief Justice's daily procedure and work schedule reinforces the extent of his resolve and dedication to the letter of the law. Again in this august position, Warren improved the working functions of the office by rearranging the presentation and consideration of cases. We are impressed that the quantity of cases dealt with by the Warren court was great during the sixteen years of its tenure; the quality of the decisions was also monumental.

Warren here tells us that the most important case decided during his Chief Justiceship was *Baker v. Carr*, the reapportionment of states' legislatures by population, important because of the far-reaching effects of serving the democratic ideals of the nation. Other cases of equal or more furor from the general public were ones dealing with segregating school children by race *(Brown v. Board of Education)*, prisoners' constitutional rights *(Miranda v. Arizona)*, the unconstitutionality of school prayer, and wire-tapping. In retrospect, these decisions now seem to most Americans to be modest affirmations of basic human rights, but at the time, the clamor was immense from several dissident sectors of the citizenry. These memoirs do not attempt to answer all criticisms; they do clarify main reasons for major decisions, and declare Warren's honest opinions as to the fairness of these decisions. The chapter subtitled "The Court and Its Castigators" may have once been intended to confront the most punishing of its critics, and some have been vindictive, but this chapter now contains very little actual rebuttal. Perhaps had the Chief Justice lived long enough to complete and publish these memoirs himself, this chapter might have pursued some criticisms more tenaciously. Perhaps not. The final chapter, on the Special Commission for the investigation of President Kennedy's assassination, is not retaliative of the myriad critics of the Commission's report. Warren simply, deftly, and most convincingly acts as though he were again a prosecutor, laying out the salient facts about the case.

Given the highly controversial nature of many of the Supreme Court cases and of the findings of the Warren Commission, one might have expected to learn of Warren's many trying moments of decision (if not indecision, which somehow does not seem to apply to him), but he was not characteristically dependent on others' opinions to encourage him in his endeavors, nor was he a man to confide inner feelings publicly, so that it would not be in character to expect such revelations now.

What was in character for him was to face things squarely and to accept his mistakes, such as deeply regretting his own advocacy of the removal of Japanese-Americans from their property in 1942, even though all Californians were then convinced of such a necessity as a wartime security measure. It was also typical of him to share his successes, as he does throughout his book, with associates whom he praised, appreciated warmly, and sponsored, from his district attorney days right up to his Supreme Court years.

In regard to the many "startling insights into the workings of government and the personalities of noted figures" which the book jacket publicizes, one will be disappointed at their dearth. There are only occasional remarks about other figures: Dewey lacked warmth during their campaign; President Eisenhower should have been more understanding of the reasons for Supreme Court decisions and should not have criticized Warren for having allegedly changed after his appointment as Chief Justice (as a matter of fact, Warren was characteristically consistent in his attitudes throughout his career); Attorney General Mitchell once made a circuitous attempt to influence a Supreme Court decision, the only such attempt in all of the sixteen years of the Warren court, a fact which speaks particularly well for the court, and particularly ill of the Nixon administration team. But, for all of these brief asides, these memoirs are in no way an exposé. If some readers are unsatisfied at this fact, perhaps they, and we, can take heart at the realization that such tactics would surely have demeaned what stands now as one of the most positive legacies of political and judicial accomplishments of any American in recent history.

Earl Warren's *Memoirs* are a thoughtful, clear, and forthright extension of his own personality and a just presentation of his public service record. A final lesson we are only now realizing from this record concerns the fickleness of public opinion and that right has a way of prevailing, as witnessed by Warren's current reevaluation by cooler heads examining and declaring his superiority as a public figure. There could be no fitter recipient of fair judgment.

Anthony Lamb

MISSING PERSONS AND OTHER ESSAYS

Author: Heinrich Böll (1917–   )
Translated from the German by Leila Vennewitz
Publisher: McGraw-Hill Book Company (New York). 281 pp. $9.95
Type of work: Essays

A collection of essays spanning more than two decades of social, political, literary, cultural, and personal commentaries

Fifteen books of fiction by the Nobel laureate, Heinrich Böll, are already available in English translation and are now joined by this volume of nonfiction prose. Contained in the volume are twenty-nine essays, reviews, speeches, and miscellaneous pieces which were selected by the translator in cooperation with the author from more than twenty years of essayistic writing on a wide variety of subjects. The selections are organized in three categories in the book: Essays, Reviews, and Miscellany. One could quarrel with this division since some of the items under Essays are as much literary reviews or more so than some of the reviews which digress from the work at hand to long essayistic passages on aesthetic, sociological, or political subjects. The Miscellany contains Böll's Nobel lecture before the Swedish Academy, as well as two other addresses at awards festivities. This section, furthermore, contains Böll's forwards to two books, his response to a questionnaire, and his personal reaction to the occupation of Czechoslovakia by Soviet troops.

The difficulties of categorizing are, however, insignificant, since the real value of the book lies in its breadth of selection and the variety of items enclosed.

The volume in many ways mirrors Böll's entire literary work, in which it would be possible—and indeed critics have often done so—to point out weaknesses, banalities, and places where the author apparently loved his characters more than art and was willing to compromise the latter to ease the fate of the former. However, taken as a whole his work holds an impressive position in postwar European literature as evidenced by Böll's selection for the Nobel Prize for literature in 1972 as well as by the great popularity his work enjoys in both West and East Germany and in translations abroad.

The work at hand affords a valuable insight into the workshop and the mind of its author. It presents some of his thoughts, concerns, and priorities in a somewhat different mode than the fictional works and thus is not only interesting reading but also an important tool for the Böll scholar.

In spite of Böll's large volume of literary production and the wide variety of themes and situations dealt with in his works, it is not difficult to point out some major recurrent themes in his opus. One of them is the war and its influence on the generations touched by it. In the essay "Trying to Close the Gap," Böll states that all his novels attempt to close the gap "to all that is inexplicable" in recent German history. The complaint by critics and commentators that Böll is overly preoccupied with World War II is broached in this same essay and an attempt at refuting this criticism is made by asserting that every novel, except for the

Utopian, even the so-called contemporary novel, is historical if for no other reason than that of the inevitable time lag between writing and publishing. In apparent self-defense Böll also points out that Tolstoy was even further removed in time from his material when writing *War and Peace* than contemporary authors dealing with World War II.

In the essay " 'In Defense of Rubble Literature,' " Böll again deals with the same criticism leveled against him, and with the reproachful labeling of his literature as being one of "war, homecoming, and rubble." Such labels are not incorrect, but reproaching postwar authors for writing about what they have seen is, in Böll's opinion, reprehensible since "a sharp eye is one of a writer's essential tools." As an example of writers and readers who have played blind man's buff, Böll discusses the French aristocracy, which was taken aback by the revolution because it had lived in idyllic seclusion and was supported in its notion of peacefulness by the authors of pastoral novels and plays. Another example presented by Böll is Adolf Hitler, who in his work *Mein Kampf* did not portray the world as it was but in "the distortion created by his inner self." The effect of his distorted view of reality needs no elaboration.

On the other hand, Charles Dickens wrote about what he saw, and his books were read and caused a reappraisal and a changing of many of the reprehensible aspects of the society they dealt with. Homer, another author without blindfolds cited by Böll, is today above the suspicion of critics and commentators in spite of the fact that his writings, too, deal with war, destruction, and homecoming. Thus Böll feels no need to be ashamed of having his own work labeled a literature of war, homecoming, and rubble.

Whether this defense is considered valid or not, Böll accepts the designation and rejects the criticism implied in these labels. Thus it is not surprising that this collection of essays should contain some which deal entirely or to a substantial degree with personal memories of the war. In "The Place Was Incidental," Böll describes his revisiting a town in which he had been stationed as a soldier twenty-two years earlier. Although the town now yields no apparent relics from the war time, and although the topography of his memory no longer matches the present reality, the personal bitterness aroused by the memories is real enough. He recalls the brief visits by girl friends and wives, and the soldiers' humiliating experiences when attempting to find but a moment's solitude with their loved ones. Bitterly he reproaches a militaristic system which dehumanizes soldiers every moment they are alive, then posthumously accords them solemn honors. Who will ever write the story of those countless last embraces, before departing for the front, Böll asks, and the answer is apparent in his own literature which does not contain exciting descriptions of close combat or gripping accounts of heroic deeds on the battlefield, but looks in on life in the dreary base quarters, dirty waiting rooms, and bombed cities. Thus Böll's characters are not the ones honored by the military complex. His concern is with the unheroic little man, the downtrodden, and with those caught up in events which they often do not comprehend and over which they have no control.

In addition to the essays dealing with war memories, three items in this collection deal with Northern Ireland, and five with Alexander Solzhenitsyn, mostly before he became the *cause célébre* he now is. There is also an essay on "The Moscow Shoeshiners," Arab refugees who have found a home in Moscow where they carry out their ostensibly humble occupation with dignity and without so much as a hint of servility.

In the essay "In Defense of Washtubs," Böll responds to Curt Hohoff's sarcastic remarks about the "paupers' atmosphere" and the "washhouse smells' in Böll's literature. Böll claims to be unmoved by this reproach. An author writing in an age, he says, when two-thirds of the human race is starving would have to carry blindfolds to avoid seeing poverty. More important, Böll asserts, is his "milieu-blindness," which postulates that greatness as well as humility, and pain and joy have no social relevance, and banalities are expressed in mansions as well as beside washtubs.

In spite of these arguments, it cannot be denied that Böll's literature suffers in places from a certain flatness, from an unwillingness or an inability on the part of the author to go all the way, to carry through to logical conclusions when that would lead to extremes. Böll likes to portray himself as an *enfant terrible* who in his search for truth exposes and denounces, without fear and hesitation, the abuses of power, no matter where they may be found. However, in the central problem of postwar Germany, namely that of the war guilt, Böll has stopped short of getting to the core of the problem. In *The Clown,* the protagonist, Schnier, contemplates a trip to the United States to pose at social gatherings as an example of the remorseful German youth. He eventually drops the idea, reasoning, in typical Böll fashion, that he does not feel any remorse at all. It is ironic that one of the reasons why Böll has become such a widely read German author on either side of the Iron Curtain may be found in his awkward relationship to the truth about the guilt of the German populus in the Third Reich. At a time when eradication of Nazism throughout the population and a changing of the attitudes allowing its rise and existence was necessary, the reader of Böll's literature tends to gain an awareness of the false attitudes of "others." By focusing on the involuntary involvement and suffering of the meek in society, Böll awakens the reader's pity and places the blame on institutions or minor characters so far removed from the center of attention that the reader avoids identifying with them.

A similar attitude on the part of the author can be felt in the essay "The Gun Was Aimed at Kafka," in which Böll reacts to the occupation of Czechoslovakia by Soviet troops in 1968. This essay praises the restrained defiance of the Prague population and portrays both the Czech people and the Soviet soldiers as victims. The entire blame is placed on the Soviet Secret Service and on Muscovitism.

The ability always to see the goodness in man in spite of all his weaknesses, to see life as meaningful and worthy even in view of the defects and cruelty of human institutions has, without a doubt, contributed to the popularity of Böll's literature. This same ability may, on the other hand, have led to artistic compromises which are the causes of disputes among critics concerning the artistic merits of Böll's writings. Böll, however, is undaunted by all this. "To be disputed," he says in the review "The Poetry of Curses," "is the only possible status for an author."

In closing, mention should be made of the outstanding translation done by Leila Vennewitz. With the exception of the translation of the German word "heil," such as in "heile Welt," the essays read like originals. In the same vein the excellent design and printing of the book deserve commendation. It has almost become a rare delight to read a first printing which, like this one, is virtually without errors.

Sofus E. Simonsen

A MOMENT OF TRUE FEELING

Author: Peter Handke (1942–   )
Translated from the German by Ralph Manheim
Publisher: Farrar, Straus and Giroux (New York). 133 pp. $7.95
Type of work: Novel
Time: The present
Locale: Paris

A young man, wakening from nightmare to find he leads a completely empty existence, is driven to a desperate search for self-identity and the meaning of life

> *Principal characters:*
> GREGOR KEUSCHNIG, press attaché at the Austrian Embassy in Paris
> STEFANIE, his wife
> AGNES, his four-year-old daughter
> BEATRICE, his girl friend
> A GIRL, who works in another office in the Embassy
> A WRITER, who has already survived the kind of decision Keuschnig must make and prods him toward it

Existentialism is in many ways a philosophy of despair. It is the ultimate reaction to an age beset with such evils as totalitarianism, compulsion, conformity, overorganization, mass irresponsibility, violence, and potential annihilation. It postulates that modern existence is a meaningless absurdity polluting an indifferent universe, and it emphasizes the isolation of the individual who, because of his fundamental nature, must remain a stranger to all about him. Its themes underlie a great deal of contemporary art, drama, music, and literature: isolation, alienation, noncommunication, discord, jarring or shattering impacts upon the senses. In terms of much traditional belief, it is spiritual nihilism. It informs us that God is dead and that each person is utterly alone in a world where all semblance of meaning is illusory.

This is not to say that existentialism is without its positive aspects, for its great virtue lies in its recognition that each individual human being is unique, unlike any other person who has existed before or will exist again; that each person can shape—indeed, has the responsibility to shape—his own destiny; and that individual acts not only matter but have a direct influence upon the world in which we live. The moral and ethical implications of this concept are obvious. The slogan "God is dead" does not necessarily deny a higher power, for there are many religious existentialists. It rather means that the concept of a personal God who acts as decision-maker or problem-solver is invalid and that the individual self, once created, is given the responsibility of discovering its true nature, making choices based on that discovery, and thereby achieving life rather than existence. It must do so alone and unaided.

The difference between mere existence and what Sartre calls authenticity lies in the necessity of choice. One must choose the life he is to live; he must choose between good and evil, between truth to self and acceptance of a multitude of shams. Refusal to choose is in itself a choice and insures self-destruction. As

Sartre puts it, in one of the expressions of absurdity characteristic of existentialist writers, man is not only condemned to be free but also embodies his own freedom. In addition to the responsibility of making a choice that will give his life meaning, each individual has the additional responsibility of leaving the world a better place than it was when he came upon the scene: it is a basic tenet of existentialist thought that just as each individual influences the entire world in some way through each act he performs, so he is at the same time individually guilty of all the evil that is abroad in it. To recognize evil and do nothing about it is to make a choice in its favor. This helps to explain the obsession with mass guilt that permeates so many avenues of contemporary expression.

To be sure, the notion that meaningful decisions based upon true awareness of a unique self will inevitably lead all such selves toward world betterment is an obvious *non sequitur;* and it presents some knotty problems for those who would develop a moral or ethical system based upon it.

The message of existentialism, as transmitted through the arts, does not customarily deal with such considerations. Instead, it dwells primarily upon the emptiness of conventional existence, the agony of self-discovery, the necessity of choice, and the search for true meaning. These elements have been exploited until they have become in a sense stereotypes, and reflect a certain mystique rather than a philosophical system. The tormented individual, alone in a mad world with which he cannot communicate, is as much a stock character as Pierrot or Harlequin, or a character in classical Japanese drama. Existentialists tend to repeat the same themes over and over. Preoccupied as they are with perceived absurdities and clichés, they at times become absurdities and clichés in themselves. Yet the effect is often intentional.

With certain very notable exceptions, Peter Handke's *A Moment of True Feeling* typifies what has become the standard existentialist novel. The plot is entirely predictable: its protagonist undergoes an experience of shattering awareness which severs all ties with the world he has known and leaves it an incomprehensible and terrifying place; he endures frightful tortures while he peels away the layers of simulation from his true self; he tries to escape this responsibility through forays into masochism and sadism, violence, readaptation, disguise. He is denied the refuge provided by his former life of thoughtless conformity; the world about him is utterly alien. He contemplates suicide and almost carries it out before he recognizes and assumes his basic responsibility. This satisfies the dictum of Camus that our moment of awareness leads either to suicide or to authenticity. Handke's plot adheres to formula.

For any reader not already steeped in the existentialist literary mystique, identification with Handke's protagonist is all but impossible. This is largely because we are given no opportunity to know Keuschnig before his transformation. There is no real comparison with the former life other than a brief statement of identification that establishes him as a bourgeois stereotype, together with some description of his inability to stomach old routines: the previous existence, already unreal, becomes a mere extension of the dream or nightmare in which Keuschnig finds himself. His experience, seen objectively as terrifying, does not become a subjective experience of comparable power for the uninitiated reader. His frantic efforts to achieve identity are inevitably viewed with some detachment and become more tedious than enlightening. On this level the existentialist statement is one recognizable as such even to the uninitiated: the protagonist is isolated and his ordeal can be seen and assessed but neither felt nor shared by others: it is thus an absurdity.

For the reader with an existentialist viewpoint, the reverse is true. No preliminary background, in preparation for the transformation, is necessary. The reader slips into a familiar situation, much as one addicted to westerns drops into another shootout without the necessity of finding out what circumstances precipitated the duel. The protagonist's ordeal is comprehended automatically as a fresh restatement of scripture. This, however, is not meant to imply complete identification with him; what is true for one individual is not necessarily true for any other. His significance, to the existentialist reader, lies in the nature of his experience and in the assurance that it has taken place.

Handke's novel owes an obvious debt to Kafka's "The Metamorphosis," as it does to Camus and Sartre, particularly the latter's *Nausea*. However, Kafka's story is genuinely horrifying in a way no other writer has been able to approach, let alone equal; and Sartre has already written the basic existentialist novel so brilliantly that other efforts, including the present example, tend to suffer by comparison. This is perhaps unfortunate. There are many examples, in the various arts, of innovators whose original statements were so powerfully developed that those who followed them were left at a serious disadvantage. The innovation becomes a movement or a school of thought and expression; its themes are repeated and elaborated upon, with variations; eventually they become threadbare. This progression is inevitable, and the more definitive its original statement, the more rapidly it runs its course.

Handke is widely recognized as the most important young writer in the German language today, and some critics consider him the greatest German writer of the century. There is good reason for this assessment; his work in drama, poetry, and the novel have abundantly demonstrated his mastery of thought and language. Although some critics have referred to the present novel as a blatant rewrite of *Nausea*, it is such only in terms of its existentialist viewpoint and its plot, both of which are now conventional vehicles for expression and are, so to speak, in the public domain. It is to Handke's credit that he can take a stock item and create from it a genuine work of art that bears the unmistakable stamp of his own genius.

All successful writers have the ability to communicate, but rare indeed is the writer who can, in the fewest possible words, convey to the reader a visual image of absolute completeness and clarity. Handke is such a writer. As we follow Gregor Keuschnig through the streets of Paris, everything he sees registers instantly on our minds, down to the smallest detail that impinges upon him. If the scene or object has a malign significance, that also is imparted to us. In Keuschnig's agitated state, his surroundings partake of both reality and dream, and nothing makes sense to him. The images exemplify this: extreme but slightly distorted clarity, glimpses of human beings at their most grotesque, the impression that their actions are automatic and dictated by their surroundings, that they have no authentic reason for what they do.

These verbal crystallizations, each perfect, are enhanced by other sensory impressions transmitted with equal fidelity and often with the same impact. They are innumerable and are piled upon the reader in such profusion that the cumulative effect is overwhelming. We never quite feel what Gregor Keuschnig feels, for we too are unique and cannot experience the agonies of another self; but all his sensory impressions are ours and we can react to them. There is no impression here of the writer as filter, and communication is directly from character to reader.

In this context, it is difficult to identify other writers with whom Handke can be compared. One such is the virtually forgotten American, Ambrose Bierce, who not only possessed the same ability to convey brilliant imagery through a minimum of words but was also akin in many ways to contemporary existentialist writers and deserves reexamination by them.

Equally significant in Handke's writing is the sustained poetic mood that pervades it, and the mastery of both mood and imagery. This is perhaps best exemplified in two passages. One relates to Keuschnig's preliminary decision, the other to his state of awareness following the ultimate choice. As he moves toward the spot where he plans to commit suicide, all becomes warmth and sunlight: with the discovery of meaning, the terror is gone. After the decision is made in favor of a life that is true to himself, what he sees around him is merely grotesque; it is as though he were moving through a three-dimensional color film in which all the other people are merely animated figures of no significance.

It soon becomes apparent to the careful reader that each of these countless images is an integral part of the novel's fabric and contains an underlying validity beyond its function in building mood or emphasizing environment. Even the numerous clichés, which Handke unfortunately proclaims as such by expressing them in capitals, serve as route markers along Keuschnig's dreadful path. That the protagonist should be terrified by a baby carriage, for example, is an entirely logical insight if we remember Sartre's observation about freedom.

The existentialist premise that thinkers of a more sanguine temperament find most difficult to accept is the rejection of human attributes long considered essential: love, shared lives, understanding, and compassion. If each individual is truly unique, and if what is true for one is not necessarily true for any other, then such concepts are no longer tenable as we have known them. Keuschnig's moment of true feeling, which he must experience and then analyze on some level in order to make the choice required of him, is a brief sexual contact with a stranger. It is a moment of true feeling because neither person is expected to know or feel anything about the other, and there are no commitments of any kind; and the novel ends as a liberated Keuschnig strides purposefully toward another tryst with another unknown. He is entirely private, as his self requires him to be. He will give nothing, and will receive nothing beyond self-gratification. And, in the final analysis, self-gratification—or the lack of it—is what existentialism is all about. Athough many existentialist thinkers emphasize the moral and ethical responsibility of each liberated self to work productively in a manner true to its nature and to leave the world a better place, the *non sequitur* still applies. There is no indication that Keuschnig will ever make any such contribution. The inner Keuschnig, it would seem, was hardly worth liberating in the first place.

In spite of its undeniable brilliance and craftsmanship, *A Moment of True Feeling* does not rise far above the level of modernist statement that it typifies. It is handicapped by themes already becoming hackneyed and by stock characters already exploited to the point of satiation. It adds little to a thesis, however valid, that has been stated many times, and the essential message it conveys has acquired a certain monotony. It remains a beautifully constructed work of art; one can only wish it embodied an original concept or demonstrated a new idea.

John W. Evans

NABOKOV
His Life in Part

Author: Andrew Field (1938–   )
Publisher: The Viking Press (New York). 285 pp. $15.00
Type of work: Biography
Time: Late nineteenth century to present
Locale: Russia, England, Germany, France and America

An original, inventive biography of Vladimir Nabokov, including his family background and the social and intellectual milieu in which he grew up

> Principal personages:
> VLADIMIR V. NABOKOV
> VÉRA EVSEEVNA NABOKOV, his wife
> VLADIMIR D. NABOKOV, his father

"Do you know this man now?" As Field asks in the conclusion to this book, the question is, of course, the ultimate one to be asked of every biography. The answer in this case is not a simple one. Auden, Eliot, and Nabokov himself have long maintained that their works should stand alone, speaking for themselves. Yet scholars have long agreed that to appreciate fully a given author's imaginative scope and creative ability, a thorough and perceptive literary biography can be of immense aid. Field—in the title, throughout the book, in the conclusion—points to the inconclusive and often contradictory nature of facts, both personal and historical, and the elusive nature of trying to "capture" a real person in time and place. At moments, Field succeeds brilliantly; at points, his failures are irritating.

In attempting to write an unconventional and inventive biography, Field has created unnecessary stumbling blocks for the reader. Time sequences are often confusing, with phrases such as "but that was later" or "but that was earlier"; incidents which begin in the present suddenly drop back three or four years. Chronological problems abound. If Field wanted to avoid the usual ponderous overdating which often makes many scholarly biographies such dull reading, he should at least have added an appendix of names and events in chronological order. A bibliography of his sources would not have been amiss either, for he uses no footnotes, leaving the reader no way to check his accuracy. An index should also have been included in a book of this nature. Unless the reader marks the pages as he goes along, he will find it virtually impossible to relocate specific points without actually rereading whole chapters page by page. Library copies will, no doubt, quickly become a jungle of underlinings.

In establishing an informal, almost gossipy tone and style for the book, Field occasionally lapses into self-indulgence which seems to focus more on himself than on Nabokov, such as in his overly long, almost maudlin reaction to the death of Nabokov's young cousin Yurik. The whole first chapter is also a case in point, in which Field talks almost entirely about his long personal relationship with Nabokov and his problems with the novelist in trying to write the biography. The book abounds with this kind of self-indulgence. The full-page account of a house, of which he cannot even find a photograph, seems needlessly sentimental and long, leaving the reader with no new information. His evocation of St. Petersburg as it was in the youth of Nabokov, Field admits that even Nabokov criticized as "a dreadful macédoine." That Field's images have come straight from the poetry of Nabokov does not save the description.

Another kind of failure is one that scholars will look more kindly upon, even if they occasionally become bored with the piles of details. Field has thoroughly researched the materials for this book; unfortunately, he seems unable to discriminate between those facts which illuminate his subject and those which simply obscure it. One wonders if the time spent "guessing" when Nabokov's father first grew his mustache might not have been better employed. The long discussion of family origins and genealogy could have been heavily edited without losing the main point: the social position of the Nabokov family through two generations. The same is true for much of the introductory material about the Tenishev School which Nabokov attended—its founding, its theories, its exterior architecture. The mini-biography of Nabokov's literature teacher, Gippius, also becomes tedious. Even though Field's observations on literary influence are perceptive and persuading, the reader learns more about Gippius than he wants to know. Were this book as substantial as Blotner's two-volume biography of Faulkner, these superfluous details would not matter so much; however, in a biography this brief, the reader would appreciate less Gippius and more Nabokov.

However, better to have too much detail than too little, and much of Field's detail *is* significant and important. The Tenishev school curriculum; the reading lists; the books in the family library; the information regarding the family's political involvement—all these are important and essential to an understanding of Nabokov's intellectual and emotional development as well as his passionate determination to be a *Russian* writer, a determination which he did not give up until the 1940's, and then only with anguish. The reader will appreciate the accounts of the relationship between father and son, the early years of wealth, the first flight to escape the Bolshevik Revolution, and the successive stages of emigration. The flight continues out of political necessity when Nabokov and Véra, his wife, leave Nazi Germany for France only to be forced from Paris to America when France falls to Hitler. Field's clear and moving accounts give the reader a sharp insight into Nabokov the man, and do much to illuminate the fiction of Nabokov the writer. The patterns of the life are reflected in the writer's art.

The portrait of Nabokov's father is especially important and well executed, based not only on family memoirs, but also on accounts of contemporaries. By all accounts, the father was a remarkable man whose influence on his son is made obvious—a man of "harmony and integrity," of spirit and good humor, a loving father. He was a lecturer on criminology and literature, an expert lepidopterist, a journalist interested in abnormal psychology, a liberal politician, a man of courage and honor. When accused in print of marrying for money, he challenged the writer to a duel. Twice he was arrested for political activity. The first time it was for his attacks on the Tsar's anti-Jewish pogroms and his protest of the Tsar's dissolving the First Duma; the second time he was arrested by the Bolsheviks for his work with the Kerensky provisional government. Each time he faced his sentence with courage, attempting through letters to cheer his wife and children. His tragic death, occurring while he attempted to prevent the assassination of a colleague, shook the whole family. (The reader is never told how, when, or why the father and mother returned to Russia after perilously escaping from the Crimea under Bolshevik gunfire.) For the next thirteen years, Nabokov's mother, Elena, and the three youngest children struggled in Prague on a small Czech government pension.

Vladimir Nabokov emerges as a man much like his father—a multitalented man of "harmony and integrity," a loving son, husband, and father with a strong sense of humor, an enemy of totalitarian governments and anti-Semitism. His Berlin days were filled with jobs trying to stave off poverty; he taught everything from languages to tennis. He tried journalism, theater, and cinematography, including a bit part as a walk-on actor. Throughout these lean years he worked steadily to become an established Russian writer.

Although courted by the government to return to Russia, Nabokov, unlike many of the *émigrés*, knew that to return would mean to compromise his principles. He refused to consider the idea. Living in Berlin with his Jewish wife, Vera, Nabokov saw clearly the threat and approaching dangers of the Nazi government. After their son was born in 1937, the Nabokovs left Berlin forever, but he took his strong feelings about the Jewish persecution with him. He told Field: "There is a sense of responsibility about this theme which I think I will tackle one day. I will go down to those German camps and *look* at those places and write a *terrible* indictment." His continuing opposition almost cost him his first fulltime job in the United States—his lectureship at Wellesley. Because the United States and Russia were, at the time, Allies fighting the Axis Powers, his stinging denunciations of the Bolsheviks were not approved of by the administrations. He refused to compromise. Later the termination of his teaching career at Cornell University came over a matter of principle about the teaching of Russian.

Like his father, Nabokov from childhood exhibited a strong sense of humor and a flair for the heroic gesture. Field illustrates this quality both by describing schoolboy pranks and by writing with mature humor, underlining the quality of wit so evident in Nabokov's fiction. One of the first qualities that impressed Nabokov about Americans was their goodnatured honesty and sense of humor. Even his naturalization ceremony becomes a side-splitting roar of laughter. When his wife objects to being represented in the biography, Nabokov exclaims, "You can't help being represented. We're too far gone! It's too late!" bursting into laughter that evokes tears. Like his father, too, Nabokov once issued an enemy a challenge to a duel over a matter of honor. In Berlin, he and another *émigré* drew straws to see who would be first to hit a violinist accused in court of driving his wife to suicide. The two carried out their plan, causing a general melee.

The Field portrait is various and lovingly executed. He shows us a man of moods and interests more complex than is generally known. Since Nabokov's pursuit of chess and butterflies have often been used to make him seem something of a dilettante, Field balances the picture by showing Nabokov's lifelong love of tennis and soccer as well. His active pursuit of soccer ended abruptly in his mid-thirties when he was knocked out on the field, suffering several broken ribs. The man that emerges from this wealth of detail is the whole man—a very different portrait from the stereotyped intellectual, esthete, and dandy.

Although *Nabokov: His Life in Part* is not as illuminating or as skillfully presented as Field's early study, *Nabokov: His Life in Art* (1967), nor as thorough as his excellent *Nabokov: A Bibliography* (1973), it is a useful and informative work. Its flaws seem to result from the biographer's being too close to his subject matter, too personally involved. It is as if Field were trying to write a Nabokov novel about Nabokov: techniques which work well for the master craftsman in fiction do not serve his biographer well. Still, the book's major contributions far outweigh its flaws and disadvantages. The details and anecdotes, hardly touched on in this review, provide valuable insights into a time and place and people that might have been lost if Field had not captured them here. More importantly, of course, Field's book provides another window on the fiction of Nabokov.

Ann E. Reynolds

THE NAMES
A Memoir

Author: N. Scott Momaday (1934–   )
Publisher: Harper & Row Publishers (New York). 170 pp. $10.00
Type of work: Memoir
Time: 1934–1949
Locale: Rainy Mountain, Oklahoma; Hobbs Air Force Base; Jemez Pueblo, New Mexico

A memoir in which an established poet, novelist, essayist, and college professor recalls the influences on his early life of the two Southwestern cultures, American Indian and white, which shaped his future

> *Principal personages:*
> N. SCOTT MOMADAY, a writer and professor
> NATACHEE SCOTT MOMADAY, his mother, a teacher and author of children's books
> ALFRED MORRIS MOMADAY, his father, a teacher and artist
> JAMES MAMMEDATY, Alfred's brother
> POHD-LOHK, an old Kiowa storyteller

Among the richer themes characterizing the literature of the 1970's are the search for ancestral roots, and, as a logical counterpart, a new sense of the regional basis of American writing. *The Names* excellently combines these two qualities in a poetic evocation of N. Scott Momaday's infancy and childhood within the shaping traditions of the Southwestern Indian communities of which he is a product. As our foremost Native American writer, Momaday is in an excellent position to bridge the gap between the European American tradition in which he currently lives and works as a Professor of English at Stanford University and the tribal world of the Southwest in which he grew up. More than a simple memoir or factual autobiography, however, *The Names* is, according to its author, "an act of the imagination" through which he seeks to come to terms with his own past and to discover his identity within a larger context than that of the self. It is, in fact, Momaday's own portrait of the artist as a young man.

Appropriate to its title, *The Names* begins: "My name is Tsoai-talee. I am, therefore, Tsoai-talee; therefore, I am." For Momaday this name is the word that is in the beginning, and from which all subsequent events flow. Tsoai-talee is the Kiowa name given Momaday by old Pohd-lohk, the storyteller, who "believed that a man's life proceeds from his name, in the way a river proceeds from its source." Thus, through the magic of his Indian name, Momaday is given at once his being and his place in the fixed order of things. Meaning in Kiowa "Rock-Tree Boy," the name links him inextricably to the Kiowa past through the Tsoai or Rock-Tree which whites know as the Devil's Tower in Wyoming. Native to the Wyoming region, the Kiowas "many generations before . . . had come upon Tsoai, had been obliged in their soul to explain it to themselves. And they imagined that it stood in some strange and meaningful relation to them and to the stars. It was therefore a sacred thing."

The first significant episode of Momaday's life came when he was six months old and his parents took him to Devil's Tower, Wyoming "to be in Tsoai's presence even before the child could understand what it was, so that by means of the child the memory of Tsoai should be renewed in the blood of the . . . people." Later, old Pohd-lohk would formalize this relationship between the child and the Kiowa past by conferring upon him the name Tsoai-talee. The old man gives the child more than just a name, however. As the storyteller, Pohd-lohk keeps alive the memory of the Kiowa past by means of a book of pictographs "in which the meaning of his racial life inhered—a force that had been set in motion at the Beginning." In naming Momaday, Pohd-lohk in effect anoints him as successor to the tradition of storytelling which keeps alive the Kiowa past and assures that its cultural memories will not pass from the earth.

Though never overtly stated, a strong sense of destiny informs *The Names* and to some extent shapes the form of Momaday's work. Divided into four sections, each of which deals with a distinct period in the life of the developing artist as he grows from infancy to young manhood, the book reads more like a novel than an autobiography as it records the emergence of a sensitive and intelligent mind. Along the way, a range of people and experiences combine to shape a personality which will ultimately find identification both as an artist and as an American Indian. It is the complex vision resulting from this dual identity which gives *The Names* its particularly rich flavor.

The opening section of the book covers Momaday's infancy up to the point where he is given his Kiowa name by old Pohd-lohk. Previous to the naming ceremony, however, Momaday establishes himself in terms of the two traditions of his life by a detailed summary of his ancestors on both sides. "An idea of one's ancestry," he writes, "is really an idea of the self." In search of this idea, we learn that on his mother's side Momaday descends from a Kentucky frontier family who, in their movement Westward, incorporated some Cherokee blood into their European stock. His father, a well-known American Indian painter, is pure Kiowa and the source of most of Momaday's own Indian blood. As the histories of these two distinct clans lead inevitably toward Momaday's birth, we feel a strong sense of destiny uniting within the child the two cultures which give him his consciousness as a writer.

Like several other passages in the book, the naming ceremony is frankly imaginary. However, this episode as well as others serves to suggest that, unlike a factually limited biographer, Momaday refuses to distinguish between the truth of fact and the the truth of the imagination. It is, rather, the final effect—that is, the artistic effect—of truth that shapes his work, making it an act of the imagination. Recalling the moment when he left childhood behind forever, Momaday writes, "I should never again see the world as I saw it on the other side of that moment, in the bright reflection of time lost. There are such reflections, and for some of them I have the names." The episodes, memories, and impressions that make up *The Names* are just such bright reflections.

The second section of the book recalls the early childhood years when Momaday began developing the qualities which would ultimately define his mature personality. Though the child seems to identify most strongly with the white or non-Indian world at this point, actually he is surrounded by both cultures and gains from each. From his mother, Momaday learned the myths and legends of the European tradition, while at the same time he absorbed from his father and Indian relatives the legends and traditions of their culture. Though his mother elected that English should be his primary language, the richness of both cultures are absorbed into Momaday's life and work.

The most interesting figures to emerge from this section are his grandmother and uncle, each of whom holds an important lesson for him. Uncle James, though a sympathetic and warm character, nevertheless represents the sad portrait of a drunken Indian who cannot adjust to the world in which he must live. Momaday's grandmother, on the other hand, is so fully centered within her Indian identity that she "seemed simply to know how to be comfortable in the world." This contrast between the tragic existence of Uncle James and the stable self-acceptance of the grandmother is a theme which to some degree preoccupies Momaday. It is, in fact, essentially this relationship he dramatizes in his Pulitzer Prize-winning novel, *House Made of Dawn*. In that work, Abel, the drunken young misfit, is contrasted with old Francisco in ways similar to the relationship seen here. In each case, the acceptance of Indian identity leads to an almost mystical sense of wholeness and acceptance which brings great beauty and dignity to these old Indian figures.

Momaday's early adolescence, as recorded in Part III, was spent largely at Hobbs Air Force Base in New Mexico during the years of World War II. Composed largely of a series of recollections of a boy's world of adventure and excitement centered around friends, school, the war, and the games of childhood, Part III again suggests little strong identification with the Indian culture. Through the section, however, runs the dual themes of the development of imagination which would point Momaday toward his artistic career and his increasing discovery of himself as a unique individual. As he says of those years, "I was yet a child and I lay low at Hobbs, feeling for the years in which I should find my whole self." The section ends with an epiphany through which the young boy perceives in a mystical moment the continuity of time and space which unites in a living present, past, and future. "Time receded into Genesis on an autumn day in 1946," he writes. Shortly thereafter Momaday would begin his emotional integration into the primal world of Native American culture.

Though he lived in a number of other places, it is clear that Momaday's true spiritual home as a youngster was the Jemez Pueblo in New Mexico where he was taken to live when he was twelve. His parents accepted positions as teachers in the Jemez Day School, and the reservation became for Momaday "the last, best home of my childhood." The traditions of the Jemez people seem already to have been in decline when Momaday came to live there, and to some extent his description of the rituals and customs of the pueblo describes a dying culture. Nevertheless, he absorbed from his experience there both a strong sense of Indian culture and the powerful sense of place which is characteristic of his writing. Of his strong identification with Jemez he writes,

> the events of one's life take place, *take place*. . . . Events do indeed take place; they have meaning in relation to the things around them. And a part of my life happened to take place at Jemez. I existed in that landscape, and then my existence was indivisible with it. I placed my shadow there in the hills, my voice in the wind that ran there, in those old mornings and afternoons and evenings.

Appropriately, the final episode of *The Names* dramatizes Momaday's break with this final world of his childhood. His parents decide he should go east for his final year of high school so he will be better prepared for college. Contemplating his departure, Momaday climbs to the top of a favorite mesa where he is accustomed to go to be alone with his thoughts. Trying to descend by a seemingly easy, but untested, route, he suddenly finds himself trapped halfway down, unable to either ascend again or to descend the rest of the way down. "I believed then that I would die there," he writes, "and I saw with a terrible clarity the things of the valley below. They were not the less beautiful to me." Momaday professes not to know what happened after that, but suddenly he was sitting safely on the ground "looking up at the rock where I had been within an eyelash of eternity." Reflecting on that moment of confrontation with his own mortality, Momaday says, "I think of it as the end of an age."

Partially *The Names* is a recollection of the innocence lost in that moment of transition into maturity, but it is ultimately more than a simple record of the bright reflections of childhood and youth. Momaday recounts his mother's conscious decision to affirm her Indian heritage, "she imagined who she was. This act of the imagination was, I believe, among the most important events of my mother's early life, as later the same essential act was to be among the most important of my own." In the final analysis, *The Names* is the act of imagination through which Momaday discovers who he is and assimilates his own Indian heritage into his sense of himself as man and artist.

William E. Grant

NIGHT-SIDE
Eighteen Tales

Author: Joyce Carol Oates (1938–   )
Publisher: The Vanguard Press (New York). 370 pp. $10.00
Type of work: Short stories
Time: The present or recent past
Locale: Unspecified large northern cities and towns, presumably Upstate New York and southern Ontario

Eighteen stories which depict people whose considerable intelligence and professional competence as doctors, professors, and artists prove useless in allowing them to cope with the loneliness and fear that are part of every life

In the fifth of eighteen stories in this collection by perhaps the most productive serious young writer in North America, "The Translation," the protagonist is asked his opinion about modern art in the United States. The response is that

the contemporary pathway is but a tendril, a feeler, an experimental gesture . . . because it is obsessed with death and the void and the annihilation of self it will necessarily die . . . it pronounces its own death sentence.

Much the same judgment could be rendered by a hostile reader of Joyce Carol Oates's work as a whole. Certainly her tortured souls doomed to agonies of loneliness, frustration, and shattered illusions do nothing to deny the general opinion of her work as extraordinarily depressive in theme and content. But then, they are not intended to, if one reads the epigraph from Whitman: this is a collection for the hour that Whitman describes in "A Clear Midnight," when the soul flies into the wordless void, "pondering the themes" it loves best, "Night, sleep, death, and the stars."

Any group of eighteen stories, even those on similar themes, will of necessity be too diverse for easy generalization; the stories in *Night-Side* range in time and place from nineteenth century Massachusetts to contemporary Eastern Europe, though most are set in familiar Oates territory—Upstate New York and southern Ontario. The protagonists, like the settings, are also varied, including aging philosophers and psychologists, precocious lunatics, distraught physicians, artists and teachers, husbands and wives.

But this apparent diversity of setting and character is deceptive. For all their differences, the stories share several important characteristics. The first of these is that in none of them does anything "happen"; they are extraordinarily static in the sense of physical action, though in almost every case physical action seems imminent. For example, in one of the slighter stories, "The Giant Woman," a boy and his older brother and sister break into the lonely farmhouse of an elderly recluse who is rumored to have killed her son. The children search her pathetic belongings for the cash hoard that all eccentrics are supposed to have squirreled away; while they do so the reader waits apprehensively for the formidable and dangerous old woman to return and do something dreadful to the children—or at least to frighten them. Instead, the younger boy, the protagonist, finds the money that none of them really expected to be there, and chooses not to say anything about it. The woman never does return, and the boy is left, atypically for Oates, with a warm and comfortable feeling about himself.

Similarly in other stories our expectation of some action, usually to be dreaded, is never realized. In the short sketch "The Murder" there is no murder, though one is wished for by the protagonist and might in fact occur after the story ends; in "The Sacrifice" the only action comes in a horrible dream, though the protagonist, an elderly psychologist, is apparently hit accidentally with a stickball at the end; and in "The Blessing" the promised violence inherent in any crowd, especially one which has gathered for religious instruction and is disappointed, never materializes.

The lack of overt action does not mean that nothing transpires in these stories—merely that the most important occurrences for Oates are, in this volume at least, internal, hidden, and not, by and large, communicable. That is the second major similarity among the stories in *Night-Side:* each one depicts a character who seems to have a quality of poise or balance or certitude which is shaken by an intense perception of what he comes to see as the truth. Examples abound, not only in the stories already cited but in "The Widows," in which a mourning young widow learns that her husband had been involved in an affair with a dying colleague's wife just before his own death; in the title story, when a staid and conventional college professor receives "messages" from a dead friend; and in the last story, "A Theory of Knowledge," when an elderly professor of philosophy finds solace in aiding a small boy, thereby transcending the sterile Platonism to which he has devoted his life.

It is no coincidence that of these eighteen stories, fourteen deal with characters who might be said to live the life of the mind, as students, professors, writers, artists, or doctors. For it is the person who lives the life of the mind who will be most dramatically affected by certain "truths" that seem to recur, and which constitute the themes of the stories. Loneliness is a universal condition; death and dying seldom ennoble character; love and sickness are so closely linked as to be indistinguishable; the natural condition of things is disintegration and decay; the artist has little or no control over his creations; and intelligence— the ability to see all of the above—is of no help in dealing with any of them.

If intelligence is no help, neither is skill or compassion or dedication, all essential qualities for good doctors. Four of the best stories in *Night-Side* are about doctors: "Lover," "Bloodstains," and "Exile" are about physicians, and "The Sacrifice" is about a psychologist. In "The Lovers" a young doctor's marriage is ruined because he has invested all of his emotional energy in his patients, one of whom has physically attacked him; in "Bloodstains" a doctor of similar age (late thirties) has a similar bad case of overextended sympathies. The process has gone further in "Exile"; in this story an older doctor has gone nearly blind and insane; and in "The Sacrifice" a complacent old man, an eminent psychologist, finally collapses from the strain of recording and understanding mental aberrations, and from the recognition that for all of his expertise he has been unable to make contact with his own wife, son, or grandson.

Unlike some of the stories in this volume, including the title story, which seem overly contrived, the stories about doctors seem convincing because they have a basis in reality. Some years ago Robert Lindner wrote a celebrated book called *The Fifty-Minute Hour*, a series of dramatized case studies of his own patients, in which he described the dangers that lay in wait for psychoanalysts who were constantly exposed to mental illness. The greatest danger, Lindner explained, was that the doctor would enter into the mind and heart of the patient and assume the burden of the disease with him. By extension, something of the same thing seems to have happened to the doctors in these stories who give themselves "without restraint" to their patients, and pay the price.

Perhaps the most effective story in the volume is that of the young woman in "The Snowstorm," who denies needing any kind of help, even to herself, but who is clearly in desperate need of it. For its theme, its character, and especially for its narrative technique, "The Snowstorm" is a story that rewards close attention. The third-longest story in *Night-Side*, "The Snowstorm" is essentially an extended interior monologue. Like so many of Oates's stories, it begins simply and moves into complexity. Claire, the protagonist, is a professor of English at a university in a northern city. She is comforting a young woman, a student who is distraught over her academic and romantic failures. The girl leaves; shortly afterward Claire finds that the snow which has been falling all day has made even the university parking lot impassable, so she calls a cab. The cab is delayed so long that she begins to walk aimlessly in the general direction of her home, an apartment several miles outside the city. As she walks through the cold and deserted streets, Claire is buffeted by contrary forces: on the one hand, the assertion of her intelligence as a tool for command of herself and of others, and on the other, the denial of her loneliness. The physical effect of the snow, which is real enough, is less significant than its symbolic associations of coldness, separation, and death. The irony of noncommunication around which so many of Oates's stories are built is heightened here by Claire's profession, which requires mastery of words and ideas, and even by her name, which suggests clarity. She has come to realize that her success is based on a kind of lie that negates intelligence: she can tell anybody anything, and she will always be believed; not, however, because she is so persuasive, but because nobody ever listens. Individuality and contact are illusions: a long-distance telephone call with an ex-lover reveals only the "crackling distance between them," and all the many men she has known fade into an "undifferentiated mass," like the falling snowflakes." By denying the individual, Claire tries to deny her own unhappiness, the results of an isolation which she can intellectually prove is a condition of existence but which she cannot tolerate emotionally. The story ends as Claire admits to herself that she will, once again, allow herself to be picked up, solaced, and used by the first man who opens his door to her.

The narrative technique of "The Snowstorm" is something of a *tour de force;* Oates seems to be developing an interest in experimental styles, particularly those associated with disturbed narrators upon whose judgment the reader cannot rely. Her basic strengths, though, remain the realism of her detail, and the ways in which her details spread beyond simple realism into symbolic associations. A further example from "The Snowstorm" will serve to explain both her method and its benefits and drawbacks.

As Claire is trying to get her car out of the parking lot, the wheels spin on the ice. This is a homely detail, instantly recognizable; but for Claire it is "sickening," not because it means she has to call a cab but because it suggests motion that "hungered to be physical," to be free. Claire then recalls a newspaper story about a woman who was buried alive and who later tried to claw her way out of the coffin. The extension of the trivial detail into a matter of philosophical significance, the association of the intellectual concepts of motion and energy with the physical fact of death, and the incorporation of these perceptions in the mind of the protagonist are deftly accomplished. Oates is doing something here very similar to what Wordsworth and other Romantics did, showing how significance can inhere in the most ordinary occurrence. We learn a great deal about character and theme in this scene.

At the same time, one wonders whether the character—any character—would really think so quickly about spinning wheels in terms of frustrated energy yearning for release. The very appropriateness of the metaphor which the car becomes through the narrator's speculation seems too tidy, too calculated, too much the art which calls attention to itself. For all of the realistic details in Oates's work, the reader is not always convinced that their symbolic associations necessarily follow. Similarly with regard to character and theme, their monochromatic greys—admittedly appropriate to the hour of midnight mentioned in the Whitman epigraph—become wearying. The reader who finishes this volume will conclude that its author is a woman of considerable intelligence, understanding, and knowledge of human psychology; he will also wish that those gifts were wider in their application and less bleak in their conclusions.

Anthony Arthur

ON KEEPING WOMEN

Author: Hortense Calisher (1911–   )
Publisher: Arbor House (New York). 325 pp. $9.95
Type of work: Novel
Time: The present
Locale: New York

A novel that unfolds the drama of a man and a woman and their four children, and traces the physical and mental odysseys of each of the principal characters as they search for their own identities in journeys away from their fiery glade of a home

Principal characters:
>LEXIE, a wife and mother
>RAY, her husband
>CHESSIE,
>CHARLES,
>MAUREEN, and
>ROYAL, their children
>JAMES, Lexie's brother

On Keeping Women by Hortense Calisher is divided into five chapters or sections. Often, the writing style of this book resembles a prose poem—fluid, abstract, and beautiful. The narrative point of view, which changes from the divided self of the female protagonist, to her husband, to each of her children, to her former employer, and back to her rejoined self, is complicated and often confusing. Is the reader presented with an actual change in perspective, or is he voyaging on a mental odyssey of the female character's imagination which projects other people's thoughts in her search for her own language? If the events in the novel are told from different perspectives, then the misunderstandings and misconceptions surrounding the action in the novel are unfolded to the reader, but are kept hidden from the characters who are involved. In this way, the text resembles James Joyce's *Ulysses;* we, the readers, are allowed to view the action and to peer inside the minds of the characters, but ultimately we remain outside of the text. However, the reader is often linked to another character in the book who feels that he is on the outside, too. In mutual voyeurism, identification, knowledge, and understanding occur, in spite of the thoughts that are expressed in fragmented syllables and sentences.

In the first section of the novel, "Touching upon Youth," Lexie lies on the riverbank in front of her house while she drifts, like the Hudson, through the memories of her thirty-seven years. The only present action is her state of repose and present thoughts that involve the condition of her nude body on the riverbank. Practically all other events, characterizations, and emotions surrounding Lexie are presented in past tense—via her memory. The only experience that we as readers can share with her is her reunion with her husband. The effect of this flashback mode of unfolding herself keeps the reader emotionally stifled. The picture is too well-defined and onesided. Not that there are not various ways of interpreting this novel—quite the contrary. However, the places where one is, in Lexie's terms, "vagued out" may be due to Lexie's misconceptions, or to our miscomprehension of characters whom we rarely do see in present action.

From the nucleus of the present of "Lexie on the riverbank," several family incidents are revived from the past; however, the second generation is more complicated and intense, and has a peculiar effect upon the first. The wheel of fortune has come full circle, and some of the characters of the second generation are repeating the actions of the first. Lexie and Ray's daughter, Chessie, is seventeen and more severely schizophrenic than her mother was at this same age. Although Chessie looks like her father, she thinks like her mother. Her siblings Charles, Maureen, and Royal try to keep her under control, but cannot. Unfortunately, there is no doctor-husband to engage her into settling into normalcy; instead, her father, Ray, who understands the strong connection between his daughter and his wife, is strongly attracted to her and kisses her passionately. He is not really certain (and neither are we) when he realizes it is Chessie, not Lexie, that he is kissing.

Chessie's brother Charles has witnessed the passionate embrace, and it is through him that we see the event. Although he has a strong allegiance to his father, Charles assumes the role that Lexie's older brother James had played in her earlier life. As the guardian of Chessie, Charles tries to keep her mental explosions hidden from his mother. He views their relationship as a rival-sibling one, not a mother-daughter one. Afraid that the stronger may destroy the weaker, he copes in the best way that he can. Whether the choice is the most advantageous is difficult for the reader to discern. Once again, the sequence of events is relayed in elliptical passages of memory—neatly imprinted with external images, verbal editing, and thought organization. One of Chessie's disruptive behavior patterns reminds him of another, both of which are told to the reader in neat packages. We feel like the blot-head drawings on the walls of Chessie's studio; we receive what the character chooses to give in layered patterns of the recent and not so recent past.

Like both James and Ray, Charles has chosen medicine as his field of study, and so has his brother, Royal. It is Royal who bandages up Chessie's wrist wounds after her attempted suicide. Although he may go into psychology, at his young age he can only treat her externally from his own black medicine bag. He is not directly involved in a cyclical familial pattern since he has no prototype in Lexie's family; however, he does have one in another house. The Kellihys, who live next door, have a little girl named Dodo. Royal is paid fifty cents by the maid to bathe the child, just as another little child was given a smaller amount to bathe Dodo's aunt. Royal uses this job as a means of studying anatomy and makes drawings of the little girl's private parts. His other medical studies are quite peculiar, also. From Royal's vantage, the reader learns that Chessie and Lexie are so closely connected that even their menstrual cycles occur at the same time; Royal knows; he observes.

Lexie still lies on the river bank thinking that her children are asleep or peacefully awaking to this beautiful new day. The reader has left her there for several pages in order to catch a glimpse of the present time within the home. In it we witness Ray's misplaced passion for life and Chessie's grasp at death. Observing the children interact and discuss their plans to leave this place, the reader can also witness their observance of their mother and father now reunited by the river. Once again, there is a layered vision.

This complicated father-daughter incident is the one that pulls all of the characters of the family into the present time. It is peculiar, then, that the narrative voice which describes Ray's kissing Chessie is that of an outsider. J. J. Hoppe, the newspaperman for whom Lexie worked, describes the occurrence. The style of writing reads like a newspaper article. The sentences are uninvolved, although the action is complicated enough. Mr. Hoppe foreshadowed such an event by commenting to Lexie that she lived in a village of "unnatural acts." From this point of view, it is only natural that he should do the reporting. He, shares this information with us, but chooses to file this piece in the circular bin. He has the story, which is of primary importance to him.

Lexie's relationship with J. J. Hoppe, which evolves while Ray is recovering from an illness in Spain, is an intellectual one. In his newspaper office, they sit and discuss people and words. In a strange communion of language, the two teach each other about themselves, and some of the most delicate prose and most enlightening thoughts are revealed while the two chat in Lexie's cubicle. She, in constant search for her own mode of communication, states that very often a man and a woman may live together for years and still not know each other's glossaries. Obviously, she and Ray do not.

When she and Ray are united on the riverbank, they speak in a staccato-like conversation. After being separated for several months, they attempt to avoid conversation and try to establish an intuitive form of understanding. After a short time, they begin to speak in complete sentences; however, their most startling realizations, fears, and concerns are kept hidden in silence. We are privileged to such knowledge; their unexpressed words in their glossaries are reserved for us. They are like abridged dictionaries from which we can skim the surface of their true meanings, but yet, the view is still somehow incomplete.

Ray does not share the important particulars of his stay in Spain with Lexie. Instead, before he sees her or enters his house, he walks down the road and remembers what has been. Here, too, the reader is presented with an action, which encompasses a large expanse of time, in the past tense—another double vision. Returning from a deeply religious experience and physical convalescence in Spain, Ray recalls the conversations with his attending physician and nurse, his physical pain, and emotional distress that included his conflicting feelings about Lexie, their children, and his brother-in-law, James. Like his wife, he has sought a means to reflect upon himself, apart from her physical presence. In order to do this in such close proximity to home he has asked a bus driver to let him off one mile away from his doorstep. Whereas Lexie's memories take her to actions in close geographical proximity, Ray's recollections are enhanced by geographical distance. Now, though, his ideas seem organized, and he hopes to return to Europe. Within this walk, then, Ray's dual viewpoint of time alternates while he presently looks down at his shoes and then remembers what has been.

The patterns of conscious memory represented in the novel form a larger thematic organization in which concrete objects attach themselves and become a part of the whole. As the characters formulate their thoughts in past tense, particular possessions become a segment of their experiences, and sometimes are the symbols for the person or experience itself.

On her mental journey, Lexie carries with her a suitcase of memories filled with former attire which represents the expression of her multifaceted self. For Ray, she wears a string of pearls—a gift from him; for Kevin Sheridan, her first lover, she adorns herself in a white cashmere dress shimmering with metallic threads and divests herself of the pearls; for Day Folger, her second lover, she buys a scarlet petticoat and many other "city" outfits. These latter *écoutrements* she leaves at Day's apartment and is proud that she has done so. They belong there. When, coincidentally, Day arrives at her home with a new lover, she feels miserable and fat in a worn-out white sweater and shepherd-checked slacks. These pieces of clothing help Lexie to note the various stages of her life. She states that the first week with Ray progressed from chiffon and lace to a purple velvet dressing gown which she still wears because it is "so me." It seems appropriate now that she should be naked as she introspectively reviews her life.

Lexie's keen visual perceptions extend to others, too. Her professor's ill-fitting slacks are indicative of his unexpressed problems in his life, while Bets Kellihy's one-hundred-dollar Saks Fifth Avenue dressing gown represents her sensual decadence. Like her multitoned brown dress, Chessie has depths that can only be perceived in different moods or lighting. Less complicated than Chess, Ray still adorns himself with the cufflinks and tie pin engraved with the letters "DR." The borrowed yellow shoes he wears when he meets her are not those of a father. Ray realizes this fact before he ascends the stairs of his home where he does not act "fatherly."

For each of the members of the family their house has been the most important possession. Each has formed his own relationship with it, and they are concerned about its safety one night when a fire blazes at a neighbor's house. The Kellihys, whose parties are similar to the great Gatsby's, do not feel a strong alliance with their home. The conservatory windows are continuously being smashed, telephone wires connecting to nowhere litter their sitting room, and the floors of bathrooms, not the toilets, are receptacles for urination. When the Kellihys' garage/servants' quarters burns, it is replaced quickly by a swimming pool. Fortunately masses of bamboo and trees separate the two homes, and Lexie feels confident that her house will not be endangered by her neighbors'. This is important since every room in Lexie's home is vital to her. The kitchen is filled with thoughts of the unconditional love of children, while her upstairs ledge is a source of solitude and introspection. She sees her home as she viewed her parents' apartment; each place is a part of her entire experience of life, and each affects her self as she emerges in life's experience.

It is from this house that all of the characters escape. The children leave by the back door while their parents lie on the grassy bank. Each character has outgrown this home and needs a new environment in order to grow. Lexie, who seems unaware of her childrens' flight, thinks of her incomplete thesis. Although she is incorrect about the authorship of the Elizabethan play, *Friar Bacon and Friar Bungay,* she captures the essence of this all-important moment of time: she recalls the lines from the play, "Time is/Time was," just as Ray's bus passes.

Kathryn Flaris

ON PHOTOGRAPHY

Author: Susan Sontag (1933–   )
Publisher: Farrar, Straus and Giroux (New York). 207 pp. $7.95
Type of work: Historical criticism

Six essays which explain and deplore the inherent urge of photography from its beginning: the democratizing of all experiences and things and the leveling of all meaning by translating them into mere images

Principal personages:
ANSEL ADAMS
DIANE ARBUS
WALTER BENJAMIN
JULIA MARGARET CAMERON
WALKER EVANS
DOROTHEA LANGE
PAUL ROSENFELD
EDWARD STEICHEN
ALFRED STIEGLITZ
PAUL STRAND
FOX TALBOT
EDWARD WESTON
WALT WHITMAN

Now Susan Sontag has shown us in elegiac words how far we are enlightened or unenlightened about photography. The book itself does not include a single picture. What fills the space is a progress of six essays followed by an album of verbal insights into the picture-making mystique by famous men and women, most of them writers.

Nowhere does the author take us on a tour of the Rochester mansion of George Eastman, although she does provide an etymology of the ugly word *kodac.* Each of her paragraphs is itself a photograph, in fact; one placed after another in a long series. The arrangement is such that the same images keep showing up. And the medley of social philosophy, photography's history and aesthetics (or its absence), and the psychology of pictures as aids to misunderstanding develops on every page. Sontag does not actually write a history of cameras, but in two dozen different places we are afforded verbal snapshots of that history, while the psychology of photographs repeatedly appears on the pages.

Once inside *On Photography* we learn that the author is downhearted about the shutter business. And she will not stop saying so. While her basic indictments of photography and photographic reality are sharp, her own insatiable joy in repeating them in slight variants—who cherishes eighty-seven mugs of a clothesline thief?—makes us lose interest, even makes us wish for a photograph every five pages. Another way of evaluating Sontag's performance is provided us by our memory of the layout in Plato's cave, which she alludes to in the first and last essays. Her relentless strictures about photographers, their weapons, and their ubiquitous products amount to verbose graffiti on Plato's famous walls. In fact, if *The Republic* did not lead us to a different conclusion by the described position of the fire, for example, we might think from now on that the cave chamber was circular. For reading *On Photography* is a not-so-merry merry-go-round-and-round.

Again and again photography's predatory nature is attacked, and artistic seriousness is denied the photographer's efforts. Yet Sontag does not deal directly with a central issue: if photography transforms the world, then some aesthetic trophy is due it regardless of the vitiation of personal seeing and other social and psychical disturbances caused by the camera. As for a primary reason for her skirting of this matter, no more obvious one exists than her actual tendency to treat the entire lot of photographers as homogeneous, even as she appears to single out individual talent like Diane Arbus.

One example of a corrective to this simplicity on Sontag's part would be the November 13, 1976, number of *The New Republic,* in which Walker Evans has a perceptive say about himself just two days before his death. In place of sharper distinctions in *On Photography* Sontag restates one of her old and still sensible requests; in the final essay, as overwritten as the rest, she calls for a silence to the shutters, a plea for "an ecology not only of real things but of images as well." *On Photography* is *against* photography.

Unlike Plato's allegory in which the super student escapes the dark region, later to return, there is no exit and thus no return for Sontag's prisoner. Each of us is her victim as we are the camera's. Her numberless paragraphs seem to say that her subject is fresh and important, but each essay is just another mug of the same old clothesline thief.

No amount of brilliance, no amount of just having condemned photography and the photographers superbly will do. She zooms in from the same old angles all over again, criticizing this theory, this career, or that technique; the matter of painting versus photography, the camera's freezing of time, or the democratizing influence of photographs; or what two hundred artists and assorted thinkers have said on these subjects. On and On. Last year's art movie. Andy Warhol. Then James Agee's narrative for Walker Evans' photographs of the plight of Southern sharecroppers. And suddenly we realize that we have already seen and heard every bit of it. The effect of this prose overload is the exact effect the author deplores most about photography: a world or cave full of pictures dispossesses reality and dissociates us from it. In the photographer who snaps fifty shots in hopes of one beautiful image, however grotesque or ugly the subject, Sontag has found her mentor. But while the photographer's single beauty would reach the happy customer or hang in the civic museum or campus gallery, the author's every practice sentence faces us on the page.

Sontag's argument against photography is based on the objection that cameras and their users have developed seeing for seeing's sake. And the result of photographic seeing is dissociative seeing because of discrepancies between the way cameras and human eyes focus and judge perspective. What photographers often claim, according to Sontag, is a cleansing of the senses; the camera folk are showing us what our unseeing eyes had missed. And what we had missed may be either that camera's embellishment of the world or its equally accomplished effort to rip off the mask of the same old planet. For the camera, while it can artfully lie or be lenient, is an expert of cruelty. One fiber of this cruelty is the insatiability of the photographing eye. Thus the terms of our confinement in the cave world are changed. What we have a right to look at, what is worth looking at, amounts to a new visual code in the hands of photographers. They are the new grammarians. They give us our sense of clarity, even our ethics of seeing. We are their dialectic. It is they who decide how our pictures should look, they who prefer one exposure to another. This passivity on our part and the ubiquity of the photographic record compose photography's modern and deplorable essence. The whole thing is rankly aggressive. And the sad effect of this assault is the democratization of all experiences and things by both turning them into images and imposing standards for their consumption.

In a short life we too bend over the camera as the device that makes real whatever we are doing. A social rite, a defense against anxiety, and a tool of power and control—these are the urges supporting the mass art form photography. Clearly, most of us do not photograph for art's sake. But time eventually places most photographs, even the most pathetic, into one kind of art museum or another. For the new age of tentative faiths or stark unbelief is everywhere pledging allegiance to mere images. The image, not the thing itself, is the current preference. Plato's classical, derogatory attitude toward images as shadows has been updated and overturned. Today we ask for the copy, the image, and assign or condemn the original things and experiences to the file. And all the while this popular consumption goes on, photographers, like recent gods, give the most contradictory accounts of what kind of knowledge they possess and what kind of art, if any, they practice.

Whether the photograph is the accident worth admiring, the result of the camera as machine gun, or the result of a concept, an extension in McLuhan's terms of the photographer's select mind and eye, either way most professionals, Sontag notes, harbor an "almost superstitious confidence in the lucky accident." And whether through purpose or caprice, cameras and their folk are both the antidote and the dread disease, a "means of appropriating reality and a means of making it obsolete."

In the now classical modern style, the end of Sontag's argument is in the beginning. Ultimately, the photographic image to her is a surface that teases. Given this surface image we judge reality too simply. For this verbose philosopher camera intelligence is the opposite of understanding, which, she believes, begins with our not accepting the world as it looks.

James W. Clark, Jr.

THE PATH BETWEEN THE SEAS
The Creation of the Panama Canal, 1870–1914

Author: David McCullough (1933–   )
Publisher: Simon and Schuster (New York). Illustrated. 698 pp. $12.50
Type of work: History
Time: 1870–1914
Locale: Panama, France, the United States

A history of the Panama project, beginning with Count de Lesseps' bold and eventually disastrous venture and ending with the triumph of American enterprise

Principal personages:
> FERDINAND DE LESSEPS, builder of the Suez Canal and projector of the Panama Canal
> CHARLES DE LESSEPS, his son and associate
> THEODORE ROOSEVELT, President of the United States
> JOHN HAY, Secretary of State
> MARCUS HANNA, the Senator who favored the Panama route
> PHILIPPE BUNAU-VARILLA, French prime mover of the Canal
> WILLIAM NELSON CROMWELL, Public Relations Specialist on the Canal
> CAPTAIN ALFRED T. MAHAN, author of a classic book on Sea Power
> ALEXANDRE GUSTAVE EIFFEL, French Tower and Bridge builder
> JOHN STEVENS, the "unsung hero of the Canal"
> GEORGE WASHINGTON GOETHALS, final Chief of the Canal project

Product of Pittsburgh and Yale University, David McCullough began his writing career with *Time* and the Heritage Publishing Company. After his first book, *The Johnstown Flood* (1968), he completed *The Great Bridge*, declared worthy of the "Greatest Bridge in the World" and winner of many awards; then he tackled the Panama Canal. McCullough opens his history of the Canal by introducing Count Ferdinand de Lesseps, who, after completing the Suez Canal, was looking for another project to occupy his men and material. A passageway between the Americas had interested men since medieval times, and the French engineer was not inhibited, as Charles I of Spain was, by a confessor who warned him, "What God hath joined together, let no man put asunder." Nor did the common belief that the Pacific would pour through the ditch into the Atlantic deter him. The author remarks that the cost of working in the tropics did not frighten de Lesseps either, in spite of the report that the Panama Railroad for the gold seekers of 1847 cost one laborer for every railroad tie put down. Instead, he found records of the number of dead—from six to ten thousand—and of the total cross ties put down—74,000—to disprove the report. (McCullough continually interposes such interesting items; he tells, for example, the story of how the thrifty Railroad Company sold these dead bodies to Medical Colleges around the world, thereby accumulating enough money to build their hospital in Colon.) Next, de Lesseps held an international conference in Paris in 1879, where the delegates decided that the most efficient type of canal was one operated by locks, with the entrance located where Balboa started his explorations of the tropics in 1510, rather than at the more popular Nicaragua site. When the experts estimated the cost of the project at four hundred million francs, de Lesseps wasted no time; he ordered his company to begin selling shares to Frenchmen eager to repeat their gains from Suez investments, and headed for America to begin work.

De Lesseps' first task was to mark off a right-of-way fifty miles long and four hundred feet wide across the Isthmus. It was a formidable task. First, he faced a different sort of terrain from the flat area of Suez, making it necessary to unlearn much that the engineers had learned in their earlier dig. The laborers were faced by new dangers, including three species of poisonous snakes in the lush underbrush: bushmasters, coral snakes, and the deadly *fer-de-lance.* The climate also opposed him. He found that in the so-called dry season (mid-December through April), the four o'clock shower came so regularly that people could tell time by it. The rain poured down like a shower bath for an hour, then abruptly cleared to let the torrid sun come out and create a humid atmosphere unknown in Suez. Disease was rife. McCullough quotes a later director who identified three kinds of fever in Panama: malaria, yellow fever, and cold feet. De Lesseps could soon understand how yellow fever had helped the Haitians win their independence and discouraged Napoleon enough to persuade him to sell off Louisiana.

But de Lesseps persisted, though the funeral train departed every evening with a load of cadavers for the cemetery on Monkey Hill, Panama, and survivors clamored to go home. In spite of all hardships, on July 4, he saw the completion of his road across the Isthmus, and prepared to send his laborers in with their picks and shovels.

The author refuses to blame the French Company for the inadequacy of tools provided; he refutes the story that ten thousand snow shovels were shipped into a location where snow has never fallen, insisting that the laborers were provided with the best equipment available at that time. The shovels, only a thousand of which were ordered, were good quality flat steel shovels of proven efficiency.

McCullough begins Book Two, "The Period of Confusion" with an account of de Lesseps' forced return to Europe to protect his Suez Canal from the British during the trouble with Egypt. He left his son Charles and another inexperienced engineer, Jules Dingler, in charge of what was called "the largest and most ambitious task the world had ever known." Dingler composed a masterplan and ordered bigger machinery and more laborers; his plan called for the digging of forty-five million metric tons just to slope back the sides of the ditch—more tonnage than the total excavation in Suez.

From 1880 to 1885, canal work showed little progress, plagued by a fire that consumed much of Colón and some of the machinery being imported, and by the revolt by a disgruntled Haitian, Pedro Prestan, who was quickly defeated and hanged. These events were all part of the circumstances which the author blames for giving France a bad reputation in canal building. Canal shares dropped in value, and owners hurried to sell out. All this is narrated in the chapter "Downfall," which ends with the return to France of several Directors, and with Bunau-Varilla's rise to Director. De Lesseps also returned to France to float a lottery, under rumors that he had changed his mind in favor of locks for the canal, and was very ill. Someone sent telegrams to mayors of French cities announcing his death, a rumor he had to scotch by returning to America, this time to accompany the Statue of Liberty given by France to the United States. But all this was of no use. On February 4, 1889, the Compagnie Universelle du Canal Interocéanique declared bankruptcy. Panic and chaos followed; eighty thousand Frenchmen had lost all their savings. The National Chamber convened amid many accusations; one anti-Semitic writer even published a book blaming the "800,000 Jews in France" for the collapse. Clemenceau came under suspicion, and de Lesseps and his son were arrested. The subsequent sentence of fine and imprisonment was never carried out.

With the fortunes of the canal project at this low point, the volume moves into Book Three, "Stars and Stripes, 1890–1904." It commences with a quotation from Kipling, "The universe seemed to be spinning around and Roosevelt was the spinner." Theodore Roosevelt's arrival at the White House, says the author, signaled the most dramatic shift there since Andrew Jackson was President. Declaring that "No man ever had a better time being president than Roosevelt," McCullough traces Roosevelt's conviction that America's "Manifest Destiny" demanded a canal. He had been a close student of Captain Mahan's *The Influence of Sea Power upon History* (1890), which argued that "National greatness and commercial supremacy are directly related to supremacy at sea." Roosevelt had seen the theme confirmed in the race of the battleship *Oregon* around the Horn following the blowing up of the *Maine* in Manila, to take part in the Battle of Santiago Bay. As soon as he took the oath, he asked John Hay, author of the Hay-Pauncefote Treaty, to remain his Secretary of State, and his first message to Congress dealt with the building of an interoceanic canal.

Negotiations between Colombia and the United States began at once, but amid great difficulty, ending in the acceptable terms that Colombia would accept a payment of $100,000,000 in gold and an annual rental of $250,000, which, we are reminded, was about what the Panama Railroad was paying. In addition, the United States was to pay the reorganized Panama Canal Company for rights, concessions, tools, and the partly completed ditch.

Meanwhile the Department of Panama had elected Manuel Amador Guerrero as president, but almost immediately he was deposed and exiled by a sudden revolution. Following Latin American tradition, he organized a revolutionary junta to help regain his office. Proponents of the Panama route saw this junta as a means of getting what they wanted, especially in case Colombia refused to agree or was slow or greedy in its demands. Therefore, when Amador came to the United States, there were many who listened to his requests for help.

The author comments that Roosevelt's humor would have been tickled had he known of the secret conniving around him. Finally Amador started home with a new constitution, a proclamation of independence, and the belief that he would have North American assistance if needed to keep flying the new Panama flag he had wound around his body when entering his country. Now, what one senator called "the most remarkable revolution I have ever read about in history" was about to begin. Brilliantly and vividly, relying on the 1913 U.S. publication *Resolutions of the Committee on Foreign Affairs of the House of Representatives,* McCullough records the complicated succession of events.

On November 2, the U.S.S. *Nashville* reached Colón Harbor, on the Atlantic side, supposedly bringing the promised help. As the author records the events, Colonel Shaler, a burly American railroad man, had ordered all rolling stock of the Panama Railroad across to Panama City (on the Pacific side) as part of the conspiracy. Now he offered to transport the Colombian troops on the Atlantic side across to the Pacific, but lacking cars, he offered to send General Tobar and staff in a special train, with the troops to follow as soon as he could get cars. With the officers aboard getting nervous, he pulled the signal cord and sent the special train on its way.

At about the same time, Amador had gone to the Colombia Cuartel de Chiriqui in Panama City and by promising $65,000 in gold to the commander, Esteban Huertas, and fifty dollars in silver to each soldier, he had bought their loyalty. To much cheering, the success of the revolution was being announced in Panama's plaza just as Tobar's train pulled in. The soldiers promptly marched their former officers away to prison. The only casualty occurred when a shell shot from an offshore loyal gunboat killed a sleeping Chinese and a donkey before the ship was driven off by cannon from shore fortifications now gone over to the Republic. Meanwhile, Captain Eliseo Torres, on the Colón side, had no news of events across the isthmus. When ordered to surrender, he refused until he had consulted with his superiors in Panama, so Shaler made up a special conveyance to take him under parole across the isthmus, after his anger had been assuaged by a handful of gold coins for himself and silver pesos for his followers.

At the sight of cheering crowds in Panama and the new flag flying over the government buildings, and after some words with his imprisoned general, Torres saw that resistance was useless, and he and the prisoners made the rail trip once more, reaching Colón just as the U.S.S. *Dixie,* supposedly with four hundred marines aboard, was entering the harbor. That sight, with promised payments of $10,000 to $50,000 apiece for officers, and open barrels of silver coins in the plaza for common soldiers, persuaded them all to board the S.S. *Cartagena,* Bogotá-bound. At noon on November 6, 1901, the United States recognized the new republic and the revolution was over, although McCullough comments "without the presence of the U.S., the new Republic would not have lasted a week." He credits the dynamic solution of the Panama question to Washington.

Much remained to be done and details of subsequent action are included in the two hundred pages of Book Three, "The Builders, 1904-1914." Turnover of the French Company property to the Republic did not occur until November 11, 1904, when "the choicest region of Colombia" went to the use of the United States. The rest of McCullough's account tells what the U.S. government got and what they did with it.

McCullough's explanation of United States success in Panama was the American application of modern medical science, their ability to improvise, their methods of financing, and the size of their mechanical equipment. When James Stevens was appointed Chief Engineer of the project, the first thing he did was to send for William Gorgas, who had rid Havana of yellow fever. Fever was his great foe, so Gorgas arrived to start fumigating and killing rats. Then Stevens tripled his working force, selecting blacks from Barbados, Martinique, and Guadeloupe, who were not so lazy as the original Jamaicans. Shipments of Basques from Spain also arrived, given free passage to Panama, wages of $187 a month, and, after five hundred working days, a free return trip home. For them he provided improved living conditions and offered better food, as well as band concerts and football fields for their entertainment. He ordered gigantic equipment from the United States to be assembled on the site. The author also provides ten pages of comment on the new uses of electricity, and tells of the founding of the General Electric Company to supply parts. With no models to copy, the men improvised what they needed with the new kinds of steel, already in use in the new auto industry. McCullough's account of the size and weight of the canal locks is breathtaking.

Six months before contract date, the canal was completed, and we read of the passage of the flag-decorated tub through the first locks without a hitch; finally on August 15, 1914, the ocean-going S.S. *Cristobal* traversed the system. McCullough laments, however, that this spectacular feat was overshadowed in the press by war news from Europe. However, the canal was done; the Americans had scored a triumph. The total cost, including sums paid to Panama, Colombia, and France, was $350,000,000, with an additional $25,000,000 indemnity paid to Colombia in 1921 for loss of territory.

Because of World War I, only two thousand vessels used the canal during the first year, but in July, 1919, a fleet of thirty-three ships bound home from the war passed the locks in two days. By 1916, when channel lighting was installed, ships could use the canal day and night at the rate of one per hour, and in 1972 nearly seven thousand ships with a million tons in cargo sailed from ocean to ocean.

Willis Knapp Jones

THE PEOPLE SHAPERS

Author: Vance Packard (1914–   )
Publisher: Little, Brown and Company (Boston). 398 pp. $12.50
Type of work: Popular social commentary

A compendium of contemporary developments in behavioral and biological sciences together with comments on their possibly dangerous consequences

People shapers are dangerous. That's what Vance Packard is selling the public this time around. "Human engineers are at work in a variety of fields. They are increasing the capacity of a relatively small number of people to control, modify, manipulate, reshape the lives of a great number of other people. . . . Control is being achieved over human actions, moods, wishes, thoughts." Hidden persuaders, waste makers, status seekers, and pyramid climbers have all had their turn on the (book) rack; now those who shape people must do their stretch.

Who are the People Shapers? There are two more or less distinct groups: the behavioral psychologists and the biological scientists. *Shaping*, however, is a misnaming of the biological true-life amazing stories that Packard relates in his compendium of science news. The scientists who are busily doing research on test-tube births, embryo transplants, sperm banks, rented wombs, bionic replacements, cloning, and other forms of genetic juggling should really be called—at the risk of suggesting a sequel—*the body makers*. In any event, the attempt to bring behaviorists and biologists under the same cover does not succeed because each represents a different type of danger, and each therefore requires a different type of safeguard.

According to Packard the danger of behavioral control techniques, aside from any inherent aversion we might experience, is twofold. These techniques often produce counterresults, and they may fall into the hands of a dictator. The real danger of biological body making, again aside from any inherent aversions, rests only in the latter. The ability to create would allow a dictator to populate a nation with robotlike creatures. But when reacting to this frightening prospect, it should not be forgotten that dictators have never needed biological technology to gain power, let alone to keep it. And so the surest safeguard against dictatorial eugenics consists of preventing a Stalin or a Hitler from rising in the first place. The same prophylactic measure would, of course, eliminate the corresponding danger of behavioral controls—which leaves us with only the danger of undesired results to consider. And, as we shall see, a consideration of the question of consequences leads to the conclusion (denied by Packard) that recent managerial techniques do play a role in the shaping of people.

The first problem that a reader encounters in examining Packard's views on what he describes is in finding them. Not that they are not there. They are, strewn throughout his paraphrase-quote-reparaphrase journalistic account of a smorgasbord sequence of stories. Once found, the problem becomes one of discerning some coherent patterns that dominate the sometimes incompatible pieces of commentary. Hopefully, our discussion of results has overcome both problems.

The purpose of classroom conditioning is to encourage learning. But, says Packard, there is no indication that actual learning is enhanced by any of the behavioral modification projects he relates. Indeed, he sympathetically alludes to a whole school of educational thought that believes that "such a rigid structure in fact inhibits learning." Even the use of drugs to control student behavior, notes the author, fails to improve school performance as measured by the Iowa Test of Basic Skills. And as for the use of drugs to improve memory, the author concludes that forgetting can be beneficial because it prevents minds from being dulled by the clutter of details and lets time heal all wounds. (Though Packard evidently would be opposed to the use of drugs to *erase* memory, because a dictator could use them to make people forget about popular democratic leaders or what it was like to be free.) The upshot of these criticisms involving countereffects is that they imply that such manipulations of people would *not* be dangerous, in a democracy, if they only had the effects intended. Hence in the midst of selling his readers on the deplorable nature of human manipulation *per se*, Packard opens the door to the possibility of control that is desirable. If only conditioning and drugs really did help us to learn, to be brighter instead of duller, then we would presumably have grounds for adopting these techniques for controlling behavior. In fact Packard does recommend the "enrichment" of the environment of students (to improve their intelligence) and the offering of a morning glass of milk to them (as a calmative?). Drugs, though, are still to be avoided—"until someone comes along with a pill for wisdom."

Nowhere is the full import of Packard's counterresults argument as clear as in his discussion of the workplace. Here he sees behavior modification, of the behaviorist or humanist stripe, as desirable whenever it delivers what it promises. At Emery Air Freight, for example, a thoroughly Skinnerian program "provided daily feedback to employees on how well each of them was meeting company goals. Those doing well have been receiving huge doses of praise and recognition. . . . First results were reported as gratifying in terms of output and profitability." Fortunately for such companies, as a management trainer who teaches reinforcement strategies at U.S. Steel and Du Pont pointed out to the author, praise "doesn't cost anything." This observation, incidentally, is made by the same Skinnerian behaviorist quoted by Packard at the end of his opening chapter in the Techniques for Controlling Behavior section: "I believe that the day has come when we can combine sensory deprivation with drugs, hypnosis and astute manipulation of reward and punishment to gain absolute control over an individual's behavior." It is this alarming thought that Packard tells us to keep in mind as we look at what psychological behavior shapers are doing these days. But seven chapters later, when discussing the workplace, it seems that the author's emphasis on results has somewhat drowned out the initial alarm with Musak.

I say "somewhat" because at this point Packard takes another turn in his travels through techniques for controlling behavior. The humanistic psychological theories of Argyris, Bennis, and Maslow are now put forward as better ways than conditioning to get the job done. Behaviorism treats adults like children, and, more important, constant praise cannot overcome the dullness of a dull job. Generous applications of behaviorism (at least, without equally generous monetary rewards) were simply not enough to prevent the surfacing of discontent in the form of soaring absenteeism, high turnover, and on-the-job drinking and drug-taking. Industry needed something new, something cheap but effective, from the industrial psychologists. And the "enrichment" of the workplace, where workers are "trusted to choose the best way to do their jobs," filled the order. Packard fails to explore the potential and actual control aspects of humanistic psychology, however.

Instead he abruptly interrupts the discussion, not returning to the topic until some fifteen chapters later, safely out of the section on control techniques and snugly tucked under the next-to-last chapter heading, "New Trends That Can Enhance Self-Direction." It is here that we are finally told that "dramatic measurable evidence of results from the humanistic approach is now available," that job-enrichment raises not only the morale but also the amount and quality of production. To Packard, of course, job-enrichment is seen as an example of "*removing* manipulation to achieve higher results." But is humanistic psychology really so very different from behaviorist psychology when applied to the existing workplace? The author himself suggests a negative answer when he reports that the behaviorists' new stress on self-management, where "a subject becomes his own therapist," moves them closer to the humanists. For if self-management can be part of a behaviorist approach in psychiatry, it can also be so in industry. It need not necessarily be so, but the point is that it can; in other words, it depends on circumstances. Yet Packard fails to see this dependence. For him, the transfer of some decision-making power to workers makes them happier and more productive, period. The fact that management is shaping the environment to create happy workers who will produce better and faster without a concomitant increase in pay is totally ignored.

Also ignored is the issue of the limits of worker participation. The limits of patient participation in psychiatry are clear: the doctor determines what is normal behavior and how it is to be obtained, no matter how much "say" in the treatment he may deem permissible to grant the patient. Sometimes this determination is relatively harmless, as when the patient has the option of going elsewhere or discontinuing treatment. But when confined to an institution, for instance, all pretense of self-management is effectively dropped at the gate. In industry too, the question of the worker's limits of self-management is to be answered by looking at the actuality of who defines the environment in which the worker must work. Only then can a reasonable assessment be made as to who is controlling whom. Yet Packard, on a matter of this importance, reports on merely a single case of humanism in the plant, and that case, a General Foods factory, is probably as far removed from behaviorism as management will permit. Had his sample been less selective, he would have seen the variety of forms that humanistic psychology can take in the factory. He would have seen that nearly all forms are considerably more restrictive and closer to behaviorist techniques than the one he chose. And had he looked at perhaps the only plant where workers' participation exceeded the level of his selected case, namely, the Polaroid Corporation, with its spontaneous *ad hoc* workers' committees on worker concerns, he would surely have become aware of the present limits on worker participation. For at Polaroid the workers' "democracy" was short-lived because, as a company training director put it: "It was *too* successful. What were we going to do with the supervisors, the managers? We didn't need them anymore. Management decided it just didn't want operators that qualified." In short, when workers' democracies are set up by managers, the managers still maintain the power to alter the environment when it no longer serves to keep worker behavior under control. Someday things may change, but this is the way it is today.

Hence the "atmosphere of freedom and dignity" that Packard extols for making workers "more productive"—while at least avoiding the Skinnerian excesses that go *beyond* freedom and dignity—is in fact more atmosphere than either freedom or dignity. This means that the best safeguard against the dangerous effects of behavioral control techniques lies not only in preferring humanism to behaviorism, but also and especially in recognizing the basic similarity between both. And knowing when we are being manipulated is, in turn, the best way to guard against any form of tyranny.

What we have seen, then, is that Packard's "people shapers" nomenclature is doubly flawed, by what it includes and by what it omits. Body makers are included, and, certainly more important, humanistic industrial psychologists are not. The author simply fails to realize that under existing conditions, humanistic techniques for managing workers can only be described as people shaping. And this failure is reflected in Packard's concluding prescriptions. His belief that humanistic psychologists are wisely opposed to people-shaping in any guise is apparently the basis for his being ready to entrust humanistically oriented social and biological scientists with the authority to regulate research and control the controllers. Have no fear, we are told, "boards of wise men" selected by national science associations will do what is best and protect the public from *The People Shapers.*

What a relief. We don't need a pill for wisdom after all—just a glass of milk of amnesia.

E. Gene DeFelice

PIECES OF LIFE

Author: Mark Schorer (1908–1977)
Publisher: Farrar, Straus and Giroux (New York). 173 pp. $8.95
Type of work: Short stories and autobiographical pieces

A juxtaposed collection of tightly crafted fictional pieces and subjective, elusive reminiscences

One does not know whether to classify Mark Schorer as a critic who also wrote fiction or a storyteller who also wrote criticism. Whichever he was, this new collection of the late professor's short stories and autobiographical pieces has considerable artistic merit. At their best, the stories obey Schorer's own critical rule, as laid down in his well-known essay "Technique as Discovery": such technical skills as the control of language and the manipulation of point of view must provide fiction with the objectivity needed for achieving artistic significance, a significance that cannot be achieved by the serving up of mere hunks of raw subject matter.

Consider, for example, "The Lonely Constellation," perhaps the finest of the stories. Like many of the others, it deals with the promiscuous desires of a middle-class husband or wife, yet this particular story achieves its special comic clarity through a carefully controlled pattern of irony, both verbal and situational. A book salesman flying home from Boston in an almost empty plane weaves, within his mind, a philosophic reverie about the supposed contrast between human togetherness during World War II and our present state of dismal isolation. But an undercutting sequence of memories and events shows us that the meaning of the salesman's meditation is less philosophic than sex-starved: pretty girls singing popular love songs, the dullness of his wife and family, fantasies about the smiling airline hostesses who merge before his eyes with famous movie stars, memories of an attractive female publishing executive who rebuffed his sexual overtures in such a graceful way that he scarcely even felt rejected. At last the salesman's philosophizing collapses into the comedy of dreams, as he falls asleep and sees himself peddling his wares to a planeload of "lovely girls." He wakes and, with fuddled innuendo, requests that one of the stewardesses come sit beside him. But then, when his sexual invitation is challenged, he breaks down in tears and instead merely asks for a glass of water.

Technique in "The Lonely Constellation" is not just a surface embellishment imposed upon Schorer's subject but a method of giving his subject both meaning and value. Without his ironic control, the story would have been no more than a sensual or sentimental record of trivial eroticism. With his control, the piece becomes a pointed account of the comic incongruity between a man's self-inflating dreams and the tawdry actuality of his life. In Schorer's own terminology, "technique" here serves as the instrument of "discovery"—specifically, the discovery of an objective moral judgment of his lonely book salesman.

There are four additional stories concerning a married person's dabblings with the pleasures of promiscuity, yet each is so different that again we can perceive the supremacy, in Schorer's fiction, of technique over subject. In "Is Anything Troubling You, Dear?" the emphasis is on the self-centered blindness of a windbag of a wife who cannot perceive that her soft-spoken husband has sought relief from her in extramarital sex. "Picking Up the Pieces" describes yet another faithless husband, but the point here is the wife's concluding realization that a single passing fling has no real importance in the enduring experience of marriage. The significance, however, of "Don't Take Me for Granted" lies in the opposing attitudes of a man and his wife toward a whimsical invitation to a tryst sent by a female graduate student of the professor husband: daredevil puckishness on his part and shocked insecurity on the part of his "liberal" wife. Schorer's "The Unwritten Story" hints at a wife's infidelity during a couple's return trip to Italy after many years of marriage, yet this piece stresses the contrast between their former happiness and their present grubby estrangement. To say that these stories share a common theme would be to miss their variety of effect: satire, domestic affirmation, comic mischievousness, subtle depiction of *malaise.* This range is achieved by the author's shaping control of language, point of view, and carefully placed symbols: a blind man in "Is Anything Troubling You, Dear?," a girl practicing on the piano in "Picking Up the Pieces" and at last getting it right, a violent "crazy wind" in "Don't Take Me for Granted," a refuse-covered island in "The Unwritten Story."

Unlike the short stories, however, the autobiographical interstices in *Pieces of Life* at first seem violations of Schorer's concept of "technique as discovery." They are, in fact, chunks of undigested experience. They are not at all, for example, like the highly stylized bits provided by Ernest Hemingway between the short stories of *In Our Time.* Hemingway's interstices of war, bullfighting, and assorted other brutalities have the same self-contained ironic finality as the stories that surround them. Schorer's italicized bits have the look of mere jigsaw fragments from an uncompleted private memoir. His reminiscences flit inconclusively from his childhood in Wisconsin to his fortieth wedding anniversary. There are scattered vignettes of some poignancy and humor: grief for a run-over dachshund; a pathetic introduction to sex, at the age of only eight, by a fourteen-year-old *femme fatale;* collaboration with a youthful writer friend who sported a decadent cape and taught Schorer how to concoct weird pulp fiction; love for his wife's graces contrasted with her total lack of self-conceit. But, however touching they are in bits, these private remembrances do not add up to wholes. They are not shaped or distanced by Schorer's narrative skill. They remain "pieces of life" rather than pieces of art. Schorer was, of course, far too conscious a writer not to know exactly what these fragments were. "I hope," he observes in his introductory note, "that they provide . . . the slightly staggering dissonance of a real life beating beneath the surface of brighter, created lives." In a way, his hope is justified.

The value of the autobiographical pieces in the book lies, paradoxically, in their very lack of shape. They set off the craftsmanship of Schorer's polished stories, like rough slabs of narrative stone surrounding finished sculpture. It is as though the author wished to reveal to us the basic secret of the art: private memories of time gone by must be purged of egocentricity and submitted to the same disinterested judgment that they will get from readers who do not happen to share the writer's special prejudice in favor of his own delightful self.

For instance, Schorer's fragment about his puzzled introduction at eight years old to the mysteries of copulation is juxtaposed with "Another Country," a delicate story of awakening sexuality. The autobiographical piece is absolutely shapeless. Its longest and most vivid description is of early sexuality, yet the vignette is called "Frank" mainly because Frank was the brother of Schorer's teen-age seductress, though possibly also for the sake of a pun. The brother is described in five rapid sentences. The fragment opens with a detailed evocation of the household of Schorer's grandparents, for little apparent reason except for the fact that Frank lived nearby. And the piece ends with a brief description of a boy named Karl, whom the author later preferred to the seductress' brother. In this vignette, all seems haphazard. By contrast, "Another Country" depicts, with careful focus, the inner conflicts of a fourteen-year-old girl who is repelled yet subtly attracted by the flagrant animality of a young Greek boy in her Perugian *pensione.* An artful pattern of connected details makes the story's point clear: the girl's critical obsession with the boy's long hair and his wolfing of food, an allusive argument between her mother and father about the validity of phallic D. H. Lawrence and his book on *Etruscan Places,* the father's wise comment about the absence of "sharp lines" in an individual's developing "personality." "Technique" in this story objectifies and places the complexities of a young person's emerging sexuality, as they are not placed in the author's private fragment.

The objectified stories and the autobiographical fragments contrast just as sharply in subject matter as they do in technique. The stories are all middle-class in theme and, perhaps more importantly, all middle-aged. Even the one about the fourteen-year-old girl is framed within the perspectives of her middle-aged parents. The world of these carefully wrought stories is limited to that of professors, employees of publishing houses, and literate Americans vacationing in Europe or perhaps closer to home. Schorer's characters tend to be highly educated and sedentary couples at some mid-point crisis in their lives. This description applies not only to the five short stories that deal with marital promiscuity, but to all the others as well. In "Of Educational Value" a professor makes gentle fun of his wife's ritualistic liberalism. In "The Face Within the Face," a beautiful but frigid mother is disgusted by her son's attraction to the maternal warmth of an ugly woman glimpsed on a hotel beach. A graduate student's wife, in "A Burning Garden," longs to escape from her husband's stalled academic struggles. In "A Lamp" the tasteless absurdity of an Art Nouveau lamp parallels the empty life of a middle-aged couple adrift in tourist

Italy. The narrow range of subjects in these stories is hardly, of course, surprising, considering that their author was a professor at Berkeley or that five of the stories saw print first in the pages of *The New Yorker*, set among smart cartoons.

What is surprising is their utter difference in subject from Schorer's personal vignettes. The autobiographical pieces center around his early years in a small Wisconsin village. The division between the worlds of Schorer's reminiscences and the short stories in the collection is so sharp as to be astounding. It is possibly explained by his half-joking comment that he had no self-perspective until he changed his name from Marcus Robert to Mark at about seventeen: "I think that once I became simply Mark Schorer, I finally knew who I was. I don't think that that younger Marcus Robert (whom I never really knew and don't know now, for all my effort to recall him) ever did." We may perhaps conclude that the author was unable to be objective enough about his early Wisconsin days to convert them, through technique, into finished short stories to round out this volume. In Mark Schorer's case, the child may have been father of the man but was less clearly father of the mature artist.

Henry James made a very important distinction between the need of a writer to pick worthy subjects and the duty of the critic to limit his judgments to what the author has done with his chosen subject matter. We may speculate on the restrictions of Mark Schorer's subjects, but we should not judge his work on these extrinsic grounds. *Pieces of Life* is a rewarding collection simply because its author was highly skilled in the technical art of fiction. For once the old cliché has precise application: he was "a writer's writer." His book has much to teach to any aspiring author about how "pieces of life" may be transformed into genuine works of art.

Robert L. Selig

PLAYERS

Author: Don DeLillo
Publisher: Alfred A. Knopf (New York). 212 pp. $7.95
Type of work: Novel
Time: The present
Locale: New York City, rural Maine

An astringent satire on the banality of contemporary American society, centering upon urban terrorists who are "players" of dangerous games

Principal characters:
> LYLE WYNANT, young executive, broker at the New York Stock Exchange
> PAMMY WYNANT, his wife
> ETHAN SEGAL, Pammy's employer at the Grief Management Council
> JACK LAWS, Ethan's homosexual lover
> J. KINNEAR, chief terrorist operative
> ROSEMARY MOORE, Lyle's mistress, also a terrorist
> MARINA VILAR, another terrorist

Don Delillo's fifth novel, a mordantly witty satire on contemporary America, explores the psychology of banality. His major characters are bored—bored nearly to madness by the dull routine of their jobs, by the mechanical social forces that destroy their sense of community. To escape from boredom, they play games modeled upon children's amusements. They assume different identities, change roles. Like players consciously imitating the external semblance of character, they perform their little dramas, sometimes for an audience of fellow players, sometimes for themselves. Because they are *au fond* vacuous, devoid of character, devoid of real vitality, they stimulate their torpid spirits—however briefly and artificially—by developing roles that seem exciting, perhaps dangerous. Yet even the dangerous roles at last become banal. Even the player who assumes the identity of a terrorist becomes bored.

In his prefatory chapter "The Movie," DeLillo presents a symbolic drama that helps to explain the pattern of the entire novel. The setting is a piano-bar lounge of a modern luxury jetliner. Slightly tipsy, rudely jovial passengers press forward to listen to the pianist. From their vantage, they can watch a projection of a movie image, but they cannot hear the sound track without headsets. Instead, they hear the piano tinkling: an ironical or amusing commentary on the action. But the film itself is violent. Lying in ambush, a band of terrorists mow down with semi-automatic fire an innocent party of middle-aged golfers. One terrorist strikes a victim with a machete. Although the scene is visually bloody, the musical accompaniment is brisk, jaunty. To the bar loafers, the action is thereby rendered ambiguous, more absurd than tragic. The film stars perform their roles as terrorists or golf players, as murderers or as the murdered, with grotesque results. Inspired by the absurd scene, members of the audience also perform theatrical roles. All are players—the pianist, the inebriates, the sober viewers. Sharing the stage, their performances become confused. The terrorists, players within a play, seem mechanical robots; but equally mechanical seem the bar patrons, whose gestures are "Chaplinesque," stylized. Perceived with cool, intelligent detachment, the players' actions are grotesque, banal.

In a more complex pattern, the major characters of the novel extend the implications of this symbolic drama. A bright, attractive young couple—Pammy and Lyle Wynant—act out their lives as though they were theatrical performers. At first their roles are those of the well-matched, sophisticated, aspiring set of urbanites. Lyle, a broker at the Stock Exchange, is a rising executive type pushing his way to find room at the top. His wife is healthy, athletically firm, independent. She eats the appropriate nutritional foods, exercises to maintain a lithe, sexy body, and keeps faddishly current with the proper attitudes promoted by the media. Yet their performances are curiously shallow. Lyle practices his intelligence on routine, stultifying data. He is more a mechanical contrivance than a human being. To satisfy his wife's sexual needs, he measures his "performance" against the popular norms. Like a computer, he memorizes trivia. Lacking emotion, he spurs himself to vague lusts. But to him passion is less gratifying than games of rote memory. He is a player without a satisfactory role, a desperate man who cannot fathom the depths of his spiritual collapse.

Similarly, Pammy plays a variety of roles that are supposed to be exciting but are actually insipid. She wastes her energy working for the Grief Management Council, an agency that specializes in discovering euphemisms for the realities of suffering and death. Her job tedious, her domestic life a calculus of gropings, she cannot "stand the idea of tomorrow." At home she eats fruit while her husband stares glassily at the television set. Her life is a bore. She wants to escape, to rehearse a new role. When her homosexual boss, Ethan Segal, suggests that she accompany him and his lover Jack Law to their rustic cabin in Maine, she snaps at the opportunity to flee her former life. Always the player, Pammy rushes to her fate.

To DeLillo, one's fate—especially an urban American's—is established on the bedrock of banality, the North Star of flimflam. Lyle looks for augury in the pulsing blips of the Stock Exchange, an insane rhetoric of electronic codes. Or he watches commercials on television. Or he gawks at pornography. The signals he receives from the media are imperative but contradictory. To remain sane, he must dissociate himself from reality. He keeps his private counsel: to be selfish, secretive, self-contained. And Pammy similarly responds to the signals of the 1970's. She is vaguely frightened by a "Mister Softee" truck that cruises her neighborhood. She is sexually complaisant, socially tolerant, morally neutral. She yawns a lot. Everything bores her. America bores her.

As a moralist, DeLillo must prove that the malady of the Wynants is deeply ingrained, not a surface sickness. Simply to pick at random one effete American couple would not establish his thesis: that the banality destroying their lives is epidemic, that banality is part of America, that it is with us now. So he must give his characters new roles to play out their destinies. In Maine Pammy has the opportunity to perform as an unspoiled child of nature. It has always been a dogma of her sentimental creed that she is most nearly moral around growing things. Yet exposed to natural beauty and the simple though monotonous life at the cabin, she is bored once more. To rouse her flagging spirits, she attempts to seduce Jack. For Pammy the game at first is casual, amusing. They strip in the grassy fields and fall into each other's arms like experimenting children. But for Jack the experience is disastrous. Frightened at revealing his ambiguous sexuality, guilt-ridden at the idea of betraying his homosexual lover, he douses himself with gasoline and immolates himself. Pammy returns to New York, her game over. She stares at a sign marking a hotel for transients, grasping suddenly the meaning of her character in that word.

In her absence, Lyle has also been playing dangerous games. Like Pammy, he mistakenly supposes that he can manipulate people without hazard. He joins the least plausible of groups: urban terrorists, whose asserted object is to blow up the Stock Exchange. In spite of the fact that he lacks political or moral commitment to the cause, he plays the new, dangerous role as though it were a child's game. At first he enjoys a brief respite from boredom. Yet soon the terrorist's role takes on the banality of his former job. He learns an absurd cryptic language, plays games of hide and seek, disguises and deceptions. His actions become stylized. Just as he is controlled by his mysterious espionage boss, J. Kinnear, so he controls underlings. With Rosemary Moore and Marina Vilar, he plays with sex more to test his partner than to give way to passion. Always he tests, probes; the game of espionage is an absurd repetition of trivial amusements. Nevertheless, as DeLillo shows, the game degenerates at last to boredom. To maintain the illusion of interest in the task at hand, the player must continually change his performance. Soon he loses whatever real identity he once possessed; he becomes a cipher.

By accepting his new role, Lyle drops out of life. He loses his wife, his occupation, his country. Henceforward he will be stateless, without political convictions, without a moral center. As a terrorist, he will exist in a condition of theatrical terror, always pursuing, always being pursued. Other players, even counterespionage agents who hunt him down, will seem unrealistic, like characters in a surrealistic play. Burks, for example, probably a CIA or FBI operative, could easily exchange roles with Lyle. Although their political objectives seem different, their methods are the same. At times their objectives become confused. All that matters is the stimulation of the game.

Treating contemporary American life in terms of games theory, DeLillo is able to satirize not only personalities and ideas, but also social functions. He is concerned with the ways people interact, with their mannerisms as well as their manners. A stern moralist, the author believes that our social structure has fallen apart. Although he does not point to specific causes for this disintegration, he suggests that we have surrendered energy for comfort, passion for complaisance. We are the victims of banality. Like Conrad in *The Secret Agent*, DeLillo treats the terrorist mentality as entirely banal. For the modern terrorists of this novel, Lee Harvey Oswald is represented as the perfect games player; the terrorists are proud to remember Oswald "before Dallas." Indeed, J. Kinnear exclaims: "Lyle, chrissake, everybody knew Oswald before Dallas." Oswald, the contemporary invisible man, was all things to all people: Russian agent, Cuban paid-assassin, CIA agent, anti-Castro assassin. He was fluid, spilling over into whatever mold the imagination made of him.

Unfortunately, Lyle Wynant lacks the symbolic force of an Oswald. At best DeLillo can convince us that his characters are trivial people who try to manipulate other people for the sake of their own recreation. Yet trivial people are boring. And the author's satire at times becomes strained. His terrorists never grow to the tragic stature of Conrad's misguided revolutionaries. They are irritating, not menacing. DeLillo's art is better compared with that of John Updike, who also treats with exquisite precision the miniature catastrophes of everyday life. Like Updike, he captures with wit, grace, and definition the sharp details of American banality. Unlike Updike, he rarely pities his characters. As a result, they appear lost. For DeLillo, life in the 1970's is dangerous and bound to become more dangerous. He believes that we have been cruelly misdirected. In a key passage, he writes of Pammy:

> For years she's heard people say, all sorts, really, here and there: "Do whatever you want as long as nobody gets hurt. . . ." They said: "Whatever feels right, as long as you both want to do it and nobody gets hurt, there's no reason not to."

To DeLillo "they" have been wrong, all wrong. When we read *Players,* are we looking in a mirror?

Leslie B. Mittleman

THE POETRY OF TENNYSON

Author: A. Dwight Culler
Publisher: Yale University Press (New Haven). 276 pp. $15.00
Type of work: Literary criticism

An analysis and interpretation, organized roughly chronologically, of Tennyson's poems in related groups, whereby Culler traces the poet's view of himself as a poet

It is a commonplace of literary and cultural studies to claim for every age since the medieval period, that it is modern. Thus the Renaissance is modern because of the appearance of the modern vernacular and the disappearance of the old theologically centered universe, while the Metaphysicals are acclaimed as the first modern poets because of a blend of thought and feeling which is supposed to be characteristic of the present day. Likewise, the Neo-Classical Age is modern because here first appears the scientific rationalism so associated with the present; and the Romantic Age is modern because it rejects the materialism of the preceding age and because it springs from revolution.

There is, of course, some truth in all of this—even if it is only the truth of the difficulty of defining or describing *modern*. But if by *modern* we mean, fairly straightforwardly, an age that would be recognizable by a citizen of today, then we must admit that the Victorian Age is that age. If our modern citizen were transported, say, to the London of 1850, he might notice the absence of automobiles and airplanes, but a look around him, a glance at the newspapers, and a visit to a substantial bookshop would probably make him feel as though he never left home.

With the one exception of the possibility of total and instant obliteration by the atomic bomb, the Victorian world is our world in both fact and thought. All the problems of the big city, for example, with which we are so familiar, first faced the Victorians: the flight from the countryside, slums, welfare, pollution, property redevelopment, even traffic jams. Those intellectual issues which still bedevil us were first formulated and stated in modern accents by the Victorians: the death of God; science versus religion; technology versus the human spirit; the growth of the state and the central government; the destruction of the countryside; the growing cleavage between the haves and the have-nots.

All this is, of course, simply saying that the Victorians were the first ones who had to face squarely the results of the Industrial Revolution. The Romantic poets appeared as the Industrial Revolution appeared; they faced it, despised what they saw, rejected it, and went their own ways. But this the Victorians could not do; the Industrial Revolution (and all its works) was literally too much with them, and it was clear that it would not go away. Therefore, all the major Victorian writers, who are really Romantics at heart, albeit frustrated, must find some way to come to terms with their world, a world which, as they perceived it, was growing more and more uncongenial to poetry and art (and poets and artists), a world which listened less and less to poets and artists.

It is a cliché (but nonetheless true) that the Victorians were brilliant at analyzing the intellectual, moral, social, and religious questions of their day—and abysmally poor at providing answers, which were typically characterized by impracticality, wishful thinking, and downright silliness. But it is only an age which has learned little from the past that would think that it has done much better. It has been the common fashion for the past fifty or sixty years at least to condemn the Victorians for their compromise, for their sexual hypocrisy, for their class-ridden mores and their getting-on. *Victorian* is commonly today an adjective of opprobrium, suggesting old-fashioned and hypocritical, or an adjective of dismissal as irrelevant.

Of this age, then, Tennyson was to his own day and is to our own day, the great representative. And as the age has suffered so has he. Probably no poet stood so high in repute at the end of his life; but then he who was so bound up with his age fell with it. Much more than Browning and Arnold, he was found to be unacceptable to more modern fashions; he was held up as the representative of all that the post-World War I generation found false and objectionable in literature. His diction and imagery were not hard and clear; his portrayal of women was unreal and bloodless; he was a moral coward who waffled on the great moral issues of his day; he was a hopeless thinker; he was a prig.

Fifty or sixty years is a long time to be throwing stones; some of the glee of lambasting the Victorians has faded; Lytton Strachey is a bit old hat. As, in the course of time, such things happen, a reaction to the reaction has set in, resulting in a more sympathetic, if not absolutely exculpatory, view of the Victorian Age and its eminent men. To this reevaluation, which has in fact been under way for some few years now, Professor Culler has, with the present volume, made a major contribution. It is a major contribution because it is *not* a "defense" of Tennyson. It is a sign of the state of study of that age that Culler does not feel compelled to take up one by one the usual strictures against Tennyson and demolish them. Except obliquely, he never mentions the catalogue of Tennyson's supposed sins, but, with objectivity and knowledge, manages to look at the poet with sympathy and understanding, and in so doing expands our awareness of the sort of plight and problems that can beset a thinking and feeling man in the "modern" world.

One difficulty for a scholar dealing with a comparatively recent figure is simply the great mass of documentary material usually available, in notes, journals, memoirs, commentaries, not only by the figure himself but from his relations, friends, critics, and enemies. Culler comments at the very opening of his book: "This is a good moment to be writing on Tennyson, for the great collections of his letters and papers, so long in private hands or under restriction, are now available to the public and may be quoted." Fortunately the author has resisted the temptation to give us a work such as Finney on Keats in which the poet's imagination is followed in detail day by day and every image ruthlessly traced to the very bush in the very garden which gave rise to it. With presumed riches at his command, Culler has used them judiciously, combining them with his demonstrated knowledge of the age and a talent for close reading where appropriate.

Basically, the work traces the development of Tennyson's image of his place and function as a poet. Thus, many poems, whatever their specific subject or meaning, are read also as attempts by Tennyson to work out for himself a vision and a stance. It becomes clear that he probably never achieved a neat, clear-cut, rationally defensible definition of himself as a poet nor of the poet's function in society. Culler does show that, after youthful exuberances, Tennyson usually proposed himself as a uniformitarian and gradualist poet, mediating between vision and man. Culler cites several times Tennyson's dictum that " 'I' is not always the author speaking of himself, but the voice of the human race speaking thro' him." But Culler does not suggest that the other Tennysonian concept of the poet as apocalyptic, prophetic, even revolutionary, is therefore rejected by Tennyson. Here we see that ambiguity of which some complain in Tennyson; he seems, so they say, incapable of making up his mind. It is Culler's virtue here that he shows clearly how and why, given a man like Tennyson in an age like the Victorian, ambiguity is the only honest answer. We may not like the ambiguity, but it is doubtless wrong to expect philosophical consistency from any artist.

The organization of the book is roughly chronological, but no attempt is made to treat every poem or even every major poem. Poems tend to be treated in groups and relationships established, both within and among groups. The main groupings which Culler examines are: some early apocalyptic poems, largely juvenilia; the early pictorial and musical poems such as "Hesperides," "Lady of Shalott," "The Lotus-Eaters," and "Mariana"; "The Poet," "The Palace of Art," and the "political" poems of the 1832 volume; "Ulysses" and "Morte d'Arthur" from the 1842 poems; the "English Idyls"; "The Princess"; *Maud; In Memoriam;* the *Idylls of the King;* and a final chapter on miscellaneous lyrics. Detailed readings are provided of most of the works mentioned above. As an example of the sorts of relationships which Culler uses to illuminate, we may cite *Maud,* which is first presented as in some ways an opposite to *In Memoriam* and is then related to "Locksley Hall," "Locksley Hall Sixty Years After," and the "Ode on the Death of the Duke of Wellington." Or again, "The Princess," usually hastily and apologetically passed over by critics of Tennyson, is treated in detail and connected with "A Dream of Fair Women" and some of the earlier "English Idyls."

As an example of the sort of complete job which Culler can do on a poem and of the sorts of information he can bring to a poem, we may briefly look at his discussion of *Maud.* He first demonstrates the way in which *Maud* and *In Memoriam* are parallel in form but very different in content. He briefly sketches the relations between *Maud* and the Spasmodic poets and details the background of madness in the Tennyson family. He presents a useful brief history and background on the form of the poem, the monodrama. Then he indicates Tennyson's own comments about the poem. Finally he provides a reading of the poem in depth and detail, with side glances at "Locksley Hall," "Locksley Hall Sixty Years After," and the "Ode on the Death of the Duke of Wellington." The reader may get the impression that Culler is giving us all this information simply because he has found it out, but this is not so. The information is presented with economy and is well-integrated, and the author does not insist that this or that variety of fact is the sole key to understanding. Culler wears his learning lightly.

It is clearly impossible in such a short space to treat any single line of Culler's presentation in detail, but it is only fair to give some indication of the things to be found in the book. Among the ideas which Culler traces are the importance to Tennyson (and to the understanding of Tennyson) of "trances," of music both as sound and symbol, of the "garden of the mind," and of the values of social converse. With learning and insight, Culler has touched upon most of the traditional critical *loci* in Tennyson and has, for good measure, discussed a few not usually given much treatment: "Godiva," the "lady poems," "The Hesperides," the "English Idyls."

As indicative of the way in which Culler reorients our experience of certain traditional poems, one may mention *Maud*, in which the poet expresses the passionate morbidity which he felt infected the land, or the "English Idyls," which Culler judges to be the "most neglected in proportion to their merit" as "works of a subtle and delicate art." In the *Idylls of the King*, he emphasizes how Tennyson deliberately rationalizes events, omitting anything supernatural or magical, in order to reflect the failure of the imagination to live up to its poetic ideal. And in "The Death of Œnone" he shows how the traditional "right" reading of the poem is not enough: The three sisters of Power, Wisdom, and Beauty should never have been sundered from the first, and Paris' apparently proper choice (of Pallas) has about it ambiguities which are supported by details of the imagery of the poem. Indeed, in all these interpretations, Culler does not rest upon assertion but supports his reading, not only from the background, but always ultimately with a close look at the text.

The student of literature will find this a useful guide and an object lesson in attention to the text. The scholar will appreciate and admire the skillful integration of knowledge and the mastery of detail. And the general reader, if he still reads Tennyson, will find here, perhaps unintentionally but still usefully, a work which goes beyond its subject to suggest strongly that the modern age is not all that "modern," and that the intellectual career of a man born almost 170 years ago is not necessarily irrelevant.

Gordon N. Bergquist

THE PROFESSOR OF DESIRE

Author: Philip Roth (1935–   )
Publisher: Farrar, Straus and Giroux (New York). 263 pp. $8.95
Type of work: Novel
Time: 1930's to the present
Locale: The United States, chiefly New York and California, and England, chiefly London

An anatomy of male sexual desire, as experienced and discovered by David Kepesh, from early adolescence through young adulthood and into middle life

Principal characters:
> DAVID KEPESH, a Jewish man
> LOUIS JELINEK, his college friend, a suspected homosexual
> HELEN BAIRD, his wife
> DR. KLINGER, his psychiatrist
> ABE KEPESH, his father
> ARTHUR SCHONBRUNN, his dissertation director and departmental chairman
> DEBORAH SCHONBRUNN, his wife
> RALPH BAUMGARTEN, a poet and academic colleague of Kepesh
> ELISABETH ELVERSKOG, a Swedish girl with whom Kepesh has an affair in London
> BIRGITTA SVANSTRÖM, another Swedish girl with whom Kepesh has an affair in London
> CLAIRE OVINGTON, a young schoolteacher with whom Kepesh has an affair in New York
> MR. BARBATNIK, a survivor of the Nazi concentration camps and a friend of Abe Kepesh

In most if not all of his novels, Philip Roth has concerned himself with the description of male sexuality in what must be nearly all of its heterosexual manifestations. One might go further and specify Roth's concern as *Jewish* male sexuality as it is impinged upon by the specifically Jewish family unit, since, with his description of Portnoy's complaint, he has helped in a major way to define the American cultural stereotype of the Jewish mother and her sexually oppressed offspring. In *The Professor of Desire*, Roth examines this theme once again, by creating in David Kepesh a specifically Jewish manifestation of one of the stock sexual situations in American humor and folklore. Clergy and college professors, especially those who have problems with controlling the expression of their sexual feelings, have a central place in more than their share of jokes and tall tales. Kepesh is of the latter sort, a professor of comparative literature who finds that his study is more often than not orgasm instead of Chekhov.

The Professor of Desire, however, suggests that Roth's inquiry may be taking something of a different turn, for it is not so much the mother in Kepesh's case who is the disruptive figure, but Abe, the father. One central problem in Kepesh's sexual life is the issue of permanence in male-female relationships; he finds such relationships difficult to establish, and, once established, difficult to sustain. In contrast, it is the father who can see a woman once, decide instantly that she is the woman for him, and live with her in seemingly happy marriage for years until her death from cancer. David's mother plays a relatively minor role in this novel. She is an image of the one a father could fall instantly in love with, the one who loves order and yet is driven to distraction each year by the realities of keeping up a summer resort, the one who in the calm of winter teaches David to type, and thus opens to him the world of self-expression. Later she is the parent who dies and disappears from David's life. David's father, however, is the parent figure who intrudes over and over to break up his dreams, to wonder why medical school is out and the theater is now so important, to question David's marriage to a non-Jewish woman, to make him feel uncomfortable in his chosen profession and lifestyle. Finally, it is David's father whose enthusiastic, almost desperately energetic, delight in his son's relationship with Claire Ovington contributes to David's awareness that he cannot sustain the relationship, no matter how much happiness it has brought him.

Freud suggests that a basic struggle in everyone's psychological development is with the father, who must be fought with or fled from. In these terms, a major theme of the novel is flight, flight from the male parent manifested in a great number of minor flights. The first is from the discovery of sexual potential, which David discovers while living with two Swedish girls in London. Elisabeth shows him the power of sexual attraction; she attempts suicide at one point from fear of losing him. Birgitta, on the other hand, helps David discover the power of sexual exploration. Willing to try almost anything, she is drawn to occasional visits to a quack doctor who enjoys masturbating her, as well as to experiments with varieties of sexual expression more usually linked with the name of the Marquis de Sade. While on a journey with David on the Continent, she willingly aids him in recruiting other women to join them in bed. Kepesh's response is not to deal with the implications of Birgitta's attractiveness for him; instead, he flees decision by returning to the United States and to graduate school.

In a real sense, Kepesh had fled from school into the arms of his sturdy Swedes; he confesses that he wasted his Fulbright Scholarship. Now, having fled his two mistresses, he devotes himself to graduate study, only to flee scholarly pursuits once again when he meets Helen Baird toward the end of his graduate school career. Helen, a veteran of a series of erotic relationships in the Far East, brings with her a labyrinth of neuroses as complex in their own way as the sexual bypaths of the sensuous Birgitta. The result is that, although Kepesh does finish his work for the Ph.D., he is unable to do much with it until Helen finally flees him in a desperate return to the Orient. Stability and productiveness finally return to Roth's hero only after he has established a sexual liaison with Claire Ovington, a woman distinguished by Kepesh over and over again precisely because of her ordinariness. Rest is not to be permanent, however; the novel ends with Kepesh, faced with his father's intrusion once again, aware that he will soon be leaving Claire behind.

What can one make of all this? Roth has his admirers, certainly, and his books sell well; *Portnoy's Complaint* has become a cliché in our culture. Nevertheless, *The Professor of Desire* shares with much of Roth's work a pervasive quality of thinness, a sense of lightness, a lack of depth. Kepesh never puts down roots; opportunity frightens him, so he is constantly bouncing off in yet another direction, yet another flight from past realities and present opportunities. In much the same way, the novel itself has a superficial quality, a tendency to stay on the surface of life, of its characters, of its situations. Roth has published ten books in twenty years, and the speed with which he works shows through.

There are moving moments in the book, however, two of which come near the end. Claire and David share a house in the Catskills, for what seems an idyllic summer. The pastoral qualities are broken by visits in close succession of Helen, now remarried, with her new husband, and Abe, David's father. Helen, after some tentative forays into old times, reveals that she does not love her new husband, that she regrets so much, that she has a nightmarish awareness of how much she does not love anybody. As a result, Claire's and David's idyll is forcefully disrupted. But the result is not a deeper relationship between them, or deeper insight into their situation, but only the papering over of the breach in their relationship. Then, close on the heels of Helen, comes Abe with his friend, a refugee from Nazi concentration camps. Again there is disruption, but the result is a forcing of David back into himself, back into all his fears about the future, back into all his anxieties about his life. One is left with the contrast between the vitality of the aging father and the passivity of the still-young son.

Roth's style has energy, has the power to move the reader, but his vision of life, at least as given in this book, is finally deeply unsatisfying. What one misses is a getting below the surface, a sense of depth, a sense of richness in human life and human relationships. His characters, even his central character, seem superficial, drawn in a phrase, a sentence, and set going, never to rest, never to have much sense at all of who they are and what their lives are all about. Love in this book is rarely if ever something that brings men and women together, but is more often something that reminds them finally of their separation from each other, and of the transitoriness of human life. Many may find this descriptive of their situation. It may also, however, be the result of working too fast, of trying to get the novel done and out, of trying to produce a book that will read quickly, but be interesting enough to divert the mass of readers from the night's television fare. The novelist in our day is faced with the problem of defining his audience, of choosing between the many who will buy an evening's entertainment and create a bestseller, and the few who will spend more time and who expect more than a moment's literary delight. Roth is clearly in the first rank of popular novelists; he may please many, but he may not please long.

John N. Wall, Jr.

THE RAGE OF EDMUND BURKE
Portrait of an Ambivalent Conservative

Author: Isaac Kramnick (1938–   )
Publisher: Basic Books (New York). 225 pp. $12.95
Type of work: Biography
Time: 1729–1797
Locale: Ireland and England

A biography of Edmund Burke which investigates the psychology of eighteenth century England's most brilliant political philosopher

Principal personages:
  EDMUND BURKE, Anglo-Irish political philosopher, writer, and Member of Parliament
  RICHARD BURKE, his father
  MARY NAGLE BURKE, his mother
  JANE NUGENT BURKE, his wife
  WILLIAM BURKE, his cousin and close friend
  WARREN HASTINGS, Governor general of the East India Company
  SAMUEL JOHNSON, lexicographer and member of "the Club"
  LORD ROCKINGHAM, influential Whig magnate and Burke's patron

In his study of Edmund Burke, Isaac Kramnick offers a new and radical theory about one of the eighteenth century's most profound political thinkers. But prior to investigating Kramnick's methods and intentions—and furnishing an evaluation of both—perhaps it would be useful to look at the more commonly understood Edmund Burke and the manner in which the man and his achievements are generally perceived. Such an overview is necessary if this Edmund Burke is to be reconciled with the Edmund Burke Kramnick identifies and discusses.

Edmund Burke was born in Dublin on January 12, 1729, to a Roman Catholic mother and a Protestant father. As a youngster, Burke was removed from the Dublin home to his mother's family estate in the south of Ireland. Indeed, most of his formative years were spent away from his immediate family. After completing several years of study at a Quaker boarding school, Burke entered Trinity College, Dublin, completed his undergraduate degree, and then left for London to study law. But instead of pursuing a legal career, Burke began to publish a series of remarkable essays on a variety of subjects. In 1756 he published *Vindication of Natural Society,* a prose satire which supported Christianity and conventional theories about organized society. A year later Burke turned his attention to aesthetics and wrote *A Philosophical Inquiry into the Origin of Our Ideas on the Sublime and Beautiful,* an essay which attracted wide attention in England and Europe. In 1759 he assumed editorial responsibilities for the *Annual Register* and contributed a number of essays devoted primarily to political and economic matters. Within a relatively short time, Burke had made his presence known in London and was being courted by many of the city's influential citizens. When Dr. Samuel Johnson proposed the founding of the Club, where a select group of English men of letters could freely exchange ideas, Burke was one of the first men invited to join.

In 1766 Burke entered public life when elected to Parliament as representative for Bristol. He remained a Member of Parliament for twenty-nine years, in perpetual opposition to the ruling Tory party, and took pride in being a member of the Minority. Some governmental policies he attacked directly, voicing his objections to slavery and demanding its abolition. From 1774 to 1777 he made a number of eloquent speeches recommending that England reexamine its policies regarding the American colonies. He proposed that the Americans be given the right to represent their own interests (Burke himself was representative agent for the Colony of New York) and maintained that such measures would strengthen the ties between America and the British Empire. And he prophesied that if England did not alter its policies there would be war, a war England would have difficulty winning. In another colonial matter, Burke called for the arrest and conviction of Warren Hastings, Governor general of the East India Company, on the grounds that Hastings' administration was repressive, corrupt, and inconsistent with humanitarian ideals. Burke prosecuted the matter for fourteen years and considered his labors on behalf of the misgoverned natives in India among his most useful endeavors.

Burke was also the champion of several Irish causes, chief among them the question of Catholic emancipation. He attempted to convince the government that the Irish Catholics should be granted freedoms enjoyed by their Anglo-Irish counterparts. The hostility which existed between England and Ireland was, Burke contended, due largely to England's refusal to grant basic religious freedoms to the Irish. And he predicted violence if the British refused concessions to the Roman Catholics. The Insurrection of 1798 followed this prediction, and it paved the way for a series of reforms which England was forced to initiate.

When the French Revolution erupted in 1789, Burke wrote and published his best-known piece of political commentary, *Reflections on the Revolution in France* (1790), wherein he concluded that the consequences of this event could permanently alter the continuity and well-being of Western civilization. Burke was a firm believer in inherited institutions and traditions and intensely distrustful of violent change, egalitarian liberalism, or Jacobinic ideals. *Reflections on the Revolution in France* is Burke's most eloquent statement on the virtues of monarchy and established traditions and his most forceful condemnation of revolutionary principles.

These activities and achievements suggest that Burke was a political conservative, concerned with maintaining the *status quo* and defending the social structure and political understandings inherent in the *ancien régime.* Few critics have questioned his belief in the essential continuity between the past and the present, or the natural form of political evolution which institutions must undergo if they are to adapt to changing circumstances. In brief, Burke's political principles are founded on a sense of history and reality; and he is most commonly held to be the father of conservatism, dedicated to preserving what is best and honorable in nations while respecting their natural tendency towards change. The form of change Burke acknowledged was, however, not that imposed on men and society according to abstract theories of idealism; rather, it was an organic form, observing its own natural laws and analogous to the slow and steady growth of an oak tree, or the compromises and alterations which take place within the family unit. When he died in 1797, Burke was considered one of England's most illustrious spokesmen for conservative principles. His ideas and actions gave support to those who eyed, with increasing suspicion and unrest, the events in France which did, as Burke had predicted, alter the shape of history and man's relationship to his political and social institutions.

This is, then, the more traditional picture of Edmund Burke with which most students of political science and literature are familiar: a great political thinker reasonably comfortable with his station in life and convinced that the authority granted ruling institutions was well placed and occupied by the rightful heirs of power. But these are the very views Kramnick challenges. His study of Burke is an attempt to discover the man's latent ambivalence towards the rulers and institutions he spent much of his life defending. This defender of conservative principles was, contends Kramnick, a servant who secretly hated his masters and all they represented, who inwardly admired the progress made by the bourgeois radicals, and who went to his grave attempting to reconcile his public condemnation of liberalism with his private resentment of the aristocracy. There are, then, according to Kramnick, two Burkes: one pledged to serve his betters; the other deeply critical of the prevailing values and conduct of the ruling aristocracy. That Burke, reputed to have had the finest mind in all of eighteenth century England, should question the wisdom of his masters is hardly a startling theory. Much of his political life was devoted to animating the consciences of his superiors. Indeed, Burke is renowned for his opposition to government measures. But to portray Burke as an ambivalent radical unwittingly sympathetic to the bourgeois ethos which would undermine and replace England's social structure is, indeed, a sharp departure from previous studies of Burke.

Kramnick's thesis is, if not entirely convincing, a captivating one, although the more traditional Burkeans are likely to wince at the author's reliance on psychoanalytic investigative procedures. For example, Kramnick contends that Burke's social ambivalence is traceable to problems he acquired during his childhood. There developed between Edmund and his mother a deep affection; however, the love he sought from his father was never forthcoming. What followed, observes Kramnick, was inevitable: a young man desperately confused about his sexual identity and denied an understanding of what a proper father should be. According to Kramnick, this is one of the keys to Burke's ambivalent nature. His search for an ideal father instilled in Burke a desire to serve traditional authority; his resentment of the elder Burke helped shape Edmund's critical attitudes about authority in general.

When Burke departed for England to study law at the Middle Temple, he formed a close friendship with his cousin, William Burke. The two men lived together for five years, and after Edmund married Jane Nugent, Will moved in with the couple. Kramnick sees in this curious *ménage à trois* a strange equation which further illuminates Burke's ambivalence. Jane came to embody the traditional female, a passive mother figure; Will, on the other hand, who was aggressive, represented Edmund's father, the bourgeois-masculine side of Burke's personality. Kramnick insists that Burke needed both to maintain his own well-being: one member of the family, Jane, served to remind him of his obligations to the ruling class; the other, Will, represented his ambitious bourgeois dreams of success.

Another problem Burke faced was his Anglo-Irish heritage. He was an Irishman (a very conspicuous Irishman from all contemporary accounts) in England, a stranger in an alien land. Neither his Anglican Church membership nor his professed allegiance to existing political and social institutions could prevent the English from viewing him with varying degrees of resentment and suspicion. Kramnick briefly discusses this problem as a contributing factor in the deeply divided Burke. The more conservative reader might wish for additional exploration in this area, or feel more comfortable attributing Burke's "rage" and ambivalence to a brilliant political scientist who viewed with increasing alarm the inefficiency and corruption inherent in the system. It is true Burke defended the traditional order, but he was not oblivious to its faults; many of them he openly denounced, and some he succeeded in mending.

Some readers may have strong reservations about Kramnick's psychoanalytic approach in the interpretation of Burke's political actions. And it is possible that others will register some degree of disbelief at the author's conviction that Burke identified with the bourgeoisie and unconsciously dreamed of joining their ranks in the creation of a new political order. These are unorthodox conclusions reached by unorthodox methods. Yet despite the novelty of Kramnick's investigation, he does touch a part of Burke still unexplored. This might result in some discomfort for the student of political institutions, but it could lead to a fuller understanding of an extremely complex eighteenth century figure.

Don W. Sieker

RANKE
The Meaning of History

Author: Leonard Krieger
Publisher: University of Chicago Press (Chicago). 402 pp. $23.00
Type of work: Biography
Time: 1795–1886
Locale: Germany

A study of Ranke's attitudes toward history, and particularly of his analysis of the contradictory approaches of scientists on the one hand, and philosophers and historians on the other

Leonard Krieger's *Ranke* is a worthy successor to his previous studies of the relationship of ideas and institutions in German history in *The German Idea of Freedom* and the *Politics of Discretion.* In some ways *Ranke* represents an interesting departure from his previous works, for this intellectual biography relates the content (or discontents) of Ranke's personality to his development as a historian. Since the ideas and personality of Ranke are analyzed against the backdrop of the forces of the nineteenth century, the result is a major synthesis on the father of scientific history.

Krieger displays great empathy with his subject, even to the point of attempting to write "Rankeified" history. At the end of the book Krieger states his admiration of Ranke's devotion to painstaking research as the path to cumulative wisdom. Says Krieger, "There are no substitutes. There are no shortcuts." The author has lived up to his ideal. His study of Ranke has exhaustively explored both published and unpublished works, even Ranke's early student essays. Krieger has spared no pains to make sense of the vast amount of detail of a particularly long life in a particularly complex century.

Ranke's dictum that history be written as it actually happened *("wie es eigentlich gewesen")* has also been followed. The result is not a critical essay on Ranke as in Georg G. Iggers' fine work, *The German Conception of History.* Nor is it purely a biographical and historiographical study as Theodore von Laue's equally useful *Ranke: The Formative Years.* Krieger's book attempts to reconcile contradictory elements of biography, historical thinking, and the history of Ranke's own time. It thus aspires to the master's original attempt to synthesize the particular with the general, what Krieger calls Ranke's quest to portray "humanity's consciousness of its own interrelatedness."

Leopold von Ranke was the founder of both scientific history and the school of historicism which believed that history was the primary source of the disclosure of divine and human truths. For Krieger, Ranke was not so much an original thinker as a synthesizer. Such early nineteenth century historians as Barthold Georg Niebuhr had already stressed the critical study of documents as the core of historical science. Fichte and Hegel had already viewed history as the revelation of the ideals of spiritual and rational universal truths. What was original about Ranke was the manner in which he combined the two seemingly irreconcilable elements of particular facts and general principles and ideas. How Ranke reconciled this duality of science and spirit through his theories and methods of history is a major focus of Krieger's successful book.

Unlike Hegel and Fichte, whose starting point for the study of history was the application of philosophical theories and purposes to facts, Ranke was a nominalist. He stressed facts over concepts as the starting point of historical reality. His first concern was with historical objectivity, to tell how things really happened rather than why they happened. First the facts had to speak for themselves. Ranke's standards of judgment professed to be those of the particular period he studied. For him each age was a valuable and unique field of knowledge, equally justified in the sight of God. Ranke's God was also Luther's, a diety whose true nature was unfathomable and unchanging, who revealed his externals in history, but not his true purposes as was the case for Hegel. Ranke accordingly rejected Hegel's idea of progress. For Ranke, progress entailed humanity's growing ability to grasp the meaning of the facts of humanity's past through causal and temporal interrelatedness. Yet Krieger is quite right to stress that Fichte and Hegel influenced Ranke to the extent that history became for Ranke the study of the greatest ideas *(Hauptideen)* of the human community. These ideas or basic units of civilization assumed a primarily political form—the form of the nation-state. For Ranke as for Hegel, state power assumed a primarily spiritual and ethical character to which the individual was subordinate—shades of *The German Idea of Freedom.* Ranke sought out general relationships and connections in the life of nations such as the principles of the balance of power between states, "reason of state" or political necessity, and the trend toward political harmony and order within states. He nevertheless maintained that the study of individual events must take precedence over the concern with abstract concepts and theories, which for him constituted philosophy rather than history.

Krieger rightly views the Restoration period (1815-1830) as the formative period when Ranke came to emphasize facts as knowledge, states as ideas, and traditionalism and order as morality. By 1830 Ranke had arrived at the basic essentials of his theory and practice of historical method—that particular facts and events reveal in their relationships general truths.

Krieger's questions and answers of how Ranke arrived at his major theories and methods are often brilliant and well-documented. But a Teutonically ponderous and opaque writing style sometimes gets in the way of his orderly schema of Ranke's ideas. Indeed, the writing occasionally verges on the incomprehensible. Here is an example:

> The transcendence of the dualism and the ascertainment of his integrity ensue when application is made of his own practical recipe to himself and his career is treated historically, with his life and his historical work providing the explanatory circumstances of his various theoretical positions and softening their apparently frictional edges.

The analysis of Ranke's historical works is Krieger's most important contribution to our understanding of the historian, and it occupies the major portion of the book. One must marvel at Krieger's mastery of Ranke's historical writings, the details of Ranke's personal and intellectual development, and the intellectual and political currents of nineteenth century Germany.

Especially interesting is Krieger's description of Ranke's evolution in the period from 1815 to 1848. Ranke stemmed from the Protestant educated elite of central Germany. The academic vocation appealed to him most, for history provided the key to the understanding of religion, politics, and ideas. Krieger is not afraid to apply some of the tools of psychohistory to the study of Ranke's development as a historian. He explores the interesting idea that just as Ranke's hero Luther sought to communicate his spiritual visions to sixteenth century Europe, Ranke sought to communicate the spirit behind the historical facts to his own time. Krieger argues that history also became a means through which Ranke resolved the problems and conflicts of his personality. As a case in point, Ranke's historicism achieved a release from solitude. The lonely Ranke was a man of inaction, insignificant in appearance, socially awkward, and inept as a lecturer. He could gain fellowship by immersing himself in the great individual and collective events of mankind. He would make history by discovering the meaning of the past. Krieger goes so far as to argue that Ranke's "exultations" about documents were forms of sexual transference of the libido; the zeal of historical scholarship became sublimated sexual passion. What weakens Krieger's argument is the absence of any illustration. If there actually was an "erotic tone" or a sexual quality in Ranke's love for documents, Krieger does not specifically refer to it. Ranke was close to his more activist younger brother who was a German nationalist of the Jahn and Arndt variety. Perhaps this mildly influenced the development of a nascent national feeling on the part of the more cosmopolitan Leopold. Krieger views Ranke's marriage in 1843 to an Englishwoman as intellectually significant, as "symptomatic of interests in a larger community." This is even more speculative than the theory of Ranke's earlier libido displacement, for it seems to overintellectualize Ranke's marital and sexual experiences. But whatever the possible limitations of Krieger's arguments, he attempts in a thought-provoking way to relate the facets of Ranke's personality to his development as a historian.

What is particularly informative and convincing about Krieger's book is the close-grained account of the interaction of Ranke the historian with the events of his time. From his brief flirtation with the Romanticist and liberal salons of Berlin in the 1820's, he developed interests in the history of art and poetry and insights into the parallel development of thought and politics. But he soon turned to the more satisfying and enduring fellowship of historical documents.

The revolutions of the 1830's were an important stage in Ranke's development; these events stimulated him to connect the actions of individuals with those of groups. It was in this period, too, that Ranke first explored the existence of social history. But his interest in social and economic history was only peripheral to his political and ideological concerns. Finally, the revolutions of 1830 led him to develop Burke's theory that states must develop organically in accordance with their historical traditions rather than through the abstract and historically disruptive ideas of French liberalism. Krieger makes the excellent observation that it was to explain and resolve the polarities and problems of his own time that Ranke turned to modern history. Such major problems as he saw running through his time were the conflicts between monarchy and democracy within the states, and wars between the states. In addition to explaining these problems, the study of modern history would provide a solid starting point for historical science by providing a multiplicity of records and archives.

Ranke's pioneering *History of the Latin and Teutonic Nations from 1494 to 1514* handled the West as a unit and explored the relationships of states and institutions, but failed to develop explanations of causality other than fate or divine providence. The particular and the general remained unconnected. It was in the *History of the Popes* that Ranke first explored the relations between Christian universal and spiritual beliefs and the individual and temporal concerns of religious institutions. The author's fine analysis of *German History in the Age of the Reformation* provides an excellent illustration of how Ranke attempted to relate the particular forces and events of the period (Luther and the princes) to the larger general currents of Protestantism and patriotism. However, Krieger omitted a discussion of the revolutionary episode of anabaptism. Some comments on these events might have cast light on Ranke's treatment of social history.

By the 1840's and 1850's Ranke turned to Prussian history both in his capacity as official historian to the court of Frederick William IV, and as the upholder of the forces of order against the threat of the rising masses. He defended academic freedom to investigate the truth, but maintained in good Lutheran fashion the right of the state to censor political opinions. Though Ranke sought to relate political and spiritual forces in history, he finally, like Luther and Hegel, spiritualized the state and monarchy as God-given and historically based. Thus, he ended up infusing history with cosmic principles of conservatism and statism. These principles and concepts now threatened to eclipse his original emphasis on the primacy of facts. For was revolution any less of a historically rooted fact than monarchy? Ranke was now in danger of violating his own precepts of historical method. It became clear that he never quite sloughed off his idealist skin.

Ranke's growing preoccupation with the tensions between monarchy and democracy during his own time led him to investigate the history of early modern France, which, he concluded, saw the development of rigid absolutism that led to revolution; and of England, which he analyzed in Burkean fashion as the triumph of parliamentary government and principles. By the 1870's for Ranke (as earlier for Hegel), the unification of Prussia-Germany represented the ideal synthesis of the principles of monarchy and democracy. Krieger shows how the aged Ranke achieved his own synthesis between narrative and analysis, storytelling and philosophizing, the particular and the general—the goal of all great history writing.

In his conclusion Krieger poses the all-important question of whether our age can draw any lessons from Ranke's investigations into the meaning of history. He is right to conclude that his subject never really reconciled his goals of objectivity with the assertion of ideal truths. For his fields of interest and his paradigms of analysis were too narrow, limited to the study of political, diplomatic and religious conflicts, and affected by conservative beliefs. Such attitudes and concerns are outmoded in our own time.

It is Ranke's challenge of understanding history as the synthetic form of human experience that remains for us. Ranke's difficult methodological goal also endures: the historian must steer a careful path between the Scylla of factual knowledge and the Charybdis of general meaning to the ultimate goal of universal understanding. "Happy is the man," wrote Ranke, "who succeeds in understanding things simultaneously in the ground of their existence and in the fulness of their distinctive appearance." In our age of accelerating complexity, Ranke's quest and example of seeking the meaning of history in a grasp of the relationships between antithetical facts and concepts is as important as it was for his time. Krieger has not only written an excellent study of the development of Ranke's theory and practice of history. His work can stand in its own right as a lesson in the craft of history, in which the historian of today can emulate his exacting goals while avoiding his pitfalls and mistakes.

Leon Stein

RETURN TO THEBES

Author: Allen Drury (1918-   )
Publisher: Doubleday and Company (New York). 272 pp. $8.95
Type of work: Novel
Time: 1362 B.C.–1339 B.C.
Locale: Ancient Egypt

The exciting story of the rise to the throne of the ruthless General Horemheb against a background of the suppression of Pharaoh Akhenaten's heretical religion of monotheism

    Principal characters:
      AKHENATEN, the ruling Pharaoh when the novel begins
      NEFERTITI, his beautiful queen
      SMENKHKARA, Akhenaten's dimwitted younger brother and Co-Regent
      TUTANKHATEN (LATER TUTANKHAMON), Akhenaten's youngest brother
      AYE, Nefertiti's father
      HOREMHEB, Aye's son and successor

Allen Drury's *Return to Thebes* is the sequel to his *A God Against the Gods.* Both novels are about political turmoil at a particularly interesting period of ancient Egyptian history—the period of the unsuccessful attempt of Pharaoh Akhenaten to introduce monotheism. Drury's novel is interesting, readable fare by a popular novelist who has written a dozen books, the best known of which is *Advise and Consent,* about American politics. As one review put it, "in this novel we are able to learn about the Egypt of 1350 B.C. as painlessly as we absorbed the political world of *Advise and Consent.*" There is little question concerning the lack of effort with which we absorb the background of this novel: the atmosphere of palace intrigue, the peculiarities of dynastic marriage, the central place of ritual, the terrible contest between monotheism and polytheism. The history is painless too, but how accurate is it? How much is fact? How much legitimate conjecture? How much invention?

When a novelist writes about a historical period generally unknown to his readers, he surely bears some responsibility for historical truth. The reader cannot know that the novelist is inventing rather than dramatizing an event. Therefore, the writer is obliged to make it clear when he crosses the border between fact and fiction. In his "Introduction," Drury states his credo: "Egyptologists differ. . . . A novelist must make choices from among their conjectures, adding here and there a few of his own. This I have done, trying always to remain within the bounds of what seems *humanly logical* and eschewing those intense arguments over fragmentary details that understandably make up much of the world of professional Egyptology." Here Drury gives the impression that his alterations of history have very little magnitude; no more than the magnitude of his one example, whether Akhenaten became Co-Regent at the age of fifteen, sixteen, seventeen, or eighteen.

In fact, Drury handles history with a license which goes beyond the "humanly logical." In his narrative, both Akhenaten and Tutankhamon are assassinated. There is no evidence for these murders. Nothing is known about Akhenaten's death and the most likely conjecture is that Tutankhamon was physically frail and died naturally. Another example of Drury's handling of historical facts concerns a letter sent by Tutankhamon's widow to the enemy Hittite king. The letter, which asks him for the gift of a son in marriage, is delivered by a peasant especially loyal to the Pharaoh's memory. He arrives at the Hittite court disguised as Lord Hanis. After some hesitation, the Hittite king agrees to the proposal, only to have the son that he sends murdered by the henchmen of the ambitious General Horemheb. This startling series of events—beyond the wildest flights of a novelist's imagination—is true, according to Hittite records, but with one exception. There is no evidence whatsoever that Lord Hanis was a peasant disguised as an Egyptian lord.

The reasons behind Drury's inventions in both these cases are not hard to find. The twin regicides are designed further to blacken the reputation of the villainous General Horemheb, the novel's protagonist. As such, they are not "humanly logical" events but a means of thickening the plot and heightening the melodrama. The incident of the peasant disguised as Lord Hanis has two purposes: to underline the people's love for Tutankhamon and to add a little human interest to a plot otherwise overweighted with political intrigue.

It is this political intrigue that is at the center of the novel. In view of Drury's predilection for sheer invention, and his previous experience with modern American politics, one may wonder whether these politics have merely been projected into ancient Egyptian times. *Return to Thebes* is essentially the story of a ruthless realist, General Horemheb, who determines to be Pharaoh even though he is not in the line of succession. His ascent to the throne involves the assassination of two idealistic pharaohs—Akhenaten and Tutankhamon. Still, his aim is thwarted by Aye, his father. Finally, in extreme old age, Aye, as realistic as his son, has to allow Horemheb's succession. In Horemheb, Aye feels, Egypt "will have a stern father and a hard ruthless taskmaster." Aye is correct; Horemheb rules Egypt harshly but justly.

Horemheb—arguably the most developed character in the novel—bears an uncomfortably close resemblance to the modern stereotype of political ambition. He has a hunger for power that is unreasonable and apparently without motive. This hunger is clearly evil; it is connected with ruthlessness and the forces of reaction (in the novel, polytheism). Its punishment is the absence of love, a feeling of inner emptiness. Admittedly we can never know what motivated ancient Egyptian palace intrigue; still, we can expect an analysis that would make us less suspicious of anachronism.

The politics of *Return to Thebes* seems anachronistic also in its cynicism. The idealism of Akhenaten—"he *was* a true idealist, and so can be forgiven much"— is connected with ineffectuality and sexual deviance. Tutankhamon's more sophisticated idealism is regarded as too clever by far and is seen as no match for

Horemheb's ruthless realism.

Drury's novel also devotes a great deal of attention to the conflict between traditional Egyptian polytheism and the heretical monotheism initiated by Akhenaten and continued, by Drury's imputation, in the reign of Tutankhamon. This monotheism is regarded as little more than a precursor of Judaism and Christianity. As such it is the source of much irony in the novel. A servant of Nefertiti, Akhenaten's queen, says, "You cannot destroy what is in men's minds . . . and though many condemn what he has planted there, not all will be able to forget it. It may outlive us all." At the novel's end Horemheb says:

> The Heretic and the Beautiful Woman are dead.
> The evil concept of One God is dead, forever and ever, for millions
> and millions of years.
> The mad dream is ended.

The novelist seems little interested in the actual heresy of Akhenaten. In fact, this Pharaoh's innovations had a profound effect on Egyptian society. Akhenaten wanted to simplify theology so that it would be accessible to all people; to emphasize the equality of all men at birth, differentiated only by later wickedness; to underline the close relationship of all forms of life; and to suppress the practice of magic because that practice interfered with moral progress. Drury shows no interest in this program, except insofar as it can fuel melodramatic conflict between the progressive forces of monotheism and the reactionary armies of polytheism. The latter are crystallized in the character of the chief priest of Amon, the evil and vengeful Hatsuret.

Drury's interest in ideas and in character is rudimentary; his real interest is in the narrative line. For his vehicle he has chosen not the usual third-person narrative, but another device, which allows him to take advantage of a multiplicity of points of view. The novel is built up entirely from "soliloquys" of varying length by all of the major and some of the minor characters. In many cases these soliloquys amount to no more than a first-person narrative. For instance, early in the novel, Akhenaten awaits the quarrelsome visit of his family. In telling his part of the story, the Pharaoh does not violate any of the conventions of first-person narrative. He may comment on other characters—for instance, he calls his Co-Regent "this simple child"; however, there is never any implication that the events Akhenaten narrates did not happen exactly the way he said they happened. This is no *Rashomon,* in which different characters can have entirely different, even contradictory views of the same events.

Although these "soliloquys" are for the most part a collection of first-person narratives that carry forward the story in a conventional manner, they are occasionally used to depict the inner thoughts of one of the characters. For example, when Akhenaten learns about the death of his beloved Co-Regent, he soliloquizes: "Ah! They have killed my heart. Help me, Father Aten, help me or I shall die." The tone is wrong, bathetic—it demonstrates Drury's limitations; however, for the most part the novelist sticks to straight narrative, at which he excels. Moreover, his choice of a series of first-person narratives admirably suits the matter of his story—the plots and intrigues of each of his characters, forming as a whole the mosaic of intrigue which is the novel.

Where does the distinction of *Return to Thebes* lie? Not in its depiction of ancient Egyptian society, a depiction which is in many cases shallow and misleading, nor in the political and religious ideas with which the novel deals. These ideas are not explored at any length and are in many cases merely exploited for melodrama. The novel also lacks distinction as a study of character, though some of its characters, particularly Horemheb, Aye, and Tutankhamon, are not without interest. No; finally the novel attains distinction in the sureness of its narrative line—Drury has an exciting story to tell and he tells it well.

Alan G. Gross

THE RIVER CONGO

Author: Peter Forbath
Publisher: Harper & Row Publishers (New York). 404 pp. $15.00
Type of work: History
Time: 1482–1908
Locale: The Congo River of Central Africa

A history of the great river, from its accidental discovery in 1482 through five centuries of exploration and exploitation

> Principal personages:
> PRINCE HENRY THE NAVIGATOR, whose explorations and navigational school led the way to the discovery of the mouth of the Congo
> HENRY MORTON STANLEY, the greatest African explorer and the first man to identify and map the Congo
> KING LEOPOLD II OF BELGIUM, exploiter of the Congo

In the 1960's there appeared Alan Moorehead's books on the White Nile and the Blue Nile. More recently came Sanche de Gramont's *The Strong Brown God: The Story of the Niger River.* And now Peter Forbath has completed the story of the three great African rivers with his history of the Congo.

Three thousand miles long, the Congo River is the fifth largest river in the world. No other river stirs the imagination as much as the Congo; "the river that swallows all rivers" is the name given to it by the natives who lived along its banks. Fifteen miles across where it exits into the Atlantic Ocean, its force is so great that it has gouged a path into the sea one hundred miles long and four thousand feet deep. Forbath's story of the Congo is a tale of great courage and dark horror.

The quest for the legendary kingdom of Prester John was the motivating force behind the discovery of the Congo. Forbath writes that "no one could dream of setting out to find it because no one could dream that it was even there. Its discovery was an accident. . . ." Prester John was believed to be a direct descendant of the Magi and to rule over a splendid Christian kingdom of jewels and gold. In the fifteenth century Prince Henry the Navigator began Portugal's search for this fabulous kingdom. Establishing a school of navigation at Sagres, he sent out expedition after expedition sailing down the west coast of Africa searching for the legendary site. The expeditions continued after Henry's death in 1460, and in 1482, ten years before Columbus discovered America, Diogo Cão discovered the mouth of the Congo. The native people called the river *nzere*, which Cão translated as Zaïre. The name was used until the eighteenth century, when it was renamed after the Bakongo people who inhabited its estuary.

More than three hundred years after Cão's discovery, the river was still uncharted. Before Europeans began to explore the Congo, James Bruce had discovered the source of the Blue Nile, and Mungo Park had made important discoveries along the Niger. Finally, in 1816, Captain James Tuckey was sent by the British Admiralty on a Congo expedition; but illness and lack of supplies stopped the explorers after only three hundred miles. In the fruitless attempt, Tuckey and many of his men died.

The decades of the 1850's and 1860's were the great years of African exploration. This was the period of the discovery of the source of the White Nile by John H. Speke and of David Livingstone's great discoveries of the Zambezi River, Victoria Falls, and Lake Nyasa. In 1856 Livingstone was the first European to traverse the African continent from coast to coast, and a decade later he discovered the Chambezi, which flowed southwest into Lake Bangweolo and was the source of the Congo. Because he was ill and had spent years looking for the beginnings of the Nile, Livingstone believed that this river flowed into Lake Tanganyika and was the source of the Nile.

It was left to Verney Cameron and Henry Morton Stanley to correct Livingstone's miscalculations and make the great discoveries of the Congo. Sent out by the Royal Geographical Society in 1873 to search for Livingstone, Cameron was in Tabora in east Africa when he was told that the great missionary-explorer had died. Instead of returning to England, however, Cameron pressed onward to Ujiji on Lake Tanganyika, where natives and Arab traders told him that the Lualaba River flowed into the Congo and not, as Livingstone had believed, into the Nile. At Nyangwe on the Lualaba Cameron calculated that it was eight hundred miles to the Yellala Cataract, which was as far as Tuckey had gotten. Cameron also believed that the Congo's course took it across the equator and that, therefore, part of the Congo was always in rain and continuously supplied with water. But, like Livingstone, Cameron could not get native canoes to take him down the Lualaba.

Finally the great Arab trader, Tippoo Tib, who had earlier assisted Livingstone and would later assist Stanley, took Cameron away from the Lualaba to the Lomami River in 1874, and by 1875 Cameron had arrived at Benguelo, Angola, on the Atlantic coast, becoming the second European (after Livingstone) to traverse the African continent from coast to coast. He had not used the Congo route, but he had succeeded in filling in a large portion of the map of Africa. His observations would have a great influence upon the course of European exploration into the Congo. He was the first explorer to suggest the probable course of the great river, and the first to recognize the potential of Katanga. Cameron was a realistic viewer of Africa's potential and an enlightened explorer of central Africa.

But to the popular mind it is the name of Henry Morton Stanley that is associated with the Congo discoveries. Stanley, a newspaper reporter with the New York *Herald,* charted the remaining portion of the river—that portion that had been so long uncharted because of the cannibals on its shores and because of its dangerous cataracts, impassable by boat. Stanley, with financial backing from the *Herald* and the London *Daily Telegraph,* set out on the expedition which would make him the greatest Africa explorer that ever lived. The year was 1874.

Arriving in Zanzibar on the east coast of Africa, Stanley purchased supplies and hired porters and *askari,* the armed escorts. By November his party of over three hundred strong had left Bagamoyo for the interior. Fighting his way westward as he suffered from attacks of malaria, he pushed on to Ujiji where, five years earlier, he had uttered those now-famous words, "Dr. Livingstone, I presume?" Finally, in October, 1876, Stanley reached the Lualaba, which he compared with the Mississippi. He wrote,

> . . . a secret rapture filled my soul as I gazed upon the majestic stream. The great mystery that for all these centuries Nature had kept hidden from the world of science was waiting to be solved.

At Nyangwe on the Lualaba, Stanley hired Tippoo Tib to accompany him for three months into the interior. This was the Arab trader's first venture into the dark rain forest where smallpox, dysentery, and blackwater fever were rampant, along with attacks by aboriginies with poisoned arrows, and Tippoo Tib soon left the expedition. Stanley proceeded with 140 survivors of his Anglo-American expedition and reached Stanley Falls in January, 1877. It took three weeks to clear the seventh and final cataract of the Falls. By this time Stanley was sure that the Lualaba was not the Nile as Livingstone had believed. The next one thousand miles were covered in seven weeks of calm water and fighting natives. At Rubunga Stanley saw the first evidence of Europeans on the river since leaving Nyangwe: four ancient Portuguese muskets. On March 9, the expedition had its thirty-second and final fight with the natives. "Our blood is now up," wrote Stanley. "It is a murderous world, and we feel for the first time we hate the filthy, vulturous ghouls who inhabit it." When Stanley discovered Stanley Pool, a lake fifteen miles across and twenty miles long, he had attained the end of the longest navigable stretch of the Congo. Less than four hundred miles from the Atlantic and two hundred miles from Boma, he had proven that the Lualaba was the Upper Congo.

Stanley had been told by the natives that between Stanley Pool and Boma there were two or three falls. In fact there were thirty-two, and this watery nightmare almost cost Stanley his life and nearly destroyed the expedition in the last stage of its Africa crossing. The expedition struggled with the cataracts for five months and covered only 180 miles. Exhausted and starving to death, Stanley left the river at Tuckey's farthest point on July 30, the Isangila Cataract, and sent letters to Boma for help. Boma sent sackfuls of food and the expedition survived. Stanley had spent 999 days traveling seven thousand miles from Zanzibar to Boma. The dispatches which he sent from Boma reached the outside world months ahead of him and so, by the time he arrived in England in January, 1878, Stanley was given a hero's welcome. His fellow explorers, Burton, Grant, and Cameron, heaped praise upon him; Stanley had accomplished what they had all tried unsuccessfully to attain.

King Leopold II of Belgium was the next European in the Congo (although he never set foot in Africa). He was looking for lands to colonize and over which to exert his power, and he sent Stanley back in 1878 to build settlements, trading stations, and railroads around the cataracts at Livingstone Falls and Stanley Falls. Stanley by 1881 had succeeded in completing fifty-two miles of road from Vivi to Isangila, thereby earning for himself the native name Bula Matari, "stone breaker." He built a large settlement at Kinshasa (renamed Leopoldville) on the Stanley Pool—a settlement which is today a city of 1.5 million inhabitants. In gaining sovereignty over this territory, which he called the Congo Free State, Leopold purported to bring European goods to the natives of the Congo in trade for ivory and rubber. He established three trade zones—the Free Trade Zone, the Domaine Privé, and the Domaine de la Couronne—in order to replenish his coffers, emptied through battles with the natives and Arab traders.

But Leopold became greedy and the trade zones were used "to tear treasure out of the bowels of the land," in the words of Marlow in Joseph Conrad's *Heart of Darkness*. Leopold's greed led to horrible atrocities against the natives. To stimulate rubber production, a man's wife and children would be held hostage and kept in chains until he produced the desired amount of rubber; there was the constant sound of clanking chains in the Congo rain forest during this period. Raids were made on villages and, as one of Leopold's officers described it,

> War has been waged all through the district of the Equator, and thousands of people have been killed and twenty-one heads were brought back to Stanley Falls . . . as decoration around a flower-bed

in front of the station commander's house. "If the rubber does not reach the full amount required," the report continued, "the sentries attack the natives. They kill some and bring the hands to the Commissioner." It has been estimated that, in the twenty years of Leopold's rule, five million Congo natives were killed. When Leopold died in 1909, his estate was thought to be worth $80 million.

Reports of the atrocities eventually reached Europe through the work of the Aborigines Protection Association in England, and books like Conrad's *Heart of Darkness*. The Congo Free State was taken from Leopold and given to Belgium in 1908, at which time it became the Belgian Congo, which it remained for fifty years until the struggle for independence began. The Congo River is now called the Zaïre in a move by the native people to erase the ugly part of their history.

In *The River Congo* Peter Forbath has captured the history and the feeling of a great river, a task which he set for himself when he first stood on the banks of the Lualaba as a journalist covering the Simba uprising of 1964. His fascination with the river set him searching for a book on the Congo. Finding none, he decided to write one himself on the order of Moorehead's studies on the Nile. It was a large order, and he has filled it, using exciting prose based upon extensive research.

Richard A. Van Orman

ROBERT FROST
The Work of Knowing

Author: Richard Poirier
Publisher: Oxford University Press (New York). 322 pp. $11.95
Type of work: Literary criticism

A critical examination of the major poems of Robert Frost

The image of Robert Frost, both as poet and person, has been considerably tarnished since his death in 1963. As was the case with Hemingway and Faulkner, for example, exhaustive biographies have given him more shortcomings and flaws than the public was aware of or was prepared to accept in our "unofficial poet laureate." Of course, the reaction against Frost had set in well before his death. But the publication of Lawrance Thompson and R. H. Winnick's *Robert Frost: The Later Years, 1938-1963,* the third and final volume in the official biography, instigated some of the most irresponsible reviews and articles since Ezra Pound was awarded the Bollingen Prize for the *Pisan Cantos.* Frost was not only presented as a monster of selfishness and cruelty, but was somehow made responsible for his son's suicide and his sister's being committed to an asylum.

Admittedly, Frost is partly responsible for this sometimes hysterical reaction, for during his long career, with the help of Louis Untermeyer and other friends, he was careful to manipulate the public image of himself—which often resulted in unfortunate distortions. Then, as the various collections of letters and the three-volume biography were published, revealing his egoism, instability, prejudices and even an occasional "tendency to falsification," a change in his image was inevitable. (No doubt, his surviving daughter Lesley has not improved matters by censoring *The Family Letters of Robert and Elinor Frost.)*

In any case, Richard Poirier's often fresh and brilliant study of the major poems comes at a time when Frost's reputation is at a low ebb. His book should go far in not only cleansing but adding new luster to the tarnished image of one of America's major poets.

However, it needs to be said that, as good as it is, this is not quite the book his publishers claim. Poirier is not the first critic to emphasize Frost's sophistication and subtlety, his stressing of the "sound of sense"—or, for that matter, to point up the "submerged metaphors of sex and love-making." What Poirier does here is rescue Frost's best work from his friends and protectors who consistently stressed his popular side—his lucidity, balance, and saneness—as well as from the certified modernists who dismiss all poetry that is not written in the manner of Pound and Eliot. He also frees some of the poems from the poet's own misleading comments and asides.

The organization of *Robert Frost* is simplicity itself. After "A Preview" indicating his aims and method, Poirier takes up the major poems in a roughly chronological order—not the order in which they were published. "Beginnings" is a long chapter devoted to *A Boy's Will* (he calls it "a portrait of the artist as a young man") which includes a fresh examination of Frost's grouping of these early lyrics. "Outward Bound" focuses on the major poems of *North of Boston,* Frost's greatest achievement, revealing a continued need in the poet for freedom and form, home and "extra-vagance." "Time and the Keeping of Poetry" examines the role of time and the permanence of art, and later chapters offer helpful discussions of such late poems as "Kitty Hawk" and "Directive." Poirier is particularly effective in his analysis of what he labels Frost's "work poems," as well as those dealing with marriage.

Perhaps the critic's aims and style can best be suggested by a quote from "To the Reader":

> Frost is a poet of genius because he could so often make his subtleties inextricable from an apparent availability. The assumption that he is more easily read than are his contemporaries, like Yeats and Eliot, persists only in ignorance of the unique but equally strenuous kinds of difficulty which inform his best work. He is likely to be most evasive when his idioms are so ordinary as to relax rather than stimulate attention; he is an allusive poet, but in a hedging and off-hand way, the allusions being often perceptible only to the ear, and then just barely— in echoings of earlier poets like Herbert or Rossetti, or in metrical patternings traceable to Milton; he will wrap central implications, especially of a sexual kind, within phraseologies that seem innocent of what they carry. . . .
>
> Frost seems to me of vital interest and consequence because his ultimate subject is the interpretive process itself.

Poirier, as his *The Performing Self* made clear, is a widely read and perceptive critic. He is able to relate individual poems to works by Horace, Marvell, or Robinson; and he is particularly successful in establishing Frost in the tradition of Thoreau and Emerson, at the same time showing the influence on individual poems by such diverse poets as Yeats, Poe, Hardy, and Hopkins. (Incidentally, he rates Emerson higher than Frost.) And his relating a number of poems to the work of William James is fresh and nothing short of brilliant. For example, his discovery of the source of "Design" in James's *Pragmatism* is especially exciting—though his comparison of this great sonnet with the earlier version "In White" has been done earlier by Randall Jarrell and others.

As already noted, Poirier is not the first critic to point up the sexuality in Frost's poems, but he is the first to trace the "hidden" sexual metaphors throughout the major poems, relating them to the creative process, to Frost's comments on writing poetry, and to such minor poems as "Putting in the Seed" and "The Silken Tent." This new emphasis is clearly needed, for Frost played down this aspect of his work. He never read "Home Burial" in public, and his "The Subverted Flower," an autobiographical poem apparently about an early sexual approach to Elinor White, was rarely anthologized—though, to be sure, it is not among his memorable successes. If Poirier occasionally discovers sexual implications that Frost might not have intended, this does not undermine his point that sexuality and the making of poetry are overriding concerns in Frost's poetry and prose.

Although Poirier writes out of a devotion to and admiration for his subject that is manifested on every page, he is no Reginald Cook or Louis Untermeyer, careful to whitewash the "good grey poet." He is not afraid to show Frost, warts and all, because he knows the poet will survive in his greatest poems, and the feebler efforts should be allowed to pass into oblivion, as some already have. He acknowledges Frost's egotism and his tendency to manipulate others to his advantage. He deplores his cuteness and cracker-box-philosopher side as much as Frost's harsher critics (Yvor Winters and Newton Arvin, for instance). He also comments on the silliness of his feud with what Frost labeled "the Eliot-Richards-Matthiessen gang" and the dishonesty of some of his dealings with Ezra Pound.

But no doubt this is beside the point: Poirier obviously wants to play down the sticky, unpleasant biographical facts and focus our attention on what really matters: the individual poems. And here he succeeds brilliantly. He has helped rescue more than a half-dozen poems that are frequently ignored; for example, "The Ax-Helve," "A Star in a Stoneboat" and "Kitty Hawk," at the same time downgrading poems that have been too frequently anthologized and over-praised or have not worn well with time—"Directive" and "New Hampshire," among others. Who would have thought that anything fresh could be said about "After Apple-Picking," "Mending Wall" or "The Wood-Pile"? In general, his analyses are brief, interesting, and always illuminating—especially in his exploration of metaphors and symbolic meaning, which are his prime interests.

On the other hand, it would seem impossible to discuss "Stopping by Woods on a Snowy Evening" without a mention of John Ciardi's memorable—even newsworthy—*Saturday Review* article, or difficult to explore the sexual nuances of "Home Burial" without acknowledging Randall Jarrell's work on this great dramatic monologue. And there are other instances where Poirier's discoveries or readings are not as original as one might be led to believe.

Perhaps it is worth noting that Poirier makes no pretense of discussing Frost's whole canon. There are dozens of poems that go unmentioned—even some that would shed light on the sexuality theme he rides so hard. He barely mentions the masques and omits most of the lesser-known monologues. On the other hand, he has made excellent use of Frost's few critical essays, the numerous interviews, and the letters—especially those to Louis Untermeyer. (Nor has he been content with the latest edition of *The Collected Poems*. In a number of instances he has restored Frost's original punctuation, going behind the emendations of Edward C. Lathem.) Undoubtedly, Poirier is drawn most obviously to those poems that Lionel Trilling has said come from "the terrible Frost," and the ones that have multiple layers of meanings or ambiguous metaphors at their centers. The less subtle poems hold little appeal for him. But this is not to say, of course, that he distorts Frost's major concerns.

Perhaps the greatest weakness of this book is its style. Poirier can be wooly and almost impenetrable at times, which seems odd in one who so obviously admires his subject's classical purity. But, even so, there is little of the usual critical jargon so frequent in academic criticism. Also, the book is not as "heavy" as it might have been; Poirier lightens the tone with amusing anecdotes. And, of course, many of the quotes—and these are generously provided—from Frost's poems and letters are clever and witty.

One could also wish for a fuller bibliography. Poirier cites only ten books here, most notably the work of Lawrance Thompson and Edward C. Lathem; yet he has leaned heavily on the groundbreaking work of Randall Jarrell and Reuben Brower, as well as others. But perhaps this is asking too much, for even with its few obvious drawbacks *Robert Frost: The Work of Knowing* is a noteworthy achievement. It is without doubt the best critical book thus far on the poetry of Robert Frost.

Guy Owen

ROBERT FULTON

Author: John S. Morgan (1921–   )
Publisher: Mason/Charter (New York). Illustrated. 235 pp. $10.95
Type of work: Biography
Time: 1765–1815
Locale: The United States and England

A biography of Robert Fulton which focuses on the significance of his career in the development of technology as a science, rather than emphasizing his personal life

It is given to some people to come to the world's attention, to achieve fame and/or fortune, to succeed in unlikely endeavors, almost from the sheer force of their personalities. Such a person was Robert Fulton.

Fulton's rise from obscure beginnings to lasting world fame is chronicled here by a man who both understands Fulton's technical prowess and can wonder with us at his remarkable achievements. John Smith Morgan is a prolific writer, with many more than a dozen titles to his credit. Most of his works are of a technical nature, and his expertise in such matters acts as a solid basis for this biography of Fulton, a prolific inventor, and best known as the builder of the first steamboat.

The book is divided into three parts which parallel the three major phases of Fulton's career. The first section of the work centers around Fulton's early life and family background. There is very little direct information available in primary sources of the era, and consequently much of this section is conjectural. Morgan attempts to flesh out this sketchiness for the reader with reminders of political and social events that would have occurred during Fulton's early years and which may have been influential in his development. One wishes that Morgan had condensed much of this material, for, while probably having some bearing on Fulton's early years, much of it is superfluous to the narrative, especially for a reader with any familiarity with history.

Fulton's first career was as an artist of sorts. As a very young man, he was apprenticed to a jeweler in Philadelphia and first learned to paint the miniatures that were so popular at the time. Through his experience with the jeweler, he also discovered a whole new world of genteel people and a life very different from that of the farm and small town of Lancaster. He soon directed his restless energies toward the ambition to become a gentleman, and discovered that he could at least spend much time in the company of gentlemen by painting portraits of them and their families. He resolved to become an artist.

It was greatly by luck augmented by charm that he managed to make and to borrow enough money to reach England to begin his artistic apprenticeship. This was the first of many instances in his life in which Fulton demonstrated an uncanny ability to attach himself to a famous person, in this case the artist Benjamin West, who was well known and successful in London circles. Although West was not overwhelmed by Fulton's talent, the entire artistic adventure in London gave Fulton some personal polish and an even greater drive toward fame and fortune.

Morgan seems to have written this section of the book in a great hurry, and not edited it with sufficient care, for there are many instances in which the writing style detracts markedly from the information being imparted. Perhaps this problem resulted from the conjectural nature of much of the material in the section; nonetheless, it is regrettable.

Morgan comes more into his own element, however, in the second section of the book, which deals with something that almost constituted Fulton's second career, and was certainly his first love: the submarine. Although Fulton's name is rarely linked to the submarine except by true students of the device, he was certain at the time that his fame was to come from his inventiveness with the "plunging boat." Most of his work with it was done while he was in France, having given up his English artistic endeavors after some passing interest in the design of canals.

Morgan next sets before us the story of Fulton's attempts to "sell" the idea of the submarine in an objective fashion, but shares with the reader an appreciation for the enormous charm and ego which aided Fulton. In his drive to achieve fame and recognition he took his cause to anyone who would listen, and to a few, like Napoleon, who would not. He was not in the least shy about pushing his experiments at every opportunity, many of which he created himself. This was an intensely frustrating time for Fulton since the submarine drew moral objections from many quarters as an ungentlemanly, dishonorable form of warfare, and he had many technical difficulties with it to overcome as well. Here, as with the steamboat later, Fulton was not the only inventor working with the idea, but his ambition to make a name for himself, now that he was accepted into polite society, drove him almost as much as his technological interest in the mechanism. Some measure of success again came from his acquiring a new patron, Joel Barlow. Mr. Barlow was wealthy and well respected, and his friendship with Fulton led him to sponsor many of Fulton's projects.

One of the most amazing aspects of Fulton's personality was his flexibility. He tended to side politically with whichever country or group seemed most likely at the time to subsidize his experiments. He presented his ideas about submarines to the French as a way of crushing the English fleet even though he retained many close friendships in England. In this and the following section of the book, Morgan provides quotations of many of the primary documents from this era which, in all charity, can only picture Fulton as opportunistic rather than principled.

Fulton came upon the idea of steamboats, and his third career, almost by accident. Whle he was in Paris, casting about for the funds necessary to continue his submarine experiments, he met Robert Livingston, the new American minister to France. Livingston was very interested in fostering a practical steamboat for the Hudson River in his home state of New York. He had been connected with many early experiments along such lines but none of them had shown great practical promise. In addition, he held a monopoly from the state of

New York for the exclusive right to operate a steam-powered boat on the Hudson for twenty years if a test model could prove itself within a short amount of time.

Fulton had, while working on his submarine ideas, come across and actually tinkered with the idea of a steam-powered boat, but at the time it was not germane to his interests. With Livingston as his new patron, Fulton's interest in the steamboat was renewed. Livingston was very genteel, famous, wealthy, and powerful, and Fulton was very ambitious and flexible. Consequently, Robert Fulton soon began to devote his attention to steamboats.

In order to put Fulton's achievement into perspective Morgan digresses from time to time to give the reader some history of the steam engine and its early application in boats and other devices. Many other men were working on such projects, and, as Morgan unfolds the stories of their experiments and successes, it becomes apparent that the honors for inventing the steamboat should not go to Fulton alone. Yet it is natural, in reading through the litany of false starts on a seemingly simple application of a basic machine, to question why the inventors did not succeed. Morgan suggests that Fulton's ultimate success where others had been less fortunate centered around the fact that his was the first practical steamboat. But the question remains: why did Fulton, who was technologically bright but not by any means a genius, succeed where others had failed? The answer may lie in his great ambition for fame and the persistence which accompanied it. While most of the other inventors worked on their projects because they loved their work, Fulton experimented with the steamboat because it was the most likely way for him to attain the fame and fortune he craved. The end result was a practical success even though the motivation may have been less than idealistic.

Once his invention had proved itself a success, Fulton's interest shifted to the money that he could make from it, and he became concerned about his reputation as a ship owner rather than an inventor. As a consequence of this shift of interest, he spent much energy and money in a quest to keep the New York State monopoly rather than spread the bounties of the new mode of transportation to all who could benefit from it. Morgan recounts this change in emphasis without accusations, but does point out to the reader that these personal quirks of Fulton prevented the wide dissemination of the design to the detriment of many others for much longer than it should have. In a way, this dispassionate attitude toward the historic significance of the design is part of what Morgan attempts to applaud by calling Fulton the first of the true technologists. Morgan's emphasis is simply on Fulton's talent for gathering together devices and ideas that had been developed separately and were individually unsuccessful, and the creation of a successful whole out of them.

The final section is as much a history of the development of steam powered vehicles, particularly the steamboat, as it is a history of one man. Morgan's chronicle is well researched to include all the other important developers, and he has made extensive use of primary sources, quoting liberally from them. The lengthy quotations serve not only to impart very valuable information but to impart the flavor of the times. Fulton's mercurial character and suave public appearance shine through quotations of even the most technical nature and, set off in Morgan's objective narrative, they display Fulton's enormous persuasiveness.

Since the book was apparently written for the average layman with a limited technical background, the sections that describe each inventor and his mechanism could have been a little more fully explicated. The illustrations that are included help the reader who has little technical knowledge of steam engines to envision some of the mechanisms alluded to, but would have been more helpful had they been more numerous. It may be, however, that the author tried to avoid much technical detail so as not to inundate the reader and further to avoid emphasizing the mechanism over the man.

Morgan's emphasis in this portrait of Robert Fulton is on the significance of the inventor's career more than on his personal life. Family and friends are not depicted in depth, nor are his relationships with them. The biography is concerned, rather, with Fulton's importance in the development of engineering and technology.

Margaret S. Schoon

SARAH BERNHARDT AND HER WORLD

Author: Joanna Richardson
Publisher: G. P. Putnam's Sons (New York). Illustrated. 232 pp. $15.95
Type of work: Biography
Time: 1844–1923
Locale: Europe, England, and the United States

A biography of the celebrated actress, with special emphasis on her famous roles, her admirers among her contemporaries, and her mystique

> *Principal personages:*
> SARAH BERNHARDT, legendary French actress
> JUDITH VAN HARD, her mother
> MAURICE BERNHARDT, her son
> AMBROISE ARISTIDE DAMALA, her husband

Occasionally in the course of history individuals stand out not only because they embody the milieu in which they live, but also because the overwhelming power of their personalities shapes and transcends their milieu. In the late 1800's, which saw the emergence of the Age of Realism, as depicted in literature by Zola and James, but which also simultaneously witnessed the flowering of the Pre-Raphaelite movement in England, Sarah Bernhardt stands out as such a unique personality. Her dazzling career as one of the most celebrated actresses of all time was matched only by her lifestyle, which at once outraged and secretly delighted the prim Victorian milieu. At the same time, her love of the exotic and the bizarre perfectly reflected the emergence alongside Victorianism of the ornate Byzantine style of art and literature known as the Pre-Raphaelite Movement, which led variously to the "art for art's sake" movement, the *fin de siècle* Decadents, and Art Deco.

The illegitimate daughter of a Jewish mother and a Catholic father, Sarah was born on October 23, 1844, in Paris. Undistinguished for maternal feelings, her mother deposited the red-haired Sarah with a nurse until, at age fifteen, her parents decided her fate; she would study to become an actress. Her debut in *Iphigénie* began a career of sixty years in which she played in every classical and modern play including *Phèdre, Le Misanthrope,* and, perhaps her most famous role, as Marguerite in Dumas' *La Dame aux camélias.* So versatile were her talents that she even made a triumphal version of *Hamlet* in which she played the melancholy prince, certainly an unorthodox role in a society which decreed that a woman's place was in the home.

Joanna Richardson's biography provides the details of Bernhardt's career and begins a much-needed discussion of the reasons for the mystique that surrounded her. Perhaps the first actress to be accorded the adulation usually reserved for royalty, Sarah's mystery in part surely was due to her striking appearance. Her often unruly red hair, aquiline nose, rather pale complexion, and slim yet rounded figure made her the ideal of feminine beauty espoused by Pre-Raphaelite painters. To add to her mystique Bernhardt selected her accouterments carefully. Her gowns were often white, subtlely tapered to enhance her figure. Her home was a mad collection of Oriental bric-a-brac, bizarre pets like cheetahs and monkeys, and the elaborate metal lamps and sculptures in the style later to be known as Art Nouveau. Herself a talented painter and a sculptor whose works were exhibited at the International Exhibition of 1900, Bernhardt perpetuated her image as *artiste*, not simply artist. She was said to have studied her lines in a coffin, to have thrown offensive pets into the fireplace. In short, she was clever enough not to deny her public image as an outrageous eccentric.

Her lifestyle, what is more, went counter to Victorian prudery. Herself illegitimate, she gave birth at twenty to Maurice by Henri, Prince de Ligne. Her love affairs were never secret, yet even her notoriety did not prevent her marriage at age thirty-seven to Ambroise Aristide Damala, eleven years her junior and a morphine addict who died seven years later. Some speculate her scandalous private life included a liaison with George Sand. Others question her relationship with the Prince of Wales, later King Edward VII. Yet this lifestyle did not exempt her from a triumphal season in London in 1879 where she was lionized by society, visited by royalty, and treated to some of the most lavish reviews of her career.

Bernhardt was thus a "personality" whose charisma intrigued the public. But she was not simply that; she was also a serious, talented actress, perhaps one of the world's finest. Richardson carefully points out that it was Bernhardt who realized the importance on the stage of the pause, of silence, of correct detail, of historical authenticity. She meticulously studied, for example, how to die appropriately, whether by consumption as in *La Dame aux camélias* or by a heart ailment in *Julie*. Her ability to play male roles startled her audiences yet challenged male actors and expanded the concept of what possibilities the theater offered. Her choice of roles was also congruent with her times: as Theodora in a Byzantine setting; as La Princesse lointaine, melancholy and beautiful; Izeyl, exotic embodiment of the Baudelaire sonnet; Cleopatra, dangerous *femme fatale;* and of course Marguerite, beautiful but doomed. All were roles in which the heroine as a *femme fatale* lived intensely, perhaps wickedly, but shone with the hard gemlike flame Walter Pater deemed as the only way to live. Her professionalism, her versatility, her originality infused every role with the magic through which an audience could easily suspend not only its disbelief but apparently even its ingrained Victorian codes of right behavior.

Her life was a full one; there seemed always to be a new role, a new tour, a new lover, but in 1905, she injured her leg in a fall in Rio de Janiero in *La Tosca* when someone neglected to put down a mattress to cushion her suicidal leap in the finale. The injury led eventually to having the leg amputated in 1918 and ultimately to her death by blood-poisoning in 1923 at age seventy-nine, an event mourned officially in London and Paris.

In the last few days of her life, Bernhardt is said to have remarked to a friend, "Well, dear Tutur, when shall we decide to die?" Who was this woman who could ask such a question so fraught with humor, with resignation, with depth? Unfortunately Richardson's biography does not help the reader answer that question because its pace is too rapid. Bernhardt's inner life is revealed only indirectly, through snatches of her memoirs which Richardson quotes, through reminiscences of friends, through inferred deductions from Bernhardt's actions. One would like to know her feelings about her illegitimacy, her Jewish heritage (though she herself was a Catholic), her convent school education. What about her son's opposition to her marriage, to which Richardson refers all too briefly? The reader learns that Ellen Terry was her friend, but not what Terry thought of their friendship.

Sarah Bernhardt's inner self is only fleetingly revealed in this biography, perhaps, because the people whom she loved are not fully characterized for the reader; Victor Hugo, Thomas Edison, European royalty enter and exit without our understanding them as people. Character sketches of lesser-known figures are even more essential. We need to understand Perrin at *La Comédie-Française,* John Hollinghead who arranged her first fabulous tour in London, Damala her husband, and Ellen Terry. Perhaps the reader could know the great Bernhardt through the people who loved and admired her. And the reader would also like to know more about Bernhardt's personal habits, her favorite haunts, her tastes in food: we learn she could catnap at will, for example, and are intrigued.

While Richardson's biography moves a bit too quickly, it does do justice to Bernhardt's career and to her admirers. Lavish illustrations and photographs are fortunately collected in this . biography, and they alone would make the biography worth perusing. Bernhardt was not merely an anomalie in the age of realism, as Richardson concludes. Bernhardt understood that realism was always at war with the mysticism and medieval splendor of *fin de siècle* Decadence. Perhaps the deficiencies in Richardson's biography seem so only because Bernhardt's mystery is still unexplained by Richardson's text and the illustrations, but whether Sarah Bernhardt's mystique can be understood at all remains illusive. Like the Mona Lisa, that other Pre-Raphaelite heroine, Bernhardt may be ultimately unknowable, a splendid actress, a heterodox personality, a luminous symbol of her time.

Kathryn L. Seidel

SELECTED POEMS: 1923-1975

Author: Robert Penn Warren (1905–   )
Publisher: Random House (New York). 325 pp. $15.00
Type of work: Poetry

A collection of poetry, arranged in reverse chronological order, which represents a half-century of achievement

Robert Penn Warren's *Selected Poems: 1923-1975* represent his retrospective and evaluative view of over a half-century of productivity as a poet. At the age of seventy-three, Warren can look back on an honorable and honored career as a poet and novelist. *Promises* (1957) won the Pulitzer Prize for poetry; eleven years earlier *All the King's Men* won the Prize for fiction. In reviewing this book, therefore, we are reviewing Warren's career as a poet and his critical judgment in selecting the poems he would like to preserve for posterity.

None of this is meant to imply that Warren's career as a poet is over—far from it. In a recent *New Yorker,* he has published "Inevitable Frontier," a poem which successfully employs a highly developed conversational style to help with a smooth transition from the details of a dreamlike frontier to broad statements of conclusion. We are in a world where "all tongues are sloppily cubical" and "food is, of course, forbidden." It is also a world where

> among others, the names
> Of Plato, St. Paul, Spinoza, Pascal and Freud must not be spoken and when,
> Without warning, by day or night, the appalling
> White blaze of God's Great Eye sweeps the sky, History
> Turns tail and scuttles back to its burrow,
> Like a groundhog caught in a speeding sports car's headlight.

The transition from detail to statement is beautifully managed and the poem is of typically high quality and typically Warren.

Warren's is clearly traditional poetry. In the first place, it eschews artifice and ungrammaticality. When, as in the last sentence of "Inevitable Frontier," a construction is not completed, we can be sure it is for dramatic effect. Second, the poems impose a personal rhythm on what is recognizably scanable verse. In "Inevitable Frontier" iambic pentameter is the matrix from which each of the poem's couplets grow. Some lines are more clearly rule-bound: "The shadow of something—yourself, for instance—" Some are far less so:

> To the cafe terrace divans of ingeniously provocative design. Nevertheless all lines are the result of a fruitful marriage between traditional meter and personal rhythm.

In the third place, Warren's poems are traditional in their thematic content. Throughout his corpus there is a recurrence of the themes of identity, love, the continuity of the generations, the search for wisdom, and the effects of time. In his exploration of these themes over the years, Warren clearly shows himself to be a poet of philosophical inclination in the romantic tradition of Keats and Wordsworth. He does not rhyme platitudes like Pope; nor does he contribute elegance and personality to traditional themes, like Herrick. His lifelong interest is in transforming traditional themes into personal statements which embody poetic truths, the sum of which is a kind of poetic wisdom, parallel to and as important as philosophical wisdom.

The nature of this task—Warren's central task—makes his poetry initially obscure and forbidding. Despite the conversational, colloquial style evident especially in later years, the poems lack superficial charm and fail to ingratiate. They require repeated readings and long reflection to yield their meaning and power. Three later poems, "Old Nigger on One-Mule Cart Encountered Late at Night When Driving Home from Party in the Back Country," "Rattlesnake Country," and "Birth of Love," demonstrate Warren's method and success.

All three poems exhibit the characteristics already exemplified in the analysis of "Inevitable Journey." They are written in a conversational manner and everywhere there is in their rhythm a tension between traditional meter and idiosyncratic speech. The first two have as their theme the relationship between the effects of time and the attainment of wisdom. The third concerns the nature of mature love. In order, however, to get the full flavor of Warren's achievement, the analysis must be carried further. Throughout Warren's career, we see the progressive integration of two key elements in his poetry: abstract statement and nature imagery.

To obtain a sense of Warren's final achievements as a poet—the remarkable achievements of a man in his sixties and seventies—it is necessary to look back on the whole body of his work. For fifty years, he has used his poems to express a personal philosophy, and that use has necessitated a shift from image to abstract statement. In the early "Bearded Oaks," Warren begins:

> The oaks, how subtle and marine,
> Bearded, and all the layered light
> Above them swims, and thus the scene,
> Recessed, awaits the positive night.

After several equally gnomic stanzas, Warren concludes:

> We live in time so little time
> And we learn all so painfully
> That we may spare this hour's term
> To practice for eternity.

The poem is modern, obscure; however, its structure is like that of Longfellow's "The Village Blacksmith," in that specific observations lead to boldly general conclusions. The effect is syllogistic and the ending seems more like an appendix than an integral part of the poem.

All three of the later poems also contain philosophical statements of great generality. In "Old Nigger," for example, "We are entitled to our fantasies, for life/Is only the fantasy that has happened to us." And in "Rattlesnake Country," Warren writes, "What was *is* now *was*. But/Is *was* but a word for wisdom, its price?" In "Birth of Love," he writes, "This moment is nonsequential and absolute, and admits/Of no definition, for it/ Subsumes all other, and sequential, moments, by which/Definition might be possible." What makes these statements different from the one in "Bearded Oaks"? In the first place, they have a stature which makes them interesting for their own sake. The statement in "Bearded Oaks" is after all, merely an engaging way of stating the obvious, in the manner of Pope or Longfellow.

More important, the statements in the later poems are completely integrated into the poems themselves because the poems imitate the poet's mental process in arriving at them. "Old Nigger" begins with a present-tense narrative concerning a dance. With the line, "I can't now even remember the name of the dancer," we realize that the dance episode is a recollection. Next, there is an anecdote concerning a near-accident between a car and an old black man riding a mule cart. After the incident, the narrator goes to bed, makes love, goes to sleep, and wakes up to write out the first two lines of a conventional sonnet about the near-accident. In the two lines that follow, "As I said, Jesus Christ. But/ Moved on through the years," the callowness of the sonnet is criticized. We also see clearly that the poet is remembering from a great distance in time.

"Rattlesnake Country" is a recollection of a vacation on a dude ranch. The scene is sharply etched:

> the horsemen
> Plunge through the pine-gloom, leaping
> The deadfall—*I-yee!*—
> Leaping the boulder—*I-yee!*—and their faces
> Flee flickering white through the shadow

Until its last section, the poem seems merely narrative; but then the poet offers a philosophical reflection, which comes as somewhat of a jolt. The poem has definitely not earned the right to this powerfully expressed reflection. But then, with startling nimbleness, Warren proceeds to integrate the reflection into the poem's fabric. He recalls the eventual distressing fates of those he once knew in rattlesnake country; then in a brilliant close he makes it clear what the poem really is about—the springs of memory and of poetry.

"Birth of Love," surely one of the great love poems of the century, is simply structured. A man and a woman, probably man and wife, go for a nude swim. The woman leaves the water first and the man observes her. Two-thirds through the poem come the lines, "This moment is non-sequential and absolute, and admits/Of no definition. . . ." The lines are crucial; they transform the description, just completed, into a vision; moreover, they make the ending—an outpouring of protective love—possible and appropriate: "if only/He had such strength, he would put his hand forth/ And maintain it over her to guard, in all/ Her out-goings and in-comings, from whatever/ Inclemency of sky or slur of world's weather/ Might ever be."

Warren's use of nature imagery is always good: "hoofs on the corduroy road/

Or the foul and sucking sound/A man's foot makes on the marshy ground./ Past midnight, when the moccasin/ Slipped from the log and, trailing in/ Its obscure waters, broke/ The dark algae." ("Pondy Woods") This description from an early poem is impressive in itself; furthermore, it deepens the atmosphere of menace that is clearly central to the poem.

The description is not necessary to the poem; but its omission would lessen the poem's stature, even though it would not destroy its meaning. At the end of "Birth of Love," the following imagery of nature is used: "Above/Height of the spruce-night and heave of the far mountain, he sees/The first star pulse into being. It gleams there." In these lines, from a mature poem, the nature imagery represents nothing less than a culmination of an important theme gleaming out of darkness.

Robert Penn Warren's *Selected Poems* represents a half-century of achievement. The poet publishes his collection in reverse chronological order: we read his final achievement first; and it is indeed impressive. Here is a true philosophical poetry in which nature, recollection, and reflection are welded into verse that is initially difficult and ultimately rewarding. This is not to slight Warren's earlier achievements. Poems of the earlier years (1923–1943) can be very fine indeed: "Bearded Oaks," "Pondy Woods," and "To a Face in the Crowd," for instance. And when after a decade's hiatus, Warren resumes the writing of poetry, he can write verse as impressive as "To a Little Girl, One Year Old, in a Ruined Fortress" and "Infant Boy at Midcentury."

Alan G. Gross

SICILIAN CAROUSEL

Author: Lawrence Durrell (1912–   )
Publisher: The Viking Press (New York). 223 pp. $10.95
Type of work: Travel literature

This travel book investigates the various factors which have combined to create the unique entity that is Sicily

Travel broadens a person. At least that's what the old adage maintains, and if we are to judge by the experience Lawrence Durrell renders in *Sicilian Carousel,* we have to agree. Of course, the adage requires qualification, since the traveler has to have his perceptive powers working at full tilt truly to broaden himself. Certainly not every traveler embarking on journeys hither and yon manages to engage himself in more than merely remarking on scenery and tasting wines and foods. But be assured, Durrell does. Moreover, he is able to re-create his engagement with place so remarkably that we too are enriched by his travel.

At bottom *Sicilian Carousel* succeeds because once again Durrell whole-heartedly devotes himself to investigating the "spirit of place." Readers familiar with his *The Alexandria Quartet* will recognize this reminiscent theme, among others. Readers particularly sensitive to the influences of locale will understand Durrell's reaction when he says, "In Sicily one sees that the Mediterranean evolved at the same rhythm as man, they both evolved together. One interpreted itself on the other, and out of the interaction Greek culture was first born." Durrell's powers of seeing and making us see—the land, the people, the ruins, the aura of place—produce unique effects, so that travel becomes exploration into intellectual currents.

Thus, the consciousness evolved within a place, developed out of the characteristics of geography meshed with human history, generates an enthusiastic response in Durrell. In his *The Alexandria Quartet* he presented a kaleidoscopic vision of Alexandria through a uniquely complex form, what he called at one point a palimpsest. But unlike the earlier work, *Sicilian Carousel* reveals no great complexity, for it makes no claims to be more than a travel narrative. However, the simplicity is deceptive, and the depth to which Durrell delves in this small book allows him to unearth an understanding of life central to all of Western culture.

Durrell has been at home in the Mediterranean for some time. Previous books about Cyprus, Corfu, and Rhodes attest to his love for what he has called "that magical and non-existent land—the Mediterranean." Infected by "islomania," he claims it is the range of the olive tree which marks this region's spiritual and physical boundaries. The small bits of land set upon the pristine sea and strung together by their common Greek heritage hold countless memories for him. We are privy to his recollections as he examines Sicily in the light of those past sojourns, those past definitions of what is stimulating and comfortable for the soul (an unfashionable word for a troublesome concept).

Enriching the spiritual dimension of *Sicilian Carousel* and reinforcing the author's memories are a series of letters sent by his longtime friend Martine, now dead, but still responsible for his embarking on the current journey. Her urgings have increased his anticipation of what he will find on Sicily. She remarks key locations and often addresses herself to questions the two of them have raised in other places, at other times. Reading her letters periodically throughout the journey, he is prompted to recall those conversations long past. In a letter about Agrigento, Martine cites their discussions concerning the Greekness of Cyprus "which had never been either geographically or demographically part of Greece." She asserts that language is the key to the Greek identity, what "gave one membership of the Greek intellectual commonwealth—barbarians were not simply people who lived otherwise but people who did not speak Greek." Martine's sensitivity to place, her letters reveal, matches Durrell's. Furthermore, she was an intimate friend, a confidante reminding one of the remarkable women that readers of Durrell's *The Alexandria Quartet* have already encountered: Justine and Clea, even the forlorn Melissa. The same intense questioning and depth of feeling exuded through her letters is evident in each of those women. The relationship between woman and author is equally significant.

But Martine is a character *in absentia* despite the vivid presence of her words. Balanced against her intensity are the amusing characters who accompany Durrell on the Carousel. Less deeply explored, they nevertheless present us with a sense of diversity inherent in any randomly selected group. A French aristocrat and his wife recognize Durrell as the famous writer but discretely refrain from broadcasting his identity. They are cultured, reserved, slightly out of place in the hectic scene of a guided package tour by bus. Included also are a shy American dentist and his "saucy" wife, she being his most glamorous patient, the two having eloped. An Anglican Bishop, recently the victim of a nervous breakdown, and his wife, alternately cowed by and highly protective of her husband, seem to be sorting out the pieces of a shattered life. Another French couple Durrell consistently calls "the Microscopes" for they remind him of a very cheap pair of such instruments.

Of the single members of the group, a few stand out. Deeds is of a type dear to Durrell's heart, a military man, a gentleman used to traveling in modest style as a benefit of his "plum" job. Early, Durrell establishes that he and Deeds "had done everything together, it seemed, except meet." They had been in Alexandria, even at the same parties. Deeds had known Martine remotely, thought her a bit spoiled (an assessment Durrell admits was once true). Most important, however, is Deeds's knowledge of Sicily, his favorite island; he has valuable suggestions concerning what deserves attention, has a well-marked guidebook (indeed, a host of guidebooks), and has a certain detachment based on experience of the inconveniences and discomforts of the Carousel. At the outset he suggests to Durrell that their motley group of travelers will come to no great troubles—personalities will mesh satisfactorily.

Another remarkable character, though quite the opposite of Deeds, is Beddoes, in Deeds's words, a "dreadful feller." The dentist's lady at one point refers to him as "a pure desecrator." He has both a sharp tongue given to sarcasm and a rather shady background. His pipe is filled with obnoxious smelling tobacco, and his manners are equally noisome. He claims to have been a prep school master, "hurled out . . . for behaviour unbecoming to an officer and a hypocrite." In any case, he seems to be trying to avoid something, and eventually authorities begin to make inquiries, so Beddoes is forced to make good an escape with the help of Mount Etna.

On the other hand, Roberto is the Carousel travelers' guide, philosopher, and friend. Efficient, he is a catalyst able to unite the dissimilar members by attending to every detail of the tour. Throughout the journey he shepherds his flock from site to site demonstrating his ability to anticipate desires and capacities of the individuals in his charge. It is to his credit that things go as smoothly as they do, with only minor discomforts and a few mishaps, most notably the Bishop's fall into a hole at one of the ruins.

Durrell is a master at characterization, and his imaginary characters in *Sicilian Carousel* are wholly believable. Voice patterns, habits, foibles are all consistent evidence of the author's practiced skill at perceiving and fabricating personalities who interact interestingly. The strong identities presented perhaps lack the depth and intensity of characters in Durrell's earlier work, but this very shortcoming by comparison may make *Sicilian Carousel*'s characters more tangible as types one could expect to encounter were he to make a similar journey. Never is there a sense that any of the persons Durrell here describes is too elevated to offer a chair in a hotel diningroom. In dealing with them, Durrell is able to focus on the quite unique experience of coming to know a group of strangers and becoming a part of that group experience even as each maintains his identity. Whether commenting on the skills of Mario the bus driver or observing a budding romance between two of the travelers—a young, blond German girl and a young architecture student—Durrell develops the sense that he has traveled with these people, studied them, and reacted with warmth to their individuality.

He turns the same skill toward his descriptions of the cities the Carousel visits. Seven towns give their names to chapters in the book, but more than seven are visited. Travel between the major cities includes a number of side excursions to historic sites or picturesque villages. Visiting each place creates a special reaction in Durrell. Either from some comment by Martine or from remarks made by Roberto or some other person, Durrell will launch a discussion that will pilot us toward an understanding of some aspect of Sicily. At Syracuse, standing poised between the Roman amphitheater and Greek theater, between two dominant forces in Western history it seems, Durrell assesses their difference: "the blue infinity of sky and the white marble were the keynotes to the Greek imagination; somehow one associates the Roman with the honey-coloured or the dun." While the Greek theater expresses "a world of congruence and vital intelligence where poets were also mathematicians," the Roman amphitheater denotes "a massive eloquence which was intended to outlast eternity." Yet history treats either urge with equal indifference, and at one point Durrell notes that much has been carried away from many ancient sites to be used in more modern constructions: "what was exportable was expendable, what was beautiful had a value worth despoiling." Still, he finds, what is left makes it possible to imagine without much difficulty the appearance and nature of what went on here.

Ultimately, what has happened to Sicily is that the entire cultural progression of Western civilization has broken in wave after wave on its shores. But rather than compile a history (to use Durrell's phrase) "in yawn-making detail," he would "build something more like a companion to landscape than a real history." He finds, for instance, that the Sikels, early inhabitants of the island, are not so interesting as is imagining the state of the island when they encountered it and their reaction to that state. But to imagine this state, Durrell notes, requires great effort. For modern-day Sicily's botanical diversity is the result of importations by numerous conquerors, centuries of encroachments from various sources, and the result of a climate varied by altitude and exposure, which means somewhere on the island a new arrival could find a conducive spot. The ecological evolution of the island has its analog in the island's cultural evolution, for with every historical period and new group of peoples came changes in the face of the land. Thus, a Roman structure would be altered by later peoples; the cathedral in Palermo exhibits the synthesis of Oriental and Norman influences. Throughout the island, the juxtaposition of styles is a stimulus causing Durrell to remark upon the development of a consciousness particular to place, and to remark upon the particular parts of that consciousness.

Upon leaving the caverns of the Paradise Quarry near Syracuse, Durrell is given to consider Martine's death and a sense of panic she felt within the quarry. This leads him to a point he had previously explored: "a definition of what constitutes the tragic element in people and situations." He comes to several realizations, but one in particular is striking: "The Greeks had from early on transplanted the Indian notion of Karma to Greece, and in Greek tragedy what assails us is the spectacle of a human being trapped and overgrown by the huge mass of a past Karma over which he has no control." The hero finds what has always been there and, in so doing, reveals for us the undeniable nature of process.

So, too, the land and its people become the material of change. The modern in Sicily sits astride and beside the ancient. The traveler, in assaying the composition of his travel experience, must sift the various elements that have affected him. He must be sensitive to the delicate strands of a heritage interlocked with amazing complexity, ever creating a new formula of place. When he does this, he cannot help but broaden his understanding of his culture and of himself

Gary B. Blank

SILKEN EYES

Author: Françoise Sagan (1935–   )
Translated from the French by Joanna Kilmartin
Publisher: Delacorte Press/Eleanor Friede (New York). 179 pp. $6.95
Type of work: Short stories
Time: The present
Locale: Europe and Hollywood

Eighteen stories which trace the diversions and temptations of the beautiful and the bored from Paris to Hollywood

Critics, especially Anglo-Saxon, have been hard on Françoise Sagan. Since the appearance of her first novel, *Bonjour Tristesse,* the 1954 publication of which catapulted her into fame, reviewers have, on the whole, judged her severely. They grant that she is a gifted storyteller, but they cite the frivolity, the facileness, the clichés of situation and characterization; "brittle" is a word which recurs in attempts to describe her manner. But critical hostility notwithstanding, Sagan has made the bestseller lists with regularity for nearly a quarter of a century now. Her books are initially printed in great number, rapidly translated into foreign languages, swiftly edited in paperback, and endlessly devoured by a French and foreign public. Yet many still refuse to take her seriously: "I have practically no literary critics," Sagan herself noted in a 1969 interview *(Les Nouvelles Littéraires,* May 22, 1969, page 11). Indeed, her work is prone to be treated less as literature than as a phenomenon, a curiosity: "un accident qui dure" (an accident which endures), as a French periodical recently qualified it.

One of the things for which Sagan has been most consistently reproached is the sameness of her settings: her tales evolve against a background of vain and idle opulence. Her characters, as feckless as they are wealthy, lead existences which appear almost uniformly inconsequential. Sagan's latest production, *Silken Eyes,* published in French in 1975 as *Des Yeux de Soie* (although one of the original nineteen French stories has been dropped, apparently because of translating difficulties) represents no deviation in this respect from her numerous novels and plays of the 1950's and 1960's. It is peopled by creatures as stunning and as otiose as ever: they still drive Maseratis (at 120 mph) and wear Dior clothes; they still keep multiple residences and multiple lovers. Formally, however, this volume represents a new direction in Sagan's opus: it is her first collection of short stories. Stories so short, in fact (some of them, like *The Five Diversions* or *The Fishing Expedition,* occupy only six pages) that they may better be described as vignettes.

In the 1969 interview in *Les Nouvelles Littéraires,* Sagan asserted that her primordial literary theme is people's solitude. The present collection bears this out; in salons, in nightclubs, in automobiles, in bed, her characters remain ultimately alone. In this particular volume, the principal maker of solitude is aging. The phantoms of middle and old age haunt a fair number of the characters, separating them ineluctably from their companions. Sagan's women, who tend to be between thirty and fifty years of age, perceive themselves as incipiently and tragically old, and struggle to retain an appearance of youth and to enjoy some vestige of its corresponding prestige. A certain maturity—in chronological age if not in mentality—thus informs these tales; no major character in *Silken Eyes* recalls the perversely insouciant youth of seventeen-year-old Cecile of *Bonjour Tristesse,* or even that of Josée or Béatrice, her elders by a few years, in *Those Without Shadows.* Sagan's characters are eternally strategists, but the tactics and ruses of the short stories are devised less in the interests of passion, jealousy, or ambition—those emotions so much in evidence in her earliest works—than in the service of appearances, vanity, and style. When the gigolo, for example, towards the end of the story by that name, in an unwonted moment of tenderness looks closely into the face of his middle-aged mistress, her first instinct is to disengage herself, fearful that her makeup, so necessary to her *persona,* may be in disorder.

The subtle irony with which this moment is reported in fact pervades the volume. At least a few of the pieces are ironic and humorous to a degree that invites comparison of Sagan with the great masters of the form. *A Dog's Night* recounts a sort of Christmas miracle among the bourgeoisie: it is accomplished in the snow outside the church a little after midnight, by means of an endearing mongrel called Rover; but here the thrust of the "miracle" is entirely material, with no moral dimension whatever. In another *tour de force* entitled *The Left Eyelid,* Lady Letitia Garrett is confined by a capricious door latch, for several hours and nearly a dozen pages, in the lavatory of the *Mistral,* the fast train between Paris and Italy. At her destination in Lyon waits her adoring lover Charles, little suspecting that Lady Garrett—beautiful, regal, rich, and already four times divorced at thirty-five—is troubling to make the journey from Paris only to put an end to their affair. This preposterous incarceration—more effective, she reflects, than any psychiatrist's couch—unexpectedly and conclusively demonstrates to Lady Garrett her need for the tender and protective suitor: if only he were there, he would beat down the doors of all the lavatories in all the *Mistrals* in France until he had liberated her. Her enforced leisure thus occasions a revolution in her sentiments, and after her release occurs near the trip's end, she descends and inquires simply: "And when would you like us to get married?"

Volatility and infidelity play essential roles in this collection: these characters, like Josée of *The Wonderful Clouds,* are almost compulsively unfaithful—to their husbands, their wives, their lovers, their mistresses—although there are several exhilarating twists in the manner in which the infidelity is committed. *The Unknown Visitor,* for example, delineates the discovery by a proper English socialite wife of her husband's extramarital affair. Millicent returns early from a weekend of golf to find their country house in disarray, two dressing gowns (her husband's and her own) on the living room floor, two empty coffee cups on the kitchen table. With British control, she reasons away her astonishment and speculates calmly: Could it be Pamela? Or Esther? Certainly not Linda, her golfing companion that weekend. At last, on her bedside table, she notices a man's watch, and the nature of her husband's betrayal all at once becomes clear.

In the tale which gives its name to the collection, the infidelity is aborted. After thirteen years of marriage, Monika and Jerome have little to say to each other. Her favors are solicited during a hunting weekend by their companion Stanislas, but when Jerome oddly spares the life of a splendid chamois (to whom the silken eyes of the title belong) after pursuing it for eight hours, Monika inexplicably falls back in love with him.

Death, be it animal or human, hovers over the entire collection. It is the obscure temptation (*The Lake of Loneliness*), the comic and menacing spectre (*Death in Espadrilles*), the absurd and not altogether unwelcome conclusion to dissipated and meaningless lives (*A Stylish Death*). Two accounts of suicide (*The Corner Café* and *The Five Diversions*) suggest that a contrived and violent end (by car crash, by gunshot) is better than a life without style. Note that the two characters in question kill themselves not after the discovery of a loved one's infidelity (like Anne in *Bonjour Tristesse*), but after viewing their own cancerous insides on a physician's x-rays. The counterparts of these two suicides are the brushes with death of the animals in two other stories—the chamois of *Silken Eyes* and the magnificent Spanish bull of *The Sun Also Sets*. The latter tale, whose title is, of course, an obvious take-off on Ernest Hemingway's *The Sun Also Rises,* is a delightfully unconventional bullfight story. In both these Sagan pieces, the proud untamed beast is spared—to the satisfaction of the sportsmen's women, who seem to divine in the reprieve a justification of their own impeccable, but useless and savage, splendor.

The most sustained treatment of death is *In Extremis,* a piece which evokes the reactions of a nameless character in his sickbed one Spring afternoon, as he tries to come to terms with his own imminent demise. By its concision, its neutrality of tone, its admixture of dialogue and interior recollection, its attempt to give form to the formless, its want of anything that might be called plot, *In Extremis* recalls the "tropisms" of another contemporary French writer, Nathalie Sarraute.

The author to whom Sagan is most often compared is, of course, not Sarraute, but Colette, and there is much in the present work to justify such comparison on the thematic level. The Colette *afficionado* will assimilate the adolescent summer lovers of *The Gentlemanly Tree* to Vinca and Phil of *The Ripening Seed;* and the juxtaposition of the casual and tragic attitudes toward adultery of wife and husband in *Silken Eyes* recalls those of the couple in *Duo.* But it is in *The Gigolo* that the reminiscences of Colette are most pervasive; this is a sort of miniature version of Colette's masterful presentation in *Chéri* of the aging mistress and her young lover. Both works posit a female character of about fifty (in the original version of *The Gigolo*, the heroine's age is given as "plus de cinquante ans"; the English translation unaccountably makes her "over sixty"). She is forceful, beautiful, and sensual, and keeps a gorgeous but bestial and vapid young lover. While the liaison of Chéri and Léa endures for six years, that of Nicholas and his mistress (she is never named) ends after six months. In each case there is a female friend/rival (Charlotte Peloux in *Chéri,* Mme Essini in *The Gigolo),* who is the same age as the central character, but her physical and moral caricature, a grotesque exteriorization of her own potential for decline and deterioration. At the conclusion of each affair, the woman confronts her own irremediably old image in the looking-glass, retires shivering and nervous to her oversized empty bed and plans, come morning, to leave Paris and autumn for the South, the metaphor for warmth and rejuvenation. Since *Chéri* is a full-length novel, while *The Gigolo* occupies a mere dozen pages, it would be unfair to attempt a sustained comparison. Suffice it to say that Colette's originality in *Chéri* resides doubtless in the creation of a gigolo of mythological proportions and an abandoned older woman who achieves grandeur and nobility (it is Chéri, not Léa, who commits suicide in the sequel; she lives on into a joyous old age), while Sagan's thrust is elsewhere. The short story heroine, product and symbol of a meretricious society, is in the last analysis nothing more than her own terrifying image in the mirror, and ill-equipped, therefore, to survive the departure of youth and sexuality, let alone survive it with dignity.

The enormous geographical sweep of the stories (they range in settings from Paris to Munich, London, Scotland, Italy, Spain, and even to Hollywood) serves, paradoxically, to tie them together: the leisured class they evoke is evidently everywhere the same. Sagan has encountered in the short story a form peculiarly congenial to her talents and proclivities. The futility and emptiness of the society which she characteristically paints find a compelling echo in the economy of treatment which she here accords them. In these eighteen stories, the author conjures up with swiftness and nimbleness the vacuity and stylized *ennui* of the affluent upper class. Literary form thus parallels and reproduces both condensation of style and sociological commentary.

Joan Hinde Stewart

THE SILMARILLION

Author: J. R. R. Tolkien (1892–1973)
Edited by Christopher Tolkien
Publisher: Houghton Mifflin Company (Boston). 365 pp. $10.95
Type of work: Myths, tales, and legends
Time: Prehistory
Locale: Valinor and Middle-Earth

A posthumously published work which consists of five divisions, each narrating myths of prehistoric times from the beginning of creation to the beginning of the Third Age, which is the age of men

> Principal characters:
> MELKOR
> FËANOR AND HIS FOUR SONS
> NUMEROUS GODS, ELVES, AND MEN

These myths of creation, tales of the settling and unsettling of the early dwellers in the earth, the conflicts of power and morality, and the ascription of powers and limits of power to the vast array of beings conjured up within the covers of this book, lend to this final work of J. R. R. Tolkien a scope and philosophical range of ideas which quite transcend the narrative. Tolkien begins at the very beginning: far earlier than time, far earlier than Judeo-Christian narrations begin, for he begins with the very creation of the gods (called Ainur in this account) and their earliest development under the tutelage of God. What these gods did in the beginning was sing, and through singing created language, and out of language and music created poetry. The power and the magic of words and music are one of the several insistent themes recurring throughout this book. By songs do the Valar learn and understand, by oaths and curses do the Eldar doom themselves and their allies, and by song and epic are heroic deeds and heroic deaths remembered and rewarded.

Readers of Tolkien's book can feel comfortable with his myths, for he knows well the devices of myth creation and wields them with mastery. His myths of the trees of light, their creation, radiant beauty, destruction at the hands of Ungoliant, and subsequent partial preservation in the form of the Silmarils and the sun and moon (with appropriate myths narrated for each), are central to the entire invention of the book. Throughout the First Age, Middle-Earth lies in the dimness of starlight, while Valinor is bathed in the radiance of the trees of light. By contrast, the Unlight of Ungoliant is the most hideous and most destructive evil in the book. Even Melkor-Morgoth, who corresponds in many ways to the devil, is afraid of so black an evil. This darkness, however, is summoned forth by Melkor, who, like Milton's Lucifer, was the favorite of Eru (or God) until in his pride and independence he defied Eru and the Ainur, and was therefore punished and ostracized.

Still echoing *Paradise Lost,* the rebellious Melkor seeks to wreak revenge upon the Ainur. In his pride, independence, and anger lie the beginnings of all evil and destruction. The trees of light are destroyed by Ungoliant and the earth is plunged into darkness, alleviated finally by the light of the sun and moon. These are explained as the final products of the trees of light: a flower of silver which becomes the moon; and a fruit of gold which becomes the sun. As in Greek mythology, these are guided by a young god and a young goddess through the sky by day and night. The parallels to and echoes of Greco-Roman and Judeo-Christian mythology and legend are numerous throughout the book, and are effective devices to lend a sense of authenticity and antiquity to the narrations.

The battle of good and evil, which apparently can never be resolved nor finally won on this earth because the proponents of each side are immortal, and because both are eternally committed to their stance, is the dominant theme of the book. The myths tell how the earth and its inhabitants, including Gods, Elves, Dwarves, and Men, came into being, and how evil and destruction began. The book is not really a hopeful or happy one, because the situation does not and cannot change. Throughout the ages of the earth, good and evil must be eternally locked in battle, which is essentially a battle between the Gods. Elves, Dwarves, and Men are depicted as being largely helpless and hapless pawns in these divine power struggles. The efforts made by Elves and Men are valiant, often heroic, but always doomed by conditions and forces beyond their control or even their comprehension. The Elves are doomed by the ancient oath of Fëanor, and the Men who join them as they move into Middle-Earth are then included in the doom, which cannot be recanted. The binding power of an oath, according to the Silmarillion, is beyond morality or choice, and firmly within the realm of the absolutes.

This absoluteness, the sense of inevitability, is totally in keeping with the sense of legend and myth which Tolkien is creating in this series of narratives. It all happened long ago and in another country, when the earth was young, and the rules were somehow different. Then he adds credibility to his myths by infusions and hints of other legends and myths, and by creation of a geography that could be some place not too unlike the British Isles. He uses special devices of language to establish links to the known and credible. The words which he has created as names for places, people, and events in his mythology bear strong phonological and morphological resemblances to Old English and Celtic. His words are not really authentic terms in either of those languages, but they often could be. Aside from the invented names themselves is the special use Tolkien makes of them to imply ancient age. He will give two or three names for the same character or phenomenon or place, to convey the idea that over a long period of time the different people or Elves or Gods have adopted different words, or that the names have changed through long ages of time, because of the movement of peoples, speaking different languages, perhaps. This device is effective in conveying the impression he strives for, but is one which seems to be rather overworked in this book. It ultimately becomes tiresome to the reader to have to sort out the several names for each person, place, or event mentioned when there are so many of each encompassed within the narrative.

Another device which the author uses to convey a tone of solemnity, authenticity, and antiquity is that of mimicking Biblical phraseology and cadences in his sentences. The authors of the King James version would surely recognize a kindred spirit in the author of *The Silmarillion* and might well have congratulated him for a careful imitation of their style. It is effective in *The Silmarillion* too. The concreteness of the imagery, the measured, ponderous flow of the clauses, the slightly archaic turn of phrase, and the lack of specific time reference together with vague suggestions of length of time involved in various episodes, all reinforce the impression that solemn, ancient truths are being narrated. One might even suggest that they are being intoned, for there is so much of a regular cadence to the lines that they might well be chanted, in the fashion of bards or sages passing on the legends of the past to a younger generation.

The cast of characters in *The Silmarillion* is vast, as is appropriate for a narration of such great scope. But since such vast sweeps of time are involved, and such a range of actions and events, the focus shifts often from one character to another, and no one character or small group of characters seems to dominate the narrative. Indeed, the tales, the plots of the various books and chapters, are the real focal points of interest. The characters, while frequently potentially interesting, tend to be rather flat and onesided, lacking depth and richness of development. Neither Elves nor Men nor Gods agonize over choices, mourn over losses, nor rejoice over gains in any way that seems very moving or elicits much sympathy from the reader. It may be that the very sense of remoteness contributes to this detachment as well. The carefully contrived fiction of reporting about the legendary past has interjected a distance too great for these characters to become vivid, sharply defined personalities. Having chosen to use this style and method of narration, the author has limited his possibilities of doing one of the things a modern novelist most strives to do: depict characters with vividness, depth, and conviction. Although these characters act out their roles in this splendid drama of creation, rebellion, conflict of good and evil, and love, loyalty, hate, and betrayal, they seem more to be the puppets of doom or of God than independent creatures. And their lives and fates are rather sad on the whole. Even in Valinor, the home of the Gods, things go downhill pretty steadily. All that Gods, Elves, and Men can do is make the best of things, and be wary of the evil which is always lurking nearby.

The first division, "The Ainulindalë," is the most poetic in its language and the most abstract in its concepts. It is the story of the creation of the world and the Gods and is suitably unsubstantial and vague in its descriptions, while being very broad and general in philosophical ideas. Neither the Creator nor the created Gods assume any definite personalities or identities.

In the second part, "The Valaquenta," the powers and the nature of the Gods are revealed. The Gods are given duties to perform on the earth, and the narrative tells how they shape and develop it, and devise a suitable home for themselves. In this section some personalities emerge: Gods receive names and differences between them are revealed. They apparently settle down to a kind of familiar domestic scene as they choose mates, engender future generations, and go about their tasks in a routine sort of way. Their tasks, however, are anything but routine. They bring about the greening of the earth, create the miraculous trees of light, establish relationships with the Elves, create Dwarves, and prepare the earth for the coming of Men. But with the emergence of differences, conflicts arise. And Melkor emerges as the embodiment of rebellion and evil, disrupting the harmony of the world and the Gods.

Later Melkor cunningly causes conflicts between Elves and Gods, and thus gains allies in his rebellion. Early on he had stolen the Silmarils, the three jewels created by Fëanor, the most gifted of the Elves. These jewels had embedded within them light from the sacred trees of Valinor, and were therefore irreplaceable after the trees were destroyed by the poison of Ungoliant. The fight of the Elves to recover the jewels from Melkor is the central theme of the third division of the book, called "The Silmarillion." The battle is a hopeless cause, as the Elves cannot win against Gods, even a God turned evil, unless it is the will of the almighty Eru himself. In this third division, the concreteness of detail, the variety of characterization, and the realism of the situations and events depicted increase somewhat.

The fourth and fifth divisions of the book, "The Akallabêth," and "Of the Rings of Power," tell of the downfall of the last of the kingdoms of the Elves and serve as a link between the Silmarillion and the trilogy of *The Lord of the Rings*. Perhaps because the final shaping of this book took place after the death of the author, or perhaps because the work was composed over the course of many years, there is some sense of disjointedness, of many episodes with a lack at times of any firm links or logical connections. There is also some repetition, and the introduction of a great many figures who are never developed in any substantial way, and which serve more to confuse or distract from the narrative than to add any meaning or purpose to it.

But if this book lacks some brilliance of imagery, charm of vivid characterization, and immediacy of adventures narrated, it compensates in other ways. It has a serenity, a charming prosodic melody of line, a solemn and all-embracing philosophical acceptance of the good and evil of this earth, and a reassuring conviction that God will resolve the conflicts in the end and order will be restored. Order, harmony, serenity, peace, and obedience to God's will are the ultimate values, lost through rebellion and conflict, and irrecoverable until the end of time. The author extols the valor of the warriors, but his heart is beyond the battle, yearning after the peace to come. The divine order must surely triumph; but meanwhile, Men and Elves and Dwarves must endure lives of disorder and peril, about which they can do very little. But they do endure, and even have the hope and courage to strive to accomplish many deeds. There is a merit in their dignity and in their defiance of their fate.

Betty Gawthrop

SOMBRERO FALLOUT

A Japanese Novel

Author: Richard Brautigan (1933–   )
Publisher: Simon and Schuster (New York). 187 pp. $6.95
Type of work: Novel
Time: The present
Locale: San Francisco and a small town in the Southwest

An American humorist tries to come to grips with the loss of his Japanese girl friend; and a sombrero falls from the sky in a small town in America, eventually leading to riots, bloodshed, and mayhem

The best thing about Richard Brautigan's new novel may well be the cover: like the original hardback, the paperback edition bears the design of a reclining Japanese woman and an alluring cat whose sumptuous hair and feline beauty reproduce and extend her own. Juxtaposed with the predominantly green design, the purple lettering of the title, *Sombrero Fallout,* promises whimsy as well as complexity. "Fallout" conjures up visions of the aftermath of a nuclear holocaust, while its inexplicable pairing with "sombrero," and the latter's connotations of the mores of Spanish America and the American Southwest, startle and mystify. The adjective of the subtitle, *A Japanese Novel,* both hints at an extension of the fallout theme (Pearl Harbor?) and suggests the necessity of a reinterpretation of "sombrero": does it carry here its obsolete meaning of an Oriental parasol, rather than, or in addition to, the more common one of a high-crowned, broad-brimmed Mexican hat?

The novel proper, wherein these various allusions are elucidated in a generally more straightforward fashion than one might have anticipated, begins in a manner not altogether direct: it inscribes itself in a certain modern tradition of fiction—that of the novel which functions as a reflection on itself. This particular quality is owing, in *Sombrero Fallout,* first of all to the presence of the author, or someone rather like him, as character: the central figure bears no name, only the epithet "an American humorist." Like Brautigan himself, who authored more than half a dozen collections of poetry and as many novels before the present work, the American humorist writes "books" and has achieved fame. He is initially engaged here precisely in composing a story about a sombrero falling out of the clear blue sky for no apparent reason and landing on Main Street, in front of the mayor, his cousin, and an unemployed man. The work begins in fact with quotation marks, for its opening sentences are being written at the typewriter of the American humorist. Before the first chapter's end, the author of the sombrero story has decided against continuing it, and has carefully torn up the paper into little pieces: capriciously destroyed, then, is everything we have just read about the sombrero. Eight tiny chapters later, we return to the almost empty wastepaper basket containing those scraps of paper. They seem, to the American humorist, to have a life of their own. In fact, they decide to do just that: to have a life of their own, to go on without him.

The story of the sombrero falling out of the sky in a hot and sleepy town, then, will tell itself as the reader reads it. It is now a text entirely independent of its maker, a story ostensibly without a teller. The device of the independent text is not new, of course, but it still captivates. And as the bizarre tale evolves, the American humorist, completely separated from his aborted but still viable novel, continues prey to his own grief: his Japanese girl friend of two years has recently left him. The resulting frustration and loneliness are what impair his creativity. Two stories (apparently related only in that he who initiated the one is the chief protagonist in the other) henceforth keep pace: the recital of the snowballing events in the little sombrero town and the account of the desolate lover trying to kill an evening at home.

First the more sentimental of the two. After succumbing to tears and demolishing the first paragraphs of his story at about 10:15 P.M., our American humorist, forelorn, heartsick, worried, intermittently hungry, sulks and mopes about his apartment. He decides against going out for a hamburger (just yesterday he ate two burgers; it's too soon for another), reconnoiters the refrigerator and kitchen cabinets for eggs (knowing full well he never keeps any), considers his inordinate liking for tuna fish sandwiches with mayonnaise and his inviolable resolve to consume no more of them (tuna contains higher than normal levels of mercury), telephones an old girl friend and immediately calls her back to cancel. He is obsessed with thoughts of his Japanese ex-mistress, recalling how they met (in a bar), how she had read his books and knew who he was, how he took her home and fumbled putting the key in the lock, how they slept together that first night. (He may be clumsy, lacking in humor, and not especially handsome, but he's an exceedingly good lover; that's why the girl—very exacting on that particular score—stayed with him so long in spite of her reservations.)

Yukiko, meanwhile, is sleeping peacefully sixteen blocks away in a suburb of San Francisco, infinitely relieved to be rid at last of her insecure and neurotic companion. Next time she won't choose an author: they require too much emotional upkeep. She dreams to the purring of her black cat, dreams of her adored dead father, who committed suicide and is buried in Japan; she dreams and her hair dreams too—it dreams of being carefully combed in the morning. In her dreams there is an umbrella purchased for her in Japan (an Oriental umbrella, therefore—a sombrero?). Yukiko, in fact, sleeps through the entire novel—whose fictional time covers, admittedly, only a little over an hour. One wonders why the artist portrayed her as open-eyed on the cover. While she sleeps, the American humorist almost goes mad when he finds, then loses, then finds once again, a single strand of long, black Japanese hair. At 11:15 he is sitting with a tight grasp on the recovered strand of precious hair and singing a Country-Western song of his own spontaneous invention, about loving a Japanese woman: "She's my little lady from Japan."

"Meanwhile back in the wastepaper basket," the tale of the misplaced size 7¼ sombrero perpetuates itself. At the mayor's behest, his cousin reaches to pick it up and instantly recoils: the hat is ice-cold. Political aspirations come into play (the cousin would dearly like to be mayor someday) and he begins crying uncontrollably—like the humorist himself, whose cheeks have known a steady stream of tears since Yukiko's departure a month earlier. A crowd gathers and within a short time the curious crowd is a rioting crowd. The mayor goes mad, and arms himself along with the rest of the populace; the governor is called in, but killed en route to the scene. The town is under siege. The National Guard, and then the President of the United States himself, must intervene. War correspondent Norman Mailer arrives and demonstrates remarkable courage and perseverance in covering his story.

If the two tales which constitute the novel are themselves somewhat vapid, their conjunction is provocative and confers on them more meaning than either would have alone. Thus the distress of the American humorist both precipitates and parallels the chaos in Main Street; the death and destruction which have the wastebasket as their theater are emblematic of his own private desolation. The stories organize themselves around a series of pairs or oppositions: bathos and frenzy; heat (the temperature of the town) and cold (the sombrero); hats and umbrellas; East and West; Asian calm (Yukiko is not only taciturn by nature, she is in addition a psychiatrist by profession) and Caucasian volubility; restful and restoring sleep (the woman's, the cat's) and frantic wakefulness (the humorist's); spontaneous generation (the sombrero story) and spontaneous effacement (Yukiko's dreams); hunger (the mayor's companion's, the humorist's) and satiety (the cat's).

The evocation of Norman Mailer at the scene of the riots is perhaps typical of the kind of parody and fantasy for which Brautigan won himself a sizable public a decade ago. Whether the events are familiar or outrageous, his tone remains casual, and Brautigan affects in general to use only simple declarative sentences. There are without any doubt some delightful images (the American humorist's worries are trained white mice scurrying after him, with voices more forceful than those of the Mormon Tabernacle Choir) and some amusingly absurd speculation (does the right eye or the left start crying first?).

But on the whole it is difficult to see why his style has been described as poetic. One need look no further than the reviews quoted on the back cover of the paperback edition for examples of such pronunciations: *Sombrero Fallout* is adjudged to be not merely intricate and subtle, it is "poetry written as prose," and "structural like a prose poem" (whatever that means). Where can this poetry reside? Surely the rather silly device of repeatedly indenting for each of a succession of short declarative sentences ("The cat jumped into bed." New paragraph. "The cat lay down beside her." New paragraph. "The cat did a moment's methodical cleaning of its front paws." New paragraph. "The cat used its tongue. . . ."), so that the passage contains as many paragraphs as sentences, does not suffice to constitute poetry. Nor, certainly, can expressions which are elliptical to the point of being only marginally intelligible ("she had lost the dimensions of her existence and what she wanted out of life") be thereby qualified as "poetic." Nor, finally, does the occasional gratuitous suppression of punctuation and syntax make for poetry in prose. Brautigan is, moreover, infuriatingly repetitious: many of the eighty-five extremely short chapters (some of them a mere four or five lines, and each sporting a one-word title which accentuates the effect of brevity) begin by recapitulating what has taken place in previous chapters. Each successive movement of the novel thus involves a contraction before the expansion, so that in spite of its occupying only 187 pages, it produces at times the impression of being agonizingly slow-paced.

This new novel—where the inspiration is not always in evidence, where the fictional devices are sometimes both blatantly factitious and rather hackneyed, and where the asides are occasionally downright sophomoric ("Interesting that this fact had not been brought up until now")—seems unlikely to make many converts for its author. But those who are already sensitive to the appeal of Brautigan will doubtless enjoy *Sombrero Fallout*. It is as droll, as unconventional, as understated, as eccentric as his previous works, and it affords in places the undeniable pleasure of recognition—recognition of familiar though unwonted attitudes, of minuscule feelings and of frames of mind which the reader has experienced, though of which he may have had only a threshold awareness.

Joan Hinde Stewart

SONG OF SOLOMON

Author: Toni Morrison
Publisher: Alfred A. Knopf (New York). 337 pp. $8.95
Type of work: Novel
Time: 1931 to 1962
Locale: A town in Michigan; Danville, Pennsylvania; Shalimar, Virginia

The story of the life of a black man in Michigan from his birth to age thirty-one

Principal characters:
> MACON DEAD, JR. (MILKMAN), the principal character in the novel
> GUITAR, Milkman's best friend
> MAGDALENE (LENA) AND FIRST CORINTHIANS (CORRIE), his sisters
> MACON AND RUTH DEAD, his parents
> AUNT PILATE, his father's sister and mother of Rebecca
> HAGAR, Milkman's mistress

The title of the novel refers to a children's song which is sung in part in the opening scene of the novel, recurs at intervals later, is heard in its entirety about four-fifths of the way through, and is the litany Milkman sings for the death of Pilate in the final scene. Associated with the song throughout the novel is death, bereavement, and flying. The bereaved sing this song of loss, this ballad of the flight into oblivion of Solomon, who leapt from a high outcropping of rock to return to his native Africa, leaving a grief-stricken wife and twenty-one children. And children chant this song as part of a game, a ritual remembrance of the event of long ago. Pilate sings the refrain as a funeral dirge, and finally Milkman himself sings the song as a lamentation for Pilate's death, as a final statement of his identity, and as an assertion of his love and courage to face life or death. The novel is laced with references to the supernatural or transcendent: ghosts appear to Pilate, Solomon flies, weird sounds of monas issue forth from Ryna's Gulch, and when the once passive Milkman leaps, and even soars, to his life-or-death confrontation with Guitar, his courage and assertion of willingness to fight for his life are an almost miraculous change from his former behavior.

The underlying theme of the whole story is love—the transmuting power of love to make life worthwhile: to give people the courage to live despite grueling adversity. Counterpoised to this theme of love is that of hate, and its deadly souring effect on all who harbor it within themselves. As the Biblical Song of Solomon is a song of love, so this novel is a song of the love of people for one another, and the effect it has on making the people who love, and those who are loved, endure and flourish.

It is the anguish of his loneliness and hatred which drives the insurance agent Smith finally to seek escape through his mad attempt to fly with cloth wings from the cupola of Mercy Hospital out across Lake Superior. We learn later that he is one of the Seven Days, who have dedicated their lives to murder. From the development of the character, Guitar, we learn how corrosive hate can be, so that finally Guitar suspects, condemns, and attempts to execute his best friend

Milkman, who is blameless in the matter of deception which Guitar accuses him of. Guitar, who has tried to justify his murderous ways by saying that they were acts of love for his own people, undertaken only as retribution against white people for their murders of blacks, finally is murdering for anger, suspicion, greed, and even pure carelessness, as when he kills Pilate arising from her father's graveside.

In the narrative, the action develops out of the static situation of the Macon Dead family, in which the parents live in a state of continual antagonism, erupting frequently into verbal confrontations and occasionally into physical assaults against the mother by the father. The mother's passiveness is deceptive, however: she provokes the father's anger by her remarks, and the children have learned that this is so.

The parents' warfare, which has blighted both their lives, is based on their perception of their relative social status. The mother was the daughter of the most prominent black man in town, a doctor of some wealth and social connections. She grew up as the adored and adoring only child of the widowed doctor. When the young, ambitious Macon Dead appeared in town from obscure and obviously lowly origins, he sought to marry Dr. Foster's daughter to enhance his own social status and to increase the amount of money available to him to invest in real estate. In short order he became embittered by the doctor's only slightly veiled haughtiness and scorn, and jealous of his young wife's continued ardent devotion to her father.

It is a triumph of the author's character development that even though we have been told of the relationship between the father and daughter from the father's point of view (it was not sexual, and he was somewhat embarrassed by her continued childlike closeness into her later teens), when Macon Dead tells Milkman of his conviction that his wife and father-in-law had been somehow sexually connected, the reader is, like Milkman, very nearly convinced. When finally the mother tells her version of the relationship she had with her father, Milkman and the reader are finally able to fit the confusing pieces together and see the situation with compassion and with despair—despair because there is no love to heal the breach between the husband and wife, despair because the anger and outrage at being rejected have poisoned them and are destroying their capacity to love and grow.

Milkman and his sisters are used by both parents. Both want to make the children into images of their own ideals and to make them reject the values and lifestyle of their mate. The mother wants Milkman to become a doctor like her father, and even suggests that he might take her maiden name as his own last name. She wants her daughters to marry well, and will consider as suitors only professional men. Then finally, when no such suitors appear, she considers that perhaps some civil worker like a postal employee might do. The father wants his son to join him in the real estate business he owns, and is adamant that the daughters shall choose men of ambition and status.

The father's covetousness, his manipulation of his power in the community, and his inability to love people or be loved by them, drives his children and his wife and indeed everyone from any warm relationship with him. Contrasted to Macon Dead's greed, suspicion, and self-righteousness is his sister Pilate's openness, trust, and love. She is all that he is not. She lives in the utmost simplicity, with generosity, kindness, and love motivating all her actions. Macon cannot accept her love, her generosity, her ethics, nor her forgiveness. He tells Milkman, "You want to be a whole man, you got to know the whole truth"; yet he himself is the one who is constantly diminished by his lack of knowledge or acceptance of the truth. He relies instead on suspicion and conjecture. Just as he suspects his wife of incestuous relationships with her father, he suspects his sister of taking and hoarding a cache of gold. Milkman realizes the hopelessness of trying to arouse any feeling for people in his father when the father makes it plain that he has no interest in going to Virginia to renew family ties with his people. He would only like to return to Pennsylvania where he could display his wealth and power pridefully to the men who remembered him as a small boy, and who would admire him for attaining wealth and prestige.

The boy Milkman is much influenced by the people who touch his life and urge him to adopt their ways. He is essentially passive, accepting all, choosing none. He accepts his father's offer to work in the real estate business, and conducts the business according to his father's ways. He accepts his mother's friends and social position, and enjoys parties and the social contacts of the best black social stratum. He accepts the love and generosity of Pilate and Hagar, and uses them both, without reciprocating in any real way.

Milkman joins Guitar and his "lower class" group for companionship and pleasure, but while he is personally loyal to Guitar as a friend, he rejects the code of ethics which Guitar espouses. But if he rejects this code of life based on hate, he likewise rejects the love and the responsibility of love which Hagar represents. He would seem, like his father and Guitar, to be eschewing love and espousing greed and selfishness when he rejects Hagar and plots to rob Pilate. The abortive robbery whets his appetite for wealth. What had been a half-hearted, clumsy attempt at a robbery becomes, after it is frustrated, a spur to him to seek the gold wherever it may be: in the hills of Pennsylvania or in Virginia if it is not in Michigan. Then he does not want his father or Guitar to go with him. He wants to get it himself. This shift from a passive to an active stance is the beginning of a change in Milkman. Guitar notices it at once, and is suspicious, believing that his friend has decided to cut him out.

But once out of his home community, Milkman encounters kindness, generosity, warmth, welcome, and acceptance by strangers. Confused at first, he finally responds in kind. He aids the freight yard worker who needs help to lift a heavy load. He accepts the embrace of the aged Circe and suppresses his revulsion at the filth and decay in which she lives. He feels a genuine chagrin when people are affronted by what they consider to be his arrogant ways. He is challenged, and fights for his right to be in Shalimar. But he finds peace among these people when he sinks exhausted against the tree and acknowledges that they can do things he cannot, and that these people, his people, have merit and pride in their accomplishments and talents which have nothing to do with wealth or social status.

In this new knowledge, in this revelation of the truth, the desire for the gold vanishes. Nor does it return again. He has found something more precious: a genuine respect for people, which rapidly ripens into affection. He seeks to learn from his past, his forbears, and his relations living still. He enjoys Sweet as he has never enjoyed a woman before. He even tries to convince the murderous Guitar that he is still his true and honest friend.

Returning home, he learns of Hagar's death, and while he acknowledges that he never loved her and never could, he accepts his guilt and regret that he caused her such anguish. He takes from Pilate the box of Hagar's hair, and takes it home to keep, to remember his guilt and his relationship to her. Earlier Hagar had told Pilate that Milkman hated her hair, that he liked smooth, silky, copper-colored hair. The black kinky hair of Hagar is a potent symbol of Milkman's change of attitude. He has accepted his relationship to his people, though they be poor, uneducated, and strange in their ways.

With this acceptance, with this new evaluation of the worth of man and his worldly goods, he comes to see Pilate as the ideal person. Her death transforms him. He is infused with her spirit of love—her dying wish to have been able to love more people—and he sings louder and louder the Song of Solomon. It is chanted as a dirge, a conviction, and a promise. He rises, in the splendor of his love and grief, and literally soars to his confrontation with hatred and evil in the person of his friend Guitar.

The magic of flying and the association with love and loss are pervasive throughout the book. Solomon leapt from the bluff to fly back to his beloved Africa and his people there. When Jake the son of Solomon was shot, he soared five feet into the air before falling dead to earth. As he cradles the dying Pilate in his arms, Milkman observes that she could fly without ever leaving the ground. Then he flies too, in his new control of himself, in his new awareness of his power to make his life increase in all the important ways of loving and giving.

The strength and complexity of the main characters make it difficult to label them simplistically, although they certainly embody thematic concepts within their character development. For if Guitar embodies the idea of the curdling of righteous resentment into evil for its own sake, he is also the one who chides Milkman for his cavalier treatment of Hagar, and who solicitously urges him to give up smoking and drinking. Again, Milkman's father seems to have almost no warmth or affection in him, yet he becomes tender and gentle when reminiscing about his father and recalling the happiness and affection they shared when working in the fields together many years before. Even Freddie's gossipy malice hides a wistful loneliness, and Milkman's sisters turn out to have unexpected depth of character when First Corinthians finally falls in love and defies the family to be with Henry.

The world of this story is entirely black. No white characters really enter it at all. The whites exist only as a nebulous menace, a reported encounter, a faceless power. If this is possibly unrealistic, it has the artistic merit of eliminating the unessential and concentrating the story on the thematically important issues, without introducing elements which might be confusing or distracting in the development of the central idea.

Some potentially interesting and complex characters are introduced and then dropped or minimized. One could wish to learn more about them, but the story would have had to be longer to do that, perhaps without being any better, only richer in subplots and characterizations. But the novel does not need that; it has all it needs of people and events. It moves swiftly and effortlessly through its time and space, as events, encounters, and narrations impinge on the consciousness of Milkman. Then in Part Two, Milkman comes alive and begins to shape events, and to formulate his own design for living. The Song of Solomon, the song of love and flying and total commitment, has become his song, and he understands it even as Pilate did. The dialogue has such a ring of authenticity that the melody of the words is almost audible in print. Descriptive passages fit in well and are notably clear and concise.

The book ends just as the battle to the death between Guitar and Milkman is beginning. And yet the book seems complete, for the most important thing has happened. Whether he lives or dies, Milkman has become a courageous, actively committed, loving human being, indifferent to wealth, appearances, and superficialities. He is his own man, knowing what he believes, and ready to fight to the death for it, but eager to live and to seek out and share love.

This story of a life is really a story of many lives, for all his people share in Milkman's life, as he shares in theirs. And this is part of the story too, that belonging, support, and understanding are more precious than gold, and more lasting. Pilate is the strongest character in the book, by far; but this is finally Milkman's story. For he learns from her and from others, and chooses her way, although the way of the fliers is disruptive, anarchic, unrealistic, and unprofitable. Indeed, it is dangerous unto death, the story tells, but it is also the way of fulfillment and life, and Milkman chooses his way with rejoicing.

Betty Gawthrop

STORIES THAT COULD BE TRUE
New and Collected Poems

Author: William Stafford (1914–   )
Publisher: Harper & Row Publishers (New York). 267 pp. $10.95
Type of work: Poetry

A volume containing all five of William Stafford's previous books, and forty-one new poems

A crass fact which needs to be mentioned is that this book is one of the best bargains available to readers of poetry. At a time when the price of books is increasing recklessly, Harper & Row offer this magnificent collection at a price far lower than they might have gotten away with in these inflationary times. Aside from the new collection which gives the book its title, there are gathered here all the poems from Stafford's previous collections: *West of Your City* (1960), *Traveling Through the Dark* (1962), *The Rescued Year* (1966), *Allegiances* (1970), and *Someday, Maybe* (1973).

West of Your City was published in an elegant limited edition by a small press; except for a few poems which have been widely anthologized, and fourteen which were reprinted in *The Rescued Year*, the work in it has been unavailable for several years. It turns out to be a first book of great maturity, distinctiveness, and understated power; Stafford, it seems, is among those rare poets who do not publish a book before they have hit their stride. We are in danger now of taking Stafford's particular stride for granted, but it must have been come by courageously. The decade of the 1950's was a strange one for American poetry; it was the era of what George Garrett called "the phony war," the much-discussed conflict between the so-called Beats and the so-called Academics. When Stafford won the National Book Award for *Traveling Through the Dark*, there were some who applauded him for having learned something from each of the two camps, to make a poetry which was both energetically American and technically civilized. The obvious fact is that he was developing his unique style before the "phony war" was thought of. It is a style reminiscent of that of Robert Frost, an earlier loner of gentle fierceness. In meters that are never too insistent, yet never out of control, the poems in *West of Your City* record the observations of a questing spirit—evoking the past, revealing in the present many small but significant signs of where we are, and heading westward, into the future. The diction is discursive, almost conversational, but everywhere in these poems shines Stafford's amazing gift for arranging ordinary words into resonant truth and mystery: "Wherever we looked the land would hold us up."

Though *West of Your City* was out of print before it received the attention it deserved, *Traveling Through the Dark* immediately established Stafford as a poet of rare gifts and unusual productivity. As the citation of the poetry judges for the National Book Award put it, "William Stafford's poems are clean, direct and whole. They are both tough and gentle; their music knows the value of silence." True enough; and one is then awestruck to realize that these splendid poems—seventy-six of them, enough for two collections—were published only two years after *West of Your City.* As James Dickey once said, it appears that poetry is not only the best way for Stafford to say what he wants to say; it is also the easiest. This may be an exaggeration, but it is true that even in the most casual of circumstances, Stafford's utterances can have the distinctive and memorable flavor of his poetry, as when he closes a letter, "So long—I look toward seeing you everywhere."

In *Traveling Through the Dark,* the major advance over the first book is in breadth of tone. In a style that is low-key but distinctive, it is sometimes hard to find ways of breaking into humor, or of keeping all subjects from sounding as if they had equal significance. When one analyzes this potential difficulty in *Traveling Through the Dark,* one begins to think that Stafford has a talent, never quite indulged, for self-parody. That is, he is attuned to the effects he can create, and so sensitive to various modes of surprise, that even within a restricted range of word choices, he can be haunting, wistful, or slyly humorous.

"Thinking for Berky" and "Adults Only" make a useful comparison in this respect. "Thinking for Berky" is a recollection of a girl who lived outside the world the speaker knew, but who deeply touched his world in spite of that:

> The wildest of all, her father and mother cruel,
> farming out there beyond the old stone quarry
> where highschool lovers parked their lurching cars,
> Berky learned to love in that dark school.
>   * * *
> Windiest nights, Berky, I have thought for you,
> and no matter how lucky I've been I've touched wood.
> There are things not solved in our town though tomorrow came:
> there are things time passing can never make come true.

In these, the second and fourth of the poem's five stanzas, many of the qualities that make Stafford's poetry what it is are at their best. The meter is, strictly speaking, unstable; but though some of the lines are strict iambic pentameter, and others stray from that toward fourteen syllables, the rhythmical rightness of each line is firmly there, not to be quarreled with. Similarly, the rhyme is the very opposite of insistent; though the rhymes between the first and fourth lines of each stanza are solid and true, there is enough between the rhymes to keep them from being a gentle and mysterious reminder that this is utterance weighed and wrought. Within this delicate scheme, the sentences move easily from immediate description to generalization and back again, "the voice," as Richard Howard says, "never raised above the sound of one man talking to another man at nightfall outdoors." And yet there is something almost bravura in the calm statements of large truths: "there are things time passing can never make come true."

Many of the same qualities—discursiveness, directness, delicacy of meter, specificity of description, definitiveness of general statement—are to be found in

"Adults Only," a recollection of an evening at the state fair, in the tent reserved for the strip-tease act. The poem begins with a general statement: "Animals own a fur world;/ people own worlds that are variously, pleasingly, bare." The rest of the stanza recalls how those worlds came clear to "us kids" the night they found themselves in that tent. The poem ends:

> Better women exist, no doubt, than that one,
> and occasions more edifying, too, I suppose.
> But we have to witness for ourselves what comes for us,
> nor be distracted by barkers of irrelevant ware;
> and a pretty good world, I say, arrived that night
> when that woman came farming right out of her clothes,
> by God,
>
> At the state fair.

Certain lines in this stanza—the first two, the last four—are quite clearly different from anything in "Thinking for Berky." They are looser, more conversational; but only a few of the *words*—"pretty good," for example—are foreign to the diction of the other poem. The use of the word *farming* in each poem is instructive: in "Thinking for Berky" the context gives the word a hard and desperate sound, as if the parents farmed mostly with sickles and whips. In "Adults Only" the word is quirky but exact: the woman comes rolling out of her clothes like a combine out of a wheatfield.

Within a narrow, understated sytlistic range, then, it is possible to create an explosion with far less energy than would be required if one were, say, Allen Ginsberg. But the tact and finesse that control the energy must be of a very high order indeed.

In *The Rescued Year,* there are many poems which surprise only because they did not exist before; they are otherwise very much like Stafford's earlier work. As he says at the end of "Believer,"

> You don't hear me yell to test the quiet or try to shake
> the wall, for I understand that the wrong sound weakens
> what no sound could ever save, and I am the one
> to live by the hum that shivers till the world can sing:—
> May my voice hover and wait for fate,
> when the right note shakes everything.

However, in this book Stafford tries a number of things he has not previously explored very deeply. The title poem is a fine evocation of a year of happiness lived in his youth, when his father had a job in another town, and moved the family there. The poem is longer and more leisurely than most of Stafford's earlier poems. And in "Following the *Markings* of Dag Hammarskjöld: a Gathering of Poems in the Spirit of His Life and Writings," Stafford fashions a moving long sequence of related poems, the more valuable because they do not depend too heavily on the inspiration acknowledged in the title. And in "The Animal That Drank Up Sound," he creates a myth of remarkable freshness, which has yet that flavor of folklore that makes it sound ancient. The first part of the poem tells how the animal came down and swallowed the sounds of the earth, until at last all sound was gone, and he starved. In the second part, the world lay silent for months, until a cricket, who had been hiding when the animal came by, awoke to a heavy stillness, and with one tentative sound, brought everything back:

> It all returned, our precious world with its life and sound,
> where sometimes loud over the hill the moon,
> wild again, looks for its animal to roam, still,
> down out of the hills, any time.
> But somewhere a cricket waits.
>
> It listens now, and practices at night.

The boldness of this poem and others in *The Rescued Year* is carried forward into *Allegiances* and *Someday, Maybe*. The strain of odd metaphor against discursive diction is rewardingly increased: "He talked like an old gun killing buffalo,/ and in what he said a giant was trying to get out."

As always, any observation might start a poem, but in *Allegiances* Stafford seems freer to let the observation go either as far as necessary, or to let it stop when it should. Several of these poems are long, leisurely, and meditative; others are fleeting, fragmentary, but complete, like "Note":

> straw, feathers, dust—
> little things
>
> but if they all go one way,
> that's the way the wind goes.

Sometimes these small observations are gathered in bunches under one title, like "Brevities" or "Religion Back Home." These clusters of short poems make up items which are rather different from most poems; the tension between their disparateness, and their being gathered under one title, reminds us of Stafford's sense of his vocation: "The world speaks everything to us./ It is our only friend."

More and more often in *Allegiances* and *Someday, Maybe*, Stafford evokes the spirits of those whose ancestors lived here before the white man came. "People of the South Wind," for example, is a mythic explanation of where a person's breath goes after he dies; the tone is radically conversational, even for Stafford, but the effect is, magically, dignified. And the title poem of *Someday, Maybe*, "The Eskimo National Anthem," recalls a song, "Al-eena, Al-wona," that echoes often through the speaker's daily life. The phrase is translated as "Someday, Maybe." (It must be noted here that a small misfortune has befallen this collected edition: "Someday" is misprinted as "Somebody.") The poem ends with the observation that the song might be to blame if the speaker's life never amounts to anything, though it is a comforting keepsake. The paradox is gracefully concealed; it is hardly possible, in the poetic world of William Stafford, to notice so much, and still live a life that amounts to nothing.

The collection of new poems, *Stories That Could Be True,* extends the range of Stafford's apparently boundless empathy. Many of the speakers in these poems are not the observer, but the thing observed—wind, seeds, trees, ducks—and they speak of how things are with them, in a voice that is of course truly Stafford's, but which is profoundly convincing; it is a lively extension of the myth-making tendency that began to be displayed in *The Rescued Year.* It is also noteworthy that in these most recent poems, Stafford often permits himself a strictness of meter and rhyme that has been rare in his earlier work; he has usually preferred to suggest a form rather than commit himself fully to it; but there are poems here whose simplicity, memorableness, and charm are like the verses people who speak English have had in their heads from childhood. It takes a lifetime of thoughtful and ambitious work to arrive at the stage where one can write a miniature masterpiece like "At the Playground," which in its way can speak for what Stafford has been up to all along, and for what he will be looking for in the books to come:

> Away down deep and away up high,
> a swing drops you into the sky.
> Back, it draws you away down deep,
> forth, it flings you in a sweep
> all the way to the stars and back
>   Goodby, Jill; Goodby, Jack:
> shuddering climb wild and steep,
> away up high, away down deep.

Henry Taylor

THE STREET OF CROCODILES

Author: Bruno Schulz (1892–1942)
Translated from the Polish by Celina Wieniewska. Introduction by Jerzy Ficowski
Publisher: Penguin Books (New York). 160 pp. $2.95
Type of work: Short stories
Time: Early twentieth century
Locale: Drogobych, Poland

A short collection of autobiographical stories about Bruno Schulz's life in a small Polish town which combines a flair for surrealistic exaggeration with a sensitivity to physical stimuli

> Principal characters:
> JOSEPH, the narrator
> JACOB, Joseph's father
> MOTHER
> ADELA, the housekeeper

Forty-three years after they were originally published in Poland under the title, *Cinnamon Shops,* Penguin Books has reissued a small collection of short stories by Bruno Schulz, now entitled *The Street of Crocodiles.* Schulz is little known by the American reading public, and his obscurity is based upon his small volume of output (one other collection of short stories, *Sanatorium under the Sign of the Hourglass,* and a novella, *The Comet)* and upon the fact that he has been dead for thirty-five years.

The details of Schulz's death become an allegory for his life and for Poland, his native land. When he was born in 1892, Poland did not exist as a political entity. Drogobych, his home town, was in Galicia, a province of the Austro-Hungarian Empire, which had helped to eradicate the state of Poland almost one hundred years earlier. Poland achieved a brief independence between the end of World War I and the late 1930's when again it was divided, this time by Germany and Russia. When independence came again following World War II, it was not complete freedom, for Drogobych remains today in the U.S.S.R. (Perhaps because of the political domination at the time he was a child, Schulz had a fluent command of German, but all his writing was in Polish.)

In addition to being born in a "nonexistent" country, Schulz also was born into a social class with which he had no commonality. That is, theoretically he was Jewish, but neither he nor his family had real contact with the larger Jewish community in the area. Thus, it is doubly absurd that his death came as part of the anti-Semitic murders carried out by the Nazi S.S. In 1942 while outside the ghetto on an official pass, Schulz was gunned down in the street during Drogobych's "Black Thursday," a day which brought death to one hundred and fifty unfortunate persons. When evening came, a friend took Schulz's body to the Jewish cemetery for burial. Friends had urged him to escape from Drogobych, had provided him with false papers and with funds, but he chose to stay, for he preferred seclusion and isolation, even if it meant a ghetto existence.

When he was killed, a manuscript on which he was working, *The Messiah,* was given to another friend for safekeeping.

Today, Bruno Schulz, the cemetery where he was buried, his manuscript, and the manuscript's custodian do not exist; all were destroyed by the ruthless brutality, the inexplicable horror of the Holocaust.

One can only speculate, of course, whether Schulz would have produced more stories or whether he would have gained greater fame if he had lived, for writing and publishing were difficult things for him to do. He supported himself by teaching drawing in the local high school, although he preferred to create word pictures. His desire for isolation—which kept him in the out-of-the-way-Drogobych—also made him reluctant to expose his stories to public scrutiny. In fact, the works in *The Street of Crocodiles* were first written as personal letters to a friend, and it was only at her insistence that he offered them for publication. As Ficowski says in his introduction, "It was in this way, letter by letter, piece by piece, that *The Street of Crocodiles* came into being, a literary work enclosed a few pages at a time in envelopes and dropped into a mailbox."

What impressed Schulz's correspondent was a series of thirteen stories, each capable of standing as a separate unit but all linked together to describe a late-summer-to-early-spring period in the life of a small boy, Joseph, who serves as narrator. Joseph, obviously, is Bruno Schulz, just as the dry-goods shop in the stories is Schulz's father's shop. The father in the stories, Jacob, has the same name as Schulz's father. Schulz once admitted the stories could be classified as an "autobiographical novel" because one could see in them experiences and events from his own childhood. Thus, they are "true" stories, at least to that extent. "They represent my style of living, my particular lot. The dominant feature of that lot is a profound solitude. . . ."

Another dominant feature is a chilling strangeness, a multitude of peculiarities which, in the context of the stories and of the family portrayed, seem only unusual, but which, viewed outside those contexts, seem bizarre. From Jacob, who suddenly withdraws from business one day and begins his winter-long descent into madness, to Adela, the housekeeper, who supports and confronts the madness, to the mother, who attempts to ignore much of what is happening, the house is full of persons who could exist only within those walls. Surely Schulz has taken literary liberties with these strange personages, fictionalized versions of the family he knew and apparently loved.

The most unusual person is Jacob, who voluntarily confines himself to bed, where he spends weeks scrutinizing financial ledgers, making entries and corrections. Finally, when he proudly shows the books to the family, the pages are filled not with notations of profit and loss, but with decals he has laboriously pasted in. With that finished, Jacob begins to disappear—into closets, neglected and forgotten vacant rooms, and the attic—for days on end. No one attempts to stop him, no one forces him to maintain minimal contact with reality except Adela, who occasionally reprimands him, especially when he establishes an aviary of exotic creatures in the attic.

The incidents describing Jacob's bird fancying, those which detail his maniacal obsession with cockroaches and tailors' dummies, and the story of the uncle who is transformed into a bell and rings himself to death constitute almost half of the stories. At one point, Joseph admits Jacob may not have been transformed into the stuffed condor who sits bleakly staring at the family but might have turned into one of the cockroaches he was frantically killing, "leaping from one chair up to another with a javelin in his hand."

When Joseph describes his father assuming the behavior and characteristics of a cockroach, one begins to wonder if Schulz's major literary influence was another German-speaking resident of the Austro-Hungarian Empire, Franz Kafka, who died about the time Schulz began to write. It is impossible not to think of Kafka's "The Metamorphosis," which describes another human-being-become-insect, when one reads the portions of Schulz's book about the cockroaches. Schulz did, in fact, translate Kafka's *The Trial* into Polish, but that did not take place until the 1930's, before which time he showed no significant awareness of Kafka. Perhaps it is only coincidence that both men describe the strange transformation of men into insects.

If one separates these surrealistic fantasies from the rest of the book, one is left with an equally striking remainder, memories which re-create physical stimuli in striking prose. One is tempted to fill pages with extended quotations, for there is no way to write *about* Schulz's style which does justice to it. His training as an architect and his drawing-teacher profession both show strongly in the concise, deft word pictures he presents for the reader.

The first story, "August," establishes time and place for the entire volume. It is a hot, searing month Joseph describes. But instead of pages evoking images of profuse perspiration and debilitating, heat-induced fatigue, Joseph describes persons he passes in the square whose faces are obscured by a "grimace of heat—as if the sun had forced his worshippers to wear identical masks of gold." Thus the reader can form a mental picture similar to one Schulz might have drawn if he had illustrated the book (and he did provide illustrations for his second volume of stories). Some commentators have spoken of Schulz's hunger for and sensual responsiveness to physical stimuli, which is well illustrated in another line from "August." Although the sun is almost blinding in its brilliance, Joseph and his mother choose to walk in its light in order to create interesting shadows. "Thus my mother and I ambled along the two sunny sides of Market Square, guiding our broken shadows along the houses as over a keyboard."

Another section which is tightly packed with images is that of the "Cinnamon Shops," so-called because of the "dark paneling on their walls." On an ordinary summer day or a cold winter night, such shops, full of exotica from strange lands—magic boxes, incense, mandrake root, mechanical toys, parrots and toucans, strange and rare books—were usually quickly passed by. But on a night when the first breezes of spring arrived, when the snow became "a harmless fleece, smelling sweetly of violets," the cinnamon shops became "truly noble," and easily could keep a small boy from his prescribed errands. These are breathtaking images, paragraphs packed with the bare bones of long chapters. Schulz simply presents them and passes on to other things.

Not all the strange persons Schulz describes are residents of his own home, and he tells us of two others who are residents of Drogobych: Pan, the mad tramp whom Joseph discovers laughing madly in the briar patch, and Touya, "the half-wit girl," who often sleeps in a garishly painted bed in the town dump. When Maria, Touya's mother, dies, Schulz presents a unique conception of life and death. "Maria's time—the time imprisoned in her soul—had left her and—terribly real—filled the room, vociferous and hellish in the bright silence of the morning. . . ."

These ideas of a definite amount of time being allotted to each person, and of time being an independent entity which leaves the body at death, begin to create for the reader a feeling of timelessness, of time as something which has always been and always will be. Later, when discussing the puppy, Nimrod (who walked with "an awkward oblique roll in an undecided direction, along a shaky and uncertain line"), Schulz describes the dog's maturation process as being essentially an unlearned set of behaviors. That is, when faced with a new situation, Nimrod had only to "dip into the fount of his memory, the deep-seated memory of the body" where he found "ready-made within him . . . the wisdom of generations . . . of which he had not been aware but which had been lying in wait, ready to emerge."

As mentioned earlier, Schulz apparently had no strong ties to the rest of the Jewish community, to the most readily available genealogical extended family. Instead it appears—on the basis of his comments about Maria's time and Nimrod's memory—that Schulz's link is to all living creatures in a vast, Jungian-like collective unconscious. This tie to the past, to life and to living, also appears in Joseph's discovering animals in the park one snowy night which he was sure were the same animals he had seen in the display cabinets in school. Although these animals had been dead and stuffed for so long their fur was falling off, they felt "on that white night in their empty bowels the voice of the eternal instinct, the mating urge, and returned to the thickets for short moments of illusory life."

Thus, Bruno Schulz, who longed for isolation, for protection from attachments which might overpower his creative desires, in fact had the strongest of ties to all animal life, past and present, ordinary and exotic, sane and mad. This loner was in fact the most attached of persons. It is these ties, these attachments which are so marvelously re-created in *The Street of Crocodiles*.

John C. Carlisle

SYLVIA PLATH
The Woman and the Work

Editor: Edward Butscher
Publisher: Dodd, Mead & Company (New York). 242 pp. $8.95
Type of work: Essays

A collection of both critical and reflective essays about Sylvia Plath and her work

Poets have, in recent years, found the life of the poet and the experience of poetic creativity increasingly hard to sustain. The school of modern American poetry termed "confessional" has aspired to a kind of total public honesty, a public self-examination and airing of private anguish, an open leap into the anxiety of unpredetermined creative process, which has taken its toll. In all too short a time, Sylvia Plath, John Berryman, and Anne Sexton, among others, have found the step into the private blackness of self-inflicted death a choice preferable to continuing in the merciless self-scrutiny in the public eye seemingly necessary for their craft. Such tragic figures fascinate us; frequently they become more popular after their suicides than they ever were before. Each death conjures up images of the shortlived Romantic poets of a century ago. Each suicide provokes endless postmortems, endless analyses of the person, the craft, the society, to try to make sense of what to most of us seems a totally senseless act. Some of our interest comes from a sense of loss, of being cut off from a vibrant and living poetic voice; some of it may well come from a human fascination with death, especially in its self-inflicted form.

For whatever the reason, Sylvia Plath's death has created an industry of post-mortem volumes—reprintings of her work, collections of her unpublished writings and letters, and this volume, an anthology of writings both about Plath and about her work. The risk in all this is that the real achievements of Plath the poet can easily get lost in efforts to use her tragic life for a writer's own ends. A good place to begin in this volume, therefore, is not at the beginning but at the end, with Irving Howe's sensitive "The Plath Celebration: A Partial Dissent." Howe points to the dangers—that a good but minor poet's achievements will be lost in the rush to proclaim her great, that such lives as hers lead often to the sort of sweeping romantic generalization that would claim that all poets run the risk of dying young. But he also points to the real achievements, the real poetic gifts, the truly fine poetic moments. Howe's balanced approach will serve as a touchstone for the rest of the essays in this volume; like it, the best ones strive for balance and realism, while unlike it, the worst put Plath to their own uses, to rage against imagined injustices or to celebrate a black and nihilistic vision of our age.

Edward Butscher must be complimented that most of the essays in this volume are of the former kind. He has brought together seventeen of them, nine of memoirs, some written especially for this volume, and eight of criticism, all reprinted from prior sources. It is the memoirs which are the most given, in this volume, to excess. Laurie Levy's "Outside the Bell Jar" traces her own emerging sense of herself as a writer, which she credits in part to Plath's influence; but to see Plath as a kind of muse of youthful agony, is to give in to the easy temptation to make of her a personal icon. Much the same sort of thing fills Paula Rothholz's memorial poem "For Sylvia at 4:30 A.M.," where Plath's suicide becomes a protest against a world which would render her impotent and delight in her fall. We can never know what brought Plath to kill herself, but such speculation, to serve one's own ends, can only do a disservice to the private dignity of the dead.

Fortunately, all the memory-pieces are not of this vein. The best are personal reflections on who Plath was, and what it was like to know her. Gordon Lameyer's "Sylvia at Smith" gives us an image of Plath as a diligent college student, just beginning to write, eager to do well, but already troubled, already too eager to please, already too dependent on the opinions of others. Dorothea Krook's "Recollections of Sylvia Plath" presents the young American in England, at Cambridge, where she studied on her Fulbright Scholarship. It chronicles her efforts to do as well in her new studies as she did in her old, her eagerness in studying Plato, her marriage to the English poet Ted Hughes. What comes through Krook's essay is a sense of guilt, a sense that something might have been done, that some word might have been said, some time spent, that would have made a difference. It is a natural reaction, as natural as the shock with which Krook says she received news of Plath's death, and it makes this piece perhaps the best of the memoir-essays in Butscher's volume.

The other essays in this section are complimentary; notable among them are Jane Kopp's " 'Gone, Very Gone Youth': Sylvia Plath at Cambridge, 1955–1957," a view of Plath by a fellow American graduate student; Clarissa Roche's "Sylvia Plath: Vignettes from England," which describes her visit to Smith after Cambridge, and something of her life back in England; and Elizabeth Sigmund's "Sylvia in Devon: 1962," which tells of an English friendship which endured until the end. Characteristic of these essays is a sense of loss, a sense of surprise, a sense of what might have been, subsumed in a warmth of memory, which is so much better a tribute than Levy's romantic idolatry or Rothholz's angry projections. Butscher introduces this section with his own memories of his discovery of Plath's work and his increasing interest in her life. His own tone of compassionate search for the real person behind the legend establishes a useful perspective for the reader who wishes to use his work as an entry into the study of Plath.

Overall, the eight critical essays are useful and well done, balanced in their reading of Plath's work and realistic in their assessment of its quality. Pamela Smith's "Architectonics: Sylvia Plath's Colossus" locates Plath in the tradition of confessional poetry by reminding us that Plath and Anne Sexton both took a poetry class from Robert Lowell in the late 1950's. Smith's view of Plath's earlier poems, printed in the *Colossus* volume, is higher than some critics have held it. She sees them as apprentice poems, but as such they are remarkable for their formal qualities and for their use of all the resources at the poet's command. Even so, in the light of what was to come, in both life and art, they seem to keep the real passions and desperations of the author's life at a distance.

Marjorie G. Perloff, in her "On the Road to *Ariel*: The 'Transitional' Poetry of Sylvia Plath," continues what, in Butscher's ordering, is really a chronological survey of the poet's work. The subject here is the poetry of two posthumous volumes, *Crossing the Water* and *Winter Trees*, which contain poems written between *Colossus* and *Ariel*, the collection of poems on which Plath's reputation is really based. Perloff laments the casual editing of these volumes, and the fact that some of their contents are not "transitional" at all, but contemporaneous with either the earlier or the later collection. Nevertheless, she does venture some comments on the emergence of the "Ariel" style, which she finds, finally, to be more limited in range and power than many have claimed. In a lengthy essay, Gordon Lameyer, in his second article in this volume, attempts to explore what he calls "The Double in Sylvia Plath's *The Bell Jar*." This essay, like the first, is marred by an amateur attempt at literary psychoanalysis; nevertheless, it does give us some perceptive insights into Plath's moving and fascinating auto-biographical novel.

Constance Scheerer's "Deathly Paradise of Sylvia Plath" finds a profoundly paradoxical view of life at the center of Plath's work, a sense that the pursuit of life can only lead to death, that the pursuit of meaning can only lead to nonmeaning. She traces the development of garden imagery in Plath's work, a pattern of imagery that suggests, finally, that its author could survive neither within nor without the garden of the world, or the garden of her own imagination. Arthur K. Oberg's "Sylvia Plath and the New Decadence" seeks to locate her work in the grand romantic, imagistic tradition of poetry that stretches back to Smart and Blake, while Robert Phillips provides a Freudian reading, finding in Plath's relationship with her father the source of her personal despair as well as of her poetic language.

The best and most persuasive essay in this section, however, is that of Joyce Carol Oates, herself no stranger to violence and despair used as the subject matter of literature. Oates, in her "The Death Throes of Romanticism: The Poetry of Sylvia Plath," sees Plath as a genuinely tragic figure, tragic in the limitations of her vision, yet helpful for understanding the pathology of our culture. Oates sees in Plath a sense of aloneness, an experience of nature as nightmare, a divisiveness of self, which could lead only to rejection of relationships with others and with the world. This paranoid sensibility is for Oates an option in our time, and that itself is tragic. But the perception that it is not the only option is what sustains many, and enables them to turn from despair, if not to hope, then at least to life.

The image of Plath that emerges from this volume, then, is one of sadness and of loss, one of a lonely and almost pathetic figure crushed by the world she expected to crush her, perhaps even wanted to crush her. Butscher has done us a great service in putting this volume together, to help us see Sylvia Plath plain, without much of the excessive speculation and romanticizing that so easily attaches itself to such a figure. It is when we see her clearly that the real achievement of her work can emerge—a record of what it is like to be in a world that is hell, and to realize that it is, at least in part, of one's own making.

John N. Wall, Jr.

T. E. LAWRENCE

Author: Desmond Stewart (1924–   )
Publisher: Harper & Row Publishers (New York). Illustrated. 352 pp. $15.00
Type of work: Biography
Time: 1888–1935
Locale: England and the Middle East

The third major biography in a decade about the man known as Lawrence of Arabia, a British soldier, archaeologist, and author who was a legend in his own time

T. E. Lawrence, that extraordinary if enigmatic figure who captured the battle-wearied imagination of the West after World War I, once again has surfaced as the subject of a major biography. In fact, the present study by Desmond Stewart is the third major biography of Lawrence to appear in the last decade. The reasons for Lawrence's enduring reputation, however, are plain enough. Like Charles Lindbergh, he was a heroic figure in a world that became increasingly unheroic. In addition, the many uncertainties about every part of his life has made him a fascinating subject for biography. Lawrence, of course, was a legend in his own time, and, as it is with most legendary figures, he has both his defenders and his detractors. In this biography Desmond Stewart, a noted Arabic scholar, attempts to present Lawrence in a believable manner.

The basic outline of Lawrence's life is easily discernible, as it always has been. Born in Wales in the year 1888, Lawrence spent his boyhood in Oxford where his family moved in 1896. It was there that he was schooled, there that he acquired an interest in archaeology, and there that he entered Jesus College in 1907. After winning first-class honors in history in 1910, he received a post-graduate award that allowed him to join an archaeological expedition at the old Hittite city of Carchemish in Asia Minor. His knowledge of the Arabs, their customs and language, and of the area, led to his being assigned to the Military Intelligence Office in Cairo at the start of the war in 1914. By the end of the war, he had emerged as a daring desert fighter and a person deeply involved in the Arab revolt against Ottoman rule. When the war ended, Lawrence served for a while under Winston Churchill, who was then Colonial Secretary, as an adviser to the Middle East Department. After that, he spent time, under assumed names, in the Royal Air Force and in the Tank Corps, all the while gradually disappearing into self-imposed obscurity. As he became more estranged from public life, perhaps from life itself, he turned to writing and produced several books, including his famous *Seven Pillars of Wisdom.* Death came in 1935 as a result of a motorcycle crash.

Difficulties appear, however, the moment one strays beyond a basic sketch of his life. All of Lawrence's biographers prove that in him fact and fiction become entwined as soon as one begins to explore the nature of the actions and thoughts of this remarkable man. The answers to questions necessary to ask to understand the real Lawrence appear enshrouded in mystery. Was Lawrence a legend of his own making? Was he a military genius? In what way was he attracted to the cause of Arab nationalism? Why, as his legend grew, did his own self-esteem appear to fade? On an even more personal side, his biographers want to know what the fact of his illegitimate birth and the influence of his mother meant to the unfolding of his own character. Were such personal roots the source of his heroic ambition, his adventures in the desert, or of dissatisfaction with himself in later years? In fact, almost every element, either of his personality or of his accomplishments, that any biographer must explain, is questionable and debatable in nature. But this should not come as a surprise, for he was, after all, an unlikely hero of an unusual theater of operation in one of the most unsettling wars of modern times. Nevertheless, all of the basic questions that must be asked about Lawrence are included in this book, and from its pages he emerges more as a vulnerable yet skillful person than he does a romantic hero.

The great appeal of Stewart's treatment of Lawrence's life lies in the effort he makes to find the real man behind the Lawrence legend. Basically, the author sees his subject as a fallible man greatly attuned to action for the sake of its "intrinsic excitement." He attempts to puncture myths of Lawrence's reputed genius for desert warfare. Throughout the volume, he tediously delineates Lawrence's thoughts and explains the what and the how of his actions. He exposes Lawrence's supposed violent sexual degradation at Deraa as a myth. Regarding Lawrence's sexuality, a topic that has attracted previous biographical commentary, Stewart carefully investigates what he claims were Lawrence's masochistic practices, a subject that he presents with inoffensive frankness. Famously, the T. E. Lawrence of history is a man of many contradictions. For instance, he was both fascinated by death and repelled by it, and he lived a life that can only be described as both fact and fantasy. Stewart attempts to bring balance into the story of Lawrence's life by approaching his subject from the perspective of his personal development. In this he is successful.

In most respects, Stewart's scholarly approach to the myths about Lawrence enhances the realistic tone of the biography. The book, in fact, is the result of impressive research. The author consulted a wide range of documents throughout Europe and is the first biographer of Lawrence to use Arabic documents. He has consulted most of the secondary literature on Lawrence, and also has sought out the surviving Arabs who knew him. As a result of these investigations Stewart presents the picture of a man who manipulated historic fact and who promoted a myth about himself.

Lawrence's bending of the truth has long been a riddle to a number of writers who have commented on him. Stewart traces this aspect of Lawrence back to the time when it can first be documented. He cites a letter that Lawrence wrote to his principal at Oxford College towards the end of his famous "Middle Eastern Walk" in 1909 in which he began to create a myth about himself. It was, Stewart claims, the start "of a pattern which was to become compulsive." Lawrence, as presented by this author, was a man who loved mystification, concealed his emotions, yet had a flair for seeing himself "central to any situation."

Aside from correcting the record at many junctures, Stewart is particularly successful at handling two important elements of Lawrence's life. First, his treatment of Lawrence's final years (1923-1935), which he entitles "The Partitioned Soul" is perceptively handled. He describes Lawrence during these years as leading a compartmentalized life. In one compartment there was Lawrence, the professional airman and soldier; in the other, Lawrence remained secluded, hammered away at his writing, and enjoyed the company only of selected friends. Such a thought might well be central to understanding Lawrence in later life. The perspective that Stewart offers on Lawrence's reasons for writing *Seven Pillars of Wisdom* is equally interesting. That most famous of all of Lawrence's writings, the author claims, was meant as imaginative literature, not as official history. He convincingly demonstrates that it was Lawrence's ambition to write a work that, like *The Brothers Karamazov* and *Moby Dick*, would be great in spirit. His treatment of Lawrence's masterpiece is superb, and he weaves it into the fabric of the entire biography.

Other aspects of this biography, however, are less satisfying. Stewart is not at all convincing about Lawrence's attitude towards women, an important topic for someone who "never completely broke his mother's hold" and who found "the sexual bond between men and women" repugnant. He sees little of Lawrence's genius in warfare, and fails to explain why he was able to achieve the influence that was his towards the end of the war. One might wish also that the author had devoted more attention to creating a more complete context for Lawrence's efforts at the Paris Peace Conference of 1919.

More important, Stewart fails to paint a portrait of his subject with the broad and sure strokes of a master biographer. What this biography lacks in boldness, of course, is balanced by the vast amount of detailed analysis it provides. But even here a degree of essential clarity is lost. Partly this is due to Stewart's failure to keep the narrative of his subject's life from becoming snarled in the midst of an overabundance of material and rather wordy explanations that too frequently encumber his presentation; partly it is a result of the author's failure to reach what B. H. Liddell Hart, an early biographer of Lawrence, calls "his fundamental excellence." In the end Stewart sees Lawrence as a sad if not tragic figure, a man whose importance has been exaggerated out of proportion in history. His Lawrence is attractive enough as a figure to study, but he is not so engaging as to explain the source of inspiration that his contemporaries detected in him.

Beyond doubt, however, this study is a perceptive biographical inquiry. In spite of all the writing on Lawrence, he still remains something of a mystery. In contemplating him, it is difficult to avoid the idea that the man was a puzzle, the parts of which seem to resist total integration. Stewart's balanced and believable biography, which contains so much reasonable argument, separates the man from the myth. Even so, Lawrence retains his essential and enduring mystique, and he remains an extraordinary individual, the odd man out, in this mundane twentieth century world.

James D. Startt

THE THIN MOUNTAIN AIR

Author: Paul Horgan (1903–   )
Publisher: Farrar, Straus and Giroux (New York). 312 pp. $8.95
Type of work: Novel
Time: The 1920's
Locale: Upstate New York and Albuquerque, New Mexico

An eventful, swiftly paced, and richly charactered novel which is nevertheless sensitive to the various nuances of a cultured young man's coming of age under disconcerting, even violent, conditions

Principal characters:
>   RICHARD, a sensitive and artistic young college student
>   DAN, his father, recently elected lieutenant governor of New York
>   ROSIE, his mother
>   SAM DICKINSON, an idealistic young Brahmin public relations man
>   DON ELIZARIO WENZEL, a wealthy old rancher
>   CONCHA WENZEL, Don Elizario's beautiful young wife
>   TOM AGEE, the Don's Bible-quoting foreman
>   BUZ RENNISON, a handsome, amoral young drifter

Admirers of Paul Horgan's graceful and compelling art as a storyteller should rejoice. He has brilliantly ended the seven-year silence which followed his much acclaimed novel, *Whitewater.* As the third novel in the "Richard" series, which began with *Things As They Are* and *Everything To Live For, The Thin Mountain Air* is a totally absorbing, marvelously crafted work of fiction. As always in Horgan's work there are the richly realized ingredients of characterization, setting, and mood. Moreover, his plots have a strength which grows out of their subtle believability. Horgan never works to impress readers with shocking innovations; instead, he demonstrates solid mastery of the conventions of novelistic form. He writes within the same genteel structure as James Gould Cozzens or John Marquand; he is an unabashedly traditional teller of stories. His characters are real, his settings are recognizable; to read him is like looking at the hauntingly pictorial paintings of Edward Hopper, Andrew Wyeth, or Peter Hurd. He uses symbols, and he makes them work without hitting us over the head with them. He loves the physical world in which he places characters, and he describes it with such care and precision that we are there, too.

Horgan also loves and is fascinated by people, and because of this he creates truly memorable characters, some of whom we admire and would love to have in our own lives, and some of whom we fear, and would turn from in terror if we met them. Impressively, he is able to create both heroic and villainous figures equally well, balancing them in their humanity, and somehow to make us feel compassion for them all. It is a large, generous view of the foibles and beauties of humankind. Horgan has love for, and belief in, the human creature. His people are capable of nobility as well as shame. Thus Horgan seems at times charmingly out of step with most contemporary writers of fiction. To read him, however, is not an escape from awful realities, but a confrontation of reality from a stance that is armed through education, psychological and emotional insight, and reliance upon tradition. Horgan writes from a solid base of values which will strike many readers today as oldfashioned. *The Thin Mountain Air* builds a beautiful and convincing case for the resumption of those old-fashioned values. Realistically and at the same time encouragingly, he shows those virtues as losing many battles but winning the most important of the wars in the vicious conflict that life so often becomes. His characters have love and dignity; they have concern for others, and they exercise their intelligence and judgment to the best ends possible. Thus, at the end of *The Thin Mountain Air*, one has a feeling of affirmation, a kind of heightening of consciousness of the splendor of being alive, being a part of the enactment of a grand drama.

Taking place in the year he was twenty years old, *The Thin Mountain Air* is a retrospective narration by the adult Richard many years after the events took place in the 1920's. The grown man tells us he is writing from notes and journal entries he made at the time. He suggests, too, how though the passage of time may have softened the edges of some memories, it has enhanced the poignance, painful and otherwise, of others. Looking back, he spares no one among his friends, or in his family, in his honest analysis of their actions. He is equally unsparing of himself. Along the way, young Richard confronts many, comes to understand most, and even to embrace some human weaknesses. Thus, the novel's major theme is advanced. In its largest sense, *The Thin Mountain Air* is about Richard's journey toward gaining compassion, and achieving true maturity. Richard learns to love, even when love is not easy, either to give or to accept. Indeed, another of the novel's large concerns is the exploration of the many forms of love. In the space of one year he sees true love, corrupted love, misplaced love, and lust.

In his late teens, Richard lives a comfortable, cultured, and somewhat protected life. He loves the Upstate New York town in which he lives. He likes school and his studies. He jokes easily with his well-to-do, Irish politician father. Loved and encouraged by his parents, he feels close to them. Their love of him, and of each other, he accepts with gratitude but youthful lack of understanding. As he grows older, he learns tragically of another form love may take. Beginning blindly to push borders beyond himself, he falls in love with the idea of a young couple of lovers he observes living together aboard an old boat in the harbor. Richard observes them, fantasizes about them, in his mind joins them. In his imagination, theirs is a pure love like his mother's and father's. He is jolted back to his essential aloneness when he reads of the nameless couple's death by a fire aboard the old ship. Only later does he realize this presentiment of the vulnerability of love, and its inevitable brevity.

When his father, recently elected lieutenant governor, is stricken with tuberculosis, Richard redirects and reemphasizes his love toward his father. Moreover, he becomes conscious of how many other people love his father, and in what various ways they manifest it.

When the family has to move to New Mexico for his father's health, Richard is thrust against a confusing new set of attitudes toward love. He observes the strangely celibate love of an old rancher, Don Elizario Wenzel, for his breathtakingly lovely wife, a girl Richard's age. Richard comes to understand her love of the kindly old man. Astonishing and shaming himself, Richard learns about sensuality and lust, about the absence of love in the physical act, when he and a fellow ranch worker, Buz Rennison, take advantage of a lonely, love-starved waitress. Gradually, he comes to see the confusing complexity of the strengths and restrictions of love. Capping his education of the heart is his shocked discovery, shortly after his father's death, that the man he loved and admired has passionately loved another woman and kept the affair secret from Richard's mother. It is a test of Richard's maturity, of his own definition of love, of his compassion for his father, when the man shares his shame with his son. By that point, Richard truly understands, forgives his father, and increases thereby his own ability to show love for his mother.

The novel begins with Richard's memory of his father's saying, "In every life, Richard, there is something to be ashamed of . . . just as there is something noble. Never fail to be ashamed of the first, and never take credit for the second." By the end of the events in *The Thin Mountain Air,* Richard has understood to the depths his father's instructions. He grows to see himself as having been noble, and continuing to be capable of nobility. For that he is humble. He sees himself as shameful in his treatment of the waitress, and in his other failures to people who trust him, knowing himself capable of degradation. He carries his shame like a man, and he grows more understanding, more tolerant of those others around him who have similar burdens to bear.

In a sequence of events Horgan employs symbolically to make clear how well Richard learns from his father's early admonition, the boy visits Niagara Falls. As he stands watching the rushing water, his attention is drawn to an English nanny bringing twin children, a boy and a girl, up to the iron railing. Suddenly, the boy child rushes to the brink, playfully flings himself onto the railing, loses his balance and falls toward the torrent and certain death. Richard barely grasps him in time and saves the child's life. At first, this event seems unrelated to the other events in Horgan's tale.

Then, in an epilogue called "The Logic of Wishes," the mature Richard, now married and with a son of his own, is serving as an officer in World War II when he has an experience which marvelously draws the novel to a classically unified close. Stranded by fog in an English village, Richard has dinner with his female jeep driver. She, being British, talks to him, an American, of her childhood memories of America. Her name is Pamela, and she had been afraid of Niagara Falls when once her twin brother, Christopher, nearly fell over the railing into the flood. Representative of Horgan's powerful eloquence is the subtlety through which he has Pamela and Richard realize simultaneous closeness and knowledge of the gulf between each other when Richard hesitantly, modestly tells her he was the young man there that day at the falls. They are both impressed deeply with the moment's mystery, its miraculous concatenation. They are both quiet as they seek some meaning in what has happened to them. Then Pamela speaks of Christopher's brave death in a commando raid. Richard tells her his son is named Christopher. To himself he thinks of how he has always wondered what became of those two beautiful children. Richard and Pamela move blunderingly in human confusion through the moment. They are drawn close, then they move apart. Unable to understand, to explain any of the mystery of life, love and death, they withdraw into acceptance. Richard, true to his father's teaching, remains humble and grateful for the fulfillment of a crisis thus granted him. In the end he has come to accept with grace and balance both misfortune and blessing. He never forgets his shames, and he takes no credit for his nobility. He would not think to call himself noble, but Horgan sees him as a good man, tested and true.

It is this affection for man, this belief in his possibilities of transcending sordidness and squalor which consistently marks Horgan's themes. In the novel's last line, Richard quotes his mother as saying, "Wouldn't it be wonderful not to have to make the best of things?" Yet that very trait is her strength; indeed, it is what ennobles all Horgan's men and women. The strongest, the most thoughtful of them achieve dignity through doing their best with the cards life deals them.

Aside from being an enjoyable tale about fascinating people, *The Thin Mountain Air* is instructive, too, in its revelations of Horgan's sense of structure. The story moves at an astonishing pace, with Horgan cutting perfectly from scene to scene, from section to section. There is suspense and great character interest. The array of characters and events is amazingly large. Yet the overall impression one has is that the tale is being told in a leisurely, reflective, well-mannered style. This works so well because Horgan has excised all but the absolute essentials for his narrative in order to leave space for adequate explanation of them. It is a curious and wonderfully satisfying combination of speed and leisure, of action and reflection.

The Thin Mountain Air, viewed alongside much of contemporary fiction, will seem out of touch, anachronistic, at first. It does not seem fashionable among novelists today to write sensibly and with open admiration of people who respect each other, who think before they act, who have consciences and good manners, who show gratitude, who face evil with bravery. Most of all, Horgan creates characters who strive, thoughtfully and feelingly, for love, learning to give always more than they get.

Through all his concerns and traits as a novelist, Paul Horgan achieves a poetically lucid prose style of such calmness and purity that certain lines or images stay in the mind for days afterward as having been truly *le mot juste.* Reading him is like going for a slow, graceful ride in a Rolls-Royce; the real power resides in not having to show it all off. *The Thin Mountain Air* makes one wish for future books about Richard.

Thomas N. Walters

THE THORN BIRDS

Author: Colleen McCullough (1937–   )
Publisher: Harper & Row Publishers (New York). 530 pp. $9.95
Type of work: Novel
Time: 1915–1969
Locale: Australia

A romantic novel which deals with the adventures and relationships of three generations of an Irish-Australian family, the Clearys

> *Principal characters:*
> MEGGIE CLEARY
> FIONA CLEARY, her mother
> PADDY CLEARY, her father
> LUKE O'NEILL, her husband
> JUSTINE AND DANE, Meggie's children
> FATHER RALPH DE BRICASSART

Drogheda, a 250,000-acre sheep station in the Australian Outback, dominates Colleen McCullough's *The Thorn Birds,* giving the novel a center and a resting place. Although its numerous characters, most of them members of the clannish Cleary family, leave Drogheda for various reasons—to travel, to marry, to go to school or work or war—they all return to the sprawling ranch with its numerous water tanks (enough, it is said, to keep its lawns green through a ten-year drought), its yellow sandstone house, and its abundance of wisteria, bougainvillea, and roses. Constantly subjected to natural disasters, including monsoonal rains, droughts, fires, and too many rabbits, Drogheda's resources and its vitality are apparently unlimited. So are Meggie Cleary's. Meggie is celebrating her fourth birthday when the novel opens; when it closes, she is in her fifties. Beautiful, intelligent, and stubborn, she illustrates the theme suggested by the novel's title. According to Celtic legend, a particular bird intentionally impales itself on a thorn and, in the process of dying, sings a beautiful song. McCullough makes it all too clear that the legend's central idea is also that of her book: "the best is only bought at the cost of great pain," but human beings repeatedly choose both the best and the pain. As Meggie puts it, "We create our own thorn, and never stop to count the cost." While there is nothing intrinsically lamentable about this theme, McCullough's handling of it is annoyingly explicit. Not only does she announce her main idea before her story begins; she returns to it repeatedly at crucial points in the action. In the concluding paragraph she makes Meggie reflect, "I did it all to myself, I have no one else to blame. . . . We, when we put the thorns in our breasts, we know. . . . And still we do it."

But even this explicitness does not keep us from becoming interested in McCullough's characters, and especially in Meggie herself. Despite repetitious references to the heroine's "lambent" gray eyes and her "goldy" hair—one soon begins to imagine her on the cover of a Harlequin romance—we sympathize with her immediately. In the novel's first pages, the Clearys are living in New

Zealand. Meggie, the only girl among six children, receives for her birthday a new doll, which she must defend against the irreverent curiosity of her older brothers. Soon thereafter she starts school, where she must endure not only unfair canings by her teacher, but also the horror of catching lice from her best friend and the resulting humiliation of having her long "goldy" curls cut off and her head shaved. These early incidents firmly establish Meggie's character: she is loving, loyal, and stubbornly brave, and she must surely suffer.

When the Clearys leave New Zealand to go and live at Drogheda, the sheep station owned by Meggie's Aunt Mary, the child's prospects appear to improve. Drogheda offers security, steady work for her father and brothers, and the friendship of the tall, elegantly handsome parish priest, Father Ralph de Bricassart. Father Ralph is attracted at once by Meggie's beauty, although when they meet she is only nine years old; from that moment he is her friend and protector. At the same time, as Ralph observes Meggie's responses to an emotionally turbulent confrontation between her father and her favorite older brother, to the death of her baby brother, and to the deepening indifference of her stoical mother, he sees in her a maternal strength and a profound capacity to endure suffering, and these qualities too he finds fascinating. Until Meggie reaches adolescence, Father Ralph can successfully ignore the implications of his feelings for her; but when, at seventeen, she asks him whether he would marry her were he not a priest and then kisses him passionately, he realizes the danger he is in.

By now, however, we already know that Ralph de Bricassart is far too ambitious to let his love for any woman, even Meggie, interfere with his desire to rise within the hierarchy of the Church. It is his ambition, far more than the risk of being tempted to break his priestly vows, that motivates his departure from Australia. Having inherited the administration of Drogheda and a fortune from Meggie's Aunt Mary, the talented young priest leaves his parish to begin his ascendency. In the course of the novel he advances to the rank of bishop, then to archbishop, and finally to cardinal, returning periodically to Drogheda to visit the Clearys.

Father Ralph's departure leaves the affectionate Meggie in a state of extreme emotional vulnerability. With no other immediate outlet for her stubborn loyalty and her yearning for children, she marries a stockman, Luke O'Neill, who is like Ralph in appearance but in no other way. When the O'Neills leave Drogheda, it is clear that Meggie has made a mistake and that she will pay for it. And pay she does, in the alien climate of North Queensland, where Luke takes her, and through the difficult conception and birth of her daughter Justine. These events, in addition to Luke's long absences and his miserliness, contribute to Meggie's growing certainty that although she can never have Ralph, neither can she remain Luke's wife. When her suffering is at its most intense, she takes a holiday alone to rest and think. No sooner has she resolved to put her love for Ralph aside forever than he appears, and Meggie manages to "steal" him, though only temporarily, from God. McCullough treats Father Ralph's capitulation delicately, almost mystically; it is apparently too emotionally complex for the forthrightness of her other descriptions of lovemaking, though these, too, are less erotic than they are ecstatically romantic. At any rate, just past the novel's midpoint, Meggie returns to Drogheda pregnant with Ralph's child.

Perhaps because McCullough has so successfully conveyed the sexual and emotional tension between Meggie and Ralph during the first half of the novel, things slow down considerably once their love has been consummated. Meggie's return to Drogheda does, however, allow for development of the relationship between her and her mother, the mysteriously restrained Fiona. By now Fee has lost her husband Paddy, burned to death in a fire; her son Stu, smothered by a wild boar; her baby Hal, dead of croup; and her favorite son Frank, a love child who has been convicted of murder and imprisoned in England. Thus the two women's lives have been equally full of disappointments and trials, and their methods of dealing with their troubles have been similarly accepting. The parallel between Meggie and Fee helps reinforce the sense of "fatedness" about the Clearys and their actions. Like the Outback's violent weather, the forces which govern their lives are powerful and unpredictable, but, at the same time, predictably in charge.

As the novel's emphasis shifts to Meggie's children, the third generation of Clearys, both Meggie and Fiona are contrasted with Meggie's daughter Justine, who proves as she grows up to be tough and stubborn like her mother and grandmother but, unlike them, determined to alter circumstances before they can hurt her, a determination based on her perception of her mother's preference for her brother. Thus Justine, independent and willful, has her freckles removed because they stand in the way of her ambition to become an actress, deliberately wears orange and bright pink despite her fiery red hair, and just as deliberately contrives the loss of her virginity. Throughout her girlhood and adolescence, she is fiercely protective of her brother Dane, Ralph's and Meggie's extraordinarily handsome son. Despite her mother's favoritism for the boy, Justine behaves more maternally toward him than Meggie does, and the relation between brother and sister grows deep and strong.

Dane is not only splendid to look at, but he is also completely good. Early on, his religious leanings become apparent; thus, we are not nearly as surprised as his mother is when he announces, to her great distress, that he has decided to become a priest. "The utmost Enemy of women, that's what God is!" Meggie rages at Dane, before settling resolutely into calmness to save her son further distress. In a mixture of love and retribution, she sends Dane to Ralph, now at the Vatican, to be trained, still not telling him what he cannot seem to recognize: that Dane is his own son. Only a few days after the young priest's ordination, in an all too obvious echo of the thorn birds motif, Dane dies of a heart attack while swimming, with "one long and red-hot shaft of screaming agony" in his chest and the name of God on his lips. For Meggie, her son's death is the gods' final revenge on her for loving Ralph: "What more could the gods do?" she asks. "Don't tempt the gods, they love it."

McCullough clearly admires her characters for their strength and beauty, even as she visits upon them such throbbing human passions, such terrible sufferings, and such violently gory deaths. She tells their stories with so much gusto that their very resignation seems to pulse with vitality. Much of this vitality arises from the affectionate force of her descriptions of Australian landscapes, animals, and weather. Just as Hardy's Wessex assumes the significance and power of a human character, so McCullough's Outback shapes and dominates the lives of the Clearys; the two are inextricably intertwined. At the end of the novel this intertwining is emphasized with a bit of Dickensian plotting: although the station has been run by the Clearys, it is, according to the terms of Aunt Mary's will, owned by the Catholic Church and administered by Ralph de Bricassart and eventually by his legatee, who just happens to be the man Justine marries. Nevertheless, Meggie realizes that Justine, now a successful actress, will never live at Drogheda permanently, and that, as far as the Clearys are concerned, it is "Time for Drogheda to stop." After all, the sunburned and weatherbeaten "Unks," as Justine calls Meggie's brothers, are elderly, and none has married; Dane is dead. Thus Drogheda's end coincides with that of the Cleary family itself, whose identity is so bound to the land they work on that they sometimes seem to be one with its kangaroos and budgies and wilga trees.

If McCullough's handling of landscape is one source of the novel's vitality, another is her close attention to the details of daily life on Drogheda. Whether she is describing the inside work of cooking, scrubbing, laundering, and painting, or the outside work of sheep-shearing, fire-fighting, hand-feeding, and riding the paddocks, her attention to visual details keeps her characters' extravagant emotional distresses firmly grounded in dust, black flies, and back-breaking physical labor.

This realistic treatment of station life and our genuine interest in the characters make us all the more impatient with the novel's lapses into stilted dialogue and cliché-ridden explanations of motive. Sometimes the characters seem to be speaking out of a soapy television screen. When Meggie and Fiona have their first heart-to-heart talk as adults, the conversation goes like this:

> "Once you had Ralph de Bricassart it wasn't necessary to stay any longer with Luke."
> "Yes," sighed Meggie, "Ralph found me. But it didn't solve anything for us, did it? I knew he would never be willing to give up his God. It was for that reason I was determined to have the only part of him I ever could. His child. Dane."

Similarly, at Dane's funeral, which is of course conducted at Drogheda by Father Ralph, an unidentified narrative voice, perhaps that of the author, perhaps that of Ralph himself, speaks: "Sleep on Dane, because only the good die young. Why do we mourn? You're lucky, to have escaped this weary life so soon. Perhaps that's what Hell is, a long term in earth-bound bondage. Perhaps we suffer our hells in living. . . ." Since the events of the plot alone are usually enough to engage and occasionally even to move the reader, such banal explanations can only distract or, worse, irritate.

Yet the banality is somehow consistent with the book's other attractions, which are not unlike those of *Gone with the Wind:* a beautiful, strong heroine; a handsome, ambitious hero; a huge Georgian mansion; strong regional flavor; forbidden love; violent death; symbolic meteorological disturbances—not to mention the appeal of the story's luxurious length. *The Thorn Birds* is, in the fullest sense, a romantic novel, and its popularity grows sturdily out of that fact. But it is also something more: an energetic, sharply detailed account of three generations of hardworking Australian graziers, people who, as Colleen McCullough portrays them, sometimes seem to love and understand the Outback much better than they do themselves and one another.

Carolyn Wilkerson Bell

TOLKIEN: A BIOGRAPHY

Author: Humphrey Carpenter
Publisher: Houghton Mifflin Company (Boston). 287 pp. $10.00
Type of work: Biography
Time: 1891–1973
Locale: Mostly England, chiefly in and around Oxford

A biography of John Ronald Reuel Tolkien, Bosworth Professor of Anglo-Saxon at Oxford University, and author of The Hobbit, The Lord of the Rings, *and* The Silmarillion

> *Principal personages:*
> J. R. R. TOLKIEN
> EDITH TOLKIEN, his wife
> MABEL TOLKIEN, his mother
> FATHER FRANCIS MORGAN, his guardian
> C. S. LEWIS, a fellow member of the "Inklings"

J. R. R. Tolkien was always suspicious of biographies of authors—he thought they added little to our understanding of their works. At least partially in deference to those suspicions, Humphrey Carpenter, the author of *Tolkien: A Biography,* says little about the great works of imagination that have insured his subject's reputation. This biography provides the reader chiefly with the dates of the important events in Tolkien's life, and some indication of Tolkien's feelings about those events. Enthusiasts will find the book helpful and informative, but Tolkien has not found his Boswell.

Tolkien: A Biography was authorized by Tolkien's heirs. Carpenter therefore had access to family records, diaries, letters, and unpublished papers of all kinds. The profusion of records might have been put to better use by more experienced hands, but Carpenter is a novice at the task. Tolkien was a novelist, a poet, a professor, and a student of languages; Carpenter is none of these. He is a television producer for the BBC, and his previous publications consist, apparently, of a book titled *A Thames Companion,* which he co-authored. He has not had experience in writing biography, especially the biography of an important literary figure, so perhaps wisely he avoids the form and paraphernalia of a scholarly work. The book is designed for a popular audience: in its nearly three hundred pages, there are less than a dozen footnotes, most of them intended to explain British terms and customs to an American audience, such as glossing the name of the card game Patience as the more familiar Solitaire.

Not all transatlantic difficulties have been ironed out. One of these footnotes, clearly in error, concerns "The Book of Mazarbul," a battered volume that the members of the Fellowship of the Ring find in the Mines of Moria. As a decoration for his work, Tolkien made a facsimile of some pages of The Book of Mazarbul, and he wanted them reproduced in the first volume of *The Lord of the Rings;* the publisher refused because of cost. Carpenter tells us that some of those pages did finally see publication in the Tolkien Calendar for 1977. That may be so in England, but anyone who buys the 1977 Tolkien Calendar in the

United States will search for them in vain.

A more noteworthy difficulty faces the serious student of Tolkien and his writings who is forced to rely on the Tolkien biography for information not available elsewhere. As pointed out above, Carpenter had the advantage of access to a large amount of unpublished material, and he very frequently quotes Tolkien himself. Yet he does not cite the source of a single one of these quotations throughout the book, believing that references to unpublished material will be of no interest to his readers. These words are certainly an honest confession, but they show a complete misunderstanding of the practices of literary biography. In a discussion of his sources, Carpenter goes on to say that he has omitted material within the Tolkien quotations without using the marks of ellipsis to indicate the place of the omission. He states that he has very often omitted material, but that he finds the practice of marking ellipsis irritating. The consequence is that anyone who finds Tolkien expressing himself on some subject in Carpenter's biography, and suspects that the quotation comes from an unpublished source, has no assurance that the quotation includes Tolkien's complete remarks. On the contrary, there is a very good chance that the quotation gives only those parts of what Tolkien said that a British television producer thought relevant.

If the book is not of much use to the scholar, it may still have other virtues. The general reader may not worry about sources and attributions, but may simply want information about the life of his favorite author, and much of this information is provided by Carpenter. The key dates—marriages, births, deaths— are all there, and there is no reason to suspect their accuracy. Carpenter has done his work in outlining the chief events of his subject's life. But even the most undemanding of readers will appreciate skill at storytelling. Unfortunately, the initial reviews of Carpenter's book were almost unanimous: critics considered it sound but dull. Carpenter has no natural flair for telling a story, and this lack sometimes leads to strange omissions in his recounting of important relation- ships. For example, Tolkien and his brother Hilary were orphaned by the death of their mother when the boys were twelve and ten years old. (Their father had died eight years before.) In her will, Mabel Tolkien has appointed as their guardian Father Francis Morgan, a Catholic clergyman at the Birmingham oratory. Tolkien grew up with an immense respect and affection for Father Morgan—even as a young man, he stopped for a period of years seeing the woman he later married in obedience to the priest's wishes. After Tolkien came to his majority, Father Morgan had no objection to their marriage, and even baptized their first child, whose second name was "Francis" in honor of the priest. Father Morgan continued to visit the growing Tolkien family at least until the early 1930's, but despite his importance to the protection and formation of Tolkien in his early years, Carpenter does not tell us when the priest died; he does not even mention his death. If Father Morgan's death had any impact on Tolkien, we do not hear of it. And if it had no impact, it would be important to know that, too.

If the reviewers are correct in considering the book to be dull, the chief cause of that lack of excitement is Carpenter's attitude itself: he believes Tolkien's life to have been rather uninteresting. Several times the reader is warned that he will not be much interested in what Carpenter is about to tell him. And in comparison with the life of, say, Genghis Khan, Tolkien's life was rather ordinary. But in the hands of someone more sympathetic to the kind of life Tolkien chose for himself, the real excitement of that life could have shone through. It is ironic that Tolkien's biography was published in the same year as K. M. Elisabeth Murray's biography of her grandfather, Sir James Murray. That delightful book, *Caught in the Web of Words,* demonstrates that there can be a fascination to the life of the mind, even the life of one who, like Murray, spent thirty-five years in a shed in his backyard. Tolkien's life was likewise a life of ideas. For a good part of his adult years Tolkien met regularly with people like C. S. Lewis, Owen Barfield, and Charles Williams. Such a life might well be thought one of the more interesting of our times.

Even those parts of Tolkien's history that were exciting by anyone's standards are handled rather sketchily. Tolkien spent some time at the front during World War I: although Carpenter tells us that he kept a diary in France, none of Tolkien's comments on the war are given. If Tolkien expressed his thoughts about the war, if he was impressed by anything he saw in France, we do not read of it. Critics have thought that Tolkien's description of the blasted land of Mordor in *The Lord of the Rings* may owe something to his experience of no-man's-land between the sets of trenches. That opinion finds neither confirmation nor rebuttal here.

Or consider a much later incident: the unauthorized publication of *The Lord of the Rings* by Ace Books caused a furor in publishing circles in the late 1960's, but Carpenter is vague about the incident. Perhaps his publisher, Houghton Mifflin, was too much involved in the controversy to supply a completely unbiased account. The undisputed facts in the case are these: Allen and Unwin published *The Lord of the Rings* in three hardcover volumes in 1954 and 1955. Houghton Mifflin sold some hardcover copies in America in the same two years. Then, almost ten years later, in 1965, Ace brought out a paperback edition, the first in either Britain or America, which was quickly followed by the authorized Ballantine paperback reprint that same year. Beyond these few dates, much of the story depends on who is telling it. Carpenter charges that Ace printed their edition, intending to sell it without payment of royalties to Tolkien, and further states that their action was legally possible, if not morally blameless, because of "the confused state of American copyright at that time."

A substantially different version of the incident is found in Daniel Grotta-Kurska's biography of Tolkien, *J. R. R. Tolkien: Architect of Middle Earth.* Before America joined the International Copyright Convention, the laws in the United States attempted to protect the American printing industry from the wholesale importation of books printed in another country. The limit was set at 1,445 copies, a limit which Houghton Mifflin exceeded by bringing in approximately 2,000 copies of the unbound British printing. They thereby lost the American copyright inadvertently. Donald A. Wollheim, the fantasy and science fiction editor for Ace Books at the time, claims that Houghton Mifflin, thinking little of the book's chances of success, simply chose not to copyright the work in the United States. According to Grotta-Kurska, Wollheim further believes that if Ace had not acted, the book would not be in paperback at the present time. Whichever version is true, there seems considerably more confusion at Houghton Mifflin than in the copyright law: whether through mistake or conscious decision, they did not copyright the work in the United States, and from a major publishing house that was an astonishing oversight. In fact, it was necessary for Houghton Mifflin to ask Tolkien to revise the work so that it could be copyrighted as a new and different version.

Now, if the people at Ace were pirates, they were curiously dilatory ones: they waited a decade before bringing out a paperback edition. If Houghton Mifflin had any intention of authorizing their own softcover edition, that decision was a long time coming. In Britain, a paperback edition was not available until 1968. To an outsider, it appears as if Houghton Mifflin had so little faith in the work's chances that they would not have authorized a paperback edition at all had not another publisher taken the plunge and started to sell books in the thousands.

Finally, there is the question of royalties. Whatever Ace's original intention has been, Wollheim says that his company offered to put an amount equal to a standard author's royalties in a fund for a "Tolkien Prize," to be awarded annually to new writers of fantasy, although the company was not legally obligated to hand over a penny of the money from the sale of their edition. Tolkien objected to this plan, as he had every right to do, and said that if anyone were to receive payment, it should be he. According to Wollheim, Ace then agreed to pay Tolkien a sum equal to a standard author's royalty, and agreed further not to reprint the Ace edition after the remaining copies were exhausted. Wollheim argued that on every copy sold by Ballantine, the authorized paperback publisher, Tolkien shared the royalty first with Houghton Mifflin and then with Allen and Unwin; but the whole royalty from the sale of an Ace copy went to Tolkien. Wollheim contends that Tolkien made more from the sale of a single copy of the Ace version than from a copy of the authorized Ballantine edition.

It would not be worthwhile to mention all this squabbling in the publishing industry unless we reflect that it was the appearance of the Ace paperback version that made *The Lord of the Rings* a bestseller in the United States by putting the trilogy within the book budget of millions of American high-school and college students. Even Carpenter admits that Ace did Tolkien a great service. Certainly Tolkien was not fortunate in Houghton Mifflin's handling of his work, allowing it to "languish" in hardcover until forced to take action by the press of events.

Carpenter's biography is unlikely to satisfy many readers, though it has a real, if limited, usefulness to readers interested in the external facts of Tolkien's life. Those interested in the intricate connection between a writer's life and his art, or in the lively religious and literary discussions of Oxford dons and London writers who made up the Inklings, or in Tolkien's battles for curriculum change at Oxford, will have their appetites whetted but not sated here. Christopher Tolkien, who revised his father's *The Silmarillion* for publication, promised more works to come from the large store of manuscripts still unprinted. And it is safe to say that, for every work by Tolkien that will be published, there will be many more *about* Tolkien. Some of those will be the biographies that do the jobs Carpenter did not attempt.

Walter E. Meyers

UNCERTAIN GREATNESS
Henry Kissinger and American Foreign Policy

Author: Roger Morris
Publisher: Harper & Row Publishers (New York). 312 pp. $10.95
Type of work: Political analysis

An evaluation of Henry Kissinger's performance as President Nixon's Assistant for National Security and later as Secretary of State

Robert Morris worked successively as an aide to Dean Acheson during the NATO crisis of 1966, as a Foreign Service Officer on the Executive Secretariat of the Secretary of State, as a special assistant of McGeorge Bundy during the Mideast War of 1967, and as a staff member of the National Security Council under President Johnson in 1967–1968. He served on the National Security Council staff under Henry Kissinger from 1969 to May, 1970, when he resigned because of his opposition to the invasion of Cambodia. For the past two years he has been a contributing editor to *The New Republic,* where his profiles of Carter administration appointees in foreign affairs have provoked wide comment and occasional outrage.

Uncertain Greatness is not a biography of Henry Kissinger but an evaluation of his performance as President Nixon's Assistant for National Security and later as Secretary of State. It is a monumental task because Henry Kissinger dominated American foreign policy through some of the most turbulent years in our history. Any evaluation must include an understanding of his theory toward diplomacy and foreign affairs and his relationships with the foreign policy bureaucracy, President Nixon, his staff members, the press, and Congress.

Kissinger had written a number of books about diplomacy, foreign affairs, and international relations prior to joining the Nixon administration. In these books he set out the broad general theories which serve as a guide to understanding his performance as our foremost diplomat. His purpose was to maintain a favorable balance of power. Thus, there was a need for a precise calculation of interests and a self-interested approach to international relations and negotiations. Although Morris' presentation of the theory is brief, it is accurate. However, he would have been in a better position to evaluate Kissinger and his policy if he had taken the time to discuss at greater length the implications of this theory and to explore some of the criticisms of the theory as well as some of the alternatives.

In addition to his discussion of Kissinger's theory, Morris discerns three concepts that had a lasting influence on the man and his policy. They are his scorn for the bureaucracy, his faith in the establishment of a new national diplomacy, and the need to obtain domestic support so the policy would be legitimized.

Morris obviously shares Kissinger's scorn for the bureaucracy because the first chapter is a scathing attack upon the foreign policy bureaucracy and the decision-making procedure of the Johnson administration. The decision-makers are accused of being more concerned with how the policy looked than with the policy itself. The close circle of advisers is referred to as the "Wise Men" in a way clearly not intended to be complimentary. The career officers of the foreign service are described as paper shufflers who shun policy responsibility to the public and are interested only in the rights of passage and the desire to make no waves.

According to Morris, a shared distrust of the bureaucracy is one of the ties that united Nixon and Kissinger. He suggests that they both had the same fundamental attitude about the use of power in foreign policy and in Washington. They are pictured as suspicious men who were afraid others would use the tactics against them that they used. From the very beginning, Nixon had told Kissinger they would take the foreign policy from the State Department and put it in the White House.

Morris seems to have seen in Henry Kissinger the potential for reducing the power of the bureaucracy by a fundamental rewording of the foreign policy decision-making procedure. The new system as originally designed by Morton Halperin was to balance the bureaucratic forces for inaction and maintenance of the *status quo* by compelling full presidential consideration of all the available options. To Morris this was a decision-making structure designed to assure consideration of all dissenting viewpoints. The arrangement called for a body of senior representatives drawn from various agencies to conduct special reviews originated by Kissinger but approved by the President. The review board would receive from smaller working groups a policy paper covering the full range of policy alternatives. After a formal consideration by the review board and the National Security Council, the President would make his decision after deliberations of the options and the cover letter by Kissinger with his personal comments. This procedure was instrumental in placing Kissinger at the center of the decision-making process. Morris concludes that initially there was openness in the process, but ultimately the decisions came to be controlled by Kissinger and Nixon. Therefore, when they left office, things were as they had been before, and there was no permanent change or improvement in the bureaucracy. He counts this as a major failure of Kissinger. However, it is a failure largely because Morris has an exaggerated view of the inadequacies of the bureaucracy and no realistic views for an alternative.

Since the changes in the decision-making process initiated by Kissinger and Nixon put them at the heart of the process, the relationship between the two becomes vital to an evaluation of Kissinger. From the beginning of the first administration Nixon is shown as capricious and suspicious. The author explains the failure to notify Japan of the trip to Peking as Nixon's revenge for Japan's failure to live up to agreements Nixon thought they had reached. He also claims that Nixon favored lessening of tensions with the Soviet Union not because of any conviction but because of expediency.

Throughout the book Morris has great difficulty reconciling or justifying the continued close relationship between Kissinger and Nixon. For example, Morris opposed the invasion of Cambodia so intensely that he resigned because of it. How, then, does he evaluate Kissinger when he stoutly defended the action after it had been completed? He says he heard that Kissinger tried to talk Nixon out of the invasion—"Perhaps."

Just as Morris is ambivalent in his judgment of Kissinger because he did after all serve and continue to serve Nixon, he has trouble sorting out the relationship of Kissinger to the press. On the one hand, Morris knows that Kissinger spent a great amount of time wooing the press, but he was displeased when Kissinger was treated favorably by the press for policies which Morris considered faulty. He is likewise disturbed when at least on two instances he thought Kissinger stopped news stories by calling the editor of the paper. Yet Morris had noted that one of Kissinger's fundamental concepts was the need to obtain domestic support in order to legitimize policies.

In addition to showing Kissinger's relationship with the press, Morris apparently thought it important to give some flavor of the communications that took place behind the scenes. In one of the most unbelievable passages in the book, he accuses Kissinger of racism. This passage can only be evaluated with the knowledge that Morris passionately objected to the policy of the United States in regard to Nigeria. Morris recounts that Kissinger was briefed on the prospects of the slaughter of the captured Iboes by Northern Nigerian troops. He is reported to have asked how the Iboes would be recognized. When he was told that the northern tribes tended to be more Semitic in appearance and the Iboes more Negroid, Kissinger is said to have asked Morris, "But you have always told me the Iboes were more gifted and accomplished than the others. What do you mean 'more Negroid'?"

The book includes a discussion of a large number of foreign policy decisions covering U.S. policy toward China, Moscow, Bangladesh, Chile, Burundi, Cyprus, Angola, Vietnam, and the Near East. In his discussion of U.S. decisions during the uprising in East Pakistan which culminated in the state of Bangladesh, Morris is extremely critical because he thought senior officials both in the State Department and the National Security Council largely ignored the savagery in East Pakistan and relied upon the Pakistani army to quell the disturbance. East Pakistan was assisting the United States as Kissinger was making the initial contacts and preparing for the eventual visit of Nixon to Peking, and this may have influenced our foreign policy as Morris acknowledged. When Kissinger was informed by a State Department official that the new Bengali state would be an "international basket case" Kissinger is quoted as saying, "It will not necessarily be our basket case." Although Morris is morally indignant about United States policy, he is again ambivalent in his assessment of Kissinger, and remarks that the man's bureaucratic-diplomatic skill showed him at once as Nixon's man browbeating the bureaucrats and as the intrepid adviser trying to steer Nixon, the politician, past dangerous shoals. Morris devotes a page to evaluating whether the policy would be justified under the calculations of Realpolitik but concludes that Nixon and Kissinger had drifted through the Pakistani tragedy "demonstrating a shallow, parochial and cruel perspective of world policy." A serious analysis of the policy would have been more useful.

The final assessment of Kissinger in the last paragraph shows the paradox that characterizes the book. Morris concludes that for

> Kissinger's statesmanship to survive for long, the zealot for secrecy must become the advocate of openness, the master of bureaucratic maneuver, the proponent of bureaucratic reform, the seducer of the press and Congress, the critic of every such seduction, the practitioner of ruthless *Realpolitik*, the champion of a new humanity in American foreign policy.

Thus, on the one hand he seems unable to deny Kissinger's greatness, yet on the other to think that everything he did and stood for must be changed if he is to be considered great. It would have been better if Morris had arrived at a consistent evaluation of his subject before writing a book about him.

Doris F. Pierce

THE VENTRILOQUIST
New and Selected Poems

Author: Robert Huff
Publisher: The University Press of Virginia (Charlottesville). 58 pp. $6.95
Type of work: Poetry

The poet goes in search of those persons who were or are shapers of his art and life in a volume of poems that, at its best, speaks to the heart of intimate things

This, the fourth volume of Robert Huff's poetry, selected as the finest collection received by the Virginia Commonwealth University Series for Contemporary Poetry in the 1977 competition, is a generally strong and noteworthy contribution to American verse. In *The Ventriloquist,* Huff is, for the most part, searching for those persons who are or once were shapers and movers of his life: Vernon Watkins, the man who drove a Model "A" Ford with such *elan;* Cynthia Brookings, his black lover and godsend; sad Buster Keaton; Delmore Schwartz and his hovering, ever-present "bear"; but especially those whose lives forever touch his own—his mother and father. Other beings are here. There is, for instance, the ugly and magnificent porcupine shot by the author that drags its poor spilled entrails toward a private death, giving the poet, in the process, an eloquent, never-to-be-forgotten lesson in dignity, courage, and forbearance. There is the brahma bull, "That empty, humpbacked creature" who loves rodeos and spectators. With Sir Rod, a wizened old dog, the poet gives us an evocative animal correlative for his dying father who, like his canine friend, sleeps, "Twisting the same old painful parable."

Huff's verse is most strong and supple when it speaks of the wounded, the dying, and especially the dead, in poems like "The Ventriloquist," "My Father's Words," "Porcupines," and "An Old High Walk," wherein his spirits, like those of the aged ventriloquist's lark-resembling soul, take flight, allowing death and wounds, doubts and tears no dominion. His best writing is neither sullen nor melancholy, but rather, peacefully aware that, although life is long and troubled, there is meaning in it that a poet or a child or a dying porcupine can detect and hold dear.

The poet finds his stride when he addresses those people he really cares for, confessing past ignorance, asking for their sympathy, love, attention, and understanding. The voice he uses is an insistent, compelling one, asking the reader to take it seriously. But compelling though it may be, this voice is accessible because it is conversational—even at times colloquial ("Still it's a job. I mean I think that old gorilla knows / why I'm high-wired and who's leading whom"). Even an angel is addressed casually, as if it were an old friend that could help the poet sift wisdom from death's ashes. Confessing weaknesses, the poet apparently is hard-driven to know if life has importance, and the self any permanence. So from one looming figure to another he goes in these poems, hoping to confess and gain absolution for unnamed sins, to seek and find wisdom and self-knowledge from those who, in the past or present, are best able to give the answers.

From Vernon Watkins (who "kept us all from harm"), to Cynthia Brookings who manages to make him feel "cinnamon in morning light"; to Ellwood Johnson, who shares his own world-transforming abilities; to the "J.P." of "The Ventriloquist," a canny magician, Huff acknowledges his spiritual mentor whose incandescent lives and wisdom help him make his hard way with less perplexity.

Fellow artists, most of whom have gone, serve as sounding boards for the poet's musings and as silent advisers: Delmore Schwartz, William Carlos Williams, Theodore Roethke, Buster Keaton. Schwartz, whose own life turned out to be far sadder than he ever imagined, gave Huff the image of the bear; Williams bequeathed him respect for the common life: those "orchards of girls, plums, cherries, mice, / Nightcrawlers, owls, and otherwise fool cats. . . ." From Roethke, Huff learned to listen more closely to nature's denizens and by Keaton, who called Charlie Chaplin and croaked one fateful word, "mortal," he was tutored in the art of saying just enough and investing that "enough" with meaning. It is to these special people that the poet's *persona* haltingly explains what he is, what he is up to, and what baffles him.

But the finest moments in *The Ventriloquist* come when Huff (as he so often does) approaches his deceased parents, addressing them cautiously with hopes that by so doing, he will be better equipped to live. In these poems about his parents, Huff is alternately a child desiring parental guidance and a mature man able to gauge what his parents did with their lives and what they left him. When portraying his mother, Huff creates a mythic figure—one who has shuffled off mere mortality and become a kind of goddess. In "Saint Patrick's Day 1974," for instance, the poet celebrates a mother who has become an airy presence, a "sweet ghost" hovering around the "strait water" and fouled air of Detroit and offering "an Irish mumbler" a kiss on the forehead, followed by advice: "Now take care." He imagines she is going to him, baby bottle in hand, while he lies "swaddled in a fog banked / Little town up Puget Sound." Because his mother aspired to float out of the hospital where she spent her last days, praying for "one pure lift," the poet, waving his wand, gives her that "lift" and the freedom she once searched for.

"Sainte Anne de Beaupré" is another of Huff's major poems having to do with the death of his mother, yet, unlike "Saint Patrick's Day 1974," this poem has more to say about the pain and isolation of her death than about her triumph over it. Here, "Couched upon glands as soft as pillows. . . ," she lies on the hospital bed, having abandoned the many canes and crutches surrounding her. Pain is personified. It nags at her, asking for that deliverance death provides. The poet then softens his account. Death, he says, "coaxed her body off." Addressing Sainte Anne, who silently held vigil over his mother's dying, the poet attempts to find in family history—specifically his grandfather's "backward pilgrimage" into death from his home in Quebec to the copper mines of

Michigan where he ended his days—clues about his own destiny.

Huff's immediacy, his eye for detail, his emotional veracity, and his careful placement of strong, elemental language provide the poetry of *The Ventriloquist* with power and depth. In the first of the "father" poems, "An Old High Walk," one learns that father gave son "the gift of balance" with which he can walk the tightrope far above those who would maim or destroy him. Here Huff creates his best metaphor: the tightrope act wherein one must concentrate on one's art in order to survive the fatal fall. And here Huff provides the reader with the one person who, he believes, has given him an emotional fulcrum for his artist's balancing act—his father. Now, like his wife, a disembodied presence, the father is lovingly recalled by the son and affectionately referred to as "Dad."

Poised above the tumultuous, dangerous crowd, the *persona* of "An Old High Walk" worries about the "other animal," an ugly ape with "pig eyes" who may toss him and his "bear" to the floor below. A very real feeling of fear emanates from this encounter; the reader senses that the ape, whose identity is never ascertained, represents enemies of the self and soul: lust, greed, malice, jealousy, and anger. The *persona* appreciates the father's spiritual guidance which helps him somehow summon sufficient courage to stay alive above the milling mob below.

The tie binding dead father and living son is reiterated in "My Father's Words," another one of the finer Huff poems. And yet, here the father is no longer directly addressed by the poet, being spoken of rather than to. Here the poet is analytical, more fearful, more *angst*-ridden than he was previously in "An Old High Walk." Here the dead father's living words about skating under hell's leather wings make the son uneasy. In "My Father's Words," as in other poems, the poet expresses an unfocused fear of death that he likens unto a terrible ocean entering the conscious mind or a freezing of the blood. Huff conveys very tellingly his fear that death may be unpleasant and that if an afterlife exists, it too will be unsettling—even horrible. This elemental fear resounds throughout the volume: at times, the poet will speak of what, in one instance, he refers to as his "clammy ghost," a silent, sinister companion reminiscent in some ways of Schwartz's bear. Death he fears, it would seem, because it so cruelly separated him from those whom he so eloquently mourns.

What ultimately assuages his fears (the general tenor of his poetry is cheerful rather than mournful) is a capacity for love. Love, as it is found in *The Ventriloquist,* buoys the poet's spirits, making him forget hell's leather wings and the seaweed clotting of death. In its more debased form, this love is lecherous, as witnessed in "Girl Watching at Grant's Pass" or "In Defense of Pornography: A Classical Setting for Spencer Moore" wherein the poet expresses fleshly longings in voluptuous imagery. Or love can be something as ethereal as a poet's celebration of a violet ("To a Violet"), where the poet, hungry for beauty, finds beauties traditionally sung by poets still ready to inspire new song ("Now in your eye's / Lime center still the dew, same delicate, / Dark, velvet-looking streams, in miniature. . . .") Or it can take the form of the love between man and woman, the kind eloquently delineated in "A Story for Cynthia Brookings on the Birthday of Queen Elizabeth II 1968" wherein the poet can put aside his thoughts of decay and death for a time, saying, "But we are absolutely really here, / All wrapped up in each other. And the life-force is at work in "Getting Drunk with Daughter," a poem about a proud father and his young daughter at play on a beach. Huff reveals, in a descriptive poem, an encompassing love for everything from the sand castle with its "stick gate" to "our shapely neighbor" with her all-over tan to his daughter's resemblance to her mother. Though his euphoria is no doubt (as he says) partially bourbon-induced, there is a surge of genuine love for creation behind it: "Oh, I know you know I know love likes beaches —/For blood outruns the heart, no doubt. . . ."

Then, as it very often does, the awful realization comes to the poet that the day is nearly done and that a new, far more unpleasant day is nearly at hand. Nevertheless, he can say to the daughter he loves, "We'll be together"; and though "The world lies down and waits in all its ditches," he and his beloved "aren't going to let it rain."

Another sort of love is that expressed for the creatures of the earth whose lives make us reevaluate our own. The poet, after shooting a porcupine who, along with friends, was eating all of the wooden objects near his cabin, finds that he is deeply moved by a love for the wounded beast who crawls slowly into the night to die, dragging along his golden entrails, as rich as those found in a pirate's treasure. The porcupine's dignity, its remorseless facing of death—all that raw and instructive courage it displays—gnaws at the poet, and chastens him for destroying something so rare and oddly magnificent.

The poet's love of nature is perhaps most admirably expressed in "Now," the last poem in the volume, wherein the "Flocks in the sea" become, in Huff's imagination, "like negatives of stars" in the distance. Here, in this peaceful poem, Huff seems to have discovered another refuge, another place to ease his fears, for here the poet's instincts take over from his intellectual apprehensions. Some of his most vibrant metaphors—"Whacked grass impatient, wind glued on the gull"—take the reader into the spaces of sky and sea, making him one with them and one with the poet ("And there you are and I. . . .")

What is remarkable and worthy about Robert Huff's *The Ventriloquist* is his impassioned and exuberant praise for the many glories of this fleeting life, praise couched in delicate and controlled bursts of imagery. His poems (for the most part) require little unraveling and yet manage to say much about fear, doubt, and their overcoming. He brings the reader the happiness of the mundane world and like any responsible poet, makes us see things in a new way. Though his place among American poets of the first rank is far from a foregone conclusion, there is, in this volume of verse, much promise of greater things to come.

John D. Raymer

THE WALNUT DOOR

Author: John Hersey (1914–   )
Publisher: Alfred A. Knopf (New York). 238 pp. $7.95
Type of work: Novel
Time: 1972
Locale: New Haven, Connecticut

A novel about the relationship between two refugees from the campus battlegrounds of the 1960's: one an apathetic young woman, the other an obsessed young man

> *Principal characters:*
> ELAINE QUINLAN, an alienated Bennington College graduate seeking a new life in New Haven
> EDDIE MACABOY, her lover, a Reed College dropout, ex-activist, and locksmith
> GREG, her former lover
> RUTH GREENHELGE, her friend who works for a Yale professor
> BOTTSY FELDMAN, her friend, a graduate student
> HOMER PLENTAGGER, a small-time racketeer
> MERLE PLENTAGGER, his wife
> MARY CALOVATTO, Elaine's neighbor
> GIULIO CALOVATTO, her husband

"O rare John Hersey!" So Rex Stout, the late mystery writer and longtime friend of Hersey, is said to have exclaimed one evening.

Indeed, he is. Drawing on his experiences as a war correspondent for *Time* and *Life* magazines in both the Pacific and European Theaters during World War II, he began to write a steady stream of distinguished books. It was his third book on the war, *A Bell for Adano*, published in 1944 and the winner of the 1945 Pulitzer Prize for fiction, that established him as a major American writer. *A Bell for Adano* is a novel about American idealism during the occupation of Italy, written at a time when the American idealistic vision was still clear, when we still believed that we had the moral power and duty to help set the rest of the world straight. It might seem to be a slightly naïve book today, but it is a novel about its time, with the flavor of its time, and it spoke to its time. Like most of Hersey's work, it is a topical novel, but, like many of his books, it is good enough to have survived the time for which it spoke; it is an important book in Hersey's now long career for another reason. The idealism that it portrays, without denying the ugliness of war, helped establish Hersey's position as a purveyor of hope and compassion at about the time that his generation of young American writers were mostly turning in the other direction, and ushering in what might be called the age of cynicism and disillusionment into American literature.

Hersey's fourth book was nonfiction about the end of the war, and the beginning of the nuclear age. *Hiroshima*, appearing in 1946 after first being published as an entire issue of *The New Yorker*, hit the public with an impact second only to that of the first news of the bomb itself. This documentary needed none of the preaching that Hersey has sometimes been accused of doing. Its message is never spelled out—it is implicit on every page.

From these two triumphs, one fiction and one nonfiction, Hersey has gone on, never looking back, producing both fiction and nonfiction, never repeating himself, maintaining a high standard of intentions, although the books themselves, as will the combined work of any prolific writer, have varied in their degree of success at attaining those high standards.

As is probably inevitable, the standards themselves may have changed some. Hersey's idealism may or may not have diminished; it has certainly become tougher, and nowhere is this more apparent than in his latest novel, *The Walnut Door*. This novel is not completely successful, because of the ambiguous handling of its several themes, the seemingly incomplete portrayal of its two main characters, and a plot line that is too obviously manipulated and, therefore, somewhat implausible. Nevertheless, the novel is entertaining, a serious book with some funny lines that uses a very original situation to tell a story that is an unusual mixture of the love, suspense, and psychological novel.

Hersey's originality and versatility cannot be overstressed because he has never been given enough credit for them. After *The Wall,* which may turn out to be his most popular and long-lasting novel, Hersey began, with *The Marmot Drive* in 1953, to experiment by mixing symbolism with his realism. For such novels as *The Child Buyer* (1960) and the recent *My Petition for More Space* (1974), he developed his own version of Orwellian speculative fiction. *Too Far to Walk* (1966) is fantasy, an allegory putting the Faust legend into modern dress; while his seriously underrated allegory on race relations, *White Lotus* (1965), is a mixture of the fantasy and Orwellian modes. He has even ventured into the historical novel with *The Conspiracy,* and this mostly imagined account of a first century conspiracy to murder the Roman tyrant Nero turned out to be one of his best books.

Always among his varied work, even in the case of the historical novel, there has been at least one note of consistency: a direct relevance to the times. One of the pivotal characters in *The Conspiracy* is the Roman poet Lucan. Lucan has the problem of trying to decide if he should get involved; he ponders the responsibility of the writer to society. The novel was published in 1972 during a time when the controversy over the role of the press in Vietnam and other Nixon Administration problems was close to its height. John Hersey has apparently never doubted whether the writer should have a role in society. He has always been involved. It is this fact that makes it hard to evaluate *The Walnut Door,* for in some ways, this novel seems to be a testament to noninvolvement.

Hersey has always been a strongly thematic writer. *The Walnut Door* darts around the fringes of several themes without totally coming to grips with any of them. It is a gentle story about the threat of and fear of violence, an occasionally funny story about two somewhat sad refugees from the campus battlegrounds of the 1960's, a metaphorically sexual story that is not really about sex, but about the search for love and security. Like everything that Hersey writes, it is interesting, intelligent, and readable. Hersey is the consummate professional writer in the best and most honorable meaning of the term professional. His newest novel is written with style, plotted with enough precision to entice most readers to ignore certain implausible aspects, and paced with an eye to keeping those readers interested. That, it is likely to do.

It may also leave the reader a bit disappointed. Hersey has fallen short in this novel in another area in which he usually excels. He has not given the reader characters that he or she is likely to care about very much. *The Walnut Door* is less realistic, more of an allegory as is some of Hersey's better fiction; this might not have mattered, except that, since Hersey presents his themes through the method of a combined suspense and love story, it becomes a serious flaw. However glib the dialogue, however innovative the plot, however intellectually interesting the theme, such a story, to leave a lasting impression on most readers, must have at least one other element. It must have people who cast shadows, characters who somehow transcend the details of the storytelling to come into being.

Elaine Quinlan and Eddie Macaboy, the protagonist couple of *The Walnut Door,* do not cast shadows. It is hard to get at the reason why. It seems that they *ought* to be convincing. The reader is told enough about them to know that they bear convincing credentials of the college generation of the 1960's, but these credentials do not translate into a completely believable reality. It may be that the telling is the problem, that Hersey tells us too much and shows us too little about his couple. The problems that Elaine and Eddie have cannot be divorced from the materialistic, often violent society that they inhabit, or from the attitudes that they developed in college during the 1960's. Nevertheless, they are basically personal problems that are, to a large extent, self-created.

Macaboy is a Reed College dropout and former campus activist who has become an expert locksmith and doormaker with an obsession to provide security for his clients, most of whom are women living alone. He can pick almost any lock, and his methods, which would no doubt be frowned upon by the Better Business Bureau, include an occasional break-in to convince his potential customers that they need his protective services. He is something of a frustrated artist who compares women to paintings by Correggio, Mondrian, or Cezanne, who does his work while listening to Mozart or Beethoven quartets. Macaboy transfers his artistic impulses into the making of doors that, if not works of art, are certainly examples of high craftsmanship. Once he learns that an attractive young lady named Elaine Quinlan has moved into an apartment in a dangerous section of New Haven, it is obvious that their paths will cross.

Elaine is a disillusioned and alienated graduate of Bennington. After having had an abortion, she has left her lover, Greg, and, taking five-hundred dollars from their bank account, has set out for she knows not exactly where, seeking a new life. Elaine has vague pains of remorse about the abortion. She is, in fact, a vague person, which is one of the problems of the novel. Far from the activist that Macaboy has been, "for ages all her energy had gone into the hard work of being apathetic." She chooses New Haven, mainly because two of her college friends are there: Ruth Greenhelge, a former SDS leader who now works for and sleeps with a linguistics professor at Yale, and Bottsy Feldman, a graduate student who is trying to write a dissertation on Kropotkin. With the "fragments of her tentative personality," a collection of junky appliances, and a box of unread books, Elaine moves into her new apartment.

Her former lover, Greg, is a phony, a posturer of the type who would turn in his draft card because protesting the Vietnam War was the "in" thing to do, and then back down and reapply for his student deferment when he found himself in the 1A classification. There is an excellent set piece in the first-chapter introduction of Elaine in which she remembers Greg's job of two summers before when, dressed as a mechanical man complete with wind-up key on his back, he paraded with jerky motions, using lip sync to mouth a recording, while advertising a movie. Greg is more mechanical than human, and if we can find little else to admire in the apathetic Elaine, we can applaude her for leaving him.

Hersey spends about a quarter of the book's wordage with the memories of Elaine and Macaboy trying to establish—through their memories of childhood and parent-child relationships, through Macaboy's memories of life in the "Movement," through Elaine's memories of life at Bennington and with Greg—a background that will make their personalities, both slightly bizarre in different ways, understandable. He does not quite manage to do so. Macaboy, thinking of his father, describes a large part of the trouble with the memory sequences of the novel. He can remember his father wearing a certain shirt and hat, "but the features in between are blurred." It can be argued that real memories tend to be blurred in this manner. Fictional memories, however, have to add flesh to the features if we are to find them persuasive. The memories of Macaboy and Elaine seem indistinct at points of critical focus. Except for several relatively sharp pictures of Elaine's life with Greg, they give few clues as to why she should be so alienated, or Macaboy so obsessed.

Nor do Macaboy's memories of the movement give us much help. When he remembers his crusading days, or talks about them with Elaine, or has a dinner date with Greenhelge, what we mainly get is a list of names of people, places, and events: Carl Oglesby, Huey Newton, the Peace and Freedom Party, Johnson, Clean Gene, Bobby Kennedy, Martin Luther King, Jr., the Berrigans, the Tet Offensive, Spiro Agnew, the Pentagon, the Weathermen, the Black Panthers, Tom Hayden, Mark Rudd, and so on. It is especially disappointing to watch Hersey relegate the history of the 1960's to a list that everyone knows. One of his main strengths, from the occupation of Italy (*A Bell for Adano*) and the massacre of the Jewish community of Warsaw (*The Wall*), through *Hiroshima* to the Detroit riots of 1967 (*The Algiers Motel Incident*), has been to incorporate into both his fiction and nonfiction a thoroughly researched, deeply felt, morally persuasive feeling of the times. Perhaps he was overreacting to the occasional criticism that he has relied too much on journalistic elements in his fiction, and was determined not to let the history of their time overwhelm his characters. If so, one must hope that he does not continue to narrow his perspective to the point of destroying one of his basic virtues, one of the reasons why his best books are likely to survive the times about which he writes.

Another factor is that Hersey may be better at writing about large-scale events than small, individual ones; he may be more convincing when he outlines the terrible ordeal of the Jews of the Warsaw Ghetto, or the fantasy world of the racial role reversal of an entire society in *White Lotus,* than when he tries to render the more intimate plight of two rather ordinary people.

All reservations aside, this is an interesting and entertaining novel. Its lasting importance, however, may lie not so much in its qualities as an individual book, as in the question of what position it should hold in the collected work of one of our most distinguished authors.

William Boswell

WARTIME

Author: Milovan Djilas (1911–   )
Translated from the Serbo Croat by Michael B. Petrovich
Publisher: Harcourt Brace Jovanovich (New York). Illustrated. 470 pp. $14.95
Type of work: Autobiography
Time: 1941–1945
Locale: Yugoslavia and the Soviet Union

An exciting account of guerrilla warfare and the rise of the Communist Party to power in Yugoslavia during World War II

> *Principal personages:*
> MILOVAN DJILAS, one of Marshal Tito's leading aides during the Nazi occupation and Vice-President of Yugoslavia from 1945 to 1954, when he was expelled from the Communist Party
> JOSIP BROZ (TITO), Secretary General of the Yugoslav Communist Party and leader of the Partisan resistance movement during World War II; President of Yugoslavia from 1945 to the present
> DRAŽA MIHAILOVIĆ, leader of the Chetnik resistance movement during World War II and an archrival of Tito
> ANTE PAVELIĆ, Croatian fascist leader who in 1941, as a puppet of the Axis, became the head of the so-called Independent State of Croatia
> JOSEPH STALIN, dictator of the Union of Soviet Socialist Republics

The expulsion of Milovan Djilas from the Yugoslav Communist Party in 1954 abruptly terminated his long association and friendship with Marshal Tito, President of Yugoslavia. During the Nazi occupation, Djilas became one of Tito's three highest aides, and after the war he served as Vice-President of Yugoslavia until his fall from grace. Djilas was ousted from the party after having appealed for the transformation of Communism into democratic socialism. He was sentenced to a ten-year prison term in 1956 for expressing ideas contained in *The New Class: An Analysis of the Communist System,* which was published in 1957. Since his early release from prison in 1961, Djilas has written numerous other works, including additional critical studies of Communism, two novels, and three autobiographical works, of which *Wartime* is the latest.

In *Wartime,* Djilas recounts his experience as a member of the Partisan resistance movement which was led by Josip Broz, better known as Marshal Tito. Djilas describes in vivid detail how the historic, religious, and political animosities which for centuries had divided the Yugoslav people were exacerbated during the German and Italian occupation that commenced in April, 1941. Employing the "divide and rule" principle, the Nazis partitioned large areas of Yugoslavia among themselves and their Italian, Hungarian, and Bulgarian allies. Worse still, the Nazis purposely cultivated the traditional feud between the Serbs and Croatians to the point where both peoples perpetrated massacres and atrocities against the other. These tactics on the part of the Nazis served to complicate the nature of the resistance movement which intensified against them after they began the invasion of Soviet Russia on June 22, 1941.

From this point, a complicated struggle developed in Yugoslavia involving four major groups, with especially bloody fighting in those areas populated by Serbs. First of all, the Axis powers, as seen, dismembered the country, with Germany annexing the northern two-thirds of Slovenia while the remainder of the region went to Italy. The Germans then proceeded to set up Ante Pavelić as the puppet leader of the so-called Independent State of Croatia. Pavelić was also the head of a Croatian Fascist terrorist organization known as the Ustashi, which lost little time in undertaking wholesale massacres of Serbs, not only the minority in Croatia but those in the province of Bosnia as well. These murderous attacks by the Ustashi inspired the Serbs in Bosnia and elsewhere to form a resistance movement known as the Chetniks, The most disciplined Chetnik groups were those under the direct supervision of Colonel Draža Mihailović in Serbia proper. The Chetniks generally tended to be strongly Serbian nationalistic, or, in other words, anti-Croatian and anti-Communist. This position eventually led to open conflict with Tito's Communist-led Partisans, who, throughout the war, maintained close contact with Joseph Stalin, the Soviet dictator, as Djilas relates in considerable detail.

Tito's efforts in the fall of 1941 to forge a common front with the Chetniks in the struggle against the Axis proved unsuccessful, and by November of that year, the two resistance movements were openly at war with each other. They continued to fight each other until the end of World War II, caught up in what Djilas describes in his book as "the civil war within a war." Three basic reasons explain the incompatibility of the two movements. First of all, on the question of the strategy to be employed against the enemy, Mihailović adopted a cautious policy of avoiding large-scale armed resistance because of the overwhelming strength of the Germans, whose penchant for merciless reprisals against the civilian population was well known. Tito's Partisans, by contrast, believed in and practiced unremitting warfare against the enemy, no matter how great the cost as measured in their own lives or those of civilians who fell victims to Axis reprisals.

Politically, the Chetnik-Partisan feud was a continuation of the struggle during the interwar period (1919–1941) between the monarchist government and its opponents. Mihailović, a royalist officer, considered the Communists to be nothing more than lawless, atheistic criminals. The Communists, for their part, regarded Milhailović as the representative of the prewar regime they had fought for years, and feared that unless they could defeat him, the monarchy would be restored once the war ended. The restoration of the monarchy, which had ruled Serbia before it became part of Yugoslavia at the end of World War I, would of course mean the triumph of the Serbian national cause.

Herein lay a third source of friction between the Chetniks and the Partisans, for Mihailović was an ardent Serbian nationalist who called for the postwar enlargement of Serbia which, as a consequence, would completely dominate the Yugoslav state. Tito, on the other hand, advanced an all-Yugoslav program based on national self-determination of all peoples, and sweeping social reform.

This program, together with the Partisan slogan "Death to Fascism, Freedom to the People," appealed to all patriotic Yugoslavs, Communists and non-Communists alike. Djilas notes that the Partisan program generated considerable support among the younger people, who yearned for something new but who also saw in it the chance to improve their lot. With an obvious reference to his later break with the Communist Party, Djilas adds that at this time the Partisans' "concern for all didn't yet reveal a desire to control everyone."

Thus, as the war dragged on, Tito's movement became increasingly popular among the broad masses, so much so that Mihailović was driven into collaboration with the Axis occupying forces. To him, the Communists were a greater threat to Yugoslavia than the Germans, who in any case would lose the war. Since the Western Allies would not provide him with adequate assistance because of his unwillingness to engage the enemy continually, Mihailović openly collaborated with the Axis and the Ustashi in what proved to be an unsuccessful effort to destroy the Communist-led Partisans. In September, 1943, the Chetnik movement suffered a serious setback when Fascist Italy surrendered to the Allies. Djilas vividly describes the rapid decline of Milhailović's cause during the last two years of the war, a period marked by even greater Chetnik collaboration with the Germans now that Italy was out of the war. Mihailović spent the winter of 1944–1945 hiding out in northern Bosnia, while typhus and political discord combined to destroy any semblance of cohesion among the remaining Chetnik units. As the war drew to a close, the Partisans methodically closed in on the Chetniks, wiping out some seven thousand in one engagement. Mihailović escaped this disaster only to be caught by the Partisans in 1946, tried as a traitor, and executed.

The official Yugoslav historiography of World War II has defined seven main offensives launched against the Partisans by the Axis High Command. Djilas devotes an entire section of his autobiography to the two most critical of these offensives, the Fourth and Fifth, both of which were waged during the first half of 1943. In discussing these and the other offensives, Djilas catalogs the atrocities committed by the Axis occupying forces and their Yugoslav collaborators. The Partisans, too, were guilty of their share of unnecessary bloodshed, though understandably, the author deals somewhat more leniently with his comrades-in-arms than with their opponents.

The Fourth Offensive, launched in January, 1943, was the result of the decision by Adolf Hitler, the German Führer, to crush the Yugoslav resistance—meaning the Partisans primarily—before the end of winter. "Operation Weiss," as the Germans called the offensive, was thus conceived as an all-out operation, in which the Axis forces, augmented by the Ustashi and Chetniks, would mount a relentless drive on the Partisan strongholds. The Axis forces were particularly anxious to clear the Partisans from territory which they held near Zagreb, the capital of Croatia, and from certain important railroad lines vital to German communications. Tito, however, was able to break through the closing ring by hurling his forces against the Chetniks who were supposed to prevent the Partisans from retreating southward into the region of Herzegovina. The Partisans completely routed the Chetniks and captured many of their documents which revealed the extent of the collaboration between Mihailović and the Axis. As a consequence of these revelations, the British ceased providing support for Mihailović by the summer of 1943.

Undiscouraged by the failure of this campaign which ended in March, the Axis opened up the Fifth Offensive—"Operation Schwarz"—in May, 1943. This time the Axis High Command was determined that the Partisans should not escape destruction as they had so many times in the past. Axis forces in this offensive totaled 120,000 fresh troops against 18,000 tired Partisans, troops who were still recovering from their recent battles with the enemy. Employing new antiguerrilla techniques, the Germans pressed forward in a series of attacks against Tito's Partisans. It was during this campaign that Djilas slit the throat of a German soldier whom he engaged in hand-to-hand combat. Tito's forces, despite heavy losses, were able to survive this offensive, which proved to be the greatest test of Partisan strength and morale of the entire war. With the surrender of Italy in September, 1943, Tito was able to more than offset his losses in earlier battles by disarming several Italian divisions, thereby acquiring enough weapons and ammunition to increase his troops by eighty thousand.

From this time, although many bloody battles remained to be fought, Tito's movement continued to grow in strength throughout the remainder of the war. On September 6, 1944, the Russian Army reached the border of Yugoslavia. Djilas describes how at this point Tito flew to Moscow where he signed an agreement with the Soviet government regarding the operation of its troops in Yugoslavia. The agreement called for Soviet troops to be withdrawn after the cessation of military operations in liberated areas and for the Partisan-sponsored National Committee to establish its jurisdiction in these territories. Together, the Partisans and the Red Army recaptured Belgrade, the Yugoslav capital, on October 20, 1944. Thereafter, the ultimate triumph of the Partisans over the Germans was never in doubt.

In *Wartime,* Djilas provides some interesting insights into the personalities of Tito and Stalin. He describes Tito as a most effective political and military leader who cultivated personal, though not cordial, relations with his commanders. He did not encourage a significant political role for his commanders, nor did he support the military ambitions of the party leaders. In this way, Tito avoided any conflict between the party and the army, thus maintaining a balance between them. Djilas, for his part, established a close friendship with Tito during the war while serving him as a political-military adviser and as a diplomat in two missions to Moscow.

These missions to Moscow, in which the Yugoslavs sought military and economic aid from their Soviet allies, gave Djilas the opportunity to meet Stalin. Djilas' exhilaration at the prospect of flying to Moscow in April, 1944, to meet the leader of the great Slav state stood in sharp contrast to his disillusionment with the Russian Communists at the time he accompanied Tito on a second mission to the Soviet capital just a year later. The meetings that Djilas had with Stalin on the occasion of the first mission were very cordial. Stalin, according to the author, had a great sense of humor, albeit rather crude; he was, however, "a bundle of nerves which never missed the slightest word or glance," on the part of those with whom he was speaking. The cordial atmosphere which surrounded the first mission had largely evaporated by the time of the second mission in April, 1945. Stalin directed repeated barbs at Tito about alleged shortcomings of the Partisan army, and he took exception to Djilas' critical remarks made a few months earlier about the assaults of Red Army soldiers on Yugoslav civilians. Djilas stood up to Stalin on this occasion but conceded that he felt divested in front of the Soviet leader. The author's impressions of Stalin on these two occasions and at the time of a subsequent meeting with him in 1948, formed the basis of a book which he published in 1962, under the title of *Conversations with Stalin.*

Despite his split with Tito in 1954, Djilas is able to write enthusiastically about his life with the Partisans and their role in the liberation of Yugoslavia from the Axis. The general reader, however, should approach *Wartime* with at least some prior knowledge of the history and geography of Yugoslavia. Otherwise, he will fail to understand the basis for the feuds between the Serbs and Croatians, and the Chetniks and the Partisans, both of which Djilas discusses throughout the book. One particularly helpful feature of *Wartime* is a section of biographical notes in which brief sketches of the principal personages in the book are presented.

Edward P. Keleher

WILLIAM CAXTON: A BIOGRAPHY

Author: George D. Painter (1914–   )
Publisher: G. P. Putnam's Sons (New York). Illustrated. 227 pp. $14.95
Type of work: Biography
Time: The 1400's
Locale: England, Germany, and the Low Countries

A biography of William Caxton, fifteenth century English merchant, editor-translator, and England's first printer, which includes illustrations and descriptions of Caxton's eight types, a chronological list of his editions, and a select bibliography

Principal personages:
> WILLIAM CAXTON, England's first printer
> WILLIAM OVEREY, his predecessor as Governor of the English merchants at Bruges
> COLARD MANSION, partner in printing at Bruges
> WYNKYN DE WORDE, assistant and successor
> ROBERT LARGE, London mercer to whom Caxton was apprenticed
> PHILIP THE GOOD, Duke of Burgundy
> CHARLES THE BOLD, his son and successor as Duke of Burgundy
> MARGARET OF YORK, Duchess of Burgundy, wife of Charles the Bold and Caxton's patroness
> LOUIS XI, King of France
> EDWARD IV, King of England
> ELIZABETH WOODVILLE, wife of Edward IV and Queen
> GEORGE, Duke of Clarence
> RICHARD NEVILLE, Earl of Warwick (the Kingmaker)
> RICHARD III
> HENRY VII
> ELIZABETH OF YORK, daughter of Edward IV, wife of Henry VII and Queen

If, in preparing a document for the Caxton Commemoration of 1976, George D. Painter had contributed a series of painstaking corrections to all earlier biographies of England's first printer, William Caxton, his effort would have been laudable. If Painter had managed to describe every known Caxton document and edition, discussing each in relation to the people, places, and times of William Caxton, his contribution would have been considered a major achievement. That he accomplished all these goals and realized still higher purposes, investing every chapter with new conclusions and fresh ideas on the man and his work, marks his exceptional book as the standard Caxton biography for years to come.

With scrupulous care, Painter does, indeed, undertake to correct numerous errors, actual and inferential, which have found their way into previous Caxton studies. For instance, as he lays out the Bruges of Caxton the merchant and mentions the church of St. Donatian, he corrects both Blades (Donatus) and Crotch (Donatius). Where Blake is content to term the absence of issue records for 411 of 670 apprentices "an overwhelming proportion," Painter points out that the percentage, though more than half, is "not quite two thirds." While such corrections may be somewhat amusing in their meticulousness, the strikingly observant Painter is not waspish but charming in bringing "light and truth to all aspects of Caxton's career." He can be gracious—perhaps he must be gracious—even while debunking the long-entrenched lore of Caxton's care as an editor of Chaucer. But when, among his observations, Painter adds the minutiae that Duff, in his allegation about Caxton's Type 8, made "two of his rare typographical errors," it is comforting to have noted two wrong fonts in Painter.

The author's succinct investigation of the roots of the elusive Caxton-Caston-Cawston-Causton family would serve as an excellent case study for would-be genealogists. Painter knows the Domesday Book and the parish registers, medieval English place names and patronymics. Beyond these, though, he also knows English—that spelling and sound are not the same, and that both have changed over the years at different rates. He marshals all the particulars with a certain air of mystery, weaving in a village here and a family connection there to form a fascinating labyrinth of possible pedigrees. What matter that the corridors prove blind alleys? Painter invests the process itself with the compelling power of a detective story. And if his summary still fails to exit the maze, it is only Painter's own scholarly caution—scarcely the reader's—that stops him short of saying, finally, this was the place and this the line.

Painter is equally compelling in his sifting of the data on Caxton's apprenticeship to the mercers, his years at Bruges as a freeman mercer, and his service as governor of the English merchants at Bruges. He dwells at length on the implications of such documents as enrollment and issue fees and the will of Robert Large, Caxton's well-to-do-master, to establish, in the absence of early life records, delimiting dates for his subject. He shows how Easter-dating in the Flanders calendar affects the reckoning of major events in Caxton's continental years. And, based on his studied analysis of key political, social, economic, and military affairs of those continental years, Painter suggests various cause-effect relationships to explain Caxton's activities during the period.

Such grand tapping of a seemingly endless reservoir of dates, places, and events is sweetened greatly by a quiet, goodnatured, scholastic humor that filters through almost the entire book. When he describes the London district where Caxton served as Large's apprentice, Painter observes that it was not only destroyed by the Great Fire and again by the blitz, but again by postwar "concrete ziggurats." When he explains the fifteenth century expansion of English cloth exports, he adds, parenthetically, that it is "always sensible to send coals to Newcastle or owls to Athens if you can be sure of underselling the locals." His pithy appositives tell of men "comfortably rich without being disgustingly so." His sense of proportion even infiltrates the footnotes, as in his amplification on the bastards of Philip the Good.

In his depiction of Caxton's service as Governor and diplomat for the English crown, Painter lays heavy stress on Caxton's Yorkist ties. He contends, flatly, that Caxton was first brought into the governorship to be a Yorkist caretaker and that his decade of difficult negotiating of the Anglo-Burgundian cloth trade was closely allied to Yorkist policy. It was, Painter concludes, the Lancastrian restoration which caused Caxton's "exile," leading him to the service of Margaret of York, Duchess of Burgundy, wife of Charles the Bold, and, ultimately, through that service, to an altogether new career as a printer.

In the chapters on Caxton's discovery of printing as a new vocation, his years of learning the new trade, and the founding of his own press, Painter is unremitting in his quest for throwing new light in dim corners, giving close attention to clues in the Caxton prologues and epilogues themselves, and adding generous quantities of supporting evidence for his hypotheses. Thus—notwithstanding Painter's scholarly care with the rhetorical question and cautious use of *perhaps, probably, no doubt,* and *may*—Caxton's famous interview with his patroness Margaret takes place at Ghent, between February 16 and June 25, 1471, steeling the mercer's resolve to complete a translation of his first book, *Recuyell of the Histories of Troy.* Thus printer and typefounder Johann Veldener becomes Caxton's teacher at Cologne in 1472 and mentor at Bruges in 1473–1474. Thus the influence of Bruges calligrapher Colard Mansion is not simply in some technical link to the printer, but in opening up to Caxton the philosophy of creating publications by writing new translations in English. If there is any limitation in these ample postulations, it may be in the brief attention given to the significance of entrepreneurship for early printing in general and Caxton in particular. And, if there is any overstatement, it may be in Painter's readiness to term some of Caxton's obscurities "little jokes."

Painter's prose style tends toward the Gibbonesque. The comparisons are taut, as in his analysis of Caxton's decision to set up shop at the Abbey, wherein "he had good reason to prefer the protection of Court, Law and Church at Westminster to the chauvinism of unruly London." The rhetorical cadences are classical, as in noting that "the possibilities of relaxation at Bruges need to be remembered, not because we have the least reason for doubting the Printer's spotless purity, but because some scholars have wasted their sympathy on his enforced continence." And the diction is suitably latinate, witness, "disponibility."

Painter applies his expertise, garnered in a long career as Assistant Keeper in the British Library in charge of the National Collection of fifteenth century Printed Books, to explain, for both specialist and layman, many of Caxton's technical problems and decisions. In the matter of casting off, for example, Painter analyzes compositor errors to explicate Caxton's method of estimating copy. In the matter of redprinting, Painter describes Caxton's early difficulties and renders intelligible the printer's arrangement, as late as 1487, to have certain work printed at Paris because of the rubrics. In the matter of typography, Painter evaluates type change as Caxton must have—in terms of aesthetics, availability, aging fonts, and the impact of smaller type on paper costs.

Such technical matters are clarified nicely by a series of full-page illustrations, including some glass plates, showing each of the eight Caxton types and the famous Caxton device. Inclusion of the woodcut "Death Among the Printers" is useful for visualizing the explanation of both printing equipment and bookselling arrangements probable in Caxton's shops. With succinct commentary in "Notes on the Illustrations," a table describing the use of Caxton's device as evidence for dating, and a chronological list of all known Caxton editions, Painter's supporting materials form something of a handbook-within-a-book.

Perhaps the most controversial component of Painter's study, and probably the one aspect of the biography least documented or documentable, is his postulation on the mature William Caxton as Yorkist propagandist. Touching on the turbulent reign of Richard III, Painter endeavors to establish that Caxton's omission of dates or regnal years during the period represents a statement of his alignment with the Queen Mother, who was in sanctuary at Westminster Abbey, where the Caxton shop was located. Painter holds that Caxton's rush to produce *Knight of the Tower* was part of a plan to increase the value of the Queen Mother's daughters in Richard's plans. With Henry VII in power and wed to the daughter Elizabeth, Painter argues, Caxton's printing of *Golden Legend* served as a discreet reminder of the old Queen's status as mother of the Queen and maternal grandmother of the young Prince Arthur.

Clearly, this is a considerable work. If George Painter has never quite managed to make Caxton the man come to life, he has nevertheless added, on front after front, important substance to an understanding of England's first printer and his work.

Robert E. Nichols, Jr.

WINSTON S. CHURCHILL
Volume V:1922-1939
The Prophet of Truth

Author: Martin Gilbert (1936–   )
Publisher: Houghton Mifflin Company (Boston). Illustrated. 1,167 pp. $25.00
Type of work: Biography
Time: 1922–1939
Locale: Great Britain

A study of the character and public career of the great wartime Prime Minister from 1922 until the outbreak of World War II

> *Principal personages:*
> WINSTON S. CHURCHILL, grandson of the Duke of Marlborough, leading figure in British government, twice Prime Minister
> RANDOLPH CHURCHILL, his son
> LEOPOLD AMERY, a classmate of Churchill at Harrow, and member of the Baldwin cabinet, 1922–1929
> C. T. ANDERSON, Wing-Commander in the Royal Air Force
> STANLEY BALDWIN, Conservative Prime Minister, 1923–1924, 1924–1929, and 1935–1937
> NEVILLE CHAMBERLAIN, member of Baldwin government in the 1920's and 1930's; Prime Minister, 1937–1940
> ANTHONY EDEN, Foreign Secretary, 1935–1938, Prime Minister, 1955–1957
> JAMES RAMSEY MACDONALD, first Labour Prime Minister, 1924; again 1929–1931; formed coalition government with Conservatives, 1931; Prime Minister of National Government, 1931–1935
> ROBERT VANSITTART, Permanent Under-Secretary for Foreign Affairs, 1930–1938

The Prophet of Truth is the fifth volume of what must surely be not only the authoritative life of Winston Churchill but also one of the great biographical works of the twentieth century. The first two volumes were written by Sir Winston's brilliant but erratic son, Randolph, who found in them at last an expression for his very considerable but hitherto wasted talents. Each of the volumes as it appeared was hailed by the critics as a masterpiece. Tragically, Randolph died when his work was only well started (Volume II closed in 1914), and Martin Gilbert, known for his historical studies of twentieth century Britain, was chosen to carry the biography forward. This is the third of his volumes, carrying Sir Winston up to 1939, and while not perhaps equaling the achievement of the Randolph Churchill volumes, they certainly are very good indeed. With World War II, the beginnings of the Cold War, and the Churchill government of the 1950's still to be covered, the project clearly has many thousands of pages still to run. When one adds that each of the first four volumes was ultimately supplemented by two to three additional volumes of supportive documents (as will be this volume and those to follow), the scope of the biography is seen to be truly awesome—or perhaps better, Churchillian—in its dimensions.

Although part of this vast project, *The Prophet of Truth* can be read as a separate book of great interest in itself, without reference to the earlier volumes. For the nonspecialist reader, it may prove something of a challenge at times since Gilbert provides only to a minimal degree the context of British and European public affairs within which Churchill's career as politician and statesman took place. (He is better about recording events in Europe in the 1930's than about British domestic politics in the 1920's.) As a matter of practical necessity, Gilbert obviously had to focus rather narrowly on the life rather than the "life and times" of his subject. But the nonspecialist may wish to have at hand a brief summary of British history in the 1920's and 1930's to fill out his own background of Churchill's actions and opinions.

The volume opens with Churchill without a seat in Parliament for the first time in twenty-two years and about to return to the Conservative Party. The occasion for his break with the Liberals, whom he had served in high office for almost two decades, was the victory of the Labour Party in 1924 and the Liberal Party's decision to give the first Labour Government tacit support. Churchill's reaction to the growing strength of Labour is reminiscent of his extravagant and unfortunate remarks about that party in the campaign of 1945: he predicted in 1924 that if Labour were in charge of elections, law and order could not be guaranteed and the threat of such a situation would cast a blight "on every form of national life." He was, of course, completely wrong; both Labour governments of the 1920's were models of decorum and responsibility. This attitude and statement are typical expressions of one aspect of Churchill as politician. He was, as the title of the book suggests, rather given to prophecy, but these prophecies did not always prove to be the truth. In the 1920's and 1930's, he failed to appreciate the true nature of several of the most important events and tendencies of the age. He pictured the Labour Party as Bolshevik when in fact its members were essentially conservative; he dramatized the General Strike of 1926 as carrying the threat of revolution whereas its leaders viewed it as a large-scale trade union dispute; he disliked and misunderstood Gandhi and Nehru and opposed movement toward dominion status for India. (He even invested heavily in the New York stock market on the eve of the 1929 crash.) He wished always to relate individual events to a larger context, and to present that relationship in dramatic and even extravagant terms. This tendency of his mind served him well in understanding the true significance of the rise of Hitler in the early 1930's and in rallying the British nation to rearm and eventually to resist the Nazis in war. But earlier it caused men to be wary of him.

Churchill returned to Parliament in the Conservative landslide of 1924. He expected to be offered office, but to his considerable astonishment he was named to the second highest post in the government—Chancellor of the Exchequer. This good fortune he owed at least in part to his future political antagonist, Neville Chamberlain, whose position in the party was such as to command that office but who found the Ministry of Health more interesting. Chamberlain suggested Churchill almost casually to Stanley Baldwin, the Prime Minister, and the latter responded favorably. The appointment surprised the Conservative Party, the country, and even Churchill's wife, who was persuaded only with difficulty that he was not teasing when he returned home with the news.

Churchill was Chancellor from 1924 to 1929, preparing five budgets in that time, as well as putting out an official newspaper during the General Strike of 1926, helping with a settlement of the coal strike in that year, and participating in continuing discussions of foreign affairs and defense. He impressed colleagues and the public alike with his vigor and boldness and was praised as the best Chancellor in many years. Nevertheless, his achievements do not seem of great significance when viewed in retrospect. The overriding problem for Britain in the 1920's was to revive industry, still stagnating after the war, and to deal with massive unemployment. Churchill was much concerned with these problems but did little to solve them. He is today chiefly remembered for having returned Britain to the gold standard in response to demands of the Bank of England and the financial community, an event which aggravated Britain's already serious problems as an exporting nation. Gilbert helps to balance that unfavorable impression with evidence of Churchill's humane endeavors to solve problems of unemployment and make social reforms through his budgets. But his techniques were not adequate to his tasks, being strikingly orthodox. Despite this fault, the years as Chancellor were good ones for Churchill, years in which he had the confidence of the leading men of his party and an outstanding reputation as a speaker in the debates of the Commons. In fact, by 1928 and 1929, his fame as a speaker was such that members crowded in to hear him above all others; his role in the Commons was almost that of a public performer, appreciated and applauded by men of all parties.

That kind of acceptance was pleasing to Churchill. He coveted fame and wished to earn for himself a great name in the history of Britain. Yet part of his greatness of character was that he did not hesitate to take unpopular stands. In the early 1930's he sacrificed his leading position in the Conservative Party by his opposition to tariff reform and more especially by opposing the party's policy in regard to India. Between 1930 and 1935, the Labour Government and its successor National Government made every effort to conciliate the leaders of the Indian Nationalist movement, and in the India Bill of 1935 offered the subcontinent an All-Indian federation and a cabinet system of government in the provinces. Churchill disliked the nationalists and opposed granting self-government without guarantees for Indian minorities (Muslims, Untouchables) and for the Lancashire manufacturers for whom India was a principle market. Typically, he went all out in his effort to oppose radical change in India—in public speeches, newspaper articles, and a constant flow of letters to influential men. Ultimately he failed, of course, and in the process he became isolated from both the leadership and the rank and file of his party, although he was briefly the darling of the Die Hard element among the Conservatives.

An incident of 1934 which arose in the course of discussion about the future of India was particularly held against him. Rumors circulated in March of that year of a serious impropriety initiated by Lord Derby in regard to certain testimony given before the parliamentary committee on Indian Constitutional Reform. It was alleged that under pressure from two prominent members of that committee certain witnesses had withdrawn negative testimony. This act was a serious breach of parliamentary privilege, if true. Churchill came forward like a roaring lion. He had a double cause: defense of the privileges of the House of Commons, about which he always felt deeply, and building up his case against change in India. He pressed for an investigation, and once a committee of investigation was appointed, continually pressed it to be more thorough than it wished to be. Eventually, that committee found that no impropriety had been committed, when, in fact, there had been and the committee knew it: personal papers have become available in recent years which prove without any doubt that Lord Derby, a great man in the Lancashire area, had persuaded merchants from Lancashire to withdraw their objections to constitutional development in India. Churchill was right, both in defending the privilege of the House of Commons and in the substance of his charge of impropriety. But he was not prudent in bringing grave charges against leading members of his party. This was deeply resented.

The unwise actions of Churchill's only son, Randolph, also hurt him. In 1935, that willful, strong-minded young man ran for a seat in Parliament in a by-election against the official Conservative candidate on an anti-India Bill stand. He was defeated, and split the Conservative vote so that the Labour candidate was elected by a minority vote. In the following year, he ran in another by-election, this time against Malcolm MacDonald, son of the former Prime Minister, for whom the Government was trying to find a seat. He lost again. On both occasions, he entered the race against his father's wishes. The young man wished to help his father and persisted in the face of the most explicit statements of how damaging his actions would actually be. Once he had plunged in, Winston stood by him, never revealing publicly his opposition. He thus seemed responsible for his son's challenging two party candidates. This apparent defiance, along with the previous charge of impropriety against Lord Derby, gave the impression that there were no lengths to which Winston would not go in opposition to his party, and he was considered not only disloyal and irresponsible but reckless as well.

Churchill's first warnings about the Nazis and German rearmament came in 1933 and 1934 when he was vigorously opposing the Government's India policy. He thus spoke from an isolated position. On the periphery of his own party, resented by leaders and rank and file alike, he was also anathema to Labour because of his outspoken criticism of that party in the 1920's. Yet little by little as time went on he impressed his views on Parliament and the public. He had several assets which worked in his favor. First, even though unpopular, he could always command the attention of the House of Commons through his great gift of oratory. Second, he was a professional writer, supporting himself when out of office by writing not only the multivolume historical works *(Marlborough, His Life and Times; History of the English Speaking Peoples)* but also many newspaper and magazine articles each year and eventually a regular column syndicated throughout Europe and the United States. His name and his views were always before the public. Third, men in key positions in government and the armed services came to share his alarm at the Nazi menace. Despairing of the Government's policies, they provided him with secret data. Chief among his informants were Robert Vansittart, Permanent Under-Secretary of State for Foreign Affairs, 1930–1938, and Wing-Commander C. T. Anderson, Director of Training for the Air Ministry from 1934 to 1936 and then commandant of two different R.A.F. training camps in the period to 1939. From these two men, Churchill had highly reliable intelligence on both German and English military strength. There were others as well, and by 1938 and 1939 large numbers of patriotic men and women were violating the Official Secrets Act to furnish him with information they thought he should have. Even the French government made available to him their estimates of German strength. As a consequence, Churchill successfully challenged the Government's monopoly of military and diplomatic information, proving over and over that he had better data and was able to interpret them more accurately than were the officials.

He was served well in these years by both his heart and his will. It is to his eternal credit that his judgment of Hitler from the first was a moral one. He decried the suppression of the opposition parties and the trade unions in 1934; he repeatedly spoke out movingly against the persecution of the Jews; he called attention to the concentration camps. His moral indignation was especially aroused by British pressure on Czechoslovakia to yield to Hitler's demands in 1938. In these years of moral confusion, he saw the issues clearly, and his great force of will sustained him when he stood practically alone. For Churchill, the low point was undoubtedly the Autumn of 1938 during and immediately after the Munich settlement. The story of the Munich crisis is familiar, but as Martin Gilbert takes us forward day by day through these weeks with Churchill, the tension mounts and one feels his own desperate need to influence Chamberlain's actions, his hope that the Prime Minister would finally stand firm, and at last his despair at the outcome, this "sordid, squalid, sub-human and suicidal" policy. In the Commons' debate on Munich, when men of all parties were hailing Chamberlain for his great achievement, Churchill declared "we have sustained a total and unmitigated defeat." His standing in the House was never so low. Even the handful of Members who also opposed Munich did not wish to be associated too closely with him, preferring to gather around Anthony Eden or Leopold Amery.

Yet at this low point, the tide was already turning. Some newspapers began to support his views, and in the reaction against Munich, especially after Hitler took over all of Czechoslovakia in March, 1939, the public turned to Churchill. All through the spring and summer of 1939, there was widespread expectation that he would be asked to join the Government. But Chamberlain and the cabinet held out to the bitter end. Not until the German attack on Poland in September did Chamberlain yield. As the volume closes, Churchill has been appointed to the Admiralty and the War Cabinet, and the now-famous signal went out to the Fleet, "Winston is back."

Characteristically, he joined without rancor the Cabinet which had treated him harshly. One is struck over and over in the course of his career with his essential gentleness of character, his magnanimity towards opponents, his loyalty to colleagues. One of the paradoxes of his paradoxical life is the contrast between his true personality and his public image in the years before World War II. His political independence, his loyalty to his own family, his extravagant rhetoric led to misunderstandings. Martin Gilbert presents massive evidence to judge Winston Churchill as he really was. One closes this volume with a sense of having associated through its pages with a truly great man.

James E. Newman

CUMULATIVE AUTHOR INDEX

All twenty-four Masterplots Annuals—1954-1978

(Figures within parentheses indicate years; other figures indicate page numbers.)

I

CUMULATIVE AUTHOR INDEX—1954-1978

CUMULATIVE AUTHOR INDEX—1954-1978